A CONCISE HISTORY
OF ROMANIA

Also by Andrew MacKenzie

ON ROMANIA
Dracula Country
Romanian Journey

On Psychical Research:
The Unexplained
Frontiers of the Unknown
Apparitions and Ghosts
A Gallery of Ghosts (an anthology)
Riddle of the Future
Hauntings and Apparitions

A CONCISE HISTORY OF ROMANIA

Edited by Prof. Andrei Oțetea
English edition edited by Andrew MacKenzie

ROBERT HALE • LONDON

© Andrew MacKenzie. 1985

First published in Great Britain 1985

ISBN 0 7090 1865 7

Robert Hale Limited
Clerkenwell House
Clerkenwell Green
London, EC 1 OHT

Printed and bound in Great Britain by Unified Printers and Publishers Ltd., 170 Brick Lane, London E 1

Contents

Introduction 7
1. From the early inhabitants to the Dacians   43
2. The Geto-Dacians   63
3. Roman Dacia and Scythia Minor 103
4. The formation of the Romanian people . . 127
5. The emergence of the Romanian states (tenth to fourteenth centuries) 155
6. The Romanian countries in the fourteenth and fifteenth centuries 173
7. The beginnings of Ottoman domination. The epic of Michael the Brave 200
8. The Phanariot Régime in Moldavia and Wallachia. Habsburg Absolutism in Transylvania 253
9. The Revolution of 1821. The rule of native princes is re-established 283
10. The age of the *Règlement Organique* and the Revolution of 1848 in the Romanian countries 299
11. The union of the two principalities and the way in which they achieved their independence 339
12. The Romanian National State makes great strides 382
13. Romania in the First World War 404
14. Romania between the two World Wars (1918-39) 428

15. Romania during World War Two (1939-45)	472
16. Creation of Socialist Romania	498
17. Culture and Science	518
Commentary	533
Bibliography	559
Acknowledgements	567
List of Illustrations	569
Index	571

INTRODUCTION

This *Concise History of Romania* is based on documentation and mainly on *the History of the Romanian People* edited by the late Professor Andrei Oțetea, a distinguished historian who was a member of the Academy of the Socialist Republic of Romania, and compiled under the sponsorship of the Romanian Academy by a comprehensive panel of historians who were specialists in different aspects of their country's history. As stated by the authors, in their foreword to the American edition of the book in 1970, "It will be a reference book — a basis for all historical investigations". They point out that "this is the first work to have depicted the history of the Romanian people in the light of materialist-historical concepts".

Although I have no claims to be a historian, I have taken a great interest in the history of Romania since I first went there seventeen years ago. In the course of frequent visits I have interviewed many leading historians in universities throughout the country and, in particular, at the Institute of Historical and Socio-Political Studies (the Institute of History) at Bucharest. It seems to me, as a visitor from the capitalist West, that historical research in Romania is conducted with a drive and thoroughness that is most unusual. It is, as it were, that Romanian historians are engaged in putting a stamp of authenticity on their origins and nationality : not that they have any doubts about it but because of questions raised on some aspects of it in other countries, particularly Hungary and the Soviet Union. In my own research I have been greatly helped by books by two eminent British historians: the late Dr R. W. Seton-Watson (1879-1951), Masaryk Professor of Central European History at London University, and his son Professor Hugh Seton-Watson, who until recently held the chair of Russian History at London University.

Professor R. W. Seton-Watson's *History of the Roumanians* (Cambridge University Press, 1934) was, he said, "the first attempt by any British writer to give a complete survey of Roumanian history from its obscure origins down to the achievement of national unity in our own day". He added that "To some, Roumanian history may seem obscure and often inglorious: but there is a certain dynamic force in its vicissitudes, and Europe cannot show any more striking example of the corroding effects of foreign rule, of the failure of a policy of systematic assimilation and of the gradual triumph of national sentiment over unfavourable circumstances". It is a pity that this admirable book has long been out of print. I hope that the present volume will help to fill a gap in the market.

But first of all about the country. Romania, which has borders with the Soviet Union, Hungary, Yugoslavia and Bulgaria, is crossed by the 45th parallel and the 25th meridian, the latter dividing her territory into two nearly equal parts. The whole area is 91,738 square miles and the population 22 million. The country is located in the temperate zone, the climate inclining towards the continental while, with reference to Europe, Romania lies in an area of transition between the eastern and southern climes. As R. W. Seton-Watson has pointed out, "Roumanian History can only be understood in its geographical setting". A ring of mountains in the centre of Romania encloses a tableland of no great height (1,200-1,500 feet) which was formerly a seabed carved out by streams and turned into hills and dales, with a plain to the north-east and a number of well-sheltered lowlands all around. Mountains seldom exceeding 6,000 feet border the tableland. Throughout the Carpathians, including the spurs projecting into Maramureş and Bukovina, and those of Oltenia and Banat, there are only twenty peaks exceeding this height, and only five of these rise a little above 7,500 feet (Moldoveanul, the highest, is 8,347 feet). Most of these mountains do not form ramparts of sheer rock; their summits are broad, with gentle slopes and wide expanses of flat land. On these summits it becomes quite warm in summer and this is the reason why the Carpathians have no glaciers or eternal snow like the Alps but boast a much richer flora than the latter mountains and form one of the most extensive pastoral areas in Europe.

The main mountain ring is mostly surrounded by a second one, the Carpathian foothills, separated from the central massif by a succession of lowlands which in many instances look like smooth plains. Further down again are the hills, which in certain areas rise up stepwise and form wide plateaus. At the foot of the hills are the plains, the greatest of which is the Romanian Plain, whose centre, the Bărăgan, was built up from detritus of rocks on the bed of a sea. As the bed was filled, a flat plain emerged, containing salt lakes that looked like so many white patches. Judging from its flora and fauna, this shapeless plain is obviously an extension of the great eastern steppe.

Between the Danube and the Black Sea — Romania's sea front — there is a gently rolling expanse which in the north rises to the bare crests of the Măcin, a mountain much older than the Carpathians and eroded very nearly down to its base. To the east it slopes down to the Black Sea, with lagoons all along the coast; these were formerly bays used in the past by Greek sailors but are now choked with alluvium. This coast is truly a lagoon coast and, in geography, it has served as a type in the classification of all similar ones. In the course of time the map of this part of the country, like that of the Danube delta, has changed incessantly. The Danube delta, Europe's largest nature reserve, covers 5,050 square kilometres, four fifths of it in Romanian territory and the rest in the Soviet Union. The Danube meadowland has an untypical aspect. From the Iron Gates onwards the Danube has mostly a high, precipitous right-hand bank, while its left bank (the Romanian) is low, with ponds and backwaters, widespread willow woods, grasslands, and fields flooded regularly every year. This area is commonly called Balta (backwaters), and this is the name given in the past (when the river meadow, which is now being drained, was wider) to the riverside districts of the counties along the Danube in Wallachia. Beyond Călărași, the Danube branches out twice, forming two "internal deltas" between the Ialomița and Brăila backwaters, subsequently to divide into three main arms and form the delta proper.

The main environmental conditions that have influenced the early history of Romania have been its relative location in Europe, the manner in which the land was formed, and the extensive forests that have covered it all the time.

During a very long period, from the time of the Scythians to the Tartar invasion of the thirteenth century, the Carpathians and the Lower Danube were an obstacle to the nomads pushing westwards from Central Asia. The age of the great migrations of populations and of periodic invasions with the object of plunder lasted longer here than in any other part of Europe. West of the Carpathians there was more security, states were built up earlier, and civilization assumed more advanced and more lasting forms. However, despite many calamities through the ages, the territory between the Carpathians and the Danube offered its inhabitants conditions, particularly thick forests, which enabled them to stand their ground and preserve their entity throughout the territory now inhabited by the Romanians.

INTRODUCTION 11

The importance of the mountains in the life of the Romanian people can be indicated in a number of ways. The Dacians were known to the Romans as mountain people *(Dacii inhaerent montibus)* and it was natural that their offspring should continue to live primarily in that geographical environment. Those who in the past have studied the life of the Romanian people during the Middle Ages have never doubted that the natives found safety in the mountains during the age of the great migrations, for they had before them examples of the age in which they lived themselves of people withdrawing to the mountains in wartime. Such withdrawals, which were actually an old military strategy — practised, for example, by Stephen the Great — were measures taken by the administration itself. A foreign traveller, Paul of Aleppo, who himself went into hiding in the mountains in fear of the Turks and Tartars at the time of Prince Constantine Șerban (1654-8), records that the Prince sent out horsemen "to let all the country know that the people should leave their homes and withdraw to the mountains". The flight to the Carpathians was so common a thing that the same traveller points out as a specific feature that the mountaineers around Cîmpulung, Argeș and Cozia had found an important source of income in acting as carters. "When there is a rumour that the signal for flight has been given, the latter [carters] immediately come to the capital city, load the people's belongings on to wagons and conceal them in safe places known to them alone. These carters are all well known to the tradespeople."

But what drew the native population to the Carpathians was not only the need of safety from danger but also the economic value of the mountains, this being particularly true in the Middle Ages. For even if we do not lay stress on the two great sources of wealth, gold and salt, which were not to be found in the neighbouring countries, we should note that the sun-drenched tablelands of the Carpathians were often tilled up to heights of 3,000 feet. When the first principalities (Voievodate) — whose territories at the beginning spread over both sides of the Carpathians, an example being Litovoi's Principality set up in 1247 — began to expand, they first extended over the amphitheatre of heights all around, which the people never thought of as different from the mountains. The population of the hills, already dense in that period, was thus incorporated into the mountain states that were taking shape.

Next to the mountains, forests played an important role in the life of the Romanian people during the Middle Ages. In the Carpathians and in the hills, the forests, together with the rugged configuration of the territory, made it difficult for outsiders to penetrate. But the forests spread beyond the hills, sometimes very far into the plains. South of the Carpathians they divided the plain in two, making a wide barrier of the Bucharest area and in what was formerly the Vlaşca county. A dense forest crossed by small muddy streams that widened out into marshes was to be found here. During the migration period the forest of the Romanian Plain could only be crossed on foot and was impenetrable for the foreigner who did not know the paths. Like the regular armies of a later date, the horsemen of the steppe were compelled to go round it, and this difficulty, which irked them so, is shown by the name the Turanians had for the western part of the forest: Teleorman — Mad Forest.

The Danube meadow and delta, like the Siret meadowland, were to a great extent similar to the marshy forest in the Romanian plain. The food resources available for men and beasts and the shelter offered by the woods and thickets of the backwaters account for the string of sizable villages existing along the Danube, the uninterrupted life in those parts being in striking contrast to the scattered and ephemeral settlements of the steppe. Owing to the river meadow the Romanians were in closer touch with the Danube throughout their history than were the peoples south of the river. On the high southern bank mostly urban centres were to be found and their purpose in the first place was military. In the nearly five hundred years of Turkish rule the garrisons that were stationed in these towns kept the villagers away from the water. On the Romanian side of the Danube, on the other hand, the meadow was populated by farmers, shepherds who had come down from the Carpathians, beekeepers and fishermen.

Compared with this area where the native population was permanently settled, the open plain afforded living conditions that were widely different. Closely bound up with the great steppe that stretches from north of the Black Sea to the Pacific Ocean, it was an area where the migratory populations from Central Asia on their way to Europe passed through and halted, while in the eighteenth and nineteenth centuries it was the main arena of anti-Ottoman wars. The native population here lived alongside a nomad population, as it did at the time of Darius's expedition, or alone, as in the days of Alexander the Great and of Lysimachus.

In Wallachia and Moldavia the plain was the main area in which the changes of the modern epoch took place. In this area of immense landed estates belonging to the boyars or the monasteries — an area where the social environment was widely different from that of the uplands, where most of the free villages were to be found — the economic processes through which the peasantry passed after 1829 unfolded with greater intensity. The "iron yoke" of compulsory service, the peasant uprisings, and the successive land distributions were mass phenomena of considerable significance. As a consequence, while the economy of the areas that were mostly populated by free peasants and had enjoyed a privileged situation in the past, stagnated largely through lack of arable land, the plain in less than a century changed greatly owing to the "agrarian revolution" and to the "demographic explosion" which enabled the population to increase many times over large areas.

Other developments, this time exterior ones, in the political and economic geography of the Balkan Peninsula and of Europe generally, brought about a change in the relative importance of certain components of the geographical structure of Romanian territory from one period to the next. This becomes apparent when we consider the importance in the course of time of the Black Sea and of the Danube in the history of this part of the European continent.

In the hazy dawn of antiquity the Black Sea appears as inhospitable to the Greek sailors, but from the eighth century B.C. it became an area of thriving navigation. It was the age when material goods and cultural influences reached Dacia through the Dobrudjan sea-coast cities. Here, up to the fifteenth century A.D., sea trade thrived despite the crises caused by wars and invasions. By the close of the fourteenth century the two free Romanian states had their natural boundary along the Black Sea coast, and consequently Mircea the Old and Prince Roman called themselves rulers of the land down to the sea. When the Genoese were compelled to leave these waters the Black Sea became a Turkish lake and the area went through a dark period. For several centuries the Sultans' war fleets alone sailed there, apart from the ships that supplied Constantinople with products acquired under a monopoly. The Black Sea was no longer an international waterway.

In many respects the destiny of the Danube was conditional upon that of the Black Sea. In ancient times the Danube was named Istros by the Greeks and Danubius by the Romans, thus showing that there were actually two basins, each with a life of its own, with the Iron Gates dividing them. For the Greek sailors the Lower Danube provided a waterway in continuation of the sea. Little wonder, therefore, that the main Pontiac city at that time — Histria, the ruins of which are now a tourist attraction — was named after the river. When the Romans reached the Romanian part of the Danube they ruled it by means of a string of fortified towns along the steep bank and also by their fleet and the bridgeheads on the left bank, where the towns and territories were well organized and where the Roman influence had been felt long before the conquest of Dacia. The same bridgeheads preserved the influence of the Roman Empire north of the Danube after Emperor Aurelian withdrew from that area.

Under the Turkish rule there was no trade on the Danube with countries other than the Ottoman Empire, and consequently an economic recession was brought about. River traffic therefore brought no profits to Wallachia and Moldavia, and when the Treaty of Adrianople changed the situation the consequences were of the utmost importance for the Romanian principalities, bringing about new orientations in politics, economy, and culture. A free Danube brought Romania nearer to Western Europe which from then on spoke of Moldavia and Wallachia as the "Danubian Principalities". The demand for Romanian wheat in the continental markets and also the need to ensure this axis of European trade, which could be jeopardized by any one great neighbouring power, caused many measures of an international character relating to the modern Romanian State and the "Danube problem" to be taken. The Danube, it should be noted, was the first river in the world for which a commission was set up to watch over the freedom of its outlets to the sea. At the same time the new importance of the Danube wrought many transformations in the Romanian economy during the period of its renaissance.

Consequently, the Danube, the Black Sea, and the Carpathians are the three elements which, together, account for the original features and the unity of the territory on which the Romanian people was formed and developed.

Romanian history is not a chronicle of kings and queens such as British children, learning the history of their own country, once had to commit to memory. True, there were Dacian kings, but the last of these, Decebalus, took his own life when his forces were overwhelmed by the Roman Emperor Trajan in A.D. 106. When the Emperor Aurelian withdrew from Dacia in A.D. 271 a long period of chaos followed until the separate principalities of Wallachia and Moldavia emerged in the fourteenth century. These two principalities merged under A.I. Cuza in 1859 and he may be said to be the first prince of Romania. His reign, however, was brief; he was deposed, and in 1866 Prince Charles of Hohenzollern Sigmaringen, an officer in the Prussian army, was elected Prince of Romania. He was crowned king in 1881. His descendant, King Michael, abdicated in 1947, so the reign of the Hohenzollern kings may be said to be a comparatively brief one.

So far we have talked about Wallachia and Moldavia: the third and largest Romanian province, Transylvania, did not come under Romanian control until after the end of the First World War. Before this Transylvania had been part of the Hungarian kingdom, and earlier had been under the sway of the Ottoman and Habsburg empires, but the Romanians, who had been there from the earliest times, regarded Transylvania as their own land; indeed, Prince Michael the Brave was in 1600 briefly prince of Wallachia, Moldavia *and* Transylvania. Controversy about Transylvania, which many Hungarians regard as a Hungarian province taken from them because they were on the losing side in the First World War, still continues, with Hungarian *émigrés* in Europe maintaining that the Hungarian minority there is persecuted, so it is worth while looking at this dispute in some detail. Romanian histories say one thing and Hungarian histories another. Therefore I think it is important that an independent voice should be heard and for this reason I quote that of R. W. Seton-Watson, who, of all western commentators, was the best informed.

Pointing out that "We are dealing with perhaps the most obscure corner of Western history" and that "There is simply no parallel for the mysterious silence which surrounds the Romanians following the thousand years following the withdrawal of Aurelian and his legions — a period in which there are neither chronicles nor charters nor archaeological remains", Seton-Watson said that the Romanians claim that they are the true descendants of Trajan's colonists, that Transylvania is the cradle of the race, and that historic continuity has never been lost. In their view the withdrawal during Aurelian's reign only affected the military and official classes ; the bulk of the population remained behind, and though doubtless much reduced through long centuries of anarchy and modified by intermarriage with various invading tribes, managed to preserve its racial identity, withdrawing in moments of extreme stress into the remote fastnesses of the Carpathians.

"The Magyars in their turn argue that the continuity is a myth ; that the abandonment of Dacia by the Roman element was complete ; that in any case Romanisation of the provinces cannot really have struck very deep in so short a period as 163 years [more exactly 165 years], and that of the colonists who originally crossed the Danube, the great mass were not of Roman blood at all. Arguing from the large admixture of Slav elements in the modern Romanian language, they lay greater stress upon the Slavonic than upon their Latin origin. They point to the absence of any records showing them to have occupied their present territory during the Dark Ages, and proceed to argue that the Romanians of today are descended from nomadic Balkan tribes who only crossed to the north bank of the Danube in the thirteenth century, and then gradually overflowed into Transylvania, in response to the welcome extended by the Hungarian kings to foreign settlers."

Seton-Watson maintains that we may safely dismiss such arguments as are based upon the absence of early records. Much has been made by Magyar historians of the fact that the first charter containing any reference to Romanian inhabitants of Transylvania dates from the year 1210. But here it is necessary to point out that the same profound obscurity surrounds the history of *all* the inhabitants of Transylvania till the beginning of the thirteenth century.

"The lack of records is due to a double cause — that throughout these south-eastern territories really ordered life can only be said to begin after the twelfth century, and that the terrible Mongol invasion which devastated Hungary in 1241 is responsible for a wholesale destruction of such records as existed.

"Meanwhile it is obvious that the Romanian claim of pure Roman blood is untenable : in 163 years [more exactly 165 years], the old Dacian element cannot have been wiped out, and must clearly form the lowest stratum of Romanian nationality. At the same time it is impossible to travel very long in Romania, and *especially* in Transylvania, without coming across strikingly Latin types among the peasantry ; and the Romanian language, for all its Slav admixture, is essentially Latin in texture."

In present-day Romania the "strikingly Latin types" observed by Seton-Watson more than fifty years ago may now be seen among the waiters and waitresses in tourist hotels. In my most recent visit to Transylvania (1983) I also saw waitresses whose features reminded me of those depicted on Greek vases in museums.

Seton-Watson maintains that the Romanians are Romanized Dacians, infiltrated with Slav and to a much lesser degree Tartar blood.

But what of the theory that the Romanians only reached their present home in the thirteenth century ? Seton-Watson discusses the Romanian and Hungarian points of view and decides that "the weakness of the whole theory soon begins to emerge if we ask its [mainly Hungarian] authors to explain what on their showing became of the Romanians during the period of nine centuries which elapsed during their withdrawal by Aurelian and their reappearance as a budding state in the thirteenth century. It cannot be maintained that they continued to inhabit Moesia after it was rechristened Dacia ; for we know that province to have been submerged by Slav invasions and to have reemerged long before the period in question as one of the most purely Slavonic states in Europe. There is probably no other Roman province in Europe where so many important towns so completely lost their former character and even name. Thus the very theorists who have banished the Romanians from Transylvania for lack of records, are driven to admit an even more complete and far more perplexing lack of records regarding the Romanians in their alleged Balkan home [the two Moesias were the territory of Bulgaria and part of Yugoslavia of the present day].

"But quite apart from this, the theory involves six quite distinct stages of emigration — first, the settlement of Dacia by the Romans ; second, complete withdrawal to the south of the Danube and eventually to the Pindus region ; third, a re-settlement by the Romanians in Moesia and other Slavized Balkan territories ; fourth, a return of these populations to the north of the Danube through Wallachia into Transylvania, in the early thirteenth century ; fifth, a re-migration from Transylvania into Wallachia at the close of the same century ; sixth, the gradual migration of Romanians from the south into Transylvania ever since that time. The last process is the only one of the whole chain which is susceptible to complete historic truth."

Seton-Watson says that without desiring to dogmatize on a subject which has been rightly described as "an enigma of the Middle Ages", he ventured to think that a much more *logical* and *simple* explanation was provided by the assumption that the modern Romanians, who fell into two main groups — the so-called Daco-Romanians and Macedo-Romanians — owed their survival in each case to the shelter provided by high mountain ranges, inhospitable and difficult of access in early times — in the south the Pindus, in the north the Carpathians. Transylvania stood out as a mountainous island on the physical map of Europe, surrounded on three sides by great plains. "What more natural than that it should serve as a refuge during the long centuries of invasion, and that the survivors should issue forth into the plains when at last the tide of invasion began to subside?"

R. W. Seton-Watson might have added that the thick forests of that time could also have served as places of refuge for the local inhabitants. His son, Professor Hugh Seton-Watson, says in his *Eastern Europe 1918-1941* (Cambridge, 1945), that:

> The proportion of Romanians or Dacians to Hungarians in these earlier centuries is the subject of acrimonious controversy between Hungarian and Romanian historians, the former claiming that the Romanians did not enter Transylvania until much later. In the absence of conclusive evidence it seems reasonable to suppose that a substantial Dacian population remained there uninterrupted, but whether it always outnumbered the Hungarians it is impossible to say.

R. W. Seton-Watson has referred to the absence of "archaeological remains" as clues to what happened in Romania, as it is now called, after the withdrawal of the Romans, but the book from which I have been quoting was written fifty years ago, and since then a great deal of "spade work" has thrown new light on the settlements that survived during the centuries that followed the withdrawal. When I was in Cluj-Napoca, the capital of Transylvania, in 1982 Dr. Hadrian Daicoviciu, Director of the Museum of the History of Transylvania, told me that more than a hundred archaeological discoveries had proved "beyond any doubt" the continuation of the Dacian element in the population under Roman rule and another 150 archaeological discoveries after the withdrawal of the Romans showed the continuation of this Dacian element, in addition to that of others who had entered the territory.

In the summer of 1980 an important archaeological discovery at Alba Iulia, an important centre in Transylvania, brought to light important new evidence of the continuation of the life of the inhabitants of this area after the withdrawal of the Romans. When a burial ground was excavated 450 cremation and inhumation graves were found — 75 belonged to the second and third centuries, 195 to the 7th-10th centuries and 180 to the 11th and 12th centuries. The inventory of the graves, as well as the complete absence of weapons, proved that the graves belonged to a peaceful, sedentary population of land-tillers and animal breeders, as the 7th-12th century Romanian population was. Dr. Ştefan Pascu, a member of the Romanian Academy who is a specialist in the medieval history of Transylvania — I have discussed Romanian history with him a number of times — described the discovery of the graves as "one of the most valuable archaeological finds made in Romania during the last few years. This is the first time that such a large number of graves has been discovered in a limited area. Likewise, we have noted that the graves belong to various periods, lying over Roman graves. The finds at Alba Iulia elucidate numerous questions and bring new data regarding the history and continuity of the Romanian people. It is known that very few data about the seventh and eighth centuries were available. This was the main reason that made several foreign historians question the continuity of the Romanians in the Alba zone. This necropolis belies once and for all such erroneous theories".

We should now consider the relationship of the Hungarians and Romanians in Transylvania throughout the centuries because only in this way is it possible to assess the validity of present-day agitation by Hungarian *émigrés* and others about the treatment of the Hungarian minority in Transylvania, the largest minority, incidentally, in Europe. According to the 1977 census, Hungarians, who number 1,706,874, comprise 7.9 per cent of the population. Most of them still live in Transylvania. It is not a matter of dispute that under the Ottoman, Austrian, or Hungarian overlordship Romanians in Transylvania were always in an inferior position, being regarded as an inferior race to the Hungarians, who considered themselves to be "noble". In discussing this problem I prefer to quote Western commentators. On page 377 of his *History of the Roumanians* R. W. Seton-Watson refers to "The outrageous treatment meted out to the Roumanians of Transylvania by successive Hungarian governments" and also to the "racial fanaticism" of the Magyars (p. 471). An earlier traveller in Transylvania, Charles Boner, author of *Transylvania : its Products and its People* (London, 1865) said that :

> With the Hungarian, every question becomes crystalised into one of nationality : this warps his judgement, for he thus regards even those which are most diverging from one sole special point of view. Argument is then at an end, and a rabid state begins... Owing to this extreme party feeling, the Hungarian is not at all reliable in his statement of a case ; circumstances which tell against him are left out altogether. All relate their story in one way, and keep to it. They do not observe the same honesty in dealing with political questions as they would consider themselves bound to do in transactions of social life...

Boner was discussing Hungarian-Austrian relations in regard to Transylvania more than a century ago but

INTRODUCTION 23

they could equally apply to Hungarian-Romanian relations today. The Hungarian government itself is not directly involved in the agitation about Transylvania carried on by *émigrés* but it cannot help being affected by them, as I will point out a little later in this Introduction.

When Transylvania was incorporated into Hungary in 1865 the plight of the Romanian majority was at its worst. A rigorous campaign of Magyarization was carried out. The Budapest parliament voted for the Magyarization of the names of Transylvanian towns and villages. Romanian family names were Magyarized extensively. Railway stations were given Hungarian names. The Romanian Press was banned and so was the use of the mother tongue in Romanian schools. As R. W. Seton-Watson points out in his history

> The Romanian language was not tolerated officially. Public notices, and even danger warnings, whether on a railway, in a post-office or on the streets were exclusively Magyar. Expulsions were frequent, from schools or seminaries, of young men who dared to use their mother tongue or to speak it "ostentatiously" in the streets, Official sanction was persistently withheld from the formation of Romanian societies. There were continual incidents due to the prohibition of Romanian songs or national colours.

Among those who protested against this persecution of the Romanian population of Transylvania was the great Russian writer Leo Tolstoy. R. W. Seton-Watson points out that some years before the First World War, at Brad, a small girl of six was arrested by gendarmes for wearing Romanian colours in her hair : father, mother and nurse were fined and sent to gaol for three or four days, and the father was suspended from his post as secretary of the commune.

These measures were strongly opposed by the Romanians in Transylvania but there was little they could do about it until the end of the First World War enabled them to break their chains. The situation of the Romanians then, and that of the present-day Hungarian minority in Romania, principally Transylvania, who are taught in their own language, have their own opera house and theatres, newspapers, books and broadcasts in Hungarian, and their own representatives in the Grand National Assembly (Parliament), could not now be more different. Another disadvantage of the Romanians under Maygar rule was that they were not entitled to settle in towns or practise certain trades.

There were three privileged nations in Transylvania under Hungarian rule: the Magyars themselves, the Szeklers and the Saxons. The Szeklers (Székelys in Hungarian) have had their origin ascribed to the Huns, Avars, Pechenegs, Khazars and other early races, but they are probably a Magyarized Turki people. They were used by the Magyars as border guards, and like the Hungarians themselves, were classed as "noble" in the technical sense, which meant that they were exempt from taxation. The third group, the Saxons, were given special privileges as an inducement to settle in Transylvania. There has been a German presence in Romania for 800 years.

The Romanians in Transylvania ("despised helots" in R. W. Seton-Watson's words) belonged, in the main, to the Orthodox faith, which was not among the "four received religions", namely the Evangelical (Reformed or Calvinist), the Lutheran or that of the Augsburg Confession, the Roman Catholic, and the Unitarian or Antitrinitarian. Under the Hungarians before the Reformation, and the Habsburgs later, strong efforts were made by the authorities to persuade the Romanians to embrace Roman Catholicism, but as they saw this as the religion of their masters, they resisted. Eventually, many of the Orthodox were persuaded to form the Uniate Church which was under the Holy See but in which the liturgy and canon law remained untouched, as also the marriage of the clergy, the wearing of beards, the internal arrangement of churches and similar points of external detail. The union was legalized by an imperial diploma of Leopold I, issued on February 16, 1699, announcing that the Uniates were to enjoy the same Christian freedom "as the members of the Latin rite", and enjoined respect for the new privileges upon all officials and prelates of the principality.

The census of December 29, 1930, shows that there were 1,426,000 members of the Uniate (Greek Catholic) Church in Romania, second in number only to the Orthodox (13,200,000) and before the Roman Catholics (1,200,000). In fourth place were the Calvinists (720,000). However, the Uniate Church disintegrated after the Second World War and is not shown in statistics of the main denominations.

As I point out in *Romanian Journey,* the religious situation in present-day Romania requires some explanation. According to the Constitution, freedom of religious worship is guaranteed to all Romanian citizens. The largest Church in Romania is still the Orthodox, to which eighty per cent of the believers belong, followed by the Roman Catholic (1,300,000 members) and then by the Reformed (Presbyterian), with between 700,000 and 800,000 members, an indication that this Church has maintained its strength during the past fifty years. The bulk of the worshippers at Roman Catholic and Reformed Churches are Hungarians. A decree acknowledges freedom of organization for fourteen religious bodies: the Romanian Orthodox Church, the Armenian Gregorian Church, the Old Rite Christian Church, the Evangelical Church, the Lutheran Synodal Presbyterian Church, the Reformed Church (Calvinist), the Unitarian Church, the Christian Baptist Cult, the Seventh Day Adventist Cult, the Pentecostal Cult, the Christian Cult according to the Gospel, the Jewish Cult and the Muslim Cult. The Serbian Orthodox Vicariate also operates within the law.

These Churches (or Cults as the Romanian Government terms them) have advantages which are unknown to their counterparts in the West. Not only does the State pay one-third of the salaries of the clergy but it repairs their churches, usually with the help of the congregation, and it also builds new churches for them. The Reformed Church has been particularly helped in this way during the past thirty years. But what about churches which do not come within the favoured fourteen? They are not recognized but they still have freedom of worship. Some of the smaller evangelical churches have complained about rough treatment by the authorities, but where there have been incidents of this kind, I am told, the dispute was not about religion but about some other matter, such as the right to emigrate to the United States. The only thing that the law prohibits with regard to religious bodies is proselytism, "which affects mutual relations and violates the faithful's conscience".

According to an official booklet:

> None of the religious bodies is prevented from carrying out its missionary-pastoral work. Whereas in the period between the two World Wars, the neo-Protestant cults, for instance, were regarded as simple "religious associations", being often called sects and treated as such; during the decades of new life in Romania they have achieved the status of cults being totally equal with the others. The number of their members has increased considerably. Thus, if in 1938 the number of Baptists in Romania was approximately 43,000, today it exceeds 120,000.

In the course of my research I have interviewed bishops in the Roman Catholic, Reformed, and Lutheran Churches, a Muslim Imam, and members of the Orthodox clergy. All confirmed that there was not religious persecution and that relations between Church and State were good.

INTRODUCTION

The cause of the Hungarian minority in Romania has been taken up by the Minority Rights Group, which has published "The Hungarians of Romania" by Mr George Schöpflin, Joint Lecturer in the Political Institutions of Eastern Europe at the London School of Economics and East European Studies, London University. Among the main grievances he outlines the merging of the Hungarian Bolyai University with the Romanian Babeş University in 1959 and the reorganization, later abolition, of the Hungarian Autonomous Province. But it is on the international aspect that Mr Schöpflin is most interesting. He says that

> The Transylvanian question has been enormously complicated by its international ramifications. It is probably no exaggeration that the absence of good will, which is so characteristic of the situation, derives above all from a persistent Romanian fear that the question has not been irrevocably settled and that one day, using the existence of the minority as the pretext, the Hungarian state may once again claim the province. No amount of disclaiming from Budapest can dispel this sense of insecurity... This fear has been exacerbated by the invisible role that Transylvania has played in the triangular relationship among Romania, Hungary and the Soviet Union. Just as the Hungarian state argues that it has a certain *locus standi* vis-à-vis the Hungarians of Transylvania, so the Romanian state claims a similar status vis-à-vis the Romanians of Bessarabia, the Moldavian SSR in the Soviet Union, to whom the status of Romanian nationality is entirely denied by the Soviet authorities [Bessarabia has at various times been in Russian and Romanian hands but was annexed by the Russians in 1944]. The Kremlin has thus used two latent irredentist issues to exert pressure on Romania and to ensure Hungary's loyalty. On a number of occasions in the past, the Soviet Union has tacitly encouraged the Hungarian party to express criticism of the Romanian party in international communist terms — criticism that was automatically translated by public opinion in both states as criticism in national terms, i.e. focused on Trans-

ylvania... The developments of the last few years have unquestionably aroused opinion in Hungary — often grossly misinformed — to the point where it is acting as a major source of pressure on the Budapest government to do something about Transylvania; and it is inevitable that the Soviet Union should be drawn into this dispute, with serious consequences for Romania.

It seemed to me, after considering the views of both sides in this dispute, that the best way to find out what the Hungarians in Romania thought of their treatment, good, bad, or indifferent, was to go there and ask them rather than rely on statements made abroad by Hungarians or Hungarian sympathizers. My latest visit was made in 1982-3 ; earlier visits were made in the 1960s and 1970s. The results of these surveys are published in *Romanian Journey*. The many Hungarians I spoke to rejected the views of the *émigrés*, denied that they were at a cultural disadvantage, and said that they had the same career opportunities as other members of the community. I paid particular attention to the views of the editor of the leading Hungarian daily paper *Elöre*, Mr Silagy Desideriu, and other Hungarian journalists because, from letters by readers, they are in a better position than most to know what people think. In brief, the Hungarians in Romania do not complain about their treatment. If they did I would say so and give their reasons for the complaints.

The Romanians have little doubt that the Russians are adding fuel to the fire in the continuing dispute about the status of Hungarians — or rather Romanian citizens of Hungarian descent — in Romania. In order to understand the reason for this it is necessary to go back to the early 1950s. In his book *The Imperialist Revolutionaries* (London, 1980) Hugh Seton-Watson said that Romania was the country in which in the 1950s the process of destruction of national culture went furthest ; the national hatred of Romanians against Russians was second only to that of Poles. The Soviet rulers forced the Romanian communists not only to break off cultural relations with France and Italy, but also to rewrite Romanian history and to remould the Romanian language. The aim was not merely to extol communism and the Soviet régime, but also to show that Romanian culture was mainly Slav, and that the brief historical benefactor of the Romanians had been "the great Russian people". Russian was also given first place among the foreign languages taught in Romanian schools. The results were profoundly counterproductive. "In 1963 conflict between the Romanian and Soviet communist leaderships were brought about by economic causes : the Romanians bitterly opposed a plan for economic specialization within the 'socialist camp' that (whatever its merits in economic theory) would have frustrated the Romanian communist plan for large-scale and diversified (even if economically less rational) industrialization. They were able to resist Soviet pressure because the Soviet leaders were preoccupied with their quarrel with the Chinese communists, with whom the Romanians succeeded in maintaining independent contacts. Once the conflict had broken out for economic reasons, it developed cultural and political aspects, which were tolerated by the government. Writers and literary critics busily re-Latinized the language, and historians rectified the re-writing of history. There were even occasional public mentions of the Bessarabian question. In the Moldavian SSR, as this territory — divested of the regions of Ukrainian population at its northern and southern extremities — was called, the Soviet authorities had fostered the myths of a separate Moldavian nation and Moldavian language. These absurd historical distortions infuriated all thinking Romanians, and suitable quotations were found from Karl Marx to show that he had considered Bessarabia a victim of the Russian tsars."

The plan for economic specialization to which Professor Seton-Watson refers was for Romania to become the granary of the East European bloc dominated by Russia while industrialization proceeded elsewhere. It is interesting to see history repeating itself here, because Romania was used for precisely the same purpose by the Ottoman Empire. The Romanians could not then resist the Turkish demands but they did the Russian in the language of orthodox Marxism. It was obvious to the Romanians that if they filled the role assigned to them by the Russians they would become a client state, relying on raw materials that could be cut off at any time if they stepped out of line. Tension between the two countries increased after the invasion of Czechoslovakia by the Soviet Union and her allies in the Warsaw Pact in 1968, Romania alone abstaining, although a member of the Pact, mainly on the grounds that no country has the right to interfere in the affairs of another country. For a time it looked as if Romania would herself be invaded but the threat receded, although it has been revived at least twice to my knowledge. There has, of course, to be some reason given for Russian intervention in the affairs of another country, and this usually takes the form of an "invitation" from some dissident element. The Romanians are only too well aware that an "invitation" could be manufactured on the pretext that the Hungarians in Romania were being persecuted, so they have taken the greatest care that such an opportunity is not presented. Despite this, reports still appear in the Western Press about alleged persecution of the Hungarians in Romania. Examples are "Hungarian protest at 'extinction'", from David Blow, in Vienna, in *The Times* of November 22, 1982, and "Unrest in Romania" by Lajos Lederer, a Hungarian, in the *Observer* of February 6, 1983. Mr Lederer's story started "Hungary's bad relations with Romania have deteriorated further because of increased persecution of the Hungarian minority in Romania." I visited Romania after this story appeared and could not find any evidence for the allegation. Rather more sensational was a report, published in a number of papers in the West early in February, 1983, that there had been a revolt in the Romanian army and even an assassination attempt on the life of President Nicolae Ceauşescu. In the *Guardian* of February 8, 1983, Hella Pick, the paper's specialist on Eastern affairs, said that "Reports first emerged on Friday saying that there had been an attempted military coup in Romania in the second half of January, and that a number of army officers had been executed after the plot was uncovered. An alternative version says that there was an assassination attempt against the President himself. By yesterday afternoon, U.S. officials were saying that one or another of these plot reports had arrived in Washington from at least 10 different sources, but none had been substantiated. In London the Foreign Office had no independent evidence to support these reports..." One report said that a number of generals had been executed and others arrested. I made my own inquiries at a high level in Bucharest and was assured that there was no truth in these reports of an army revolt. The President had the rank of General in the Romanian army, I was told, and he had strong personal support in the army. Within a day denials came from Romanian embassies in Western Europe. In London an Embassy spokesman said "There is no truth in such reports, which are the fabrications of anti-Romanian circles, and should be seen as a dirty way of smearing the Romanian leader" (The *Guardian* of February 9).

Within a few days speculation ceased when it was realized that the story of the coup was an invention. What I found particularly interesting was the statement that reports of the "coup" had arrived in Washington "from at least 10 different sources". This suggests to me that the stories had been planted there. But who did the planting ? Apart from Hungarian dissidents living abroad there are Romanian dissidents, such as former members of the Iron Guard and fascists who supported the Nazis. These are comparatively powerless but the Russians, who use such dissidents, are not.

I have given these details, with source references, to see how an impression can be formed that Romania is a country where the Hungarian minority is persecuted, there is unrest, and the army is in a state of revolt. Thus an atmosphere is created in which the Russians can be seen as having the right to intervene to restore harmony in Eastern Europe. Such an interpretation, I suggest, is not only wrong but highly dangerous to the peace of the world.

What should be kept in mind is that each of these reports is untrue, but if an allegation is repeated often enough — that of the persecution of the Hungarians, for instance — it can come to be believed by people who are not in a position to make their own inquiries. Certain writers who have been invited by the Romanians to make their inquiries on the spot to test these stories about a persecuted minority have refused on the grounds that "they have their own sources". It would be interesting to know what they are.

The irritation of the Russians with the Romanians is understandable from the Russian viewpoint. Romania has her own foreign policy and has refused to take sides in the dispute about leadership in the communist world. She has kept a friendly relationship with China and, nearer home, with Yugoslavia, that maverick in the communist camp. Unlike Yugoslavia, Romania is a member of the Warsaw Pact but it is a membership with a difference. She will not allow military manoeuvres on her soil nor allow the passage of other Warsaw Pact troops through Romania on the way to Bulgaria, the only other country in the East European bloc not to have Soviet troops stationed there. Understandably, the Romanians feel that if ever the Russians were allowed to take part in military exercises on her territory some excuse might be found to allow them to stay. Romania is the only East European bloc country to maintain diplomatic relations with Israel following the 1967 Israel-Arab war. This has allowed her to use her influence in bringing both sides together, as in the Camp David talks, where President Ceaușescu played a key role in the background.

The Soviet Union has found Romania an awkward ally in matters of defence. For instance, Romania will not allow missiles to be placed on her soil. While other members of the Warsaw Pact have increased their military budgets Romania decreased hers by 10 per cent annually and has now frozen the amount to be spent on arms. Demonstrations for disarmament have been given official support.

While relations between Moscow and Bucharest are fragile, Romania has taken great care not to allow herself to be wooed by the West because, if she were to succumb, that would attract quicker retribution from across the border than any other course of action. Romania, under the shrewd leadership of President Ceaușescu, has seen what can happen when a Socialist East European state has both liberal and "hard line" elements in it : Russian pressure is exerted to smother the liberals and to promote the hard liners, with pro-Moscow sympathies, to the seats of power. Romania does not have such conflicting interests in the higher echelons of the Communist Party and the Government. There is strict internal control with a surprisingly liberal foreign policy, as an Austrian diplomat once pointed out to me in Vienna. Government is on orthodox Marxist lines.

In recent years, under the influence of tourism and Western films and television serials, the régime has become much more relaxed than it was. Further relaxation can be expected if the international situation does not deteriorate.

I have dealt with some of the problems facing modern Romania in detail, and in advance, so that as the pages that follow are turned the reader can understand better what gave rise to these problems. A knowledge of the history of the Balkans is necessary before one can understand what is happening there today. A reader of some of the quality papers can be grossly misled by what he is told about the sufferings of Hungarians in modern Romania, or rather what *émigrés* are saying about the alleged suffering, if he did not know about the real suffering of Romanians under the Hungarian, Ottoman, or Austrian heel for centuries. Old wounds take a long time to heal. But heal they will if the different races of the Balkans are allowed to live together in peace without interference from beyond their boundaries.

It also needs to be pointed out that the industrial revolution in Romania only dates from the end of the Second World War and that until comparatively recently Romania was a very poor country. Although the soil is rich and she is comparatively well endowed with oil resources and minerals, Romania has been grossly exploited by foreign powers. There was also exploitation of the peasants by the landlords. Discussing peasant clothing and food standards in his book *Eastern Europe 1918-1941* Hugh Seton-Watson said that the food of the peasant population of Eastern Europe was most unsatisfactory. The smallholders hardly ever touched meat. In Romania the food of the masses is "mamaliga", a maize polenta, which is made more tasty by the addition of cheese or onions when these are obtainable. The Eastern European countries have a wealth of excellent national dishes of grilled meat and meat-and-vegetable stew, which delights the enterprising foreign visitor, but the latter did not usually realize that these dishes, although "national" in the sense that they are specific to particular countries or regions, did not reach a very large part of the "nation". The peasant masses seldom tasted them. Bad bread, cheese, onion and paprika were all that came their way for most of the year.

On matters of infant mortality and public health, Professor Seton-Watson pointed out that infant mortality in Eastern European countries was from three to four times higher than in Holland. "It is highest of all in Romania, and of the Romanian provinces the worst is Bessarabia [annexed shortly after this was written by Russia]. Tuberculosis is the scourge of the peasant masses. It is high in all the countries under review, particularly in such miserably poor regions as Montenegro. In the Romanian plains of Wallachia and Moldavia a disease called pellagra is not uncommon. It is due to bad nourishment, and seems to be connected with the unvaried consumption of badly prepared maize flour. It is occasionally found in other European countries such as Italy and Spain, but much the highest rate of occurrence in Europe is that of Romania."

I could give other examples of great poverty and hardship from Professor Seton-Watson's book but these will suffice. He is referring, of course, to conditions as they were forty to fifty years ago, but they are much improved today. I have eaten in Romanian households in various parts of the country, sometimes arriving unannounced with my guide, and can testify that something much better than mamaliga now comes out of the pot.

Western visitors uninvolved in local disputes have, in the past century, provided some of the best evidence of conditions as they were in Romania, and this helps us to gain a historical perspective. Mrs Emily Gerard, the English wife of the Austrian commander of the cavalry brigade in Transylvania in 1883, said in *The Land Beyond the Forest* (London and Edinburgh, 1888) that "Of pride the Romanian has little idea as yet. He has too long been treated as a degraded and serf-like being." But she also said that "It is scarcely hazardous to prophesy that this people have a great future before them, and that a day will come when, other nations having degenerated and spent their strength, these descendants of the ancient Romans, rising phoenix-like from their ashes, will step forward with a whole fund of latent power and virgin material, to rule as masters where formerly they crouched as slaves."

A distinguished Irish scholar, Dr. Walter Starkie, has pointed out that "Transylvania has always been separate from Hungary in its traditions, though the Magyars were in the ascendancy ; it has always been a centre of toleration and religious liberty in comparison with other parts of the country. But this toleration extended only to the Magyars, Saxons and Szekels (Szeklers). The Wallachs were considered to be a subject race, for they were not of noble blood, according to their masters" (*Raggle-Taggle. Adventures with a Fiddle in Hungary and Rumania*, London, 1933).

The late Lord Snow (C. P. Snow) said in his foreword to William Forwood's *Romanian Invitation* (London, 1968) that

> Romania is unique. It lies in the heartland of Slavonic Europe, but it is quite different from the Slav countries — and I can say that, since I know the Slavs and love them. The Roman legions left their own Latin language in Romania, the most remote Latin outpost of the Empire. They left more than that. To this day, Romania not only speaks a language very much like Italian, but has a population which possesses the sparkle, the intelligence, the physical appearance that one meets in Tuscany and the Lombard plain. In the long run they have everything — natural riches, great scenic variety, widespread education, gifted people — which will make for a brilliant future.

R. W. Seton-Watson ended his *History of the Roumanians*, written between the wars, with the statement that

> Gigantic problems of reconstruction confronted the new country, and after fifteen years are still to a great extent unsolved. Two generations of peace and clean government might make of Roumania an earthly paradise, for she has great natural resources

and all that is necessary to a well ordered economy. But her chief asset is the Roumanian peasant, who amid adverse political surroundings has shown a virility and endurance that border on the miraculous.

Professor Hugh Seton-Watson added in *Eastern Europe 1918-1941* that

> The process of decay has gone further in Roumania than in other parts of Eastern Europe. No progress will be made until the old governing class disappears, and a new one is trained to take its place. The period of transition will be long and bloody, but when it is accomplished the great energies and qualities of the Roumanian people, the second most numerous and perhaps the most naturally talented in all Eastern Europe, will assure to it that honourable position which it has not yet been able to attain.

The "old governing class" disappeared a few years after this book was written. It is still too early to evaluate the total performance of the new régime, but one can say, without fear of contradiction, that the country has been transformed. But economic problems have been only partly solved : delay has been caused by the aftermath of the Cold War and by a world recession. In my Commentary at the end of the book I will deal with some of the problems and prospects of present-day Romania and this will, I hope, contain material needed for a history of the country to be written in the future. The views expressed in this Introduction are my own and it should not be thought that they have been unduly influenced by historians whom I have interviewed in Romania. Whenever possible I have chosen to quote the words of Western commentators because they cannot be accused of nationalistic bias. I am indebted to Mr I. Donat, a researcher at the Institute of History in Bucharest, now retired, for the passages on the geography of Romania, taken from his Introduction to *The History of the Romanian People*.

In my Commentary at the end of the book I refer to the disparaging remarks about modern Romania made by some *émigrés*. However, this is not the whole of the story. There are *émigrés* who retain a deep affection for the land of their birth, and its history, and this was shown by the 150 people, mostly academics, from twenty countries who attended, in September 1983, an international symposium in Vienna. It lasted for five days and marked the part Romanian armies played in the second siege of Vienna by the Ottoman Empire in 1683. It was the 300th anniversary and was celebrated in some style, both by the Austrians and visitors from abroad.

The symposium was held under the title "Cantacuzino" — The Romanians-Europe' Defenders —, the Prince concerned being Şerban Cantacuzino, ruler of Wallachia. He led an army of 4,000 men from Wallachia. In addition, there were armies of 2,000 men from Moldavia, led by Prince Gheorghe Duca, and 6,000 from Transylvania led by the Hungarian Prince Michael, or Mihail Apafi (sometimes spelt Apaffy). The Christians, who were bound by treaty with the Turks to assist their armies, were most unenthusiastic allies, doing all they could to assist the defenders. Their activities were confined to engineering operations : bridge building, cutting wood, and transport. When they were forced to take part in attacks on the city the assaults usually petered out or were unsuccessful in some other way. What was more important was that the Romanians managed to get a steady supply of intelligence information about Ottoman troop movements to the besieged.

In an official booklet published by the Federal Press Service in Vienna in 1982 to mark the 300th anniversary of the siege the following year it is stated that "The Turks' Christian auxiliaries proved the weak point in the besiegers' forces. Some of their carters were caught selling cattle to the townsmen. They received three hundred strokes of the stick."

It is now known that there was a fourth Romanian Army, part of that of John Sobieski III, King of Poland, who led an army of 36,000 men, of which 4,000 Romanians comprised the Light Cavalry section. This information has been obtained recently from Polish sources by Dr. Constantin Rezachevici, of the Institute of History, Bucharest, and, naturally, these Romanians, fighting with the Poles, played a more heroic role, in keeping with their character, than their fellow countrymen, who, forced to follow the Turks, were more engaged in sabotage than fighting.

The Polish army played a vital part in the relief of the siege. The Turkish army consisted of about 250,000 fighting men and 60,000 baggage train. They achieved some limited successes but were unable to breach the walls. In the final stages of the siege Count Ernst Rudiger Starhemberg, the garrison commander, had no more than 4,000 very exhausted men at his disposal. By September 11 between 65,000 and 80,000 men of the relieving force were concentrated on the ridges of the Vienna woods to do battle for the city.

The Turks had, unwisely, left the heights around the city unoccupied. The Polish horse held the extreme right flank. Contrary to every basic rule of strategy, Kara Mustafa, the Turkish Grand Vizir did not face the relieving force with all his available strength. Instead he decided to fight on two fronts by continuing to let 30,000 Janissaries batter against the walls of Vienna. The advance, when the battle began on the morning of September 12, was initiated by the cavalry on the left. About four o'clock the relieving army broke into the Turkish camp. The Grand Vizir precipitately abandoned the field. The remainder of the Turkish army took to disorderly flight eastward. Instead of pursuing the defeated foe, Sobieski allowed his troops to loot the enemy's camp. He himself captured Kara Mustafa's own complement of tents. The enormous value of this piece of booty is known from the letters he wrote to his wife immediately after the battle. It is safe to assume that the Romanian cavalry were among those who enriched themselves on goods captured from the Turks. News of the pillage by the Poles and Romanians was received very sourly because other units were only allowed next day to fetch their share.

I took part in the symposium on the siege in Vienna and attended a moving ceremony in a suburb in a spot that was once wooded (the Schönbrunn Woods) and where Prince Șerban Cantacuzino left a monumental cross as a symbol of the Anti-Ottoman victory. This cross was later destroyed, but a replica of it now stands in a shrine. A bronze bust of the Prince was unveiled by the Romanian Orthodox Archbishop of Paris, Adrian Hrițcu, who is responsible for the Romanian Orthodox churches outside the country.

The victory of the Allied army effected a crucial change in European politics of the expiring seventeenth century. With its defeat before the gates of Vienna the Ottoman Empire reached the limits of its power and boundless expansion. What followed was incessant retreat. The beneficiaries of this repulse were not only the Habsburg state, able decisively to broaden its basis, but Tsarist Russia too. Romania was not able to benefit to a corresponding extent, if at all, but in the siege of Vienna the Romanians were able to demonstrate that they were indeed Europe's defenders, just as they were through the exploits of Mircea the Old, Stephen the Great and Vlad the Impaler against the Turks.

The next symposium for the group which organized the event in Vienna was arranged for August 1984, in Toronto, Canada.

The concluding chapter of this book before my Commentary deals with culture and science. This, to the Western reader, may seem out of place in a history book but anyone in a country in the Eastern Bloc would not share this view. Culture is seen as an essential part of national life; indeed, it is regarded as a manifestation of it. For this reason, folk dancing is encouraged and there are many more groups of folk dancers and singers in Romania than there are in, say, the United Kingdom. Young people have their rock groups, but if they attend a country wedding they will follow the bridal procession dancing the *hora*, a traditional folk dance.

Romania has a number of "firsts" in inventions, some of which are given in the chapter on culture and science. For instance, a Latin manuscript of 1395 at the National Library in Paris records the first use ever of explosives in mining "in the area lying between Hungary and the mouths of the Danube", therefore in Transylvania. To facilitate conveyance of gold ore from the mines in the Apuseni Mountains in the sixteenth century, Romanian carpenters made a railway car completely of wood which was the first railway vehicle in the history of technology. "The car of Brad" is exhibited at the Museum of Transport in West Berlin. In 1453 Orban the Dacian, a cannoneer in the service of the Ottoman Empire, made the first high-power cannons, thus opening the history of heavy artillery. Between 1529 and 1555 Conrad Haas of Sibiu devised the first multiple stage rockets in the history of technology equipped with delta-shaped wings. In 1857 Bucharest was the first town in the world to use kerosene for public lighting and in 1884 Timișoara was the first town in Europe to have its streets lit by electricity.

Romanian scientists have made some notable discoveries in medicine. In 1889 Victor Babeș published, jointly with A. V. Cornil, the first systematic treatise on bacteriology showing that "there are micro-organisms that can develop substances able to stop the development and counteract the noxious character of other micro-organisms". A year earlier Babeș had discovered the group of endoglobular parasites eventually named *babeși*. In 1909 the Romanian physician Constantin I. Parhon jointly with M. Goldstein published in Paris the first treatise on endocrinology in the world. The physiologist Nicolae Paulescu did notable work in Paris on the preparation of a pancreas extract which culminated later, and in another country, in the discovery of insulin. In 1942 Ştefan Nicolau organized in Bucharest the first chair of microbiology in the world. Other instances of the creative powers of the Romanians could be given but these will suffice.

The chapters that follow were written by a panel of Romanian historians, but here and there I have added a few sentences of explanation where these were necessary. When I have quoted from the works of British or other historians or scholars I have made this fact plain. I have made some additions to the chapter on culture and science in Romania and to the chapter on the creation of Socialist Romania.

Readers should remember that Muntenia is an old name for Wallachia and Pannonia an old name for the area covered by contemporary Hungary.

CHAPTER ONE

FROM THE EARLY INHABITANTS TO THE DACIANS

ROMANIA'S territory was already inhabited when, physically and spiritually, man was evolving from his animal condition, a phenomenon which occurred throughout the Pleistocene period of the Quaternary geological era. This period began some three million years ago and ended about ten thousand years ago. As regards climate, the Quaternary era witnessed repeated glaciations.

The period between man's appearance in the Carpatho-Danubian area and the beginning of Geto-Dacian political formations is the age when the primitive commune, the socio-economic formation of the longest duration, was formed and developed. The primitive commune was based on common ownership of means of production; as the process of social differentiation intensified, the principle of kinship was replaced by the territorial principle. The progress made by the forces of production, the invention and improvement of farming implements, the working of copper, bronze, and iron, among other factors, induced changes in the social pattern so that the first antagonistic classes in history made their appearance at the close of this period.

1. Early Inhabitants. The Stone Age

RECENT finds on Romanian territory and around it show that the Carpatho-Danubian area was long ago integrated in the wide geographical area over which the early stages of the anthropogenic process unfolded.

Primitive chipped stone tools discovered in the lower reaches of the River Olt, for example, in the valley of the River Dîrjov, a left-bank tributary, and at Bugiuleşti on the right bank of the Olt, strongly favour the assumption that early *homo erectus*, who represents the second stage of anthropogenesis, lived also in this country in the course of his peregrinations.

A denser and more permanent population of the Carpatho-Danubian area and of the surrounding territory is found after the next "leap" of anthropogenesis which turned *homo erectus* into the more developed type of man, the Neanderthal type. Neanderthal man settled on this territory, dwelling in caves (for example, at Ohaba-Ponor in Transylvania, Baia de Fier in Oltenia, Cheia and La Adam in Dobrudja) as well as in the open air (for example, at La Izvor, Ripiceni village, on the River Prut). Over most of Romania's territory we find traces of his activities at the beginning of the last glaciation (conventional date : ca. 70,000). Neanderthal men consequently constitutes the first denser human population in Romania.

The presence of so-called *homo sapiens fossilis* (fossil intelligent man) some 35-40,000 years ago is recorded on the European continent. Romania's territory was intermittently traversed and inhabited by such fully evolved men in various stages of cultural development. They were now organized in maternal clans founded on kinship, the first form of crystallized society.

Having reached a high technical level in the working of stone tools by flaking, and of bone, horn, and ivory tools by cutting and polishing, *homo sapiens fossilis* attained an advanced stage of the still primitive hunter and food gatherer's economy. The skull found in the Cioclovina cave in Transylvania is a reliable testimony to the existence of fully evolved man on Romania's territory.

The essential differentiation wrought at the time is the division of mankind over wide geographical areas into three great fundamental races (white, yellow, and black). Romanian territory has been integrated in the Eurasian area of the Europoid (white or leucodermous) race.

The end of the last glacial (Würm) subcycle is the beginning of the present-day geological period (the Holocene). Seriously affected by the effects of glaciation owing to its northern position, Europe underwent profound transformations in its climate, its physical and geographical aspect, its fauna and flora. In this period, man, now fully evolved and having to live through conditions which made great demands on his inventiveness and powers of adaptation, changed from a creature who took his food from nature's reserves directly (by hunting or food gathering) into a quasi-creator of his food sources, by growing plants and raising the animals he had tamed. Archaeologically, he passed from the Palaeolithic stage (the Old Stone Age) to the Neolithic (the New Stone Age).

The New Stone Age on Romanian territory, as elsewhere, was an age when these places were densely and permanently populated, for this was now possible owing to the new forms of a complex productive economy (the growing of plants and the breeding of domesticated animals) which increasingly favoured the sedentary way of life. In the fourth millennium B.C. Romania and the surrounding regions seem to have become the homeland of Neolithic tribes which were to remain at this stage until the second millennium B.C.

During that period the early primitive plant growers and animal raisers who inhabited these places developed a material and spiritual culture which was among the most advanced on the continent of Europe. The first flow of Neolithic "settlers" in the area between the Tisa and the eastern Bug reached here from the south by crossing present-day Serbia and Bulgaria. They brought with them a fairly advanced Neolithic culture (named the Criş culture on Romanian territory), with a comparatively well developed pottery, including painted ware characteristic of the evolution of the whole Neolithic period in Romania and, at the same time, proof of its high level. Against this background, the Mediterranean racial type (as a sub-branch of the great Europoid race) prevails in this part of Europe and has preserved its predominance over Romanian territory to this day.

The movement and mixing of tribes and the contacts between cultures continued in the Neolithic period, though over more restricted geographical areas and with more limited effects. On Romania's territory we further find that populations and cultural elements continued to intrude from the south (the Balkan Peninsula) from where cultural innovations unceasingly penetrated, and also from the north-west, with Europe's continental core exerting pressure.

The mixture of tribes and cultures brought about the development of a widespread and mature Neolithic culture on Romanian soil under the continued southern cultural influences that reached this territory through the Danube plain. Neolithic cultures are characteristic of these areas. They are all distinguished through the high level of the technique of painting on burnt-clay vases. Neither the Carpathian ranges, whether western, southern, or eastern, nor the great gap of the Lower Danube constituted impassable frontiers, but, on the contrary, were avenues of life and culture which extended unhindered on both mountainsides and both banks.

The fundamental unity of the variegated aspects of the mature Neolithic culture within the framework of the Carpatho-Balkan regional block showed prolonged stability. The general level of culture then attained relied on the remarkable development of the two main branches of the economy — plant cultivation and stock breeding — as well as on advanced exploitation of other resources available in the territory, from among which the first metals to be worked played the most important role, as will be seen later. The gold nuggets of the gold-bearing deposits of Transylvania, like the gold dust in the sands of the streams, soon drew the attention of the Neolithic population who engaged in fairly remote intertribal exchanges right from the beginning.

Sheep, goats, cattle, and pigs were the animals mostly raised and over the widest areas, while as regards plants the primitive species of millet, wheat, and oats were soon superseded by species improved through cultivation and selection. More rational tilling of the high-quality arable land in these parts (*chernozem*) and more competent selection of the cultivated species account for the prosperity of the tribes that were bearers of the aforementioned Neolithic cultures. The data available on the intensive religious life of the population (idols, shrines, magic practices) show that it was almost exclusively centred on the fertility cult.

2. The Copper and Bronze Age

THE working of native copper was of great importance and yielded rich results ; in the Late Neolithic period it assumed considerable proportions. Copper was generally the first metal to be used by ancient man, and not only for ornaments, like gold, but also as raw material for tools. In Transylvania, Oltenia, and partly in Dobrudja, there existed and still exist substantial copper ore deposits.

Bronze metallurgy was introduced during the period of transition from the third to the second millennium B.C., consequently around the year 2000. That moment was an important turning point in the history of Europe, for it involved not only the penetration and development in these parts of the first complex metallurgy (bronze metallurgy) but also a profound ethnic and especially linguistic transformation as a result of which the foundations were laid for the formation of the peoples speaking Indo-European languages. In the Carpatho-Balkan area these were the first stages in the formation of the Thracian tribes.

The events which occurred on the territory of present-day Romania at the end of the Neolithic period are among the most reliable indications in support of the view that, on the one hand, the Neolithic populations of these regions did not speak Indo-European languages (as certain theories still contend), and were consequently pre-Indo-European from this point of view, and, on the other hand, that "Indo-Europeanization", or adoption of Indo-European languages, occurred as a consequence of the infiltration of new peoples from the east, in the last resort from a vast Eurasian area that stretched from the Lower Volga across the Aralo-Caspian steppes to the Yenisei in south-west Siberia. According to the latest investigations, it would seem that these regions were "the primitive homeland" of the peoples speaking Indo-European languages and that it is from here that their westward expansion began around 2400-2300 B.C., as approximate but well-grounded calculations have established. They were groups of semi-nomadic herdsmen with a social structure and a material and spiritual culture that differed from those of the old Neolithic population into whose territories they penetrated. And their anthropological type was also different. The pastoral character of their economy, the patriarchal and stratified structure of their society, as reflected by certain particulars of rite and ritual, evidenced by their graves covered with earthen mounds (tumuli, barrows), with the corpses strewn with red ochre; the use of the domesticated horse and before long of the first four-wheeled vehicles borrowed from the Mesopotamian East (the wheels were of compact wood and spokeless); their warlike aggressiveness heightened by the use of the stone battle axe and of the dagger (made of stone or metal) — are all strikingly different from the way of life of the Neolithic population of the Carpathians and of the Lower Danube. It is at the end of the Neolithic period that the mound-covered graves of this foreign population appear, from the Dnieper to the Danube plain and subsequently as far as eastern Hungary ; and such graves have also been found in Dobrudja and in northern Bulgaria.

However, the archaeological observations now available prove that the old Neolithic population was not destroyed or totally expelled by the newcomers, but that there was co-existence and intermingling, so that the local substratum was linguistically assimilated, itself assimilating the newcomers' culture in course of time. The process undoubtedly lasted several centuries and was of a complex character, part of the settled Neolithic population being dislodged and moving with the migration of the mobile groups of herdsmen over great distances, for considerable hordes of those herdsmen traversed the Carpatho-Danubian territory on their way to the west, that is, towards Central Europe, and also, and especially, southwards towards the Balkan Peninsula, Greece and the Aegean Sea, and generally towards the warmer districts of the eastern Mediterranean. The latter groups established liaison with the areas where the Cretan (Minoan) civilization had flourished or where the impact of that civilization had spread (in Greece proper and the islands). It was thus that a cultural "counter current" came into being, elements of a higher culture being transmitted from the more evolved southern regions to the northern ones, where the new ethnic, linguistic, and cultural synthesis took place.

At the end of the Neolithic period certain groups retaining a pastoral character spread over wide areas in Oltenia, Banat, and the Transylvanian plateau, as bearers of the Coțofeni culture. Gradually the unification process of the tribes in the regions outside the Carpathians began to take shape, so that Muntenia, Oltenia, and south-east Transylvania appeared to be occupied by the great union of Glina III tribes ; Moldavia and Dobrudja were occupied by a kindred union of tribes (Foltești) ; while on the Transylvanian plateau the group distinguished by their "dotted earthenware" was consolidated. They were all tribal unions, at times of a more marked pastoral character, at other times more agricultural. These unions were made up of various elements that had come into contact during the stage of great dislocations and were each, to a different extent and through various channels, affected by the southern cultural counter-current. Underlying it all were the traditions of the local Neolithic substratum, the ethnic and cultural contributions of the eastern nomads, and the abundant influence of southern cultures. Whatever came into being at that time outside the Carpatho-Balkan area — new syntheses generated by the same events — assumed a different aspect and encroached on this area only partially in the marginal regions. Consequently, it would appear that the regional Carpatho-Balkan bloc resumed its old individuality within the framework of the new world that was coming into being in Europe, its specific features causing it to stand apart from the surrounding regions and defining its proper Indo-European character. Subsequently, no other movement of populations was totally to dislodge the population now settled within this area. Therefore, considering that when the first scanty rays of historical records light up this area, and the presence of Thracian tribes is revealed in these parts, we must conclude that during the period under study, around 2000 B.C., the homeland of the Thracians was built up here, and from them Daco-Getian tribes were later formed in the Carpatho-Balkan area.

For about four centuries, from the seventeenth to the thirteenth centuries B.C., these tribal unions were constituted and consolidated, developing in conditions of comparative stability and peace by exploiting gold, copper, salt, pasture land, and fields. From the sixteenth to the fifteenth centuries B.C., they kept up close contact

FROM THE EARLY INHABITANTS TO THE DACIANS   51

with the early Greek world, which was fully constituted at the time in the Mycenaean civilization; they most probably exported gold and received in return quality weapons and ornaments. As has lately been shown, this was the age when the Balkan-Carpathian area was the greatest gold storehouse in Europe and when it also turned its scantier silver resources to good account.

The Thracian communities of the Bronze Age proper, well organized and usually grouped around some elementary fortifications, were in the second millennium a most flourishing European unitary centre, with a great variety of regional aspects and close mutual political and economic relations.

This was a situation that changed as a result of new displacements and new clashes of tribes, initially occurring at the two extremities of the Carpatho-Danubian bloc, the Western and Eastern extremities, its ethnical and cultural pattern being thereby modified to a bigger or smaller extent, without the bloc being wholly dislocated. It was only when these new protracted upheavals, with the intermingling of tribes they involved, had come to an end that the Geto-Dacian tribes were formed out of the early Thracian mass of the Carpatho-Balkan populations of the Bronze Age.

The developments considered here are the continental-European preliminaries to the so-called "Aegean migration", at the same time including the process of full separation, and of migration to their European settlements, of the great Indo-European peoples of antiquity — the Celts, Italics and Illyrians to the West, the Scythian-Sarmatians to the East, and the Balto-Slavs to the North. Together with them, new waves of continental-European populations were ultimately to make their way towards Greece (the Dorians) and towards Asia Minor (the Phrygians and the Armenians).

On the continent of Europe the "Aegean migration" appears to have begun in the fourteenth century B.C. with a southward and eastward movement of the powerful Central European group, known during the middle period of the Bronze Age as "the tumular grave culture", which penetrated into eastern Hungary and northern Yugoslavia. In Romania, it is interesting to note that the western "proto-Thracian" groups — Otomani in Crișana and Periam-Pecica in Banat — although pressed upon and themselves pressing on towards the east (towards the centre of the Transylvanian plateau and Oltenia) stood their ground and were even drawn, as important participants, into the process whereby a new cultural synthesis was formed in the basin of the middle Danube and the Tisa — a process which was soon to lead to the birth of the so-called early Hallstatt culture in the twelfth century B.C.

A different process occurred in the eastern area of the Carpatho-Danubian bloc, where a new westward pressure was exerted (similar to that which impelled the first Indo-Europeans into Europe around 2400 B.C.). The pressure was again started in the Middle Volga area, where in the meantime the populations that practised tumulus burial had developed in the Bronze Age into a group known as "the wooden structure tomb" group (*srubniie* in Russian), those populations almost undoubtedly representing the Iranian Indo-European branch. In their westward drive, this group reached the Dnieper, probably in the fourteenth century B.C., thus contacting the Carpatho-Danubian elements, themselves pushing eastward owing to the aforementioned western pressure. The Monteoru group, the most active in this "encounter", assimilated the eastern elements in a first stage and was dislodged in the following stage (thirteenth-twelfth centuries B.C.) when it again switched over to a predominantly pastoral way of life and changed its culture and partly its ethnical character, by mixing with the new eastern elements.

Archaeology makes it clear that about the thirteenth century B.C. a new cultural and ethnic synthesis took place between the Dnieper and the western Carpathians on the basis of the local Bronze Age cultures (mainly the Monteoru, Costişa, and Wittenberg cultures) and of certain eastern elements of the "srubnoi" complex. Archaeologists have named that synthesis Noua (on Romanian territory) and Sabatinovka (in the U.S.S.R.). Certain types of eastern bronze metallurgy practised in the Urals and the Caucasus centres thus penetrated into the Carpatho-Balkan area, primarily in the extra-Carpathian area. Consequently, it is quite clear that the new Noua-Sabatinovka complex was primarily formed on the basis of local Carpatho-Danubian elements and that contact with the groups that came from the east means that the area down to the Dnieper was connected to the Carpatho-Danubian area rather than vice versa.

The geographical spread of the Noua culture, which extended north of the Carpathians to beyond the upper Dniester and assumed a special regional aspect on the Transylvanian plateau, did not reach the western provinces of Romania — Crişana and Banat — nor the southern ones : Oltenia, Muntenia, and Dobrudja.

The period considered as the end of the Bronze Age proper, whose features, in as far as they can be determined today, is primarily characterized from the economic standpoint by a return to the predominance of the pastoral way of life — though agriculture did not die out altogether — by a marked development of bronze metallurgy (and very likely of salt extraction), and a great mobility and intermingling of tribes speaking kindred languages, though the local Carpatho-Balkan ethnical and cultural set-up was not affected. Instability continued in the following centuries but it assumed a significant historical aspect when what was rightly called the counter-offensive of the Carpathian bloc began in the twelfth century B.C. Groups of warlike herdsmen and tillers of the soil living on the western fringes of the Carpatho-Balkan bloc who were making good use of the Carpathian copper ore deposits and who, on the basis of local traditions, had achieved a new society and new cultures of the Early Hallstatt type, then started from their formative area in Slovakia's Carpathians and from the regions between the Western Mountains and the Middle Danube, including northern Yugoslavia, on a powerful eastward drive, leaving their culture on their way to the groups that had formed in the "Final Bronze Age" (the Noua-Sabatinovka group and the southern Lower Danube group); they achieved a new mobile Carpatho-Balkan unity — the Early Carpatho-Balkan Hallstatt — which showed characteristic traits in material culture and, of course, in their linguistic structure as compared with the early Central European Hallstatt. Subsequent developments show that to the west of the area they occupied there was a zone of Celtic, Italian, and Illyrian populations, and in the east — for a time only beyond the Dnieper — a zone of Iranian peoples, while in the Carpatho-Balkan area material culture and the linguistic (toponymic) and historical data discernible at that time or later suggest once again that it was the Thracian bloc that dwelt here. Proof of it lies in the fact that during the disturbances at the close of the Bronze Age, populations speaking the Thracian language or populations closely related to them (Phrygians, Myssians, and Bithynians) infiltrated into Anatolia.

3. The Iron Age

IRON Age I (so-called Early Hallstatt) lasted up to the eighth century B.C. Its salient feature was a predominantly pastoral and mobile life, the population moving from their place of settlement in search of good pasture land after each season. The settlements were extensive, mostly fortified in the Carpathian area and open in the plain, and the social structure was strongly differentiated, with chieftains recalling the Greek aristocracy of the Homeric age.

The south-eastern region of this country had to a certain extent drawn apart from the rest of the Carpatho-Danubian area as early as the final Bronze Age transition period, forging closer connections with the Balkan area. This points to an accentuated differentiation among the Thracians, if not to the very beginnings of differentiation (which might have come about when the Indo-Europeans first infiltrated here at the close of the third millennium B.C.). The Cimmerians, a people akin to but not identical with the Thracians, lived north of the Black Sea. In the last decades of the eighth century B.C. they began to withdraw from those parts and were replaced by the Scythians. By the year 600 B.C. the latter people had settled down along the Dnieper, as shown by archaeological evidence.

The Cimmerians seem to have been either a column of the Thracians which had remained in Eastern Europe at the time of the first Indo-European migration, or Thracian groups which had expanded eastward from the Carpatho-Balkan area at an earlier date (fourteenth century B.C.) or more recently (tenth and ninth centuries B.C.).

The Cimmerians were dislodged at the end of the eighth century B.C. by the Scythians, themselves pushed across the Volga from the east by other Iranian peoples. But while it is well attested that the Cimmerians had crossed the Caucasus into Urartu and Asia Minor, their westward penetration into the Carpatho-Danubian area in the eighth century B.C. is still controversial. It is most characteristic that around the supposed date of the clash between the Cimmerians and the Scythians, a number of complex and significant transformations and phenomena occurred in the Carpatho-Balkan area, though the culture and ethnical features of the Carpatho-Balkan Thracian stock clearly continued unimpaired.

During the latter half of the eighth century B.C., the Carpatho-Danubian Early Hallstatt culture underwent a number of transformations that entitle us to speak of a new period : the Middle Hallstatt. This was a comparatively short period lasting from *ca.* 750 to *ca.* 600 B.C. and ending the age of predominance of the pastoral way of life, which had begun at the close of the Bronze Age with a new expansion of this way of life. Greater mobility of the tribes once again brought about increased cultural unity throughout the Carpatho-Balkan area.

The uniformity of the cultural aspect has become known owing to the recent research of Romanian archaeologists, and was named the Basarabi culture after the finds made at Basarabi near Calafat. Obviously this culture is directly developed from a prior local stock and has given rise to all the subsequent groups of the period of full consolidation of the Geto-Dacian tribes.

During the period characterized in the wide Carpathian area by the local synthesis of Basarabi of great cultural and ethnic uniformity, the Greeks began to settle on the western and northern coasts of the Black Sea.

This is the first time that the age-old connections of the Carpatho-Danubian area with the centres of advanced civilization east of the Mediterranean and in the Aegean — connections which had formerly been established over great distances and through the intermediary of the intervening regions and populations — became direct connections, the Mediterranean civilization in its highest form, the Hellenic, being transplanted to the south-eastern maritime border of the Thracian lands.

As early as the mid-seventh century B.C., the second "wave" of the Hellenic colonization movement had dotted the coast of the Mediterranean with Greek towns. This time the wave swept over the western and northern coasts of the "landlocked sea" which the local population had named the Black Sea, this being interpreted by the Greeks as inhospitable *(axeinos)*. However, the sea soon became a Greek sea and "hospitable" *(euxeinos)*.

The Greek colonists — farmers and traders — reached Histria (at the far end of the Sinoe Gulf) and Olbia (in the Bug estuary) in the mid-seventh century B.C., coming from the Ionian Miletus in Asia Minor. Other Ionians from the same metropolis were to settle at Tomis (present-day Constantza) and Tyras (Cetatea Albă), probably in the next century, while at Callatis (Mangalia) Dorian Greeks settled, having come from the Pontic Heraclea on the southern, Anatolian, coast of the Black Sea. In the course of time a string of such colonies developed along these coasts, a phenomenon which is of considerable importance for the history of these districts. The Greek colonies became an integral part of the history of the Carpatho-Balkan area, acting as intermediaries between the mother cities that boasted a highly developed civilization and the "barbarian" world where they took root, at first through economic links and then through their political connections with the natives and their influence on the local Thracian society, which they guided towards higher forms of sociopolitical organization. On the other hand, the local Thracian environment also set its mark on the historical development of these towns : in the course of time the tribal unions of the native population, as part of which the tribal aristocracy now found new economic possibilities and a suitable political ground for consolidation and development, became "protectors" of the Greek colonies, levying "tribute" on them.

Owing to its nature and orientation, Greek colonization was restricted to the narrow strip of coast where they first occupied the land by force of arms or by understanding with the local tribes. Inland, the Greeks penetrated only as traders, which they did to great distances, first as middlemen for the goods brought from their remote homeland with which they had maintained close connection, and later by selling their own artisan production while exporting overseas the surplus of the native production obtained by barter, or the products of their work as fishermen and farmers.

The pressure and expansion of the Scythians after they had crossed the Dnieper in the sixth century B.C., were of an altogether different character. Warlike nomads organized in a tribal union of herdsmen accustomed to keep the stable agricultural population under their dominion and to exploit them, the Scythians proper ("royal" Scythians) now grazed their flocks on the steppes north of the Black Sea, making predatory excursions in order to ensure the safety of their nomadic life and to enlarge their basis of exploitation. They were in the main Iranians, with a possible Mongoloid infiltration into their leading stratum.

In the first half of the sixth century B.C. an eastern population infiltrated into the Carpatho-Danubian area. What distinguished it from the local population was, in the first place, its different burial rites (level inhumation or within barrows) with the horse, or part of it, being laid in the grave. Its armament was also more constantly and more completely Scythian. This population, traced only quite sporadically in the rest of the country, settled mainly in the upper Mureș basin (with the two Tîrnava Rivers).

As a result of this eastern infiltration, of the raids, and of the continuous Scythian threat, the local population, indubitably descendants of the preceding Basarabi culture, judging by their material culture and their burial rites (cremation), was found to be differently distributed geographically around 550 B.C. In the first place, the extra-Carpathian regions of open plains appear to be nearly (but not quite) emptied of population throughout the period under discussion, which is Late Hallstatt (ca. 575-ca. 350 B.C.). It was only along the banks of the Danube that the population was denser.

În the extra-Carpathian area of the country, in the central Moldavian plateau and as far as Dochia, on the outskirts of the town of Piatra Neamț, there are impressive strongholds of earth and stone covering large areas and standing on high ridges. These strongholds built by the local population against the Scythian threat have only recently been identified and have been only partially studied on account of the large areas they occupy (18 acres at Moşna in the Jassy county and 90 acres at Stînceşti in the Botoşani county). From the mid-sixth century to the third century B.C., a chain of strongholds, of which twenty perhaps have been identified so far, made of Moldavia's central plateau an advanced bridgehead of the Geto-Dacian world, which proved to be storm-proof. In times of danger, the population in the open settlements would withdraw into those strongholds, taking their belongings with them. These strongholds were consequently for times of stress, but discoveries show that they also served as places of residence of the tribal aristocracy.

In the west of the country, the Thracian population which had partly mixed with the eastern "Scythian" population, mostly lived in the Tisa plain. In the north, the same Thracian population was to be found in the sub-Carpathian Ukraine and in east Slovakia.

It is from this Late Hallstatt stock and against its background that the tribal unions known in written historical tradition (Herodotus, Thucydides) as Getian and later as Dacian arose in the Carpatho-Balkan area, with their high culture at the level of Iron Age II (Latène Culture, after the name of the corresponding culture created by the Celts in Western Europe) — a culture which is the effect of assimilation by the autochthonous stock of the influence of Mediterranean civilization transmitted by the Greeks. This was an organic and a fairly slow process beginning in the fifth century and reaching full maturity in the first century B.C., in Burebista's time. During Decebalus's period there is further progress, which brings this culture to a stage approaching civilization (of the slave-owning type).

The transformation process of production relations within Geto-Dacian tribes, which also brought about a switchover to a new, specifically Dacian culture of the Latène type, was gradual and complex, as it was also in the rest of Europe, among the Celts and the Illyrians.

It began everywhere in the southern regions, which were nearer to the Greek world. In the Carpatho-Balkan area, it is first attested in the southern Thracian area, south of the Balkan range. When the population of the Danube plain partially withdrew in the sixth to the fourth centuries B.C. the Geto-Dacians retreating to the hills and the tablelands, and also along the Danube, the Getae on the south Danubian pre-Balkan platform — the Vrața and Dobrina-Varna groupings — were only for a short time, and not completely, separated from those in the Carpathians. For this reason it is not right to name the former southern Thracians and the latter northern Thracians. Ultimately, it is only the tribes south of the Balkans, where the state of the Odrysi was set up in the first half of the fifth century that should be considered as southern Thracians. The new, specifically Geto-Dacian society and culture were first effectively organized as a result of these contacts on the pre-Balkan platform and in the plain north of the Lower Danube in the latter half of the fourth century B.C. Advanced agriculture was then practised, wheel pottery and other crafts were separated from agriculture and stock-breeding, and the aristocracy was consolidated, "kings" *(basilei)* standing out from its ranks. The names of these kings are mostly unknown; there was one, however, who encountered Alexander the Great in the Danube plain in 335 B.C., another from whose supposed grave the silver horse trappings in the "Craiova treasure" are assumed to have been obtained, and yet another buried in the Hagighiol barrow in the Tulcea county in the second half of the fourth century B.C.

It is from this background that Dromichaites, who defeated Lysimachus, the Macedonian King, at the turn of the third century B.C. was to rise; it is this world he will represent.

It is clear that the decisive role in the rise of Geto-Dacian society to the higher stage of Iron Age II cannot be attributed to the Scythians. The Scythians, warlike nomadic herdsmen, remained at the level of the Late Hallstatt up to the fourth century B.C., importing Greek luxuries but being unable to produce them or improve on them. There is no significance in the fact that as early as the sixth century B.C. the Getae had partially adopted the armament and the battle tactics of the Scythians (and this could have been brought about partly through the intermediary of the Cimmerians).

These two great peoples of Europe in those days — the Celts (Gauls) and the Geto-Dacians — came into contact, exerted mutual cultural influence but from the latter half of the fourth century B.C. they came to grips. The vast migrations and conquests of the Celts encompassed Pannonia down to the Adriatic but were compelled to give a wide berth to the Dacian bloc in the Carpathians, though not without infiltrating into the peripheral districts of that bloc. The most powerful infiltration was in Crișana, in north-west Dacia, where Celts settled in great numbers as early as the fourth century B.C., overlapping the Dacians and mingling with them. It is from Crișana that Celtic groups penetrated along the valleys of the Someș and Mureș into the Transylvanian plateau up to the Tîrnave valleys as well as into the neighbourhood of the Bîrsa plain, while other groups were to skirt Dacia in the north and pass through sub-Carpathian Ukraine and southern Poland in order to reach the valley of the Dniester in stray bands whence they went further to the northern coast of the Black Sea. Outside the Transylvanian plateau, where up to the end of the third century B.C. and in certain places even later, there seems to have been Celto-Dacian co-existence, with the Celts being fully assimilated : it is only sporadically that Celtic elements penetrated within the Geto-Dacian bloc. In Oltenia the Scordisci Celts of the Sava region infiltrated in the second and first centuries B.C., mixing with the Dacians of those parts and being also assimilated. On the same occasion Geto-Dacian culture assimilated a number of elements of Celtic culture, integrating them into its traditional source, which remained essentially unaltered in its originality. The Dacians' co-existence and intermingling with the Celts is a process of historic importance.

The fact that north-west Dacia north of the Danube, including the Transylvanian plateau, was so powerfully infiltrated by the Celts for a comparatively long period — and, as it seems, also dominated by them from the military and political points of view — is a reason for the social and cultural evolution of the Dacian people in those parts becoming later synchronous with that of the Geto-Dacians of the southern and south-eastern extra-Carpathian regions and still later acting as a decisive factor in the political and military life of the Geto-Dacian bloc north of the Danube. This branch of the Geto-Dacians known by the new name of Dacians (probably after the name of a leading tribe in the tribal union) exerted their influence from around the year 200 B.C. But, as asserted by the Roman historian Trogus Pompeius at the end of the first century B.C., *"Dacii quoque suboles Getarum sunt"* (the Dacians are also descendants of the Getae).

It is from the core of the "Carpathian stronghold" that the outburst of unifying military, political, and cultural energy was to arise during Burebista's century.

CHAPTER TWO

THE GETO-DACIANS

MENTIONED in historical records as early as the sixth century B.C., the Getae along the Lower Danube first organized themselves politically during the subsequent centuries, the most important tribal union being that headed by Dromichaites. During the third century B.C. we find the first indications of a similar union built up by the Dacians living in the mountains. During the first century B.C. an ephemeral union of all Geto-Dacian tribes took place under Burebista's leadership. Later, the tendency of the Roman Empire to establish its border along the Lower Danube led to frequent conflicts between the Dacians and the Romans, culminating in two fierce wars waged by Emperor Trajan in Dacia, which resulted in the overthrow of Decebalus's kingdom and the transformation of Dacia into a Roman province.

1. Hellenic Cities : Histria, Tomis, Callatis

BEFORE commencing this chapter devoted to the Geto-Dacian native population, we ought to dwell for a moment on the three Greek colonies of Histria, Tomis, and Callatis, which in ancient times flourished on the Getian coast of what is today Romanian Dobrudja. These trading cities — parallel with other Pontic cities, like Tyras and Olbia on the coast of the present-day U.S.S.R., and Dionysopolis (Balcic), Odessos (Varna), Mesembria (Nesebar), and Apollonia (Sozopoli) on the coast of present-day Bulgaria — maintained busy economic connections with the Carpatho-Danubian regions, exercising fruitful influence on the development of Geto-Dacian society and speeding up its progress. These are the oldest urban settlements in the neighbourhoods of the Geto-Dacian lands, and simultaneously direct centres of the High Hellenic civilization, the source of Europe's civilization. Thanks to their economic activities and their cultural impact, the territory of Romania was for the first time drawn into the orbit of world history.

Istros or Istria (Histria in Latin), the oldest of them, was set up during the seventh century B.C. (more precisely in 657) by Miletus, the famous Ionic city on the Aegean coast of Asia Minor. The site was south of the mouths of the Danube at the far end of the gulf which, owing to subsequent sand deposits, was to become the present-day Lake Sinoe. Its Greek name was that of the Danube, which Greeks and the Geto-Thracians named Istros. The Milesians set up their colony on that site mainly in order to make good use of the Danube for commercial penetration into the Geto-Dacian lands, and also with a view to profitable fishing in the Delta. Thanks to this economic background, Histria soon became a most flourishing city.

The second Greek town in Dobrudja to reach a flourishing condition in a short time was Callatis. This Doric colony which emerged comparatively late on the coast — at the close of the sixth century B.C. — had been founded by farmers from Pontic Heraclea (today Eregli on the coast of Asia Minor), a city which had previously been a colony of Megara in central Greece. The people of Heraclea raised the city of Callatis on the site of present-day Mangalia, where natural defence conditions were non-existent and where the coast had no economic value apart from its mediocre advantages as a harbour. On the other hand, the steppe around, inhabited by Getian and Scythian herdsmen, had a soil and climate most favourable to the growing of corn. The development of this city relied on its grain trade. The grain was in such demand in the market of southern Greece and grain-growing so profitable that the Scythian herdsmen in the neighbourhood gave up their nomadic life and turned ploughmen with an autonomous organization and their own kings, who issued coins minted in the shops of Callatis. The height of the city's prosperity was reached in the fourth and the third centuries B.C., when its wealth and glory exceeded that of all the other Hellenic colonies in the Left Pontus, as the western coast of the Pontus Euxinus was then called.

Although raised as early as the seventh century, possibly simultaneously with Histria, and in any case not later than the early sixth century B.C., the Milesian city of Tomis on the site of present-day Constantza, more exactly on its central promontory, remained obscure for long, being merely a place of call for the sailors who reached the shelter of this unique natural harbour on the monotonous middle portion of the Dobrudjan coast. Apart from the port, there were no economic advantages to be derived from its location, nothing comparable to Histria or Callatis, for there was no river to enable the sailors to reach the interior of the country and no native population numerous enough in its vicinity to ensure trade development. Economically, it was of service as a harbour for the needs of seagoing vessels ; it acted as a naval station, this ultimately securing its growth, prosperity, and primacy. A radical change was brought about by the advance of silt deposits at the mouths of the Danube, which being carried southward by the sea current along the coast, became an obstruction to Histria, forming underwater belts most dangerous to navigation. Many Greek traders who wished to reach the interior of the country by way of the Danube, soon developed a tendency to avoid the delta and shortened their way by transhipping the goods and taking them across Dobrudja by land. As the shortest and easiest way inland was from Tomis, this none too rich little town became increasingly favoured by the sailors who had their goods trans-shipped here, thus bringing in great profits. Traffic along this route became regular after Lysimachus's Macedonian domination established order in Dobrudja. It was then that the Danube port of Axiopolis (present-day Hinogu near Cernavodă) was created at the far end of the land route.

The city's sudden development earned it the envy of the neighbouring towns of Histria and Callatis, which tried to subjugate it around 260 B.C. Tomis was saved through the intervention of Byzantium, the powerful Megarian city on the Bosphorus (on the site of what was to be Constantinople), which had financial interests here and consequently supported free traffic in Tomis. The Byzantine fleet overcame the naval forces of Callatis while Histria had to submit to the curtailment of maritime transit in its waters and be content with the income derived from fishing in the delta, which was fairly high and where there was no competition. After this critical moment Tomis prospered without hindrance. And when Roman domination began in these parts, Ovid who had been exiled here, found a city which was already the main centre of Dobrudja. Subsequently Tomis became "the most flourishing metropolis of the entire Left Pontus", as it was described in inscriptions and on coins.

When they came under the authority of the Roman Empire, Histria, Tomis, and Callatis preserved their autonomous institutions, being considered as "allied" cities (*civitates foederatae*) and being entitled to mint their own coins (though only bronze ones), although they were closely dependent on Roman officialdom. Nevertheless, the peace Rome had established proved so favourable to their economy, it secured for them so long a period of prosperity, that their devotion to the Empire was unshakable.

Histria, Tomis and Callatis kept up their economic activities and their connections with the populations on the left of the Danube until the Eastern Roman Empire abandoned Dobrudja in the seventh century A.D., when the repeated attacks of the Avars [a nomadic people from central Asia] and Proto-Bulgars finally destroyed them after well over twelve centuries of life during which, assiduously and creatively, they had spread without interruption the values of Greek civilization on the territory of the Geto-Dacian homeland.

2. The Early Getae

WE know from ancient historical records that the territory of present-day Romania mostly coincides with that of Dacia, a country inhabited by Getae and Dacians from remote times. The populations thus named spoke the same language, had the same Thracian origin and the same culture, and shared between them the Carpatho-Danubian area, a large geographic unit.

The only difference between the Getae and the Dacians was the region they occupied, the former living in the plains south and east of the Carpathians, primarily on the two banks of the Lower Danube, while the latter held sway over the mountainous regions of Transylvania. When the ancient Greek writers wished to name all the tribes of Dacia by one name, they preferred to call them Getae, these having been known to them for a longer time than the Dacians, as they were nearer to the Hellenic cities along the coast of Pontus Euxinus. On the other hand, the Romans called them Dacians for they had been in more frequent contact with the latter people owing to their westerly position. During the modern period the double name — Geto-Dacians or Daco-Getians — is generally used as more convenient, for it expresses the fundamental unity of the two populations while taking the regional individuality of each into account.

Herodotus, the Greek historian, said that "the Thracians were the greatest of all peoples after the Indians," and that "had they been under a single leadership and with a unitary consciousness, they would have been invincible and by far the most powerful of all peoples." They were divided into many tribes, which lived independently and seldom formed a powerful political union, and that only in certain parts of their territory.

Among the numerous Thracian tribes, three main groupings are distinguished, which with time showed distinct features according to their evolution under different geographical, economic, historic, and cultural conditions. One group of the three were the Myssians and Phrygians of Asia Minor, the second, the Thracians proper *(Thraces)* of the Balkan Peninsula (thus named in history), and the third, the Geto-Dacians, to whom should be added the North Thracian tribes of the Carpi, Costobocae, and of other populations of the northern Carpathians. There are differences between the dialects, religious practices, customs, and cultural trends of the three groups.

The oldest records mentioning the Getae belong to the sixth century B.C., while the Dacians are only mentioned in historical sources at the close of the third century B.C.

Dacia's historical records begin with the information transmitted by Herodotus on an important event which took place about 514 B.C., when Darius, son of Hystaspes, the Great King of the Persians, undertook his famous expedition against the Scythians with the purpose of bringing all the rich coasts of Pontus Euxinus under his rule. At the head of a great host, this monarch crossed the Bosphorus and Thrace towards the Danube (Istros), while the fleet of the Greeks of Asia Minor, who had been subdued by him, was sailing in the same direction along the western coast of the Pontus, also called the Left Pontus. Along the coast of southern Thrace, Darius met only three tribes, who submitted to him. However, when he had crossed the Balkans (Haemus) and entered Dobrudja, he was faced by the Getians on the banks of the Danube, who opposed him. Finally the Getae were defeated and compelled to enter the ranks of the Persian army, but Herodotus nevertheless praises their gallantry and moral discipline, describing them as "the most courageous and fairest of the Thracians". He speaks about their contempt for death, inspired by the belief that the souls of those fallen in battle were immortal. However, their brave opposition to the impressive Persian hosts depended not only on warlike virtues but also on their number. Indeed, they must have been numerous if we admit that even at that time they formed a widespread union of tribes on either bank of the Lower Danube, in the Muntenian plain, northern Bulgaria, Dobrudja, and southern Moldavia, as will appear in the following centuries.

At about the same time, the Agathyrsi in the Carpathians are shown by Herodotus to have broken away from the Scythians and to have taken a neutral stand during Darius's expedition.

At the time referred to by Herodotus, Scythian expansion had reached its maximum westward limit and, after some last thrusts, was beginning to decline, despite the victory they had won over Darius. Actually, that victory was not so much a military success (there is no mention of a battle) as the result of the climate and of the hardships encountered in the great eastern steppes, which decisive factors compelled the Persian monarch to retrace his steps.

3. The Getae of the Danube Plain ; The Tribal Union Headed by Dromichaites

EVEN though Darius had failed to reach his goal in the Great Scythia beyond the mouths of the Danube, it seemed probable that he would establish the boundary of his empire along the Lower Danube, for he had been successful against the Thracian and Getian tribes there.

However, the withdrawal of the Persian forces pursued by the Scythians and the subsequent defeats of Darius and his successor, Xerxes, in Greece made it impossible for Persian authority to be established for any length of time north of the Straits.

Conquered for a brief spell, the Thracian and Getian tribes recovered their independence as soon as Darius's forces left their land. Shortly after 500 B.C., a state of the Balkan Thracians was founded, a stable union of tribes having been organized under the rule of the kings of the Odrysian tribes, the first of whom was Teres. Teres's son, Sitalces, consolidated the Odrysian state and extended it to the mouths of the Danube, incorporating the Getae north of the Balkans, those in Dobrudja included, as well as the Scythian enclaves close to the Left Pontus. Thus Darius's wish to turn the Danube into a boundary was achieved, though not by him and in favour of his empire, but by the local Geto-Thracians in favour of the Odrysian state. The Getic and Thracian tribes of Dobrudja then became autonomous elements of this state, on the basis of mere association, according to the rules of the tribal unions in the stage of military democracy, which was then the social system of all the populations of the Balkano-Carpatho-Danubian area and of the rest of Europe.

Macedonia's emergence as a great Hellenic power in the Balkan Peninsula under the energetic rule of Philip II was not without considerable effects on these regions. After over a century and a half of existence, the Odrysian kingdom, weakened by domestic strife, was conquered by Philip in 341 B.C. and turned into a Macedonian province *(strategia)*. Following this considerable annexation, the Macedonian king felt the need of extending his authority to the Danube, which he did by force of arms.

Thus, when Philip died in 335 B.C., Alexander, his son and heir, found it necessary to undertake an expedition to the Danube, as a preliminary safety measure before setting out on his prodigious conquests in Asia. Defeated in the first clash on the River Lyginus (probably present-day Panega), a tributary of the Oescus (Isker), the Triballians under their king Syrmos, withdrew to a Danube refuge, repelling all Macedonian attacks by water. Realizing that resistance was possible mainly through the aid received from the Getae on the left bank of the river, Alexander decided to make an audacious demonstration against the latter ; crossing the Danube one night with improvised facilities, he unexpectedly attacked the Getian forces, which despite their great numbers, were compelled to leave in all speed their poorly fortified citadel on the Danube bank and to withdraw into the steppe. Alexander was cautious enough not to pursue them and to be content with the rich booty of provisions and cattle he had found in the conquered citadel, and with his important moral success. Without Getian support in the offing, the Triballians were compelled to submit to the young Macedonian king. Other populations between the Adriatic and the Danube, among them the Celts, recent arrivals in these regions, sent Alexander messengers with tokens of friendship.

The political success of Alexander's sally is proof of the impressive strength of the Getae, whom he had defied though refusing to fight them and to be inveigled in the meshes of their wily withdrawal. From the minute account of Alexander's campaign along the Danube by Ptolemy, son of Lagos, as transmitted by Arrian, we learn that the local Getae were fishermen and traders, for which purpose they use numberless one-oar boats, and also successfully practised farming. On the northern bank of the Danube, the Macedonian foot soldiers had to bend down the high wheat with their long spears *(sarissae)* aslant for the cavalry to pass.

In 326 B.C., nearly a decade later, while Alexander was at the height of his successes in Asia, the strategist Zopyrion, governor of Thrace, sought to extend his authority north of the mouths of the Danube, by undertaking an expedition in the Bugeac and beyond the Dniester and attacking the Greek town of Olbia, which was not prepared to submit to Macedonian supremacy. Repelled by that city and forced to withdraw for lack of provisions, Zopyrion shortly found himself unable to cross the Danube on his return because of the rising waters. Taken by surprise by a great army of the union of Getian tribes, he was killed together with most of his troops. Alexander's premature death in 323 cut short his plan of returning to the Danube to smash the power of the Getae.

The plan was, however, followed by Alexander's general and successor, Lysimachus, who had become king of Thrace when the Macedonian conquests were divided. His excessive levies caused the Hellenic cities in Dobrudja to revolt. Though they were supported by the trans-Danubian populations and primarily by the Getae, Lysimachus after prolonged efforts ultimately succeeded in isolating and defeating them. For nearly six years Callatis had put up an heroic resistance. Now master of the sea coast and of the Dobrudjan mainland, the Thracian king, having decided to ensure the safety of his Danube frontier, sent his son Agathocles with an army into the Bărăgan steppe across the river to subdue the union of Getian tribes under the leadership of King Dromichaites, who had refused to resign himself to the loss of his territories along the right bank of the Danube.

The expedition was a failure : Agathocles was defeated and taken prisoner. After he had ransomed his son, Lysimachus crossed the Danube with a great army in 291, but suffered the same fate as his son, persisting, as he did, in his decision to traverse the Bărăgan steppe in pursuit of the Getae who, according to their tactics, withdrew farther and farther into the steppe. Exhausted by hardships, thirst, and a low morale, the Thraco-Macedonian hosts suddenly found themselves surrounded by Getae in large numbers and were forced to lay down their arms. Lysimachus and his followers were taken to the citadel of Helis (so far unidentified) where Dromichaites's political wisdom succeeded in saving them from the massacre the Getae, intoxicated by victory, threatened them with. It is characteristic of the type of military democracy of Getian society in those days that the Getian king, whose authority over his men was far from absolute, had to resort to speeches and artful reasoning in order to repress their fury and convince them that peace with great and lasting advantages was to be preferred to futile vengeance that would bring new wars in its train. Lysimachus being released, a solemn pact was concluded on Dromichaites's terms. The alliance between the two rulers was consolidated by the Getian king's marriage with Lysimachus's daughter.

This dynastic kinship propelled the union of Getian tribes along the Lower Danube into the political sphere of the Hellenistic world, with important consequences for the development of Getian culture.

4. First Appearance of the Carpathian Dacians

THE invasion of the Galatians, which profoundly shook the Hellenistic states of Macedonia and Thrace up to Asia Minor, was an outflow of the vast Celtic migration which started in Gaul, over northern Italy and Central Europe, and penetrated into Dacian territory as early as the fourth century B.C. Celtic warriors — the Scordisci, Boii, Teurisci — settled in the vicinity of western Dacia, while other tribes infiltrated within the country as far as eastern Moldavia and Dobrudja. In their expansion, the Celts spread their specific forms of culture, named Latène after La Tène in Switzerland. Their culture was similar to that of the Geto-Dacians and at the same level, and both peoples were influenced by Greek civilization. Celtic artifacts frequently occur over the territory of Romania, mostly in Transylvania and Oltenia, where continued finds attest the presence of Celtic warriors, while in Muntenia, Moldavia and Dobrudja the finds are less frequent.

As a consequence of Celtic migrations, groupings of Germanic populations appeared in Eastern Europe towards the close of the third century B.C., and from among them the Bastarnians, coming from the eastern parts of Germany, spread along the North Carpathian foothills and settled in Galicia and North and Central Moldavia; archaeology characterizes them by a specific culture — the Oder-Vistula culture — which was first studied at Poienești in the Vaslui county in the Socialist Republic of Romania, and at Lukashovka (Orhei) in the Moldavian Soviet Socialist Republic.

The Bastarnians' invasion of Moldavia and their drive towards Transylvania over the Carpathians caused the local Dacian tribes to rise in opposition, this being the first time they are mentioned in historical records. The historian Pompeius Trogus tells of the Dacian king Oroles who, having been defeated by the Bastarnians, regrouped his forces and after reproving them, resumed the fight and repelled the enemy. Yet, this must have occurred only in the Carpathian foothills, for in the rest of Moldavia the Bastarnians dwelt for nearly two more centuries.

The battles fought against the Celts and then against the Bastarnians induced the Dacians of the Carpathians to form a durable union of tribes after the example of the Getian union along the Danube. The organizer of this new political power seems to have been a king called Rubobostes, who seems to have lived around the beginning of the second century B.C.

While the unions of Dacian tribes were being consolidated in Transylvania and in the Moldavian Carpathians, the old union of Getian tribes on the Lower Danube stood its ground during the troubled times of the invasions of the Celts and Bastarnians, and was as well-knit and strong as ever. Ultimately, a balance was established between the Geto-Dacians and their Celtic and Bastarnian neighbours, and alliances were forged, mainly with a view to joint plundering forays south of the Danube. On the Getian territory in Muntenia [Wallachia] and southern Moldavia archaeology attests that in those days there was an uninterrupted development of the local culture, with Greek influence.

The most significant historical process in the second century B.C. was Rome's eastward expansion as a consequence of its wars with Macedonia. When the homeland of Philip II and Alexander had become a Roman province in 148 B.C., the Getae and Dacians, singly or co-operating with the Celts and Bastarnians, carried on unceasing attacks against the new power that had been established in the middle of the Balkan Peninsula. Indeed they were its most implacable enemies. The prolonged resistance of the Illyrians, Dardanians, Scordisci, Triballians, and Thracians to the advance of the Romans, always found support in a Geto-Dacian alliance. Nevertheless, the Romans slowly but ineluctably strengthened their domination east of the Adriatic, showing a tendency to establish their boundary along the Danube.

It was in 74 B.C. that their forces first reached the Danube line, when Proconsul Scribonius Curio, having defeated the Dardanians, advanced as far as the Iron Gates. However, he did not dare to cross into Dacia, being, as the historian Florus states, "scared of the dark woods there". Two years later, on the occasion of the war against Mithridates, king of Pontus, who had organized a vast anti-Roman coalition, which included the populations around the Black Sea, another Roman general — M. Licinius Terentius Varro Lucullus — subdued the Greek cities in Dobrudja and advanced up to the mouths of the Danube. But, this first attempt at enforcing Roman authority in Dobrudja did not last long for in 61 B.C. Proconsul C. Antonius Hybrida, bringing about an uprising of the local Greek cities by his pecuniary extortions, was defeated not far from Histria with the assistance of the Getae and Bastarnians.

5. Burebista Unites the Geto-Dacian People

THE fruits of this victory were gathered by the Getae who were then organizing a vast union of tribes, which included all the Geto-Dacian tribes under the leadership of Burebista. The latter did not originate in Dacia's Carpathian centre : he was the head of the old union of Getian tribes on the Lower Danube. Supported by the moral authority of the High Priest, Decaeneus, he succeeded in inculcating a sense of discipline into the Getae, enforcing sobriety, forbidding them to drink too much wine and ordering them to root out the vine, which they were beginning to cultivate assiduously after the methods they had learned from the Greeks and the Thracians of the Balkans. This detail is an additional indication that Burebista had his seat primarily among the Getae of Muntenia and Lower Moldavia, whose climate, unlike that of the Dacian Mountains, is most favourable to the vine.

Argedava, residence of Burebista and of his predecessors, was probably situated on the River Argeş, the valley of which was at the time a main trade route between the Pontic cities and central Dacia, a continuation of the Danube, and consequently the natural route to be chosen by messengers coming from Dionysopolis. On the other hand, archaeological research has revealed a number of stations along this valley, proving a remarkable development in the second and first centuries B.C. — the epoch of Burebista and of his predecessors. The Getian citadel of Popeşti on the right bank of the Argeş not far from Bucharest appears to be specific to Getian development and proof of profound assimilation of Hellenistic influence. It undoubtedly had held priority over all other stations in Dacia in those times, and its central position was suitable for the residence of a leader of the united Getian tribes of the Lower Danube plains. Its identification with Argedava, the seat of Burebista's dynasty, is the most probable hypothesis based on our present-day knowledge of this matter.

In the Geto-Dacian world, made anxious by the progress of Roman expansion and realizing the need of closing their ranks to oppose it, the old union of Getian tribes seemed to be the soundest, the most powerful, the best fitted to direct Geto-Dacian tendencies towards solidarity. Thus, before long Burebista who, according to available information, was an outstanding personality, headed an impressive political formation that incorporated immense territories stretching as far as Bohemia and the vicinity of the Austrian Alps, to the Northern Carpathians, to the Southern Bug and the Black Sea, to the vicinity of the Adriatic and to the Balkans. As Greek geographer Strabo (born B.C. 63) states, the could always have at his command a force of 200,000 men.

The Getian king owed his extraordinary power not so much to force of arms as to his power of persuasion. The unification of the Geto-Dacians was stimulated by the imminent Roman threat and was facilitated by the concentration of the innumerable Geto-Dacian tribes into four regional unions, two being those of the Getae of the plains and of the Dacians in Transylvania. No data are available concerning the other two, but it can be supposed they were somewhere in the northern and eastern Carpathians, one in Maramureş and Slovakia north of Dacia, the other in Galicia and Moldavia. Once these unions had coalesced, Burebista could set about solving the problems of each by war, suppressing all the Celtic states of Central Europe, in the first place those of the Scordisci, Taurisci, and Boii in Pannonia, and extending Geto-Dacian rule over all the Danubian lands. He also subordinated to his interests all the rich Greek cities along the western coast of Pontus Euxinus — from

Olbia (in the estuary of the Bug and Dnieper) to Apollonia (present-day Sozopoli not far from Burgas). Some of these cities, Dionysopolis among them, had been for long under the Getian king's protection, but others came under his authority only when their resistance had been quashed. Olbia, for example, was completely destroyed by the Getians and there are indications that Histria also was devastated, while an inscription found at Mesembria (present-day Nesebar) clearly shows that that city at the Pontic extremity of the Balkan Mountains opposed Burebista's attack by force of arms.

While the civil war between Julius Caesar and Pompey was raging, in 48 B.C., soon after Caesar's transient defeat at Dyrrachium, Burebista sent a diplomat to Heraclea Lyncestis in Macedonia, to negotiate an alliance with Pompey who no doubt agreed to recognize the Getian king's immense conquests in return for the military aid the latter offered. However, Caesar's decisive victory at Pharsalus took place before the forces of the Getian king could reach the theatre of war. Nevertheless, Rome considered the Getian threat so serious that the Pharsalus victor decided to forestall it by undertaking a great expedition in Dacia. A mighty army had been concentrated in Macedonia for the purpose, and Caesar was all ready for war when he was murdered on the Ides of March in 44 B.C. The expedition was called off.

Soon after, Burebista himself suffered the same fate as his opponent, for he was overthrown and killed by a conspiracy of malcontents. These were most probably heads of the regional unions of tribes who wished to regain their freedom. They were unwilling to accept a permanent coalition in the form of a monarchic centralization incompatible with the spirit of tribal autonomy rooted in the tradition of Geto-Dacian society, especially in view of the fact that after Caesar's death the Roman threat was not serious enough to justify their subordination to a supreme chief. Burebista's death was followed by the parcelling out of his huge political realm; it was divided into four parts, one of them (there is no specification as to which) being subsequently divided in two.

Burebista's intention to change the shaky confederation of Geto-Dacian tribal unions — built in haste and rather as a transitory alliance — into a durable, well organized state is evidenced by his deeds. Moreover, it was the Geto-Dacian people's only chance of successfully resisting the immense bloc of Roman power. Once at the head of the great union he had built up, Burebista left his regional residence in the plain, Argedava, to found a new seat at Royal Sarmizegetusa (Grădiştea Muncelului), a stronghold built in a mountain range difficult of access.

Even though centralization, according to Burebista's plan, was unsuccessful, being too far removed from the stage of socio-political development of the Geto-Dacian tribes at the time, it continued as a military democracy, and the meteoric passage of such a powerful figure in the history of the Geto-Dacian people had profound consequences. It was Burebista who laid the foundations of the Geto-Dacian state. He forged closer connections between Geto-Dacian tribes and promoted intensive inter-tribal economic circulation, which led to a swift and uniform spread of the Getian culture of the Lower Danube throughout the Carpatho-Danubian territory under his authority. It was he who established the centre of gravity of the Geto-Dacian state in the Dacians' mountains. It might well be that the main part in the conspiracy that removed him was played by the Dacian aristocracy.

6. The Danube Getae Fall under Roman Rule

ALTHOUGH the Geto-Dacians after Burebista's death ceased to be an impressive power, for they were no longer united, their policy towards Rome during the new civil wars which followed Caesar's death was just as active and as much opposed to the representative of the Italic Peninsula. At the Battle of Philippi in 42 B.C.. Caesar's murderers were aided in their opposition to Octavian and Mark Antony by a Dacian corps headed by one Coson, whose name is to be found on the gold coins minted by Junius Brutus on that occasion. Such coins have been found in great number in Transylvania. Coson might be identical with the Dacian king Cotison who ruled south-western Dacia and who was shortly to enter into negotiations with Octavian, but historical sources do not show conclusive proof of the identity. During the Civil War of 31 B.C., which ended with Mark Antony's defeat at Actium, Octavian had no Geto-Dacian ally on his side. On the other hand, his rival, who represented the East, had been supported by Dicomes, a king of the Lower Danube, who, though prepared to resume Burebista's policy and despite the subsidies he had received, did not take part in the fight. Events were too quick for him, as formerly at Pharsalus, and the war ended before the Getian corps arrived. Actually, it was a naval battle that decided the destinies of the war. The latest observations seem to point to Moldavia's Carpathian foothills as the seat of King Dicomes.

Undisputed leader of the Roman power after Actium, Octavian sought to establish a firm boundary along the whole course of the Danube for the empire he was organizing. The occasion to do so arose sooner than he expected in the territory at the mouths of the river, for he had to face a great migration of the Bastarnians into the Balkan Peninsula. Octavian sent M. Licinius Crassus, Proconsul of Macedonia, against the aggressors. The Proconsul had to wage war for two wearisome years (29-28 B.C.) before he could break the resistance of the Thracian populations, crush the Bastarnians and conquer the whole peninsula up to the Danube. Among the Getians on the right bank of the river, he had a devoted ally in the local king, Roles, who had suffered great losses at the hands of the Bastarnians. On the other hand, in the middle of the present-day territory of Dobrudja, the Roman general came up against the fierce resistance of the Getian tribes headed by Dapyx. After defeating Dapyx, who committed suicide, Crassus attacked the Getian tribe in northern Dobrudja headed by Zyraxes, ending the war with the conquest of the Danubian city of Genucla, where he recovered the trophies taken from the Romans thirty years earlier following the defeat of C. Antonius Hybrida. The Romans entrusted the newly conquered land to the Odrysian kingdom of Thrace, which was revived as a client state. Octavian, who had in the meantime become emperor under the name of Augustus, did not deem these regions to be sufficiently safe to install direct Roman administration there.

Dobrudja and the other territories on the right bank of the Danube were thus incorporated in the sphere of Roman authority. This was a great blow to the old union of Getian tribes which, greatly weakened after Burebista's death, had its territories limited strictly to the Danube border and was squeezed between Thraco-Roman authority on one side and the Sarmatians on the other. The latter were Iranian nomads kindred to the Scythians. Having overrun all the vast steppes north of Pontus Euxinus, they had now reached the mouths of the Danube. In the end, a balance and even a partnership was established between them and the Geto-Dacian populations, who joined them in their plundering raids in the Roman-protected Balkan countries. The fact is that the Getians of Muntenia and Moldavia ceaselessly made such raids, creating an atmosphere of terror in the territories subject to the Thracian kingdom. The poet Ovid, who was exiled by Emperor Augustus to Tomis between A.D., 9 and 18, gives in his works impressive testimonies of the precarious life of the inhabitants of Dobrudja in those days under the constant threat of trans-Danubian attacks. Augustus took a number of energetic measures to put an end to this state of affairs and to consolidate his boundary along the Danube. While a great uprising of the Illyrians in Dalmatia and Pannonia (the area covered by contemporary Hungary) was suppressed after a long war (A.D. 6-9), Consul Cn. Cornelius Lentulus crushed a Getian army which had overrun the territory south of the Lower Danube and enforced a pact on the Sarmatians under which the latter agreed to keep far from the mouths of the Danube. Soon after these successes, from about A.D. 9 to 11, the Roman general Sextus Aelius Catus crossed the Danube into the Muntenian plain and after several bloody battles during which no fewer than three local kings fell, suppressed the union of Getian tribes and compelled the population to pull down their strongholds and leave the territory. Some 50,000 Getians settled in what was to be the Province of Moesia, as subjects of the Roman Empire. Archaeological research carried out in the main Getian strongholds of that area — Zimnicea on the Danube, Popești on the Argeș, Piscul Crăsanilor on the Ialomița —, where there is no further proof of habitation after the early years of our era, leaves no doubt that the measures taken by Aelius Catus were uncompromising.

This is an event of outstanding importance. The old political formation of the Getians on the Lower Danube, which had been a strong and flourishing body for so many centuries and a source of progress for Geto-Dacian culture, was now totally stamped out. The Getians who had been outside this area, for example at Tinosul further north on the River Prahova on the outskirts of the Carpathian foothills, were not a Getian force, for they were dependent on the goodwill of the Romans. And even the Getians of Moldavia, who were still free, were unable to undertake anything of note on their own.

Following their great success, the Romans continued to consolidate still more intensively their frontier along the Danube. In 46 Emperor Claudius considered the moment ripe to suppress the Odrysian kingdom and to establish there a Roman provincial régime. The territory south of the Balkan Mountains then became the province of Thrace while the territory along the Danube, Ripa Thraciae, comprising also Dobrudja, was incorporated into the province of Moesia. The latter province founded by Emperor Tiberius in A.D. 15, occupied more or less the territory of present-day Serbia and also the lands of the Triballians. Now it was extended all along the Lower Danube down to the sea.

7. Geto-Dacian Culture

GETO-DACIAN culture was on the ascendant. Its beginnings had been in the Getian area along the Danube, on the basis of Geto-Dacian elements but under the impulse of Greek influence. Later, it assumed its own creative impetus and aspect, and spread over the entire territory occupied by the Geto-Dacians when Burebista united them. After the death of the great Getian king, far from ceasing its progress, it reached full maturity during the first century A.D., at the time when the Dacian state at Sarmizegetusa assumed political prominence in the Carpathian territories.

As a result of demographic growth and of economic development, the Geto-Dacian settlements became very numerous between the third and the first century B.C. and also in the first century A.D., as attested by archaeological research. Apart from the purely rural settlements which occupied convenient places in the valleys, on river terraces and in forest glades, there were fortified settlements whose frequency is truly impressive. The latter were densely populated places of the oppidum type — named *dava* by the local people — genuine economic, political, religious and military centres of the tribes : budding towns and actually performing the functions of towns. Although they did not resemble the Greek-Roman towns, Greek authors do not hesitate to speak of them as *polis*, a term they also use for the urban localities of the Mediterranean world. Such

Geto-Dacian centres had emerged at places important for economic and strategic reasons : crossroads, fords, mountain passes, places where valleys met or where transport means had to be changed. They were situated on dominant heights in isolation, and natural defences were supplemented by ditches, vallums, and stockades. Beginning in Burebista's time, stone walls of an improved technique reinforced with timber were built in the capital in the Dacian Mountains with the assistance of craftsmen enticed from the Roman Empire, primarily Greek ; walls were also built according to local concepts based on Celtic influence.

In the settlements of the Danube plain, where there were no stone quarries, all structures were made of wood and clay, which were also basic materials for most of the dwellings in the west of Dacia. The houses were usually built above the ground and consisted of one or several rooms. They had an earthen floor and roofing of straw, reeds, or boards. Roofing tiles were currently used in the settlement of Popeşti on the River Argeş. In this important Getian settlement of Burebista's time, a large conglomeration of houses with many rooms, each designed for a special purpose, has been found. It undoubtedly belonged to the head of a tribe or of a tribal union. It spreads over more than 6,000 sq.ft., and includes a large rectangular structure with sacred hearths inside and an apse along the north-western part. Places for religious use similarly shaped and oriented were also to be found in the Dacian cities on the tops of the Orăştie Mountains.

At Grădiştea Muncelului, on the mountain where Sarmizegetusa Regia was situated and where the main shrine of the Geto-Dacians was to be found, there were stone circles and aligned wooden poles with discoidal stone pedestals, and in the centre of the most sacred of those circles there was a structure with an apse as described above. The principal circle had a 90-ft. diameter and consisted of two rows of parallelipipedic andesite blocks placed close to each other, the row towards the inside consisting of thirty groups of six uniform blocks each, followed by a seventh lower and broader block. This order has been interpreted as a symbol for the half-year calendar connected with the sun rite.

For ages the Geto-Dacians had been known to be greatly devoted to their god, Zamolxis, who was worshipped in caves and on the heights. They believed that death in battle secured eternal life. Their religion was Uranian, solar and henotheistic, belief in other deities, apart from the main one, being admitted. The Geto-Dacians were famed for their magic practices and their medical art based on wide knowledge of healing herbs. Generally they attached no great importance to funeral rites. Compared with the number of their settlements, few graves have been found, and those hardly ever grouped in large cemeteries.

The Geto-Dacians' main pursuits were agriculture and animal husbandry, whereby they procured their means of subsistence as well as goods sought after by Greek traders who gave in exchange the products of their art and crafts. In the Geto-Dacian settlements explored so far, iron implements (ploughs, shares, hoes, spades, sickles) have frequently been found. Grain was usually kept in holes in the ground, but starting from the first century B.C. big burnt-clay storage jars *(pithoi)* were used for the purpose. A large number of these have been found at Popești dating from Burebista's time, and in the strongholds in the Orăștie Mountains of a later period. Apart from wheat and rye, the Geto-Dacians ate millet. Their animals were cattle and sheep, pigs and goats and also horses, animals of prime necessity in transport and in battle. Hunting, fishing, and bee-keeping were additional pursuits.

Besides their work to procure food, the Geto-Dacians practised various crafts. Very many iron objects have been found in their settlements for the working of wood and metals. Their tools were of various types, for fairly evolved crafts : smith's work, bronze-casting, and the production of personal adornments out of precious metals after Greek models. Beginning in the third century B.C., there is a sign of greater commercial activity : the minting of coins imitating the Macedonian and Thasos types. In the first century A.D. they counterfeited the Roman Republican denarii but the silver content was occasionally higher than that of the original coin. For the purpose they used directly moulded dies.

The most representative category of products showing the progress achieved by Geto-Dacian culture is earthenware. The main centre of manufacture was in the city of Popeşti on the Argeş whose earthenware shops ranked foremost in the Geto-Dacian world not only in the production of common pottery but also of big storage jars and amphorae imitating those of Rhodes.

Inside the country trade was carried on by local people, while outside the country the Geto-Dacians traded with the Greeks and Romans. In their settlements Greek, Macedonian, and Roman coins are frequently found, mostly silver coins and occasionally some of gold and bronze. Counterfeit coins are also to be found. There are moreover countless imported goods of various categories : tools, weapons, personal adornments.

The Geto-Dacians dressed in woollen and hempen fabrics, and in winter they also wore furs. The reliefs on Trajan's Column and on the Adamclisi Monument give a correct picture of their dress and physique. Their weapons were spears, straight or curved swords, shields, and arrows. The Getae of the plain, once under Scythian influence, were mounted archers of repute. Spurs and arrowheads have been found in their settlements in large numbers.

Though the Geto-Dacians had made great progress in practical life, they were faithful to their old traditions in their spiritual life. Their religion still called for human sacrifices, a trait common to other European populations at that time. They did not know how to write ; the Greek amphorae they imitated from the Greek ones bore a seal but no letters. Neither is there any writing on their coins, which were imitations of Macedonian models.

Most of the Geto-Dacians' artifacts belong to the ornamental category. Without excelling, they gave proof of good craftsmanship as shown by their jewellery and earthenware. Their bone tools are engraved with fine geometrical motifs. The human figure is only represented by primitive bronze or clay semblances for religious or magic purposes (as a defence against evil spirits).

The progress of Geto-Dacian culture was part of their evolution from the tribal stage to the slave-owning system. It was a period of military democracy when constant wars of plunder were waged and the trend towards individualism and social differences appeared. Beginning in Burebista's time, the Geto-Dacians were enjoying all the essential conditions for the organization of a state; the productive forces and production of goods had developed (archaeological finds are sound proof of the above statement); division of labour, as attested by the development of crafts and trade, had been accentuated; private property had gradually appeared, to begin with ownership of mobile goods, then land ownership; labour was carried out by slaves, who were also an object of trade in great demand in the Greek and Roman markets; social classes, and no doubt the conflicts that go with them, had appeared. The aristocracy — the *pileati,* in Dacian *tarabostes* — are shown in ancient images wearing bonnets *(pileus)* in contradistinction to the common people *(comati)* who wore their hair loose without any headdress. The state, whose centralizing organization was vaguely put together under Burebista, gradually brought under its sway the whole territory of the Dacian mountain tribes, to assume the robust aspect it had in the time of Decebalus when it showed so manifestly its cohesion, power, and aspirations towards a higher stage of civilization before being suppressed by the Romans.

8. Decebalus's Wars against the Romans

DEFEATED in all their attempts to oppose encirclement by the Romans and almost wholly isolated after the fall of the Getian power, the Dacians of Transylvania were for a long time on the defensive in their mountainous country following the reign of Augustus. However, the civil war which raged in the Roman Empire from A.D. 69 to A.D. 70, after Nero's death, was an occasion for them and for the Sarmatians to resume their attacks south of the Danube. Even during Nero's reign, in the winter of A.D. 67-68, the Roxolan Sarmatians had crossed the Danube into Dobrudja and, taking two auxiliary Roman cohorts by surprise, had slaughtered them. Encouraged by these easy victories and by the aggravation of domestic affairs in the Empire, they returned to northern Dobrudja in greater numbers the following winter. M. Aponius Saturninus, Governor of Moesia, was prompt to retaliate : his legions fell on the invaders' armoured cavalry *(catafractarii)* and completely smashed them as their horses could not move freely on account of the slippery ground. At the close of the year 69 when Aponius had taken his forces to Italy to support Vespasian against Emperor Vitellius, the Dacians also went into action, devastating a number of Moesia's districts. Their advance was only repelled by the unexpected intervention of an eastern legion which was crossing Macedonia on its way to Italy. Soon after, early in 70, when Vespasian had been proclaimed Emperor, the Sarmatians again crossed the Danube into Dobrudja with overwhelming forces. When the new governor of Moesia, C. Fonteius Agrippa, sought to oppose them, he was killed with the greater part of his legions. His successor, Rubrius Gallus, finally succeeded after fierce fighting in putting them to flight.

It was through this legate that Vespasian re-established Roman order along the Danube. Moesia's boundary was greatly reinforced, the legions in the province were increased to four, and the military fleet on the Danube, which had been active ever since Augustus's time, was reorganized. Following these measures, the Dacians were persuaded to conclude a peace treaty with the Empire, which they observed faithfully for fifteen years. An inducement to this end had been the periodic payment made by the Romans. It was only in 85, under Emperor Domitian, that they tried to take advantage of the difficulties this son of Vespasian was encountering along other frontiers, by claiming that their subsidy should be increased. Their claim was rejected. This is a possible interpretation of a statement reported by Jordanes after Dion Chrysostom, contemporary with these events, to the effect that the Dacians had broken the pact "concluded earlier with other emperors", "because they feared Domitian's stinginess".

Unexpectedly the Dacians overran Moesia, inflicting a disastrous defeat on the Romans. The forces that stood in their way were slaughtered, together with the governor of the province, C. Oppius Sabinus. Domitian was alarmed and hastened to the Danube. Following the measures taken by him, the invaders were driven back across the river. In 86 the province of Moesia, being considered too big to carry out the military duties devolving on it, was divided in two : Moesia Superior, west of the River Ciabrus (Tzibritza), more or less present-day Serbia, and Moesia Inferior in the east, which incorporated the land of the Triballians, the former Ripa Thraciae, most of present-day Bulgaria and the whole of Dobrudja. The two provinces were ruled by a governor who had a consulary rank and was entitled *legatus Augusti pro praetore*. Each governor had an army made up of two legions and of auxiliary forces. Cornelius Fuscus, the praetor's prefect, was put in command of a great army that was to undertake reprisals in Dacia. Sure of victory, Domitian returned to Rome without waiting to see the results of the expedition.

Aware of the danger but considering himself too old to face the Romans, Duras, King of the Dacians (also called Diurpaneus), abdicated in favour of Decebalus, son of Scorilo, who had ruled before him. Decebalus was endowed with exceptional military and political qualities and proved well able to meet the emergency. Cornelius Fuscus crossed the Danube on a pontoon bridge in the summer of 87 and sought to reach the centre of Dacia by the shortest route which ran through Banat along the Bistra Valley towards Sarmizegetusa. Being impulsive and venturesome, brave but rash, the exact opposite of his skilled and cautious Dacian opponent, he let himself be drawn into the trap the latter had laid for him, and with his army met his death in a fearful slaughter which may have taken place in the Tapae Pass (the Iron Gates of Transylvania). This was one of the most memorable of the disasters inflicted on the Romans. The banners, war engines, and weapons which had fallen into Dacian hands were taken to one of the strongholds in the mountains around Sarmizegetusa.

Decebalus was in no haste to take advantage of his success by a new invasion of Moesia, where he would have run the risk of compromising the glorious prestige he had won. In his wisdom, he used this prestige to strengthen his authority within the country and to win allies outside it. He realized that the Roman Empire had vast resources and that a new Roman offensive against the Dacians was to be expected. Aware of the superiority of Roman civilization, he sought to entice craftsmen and deserters from the Empire by every possible means so that he might build strongholds and war engines and initiate the Dacians in Roman military tactics.

Domitian reacted promptly and energetically. A new army of impressive proportions was formed and an able and experienced general, Consul Tettius Julianus (who had participated in the victory won by Aponius Saturninus in Dobrudja against the Roxolans in 69) was put in command. Julianus crossed the Danube, possibly at Drobeta, in 88 and taking the straight way through Banat in order to penetrate into Transylvania by way of the Bistra Valley, he defeated Decebalus's forces at Tapae, the same place where Fuscus's disaster had occurred the year before. Vezinas, a Dacian dignitary, second in rank after Decebalus, was only saved from captivity by pretending death and getting away from the battlefield during the night. Following this defeat, Decebalus gave proof of outstanding military ability — more than on the occasion of his former victory, for he succeeded in circumscribing the consequences of defeat and delaying the enemy's advance. What was left of his forces regrouped and withdrew in good order inside the country. Frontinus reports that in order to gain freedom of movement and to check Julianus's advance, even though only for a brief time, the Dacian king ordered that branches should be lopped off some of the forest trees, and clothes and weapons be put on the trunks to give the Romans the impression that a great army had come to replace the vanquished one. For a time his stratagem was successful, but ultimately the Roman forces reached the neighbourhood of the mountains clustering about Sarmizegetusa. Decebalus asked for peace.

Domitian's first impulse was to refuse the request and continue the war until all Dacian forces had been crushed, but having been defeated in the meantime by the Quadi and the Marcomanii at the Pannonian Danube, he consented to a compromise peace in A.D. 89, the Dacian king thereby becoming a client of the Roman Empire in exchange for an annual stipend and assistance offered him in the way of craftsmen skilled in the building of cities and of war engines. Decebalus did not pay homage to the Roman emperor, but sent his brother Diegis instead. The latter being heir presumptive (according to the agnatic rule of succession to the throne) he was fully entitled to represent the Dacian state. Domitian permitted the substitution and was also content to have merely a symbolic implementation of the stipulation that the Dacians should return the trophies taken from the Romans at the time of Fuscus's disaster.

The peace of 89, being equivocal, aroused deep discontent among the senators in Rome who were in fierce conflict with Domitian. This unfavourable view is the only comment that has come down to us. And yet the peace was not so unfavourable to the Romans. Decebalus had lost much of his independence and was closely bound up with the interests of the Empire to which he was doing good service not only by abstaining from acts of hostility but also by watching the neighbouring populations and inducing them to assume a similar pacific stand. It is undeniable that he faithfully observed the pact throughout the rule of Domitian and of Nerva until Trajan's war, which was solely the latter's initiative.

Even though Decebalus seemed to be docile at the time, the growing prosperity of the Dacian state and the consolidation of its forces filled the Romans with well-founded fears for the future. With the assistance of the craftsmen the Romans had procured, the mountains around Sarmizegetusa had been turned into a formidable system of fortifications whose advanced techniques were designed to make Decebalus unconquerable not only by trans-Danubian neighbours (for in Domitian's pact this was the reason for the subsidy paid to him) but also by the Romans. Consequently, as soon as Emperor Trajan ascended the throne in 98, he made it his aim to suppress this highly dangerous centre. Trajan was a military man and shared in every particular the views of the Roman senators. Moreover, the conquest of Dacia was to bring substantial economic benefits to the Empire.

After detailed preparations, war was declared by the Romans in the spring of 101 without any provocation from the Dacian king. Unlike Domitian, Trajan enjoyed a most favourable strategic position : he had immense forces which were well organized and under the command of an outstanding general — himself ; there were no other involvements along the Empire's frontiers ; he had full freedom of action, and had started hostilities at the moment and place chosen by himself ; his opponent, however, had restricted possibilities, his forces being small in number, and he was almost isolated and compelled to be only on the defensive in his fortified mountains. However long and gallant Decebalus's resistance in the mountains, his downfall was a certainty to the Romans from the beginning of the campaign. And yet, the Romans won only after two hard-fought wars carried on over a period of six years, and the efforts and risks of the Roman army were immense. Trajan had to face the severe geographic conditions of the theatre of war around Sarmizegetusa, the gallantry and discipline of the Dacian people, and especially the energy and wisdom of their king, Decebalus.

Far from passively awaiting the threat, Decebalus sought to counterbalance the inferiority of his forces and the difficulties of his position by wise and audacious moves. He made an alliance with the Dacian, Sarmatian, and Germanic populations north of the Carpathians, primarily with the Suevian Buri of Slovakia and Maramureș, whom Tacitus mentions in his works, and, no longer isolated, built up a vast plan whereby he meant to take advantage of Trajan's offensive tactics. When the huge Roman army had penetrated deep into Transylvania's mountains, Dacia's allies were to spill into Dobrudja in large numbers — in the regions farthermost from the Carpathians — and, taking advantage of the poor Roman defence in those parts of the frontiers, were to make speedily for the Balkan provinces in order to intercept Trajan's communications with the rest of his Empire and strike at him from behind while Decebalus undertook a counter offensive. Thus encircled, the Roman army would have been threatened with unprecedented disaster. The success of the plan largely depended on perfect co-ordination of the moves of heterogeneous forces placed at an enormous distances from one another, as well as on complete secrecy of the allies' intentions, on cunning, and constant misinforming of the Roman emperor. It was of the utmost importance that operations in the Dacian Mountains should be prolonged by every possible means until winter, for the hard frosts of this part of Europe would facilitate the allied invasion along the Lower Danube while locking the Roman fleet at Drobeta which would otherwise have been an excellent instrument for rapid Roman moves inside Dacia. Decebalus and his allies faithfully carried out what had been demanded of them by this grand plan. But skill alone was not enough. The mildness of that winter's frosts was in favour of the Romans and compromised everything.

At the beginning of the war in the summer of 101, the Romans took the initiative. Two armies, coming from Moesia and Pannonia respectively, crossed the Danube by pontoon bridges at both ends of the Cazane defile, one under the command of Laberius Maximus, governor of Moesia Inferior, at Drobeta, the other under Trajan, at Lederata. Skirting the Banat Mountains, Trajan advanced along the valleys of the Caraș, Cernovăț, Bîrzava, and Pogăniș, and Laberius along the valleys of the Cerna, Belareca, Domașna, and Timiș, the two armies meeting at Tibiscum not far from present-day Caransebeș, having been offered no resistance. No sooner had Trajan crossed the Danube and started on his expedition through Banat, than a messenger brought him a communication written in Latin letters on a mushroom, asking him to stay his advance and make peace. The message was from the Buri and the other allies of King Decebalus. By thus warning Trajan that the Dacians were not isolated but enjoyed the support of numerous warlike populations, Decebalus hoped to induce the Roman emperor to start negotiations for peace or at least to overhaul his war machinery, which would have enabled the Dacian king to gain time. But Trajan continued his march onwards. Having joined forces at Tibiscum, the two Roman columns advanced along the Bistra Valley towards Sarmizegetusa.

It was at Tapae, the narrow, forested place now called the Iron Gates of Transylvania, that Trajan first met resistance. Having abstained from hostile acts so far, Decebalus decided to give battle thinking that even if the day went against him it would delay the enemy's advance. Topographic conditions here were unfavourable to the deployment of the Roman's superior forces. The clash was fierce but shorter than expected. Only the auxiliary Roman forces fought, for the battle was won before the legionaries had cause to intervene. With a violent storm raging and impressed by the death of a Dacian chieftain struck by lightning, the Dacians abandoned their positions and withdrew, though in good order. They had been defeated by the elements and their superstitious fears rather than by the superiority of the Romans.

The Roman army in pursuit of the Dacians occupied the Hațeg country and penetrated into the Orăștie Mountains by way of Boșorod and Costești. In one of the Dacian citadels, the Romans recovered the booty taken by Decebalus on the occasion of Cornelius Fuscus's disastrous expedition. It should be recalled that after the peace negotiated with Domitian in 89, this booty had not been returned by Decebalus. Simultaneously a wing of the Roman army under the command of Laberius Maximus undertook an expedition along the Luncani Valley south-west of Sarmizegetusa (Grădiștea Muncelului) where he conquered by a surprise attack an important citadel, possibly on the site of present-day Piatra Roșie; he also captured Decebalus's sister. The Roman advance over the mountains was very slow on account of a variety of difficulties and primarily because of the resistance of the Dacians, who withdrew towards Sarmizegetusa only by slow degrees, never abandoning a position without fierce fighting and destroying everything they could not carry away with them. In order to gain time, Decebalus sent the emperor a great deputation of his allies headed by Buri foot soldiers and Sarmatian horsemen, to bring to his notice that they, too, would go into action if he did not cease hostilities. Trajan refused to deal with them but was soon met by another delegation, this time of lower class Dacians, *comati*, who handed him a request for peace direct from Decebalus. The Roman emperor again refused the request, which was ostensibly insincere as it had not been transmitted by the representatives of a class possessing political responsibilities. However, all this served the dilatory purposes of the Dacian king. Winter was coming and military operations would cease without any decisive result having been obtained by the Romans. Nevertheless, they were so near the main target of the war, Sarmizegetusa, and Decebalus's position seemed so desperate that they could spend the winter looking forward to the promising prospects of the following spring.

But the Romans' dreams were rudely shattered, for at the height of winter unexpected news reached them that the bulk of Decebalus's allies had crossed into Dobrudja and the remaining territory of Moesia Inferior and were attacking the weak auxiliary Roman garrisons along the Lower Danube. It was only then that Trajan realized how serious had been the threat made by the Buri and their allies. His victorious advance into the Dacian Mountains could end by being a dangerous trap if the Dacian plan were carried out. The initiative had passed into the hands of his able opponent without his being aware of it. The emperor had to readjust things without delay in order to meet this unexpected situation. Leaving behind only sufficient forces to keep the positions that had been won, he took the bulk of his army to Drobeta where his fleet was stationed. Fortunately for him, winter was surprisingly mild that year. The reliefs on Trajan's Column — that precious document that gives a full account of the Dacian Wars in eloquent scenes — show how on the Daco-Sarmatian coalition crossing the Danube, the crust of ice being thin broke under the weight of some of their cavalry and caused a grievous disaster. Trajan is then shown in the early months of 102 embarking his forces and impedimenta and floating swiftly on the ice-free waters of the Danube. Having disembarked in one of the ports of Moesia Inferior, possibly Novae (Shishtov) or Sexaginta Prista (Ruse), he made for the interior of the province at the head of his cavalry and defeated beyond recovery the Sarmatian horsemen, after which he took all his forces to the Shipka Pass and caught up with an important Dacian army not far from present-day Tirnovo, which he surprised during the night and crushed after savage fighting. Here he ordered that a citadel — Nicopolis ad Istrum, present-day Stari Nikiup — should be immediately built. This victory made communications between his army and the rest of the Empire safe, while Decebalus's plan was dealt its first blow.

Nevertheless, the plan still held good for the counter-offensive of the Dacian king in the Transylvanian mountains after Trajan's departure ended with the defeat of the Roman forces while the main column of Decebalus's allies, the most numerous and strongest, was advancing from northern Dobrudja to the Balkans. Trajan went to meet them with all his forces. The clash that took place on the Adamclisi Plateau in the forested steppe of south-western Dobrudja was a complete slaughter. This is the battle that is the most extensively represented on the Column. All the Roman forces took part in it: auxiliaries, legionaries, pretorians, the emperor's personal guard, the Roman war engines; the enemy were slaughtered indiscriminately and for the first and only time wounded Romans belonging to the auxiliary forces as well as to the legions are shown. It was a victory won by the Romans but at the cost of an immense sacrifice. The Column shows barbarians in flight or captured in great numbers, and it also shows Trajan delivering a speech to thank his men and handing out rewards.

The mutilated text of Cassius Dio refers to this battle and not to the easy victory won at Tapae. It says : "Trajan saw many wounded among his men and killed many of the enemy, and as bandages were insufficient he is said not to have spared his own clothes, which he tore into strips to bind the wounds ; for those who had died in battle he ordered that an altar be raised and services to their memory be officiated every year." This altar was discovered at Adamclisi, where the battle was fought. The foundations and steps form a square with sides of 36 ft. still above ground, while what is left of the wall discovered among the ruins entitles us to conclude that they were about 18 ft. high, all covered with the names of the Roman soldiers fallen in battle, whose number is estimated to total nearly 4,000, an enormous figure for a victorious army.

At Adamclisi, Trajan was on the brink of catastrophe but this made his victory all the more important, since Decebalus's plan was now definitely beyond realization and Trajan was indisputable master of the destinies of war. Decebalus's victory over the forces Trajan had left in the mountains now lost its significance. The Roman emperor commemorated his victory in Dobrudja not only by the altar and the mausoleum mentioned above but also by a monumental trophy inaugurated in A.D. 109, whose impressive ruins — a cylindrical mound of compact concrete nearly 36 ft. high and 90 ft. in diameter — still towers over the Dobrudjan steppe.

Apart from the three monuments raised on the battlefield, there is a fourth commemorative structure at Adamclisi : the citadel in the vicinity founded at the time by the veterans who had fought in the battle and significantly named Tropaeum Trajani. Obviously the destinies of Trajan's wars in Dacia had been decided on the Lower Danube. The campaigns that followed were extremely hazardous and Decebalus's resistance fierce, but after Adamclisi Dacia's final fall had become inevitable.

Immediately after the Adamclisi victory, Trajan re-embarked his forces, sailed up the Danube and returned to the Transylvanian mountains to resume his advance towards Sarmizegetusa. Operations had to start from scratch as during his absence the positions occupied the year before had been lost to Decebalus. After fighting fiercely throughout the summer to conquer the numerous fortified mountain tops of the Orăştie range, the Romans finally found themselves in the vicinity of the Dacian capital. The Moorish prince Lucius Quietus and his African cavalry having surrounded this almost impregnable citadel by surprise, Decebalus decided to ask for peace and to accept all the conditions that might be set by the victor. It was for him the only means of preventing the extinction of the Dacian state while hoping for more favourable prospects in the future. On the other hand, Trajan, too, was obliged for the moment to give up some of the plans made at the start of war, for he could not demand fresh efforts of his men, exhausted by two years of uninterrupted campaigns. At the close of A.D. 102, a solemn peace was concluded, but the terms were very hard on the Dacian king who had to hand over all the war engines, all the Roman craftsmen and deserters in his service, and take upon himself not to accept others, to dissolve his citadels, his capital included, and to maintain only such foreign relations as approved of by Rome. As a security, a permanent Roman garrison was left in the Dacian state, namely at a place in the Haţeg country where later the colony named Ulpia Sarmizegetusa was to spring up. Trajan returned triumphantly to Rome.

It was a two years' peace. Neither of the opponents could consider the peace otherwise than as a truce. Trajan made intensive preparations for a second war. A bridge was built over the Danube at Drobeta (present-day Turnu Severin) by the skilled architect Apollodorus of Damascus. On the other hand, well aware of the catastrophe ahead of him, Decebalus decided to violate the peace conditions which had been intended to cripple him. He again began to entice craftsmen to come from the Roman Empire, to rebuild his citadels, and seek allies. Then, early in 105 he started hostilities by a surprise attack on the Roman garrisons in the vicinity of his capital, though without success. This he did to forestall the Romans and obtain freedom of action. Longinus, commander of the occupation forces, sought to enter into negotiations in order to gain time for Trajan, now on his way to the Danube with the bulk of the Roman army. Longinus was captured by a cunning trick but his heroic suicide brought to nought Decebalus's plan for exacting easier terms from Trajan in exchange for the release of such a valuable hostage. The Dacian king then resorted to extreme measures, paying for the assassination of Trajan. The emperor had in the meantime reached the banks of the Danube. In this attempt, too, Decebalus failed, for the plot was discovered. Considering Decebalus as lost, his allies of the first war, who had been defeated at Adamclisi, broke with him and concluded a pact of friendship with the Roman Empire. Furthermore, a message the Dacian king had sent to Pachorus, King of the Parthians, proposing that he should attack the Roman Empire in the east, was left unanswered. Seeing no way out of the deadlock, Decebalus decided to fight on alone to the last, his one aim now being to prolong the combat for as long as possible and to give the enemy forces more than they had bargained for.

The events of the second war are not easy to interpret on Trajan's Column, for they are not complemented by written records. It is probable that in order to completely encircle the Dacian forces, the Romans attacked Dacia simultaneously from several directions: through Banat, along the valleys of the Rivers Jiu and Olt, and also perhaps through southern Moldavia and eastern

Transylvania. The main action, however, was fought in the Orăștie Mountains in the spring and summer of 106. All the citadels on the mountain tops were conquered one after the other with great difficulty, and Sarmizegetusa itself was finally surrounded. Opposing the Roman assaults with epic gallantry, the capital only fell when its water supplies were exhausted and its last defenders had died of thirst. At the last moment, Decebalus and a group of noblemen succeeded in making their way on horseback along secret paths through the Roman ranks in the hope of building up new centres of defence against the invaders in other parts of Dacia. But finally surrounded by the enemy, Decebalus stabbed himself with his curved dagger to avoid being taken prisoner. His head was shown to the Roman troops and then taken to Rome and exhibited on the Gemoniae Steps before being thrown into the Tiber so that the people of the Urbs should know that their great adversary was really dead and that the bitter wars against him were at an end.

After the fall of Sarmizegetusa Regia the Romans took every measure to preclude that this sacred place of the Dacians should serve to arouse the people of Dacia in future : they deported the population of the region to other parts of the country, destroyed the religious monuments of the shrine and for a long time kept a garrison in the conquered citadel. In 106, the year of victory, the Dacia Decebalus had ruled was proclaimed a Roman province. Trajan remained for nearly a year after that in what had been the theatre of war in order to organize the province. Colonia Ulpia Trajana, subsequently to be called Sarmizegetusa, was to be the main city of the new province. It had been founded in the Hațeg country at the place where Longinus's garrison had formerly been stationed, and was more than thirty-five miles away from Decebalus's Sarmizegetusa Regia in the Orăștie Mountains.

Dacia's conquest by the Romans was a decisive event in the history of Romania, for intensive Romanization of the province in the years that followed laid the durable foundations of the Romanian nation, descendants of the worthy Geto-Dacian people and heirs to the inestimable values Rome implanted in the country.

CHAPTER THREE

ROMAN DACIA AND SCYTHIA MINOR

TRAJAN'S victory over the Dacians, a hard-won victory, was the crowning of Roman efforts to consolidate their Lower Danube boundary. By conquering Dacia, the Roman Empire had reached the height of its expansion. Situated in the centre of the arc formed by the Danube between the Pannonian Plain and the Black Sea, this Carpathian bastion which had been for a long time not only a basis of Dacian power but also the rallying point of the various peoples of South-east Europe against the Roman Empire, had now become a Roman possession and a means of imposing the strategic superiority of Rome on all the peoples of this entire area. A Romanized Dacia consolidated the Roman element in East Europe and laid the foundations from which emerged the Romanian people.

1. Organization of the Province of Dacia under Trajan

THE part Dacia had to play in consolidating Roman domination along the Danube was of such importance that Trajan took great pains to make of the country a durable Roman outpost. Immediately after his final victory in 106, which gave him mastery over the whole of Dacia (*Universa Dacia*), the Roman Emperor began to organize the land he had conquered.

At first *Provincia Dacia* was confined to the inter-Carpathian areas of Decebalus's former kingdom, such as it had been after the peace with Domitian in 89 and with Trajan in 102. The lands beyond these confines, which had formerly been part of the great Geto-Dacian homeland, had come under Roman authority before that, as annexes to the provinces of the right bank of the Danube. Banat and West Oltenia (where the Drobeta bridge was to be found) were part of Moesia Superior, while the rest of Oltenia, together with Muntenia, Lower Moldavia, and part of South-east Transylvania along the River Olt (from Turnu-Roşu to Oituz) had been occupied by forces from Moesia Inferior. Dobrudja (Scythia Minor) was also part of that province. Soon after 106 part of these territories were to be incorporated in the new province of Dacia. North Transylvania, Crişana, Maramureş, and most of Moldavia were outside the boundaries of Roman domination, the populations of those parts being bound to the interests of the Empire merely by pacts which secured their autonomy.

The very first year the new province was settled with considerable masses of Romanized elements brought over from all parts of the Empire *(ex toto orbe Romano)*. It is perhaps the only instance in Roman history of such substantial official intervention in a Romanization process. Trajan was anxious to create within the shortest time a Roman country in a territory which had formerly been a great threat to Roman peace. A large part of the native population, now disarmed and disorganized, had remained in regions determined by the victors, to whom they had officially submitted. Having become sparse after the two wars, which had taken a heavy toll of human lives, and after the emigration of the more active political elements to the Northern Carpathians, the Dacian population was below the new Roman colonists in point of civilization as well as socially. The best land and the more important economic positions were given to the new arrivals.

The Roman elements in Dacia developed in close unison with those of the neighbouring provinces, primarily those of the two Moesias and of Illyricum. The native population, naturally attracted by the higher standard of life that was rapidly developing in their midst, began to value its advantages and to adopt the forms of Roman civilization. Romanization was being carried out in the same manner in the intermediary regions between Transylvania and the Danube, that is in Banat and Oltenia. Towards the end of Trajan's rule at the earliest, a territorial reorganization was carried out. The whole of Oltenia, together with a strip of land south of the Transylvanian reaches of the River Olt, was made into a separate province, named Dacia Inferior. The other Dacia, made up of Decebalus's former kingdom enlarged through the incorporation of Banat, was named Dacia Superior. The two Dacias were two successive creations and not the result of the division of the province set up in 106, as it is usually believed.

Trajan did not attempt to incorporate within the Roman Empire all the Geto-Dacian lands, which showed such natural, harmonious unity. Muntenia and Lower Moldavia always remained outside the Roman provincial régime, although their importance in the communications between Dacia and Moesia Inferior, primarily with the cities along the Dobrudjan coast, was evident. This apparent anomaly is to be accounted for by military reasons. The necessity of ensuring the defence of the Empire along the Lower Danube was the essential aim of Roman policy in this part of Europe. While the Danubian *limes* (frontier) was weakened in Banat and Oltenia where the main support was the mountain ranges of Dacia Superior and the Olt Valley, the situation was different in the lower reaches of the Danube, where the river was an impressive and continuous obstacle, invaluable in these regions of flat land. Incorporation of Muntenia and Moldavia in the Dacians' provincial organization would have raised strategic problems impossible to solve on what was one of the frontiers most threatened from the north-east. Consequently, Trajan had to be cautious and preserve the Danube line of military defence while assigning to

Muntenia and Lower Moldavia the role of exterior safety areas depending on Moesia Inferior but non-colonized and non-urbanized.

The military, political, and administrative organization of wide scope imposed by Trajan along the Lower Danube spread not only over the various regions of Dacia but also over the provinces along the right bank of the Danube — the two Moesias and Thrace — where many towns were founded by the same emperor. From among them Oescus (Ghighen) on the Danube, facing Oltenia, was raised to the rank of a *colonia*.

It was Dobrudja which profited most by the new Roman order installed after the conquest of Dacia. Considerably reinforced by military troops, surrounded only by regions which in different ways depended on Rome, this area between the Danube and the Black Sea was to live henceforth through a long period of peace and thus attain a high standard of civilization.

Having made sure that the measures he had taken in Dacia and in the neighbouring provinces were effective, Trajan returned to Rome in 107 and celebrated his triumph with great pomp. He bolstered the finances of the Empire with the immense treasures captured in Dacia, and had the sumptuous Forum that bears his name built in the centre of Rome, with the Trajan Column towering in the middle of it. This commemorative monument preserved to this day gives the history of the great Dacian wars carved in relief spiralwise. The building of the Column was started in A.D. 113.

2. Consolidation of Roman Rule

AFTER waging another war in the east against the Parthians from A.D. 114 to 117, Emperor Trajan died on August 11, 117, at Selinunt in Cilicia. His successor, Hadrian (P. Aelius Hadrianus), a nephew whom he had adopted at the last moment, proved a worthy continuer of his work. With a lucid, realistic mind, Hadrian realized that the Roman Empire had reached its utmost limits of expansion in relation to its forces and resources, and that an attempt to exceed those limits could only lead to dangerous involvements. Consequently, his first move was to make peace with the Parthians and abandon the new provinces which Trajan had hastened to create in Armenia and Mesopotamia at a time when military conditions were still precarious.

Hadrian was an excellent soldier and gave much attention to the organization of the army. Whenever necessary, he acted energetically in defence of the Empire.

As early as in 117 the Roxolan Sarmatians north of Pontus Euxinus, encouraged by the difficulties the Romans were up against in the Parthian wars and by the absence of part of the Danube garrisons, began to stir, demanding that the subsidies paid them by the Empire should be increased. After Trajan's death, they found the moment ripe for increasing their threat and, as a first move, they prompted their Iazygian kinsmen on the Tisa plain to attack Dacia. Hadrian met the situation with the utmost promptness. He immediately sent back to their garrisons the Dacian and Moesia Inferior forces which had participated in the Parthian war, and then came to the Danube in person. His energetic intervention resulted in a conciliatory attitude towards the financial claims of the Roxolans, and peace was restored in eastern Dacia without the necessity of resorting to arms. The new treaty concluded on this occasion was so satisfactory to both sides that the Roxolans observed it for a long time.

When peace had been re-established, Hadrian gave his attention to the two Dacias and to Moesia Inferior, now sufficiently consolidated to take upon themselves the reorganization measures suggested by his defensive policy. In Dacia Superior only Legion XIII Gemina remained with a garrison at Apulum (present-day Alba Iulia).

Legion IV Flavia was removed to Moesia Superior, more precisely to Singidunum (Belgrade), a point of junction between the two provinces from where it could more efficiently watch the Iazygian populations in the west. With a view to economizing his forces, Hadrian did away with the auxiliary garrisons in Muntenia for which there was no point in their remaining now that Provincia Dacia had been consolidated. On the other hand, the *limes Alutanus* was greatly reinforced. Hadrian also directed that the woodwork of Trajan's bridge at Drobeta should be destroyed for the services this grand structure afforded could not compensate for the danger of its falling into enemy hands in the event of a surprise invasion and of its allowing an easy penetration into the Empire.

An indefatigable administrator, Hadrian spent most of the twenty-one years of his principate (117-38) journeying throughout the Roman provinces in order to inspect them. Apart from his military intervention of the year 118 at the time of the Sarmatian disturbances, he travelled across Dacia and Dobrudja in 123-4, his aim being to see that the Roman forces were properly trained and the administrative bodies were functioning satisfactorily. His visit made a considerable contribution to the economic development of the provinces, such as the consolidation and maintenance of roads, the building of public works, and the development of urban centres. It was during his principate that certain Dacian towns, such as Napoca (present-day Cluj) and Drobeta (Turnu Severin) were given the title of *municipium*.

The political and military order established by Hadrian along the Lower Danube was continued by his successor, a peaceful emperor and an excellent organizer, T. Aelius Antoninus Pius (138-61), Hadrian's foster son, under whom the Roman world reached the culmination point of its stability and progress. It was, however, a time when frequent mild disturbances occurred in the provinces, showing discontent with the strict taxation system of the Romans and foreshadowing a mounting social crisis, despite the economic prosperity and the high living of the well-to-do classes.

Disturbances also occurred in Dacia, the free Dacians beyond the borders of the province harassing and carrying on attacks. Their dependence on the Empire was merely political and, as they enjoyed full liberty of organization in their territories, they could at any time contest it. An attack on the province recorded to have occurred in 143 was easily repelled, but another of greater proportions took place in 156-7 when the provincial army was obliged to wage a systematic war against the offenders. Finally, the free Dacians were driven back beyond the frontier along the valleys of the Someş River.

The inroads of the free Dacians into Dacia were the only warlike events to occur in the Carpatho-Danubian provinces under Antoninus Pius. At the time Dobrudja, undisturbed by foreign threats, enjoyed a flourishing state, as never before in its history. This region, which was the centre of gravity of the whole Moesia Inferior, with the most numerous and most important garrisons and a busy economic life, had become profoundly Roman. The inscriptions and constructions of Dobrudja of Antoninus's time are proof of the prosperity of the cities as well as of the countryside down to the most out-of-the-way places.

Under Antoninus Pius's successor, his foster son Marcus Aurelius Verus, the Roman Empire experienced fearful trials, in contrast with the comparative peace it had formerly enjoyed.

During the first year of his principate, in 161, Marcus Aurelius had to organize an expedition against the Parthians who had attacked the eastern provinces. A great army which also included troops from the Danube regions, namely Legion V Macedonica stationed in Dobrudja, was sent eastward under the command of his foster brother Lucius Aurelius Verus, the co-regent emperor. After five years of struggle, the Parthians were defeated and compelled to make peace. Hardly had that war ended when another of far greater proportions and much more dangerous broke out in Europe along the higher and middle reaches of the Danube. In 166 all the Germanic populations beyond the river, and primarily the Marcomanni and Quadi, forced their way across the Roman frontiers and, having overrun Pannonia, reached as far as northern Italy. Shortly after, in 167, the free Dacians also overran the province of Dacia, while other populations of the northern Carpathians such as the Bastarnians and the Costobocae, were preparing to take action. The situation was extremely serious, for the attacks were simultaneous and placed the Roman army at a distinct disadvantage. The monolithic force of this army was now for the first time counterbalanced by an immense coalition of forces which included all the trans-Danubian populations, from Vindelicia to the Iazygian steppe and to the northern Carpathians. This was not due to an understanding among these populations, who had always lived in discord ; it was a spontaneous and uniform effect of the pressure of the Goths who, possibly on account of the growing severity of the climate, had left their Scandinavian territories, crossed the Baltic, and were slowly but in great numbers making their way southward, thus driving the local peoples in the direction of the Roman Empire.

At the time a frightful plague, which the Roman forces had brought from the East, was becoming increasingly virulent in the Empire. Marcus Aurelius controlled the panic in Rome and took prompt measures to cope with all difficulties. The main military efforts were concentrated against the Marcomanni and Quadi, troops having been brought from all parts of the Empire. In 167, the Roman army under the command of Marcus Aurelius, assisted by his brother, took the offensive. After a year's fighting the provinces which had been overrun were liberated and the aggressors driven back across the Danube. At the same time peace was re-established in Dacia where the free Dacians in their plundering raids had reached as far as the gold-bearing areas in the Western Mountains and the neighbourhood of Sarmizegetusa.

The victory of 168 did not in any way remove the possibility of further invasions. On his return to Rome, Marcus Aurelius made preparations for a new offensive, resorting to emergency measures in recruiting soldiers and procuring funds. The war was resumed in 169 and lasted for five years. It was waged along the left bank of the Danube, in the mountains held by the Marcomanni and the Quadi, and in the steppe of the Iazygian Sarmatians, and was attended by many trials, Roman successes alternating with defeats. Generals of great ability lost their lives in disastrous battles, among them being M. Claudius Fronto, Dacia's consular governor, who had participated in the battles fought against the Iazygians as chief of the forces of his own province and of Moesia Superior. Ultimately, the Roman armies, encouraged by the Emperor's perseverance, succeeded in putting down all resistance and the barbarians submitted one after the other : the Marcomanni in 172, the Quadi in 174, and the Iazygian Sarmatians in 175.

In 170 the Costobocae (Dacians of the northern Carpathians) had overrun Dobrudja and penetrated as far as Greece. Finally defeated, they were settled as *dediticii* (unconditional subjects) in various provinces in the centre of the Empire.

Despite the great trials the whole of the Empire was experiencing, the Carpatho-Danubian provinces generally maintained the prosperity they had enjoyed under Marcus Aurelius. The peace with the Marcomanni, Quadi, and Iazygians was not of long duration. Around 177 these populations again rose in arms against the Empire. In order to sow discord among them, Marcus Aurelius concluded a new peace with the Iazygians, setting conditions more favourable than the preceding ones, among other things entitling them to maintain relations with their Roxolan kinsmen in the East by crossing the province of Dacia, with the approval of the Roman authorities every time. Having thus solved the Sarmatian problem, Marcus Aurelius concentrated all his forces against the Marcomanni and Quadi, whom he reduced to total capitulation after some resounding victories. The emperor was planning to make a new Roman province of their land and to remove the boundary of the Empire along the line of the northern Carpathians, thus solving a difficult problem for the Empire, when he died on March 17, 180. His successor was L. Aurelius Commodus, his own son, who had been sharing authority with his father since 177. Disorderly and frivolous, without any serious thought for the State, and far from inheriting his father's outstanding talents, Commodus made haste to return to Rome, giving up the idea of a new annexation to the Empire and making a peace such as the defeated barbarians had never dreamed of. However, thanks to the great victory won by Marcus Aurelius, the peace was effective and lasting, definitely putting an end to the long and troublesome wars against the Marcomanni.

Under Commodus's rule a number of conflicts with the Buri and free Dacians were decided. Hostages and prisoners were taken from the Buri — Decebalus's allies of old bordering on Dacia — and the obligation was laid on them to make a desert area 40 stadia (four and half miles) wide along the Roman frontier. The same obligation was laid on the Vandals and Iazygians. At the same time thousands of free Dacians were settled, probably within the Dacian province, as *dediticii*. Later, ca. A.D. 184, an army under the command of D. Claudius Albinus and C. Pescennius Niger took the offensive in the north of the province against other free Dacians and neighbouring populations, compelling them to observe the peace of the province.

The Danube provinces were within the focus of Emperor Septimus Severus. Inspired by monarchic tendencies, Septimus Severus strengthened his dynasty, which continued his policy after his death. His son, M. Aurelius Antoninus, also named Caracalla (211-7), travelled through Dobrudja and Dacia as far as Porolissum. On that occasion he renewed the Roman pacts with the free Dacians, from whom he took many hostages. His successor, the usurper Macrinus (217-8), was to release those hostages in the hope of winning a more lasting friendship.

It was under Caracalla that the famous Edict named Constitutio Antoniniana was issued, extending the right of Roman citizenship to all the free townsmen of the Empire. Although the Edict was inspired by fiscal reasons, the aim being to levy taxes from which the *peregrini* (the inhabitants who were not Roman citizens) were exempted, its effects promoted Romanization, for a large number of people became Roman citizens, the consciousness of solidarity with the Roman people thus becoming more widespread and being strengthened, while the Romanization process in the provinces that had already been won over by Latin civilization was speeded up. This was the case of the Danubian provinces, including Dacia and Moesia Inferior. But there was another consequence of the Constitutio Antoniniana : the titles of *colonia* and *municipium* lost their value for, being based on the degree of Romanization of the inhabitants of certain towns in contrast to other settlements where the peregrines prevailed, these titles lost their sense when everywhere there were only equal citizens. Actually, after Caracalla these titles fell into disuse and were given only exceptionally to towns as ornaments, without any practical use.

Under Caracalla's successors — Macrinus, Elagabalus (218-22) and Severus Alexander (222-35) — Dacia, like, the other Danubian provinces, enjoyed a period of peace. Severus Alexander showed special solicitude for Dacia. It is to be observed that, particularly under the rule of Elagabalus, an adolescent who was also high priest of the Syrian god Baal, Eastern religious rites spread widely throughout Italy and the Latin provinces of the Empire. Among the soldiers and traders of Eastern origin living in Dacia and Scythia Minor such rites had been practised for many years.

3. Roman Civilization in Dacia

THE last stage in the ascension of the Roman Empire now being under consideration, we should dwell for a moment on the essential aspects of Roman slave-owning civilization as it developed in Provincia Dacia.

Archaeological finds in the Roman cities of Dacia prove that the latter had attained a remarkable level of development. The streets were paved and provided with a drainage system ; there were central markets (forums) surrounded by *portici* and shops, and there were also temples, public buildings for administrative purposes, private homes, shops, warehouses, and large public baths. Close to the city there was often a great amphitheatre. Water was brought from springs by means of aqueducts. Around the *castra* there were baths and sometimes amphitheatres for the use of the soldiers and of the civilian population of the neighbouring *canabae*. Outside the towns large and complex country houses *(villae)* have been found. These were isolated on large landed estates. From the great military roads which crossed the province from end to end linking the towns and *castra* between them, there have been left in places big slabs of hard stone laid over a bed of gravel and sand. The roads were marked with milestones indicating the distance to the nearest locality in thousands of steps *(mille passuum =* 1348.11 yd.) and at every stage (*ca.* 12-15 miles) there was a *statio* or a *mansio* with watch and maintenance posts, inns, relay horses, stores of military provisions, etc. Where the cities ended, funeral monuments bordered the roads. They were of lime or marble and carved on them were inscriptions, the portraits of the buried dead, and mythological symbols.

The great development of Dacian cities is to be accounted for by the busy economic activities carried on in Dacia from the very first years of its transformation into a province. The main pursuits in the country were farming, stock-breeding, and mining. In farming small and medium farms predominated. They were owned by veterans, civilian colonists brought over from other parts of the Empire, and also by the subjected Dacians. It was only later, in the third century, as the general crisis of the Empire was aggravated and the masses were impoverished, that great landed estates were built up at the expense of the smaller farmers. There were also large imperial estates consisting of arable land, pastures, and forests which were leased out. On the large estates both slaves and free workers did the work, the latter being paid in cash or in kind from the products of their work.

The transport of goods was facilitated by a dense network of roads and by the use of rafts plying along the rivers, especially the Olt and the Mureș, not to mention the intense sailing on the Danube. In the towns, commerce and the crafts were the main economic activities. Many traders came to Dacia from the East, being drawn thither by the country's wealth. In their turn Dacian traders took their wares to other provinces of the Empire. There were banking transactions in Dacia, with credit companies or individual usurers. The Roman coins in current circulation in the province were of silver and bronze, and exceptionally of gold. In the third century a mint in Ulpia Sarmizegetusa minted imperial coins of bronze with the symbols of the province.

The crafts were of great variety, relying for the most part on local raw materials. Vestiges and indications have been found everywhere attesting to the existence of shops where metals, wood, fabrics, and hides and skins were processed.

Taxation, a most oppressive aspect of Roman administration, was the mainspring of abusive practices. There were onerous toll gates *(portoria)*, taxes being levied on goods at every turn : on their entering the province, on being conveyed along the highroads and over bridges, and on their entering the towns. Freedmen and slaves made up the very numerous personnel of the toll gates, serving their patrons and at the same time deriving handsome benefits for themselves. On the other hand, abusive practices were also current in the recruiting of men for work and the requisitioning of tools and provisions, duties which the imperial clerks and the army laid in an arbitrary manner upon the villages lying in the vicinity of the highroads. Despite the measures taken by the imperial authorities, such abusive practices could not be checked, and the crisis the Empire went through in the third century increased them.

Production relations were those specific to a slave-owning society. In Dacia, too, as all over the world in those days, society was divided into antagonistic classes : primarily the slaves and their masters. But there were great social differences within these two main classes. Among the free citizens the great plutocrats emerged from the multitude of poor workers. Moreover, all slaves were not subjected to the same conditions. While those working in the mines and in the fields were cruelly exploited, toiling to exhaustion, those slaves who supervised the former or were assigned various administrative or fiscal duties, enjoyed fairly favourable conditions, which the free paupers often envied. Freedmen *(liberti)* were often appointed to public functions of some responsibility.

Wealth, primarily agricultural wealth, was being concentrated in the hands of a minority. The small landowners, when dispossessed, increased the ranks of the poor workers who offered their labour for an insignificant wage. Foreign wars, which were very frequent during Marcus Aurelius's principate and after him, were to aggravate the crisis, increasing taxation excesses, abusive practices, ordeals, and requisitions, and generating discontent, resistance, and uprisings. Although insufficiently attested in Dacia, these were general phenomena which must have existed here as in all the other provinces. Inscriptions have been found in Dacia that spoke of *latrones* (robbers, outlaws) whose frequency in the second and third centuries throughout the Empire is proof of deep-going social unrest. It was only when faced by the invasions from beyond the borders that all the inhabitants of the province became to a certain extent one, for the enemy, being out to plunder and enslave, made no difference between those they met on their way. This was not real social solidarity but simply the result of a temporary identity of all before a common threat. On the other hand, many of the paupers who were beyond the invaders' fury sought to take advantage of the exploiters' difficulties, robbing them or, if they were slaves, making their escape.

It should be remembered, however, that these acute aspects of the social contradictions became characteristic and preponderant only during the great crisis of the mid-third century and that in the preceding period, under the rule of the emperors of the Antonine and Severan stock, there was sufficient balance to allow the splendid Roman civilization to flourish in Dacia. Apart from rapid economic prosperity, we should note the high level of cultural progress in the province. All the inhabitants, irrespective of their ethnical origin or social status, spoke only Latin among themselves and with the authorities. Education through schools and other means, was widespread. Writing was in general use, as proved by the many inscriptions, of which some 3,000 (all Latin, with the exception of about 35 in Greek) have been discovered so far. The waxed tables preserved in a mine at Roşia (Alburnus Major in Roman times) show that writing was in daily use even among the lower strata of the population whenever deeds, even though insignificant, were required.

The religious beliefs of the province were cosmopolitan, like the origin of the inhabitants who gave expression to them in inscriptions. A great variety of gods were worshipped in Roman Dacia, most of them Italic : Jupiter Optimus Maximus, Juno, Minerva, Mercury, Apollo, Diana, Venus, Mars, Liber, Libera, Silvanus, Hercules, etc. In the order of frequency, next follow the mystic Eastern gods brought over by soldiers and traders from Asia Minor, Syria, and Egypt : Mithras, Cybele, Isis, Serapis, Jupiter, Dolichenus, etc. Most widespread was the cult of Dionysos, an old Hellenic god. With so many cults in vogue, Eastern and Hellenic deities frequently fused with the Roman ones. Inscriptions show that gods specific to the province were also honoured, among them Dacia, Terra Dacia, Genius Daciarum, Dii et Deae Daciarum. On the other hand, the old Dacian religious concepts crop up under the name and forms of Roman divinities : Liber, Libera, Diana Augusta, Diana Regina, Silvanus, Nemesis. It is also from ancient local beliefs that the cult of the Danubian Horseman was derived, marble or bronze sculptures of which are to be found in all the provinces along the Danube, and primarily in Dacia. The Thracian Horseman, a divinity specific to Thrace and Moesia Inferior, is also frequent in the Carpathian province. Christianity, which at the time of Dacia's occupation by the Romans was still in the illegal stage, is not met with north of the Danube before Aurelian. It was only in the fourth century that it penetrated intensively into Dacia. In Dobrudja, however, it is attested earlier and with sufficient force, for on the occasion of the various persecutions there were many martyrs in that region.

This is but a brief survey of the main aspects of Roman civilization in Dacia. It was under the aegis of this civilization that the intensive Romanization process took place, as a prerequisite to the formation of a Romanic people north of the Danube : the Romanian people. The civilian population brought over by Trajan and the army were basic factors in that process.

When discharged after around twenty-five years' service, the legionaries and auxiliaries became veterans, and received Roman citizenship together with considerable juridical and material benefits. Most of them did not return to their place of origin but settled in Dacia where they had spent such a long span of their lives and where they had illegitimate families which were subsequently recognized officially (they often lived with Dacian women) and where they could do well for themselves, especially as landowners and often as outstanding members of town councils. The army thus played an active and fundamental part in Romanizing Dacia, being also the main factor in the social rise of the native population and its participation in the development of Roman civilization in the province. The Dacians did not maintain an obstinately hostile attitude towards the victors but took part in the new life that flourished in their country. From their midst the Romans recruited many auxiliary troops sent to other parts of the Empire, and the Dacians also increasingly provided men for the Roman legions and auxiliary forces in their own province, particularly after the introduction of local recruiting under Hadrian. The populations from beyond Dacia's frontier colonized in the middle of the province after Marcus Aurelius, also provided recruits.

Dacia's population — apart from the native elements who were numerous but who seldom showed prominence in inscriptions — was based to a great extent on the Latin-speaking colonists brought over by Trajan *ex toto orbe Romano*. Most of them came from the neighbouring provinces : Moesia Superior, and Moesia Inferior, the two Pannoniae, Dalmatia, Noricum, Raetia, the two Germaniae, Gaul, Hispania, and Africa. The less numerous colonists brought from provinces where Hellenic culture prevailed — Thrace, Macedonia, Asia Minor, Syria, and Egypt — adopted the culture of the rest of the population and also became factors of Romanization once they had settled in these parts. The traders and craftsmen coming to Dacia from the East on their own initiative behaved in the same way.

4. Imperial Administration abandons Dacia

IN view of the balance of power at the time, Aurelian decided that Dacia needed to be evacuated. The evacuation probably took place in 274-5, when strategy demanded that a shorter boundary be established along the line of the Danube, as it had been before Trajan.

The withdrawal of Aurelian from Dacia had important consequences in the formation of the Romanian people, though it was a further sign of the decline of the Romans that the authorities should withdraw from a profoundly Romanized province which for over 165 years had been a powerful outpost *(propugnaculum)* of the Empire and of Roman civilization projected into the world of the barbarians. The migrations which during the previous century had filled the plains around this Carpathian bastion with numerous warlike populations, had totally changed the balance of power along the Danube. The Empire, now without internal resources as a result of the crisis it had undergone, had to economize its forces by cutting down the long perimeter of Trajan's province and resuming the defensive line along the Danube. Under the new conditions, Dacia was of no use to the Empire from a military point of view. It was no longer efficient in defending the Danubian frontier; on the contrary, it jeopardized it, disjointing the boundary and depriving it of important forces required within. The great barbarian forces skirted Dacia fearlessly to attack the provinces of Illyricum and Moesia. Withdrawal from Dacia did not mean that the strategic position before Trajan was being reverted to. Even without Roman forces, Dacia, with most of its population Romanized, did not consider itself as separated from Rome. And the Empire was still powerful enough not to allow a new enemy force, like that of the Dacians of old, to overrun the territory of its former province.

Aurelian evacuated Dacia in good order, unhampered by the barbarians who had been beaten and reduced to a state of peace all along the Lower Danube. The forces of the province crossed to the right bank of the river : Legion XIII Gemina occupied the *castrum* at Ratiaria (Archar) while Legion V Macedonica returned to its old garrison at Oescus (Ghighen). The administrative officials were withdrawn simultaneously with the army and were followed by the rich and by a part of the townspeople, who were settled between the Danube and the Balkans. On these territories a new province was founded. It was named *Dacia*, not only as a consolation to Roman prestige but also because its army, its administrative machinery, and the foremost social elements of the population were identical with those of the province that had been abandoned. The new Dacia lay along the Danube contiguously with what had formerly been Dacia Inferior. Probably the Dacia of Aurelian was already from the beginning divided in two provinces which were later attested to : Dacia Ripensis along the bank of the Danube, with Ratiaria as its capital city, and Dacia Mediterranea in the middle of the country, within the Balkan Peninsula, with Serdica (Sofia) as its capital city.

Ancient records preserved from sources of later date are extremely sparse concerning Dacia's evacuation. Indeed, the event has but a mere mention. However, there is nothing to justify the contention of certain modern researches that evacuation had meant total depopulation of the Carpathian province and that the Romanian people of today came from south of the Danube during the Middle Ages. This is not proved by even the vaguest record. The existence of the Romanian people exactly on the territory formerly taken up by Dacia is in open contradiction to such views. To deny the continuity of the Romanian people on the territory of their homeland is to fly against the logic of the general realities of human life and the natural course of things. The territory of the Dacia of Aurelian had neither the area nor the resources of Trajan's Dacia, and neither was it, being without a population of its own, able to receive all the inhabitants of the trans-Danubian province to the last man. An important increase in population in Aurelian's Dacia would have caused new towns and villages to be created. But there is not the faintest proof of such an increase in the number of localities in the new province between the Balkans and the Danube : archaeology, written records, and toponymy give no indication to this effect. The number of people withdrawn from Carpathian Dacia was small enough for them all to find place in the previously existing settlements beside the local population. On the other hand, the land in Aurelian's Dacia, which, we should recall, was the property of the local landowners, could not have satisfied large numbers of new arrivals from north of the Danube either in quantity or quality.

We might therefore conclude that Roman officialdom evacuated only what strictly belonged to them : the army and the officials and also what they felt in duty bound to protect first and foremost : the great landowners, the traders, and the rich, that is the holders of the main means of production. As to the masses, especially the peasants who felt bound to the land, they were content to remain in their fields and pastures for they had no vital reasons for leaving them. Official protection did not seem to be indispensable to ploughmen and shepherds who, during the various invasions of the past century, had so often been compelled to shift for themselves, as the soldiers and townspeople, besieged in their cities, had been unable to help them. The Daco-Roman peasants had become used to insecurity under barbarian pressure.

No greater evil could threaten them when left to themselves. It is through them that Romanism was perpetuated north of the Danube, to become the lasting foundation of the Romanian people.

Being abandoned by official bodies did not amount to being isolated from the rest of the Roman world. On the contrary, economic, spiritual, and even political connections between the Empire and the former province left of the Danube continued. And when Christianity became the privileged religion of the Empire in the fourth century, after three centuries of clandestine proselytism, missionaries were sent to Dacia who effectively helped to consolidate the Roman elements there. All the basic religious terminology in Romanian is of Latin origin. No migratory population exerted any influence liable to compete with that of the Empire on the Daco-Roman population left in Dacia.

Abandoned Dacia had not been ceded to anyone. Officialdom continued to consider it as a territory belonging to the Empire, as had been in former days the unoccupied and uncolonized territories of Muntenia and Lower Moldavia. As long as there was an imperial army along the Danube no foreign people could make of the Carpathians a centre of their power. The free Dacians and the Sarmatians, who immediately settled in the abandoned province, maintained their old connections with the Empire — a kind of conditional dependence —, and finally fused with the mass of the local Daco-Roman population. The later barbarian forces, such as the Goths, Huns, Avars, etc., exercised political supremacy over the Daco-Romans, but from a distance, their centres always being outside the Carpathian arc. The Danube, once again a strategic frontier, never separated the people living on its two banks. They were to continue to develop along the same lines even after the final collapse of imperial domination along the Danube in the seventh century.

The survival of the Roman element in Dacia as well as over vast territories on the right bank of the Danube —

for instance in Scythia Minor — under most adverse conditions, is the most lasting success of Roman civilization and one of the most vivid examples of the active, decisive part the Roman Empire played in promoting progress in ancient times.

5. The Roman Province of Scythia

WHEN Dacia was evacuated, Dobrudja, which had become a separate province under Diocletian, officially named Scythia, remained under imperial rule. The administrative boundary of this province separated it from what was left of the former Moesia Inferior (Moesia Secunda). It coincided with the geographical boundary between the Southern Dobrudjan steppe and the pre-Balkan forests of Deliorman.

When the capital of the Empire was removed from Rome to Byzantium (Constantinople), there was increased interest in defending the Lower Danube which had a direct impact on the new capital. Constantine the Great strengthened the Danube frontier. In Dobrudja the city of Tropaeum (Adamclisi) was rebuilt from its foundations in 316. It was then that the great walls whose ruins can be seen to this day were raised. In 324 Constantine repelled an attack of the Goths and of the eastern Sarmatians whom he pursued across the Danube and into today's Muntenia [Wallachia], defeating them in a battle where the Sarmatian king, Rausimodus, fell. After a new victory north of the Danube in 332, he forced upon the Goths a peace under which the latter agreed to recognize the authority of the Empire and to supply contingents to the Roman army. Constantine moreover established bridgeheads on the left bank of the Danube, from Bărboși in Lower Moldavia to Dierna (Orșova) in Banat. A vast protection area, which comprised part of Banat and Oltenia and the whole of Muntenia's plain, was created beyond the Danube frontier. At Sucidava (Celei) a permanent wooden bridge was built over the river and one of the old Roman roads leading to the Carpathians was repaired. These are measures which evidence the Empire's constant care to keep the territories of the former Dacian province within its grasp.

From among Constantine's sons and successors, Constantius II attached great importance to the defence of the province of Scythia which, having been like a gate giving access to trans-Danubian invasions, was turned into a strong bastion of the Empire with many garrisons.

From among the developments worthy of mention that took place in the province of Scythia in the centuries that followed, is the great rebellion of Vitalianus, a local general of Thraco-Roman origin and a native of Zaldapa (Abtaat). Being in command of the forces of the province, he rose against Anastasius, the then Roman Emperor of the East, in 513. The immediate reasons of the uprising were religious, Vitalianus, a staunch orthodox, opposing certain sectarian tendencies at the court of Anastasius. Actually, however, the wide participation of the troops and population of the province in his undertaking is to be accounted for by the discontent aroused by the financial levies. Heading an army of 50,000 soldiers and Thraco-Roman peasants and also having at his disposal a fleet with its base at Acres (Cape Caliacra), Vitalianus attacked Constantinople, the capital of the Empire, several times but without success. After seven years of virulent fighting, the conflict was brought to an end by the succeeding emperor, Justinus, who after smoothing out the religious divergences and easing the burden of taxation, enticed the rebel general to Constantinople in 520 where great honours and dignities were conferred on him, after which he mysteriously disappeared. Vitalianus has gone down in history as one of the most remarkable of the men coming from the Roman population of ancient Dobrudja.

Under Justinian (527-65), Justinus's successor, the province of Scythia lived through a period of economic and cultural advance, and had new fortifications built on its territory. At the same time its church was given a powerful impetus. Monumental basilicas were erected in various localities. After his death, however, the defence of the province was tested by the constant attacks of superior forces, especially those of the Avars.

In 584 Dobrudja was laid waste, the Avars conquering and destroying towns such as Tropaeum and Zaldapa in Scythia and Durostorum and Marcianopolis in Moesia.

Ruined and now largely rural, the province of Scythia continued for a time to be listed among the Empire's possessions, there being a few towns left on the coast and a number of imperial garrisons inland, but before the end of the seventh century even these semblances of the urban civilization of former days disappeared under the blows dealt by a new Turanic people, the Proto-Bulgars [Turanic people have their place of origin in Central Asia].

CHAPTER FOUR

THE FORMATION OF THE ROMANIAN PEOPLE

ABANDONED by the troops and the administration of the Roman Empire, Dacia was to weather the storms of the peoples' migrations, now and again finding support and stimulus in the Empire. Continuing to live on Dacian territory, the Daco-Romans were to survive the Germanic and Turanic rule in these parts, adjusting themselves to circumstances and taking advantage of the varied geographical features of their ancient homeland. The tenacity specific to the tillers of the soil and to stock-breeders enabled them actively to preserve the ethnical imprint due to their descent from the Dacians and the Romans. And even though adverse historical circumstances prevented them from keeping intact the heritage of their early formation, they were able to preserve to the end what was most valuable in it : the Roman strains rooted in a Dacian background.

1. Continuity of Daco-Roman Population in Dacia (The Proto-Romanians)

THE circumstances that brought about the evacuation of the province of Dacia by Aurelian and the political and strategic concepts on which it was based, as shown in the preceding chapter, for a long time made for a continuation of relation between the Empire and the population north of the Danube, and the unfolding historical process concluded with the emergence of the Romanian people in the historical arena. After Dacia's abandonment, written records concerning these regions became ever less numerous until they ultimately ceased to exist, the very rare ones found referring solely to situations and developments arising from the clash between the barbarians — migratory peoples — and the Empire. Consequently, for a long time modern research was unable accurately and wholly to understand the historical process of events in ancient Dacia between the close of the third and the tenth centuries A.D. The concept according to which no historical fact can be established without written records, and the tendency to exaggerate the importance and the part played by the migratory peoples, caused certain historians to evolve a theory according to which for long centuries the territory of ancient Dacia had foreign peoples settled on it, occupying the homeland of the Dacians one after the other, and living in it as masters, they had swept away every vestige of autochthonous life, Dacian or Daco-Roman. More recent research, however, relying mostly on archaeological finds, has proved the existence of many facts and historical events unrecorded in texts or misinterpreted by them ; and that the importance and role of the migratory peoples had nowhere been great enough to induce total extinction of the native, whether Pre-Roman or Roman, traditions. In the light of recent research, the history of ancient Dacia in the period of the peoples' migration is no longer a succession of inroads by the Germanic and Turanic peoples, but the final period of the Romanian people's formation over the vast area of what was free Dacia in ancient times.

The process whereby the Romanian people and their language were formed, was a long and complex one. Geographically as well as historically, there was in that process, as for all peoples that were formed in Europe at that time, fluctuations which cannot be specified in every detail but whose general line of development is clearly to be perceived and whose results — the presence of the Neo-Latin Romanian people in these parts — is a scientific reality which cannot be ignored. The latest research has invalidated the concept according to which the Romanian people had been formed solely south of the Danube, with an original "hearth" restricted to certain regions, from which they had proliferated. That concept was founded on the close kinship (by no means an identity) between the Romanian dialects wherever they might be spoken, a remarkable fact, undoubtedly, and a very rare phenomenon. But for the Romanians this might be accounted for by their way of life, the elementary level, whether agricultural or pastoral, which historical circumstances and uninterrupted foreign domination had forced on the Proto-Romanians during the period of transition to feudalism. Another explanation might be the close relationship maintained between the various branches of Roman descendants in Eastern Europe. The words of Albanian origin found almost unaltered in the Romanian language have for a long time served to prove that the Romanians' homeland had been in the west of the Balkan Peninsula. The latest scientific investigations, however, prove that most of these words (among which : barză — stork, brad — fir tree, brîu — waist band, brînză — cheese, a bucura — to rejoice, copac — tree, copil — child, groapă — pit, viezure — badger, mal — bank, mînz — foal, mazăre — peas, moș — old man, vatră — hearth) are the heritage of the Dacian language which is thus attested as an influence on the Romanians' language, just as the seventy-odd Celtic words in the French language are proof of the Celtic foundations of the French people.

Thus considered from a strictly ethnical point of view the Romanian people prove to be descendants of nearly all the Roman-based populations of Eastern Europe (the descendants of the Romans of the eastern part of the

Roman Empire), which in their turn incorporated the Romanized Geto-Dacians as basic elements. In the first chapter of this book it was shown that as early as the end of Iron Age I, the one and same Geto-Dacian population was living in the area extending from the Balkan Mountains to the northern Carpathians. Recent linguistic research has confirmed this conclusion. Apart from which, the Romans repeatedly removed Dacians north of the Danube to Moesia or to South-Danubian Dacia. And it is also known that the Romanization process involved only the provinces spreading southwards down to the Balkans, to the so-called Jirecek Line, named after the scholar who in 1902 established the limit of Romanization, to be later confirmed with certain important changes by recent research.

Thus, it is obvious that the formative process of the Romanian people in its first stage consisted essentially in the Romanization of the Geto-Dacian population. This historical truth means that the foundations of the Romanian people are rooted in Romanization and in the Dacian people, for — we repeat — it is proved that the population subjected to Romanization in this part of Europe, primarily a rural population, which remained after the decline of town life, was in the first place Dacian, both in Dacia and in Moesia. Having been Romanized, the Dacians went out of the historical picture.

Within the Dacian territories, Romanization did not stop when Dacia was abandoned by Aurelian, but continued until the early seventh century A.D. when the Danube ceased to be the Empire's boundary. All this time Romanization intensified, for Latin began to become the official religion of the Empire and was spreading by means of preaching and religious services held in Latin. The fact that this new stage of the Romanization process (after A.D. 274-5) made a full impact on the South-Danubian area and was less effective north of the Danube is only of episodic importance for the formative process of the Romanian people, because ethnographically, and for a long time also politically, as will be seen hereafter, the Danube was no real boundary.

It was thus that a Romanic people, mostly of Dacian origin, arose over extensive areas before the early seventh century under definite historical conditions. They were different from those born in other parts of the vast Roman Empire (in Spain, Gaul, etc.) and certain scholars have inclined to consider this people already Romanian, for they gave it that name. The transformation undergone by phonemes in the phrase *torna, torna, fratre* [1] as pronounced by a native south of the Danube in A.D. 578 and preserved by the Byzantine chroniclers Theophylact and Theophanes, shows that even at that time, from the language point of view, we could speak about a Romanic people different from the other Romanic peoples of those days; we will call them Proto-Romanians. We could, therefore, speak about two main stages in the formation of the Romanian people: Romanization, which gave rise to a Romanic people (the Proto-Romanians) and active preservation of Romanization, which also comprised assimilation of the migratory populations and resulted in the completion of the formative process of the Romanian people. Assimilation of the migratory elements by the masses of Romanic population north of the Danube is proof of its demographic and cultural superiority.

The first stage began simultaneously with the Romanization of the Balkan Peninsula. Economic contacts between the territories south and north of the Danube and the constant displacement of the population which preceded Dacia's occupation by the Romans, created favourable conditions for Romanization. Romanian ethno-genesis consequently relies on two fundamental elements: the autochthonous Geto-Dacian population and the Roman and Romanized colonies. Up to the early seventh century,

---

[1] *Fratre* stands for *frater* in classical Latin, so that the phoneme here is already Romanian.

the Roman elements spread over a vast part of the Carpatho-Balkan territories in Eastern Europe, making up a well-knit whole.

When the Danube frontier fell, a new stage began in their development. Although connections between the territories south and north of the Danube continued, a process of differentiation began between the Romanian populations in the Carpatho-Danubian territories and the Romanic populations south of the Danube, the former's language developing its first specific features.

After the Slavs had settled in the Balkan Peninsula, North-Danubian Dacia became the centre of gravity of the Roman elements of Eastern Europe.

The Romanic population north of the Danube (Proto-Romanians) was consolidated through additions of Romanic elements from south of the Danube and through the assimilation of the migratory elements who settled on the country's territory. As can be deduced from many archaeological, linguistic, and written testimonies, the formative process of the Romanian people and language ended between the ninth and the early tenth centuries A.D.

The first historical problems concerning the developments that followed Dacia's evacuation are the fate of the former province and its population. The view that the entire population had been evacuated, admitted at times despite the impossibility, both in theory and in practice, of such a measure being taken under the conditions prevailing in those days, is closely bound up with the necessary inference that the Visigoths had occupied the abandoned province. Some such inference is certainly to be made, for it is impossible to imagine that a region so rich in natural resources could have remained uninhabited. Nevertheless, a number of well established historical and archaeological facts invalidate the aforementioned theory.

The first fact is that a large part of the Romanized Dacians remained where they were.

Many finds — coins, hoards of money, town buildings that continued to be inhabited — attest the continued life of an important part of the old population, which preserved its connections with the Empire during the period immediately following the official evacuation, as proved by the following fact : in the Roman city of Napoca (present-day Cluj) bronze coins bearing the imprint of Aurelian's immediate successors — Emperors Tacitus (275-6), Probus (276-82) and Carinus (283-5) — have been found amidst the ruins of Roman buildings. For a later period, two finds are of outstanding importance. The first are the ruins of the former town of Apulum (Alba Iulia) with a Roman cemetery of an *urban character* dating from the fourth century A.D., where bronze coins of the time of Constantine the Great (306-36) have been found, and also exclusively Roman grave goods and scattered coins from the whole period extending from Diocletian (284-305) to Gratian (A.D. 375-83). We have here a resumption (to say the least) in the fourth century A.D. of forms of urban life with the attendant influx of Roman coins and of craftsmanship bearing the imprint of the Romans. A second find is the *rural* Daco-Roman cremation cemetery of Bratei (Sibiu country) on the bank of the Tîrnava Mare River. This is a cemetery of 400 graves and was used at the close of the fourth century and the early fifth century A.D., consequently during the invasion of the Huns. This means that a century after Roman troops and Roman administration had left Dacia, the provincial population here lived a stable life. The same cemetery also proves, though retrospectively, how real the Romanization of the Dacians was, for apart from a small number of graves that follow the traditional Dacian rituals, all the others show that the Roman provincial rituals were observed.

Archaeological excavations consequently attest the existence throughout the Dacian territory, after the withdrawal of Roman authority, of a Daco-Romanian material culture which was to develop without intermission for a millennium. The continuity of material culture is eloquent proof of ethnical continuity.

Another fact of major importance, referred to in the preceding paragraphs, is that groups of free Dacians — and not Visigoths — infiltrated into abandoned Dacia (abandoned and not ceded to a barbarian people). In the third century A.D., those free Dacians were arrayed on the north-western, northern, eastern and south-eastern frontiers of the province of Dacia while in Muntenia [Wallachia] and Moldavia they were living under the name of Carpi between the frontier and the territories of the Visigoths, who had settled further east. Historical and archaeological data leave no doubt about this and, in the order of things, it is quite natural that the former Roman province of Dacia should have received a new influx of Dacians after being evacuated. Indeed, the first problem the Roman Empire had to tackle after its withdrawal from Dacia is that of the Carpi Dacians east of Dacia; they were defeated by the energetic emperors Diocletian and Maximian in a number of battles and removed to Moesia (mainly Dobrudja, especially along the Danube) and to Pannonia, where it was supposed they would be Romanized in time. This occurred from A.D. 295 to 297. Diocletian again reinforced the Danube frontier and the later Roman chronicles mention reassuringly that the *whole* people of the Carpi had been removed within the Empire — which was obviously an exaggeration.

Consequently, on the one hand the free, independent Dacians were left by the Romans or driven by them to enter an area which removed the danger they represented for the Empire; on the other hand, it was only after the power of the Carpi had been brought to nought that the Empire could see its way to an understanding with the Goths, who were considered less dangerous than the Carpi.

2. The Goths in Dacia

THE image built up of the Goths being at every moment and at any cost the enemies of the Roman Empire needs to be revised in the light of certain incontestable facts. It is proved that the relations between the Goths and the Romans relied on political realism and involved mutual concessions and aggressions. After A.D. 295-7 the Visigoths penetrated into Moldavia and Muntenia and it is certain that at least after 323 they were considered as *federates* (barbarian allies) of the Roman Empire, which enables us to infer that there was a certain toleration on the part of the Empire when they were allowed to spread to the Eastern and Southern Carpathians and to the Lower Danube. Another fact which confirms this inference and proves at the same time that the Empire had not lost all interest in its former possessions north of the Danube is the Visigoths keeping away from the territories of the former Roman province of Dacia (the Transylvanian plateau, Oltenia, and Banat). And when in A.D. 332, they tried to overrun those territories starting with Oltenia, Emperor Constantine the Great, who had built the stone bridge over the Danube at Sucidava (Celei) in 328, had them attacked from the rear and defeated them. Thus the Visigoths, during most of the time they spent in these territories, kept watch over the Danube boundary of the Empire, defending the provinces of Moesia Inferior and Thrace and ultimately, even the new capital, Constantinople. This they did as mercenaries, thus establishing with the Romans a precarious but durable balance of forces not devoid of mutual fear. Another fact specific to the situation in North-Danubian Dacia after it had been abandoned was the direct intervention of the Empire for some time, which considerably extenuated the effects of Roman withdrawal from Dacia. It is just possible that Aurelian himself may have maintained a number of bridgeheads left of the Danube; however that may be, it is certain that Constantine the Great and his successors saw that the new frontier was well defended, maintaining Roman forces at the bridgeheads at Orşova (Dierna), Turnu Severin (Drobeta), Celei (Sucidava) and possibly at Constantinians Daphne facing Turtucaia, and at Bărboşi on the River Siret in Southern Moldavia as well as in other smaller strongholds on the northern bank of the Danube.

Archaeological research and the interpretation of written records in the light of archaeological finds have proved that the Visigoths lived for a time in Moldavia (mostly in Eastern Moldavia and very little on the central plateau) and in Muntenia, up to Vedea to the west, and that they were to be found in large numbers along the Danube, between Teleorman and Călăraşi. The Gothic cemeteries at Sînziana on the Mureş, at Tîrgu Mureş and at Palatca not far from Cluj, which were considered as proof of the penetration and settlement of the Visigoths in Transylvania, were ultimately found to belong to the latter half of the fourth century, certain Visigoth "garrisons" having possibly been asked by the Romans to occupy the upper Mureş line and the "Gate of the Someş" against a threat from the north-west (possibly from the Vandals) or an early infiltration of other Goths, the Gepidae, from the north-west through the "Gate of the Someş". The infiltration was stopped on the Mureş River.

3. Early Christianity among the Daco-Romans

THE aforementioned developments made it possible for Roman civilization to continue its impact on Dacia in the fourth century and this is reflected by the penetration and wide circulation of Roman coins, including a large number of small bronze coins; by the considerable imports of Roman products, including a great deal of common earthenware, though part of it may possibly have been made in Dacia, and by the material culture of the local population and of the Visigoths, which bears the distinctive imprint of Roman influence. The specific Germanic elements are few in number and restricted to personal adornments.

The fourth century A.D. is the century when the Christian religion was recognized (by the Milan Edict of 313) and then the faith was forced upon the peoples of the Roman Empire until it finally became a State religion. Though it is not exactly known how Christianity penetrated among the Dacians and Daco-Romans, for there is no definitive proof of the existence of missionaries preaching the new religion, it is a fact that Christianity did penetrate among them. The only region for which we have direct, authentic records concerning the making of converts to Christianity is the extra-Carpathian area of this country, contemporary texts describing in detail the missionary work (in Greek, Latin, and Gothic) of Gothic Bishop Ulfilas who translated the Bible into Gothic. Also described are the savage persecutions of the Christians perpetrated by some of the Visigoth chieftains headed by Athanarich, and the martyrdom of Saint Sava drowned in the River Buzău and of other less known martyrs.

The Visigoths only embraced Christianity (the Arian rite of Greek tradition and using the Gothic language) after A.D. 378, during the reign of Emperor Theodosius I. The lack of Christian objects in the territories dominated by the Visigoths is, therefore, easy to explain, for the Christians did not dare to practise their faith openly. On the other hand, in the former Trajanic Dacia, Christianity (non-Arian and Latin) could spread at will, thus accounting for the original Latin fund of basic Christian terminology in the Romanian language (cruce — cross, sînt = sfîrnt — Saint, Dumnezeu — God, biserică — church, înger — angel, etc.). This is further proof of the fact that the Visigoths never lived or ruled in the former province of Dacia.

4. Dacia under the Huns' Domination : The Gepidae

THE conditions described above suddenly came to an end in A.D. 376. The Huns, a mixed Mongolian population of Asian origin and speaking a Turkic language, led by nomadic herdsmen and warlike horsemen, defeated the Goths and set up a reign of terror, but also of order and political stability, in Eastern and Central Europe for approximately eighty years. This was the first time Asian hordes had overrun Europe, beginning the stormy period of the "peoples' migration" on this continent. Although the action and the role of the Huns were merely episodic, they had serious consequences over the years on the political, military, and ethnical set-up in which Dacia was involved. The weakening of the Eastern Roman Empire through the hard blow dealt it by the destructive plundering raids of the Huns, the fall of the Western Roman Empire as a more remote consequence of their invasion, and the access given to other similar Asian peoples to the heart of Europe, are events which had a sharp impact on the destinies of Dacia too.

The Huns, who kept to their nomadic way of life throughout, never settled on Dacian territory for any length of time. Any settlement of theirs was only temporary, as a base for their attacks and for the exploitation of the local population in the plains (North-east Moldavia, the Danube Plain, the Tisa Plain). Their domination in Dacia depended upon raids carried out mostly through the intermediary of their Germanic allies, primarily the Ostrogoths and the Gepidae. Among the immediate effects of the Huns' invasion was in the first place the emigration in two stages of the Visigoths from Dacia : the pro-Roman group in 376 and the traditionalist "pagan" group of Athanarich in 381, after a short period of settlement in the so-called Caucaland, on either side of the Buzău Mountains. It is from this time that date the hoards of Roman gold ingots found at Crasna and

Feldioara and the coins and personal adornments at Valea Strîmbă in the Odorhei country, all situated in Transylvania. The great gold treasure containing pagan cult objects at Pietroasa in Muntenia is also supposed to have the same origin. Another consequence was the winding up of the Roman bridgeheads north of the Danube by A.D. 447. Under the aegis of the Huns, large portions of Dacia continued under Germanic domination (a Gothic domination, specifically Ostrogoth and Gepid). The compromise reached between the Huns and the Eastern Roman Empire, especially under the rule of Attila (A.D. 434-53), with constant negotiations and mutual embassies, created a *modus vivendi* also for Dacia's population, "deserters" and prisoners coming and going either way, and this made it possible for Dacia to survive despite exploitation and precarious living. It is probable that during the worst periods of Hun invasions, the native population took refuge in hiding places — forests and high districts which the Huns, a people of the steppe, usually avoided. But those periods alternated with periods of peace, when the Empire came to an understanding with the Huns, paying them subsidies as federates and allowing them, as the Goths had formerly been allowed, to buy things at the border fairs of the Empire.

Immediately after Attila's death, in A.D. 454, when a Germanic coalition headed by a Gepid king, Ardarich, formerly Attila's close collaborator, crushed the armies of Attila's sons, the power of the Huns disintegrated. The Huns then dispersed and history speaks of them little more.

From among the barbarians who benefited by the new situation in the Carpatho-Danubian area were primarily the Eastern Goths (Ostrogoths) and the third, more western Gothic branch known by the name of Gepidae. The latter had appeared north of Dacia about the mid-third century A.D. and after living under Hun domination, became independent and somehow inherited the

Huns' domination over Dacia. The facts recorded in the
first decades of the sixth century by the chroniclers
Cassiodorus and Jordanes concerning their occupation
of Trajanic Dacia up to the Eastern Carpathians and to
the River Olt, are invalidated by archaeological finds and
by the other written records. For however obscure the
records showing the situation in Dacia, one thing stands
out clearly, namely, that up to A.D. 471 the Ostrogoths
— settled in the Empire some time before as federates
in the provinces of Pannonia, though a number had
remained in the present-day territory of the U.S.S.R.
when the Huns overran Europe — did not allow the
Gepidae to infiltrate into Dacia. This "strategic balance"
enabled the native population to remain for a time under
Germanic rule, primaarily Ostrogoth rule, but generally of
a non-specified character. Restricted groups of Ostrogoths,
possibly those who had been for a little longer time in
Moldavia (a small cemetery of theirs has been discovered
at Botoșani) and were only passing through Transylvania
(where only isolated graves or small dispersed groups of
Ostrogoth graves are to be found) kept watch over Dacia's
territories which they had probably often traversed in
their efforts to regroup themselves in Pannonia when
arriving from the East.

Beginning with Emperor Anastasius (A.D. 491-518), and
after the departure of the Ostrogoths from the Balkan
Peninsula, the Eastern Roman Empire began a drive for
restoring the South-Danubian provinces and establishing
a firm boundary along the Lower Danube. This drive
reached its culmination during the reign of Justinian I
(A.D. 527-65).

The Gepidae, subjected to the powerful impact of the
civilization of the Eastern Roman Empire, which for
another century was to continue to use the Latin
language, had this impact transmitted to them partly
through the agency of the Daco-Romans in Dacia, which
far from having become a Gepid country, as it had not
become a Gothic country, was developing its Romanic

traditions, these being revived by the new powerful radiation of the civilization of the Eastern Empire. Justinian rebuilt and reoccupied the bridgeheads left of the Danube and organized the Christian Church in those districts.

Muntenia and Moldavia, which were dealt a heavier blow by the Huns' invasion and exploitation, also revived under the new conditions as early as the end of the fifth century. The population in these parts kept up the traditions of the third and fourth centuries and is known to have lived in fairly large numbers in open settlements, primarily in the Danube Plain but also as far as the Carpathian foothills. Archaeological investigations have found such settlements everywhere, from Ipătești on the Olt to Dulceanca on the River Vedea, as well as in Bucharest, at Tîrgșor not far from Ploiești, and Budureasca close to Mizil and up to Botoșani near Suceava.

The political and strategic conditions spoken of above account for the fact that the Carpatho-Danubian regions were generally, though not completely, unaffected, in any case not directly affected, by the storms that broke out at this time in the steppes north of the Black Sea, again threatening the Byzantine Empire as well as Dacia. From what was left of the Huns who had withdrawn from Pannonia, and of other kindred nomadic peoples newly come from Asia, a new nucleus of warlike nomadic herdsmen known by the generic name of Bulgars had been formed. To differentiate between them and the Slav Bulgarians of today, who bear the name, we will call them Proto-Bulgars. The Proto-Bulgars began their plundering raids against the Eastern Empire in A.D. 493, taking along with them Slav groups as from the beginning of the rule of Emperor Justin I (A.D. 518-27). The Slavs may have come from their original homeland lying between the Vistula, the Pripet, and the Middle Dnieper down to the northern and eastern borders of Dacia. The Slavs known as Anti and Sclavini undertook an endless series of plundering raids in the Balkan Peninsula, where the defence of the Empire had been weakened, principally because the Byzantine armies had been concentrated in Italy to win back that part of the Empire from the Ostrogoths. Most of the raids were organized by the Proto-Bulgars and were under their leadership, though in 551 the Gepidae raided as far as today's Serbian reaches of the Danube. However, neither the Proto-Bulgars nor the Slavs settled for any length of time in Dacia and their hordes seemed to have traversed Dacia only in part while on their way towards the Empire. This was the first time that the extra-Carpathian regions of Romania came to know the Slavs, warlike hordes which made it their aim to penetrate into, and plunder, the Empire.

5. Avar Domination.
The Slavs settle in Dacia

AS a result of events that took place between 558 and 568 we find a changed situation. A new Asian conglomerate, which has gone down in history under the name of Avars, defeated and subdued the Proto-Bulgars north of the Black Sea and, taking with them part of the Proto-Bulgars, made their appearance along the Empire's boundary at the mouths of the Danube. The Avars, a nomadic people who originated in Central Asia, had been driven here by the expansion of the western Turks. Overrunning and plundering the country, the Avars at first claimed the right to settle in Dobrudja, which was imperial land. In the meantime the Gepidae were putting up fierce resistance to the Germanic people of the Longobardi who, coming up the Elbe through today's Czechoslovakia, had in A.D. 526 arrived south of the Danube, in the former Roman province of Pannonia. By 546 the Longobardi had mainly occupied Pannonia. Undoubtedly they had come as "federates" of the Empire, in which capacity they were soon in conflict with their neighbours and competitors, the Gepidae. The political and military entanglements west of this country were smoothed out in 567 when the Avars, deprived of all subsidies by Emperor Justin II, immediately after Justinian's death in 565, crossed into Pannonia, forged an alliance with the Longobardi and crushed the Gepidae. The Empire took good care to retrieve the stronghold of Sirmium. In 568 the Longobardi went to Italy and what was left of the Gepidae fell under the domination of the Avars who settled in Pannonia, thus creating a new political and strategic situation over wide expanses from the North Pontic steppes to Central Europe. This put an end to Germanic domination in this part of the world and opened the way to the Slavs towards the Danube and the Save boundary. Complex consequences ensued for Dacia. In the first place heavy and lengthy fighting broke out between the new military power north of the Danube and the Byzantine Empire. Under the pressure of Avar attacks, combined with those of the Slavs, the Empire's boundaries firmly maintained along the Danube and the Save until now, were breached in A.D. 602. Before that date, however, faced by a more serious danger — for the Avars' domination here was harsh — the Empire had endeavoured to hold the frontiers and at the same time to create stable conditions, as far as possible, in the former Roman possessions beyond the borders.

In the second place, the Avars organized the territory they inhabited or dominated according to Asian traditions, so that their nomadic and warlike tribes settled in the plains of the Middle Danube and of the Tisa, lining their central territories with dependent peoples whom they kept in obedience by means of garrisons and punitive raids.

Avars never lived on Dacian territory, the western plains of Crișana and Banat excepted. On the Transylvanian plateau a few groups of Gepidae settled — in different places from those they had occupied between 480 and 568 — on the Mureș, where cemeteries dating from that time have been found at Bandul de Cîmpie, Unirea, and Noşlac. This time an outpost advanced along the Tîrnava Mare River, as proved by the Bratei cemetery. These Gepid "garrisons", who used their own weapons, had adopted the armament and horse trappings of the Avars, and were at that time for the most part Christians (of the Arian rite) and in the service of the Avars, most probably held the native Daco-Roman population in subjection and temporarily kept in check the Slavs' expansion to the north-west of Transylvania. In Eastern Transylvania, up to the higher reaches of the Tîrnava Mică River and in Moldavia, the Slavs most probably penetrated again according to the general dictates of the Avars. In Muntenia and Oltenia there seems to have been something of a Slavo-Avar domination, with the natives prevailing from the ethnical standpoint for, in the settlements discovered in those parts, Slav elements are in a minority. In Moldavia and Eastern Transylvania the native population seems also to have been in a majority. It is clear therefore, that as part of the organization effected by the Avars, the Slavs did not initially colonize the whole of Dacia, nor the uninhabited regions : whenever they settled for any length of time in certain parts of Dacia, they found themselves among the native population who assimilated them.

It is likely that the Slavs who settled in Dacia were fractions of tribes which had broken away from their home organizations and, having settled among the Proto-Romanians, had ultimately to adopt the local traditions of the village communities. No name of any Slav tribe living in Dacia has been preserved, thus proving that they had neither the possibility nor the time to organize themselves into tribes occupying their own territories, as they are known to have done south of the Danube in the seventh century.

The Slav settlement and Avar domination generally, brought about a lowering of the standard of living and of material culture in Dacia, and this is more obvious in

THE FORMATION OF THE ROMANIAN PEOPLE 145

the regions where the Slavs were to be found in larger numbers — a phenomenon that was further aggravated after the connections with the Byzantine Empire were severed. The crafts and trades were checked in their progress, and there was a process of return to a rural life and to natural economy.

During the period between the penetration of the Avars and Slavs north of the Danube and the fall of the Empire's boundaries in A.D. 602, a period of frequent plundering of the Empire up to the Adriatic, the Black Sea, and southward into Greece took place, the Avars and Slavs bringing back to their original territories, apart from booty, a number of prisoners.

From A.D. 593 to 602, having ended the Persian war, the Byzantine Empire under the energetic rule of Emperor Mauricius Tiberius endeavoured to wipe out the Avaro-Slav threat by undertaking a number of military campaigns in Muntenia, north of the Danube, against the Slavs, and around Belgrade to beyond the Tisa, against the Avars. Despite the victories won by the imperial armies, no real success was obtained on account of the weakness of Byzantine society. The armies fighting along the Lower Danube against the Slavs rose in rebellion, and Mauricius Tiberius was overthrown and killed, being superseded by Phocas, the rebel officer (A.D. 602-10). In the chaos that ensued, the Danube and Save boundary fell and the Balkan Peninsula stood open to the Slavs who thereafter swept across the Danube and settled in the dioceses of Thrace and Illyricum. After that Dacia lost contact with the Empire and no more records concerning it appear in the Byzantine chronicle. At the same time numerous Slavs moved from these parts into the Balkans.

The Balkan Peninsula being overrun by the Slavs who settled there, the Avars helping them by destroying the Byzantine cities after which they would return "home", was of special significance for the Roman population south of the Danube. It is not very clear how the defeat of the Slavo-Avars beneath the walls of Constantinople in 626, the weakening of Avar domination, and the uprising and southward drive of the Serbo-Croatians affected Dacia. It is most probable that this region kept outside the turmoil that prevailed further west and that the Daco-Roman-Slav population throughout Dacia as well as the Gepidae in the pay of the Avars, installed in North-west Transylvania, continued very much as before.

On the other hand, a new storm was gathering in the east. A group of western Turks from Asia, known under the name of Khazars, threatened the Proto-Bulgars occupying the territories between the Volga and the Don. Finally, despite the diplomatic interventions of the emperors of Constantinople, Asparukh or Isperikh, one of the sons of the great Bulgar Kaghan, Kuvrat (or Kurt), took his armed people westward and penetrated into the north-eastern part of Bulgaria in 681, after crossing Dobrudja and defeating the Byzantine armies sent against him. At the same time another group of Avars newly come from Asia, joined those in Pannonia, thus swelling their ranks. "A second Kaghanate" of the Avars was spoken of from that time onwards.

Asparukh's nomadic and warlike Proto-Bulgars founded the so-called "First Bulgarian Empire" in the north of today's Bulgaria, where they came upon the Slavs and Daco-Romans.

There are no definite records concerning the fate of the Daco-Romans between the Balkans and the Danube, but it is probable, as indicated by archaeological data, that they had had to move on to different parts. Some must have remained among the Slavs and the Proto-Bulgars, transmitting to them the traditions of an ancient civilization and being ultimately Slavicized, while others had taken refuge in the mountainous districts of the Balkan Peninsula, grazing their flocks in the mountains and preserving their ethnical identity, and yet others may have been driven to the left bank of the Danube where they joined the other Daco-Romans.

On the other hand there is nothing to allow us to suppose that the Proto-Bulgars were dominant north of the Danube at this time or had settled there. On the contrary the Carpatho-Danubian area appears to have further remained under the Avars' indirect control, and the Avars to have remained the enemies of the Proto-Bulgars as they had been for a long time, and to have maintained a "sphere of-interests" frontier along the Danube and the Save.

For more than a century — approximately between A.D. 680 and 796/803 (when Avar domination came to an end) — there was comparative peace in Dacia, and the country was able to develop unhindered from the demographic standpoint under the conditions explained above. Byzantine influence was now eclipsed, though still faintly exercised through the medium of the Proto-Bulgar, Slav, and Avar peoples. Hardly any Byzantine coins now reached the country. The Avars did not settle in the Transylvanian plateau or in the remainder of the southern and eastern Dacian territories. Their raids were isolated, as proved by an almost total lack of archaeological vestiges, in striking contrast with the frequency of such vestiges west of the Western Carpathians.

6. The Completion of the Formative Process of the Romanian People (seventh to ninth centuries)

THE living standard and material culture during the period now under consideration (680-803) show that a new evolution was in the ascendant as well as a vast unification process which gradually brought together the area between the Balkan Mountains and the Northern Carpathians. The fundamental factors were the Daco-Roman traditions north and south of the Danube, the participation of Slav elements, and a fresh impact of Byzantine civilization. The foundations were thus laid for a specific Balkano-Carpathic material culture, the Dridu culture, so-called after the great settlement on the River Ialomiţa. It was in the eighth century that the Dridu culture developed, based on the evolution of the Bratei, Ipoteşti-Cîndeşti, and Botoşana autochthonous cultures. The constituting elements were mostly of Daco-Roman origin, and their existence has been attested without interruption from the period of the Roman rule to the founding of the Romanian feudal states. Essentially Romanic and autochthonous, the Dridu culture, judging only by the finds made so far, covered nearly the entire territory where the Romanians live today as well as certain districts south of the Danube. It was the only local material culture known in the Carpatho-Danubian area from the eighth to the eleventh centuries.

Being the only material culture, its spread over the entire territory of present-day Romania from the eighth to the eleventh centuries, indicates that the Dridu culture belongs to the Romanian population, as has now been attested by written records. In this period the first political organizations appeared under the aegis of that culture.

The Proto-Bulgars, who had crossed south of the Danube during the latter half of the seventh century, had been a minority of nomadic, mounted herdsmen superimposed on the Daco-Roman stock and, like the Avars, brought no fundamental additions to the cultural medium they found in their new homeland, apart from their nomadic ways of organization, their armament, and horse trappings. The Slavs, on the other hand, had come to these parts with an archaic culture which they developed and enriched in the new surroundings through contact with the Romanized population and the Byzantine civilization, though preserving their own structure and traditions in their spiritual culture. Their material culture in the Balkano-Carpathian area assumed a special aspect nowhere else to be found in the Slav world of Europe in those days, and this proves that the decisive factor was the local Proto-Romanian environment.

The stable settlements, whether agricultural or pastoral, like the cemeteries of the North-Danubian population who, following the developments around the year 680, came to be the bearers of the initial phase of the Dridu culture, are frequent throughout Dobrudja, Muntenia, [Wallachia], Oltenia, and South-east Transylvania. They are mostly to be found in the plains, and only a few of them in the low sub-Carpathian foothills, representing a local development of the preceding cultural environment. This is not to be accounted for by a substantial and sudden immigration of a new population. Avar domination over the North-Danubian areas and the non-existence of Proto-Bulgar expansion in this direction in the eighth century, rule out such a hypothesis. Even south of the Danube this culture was formed after the year 680 ; in Western Transylvania the powerful Proto-Romanian centre around the Western Mountains has not yet been sufficiently studied.

In Moldavia evolution took the same course beginning with the eighth century, the Slav elements of archaic tradition there being assimilated at a swift rate beginning with that period.

The co-existence of Proto-Romanians and Slavs is now attested throughout Dacia's territory as is also the slow process of the Slav's assimilation. The rate of advance of that process varied from region to region but no rigorous marking out is possible at the present-day stage of research.

The change in the political and military situation in the Balkano-Carpathian area at the close of the eighth century following the final defeat of the Avar power at the hands of the Frankish armies of Charlemagne in the years A.D. 791-6, with the remainder of the Avar forces being driven across the Tisa where they were destroyed by the Proto-Bulgars of Tsar Krum about A.D. 803, affected only slightly the life of the Dacian population. Avar domination was superseded by Proto-Bulgar domination, the later being far more shadowy than the former, for the Bulgarian Empire was fighting the Byzantine Empire in the south and moreover, as feudalism was becoming more firmly established during this period throughout Dacian territory, domination assumed the form of feudal dependence of the local leaders on the Bulgar Tsars. Naturally, it was the Slav leaders who were again mostly connected with the Tsars, as shown also by the feudal titles of *boier* (boyar) and *jupan* (gentleman) which come to us from the Proto-Bulgars through the Slavs. On the other hand, starting about the mid-ninth century, particularly after the Bulgarian Empire had been converted to Christianity, the Bulgars were becoming increasingly Byzantine, irrespective of the fact that Tsar Simeon (A.D. 893-927) strove to take the place of the Constantinople emperor, or perhaps for that very reason. The fact is that no Proto-Bulgar colonization is attested in Dacia, and neither was there any garrison of the tsars established in these parts.

The political situation also bore a different aspect in Central Europe after the defeat of the Avars because the Frankish kingdom of Charlemagne, having occupied Pannonia, had spread its domination and influence up to the Rivers Tisa and Timoc, and the Moravian principality, founded in present-day Czechoslovakia at the time, eager to draw away from the German threat, initially received Christianity and a civilizing impact from the Byzantine Empire.

Thus in the ninth century, before the arrival of the Hungarians, an unstable balance of forces existed in the regions west of Dacia between the Frankish kingdom, the Moravian principality, and the first Bulgarian Empire.

It is plain that in the ninth century Dacia, guarded east and west by the Bulgarian Empire, the latter being determined to maintain its sphere of interests, continued its domestic development without being actually under another people's rule but being only controlled, as shown above. Its development consisted in a continuation of the process whereby the Slavs were being assimilated (as the Proto-Bulgar conquerors were being assimilated by the Slavs in the south) and in the spread of feudal organization.

The Proto-Romanian and Slav population was being locally organized on the basis of a process of economic and social differentiation. A new, most intensive development of iron metallurgy with use of the poor, but easily accessible, local ores, as well as the development of agriculture and stock-breeding, increased social differences in the communities, as shown by the discoveries made in many settlements and in some of the cemeteries of those days, primarily in that of Obîrșia in the Dolj country, where Christianity is proved to have been practised by the population in the ninth century. This is also the time when the foundations were being laid for the principalities of which only a few are mentioned in the extant historical records of the following century.

7. Arrival of the Magyars

IN 896 the Hungarians, a people of Finno-Ugric origin mixed with, and led by, Turkic groups, made their way towards the Hungarian plain of today from the steppes north of the Black Sea, being driven from there by the Pechenegs. For a short time during the ninth century, they resided in the so-called Atelkuz ("between rivers") in the eastern part of Dacia and skirted it to the north, as archaeological finds have clearly proved. The Hungarians military raids in the north-west and west of the Transylvanian plateau during the first half of the tenth century, after having wiped out the Moravian principality and the Proto-Bulgar-controlled political organizations in Crișana and Banat, created a new situation in these regions, which was to terminate after 1001 with the gradual conquest of Transylvania and the implanting there of foreign colonies. The Magyars took little time to assimilate the Slavs they had found in the plains of the central part of their new homeland, and the political predominance of the Slavs on the Transylvanian plateau also came to an end at this time.

In close connection with this situation is the wide expansion attested in the early years of the century, of the native population, bearers of the Dridu culture : on the Transylvanian plateau this culture reached the Mureş line (Blandiana, Sebeş, etc.) The fact that the oldest material culture of the Maramureş Romanians — archaeologically identified at thirteenth century Siliştea Veche in the Romanian village of Sărăsău on the Tisa, and continued in the culture of the fourteenth century princely villages of Dragoş and Bogdan, for example at Cuhea — obviously originated in the Transylvanian culture of the eighth-ninth centuries and in the Dridu culture, confirms the fact that the Romanians had been in Maramureş for centuries and that the aforementioned cultures were really Romanian.

In the extra-Carpathian regions, the Pechenegs — a new group of nomadic and warlike Asian herdsmen who had come from beyond the Volga and the Urals as a first echelon of a larger group that was to include the Udi and the Cumans — put an end to Proto-Bulgar domination and for the first time created conditions that resulted in the decline of the political power of the Slavs. In the tenth century, as previously on similar occasions, no destruction or expulsion of the native population over wide areas is attested. The demographic expansion of the population in the same century is proved throughout Moldavia. Even the native settlements in the territories east of the River Siret in Moldavia, continued to exist until the first half of the eleventh century, as proved by the Byzantine bronze coins found there. It was only around A.D. 1027 that the Pechenegs were to take their flocks and herds and their warlike horsemen to the plains of Romania on the occasion of their first independent raid into the Byzantine Empire.

It is not improbable that the Byzantine Empire endeavoured to forestall the Magyar threat, as suggested by the Byzantine stone strongholds built at Slon in the Buzău Mountains immediately after 971. Byzantine coins which had again begun to infiltrate north of the Danube and even up to upper Moldavia in the early years of the tenth century, now reached extra-Carpathian Dacia in large numbers, as did also Byzantine craftware and other goods. A rapid development of the settlements of the native population has been ascertained. These developments and the domestic phenomena accompanying them in Dacia, marked the final stage of the ethnogenetic process, which also showed a tendency towards maximum extension over the territory of ancient Dacia. The mention made of the Vlachs (Romanians) in the Balkans by a Byzantine source of the eleventh century referring to developments in A.D. 976 and the fact that such remarks subsequently increased in number, is of outstanding significance when compared to the mentions made from the eighth to the eleventh centuries on the Romanian population north of the Danube, designated as Blasi in the chronicle of King Béla's Anonymous Notary (early tenth century), Volohi in the Old Russian chronicle (late ninth century), and the country Balak in the Armenian geography (eighth-ninth centuries). Vlach being the generic denomination then given by the Germans and Slavs to the Romanic peoples, the last two mentions cited above cannot be used to establish the moment when Romanian ethnogenesis ended. The final moment of that process might be considered to be the time when the last Slav groups were assimilated. It should be noted that Vlach was the name given to the Romanians by other peoples in the Middle Ages, though the Romanians themselves have always called themselves Romanians.

As the Romanian people was formed, so was the Romanian language built up over the same territories but under conditions differing from those in which the neo-Latin western languages developed.

The Romanian language is directly derived from popular Latin, whose grammatical structure and main vocabulary it has preserved. Apart from a Latin basis, the Romanian language has preserved elements of the Daco-Getian idiom.

While in full process of formation in the seventh and eighth centuries, Romanian incorporated a considerable number of Slav words which have become part of the vocabulary of common use. Its specific features emerge from the seventh to the ninth century, after which the Daco-Moesian Romanic language became the Romanian language.

The Romanian people thus concluded their eventful ethnogenesis under new historical circumstances : the Empire had again spread to the Danube and beyond it, resuming its traditional policy in Dacia, which implies continuity of a culture showing Romanic features. The Byzantine Metropolitan John Mavropous did not exaggerate when, in 1047 in connection with the Pechenegs, he said : "As a matter of fact they had conquered the country they lived in, plundering it after having chased away the old inhabitants who were weak and *for whom the old Emperors had been most solicitous...*"

It was under such auspices that in the difficult and complex situation arising from the settlement of the Magyars in the west of the country and the overflow of the Pechenego-Uzo-Cuman wave east of Dacia, the Romanian people were to build up their own forms of feudal life with a Byzantine Danube acting as a safety factor for at least two more centuries.

CHAPTER FIVE

THE EMERGENCE OF THE ROMANIAN STATES (TENTH TO FOURTEENTH CENTURIES)

WITH the conclusion of the formative process of the Romanian people, Romanian feudal society began to be built up and the first political bodies emerged. Feudal institutions on the territory inhabited by the Romanians were naturally influenced by those of the neighbouring states where feudal relations were more advanced: the Byzantine Empire, the Second Bulgarian Empire (at the close of the twelfth century), and the Hungarian kingdom. The successive waves of Turanian invaders — Pechenegs, Udi, Cumans and Tartars — and the devastation and dislocation of the population they caused, slowed down the evolution of Romanian society; their political domination was like a pall over the people on the banks of the Lower Danube, accounting for the sporadic and sparse information Byzantine and Western records of that period provide about the Romanians. At the close of the thirteenth century and early in the fourteenth, the decline of the "Golden Horde" Tartars, the unrest in the Bulgarian state and the struggle for the Hungarian crown caused the influence of the three states which disputed the supremacy east and south of the Carpathians to ebb away. And then, with the coming to fruition of the domestic process of feudal relationship, the Romanian states emerged in a chain along the Carpathians. The anti-Mongolian struggle and the endeavours to free themselves of the Hungarian king's suzerainty made it easier for such princes as Basarab and Bogdan to unify the country, and ultimately two Romanian states — Wallachia and Moldavia — appeared in the political geography of South-east Europe, alongside the older Transylvanian principality.

1. Social and Economic Prerequisites of the Emergence of Romanian Feudal States

ALTHOUGH written information about the Romanians in the ninth and tenth centuries is sporadic, archaeological excavations enable us to form a picture of their way of life and social structure. The Romanians of that period lived in villages or even in groups of villages, the Romano-Byzantine strongholds along the Danube offering the only examples of urban life.

Farming, stock-breeding, and some crafts were their main pursuits, the most widespread of the crafts being pottery-making. The many imported articles found here, the most frequent being Byzantine amphorae, are to be accounted for by trade with the strongholds along the Danube and the more important Byzantine centres in the Balkan Peninsula.

The social structure of the Romanian population relied on a territorial or village community. The members of a community owned a certain area, which was parcelled out into holdings, and used the grass land, pasture land, forests, and streams in common. The leading bodies of territorial communities were the general assembly, the council of the aged — "people good and old" — and the military chieftain *(Jude* or *Cneaz)* whose authority, at first limited to periods of emergency became permanent with time.

Taking advantage of their position, the leaders of the communities compelled the common people to work for them in a variety of ways and to give them part of the products of their work. Usurping the titles of ownership of the community, the chieftains gradually became a landed aristocracy and enslaved part of the peasantry under their jurisdiction.

The emergence of feudal states against the background of the territorial communities that spread over the Carpatho-Danubian area was the result of a lengthy process of development of local economic forces, which made it possible for an aristocracy to be fashioned. The aristocracy relied upon the exploitation of the free rural communities at first, and later upon the enslaved peasantry. Although information concerning the economic life in Romanian territory from the tenth to the fourteenth century is but scanty, it reveals a progress in production and trade and points to the decisive part played by economic and demographic factors in the genesis of Romanian feudal society.

The records available on the Lower Danube regions show that in the latter half of the tenth century this was a densely populated area carrying on a busy trade.

In the thirteenth and fourteenth centuries the presence of Genoese traders at the mouths of the Danube around Vicina and Chilia (old-time Lycostomo) is proof of the wealth of the local chieftains, who bought Italian cloth, offering grain, wax, and honey in exchange.

The districts at the foot of the mountains in Oltenia and Muntenia, as described in the diploma of the Knights of St. John in 1247 also appear to have made notable economic progress; many flour mills and natural fish ponds alongside fields and grassland, point to a mixed economy, including the products of husbandmen and stock-breeders, which provided the incomes of the landowning class *(majores terrae)* and of the Hungarian crown. In 1330, Basarab I offered King Charles Robert 7,000 marks in payment for peace. This shows the economic power of the country over which the Romanian prince ruled.

Turanian invasions checked the economic development of the Romanians, but the rise in production and productivity brought about by technical progress and demographic growth, made it possible for the country to overcome its vicissitudes, and intensified social differences in the communities. The heads of the communities strengthened their economic power and political authority and insisted on the privileged position they had reached. The most important means of reaching that goal was the state, and consequently a state was created.

2. The First Romanian Political Organizations in Transylvania, Dobrudja, Wallachia, and Moldavia

DURING the ninth and the tenth centuries the native population of Transylvania and Banat practised agriculture and stock-breeding as well as a number of crafts and mining. Economic development brought about the emergence of an aristocracy *(nobiles)* — landowners possessing large flocks and herds and exercising their authority upon the people living on their domains. It is against this socio-economic background that the first Romanian political formations were organized in this area. The results of the latest archaeological research added to written records give a clear image of those political organizations. Between the Rivers Someş and Mureş in Crişana, there was the dukedom (Voivodeship) of Menumorut, with the citadel of Biharea as its centre; another dukedom was to be found between the Mureş and the Danube. The latter was headed by Glad, whose residence seems to have been the citadel of Cuvin between the Timiş and the Danube. On the Transylvanian plateau between the gates of the Meseş and the sources of the Someş, was the dukedom of Gelu whose residential city was Dobîca, where a strongly fortified citadel has been found with many imported articles and Byzantine coins.

In the first half of the tenth century, these dukedoms strongly opposed the attempts made by the Hungarians

THE EMERGENCE OF THE ROMANIAN STATES 159

in the Pannonian plain to conquer Transylvania. The battles, and the determination shown by the local people in their defence, are described in the chronicle of King Béla's Anonymous Notary — *Gesta Hungarorum* — compiled towards the close of the twelfth century on the basis of written records that have been lost and of oral tradition. Only after thirteen days' fighting was the citadel of Biharea conquered from the Romanian Prince Menumorut. On the Transylvanian plateau, after Prince Gelu had fallen in battle, the Magyars had to come to an understanding with the heads of the local population, which is proof of the power of this political body.

Apart from the principality mentioned in the chronicle of the Anonymous Notary, archaeological research proves conclusively the existence of other political formations with powerful centres, as, for example, the principality in the Middle Mureş district with Ţeligrad and Bălgrad as its centres, as well as the political formations in the Bîrsa, Făgăraş *(Terra Blachorum)*, Amlaş, Haţeg, Ouaş, and Maramureş country. These do not appear in the aforementioned chronicle, as Hungarian expansion had not yet made contact with them.

After the first wave of Hungarian penetration into Romanian territory, the political formations here continued to develop and be consolidated. Gelu's principality, now under the leadership of his successor Gyla (Jula), is described as "a very extensive and very rich country" *(Regnum latissimum et opulentissimum)*. Gyla's refusal to submit to the authority of Stephen, the Hungarian king, and to turn Catholic, brought about an armed conflict, as a result of which Gyla was taken to Hungary in captivity together with his family and his treasure store.

In their struggle for independence during the tenth century the local leaders sought help from foreign powers interested in supporting them in this endeavour. We might conclude from *The Legend of Saint Gerhard* that Ahtum, Glad's successor and ruler of the territory between Orşova and Mureş, maintained connections with Byzantium via

Vidin early in the eleventh century. Having a powerful army at his command, Ahtum opposed the Hungarian king in the matter of levying duty on the salt transported by raft on the Mureş to the Pannonian plain. Political organization similar to those in Transylvania also existed in other parts of the country in the tenth century. Political developments were hindered by Hungarian expansion and by the new wave of Turanian peoples who invaded Romanian territory in the period from the eleventh to the thirteenth century.

Coming into contact with the Romanian population, some of the Pechenegs, Udi, and Cumans abandoned their nomadic way of life and in the course of time were assimilated. Infiltrating into the ruling class, they contributed to the consolidation of the local political organizations by using their power and their connections among the conquerors. [1]

In Transylvania, despite the victories won by King Stephen I, Hungarian rule over West Transylvania and Banat suffered fluctuations and this was further accentuated by the Pecheneg attack and the crisis which the Hungarian kingdom underwent. For half a century Romanian political organizations developed outside the authority of the Hungarian crown, and this accounts for the name given to the district : Ultrasilvana, Transilvana, Erdeelu (country beyond the forests).

During the latter half of the twelfth century and the first quarter of the thirteenth the conquest of Transylvania by the Magyar feudal kingdom was complete. The

---

[1] As a result of prolonged co-existence with the native population, the Pechenegs and Cumans left their mark in toponymy and the vocabulary of the Romanian language. Peceneaga, Cicineagul, Pecenişca Beşinău, Beşenova, and other place and river names are derived from the Pechenegs, while of Cuman origin are place names such as Cumani, Comana, Vadul Cumanilor. Comarnic, and Comăneşti, and the names of rivers ending in-ui : Bahlui, Covurlui, Desnăţui, Călmăţui, etc., and the names ending in-abă : Toxabă, Tîncabă, Basarabă, etc. It is also from the Cumans that come a number of words such as : cioban (shepherd), beci (cellar), cătun (hamlet), duşman (enemy), etc.

THE EMERGENCE OF THE ROMANIAN STATES

extension of Magyar rule to Transylvania brought about certain changes in the ranks of the ruling class as well as among the peasantry : certain local chiefs entered the ranks of the ruling élite of the conquerors' society and the process of dispossessing and making serfs of the peasant communities was intensified.

The districts along the Lower Danube, where Byzantine influence was stronger than elsewhere in Romanian territory, were of exceptional political and economic importance during the eleventh century despite the adverse conditions created by the invading peoples. In Moldavia also a number of documents of the eleventh century and of a later date illustrate the important role played by Romanian political organizations on certain occasions. For example, the Polish sources on which Dlugosz's Chronicle relies point out that in 1070 the "Wallachians" fought alongside the Ruthenians and the Pechenegs in support of Vyceslav of Polotsk and against Boleslav, King of Poland.

The policy of expansion of the Hungarian kingdom south and east of the Carpathians was inaugurated by King Andrew II (1205-35) when he called upon the Teutonic Knights to become the instruments of his policy. The extension of the authority of the Hungarian crown and the attendant Catholic proselytism were a threat to the Romanian political organizations built up in the shadow of Cuman domination or through Romanian-Cuman co-operation. The response of the native population was in line with the reaction of the Orthodox world against the political and religious offensive of the Hungarian kingdom. Thus, an alliance was formed between the Romano-Bulgarian state and the Nicaea Empire. The conflict between the Bulgars and the Magyars in 1230 was along the same line. It ended with the victory of the Hungarian kingdom, following which the Severin Banat was set up on the north-western border of the Bulgarian Empire. This was assigned the task of guarding the frontier. It included the eastern part of the Timișan Banat, which preserved the name and also transmitted it to the present-day Caraș-Severin county. The Severin Banat also included a strip of Oltenia, which accounts for Oltenia being sometimes called the Severin county.

With the Magyar kingdom and the Bulgarian Empire at rivalry, the Romanian leaders, first those east of the River Olt and subsequently those of Oltenia, acknowledged the suzerainty of the Hungarian king in order to safeguard their privileges.

The process whereby Hungarian suzerainty was being consolidated was interrupted by the great Tartar invasion of 1241 which was followed by a comparatively long Mongolian rule over a considerable part of Romanian territories (Muntenia and Moldavia). The rate of economic development was thus slowed down but never interrupted altogether.

The diploma whereby Béla IV, King of Hungary, bestowed the Severin county and "the whole of Cumania" upon the Knights of St. John in 1247 is of considerable importance as a measure of the development level reached in the territory between the Carpathians and the Danube in the mid-thirteenth century.

The diploma shows that the main branches of the economy were farming, stock-breeding, and fishing. Large estates had been formed and social differentiation into distinct classes was in process of consolidation.

Politically, the country was organized into principalities. Along the Olt were the principalities of Ioan and Fărcaș and also Litovoi's principality, which included the Hațeg country, while on the left bank of the Olt Seneslau's principality was to be found. Though they were dependent on the kingdom of Hungary, the principalities enjoyed a certain autonomy which the Knights of St. John were to observe.

Economic connections, facilitated by the development of boroughs and the emergence of a number of towns drawn into the international trade circuit thanks to the trade routes, supported the unification process of Romanian political organizations.

During the latter half of the thirteenth century an inclination to sweep aside Magyar suzerainty became manifest south of the Carpathians, assuming the form of armed struggle. A first attempt was made by Prince Litovoi, most probably in 1279. Litovoi died on the battlefield and his brother, Bărbat, was taken prisoner and ransomed on payment of a large sum of money. The military and economic power of the Romanian principalities, which were not far removed from independence, is proved by the struggle they waged against a powerful state and by the payment of a considerable ransom for a leader.

As early as the thirteenth century, the Hungarian kings endeavoured to extend their sway east of the Carpathians. In order to make better use of Transylvania's natural resources and to strengthen their domination over that principality, the Hungarian kings encouraged the immigration of Magyar, Szekler, and Saxon colonists who were to settle in the principality alongside the native Romanian population. The Saxons came from Flanders, Luxemburg, and Saxony. For a short period, the Order of the Teutonic Knights was also brought to Transylvania. The settlement of other peoples side by side with Romanians created a certain solidarity among the masses producing material goods, irrespective of their ethnic origin and let to mutual influences and to economic development in Transylvania. A number of strongholds were erected to defend the principality and around the stronghold the counties — administrative units — were built up. The Hungarian kings gave the Saxon colonists economic and administrative privileges so that they were able to carry on a lively political and economic activity and to organize themselves in administrative units of their own, which they called *sedes* (seats).

When Transylvania was reduced to subordination by the Magyar state the process whereby the peasantry was brought into serfdom was intensified. The communities of free peasants were taken over largely by the king and the aristocracy around him, the Catholic clergy, and those natives that had rallied round the royal power. Large landed estates were formed and the obligations of the peasantry towards the landowners increased. With large incomes came political power so that the nobility obtained considerable privileges from the kings, and the privileges were laid down in the Golden Bull of 1222, which was confirmed in 1231. Large-scale grants of immunities, particularly at moments when the central power underwent a crisis, accentuated the process of feudal fragmentation. In order to keep the great nobility within bounds, the kings sought the support of the lesser nobility into whose ranks members of the lower strata were raised. Gradually two categories emerged in the nobility, with different socio-juridical status and different interests : the great nobility termed *potentes* or *iobagiones regis* (a word which in time came to be applied to the peasantry dependent on the landowners) and the gentry : the *servientes* or *familiares*.

Among the peasantry there were three categories in the thirteenth century : the free peasants, the dependent peasants, and the slaves.

The free peasants lived in village communities located mostly in the peripheral districts of Transylvania where no large estates could be formed and where the nobility's attempts to enslave the peasantry met with much resistance. These peasants sought to preserve their freedom by assuming military obligations.

Among the dependent peasantry there were three categories with a different economic and legal status : a) the dependent peasants proper, who came to be called serfs, and who had the use of a plot of land (termed *sesie*) which they tilled, and for which they contributed labour service and money payment; these peasants could bequeath their own homestead; b) the *jeleri*, free landless peasants; c) the servants engaged in work around the landowner's home.

The lowest social category were the slaves, entirely at the mercy of the landowners.

In the thirteenth century the process of separating the crafts from agriculture and the setting up of towns was moderately advanced. The towns of Sibiu, Alba Iulia, Cluj, Oradea, and Rodna are mentioned in the first half of the thirteenth century. They were mostly destroyed by the Tartar invasion; they were rebuilt in the latter half of the thirteenth century and grew in the following century.

Mining went ahead in the thirteenth century. As well as the natives, the colonists — foreign "guests" who enjoyed great privileges — also worked in the metal and salt mines.

The constant tendency of the landowners to extend their estates by taking over the land of the free peasants' communities, and the increased obligations of the peasantry towards the state and the noblemen, and, for the Catholics also towards the Roman Catholic Church, no less than the exactions of officialdom, caused the peasantry to rise in revolt, their revolt often assuming the form of flight and outlawry.

The peasants' struggle to keep their ancient liberty and the deep-rooted traditions of the native organizations, set their seal on the evolution of feudal relationships in Transylvania, which showed a tendency towards a specific form of organization, a *regnum Transylvaniae* distinct from Hungary. Certain leaders of Transylvania such as Stephen, son of King Béla IV, and the princes Roland Borșa and Ladislau Kan, assumed royal prerogatives and endeavoured to carry on an independent policy.

3. The Romanian States — Wallachia, Moldavia, and Dobrudja — are organized

INTERNAL developments and a number of changes in the international situation enabled the Romanian leaders south of the Carpathians to found an independent state at the turn of the thirteenth century. The critical events that the Tartar Empire went through after the death of Nogai Khan and the disturbances that broke out in Hungary with the extinction of the Arpad dynasty, caused the feudal landowners south of the Carpathians to rally round Basarab, a prince of the Argeş district, whom they elected as Grand Voivode and Prince (1317-52). Under circumstances which are as yet insufficiently known, Basarab unified the territory between the Carpathians and the Danube, thus being the founder of Wallachia, which under him played an important part in South-east Europe. At the request of Michael Shishman, the Bulgarian tsar, he took part in the battles fought in the Balkan Peninsula when the Byzantine Empire was on the downgrade. In 1323 Basarab assisted the Bulgarian tsar against Byzantium, and in 1325-8 he won several victories against the Tartars, thereby extending his authority eastward up to the vicinity of Chilia. The district north of the Danube mouths, which Basarab incorporated in Wallachia, kept that prince's name. In 1333 Basarab again supported the Bulgarian tsar, but this time in the latter's struggle against the Serbian prince Stephen Urosh III, with Byzantium as an ally. The allied army was defeated at Velbujd (Küstendil). In an effort to check Magyar expansion over his country, Basarab formed matrimonial and political ties with the Bulgarian and Serbian rulers.

He occupied part of the Severin Banat, which was one of the main directions of Magyar expansion. The campaign undertaken by Hungary in the autumn of 1330 was intended to subordinate Romanian political bodies to Saint Stephen's crown and to suppress their autonomy.

The Hungarian king, Charles Robert of Anjou, organized an expedition to Wallachia "in order to recover the confines of the kingdom, which Basarab ruled over without any right." At Posada (November 9-12) Basarab won a brilliant victory against his former suzerain, causing the expedition to fail of its purpose (the site of the Battle of Posada is the subject of controversy among historians).

Basarab's victory made Wallachia independent and favoured its development. The unity and stability of state life were enhanced and Wallachia entered upon a period of prosperity, the population becoming more dense and trade more active. Favourable socio-economic conditions promoted the development of art. It was during the reign of Basarab that the erection began of the Princely Church at Curtea de Argeș — a splendid monument of Romanian medieval art.

Basarab well deserved to be called "the Great" for he achieved great things : he liberated the territory of Wallachia from Tartar domination, shook off the suzerainty of the Hungarian crown, organized the state, and created a dynasty which was to ensure the stability of this new political order.

Basarab's son and successor, Nicholas Alexander (1352-64), continued his father's policy and succeeded in strengthening the political position of Wallachia and at the same time his dynasty. He maintained friendly relations with the neighbouring rulers and married one of his daughters to Strachimir, the Bulgarian tsar at Vidin, another to Stephen Urosh, the Serbian prince, and yet another to Duke Ladislau of Oppeln, Hungary's Palatine. Fighting alongside Louis of Anjou, the Hungarian king, against the Tartars, he completed the work of his predecessor, liberating new territories from under their sway.

With the approval of the Patriarch of Constantinople, Nicholas Alexander, in 1359, founded the first Metropolitan Church of Wallachia at Curtea de Argeș, thus laying the foundations of church organization in his country. The church became a great supporter of the dynasty. Jachint, former Metropolitan of Vicina, was the first Metropolitan "of all Ungro-Vlachia". Subsequently, the Metropolitan of Wallachia was granted the power of jurisdiction over the Romanians in the Hungarian kingdom with the title of "Exarch of the Highlands".

Nicholas Alexander also continued his father's work in the erection of churches. During his reign the Princely Church at Curtea de Argeș was completed and the old church of the Cîmpulung Monastery was erected. It is there that his grave was found. The inscription on the gravestone calls him : "The great and only ruler, Prince Nicholas Alexander, son of Prince Basarab the Great".

It was Nicholas Alexander who initiated the policy of the Romanian princes of supporting the Orthodox Church in the Balkan Peninsula by means of gifts, particularly landed estates. Nicholas Alexander himself endowed the Cutlumuz Monastery on Mount Athos.

Nicholas Alexander's successor, Vladislav Vlaicu (1364-77), further organized the country and promoted trade and cultural life, endeavouring at the same time to curb the centrifugal tendencies of the boyars (the feudal landholding nobility). For the first time Romanian coins — they were of silver — were minted, with a Latin inscription. On January 20, 1368, the prince issued a diploma written in Latin to confirm the ancient trade privileges that the citizens of Brașov had been granted in Wallachia. The prosperity of the country and the increase in population induced him to demand that the Constantinople Patriarchate set up a second Metropolitan Church at Severin (the first was at Argeș). His request was granted by the synodical act of October, 1370. Religious life became more vigorous through the introduction of monasticism by Nicodim, a monk from Serbia, who founded the Vodița Monastery. The oldest document extant concerned with internal affairs (1374) is that

THE EMERGENCE OF THE ROMANIAN STATES 169

whereby the prince endowed the monastery. Following the example of his father, Vladislav also endowed the monasteries on Mount Athos. For the Catholics in Wallachia and for those in the territories under his rule on the other side of the Carpathians, a bishopric was founded with its seat at Argeș, where the ruins of an old Catholic Church — Sîn Nicoară — are still to be seen.

During the last years of his reign, Vladislav fought against Hungary and died fighting against that kingdom. His successors, Radu I and Dan I, continued the struggle against Hungary. By tradition Radu is known as Radu the Black and was for long considered as the founder of the country.

The second Romanian independent state, Moldavia, was formed east of the Carpathians by the union of the existing political organizations, as Wallachia had also been formed. An important part was played by the Romanians who came down from Maramureș.

Increased domestic trade favoured by the emergence of towns, big and small, as well as intensive transit trade, helped to build up the economic unity of Moldavia. A deed issued by the Papal Chancellery on October 4, 1332, mentions a local leader who had usurped the rights created by the Hungarian kings for what had been the Cumans' bishopric. It stated that "the estates, property and rights of the Milcovia Bishopric" had been taken over by "the powerful people of those parts" (a *potentibus illarum partium*).

The participation in 1325 of a Romanian army recruited on Moldavia's territory, together with Polish, Ukrainian, and Lithuanian armies, in hostilities against the Margrave of Brandenburg, is another indication that the power of the leaders east of the Carpathians had been strengthened.

The unification of the political bodies on Moldavian territory was brought about by their struggle against foreign invaders, particularly the Tartars. The victories won by Basarab against the Tartars from 1325 to 1328 strengthened the desire of the Romanian leaders in Moldavia to free themselves of Mongol rule. And when in the fifties of the fourteenth century the Hungarian King Louis of Anjou set out on an expedition designed to remove the Mongol pressure from the boundaries of his kingdom, he found full support among the Romanian population.

Following the victories won, a march (a fortified border district) was founded in Moldavia in 1325-53, which subsequently was to develop into an independent Moldavian state. Dragoș, Voivode of Maramureș, who had distinguished himself in the battles fought against the Tartars, was appointed as head of that state. The ties between Transylvania and Moldavia, and especially between Maramureș and the north-western part of Moldavia, whose ethnical and cultural unity was of long duration, were thereby strengthened.

The dependence of Dragoș and his successors on the Hungarian crown, much against the local political trends towards independence, caused dissatisfaction among the native rulers, who decided to overthrow both Dragoș's dynasty and Hungarian suzerainty. As in the struggle against the Tartars, the Romanian population of Moldavia was supported by the political leaders of Maramureș who opposed the policy of the Hungarian kings whose aim was to suppress self-governing states and form counties under Hungarian administration. Heading the Maramureș resistance was Voivode Bogdan ; he was described as an "infidel" in the Hungarian records of 1343.

Defeated in his attempt to end the subjection of Maramureș to the Hungarian crown, Bogdan joined the movement in Moldavia, and was elected by the Moldavian boyars as leader of the local forces opposed to Hungarian policy. Taking advantage of the fact that Louis of Anjou, King of Hungary, was engaged in a war against Venice and was moreover concerned with the problem raised in the Balkans by the death of Tsar Stephen Dushan (1355),

Bogdan removed from the Moldavian throne Dragoş's successor, Balc, son of Sas, and in 1359 laid the foundations of an independent Moldavian state.

The Hungarian kings' attempts to reduce to obedience "the Vlach rebels who had diverged from the path of fidelity" were brought to nought by the latter's resistance. King Louis was forced to give up his plan of subjecting Moldavia to the Hungarian crown and to be content with confiscating Bogdan's property in Maramureş, which he bestowed on Voivode Balc who had been driven out of Moldavia.

Under Bogdan, Moldavia extended its territories, incorporating other political orders east of the Carpathians, and the Hungarian kings ultimately accepted the situation.

The independence of Moldavia won under Bogdan as well as its development and unifying process under the princes of his dynasty induced the following generations to ascribe to Bogdan the foundation of the Moldavian state.

It was also in the fourteenth century that Dobrudja became a state playing an important political part in the Balkan Peninsula. The nucleus of the Dobrudjan state was the "Cavarna Country" [the area covered by present-day Bulgaria and Dobrudja] mentioned in a diploma Tsar Ivan Asen II of Bulgaria granted to the people of Ragusa. Halfway through the fourteenth century the unrest prevailing in Byzantium as a result of the struggle for the throne made it possible for Dobrudja to strengthen its autonomy.

In 1346, Balica, its leader, fought in Byzantium and was awarded the title of Despot. After his death Dobrotich succeeded to the throne of the Cavarna Country, first as a vassal of Byzantium and later as an autonomous ruler recognized by Emperor John V Paleologus against whom he had fought for the territory south of Varna.

Dobrotich extending his authority to the Danube, Dobrudja was drawn into a long war against the Genoese who had created factories at Vicina and Lycostomo and wished to make sure of a trade monopoly in that region. In order to cope with the resistance of the Genoese traders who had the Ottoman Empire for allies, Dobrotich strengthened his political organization which became one of the most important factors in the Balkan Peninsula after 1371.

It is not known under what circumstances the Dobrudjan state passed from Dobrotich to his son Ivanko, mentioned in historical records with the title of Despot. Like his father. Ivanko minted his own coins, which were made of copper and inscribed in Greek. This is a sign that he was an independent ruler. In 1386 he made peace with the Ottoman Empire and the following year he concluded at Pera a peace and trade treaty with the Genoese. In 1388 a great Turkish expedition headed by Vizir Ali Pasha threatened to turn the territory between the Danube and the sea into a *pashalik*. The energetic intervention of Mircea the Old, the Wallachian prince, removed that threat and Dobrudja was united with Wallachia.

Shortly before the Battle of Nicopolis, Dobrudja was subjected to Turkish rule but was again conquered by Mircea the Old in 1404.

There are few historical records available for the period between the tenth and the fourteenth centuries but, nevertheless, it is known that certain political formations played a decisive part in the development of the Romanian people who gradually assumed a historical identity ; their political organization developed and they themselves asserted their own identity and originality after having led an anonymous life as a result of the superposition of foreign rule on autochthonous political realities.

CHAPTER SIX

THE ROMANIAN COUNTRIES IN THE FOURTEENTH AND FIFTEENTH CENTURIES

THE establishment of Wallachia and Moldavia as feudal states was of decisive importance for the Romanian people, who, being organized in independent states, were safe from the danger of incorporation by the neighbouring powers or the migratory peoples, and could follow their own path of development, asserting their creative talents. Demographic and economic development as well as social and military organization ensued. The new state organization strengthened internal unity and enabled the two countries to resist the permanent tendencies of the great neighbouring states towards expansion. Unlike the south-Danubian states, which collapsed under the Ottoman conquerors, the Romanian countries resisted their offensive and retained their political entity. A number of outstanding figures embodied this resistance and ably coped with the problems of the Romanian people.

1. Economic Life

THE economic features characteristic of feudalism were a natural economy, each estate endeavouring to produce everything required, and a low technical level. When the productive forces developed and the social division of labour intensified, the towns assumed ever greater significance as centres for the advancement of the crafts and of trade.

The main resources of the people in the Romanian countries in the fourteenth and fifteenth centuries were derived from agriculture, the growing of the vine, animal husbandry, bee-keeping, fishing, forestry, and the wealth of the subsoil. Agriculture, the main production branch, was practised particularly along the river valleys and on the hillsides, where the population was more dense. The Danube plain, frequently laid waste by the nomadic peoples, was mostly forested and the population sparse. Agricultural implements were primitive and did not allow of widespread crops and a large output. The most important technical progress made at the time was the use of the iron ploughshare that turned the furrow, in place of the wooden one, which merely scratched the earth. As most of the country's territory was wooded, the land had constantly to be cleared. Fire was often used for the purpose as were also picks, spades, and ploughs, to prepare the soil for crops of millet, wheat, rye, and oats. The first crop after the clearing was usually fairly abundant, the crop of the second year medium, while the third-year crop was poor, so that the peasants were compelled to sow the seed on newly-cleared land after the third year.

Vine-growing had been practised widely in the country time out of mind. In the fourteenth and fifteenth centuries it brought considerable incomes to the feudal lords and to the administration, and a number of taxes were levied on it, one of which, the *perper,* so-called from the Byzantine coin *hyperperon,* was the first tax in cash known to have been paid in Wallachia. Wine was one of the Romanian products that was being exported in those days.

The breeding of cattle, horses, sheep, and pigs was a main source of income in the Romanian countries. Foreign observers who had the occasion to visit these parts were impressed by the number and quality of the livestock. One of the first trading privileges granted to the towns of Braşov and Lvov by the ruling princes of Wallachia and Moldavia showed livestock to be a main export.

Bee-keeping, like fishing, which was mostly practised in the Danube backwaters rich in fish, no less than the forests with the products and game they yielded, were sources of food for the population and brought in considerable incomes. Honey and wax, fish and forest game were important export articles.

The riches of the subsoil were being exploited mostly in Transylvania. Salt, gold, silver, and iron were mined in large quantities. In Wallachia and Moldavia salt mining was practised on a large scale for home consumption and for export to the whole of the Balkan Peninsula as well as to Poland and the Ukraine. In Wallachia salt was obtained from Ocnele Mari, and copper was mined at Bratilov not far from Baia de Aramă during the reign of Mircea the Old.

The crafts were unequally developed over the Romanian territory during the fourteenth and fifteenth centuries. In Transylvania, less exposed to devastating Turkish and Tartar inroads, the crafts and towns reached a higher level of development than in other parts. In most Transylvanian towns, though not in Wallachia and Moldavia, the craftsmen were already organized in guilds in the fourteenth century. There was a busy trade in craftware which went from Transylvania to the territories east and south of the Carpathians.

Unlike the towns of Transylvania — Brașov, Bistrița, Cluj, and Sibiu — the towns of Wallachia and Moldavia long preserved the basic elements of a rural economy, being primarily trading centres and not craftware producers.

The towns of Brașov, Sibiu, and Bistrița, three Transylvanian trading and craftware centres along the border, were the places where Transylvania, Wallachia, and Moldavia came in touch commercially. While Sibiu mostly traded with Wallachia, and Bistrița almost exclusively with Moldavia, Brașov, owing to its position, was the trading centre of all three Romanian countries.

As town life developed south and east of the Carpathians and the number of local traders increased, the ruling princes of Wallachia and Moldavia realized what advantages could be derived from the prosperity of the towns, which were actually directly subordinated to them. Towards the close of the fifteenth century, the international treaties concluded by Moldavia and Wallachia show that the administration took note of the demands of the townspeople. After 1485 special clauses provided protection for traders.

Owing to their geographical position, the Romanian countries benefited as a result of transit dues. It was through Transylvania and Wallachia that the trade routes linking Western and Central Europe to the Pontic shores and the Balkan Peninsula passed, while the routes linking the Baltic to the Black Sea went through Moldavia. The Romanian territory being now integrated in the circuit of medieval trade, the towns of Chilia and Cetatea Albă played a most important part in the development of Moldavia, Wallachia, and Transylvania.

Traders from the Levant and from Transylvania sold overseas goods and spices south and east of the Carpathians while from Western and Central Europe came cloth, linen, weapons, and farming implements. Foreign traders bought cattle, horses, hides and skins, wax, salt, fish, and other goods from Wallachia and Moldavia.

Like domestic trade, transit traffic was subjected to numerous taxes levied at the border or inside the country. The proceeds went to the ruling princes, to the monasteries or to the boyars.

Monetary circulation was considerable in the Romanian countries during the fourteenth and fifteenth centuries as a result of domestic and foreign trade and of transit traffic. Romanian silver coins *(aspri)* circulated apart from foreign ones : perpers, ducats, florins, groschen and zlotys. Romanian coins were first issued in Wallachia under Vladislav Vlaicu (1364-77) to be continued up to the time of the rule of Radu the Hand-

1. Neolithic statuette.

2. Neolithic statuette. ("The Thinker").

3. Dacian Prayer Centre in Sarmisegetuza.

4. Dacian Helmet from Coțofănești Hoard.

5. Battle scenes on Trajan's Column.

6. A Dacian Peasant.

7. Bust of Trajan

8. Stephen The Great's Statue at Jassy.

9. Voroneț Monastery.

10. The Three Hierarchs Church at Jassy.

11. Vlad the Impaler.

12. Vasile Lupu, Copperplate by Willan Hondias after Abraham van Vestereldt, 1651.

13. Demetrius Cantemir, Copperplate by Christian Fritsch, 1745.

some (1462-75), while in Moldavia they were minted for the first time under Petru Muşat (1375-91) to be continued up to the reign of Ştefăniţă (1517-27).

2. Social Structure

THE salient feature of feudal production relations is the fact that the main means of production — land — belonged to the landowners, whether laymen or churchmen. The peasants only held the lots received from the feudal landowners, tilling them with their own implements; in exchange for the land the peasants worked or paid in cash (labour services, the title, and taxes paid in cash).

The boyars' landownership, which existed before the independent Romanian states emerged, was termed *ocină* or *baştină*. It could only be confiscated by the ruling prince in the event of betrayal or disinheritance.

When the ruling princes made their appearance, conditional landownership was also created, resulting from the princes' donations for "right and faithful service".

In their turn the great boyars were also entitled to make a gift of lands, thus creating vassals (servants) who made up their military hosts.

The estates of the monasteries originated in the gifts of the ruling princes and were subsequently extended by donations, purchases, and usurpation until the monasteries ranked among the greatest feudal landowners of the country.

It was the landowners' aim to extend their estates and, at the same time, to increase the number of dependent peasants who were to till them. The enserfed peasants owed labour to the landowners as well as payment in produce. In order to compel the peasants to carry out their obligations, the landowners had servants who saw that their tasks were carried out.

The owners of large estates enjoyed the privilege of feudal immunity so that no state bodies could infringe upon their estates. The princes' prerogatives consequently passed on to the landowners, who were entitled to levy taxes, administer justice, and convene their vassals in the event of war. Starting from the latter half of the fifteenth century, the princes' administration sought to restrict immunity privileges.

A feudal estate was made up of three parts : seigniorial land, which belonged to the landowner and which the dependent peasants had to till by performing labour service ; the plots tilled by the peasants, in exchange for which they paid a tithe ; and the common land (grass land and forests). During the fourteenth and the fifteenth centuries and even later, the peasants' holdings made up the largest part of a feudal estate in Wallachia and Moldavia. The seigniorial land was very small compared with the area taken up by the peasants' holdings.

On the feudal estates there was a considerable number of gipsy slaves in Wallachia and of gipsy and Tartar slaves in Moldavia.

In the early years after the organization of Romanian feudal states, the dependent peasants were called by names of a general character *(liudi, siraci, siromabi, borani)*, names which were applied to all the unprivileged.

From the fourteenth to the sixteenth century, and possibly also before that period, there was close connection between the dependent peasant and the land he was entitled to use. Provided he fulfilled the obligations incumbent on him, the peasant could not be driven from it. With the passage of time, with the landowners systematically usurping the age-old rights of the peasants, the connection between peasant and land was loosened and personal connection with the landowner was tightened. From the fourteenth to the sixteenth century the dependent peasants still enjoyed the right to leave the estate.

The peasants were also obliged to pay taxes and to do military service. Documents frequently speak of taxes *(biruri)*, which the ruling princes hardly ever ceded to the boyars. With the passage of time these became the greatest burden. In the sixteenth century, particularly in the latter half of that century, the word *biruri* was used for all taxes and cash contributions levied by the ruling prince.

3. The Bobîlna Uprising

IN the Romanian countries the struggle of the peasantry against feudal exploitation assumed various forms : petitions, refusal to work, refusal to pay taxes, flight. In Transylvania, where the peasantry was more cruelly exploited than south and east of the Carpathians, the class struggle also assumed the form of rebellions, which culminated in the Bobîlna uprising.

The main cause was the aggravation of feudal exploitation : increased obligations towards the landowners, increased taxes to be paid to the State and to the Church (the "nona" tax was then introduced, this being a tax paid by the peasant, one tenth going to the Church and one ninth of what was left to the feudal landlord), and cancellation of the right to change one's place of habitation. Discontent flared up as a result of Bishop Gheorghe Lepeș's demand that the outstanding taxes should be paid in a new "big and heavy" coin. Hussite ideology penetrating among the rural masses of Transylvania intensified the resistance and offered a programme of struggle and the tactics to be used in the struggle.

In the spring of 1437 the peasants, both Romanian and Hungarian — with leaders whose names have gone down in history, among them Mihail Românul, Anton Nagy (Anton the Great), Pavel of Voivodeni, "the standard-bearer of the community of Hungarian and Romanian inhabitants" — won a great victory at Bobîlna over the nobility, whom they compelled to negotiate on their own terms. At Bobîlna an understanding was reached between the peasants in revolt and the noblemen, providing, among other things, the right freely to change one's place of habitation, abolition of the "nona" tax, and annual control of the noblemen's observance of these provisions by the peasantry's representatives. After Bobîlna the nobility consolidated their forces and at Kapolna (not far from Dej) on September 16, 1437, concluded the so-called *Unio trium nationum* with the leading strata of the Saxons and Szeklers. The privileged social classes united against the peasants in order to put down any revolt and to keep the peasantry in their existing condition. The Kapolna Union became the basic institution in the constitutional organization of Transylvania. It was in force until the revolution of 1848. Excluded from the Union, the Romanians, who formed the majority of the population, were treated like a "taxable mob", merely tolerated by the others.

The Kapolna Union caused the uprising to flare up again. Although less numerous now, when many had returned to their homes, the peasants battled afresh at Apatiu on October 6, 1437, but the struggle yielded no decisive result. A new understanding between the peasants and the nobility established less favourable conditions for the peasants. The dissatisfied peasants resumed their struggle, being supported by the miners and the townspeople of the lower classes, and succeeded in taking some important towns : Dej, Turda, Aiud, and Cluj. The privileged classes concentrated their forces and with the support of the Hungarian king the uprising was suppressed. The leaders were hanged on the hill facing the town of Turda. Many of the peasants were mutilated.

As in other peasants uprisings, the peasants were defeated after Bobîlna because of poor organization and lack of leaders. Their defeat once again showed that the peasantry cannot liberate itself by its own forces.

4. Political Organization

THE structure of feudal society determined the forms of political organization. On the upper rung of the hierarchical ladder was the ruling prince or Grand Voivode in Wallachia and Moldavia and the Voivode in Transylvania, followed by the great boyars or noblemen. Considered as the supreme master of the whole country, the prince possessed all public power: executive, judicial, legislative, and military. He exercised his power through the agency of his officials, who did not yet have any definite attributes, for they also fulfilled judicial, administrative, and fiscal duties.

Succession to the throne of Moldavia and of Wallachia was hereditary, though not in the order of primogeniture, for the boyars could elect any member of the ruling family to succeed the late ruler. The system enabled the boyars to contest the prince's authority and made it possible for foreign powers to interfere in internal affairs.

The prince's power was supported and controlled by the Prince's Council, made up of the great landowners, whether they held any office in the state or not. Gradually, however, the Council came to be made up of state officials only. At first they were recruited from among the *familiares* in the prince's immediate environment, who fulfilled personal functions, such as the High Steward and the Cupbearer. All important deeds — the donation of estates and whatever concerned foreign relations — were discussed by the Council and confirmed by the Council members.

In the course of time public offices were defined and domestic duties were separated from the public ones. The number of offices then increased and the attributions were limited.[1]

For their services the dignitaries received part of the taxes and fines levied by them for the account of the ruling prince.

Transylvania preserved its status as a principality (voivodeship) even after it had merged with the Hungarian kingdom. A prince (voivode) with supreme administrative, judicial, and military duties was at the head of Transylvania until it fell under Turkish suzerainty in the sixteenth century.

---

[1] The most important court officials were : the *vornic* (palatinus — Court Marshal), the leading official of the prince's court ; the *logofăt* (cancellarius — Chancellor), the most important officer in the prince's chancellery ; the *vistier* (thesaurarius — Treasurer), who kept the accounts of the prince's incomes ; then followed the *spătar* (gladifer — Swordbearer), bearer of the prince's sword during ceremonies ; the *stolnic* (dapifer — High Steward), who had the prince's table and his guests in his care ; the *paharnic* or *ceaşnic* (pincerna — Cupbearer), who procured wine for the court ; the *comis* (comes stabuli — Equerry), who looked after the prince's stables and equipages ; the *postelnic* or *stratornic* (cubicularius — Chamberlain), who had the care of the prince's private apartment. During the first stage of organization of the prince's court, these officials were to be found in the Prince's Council beside the great boyars who held no offices, and side by side with the territorial officials : the *pîrcălab* (castelanus) and the *starost* (capitane). The *ban* was one of the territorial officials of great importance in the history of Wallachia. He is first mentioned as a member of the Prince's Council in the reign of Mircea the Old.

In fifteenth-century documents other officials who held various functions at the prince's court are mentioned as members of the Council besides the great officials. Among them was the *clucer*, who held the keys of the provisions storehouse ; the *sluger*, who saw that the court was supplied with meat ; the *pivnicer*, who supervised the prince's cellars ; the *cămăraş*, who was in charge of the mint and later of the personal estate of the prince *(cămara)* ; the *medelnicer*, who looked after the prince's table services and laundry.

During the latter half of the fifteenth century, while the central power was being strengthened, the office of *armaş* was set up, the armaş being the executor of punishments decreed by the prince. During Stephen the Great's reign, a most important official was the Suceava Gatekeeper *(portar)*, who headed the army.

In the course of time the power of the voivode varied according to the ratio of forces between him and the king of Hungary. When the central power underwent a crisis there was a tendency for the Transylvanian princes to free themselves from regal authority and to look towards the creation of a dynasty : from 1344 to 1376, with short intermissions, six members of the Lackfy family held the dignity of voivode and between 1415 and 1437 there were two members of the Csaky family.

General assemblies (general congregations) were usually of a juridical nature in Transylvania, and seldom tackled economic or administrative problems. They were usually convened by the voivode, though the king, and occasionally the vice-voivode, were also entitled to convene them. Like all similar assemblies in the Middle Ages, they had a pronounced class character and the enserfed peasantry was never represented. Although the Romanians made up the majority of the population, they generally did not participate in the assembly, for most of them were serfs. And even Romanian gentry and other free men were rarely mentioned at the assemblies of 1291 and 1355.

In Wallachia and Moldavia the ruling princes exercised their control of free villages and of the estates of the lesser boyars through the agency of the county bodies.

The towns, whether big or small, were comparatively autonomous, being administrated by elected bodies.

The territory of Transylvania was divided into counties headed by *comites,* who were at first appointed by the voivode. By the close of the fourteenth century the counties, as also the other administrative centres, such as the Romanian districts and the Szekler and Saxon *sedes,* were already well organized. Romanian districts were organized according to their age-old laws *(jus Valachicum)* which the Magyar rule was compelled to observe.

In Wallachia and Moldavia the supreme judge was the ruling prince, who was alone entitled to pronounce capital punishment and to decide the suits between landowners. The boyars and monasteries, holding the privilege of immunity, exercised the right of judging labour conflicts. The free peasants were judged by the representatives of the community or, like the townspeople, by the prince's dignitaries.

So far as penal law was concerned, vestiges of the ancient clan customs were preserved for long : relatives were entitled to avenge a member of the family, and on the other side the head of this one could be ransomed from the relatives.

An old legal practice mentioned in documents was the use of witnesses under oath, especially in peasant suits, such evidence being decisive. As the feudal régime consolidated, the right to bear witness was held only by free people and by landowners.

The army was made up of the prince's men and of the men of the great boyars, who recruited them from their estates, as well as of other peasants and of townspeople. The men of the prince and of the boyars formed the bulk of the army.

In Transylvania Romanian gentry and voivodes played a most important part in the battles waged against the Turks at the close of the fourteenth century and in the fifteenth century. The towns had to recruit men for the army, though from the end of the fifteenth century a sum of money could be paid instead.

In the event of a great threat such as Turkish invasions, the "great army" was convened by the prince. This amounted to mass recruitment, a system applied especially by Iancu of Hunedoara, Vlad the Impaler, and Stephen the Great.

The equipment and armament varied with social position. The boyars and great noblemen were equipped like the western knights in mail shirts and armour and carried shields. They fought on horseback with swords and spears. Foot soldiers mostly fought with bows and sometimes with spears and swords ; the peasants called upon to enlist fought with scythes and picks. To besiege strongholds catapults were used which discharged stones against walls and their defenders. Halfway through the fifteenth century firearms began to be used : mortars made of cast-iron or copper with bombs of stone or iron. The Transylvanian towns, especially Brașov and Sibiu, were important producers of mortars.

The defensive system relied to a great extent on strongholds, whether those inside the country (Neamț, Suceava, Poienari, Ungurași, Ineu, Cetatea de Baltă, Deva, etc.) or those along the borders (Hotin, Soroca, Chilia, Cetatea Albă, Tighina, Severin, Giurgiu, Turnu, Bran, etc.). The strongholds were built of large stone blocks, with ramparts and bastions.

5. Struggle Against Ottoman Expansion

DURING the reign of Mircea the Old (1386-1418) the Ottoman Empire, now including most of the Balkan Peninsula, reached the Danube line, thus threatening Wallachia. Mircea the Old was the first of the Romanian princes who, by their struggle and sacrifices, even in defeat, saved the Romanian countries from sharing the fate of the other Balkan states which the conquerors turned into *pashaliks*. The example set by these princes nurtured the flame of independence which inspired the struggle and policy of the Romanian people through the ages. From the beginning of his reign, Mircea the Old established good relations with Moldavia : he intervened in the struggle for the throne thereto and brought about the ascent of Alexander the Good. The political disturbances in the Hungarian kingdom enabled him to extend his authority in Transylvania, where he enlarged the fiefs of his forerunners. He also incorporated Dobrudja, Wallachia thus reaching its greatest ever extension. In 1404-06, Mircea titled himself "I Mircea, Grand Voivode and Prince of all the Ungro-Vlachia Land and of the parts beyond the mountains and towards the Tartar territories, the Almaş and Făgăraş, Duke and Prince of the Severin Banat and on either side over the whole Podunavia and also as far as the Great Sea, and master of the Dirstor citadel."

Mircea strengthened the power of the state and organized the different high offices, promoted economic development, increased the state's revenue, and minted silver money that enjoyed wide circulation not only inside the country but also in the neighbouring countries. He gave the merchants of Poland and Lithuania trade privileges and renewed those his predecessors had given to the people of Braşov. Mircea the Old could thus afford to increase his military power. He fortified the Danube citadels and strengthened "the great army" made up of townspeople and of free and independent peasants. He also proved a great supporter of the Church. He raised the splendid church at Cozia after the model of the Krusevac Church in Serbia and endowed it generously, as he also did other churches and monasteries.

While organizing the country, he also took good care to form a system of lasting alliances that might enable him to defend the independence of the country. Through the intermediary of Petru Muşat, ruling prince of Moldavia, he concluded in 1389 a treaty of alliance with Vladislav Iagello, King of Poland. The treaty was renewed in 1404 and 1410. He maintained close relations with Sigismund of Luxemburg, the king of Hungary, relying on their common interest in the struggle against Ottoman expansion.

His interventions in support of the Christian peoples south of the Danube who were fighting against the Turks, brought him into conflict with the Ottoman Empire. Mircea the Old was repeatedly victorious in the battles he fought against the Turks: at Rovine on the River Argeş in 1394 and later in 1397 and 1400. He was a master of military tactics and showed great gallantry, which inspired his troops. He can be considered to rank among the great army commanders of his time. As a result of his victories against the Turks, the position of Wallachia was assured and the expansion of the Ottoman Empire in Central Europe was temporarily checked. The German historian Leunclavius described him as "the bravest and ablest of the Christian princes".

The defeat of Sultan Bayazid Ilderim by Timur Lenk (Tamerlane) at Ankara in 1402 opened a period of anarchy in the Ottoman Empire and Mircea took advantage of it to organize together with the Hungarian king, a campaign against the Turks. In 1404 Mircea was thus able to impose his rule on Dobrudja again. He moreover took part in the struggles for the throne of the Ottoman Empire and enabled Musa to ascend that throne. It was at this time that the prince reached the height of his power.

From 1414 to 1417 the Ottoman Empire resumed its attempts to expand north of the Danube. Mircea the Old facing by himself an enemy that possessed forces greatly superior to his own, decided to pay the Ottoman Porte a tribute to regain peace, though without any vassalage.

In the first decades of its existence as a state, Moldavia had to face Hungary's repeated attempts to re-establish her suzerainty over the territories east of the Carpathians. The ruling princes of Moldavia endeavoured to parry the threat with Poland's support.

Lațcu (1365-74) succeeded to the throne after Bogdan, the creator of the Moldavian independent state. In 1370 he had to cope with the joint Polish-Hungarian threat as Louis I, King of Hungary, was elected King of Poland as well. In order to weaken the pressure of Hungary, Lațcu turned Catholic and came into touch with the Pope. It was a purely political move and consequently the Catholic religion in Moldavia did not survive Lațcu's reign. Lațcu himself was buried in the Orthodox Church at Rădăuți.

Laţcu's successor, Petru Muşat (1374-91), taking advantage of the deterioration of the Polish-Hungarian union following the death of King Louis in 1382, tried to shake off Hungarian pressure by creating friendly relations with Poland. The Treaty of Lvov concluded with Poland in 1387 offered Moldavia support against the Hungarian threat.

Petru Muşat attached great importance to economic, administrative, and religious organization. He was the first to mint Moldavian silver coins and during his reign the country's revenues increased considerably thanks to domestic trade and transit tolls. In 1388 the Moldavian prince lent the king of Poland 3,000 silver rubles, for which he was given the Halicium territory (Pokuţia) as security. He founded the Moldavian Metropolitan Church and placed his relative Iosif at the head of it. Although it was canonically recognized by the Constantinople Patriarchate only much later, the Moldavian Metropolitan Church helped to strengthen the power of the ruling princes.

The reign of Roman I (1391-4) and of Stephen I (1394-9), though of short duration, covered two important moments in Moldavia's history. Under Roman I Moldavia's boundaries reached "the sea shore", while under Stephen I Sigismund of Luxemburg, King of Hungary, was defeated at Hindău and his attempts to reduce Moldavia to subjection came to nought.

Brought to the throne with the support of Mircea the Old, Alexander the Good (1400-32) gave Moldavia a long period of economic prosperity while his feudal state was consolidated and its international prestige enhanced.

From the very first years of his reign, Alexander the Good realized that it was in the interest of the Moldavian state to continue the policy of co-operation with Poland. The Moldavian armies repeatedly fought alongside those of the Polish and the Lithuanian ones against the Teutonic

Knights, gaining distinction at Grünewald in 1410 and at Marienburg in 1422.

His economic and military power enabled him to evade the consequences of the Treaty of Lublin concluded by Poland and Hungary in 1412, which stipulated that Moldavia was to be divided if Alexander the Good did not provide the Hungarian king with military assistance against the Turks. Subsequent attempts on the part of Sigismund to re-establish Hungarian suzerainty over Moldavia failed.

Alexander the Good took interest in the political situation of Wallachia and succeeded in helping certain princes to the throne : Prince Aldea, for example, added to his name that of his protector and called himself Alexander Aldea. His policy was followed by all the great Moldavian princes who tried to make of the leaders of Wallachia devoted allies in the struggle against the Turks.

Like Wallachia after Mircea the Old, Moldavia went through a period of internal struggles at the death of Alexander the Good. The country's capacity of resistance was thus weakened and this paved the way for foreign intervention.

When Ottoman pressure increased in the fifties of the fifteenth century, it was Transylvania under the leadership of Iancu of Hunedoara (1441-56), John Hunyady or Hunyadi to the Hungarians, that played an important part in the struggle of the Romanian countries against the Turks, with a military confederation of the three countries ensuing as a result. In 1438 Iancu of Hunedoara, who was Romanian by race, was Ban of Severin ; by 1441 he had become Voivode of Transylvania and Comes of Timișoara, as well as a tried fighter against the Turks, whom he had defeated repeatedly. From 1442 onwards Iancu of Hunedoara intervened in the internal policy of the two Romanian countries, placing princes on their throne in order to ensure that Moldavia and Wallachia would assist him in his anti-Ottoman struggle. In

1448 he was ceded the citadel of Chilia, one of the key positions of the anti-Ottoman front, in exchange for the support he had given Peter II to gain the Moldavian throne. Master of Chilia, Iancu of Hunedoara could control political developments in the territories of Moldavia and Wallachia.

With an eye to the innovations in military tactics and techniques, Iancu of Hunedoara created a fighting system under which the bulk of the army was made up of popular elements ; he introduced the Hussite tactics of the camp built up of linked wagons, and created a wide system of alliances with the neighbouring countries in the struggle against the Turks.

After having defeated a number of Turkish plundering hordes, Iancu of Hunedoara tried to liberate the Balkan Peninsula from the Ottoman yoke. In 1443 he organized a great expedition against the Turks, the so-called "long campaign", and succeeded in crossing the Balkans and reaching Sofia. The crusade organized the following year (1444) was insufficiently prepared, however, and led to the Varna disaster when the king of Hungary met his death. In 1448, using forces from all the Romanian countries, Iancu of Hunedoara, now governor of Hungary after King Vladislav's death, again tried to strike at the Turkish possessions south of the Danube. The decisive battle was fought at Kossovo where the Turks were victorious.

In the years that followed, internal difficulties prevented Iancu of Hunedoara from undertaking new military actions against the Porte. The truce of 1451, which also involved the Romanian countries, was merely a respite during which new campaigns were being prepared, as shown by the negotiations carried on with Byzantium in 1452.

The last great victory of the brilliant Romania commander was occasioned by Sultan Mohammed II's attempt to overcome the resistance of the Hungarian kingdom at Belgrade. On July 21-22, 1456, the Ottoman army which was besieging the town suffered a great defeat and was compelled to postpone its advance towards Central Europe. Shortly after this victory Iancu of Hunedoara died from the plague. Thanks to his brilliant resistance, Iancu of Hunedoara delayed Ottoman expansion towards Central Europe for more than half a century.

Moldavia had bowed to the Porte, as decided by Petru Aron, the ruling prince, and the Moldavian boyars at Vaslui (1456), and Iancu of Hunedoara had just been victorious at Belgrade, when Vlad the Impaler grandson of Mircea the Old, became ruling prince of Wallachia. While the decision made at Vaslui aggravated the situation of Wallachia, the defeat of Sultan Mahommed II under the walls of Belgrade had shown the efficiency of firm and organized resistance to the Ottoman invaders. But after the death of Iancu of Hunedoara, with Serbia being turned into a *pashalik* in 1459, Ottoman pressure increased along the Danube and became a direct threat to Wallachia's independence. In the military duel ahead of him, Vlad decided to take the initiative.

Before declaring war upon the Porte, Vlad the Impaler undertook some bold political measures. In order to strengthen his authority he restricted the political and military power of the great boyars, created a powerful army, and supported the local traders. In order to restrict the competition of Saxon traders, "border fairs" were set up, where foreign traders sold their goods. Vlad moreover took military action against the Saxon traders, plundering the Bîrsa country a number of times.

The conflict between the prince and the great boyars — a consequence of the prince's centralizing policy — assumed violent forms, the prince suppressing a considerable number of his opponents. A permanent army recruited from among the court officials and the peasants and subordinated to the prince's authority superseded the private troops of the great landowners.

In 1459 Vlad refused to pay tribute to the Porte and in the winter of 1461-2 he attacked and destroyed the Ottoman garrisons on both banks of the Danube, from Zimnicea to the mouths of the river. An expedition headed by Sultan Mohammed II himself ensued. According to the Byzantine chronicler Laonic Chalcocondil, the Sultan had at this time the most powerful armies the Turkish Empire had been able to muster since the conquest of Constantinople. Vlad used the conventional tactics of the Romanian princes : laying waste the territory before withdrawing, and harassing the enemy. In the night of June 16, 1462, Vlad attacked the Sultan's camp and the success he thus won built up his Europe-wide fame. The Sultan occupied the capital city of the country — Tîrgoviște — which had been abandoned by the Wallachian prince, but without any political and military effect. By June the Ottoman army was withdrawing in disorder under the repeated blows of the Romanian forces.

Vlad the Impaler's victory could only have been effective if supported by a coalition of the forces of the Christian states. In the summer of 1462 the Turks resumed their attempt to subject Wallachia, this time with new tactics ; it was no longer the Sultan that headed the forces along the Danube but Vlad's brother Radu the Handsome, a docile instrument of the Porte, who had no intention of striking at the position of the great boyars. The betrayal of the boyars and the hostility of Matthias Corvinus, King of Hungary, brought Vlad's rule to an end. The Romanian prince crossed the Carpathians and was imprisoned at Buda.

Vlad the Impaler had won European fame. His feats of arms, his energy, and the sternness with which he put down all opposition, placed him among the outstanding political figures of his age, although he became the prototype of the bloodthirsty tyrant under the name of "Dracula". It was King Matthias Corvinus, youngest son of Iancu of Hunedoara, who was mainly responsible for blackening his name, for he wished to compromise the Romanian prince whose anti-Ottoman policy showed clearly that the Hungarian king had cancelled his plans for an anti-Ottoman crusade. However, we should not overlook the role of the Saxons, who had suffered under Vlad's raids on their towns, for their part in spreading tales of terror. For the Romanian people Vlad the Impaler was a remarkable statesman and leader who defended the independence of their country. He remains, however, a controversial figure because of his cruelty. R.W. Seton-Watson says that "From the distinctly inadequate material at our disposal it is impossible to avoid the conclusion that Vlad was a man of diseased and abnormal tendencies, the victim of acute moral insanity."

6. The Rule of Stephen the Great (1457-1504)

CHRONICLER Grigore Ureche described Stephen as "a well balanced man, not in the least slothful, who knew how to cope with his work and could be found where you least expected him to be. Master of the craft of war, he went wherever he was needed so that seeing him his men would not disperse and for that reason there was seldom a war that he did not win. And when others defeated him, he did not lose hope for, when vanquished, he would rise above his vanquishers.". Stephen, the grandson of Alexander the Good, reigned in Moldavia for half a century, strengthening the country politically, defending its independence and making of it one of the main political powers of Eastern Europe.

The fundamental problems Stephen was called upon to solve were : to do away with feudal division, centralize the state, and defend the country's independence. Outstanding political ability, mastery of the military art, and great determination were the gifts that helped

Stephen to carry out these aims and brought him success. The political, diplomatic, and military measures taken by the Moldavian prince were part of a unitary system which was grounded in a broad concept of politics.

When he ascended the throne of Moldavia, the country had gone through a quarter of a century of internal struggles during which the great boyars had strengthened their position while Hungary and Poland had found the means of enforcing their suzerainty by installing their protégés on the throne. The boyars fought against Stephen's centralization programme for they were used by now to having a nominal ruler on the throne. The opposition of the great boyars induced Stephen to find allies among other categories of Moldavian society: the lesser boyars, the townspeople, and especially the free peasantry. Stephen was thus able to build up a powerful army that enabled him to dispense with the troops of the great landowners and to cope with the threats from abroad. In implementing his centralization policy he had the support of "the brave", men of great worth risen from the people. The policy of the prince was radically changed, as shown by the system of remuneration: it consisted of incomes derived from the fines levied in the capacity of dignitaries of the ruling prince. The central authority now no longer bestowed prerogatives for the benefit of people who were thereby rendered immune. Privileges were granted to those who assisted the progress of the centralization policy. Throughout Stephen's reign, the great boyars systematically opposed the measures he took, for they were a threat to their political and military position. The struggle between the prince and the great boyars either assumed violent forms or was carried on by devious ways. The more important episodes in the opposition of the great landowners were the boyars' betrayal at Baia; the internal crisis of 1485-6 and Stephen's defeat at Scheia which ensued from it; the boyars' opposition when Stephen named Bogdan as his successor and the energetic reprisals that followed. There was now a contradiction between the development of Moldavian society and feudal division, which had become anachronistic. Stephen's domestic policy provided Moldavia with the means of opposing the expansionist trends of the great neighbouring powers and also of asserting itself in the international arena.

Immediately after ascending the throne Stephen started a military action in the outlying regions of Poland. This he did in order to strengthen his power and to avert the danger of new Polish interference for the benefit of the prince who had been removed from the throne. Stephen's inroads caused King Casimir of Poland to give up his plan of bringing Petru Aron back to the Moldavian throne by armed intervention and simultaneously to abandon his plan of interfering in Moldavia's internal affairs. Though Stephen accepted Polish suzerainty according to the Overchelăuți Treaty of 1459, he gradually restricted it during his reign.

The attempt made by Matthias Corvinus, King of Hungary, to use Petru Aron, who had left Poland for Transylvania, against Stephen, opened a period of conflicts in Moldo-Hungarian relations which culminated in the Hungarian king's campaign of 1467.

This campaign was not only due to Stephen's repeated inroads in the Szekler districts as reprisals against the support given by the Hungarian king to Petru Aron. Matthias Corvinus had far more valid reasons : in 1465 the Moldavians had occupied Chilia and in 1466-7 Stephen had supported the separatist movement in Transylvania. Furthermore, the Hungarian king was determined to impose Magyar suzerainty on Moldavia.

In the second half of November, the Hungarian army entered Moldavia along the banks of the River Trotuș and subsequently occupied and burned down the towns of Bacău, Roman, and Neamț. Faced by an adversary of superior numerical force and mistrusting his boyars,

Stephen withdrew to the north of the country. During the night of December 14, the Moldavian prince attacked the Magyar army by surprise at Baia, cutting it to pieces, and compelled Matthias, who had been wounded during the battle, to leave the country in great haste.

The victory at Baia was not exploited because of the treachery of a great number of boyars : a plot with the Great Vornic (Court Marshal) among its leaders was in preparation. Stephen discovered it and the reprisals that followed showed his determination to put an end to boyar anarchy.

Stephen's campaigns in Wallachia were the prelude to a great anti-Ottoman war which he undertook in order to avert the danger of his country being enslaved by the Porte. His hostilities against the Porte began when in 1473 he placed Laiotă Basarab on the throne of Wallachia, entrusting him with the mission of enlarging the anti-Ottoman front and of ensuring Moldo-Wallachian unity of action.

The struggle against the Ottoman threat made Moldavia a factor in one of the dominant problems of the fifteenth century, giving its activities European significance. This accounts for Stephen's extensive international relations and for the wide response his feats of arms called forth.

Stephen's anti-Ottoman activities began within the comprehensive coalition which included Venice, Hungary — now more friendly to Moldavia — and Uzun Hasan's Turkish State. The coalition acted under the aegis of the Pope. In 1472 Stephen had entered into relations with the Turkic Khan, while in 1474, through the intermediary of Venice, he asked Pope Sixtus IV's support in his anti-Ottoman struggle.

It was also in 1474 that Stephen rejected the demand of Sultan Mohammed II that Chilia and Cetatea Albă should be ceded to him and refused to pay tribute to the Porte, thus openly severing relations with the latter. Early the following year an immense Turkish army under

Soliman Hadamb, *beglerbeg* [military commander] of Rumelia, marched into Moldavia. On the morning of January 10, 1475, Stephen took the Ottoman army by surprise at Podul Înalt, not far from Vaslui, inflicting a serious defeat on it. The widow of Sultan Murad II pointed to the seriousness of the defeat when she asserted that "the Turkish hosts had never suffered a more serious defeat". The victory called forth fervent response throughout Europe. The Pope wrote to the Moldavian prince : "Your feats of arms have made your name so famous that it is on everyone's lips". The Polish chronicler Jan Dlugosz described the Moldavian prince as "the worthiest to be entrusted with the duties of command and leader against the Turks".

But the Ottoman Empire could not accept a defeat which threatened its strategic position in South-east Europe and in the basin of the Black Sea. Stephen himself warned the European powers that a new military campaign against Moldavia was inevitable and that a common action of the Christian states was necessary.

In the summer of 1475 an Ottoman fleet entered the port of Caffa, an important Genoese colony in southern Crimea, and conquered it. This had serious consequences for Moldavia. Henceforth, and for a long time to come, the Tartars in the Crimea, now dependent on the Porte, became the latter's political and military instruments.

With the Ottoman power installed in the Crimea, Stephen had to face a great threat. This induced him to strengthen his relations with Matthias Corvinus, whose suzerainty he recognized in the summer of 1475, though the act concluded on the occasion was more in the nature of a treaty of alliance.

In May, 1476, Sultan Mohammed II launched an expedition against Moldavia which was one of the greatest the Ottoman Empire had ever undertaken. Stephen withdrew, evading battle in the open field and laying waste the territory. Simultaneously, the Tartars overran the country, which compelled the Moldavian prince to divide his forces. Stephen said at a later date with reference to the Turks' attack: "They found me alone, with all my soldiers scattered about the country to protect their homes." With only his courtiers about him, Stephen tried to oppose the Turks at Valea Albă on July 26, 1476, but was defeated. The Sultan, however, did not succeed in his aim politically for he was forced to leave Moldavia because of the stubborn resistance of the strongholds as well as because of the plague and famine which were playing havoc with the Ottoman army. Furthermore, he had been informed that an army corps was soon to come from Transylvania. The allied Moldavian and Transylvanian forces then took the offensive, entered Wallachia and placed Vlad the Impaler on the throne. Vlad, however, was soon to be killed by the boyars. In the years that followed Stephen endeavoured to control the situation in Wallachia in order to co-ordinate the two countries in their anti-Ottoman struggle.

International developments after the death of Mohammed II enabled the Ottoman Empire partially to reach its aims in Moldavia : in 1484 the Turks occupied Chilia and Cetatea Albă, important economic and strategic centres, as a result of a surprise attack. In the years that followed Stephen endeavoured to win back these two cities with the support of the Polish king, Casimir, who demanded in exchange that Stephen do homage personally and consequently accept rigorous vassalage. In the autumn of 1485 at Kolomea, Stephen took a vassal's oath, which he had evaded doing for a quarter of a century.

Polish support, however, proved insufficient to enable Stephen to win back the two cities. And when Poland made peace with the Turks in 1487, the Moldavian prince was placed with an accomplished fact and in his turn had to pay tribute to the Porte. This was in fact a redemption of peace.

When the rivalry between Poland and Hungary increased, Stephen sided with the Hungarian kingdom. He received from King Matthias Corvinus two important fiefs in Transylvania : Ciceu and Cetatea de Baltă. With the Moldavian princes in possession of these fiefs, the connections between Moldavia and Transylvania grew closer. Faced with the hostility of the Polish king, Stephen strengthened his alliance with Ivan III, Grand Duke of Moscow, and through the intermediary of the latter, with the Tartar Khan of the Crimea, Mengli-Ghirai. John Albert, Casimir's successor, despite the warnings of his brother Vladislav, now King of Hungary after Matthias Corvinus's death, intended to reduce Moldavia to subordination and even to install one of his brothers, Sigismund, on the throne. Under pretence of an anti-Ottoman campaign, the Polish king marched into Moldavia at the head of a great army, making for Suceava (1479). The stubborn resistance of that stronghold and the fear of being attacked by the superior forces of Stephen's allies caused John Albert to change his plans. On the way back to Poland, the Polish army suffered a serious defeat in the Cosmin Woods. Two years later, through the intermediary of the Hungarian king, Stephen concluded a treaty with Poland which ended juridically also the situation created by the homage he had paid at Kolomea. Moldavia's position was now better than it had ever been. The attempts made by three great neighbouring powers — Hungary, the Ottoman Empire and Poland — to subjugate it had failed. On July 2, 1504, the man whom contemporaries described as "most subtle and skilful in the craft of war" and who had fought 36 battles in defence of his country, 34 of which he had won, passed away after having written the most splendid page in Moldavia's history. To all his successors, Stephen was a symbol of justice and independence. R. W. Seton-Watson comments that "Unhappily Stephen was the last of the heroic breed, and none of his successors proved even remotely worthy of him. On his death there was marked and rapid decay, and we find ourselves in a new and inglorious epoch."

CHAPTER SEVEN

THE BEGINNINGS OF OTTOMAN DOMINATION.
THE EPIC OF MICHAEL THE BRAVE AND ITS HERITAGE

THE beginnings of Ottoman domination in the first half of the sixteenth century opened a new chapter in the history of the Romanian countries. The vigorous progress of the preceding century was checked by Ottoman expansion, which brought its influence to bear on the life of the Romanian people in all spheres. The great boyars extended and strengthened their power by enserfing free villages and increasing feudal impositions. The trend was for the nobility to seize all political power and to rise above the prince's authority. With Turkish domination assuming ever more oppressive forms, the three Romanian countries reacted by repeatedly participating in anti-Ottoman campaigns. This policy culminated in the epic of Michael the Brave at the end of the century.

1. The Peasant War headed by Doja

MOSTLY owing to its more advanced economic development, Transylvania was in the early years of the sixteenth century the arena of class conflicts of a wider scope than anything Moldavia and Wallachia were witnessing at the time. In Transylvania the serfs' obligations were more oppressive than those in the two other Romanian countries. The development of the towns and intensified trade stimulated the growth of agricultural production and brought in its train increased feudal obligations. The peasantry reacted vigorously against the new conditions and was joined in its struggle by other sections of society impelled by their own interests. Preceded by successive movements of a local character over the space of a quarter of a century, the uprising of 1514 was to involve wide territories in Transylvania. It was a joint struggle of the Romanian and Hungarian peasantry, of the oppressed Szeklers, the poor sections of society in many towns, the workers in the salt and metal mines, and even certain rich townspeople and members of the lesser nobility, against the mighty magnates. The uprising started at Buda in Hungary and the occasion was the recruiting of an army for the crusade against the Turks : the serfs were offered the prospect of freedom if they enrolled in the army. The crusade was proclaimed in April, 1514. At the Rakos camp some 40,000 men, according to contemporary estimates, had gathered under the command of Gheorghe Doja, a Szekly captain of some military prowess, according to R. W. Seton-Watson. The noblemen opposing the continuation of enrolment, together with the treatment meted out to the families of those that had enrolled, turned the anti-Ottoman campaign into a struggle against feudal domination. While the uprising was extending throughout Hungary and Transylvania, spontaneously or stirred up by Doja's men, the main army of the rebels advanced along the valley of the White Criș and of the Mureș towards Lipova and from there to Timișoara, where powerful forces of the nobility had entrenched themselves. Although the rebels won a number of victories, the more important of which were those of Nădlac and Cenad, and although they had made their way into some big towns such as Arad, Cluj, Sighișoara, and Bistrița, the town of Timișoara resisted the siege. New forces sent from Buda or brought over by John Zapolya, voivode of Transylvania, came to the rescue of the nobility and on July 15 Doja's army was defeated. Five days later Doja was tortured to death :

he was bound naked on a red-hot iron throne while his flesh was torn from his body by tongs, and fed to some of his followers who were forced to eat the flesh from his still living body! The other leaders of the rebel army were each subjected to various tortures. The peasant resistance, with battles being fought at Cluj and Biharea, for example, was defeated throughout Transylvania.

Having inflicted cruel punishments on the participants in the uprising, the dominant class took advantage of the victory to issue regulations to be in force a long time. The Diet that met at Buda decided that the serfs should do labour service for 52 days a year (the convention of 1437 had stipulated only one day a year) and that the right of changing one's place of habitation should be abolished, "full and eternal serfdom" being enforced. This was the last step of enslavement. The Tripartitum Code, also named the Werböczi Code after the person who drew it up, sanctioned these measures. Actually the Code was not applied in Transylvania, where the serfs had a fewer number of days to contribute during the first half of the sixteenth century, and it was differently carried out in every part of the country. The legislative measures instituted after the failure of the 1514 uprising aggravated the economic and juridical situation of the peasantry. They were part of the process whereby their exploitation was intensified and their servile dependence was tightened — a process characteristic of the districts east of the Elbe. The savage reprisals and the tasks enforced upon the peasantry were to make it impossible for them to co-operate with the ruling classes in the defence of the kingdom against the Ottoman power, at the time in full process of expansion. And the disaster that followed the defeat sustained at Mohács in 1526 is to be accounted for by the lack of support from the peasantry no less than by the lack of unity and determination of the nobility.

2. The Romanian Countries in the New Stage of Ottoman Expansion

THIS was the time when the Ottoman Empire was ascending towards its greatest heights. With the conquest of Eastern Anatolia, Syria, and Egypt under Selim I (1512-20), the Empire had doubled its territory, which now spread into three continents. Holding hegemony in the Mediterranean and expanding towards Central Europe, the Ottoman Empire came into a centuries-long conflict with the Habsburgs and this brought about a Turkish-French *rapprochement*. The struggle of the Habsburg and Ottoman Empires for Central Europe gave the Romanian countries the opportunity of renewing their fight for the recovery of independence.

The conquest of Belgrade in 1521 opened to the new Sultan, Suleiman I, the way towards Central Europe. During the first campaign, Suleiman brought the boundaries of his empire to the Danube and the Drave; in 1526 he defeated the Magyar army at Mohács and three years later, in 1529, he reached the ramparts of Vienna. In Hungary the death of King Louis II, who had fallen at the Battle of Mohács, brought about a fierce struggle for the throne, the nobility being divided into supporters of John Zapolya, voivode of Transylvania, and of Ferdinand of Habsburg, brother of Emperor Charles V. While Ferdinand established his sway over the western and northern districts of the kingdom, John Zapolya, with the support of the Ottoman Porte and paying it tribute, succeeded in keeping the largest part of Hungary and the whole of Transylvania. But as Ferdinand was still bent on ruling the entire kingdom, Transylvania was often the theatre of war between the two competitors. The struggle finally ended in 1538 when, in accord with the Treaty of Oradea, the Habsburgs were appointed heirs to Zapolya. When Zapolya died in 1540, the Sultan appointed the latter's son, John Sigismund, to the throne, and a year later, as a result of Ferdinand's attacks,

Suleiman annexed the Hungarian territories that had been under Zapolya's sway, creating the Buda *pashalik* in 1541. There were now two Hungaries, one under the Habsburgs and the other under the Turks. John Sigismund, under the suzerainty of the Porte, kept the principality of Transylvania, which included the western districts of Banat and Crişana as well as certain counties of Hungary proper. This was the beginning of a new epoch in the political history of Transylvania, which had become a vassal of the Sultan and had been detached from the Kingdom of Hungary, this being in keeping with its ancient tendencies towards autonomy. But Banat was annexed by the Turks in 1552 and organized into a *pashalik*, with Timişoara as its capital city. Part of Crişana was also incorporated in the *pashalik*.

Hungary's defeat at Mohács and the transformation of Transylvania into a vassal of the Porte weakened the anti-Ottoman resistance system on which the struggle for independence of the Romanian countries had relied in the fifteenth century.

For more than three decades after Stephen the Great's death, Moldavia maintained with the Porte the relationships established through the struggle carried on by that great prince, although the tribute paid to the Turks had been increased under the reign of Bogdan III the One-eyed (1504-17). The latter's successor, Ştefăniţă (1517-27), a nephew of Stephen the Great, evaded the request of sending his forces to Transylvania to assist the Sultan's troops; he defeated the Tartars in 1518 and even routed a Turkish army that was returning from a plundering foray in Poland (1524). The messengers sent by the Moldavian prince to the Polish king in 1522 voiced Moldavia's wish to be independent. As in the days of Stephen the Great, Moldavia was spurring on other countries to undertake a joint struggle in defence of the solidarity interests of the Christian states.

With Wallachia's growing dependence upon the Ottoman Empire, the threat to Moldavia became more and more serious. Yet efforts were still being made in Wallachia towards an anti-Ottoman orientation with the help of Transylvania and the Hungarian kingdom, and even towards incorporation into a wider international campaign. But these efforts could come to nothing with the presence of the Turks in their strongholds along the Danube, the constant struggle for power among the boyars, the conflicts between the latter and the ruling prince, and the Turkish support given to one or the other faction wishing to place a certain prince on the throne. The years during which Neagoe Basarab (1512-21) ruled the country, in contrast with the short reigns that preceded and followed him, stand out as a period of internal stability and of important cultural growth, while in the field of foreign relations Wallachia carried out its obligation towards the Porte, accepted the suzerainty of Hungary, to counterbalance Ottoman influence, and established contacts with Poland and even with Venice and the Papacy. Christian solidarity, however, did not assume the form of an anti-Ottoman struggle. There was only a cultural impact throughout the Orthodox countries of Eastern Europe.

After Neagoe Basarab's death, the Turkish governor of Nicopolis attempted to appoint Turkish dignitaries in Wallachia as a prelude to turning it into a *pashalik,* but the plan met strong opposition headed by Radu of Afumaţi (1521-9) who was assisted by the voivode of Transylvania. The many battles fought against the Turks along the Danube from 1522 to 1524 were the last tenacious efforts made against the Turks in Wallachia. In the end Radu himself accepted the princely dignity from the Sultan, though his being recognized by the Porte meant that the Sultan was compelled to accept a situation created by local forces.

Despite the adverse domestic and foreign conditions of the first decades of the sixteenth century, Wallachia made some progress in state organization, in particular during the reigns of Radu the Great and Neagoe Basarab.

In Moldavia, Ștefăniță's coming of age unleashed a conflict between the great boyars, who had ruled after Bogdan's death, and the young prince, who intended to assert his authority. The first stage of that conflict was marked by the beheading of Luca Arbore in April, 1523. In the autumn of the same year the boyars attempted to depose Ștefăniță by force of arms. The prince, however, defeated the rebels with the aid of the lesser boyars and the free peasantry and secured undisputed sway.

The policy of strengthening central authority, of developing the state machinery and curtailing the privileges of the great boyars was also carried on with remarkable consistency by Ștefăniță's successor, Petru Rareș (1527-38), an illegitimate son of Stephen the Great, described by R. W. Seton-Watson as one of the most curious figures in Romanian history. For a decade Moldavia again became a factor of importance in international policy. Petru Rareș's dominant idea was to defend Moldavia's independence, which meant opposition to the Ottoman Empire. But allowing himself to be drawn into the conflict between Ferdinand of Habsburg and John Zapolya in Transylvania, and resuming the struggle against Poland for the possession of Poquția, he split up his forces. He first sided with Ferdinand of Habsburg, then, during the campaigns he undertook in 1529, he assisted Zapolya, whose rule was ensured by the victory the Moldavian hosts won at Feldioara. As a result, the old possessions of the Moldavian princes in Transylvania were extended and the influence of Petru Rareș was felt in that province. It is not unlikely that the thought of ruling the whole of Transylvania occurred to him at the time.

The conflict between Petru Rareș and the Ottoman Empire began as a result of the assassination of Suleiman's envoy, Aloisio Gritti, followed by an alliance with Ferdinand in 1535 and by instigations to a general struggle against the Turks. But this son of Stephen the Great had many enemies : both the Moldavian boyars and the Polish king complained about him to the Sultan. The campaign of 1538 pinioned him between three enemies. With prompt moves, Petru Rareș defeated the Tartars at Ștefănești, obtained from the Poles the promise that they should withdraw from Hotin, and was preparing to face Suleiman's attack as his father, Stephen the Great, had done. His resistance was, however, ineffectual owing to the betrayal of the great boyars who went over to the Sultan's camp and accepted Ștefan Lăcustă (Stephen the Grasshopper), so called because of a symbolic plaque of these insects during his brief reign, as ruling prince. This was the first Moldavian prince appointed by the Porte. A Turkish garrison was left with the prince and a district between the Rivers Prut and Dniester in the south-east of the country was subjected to the authority of the Turkish governor at Cetatea Albă. The town of Tighina then became a Turkish stronghold and a few years later the town of Brăila in Wallachia was also annexed by the Ottoman Empire.

The defeat of Moldavia in 1538 by the Turks, without any battle being fought, meant an end to her independence. Petru Rareș, when resuming the throne three years later, continued to nurture his plans of freedom though he was unable to carry them out. The fall of Moldavia enabled the Porte to increase its sway over Wallachia. And when Transylvania passed under Turkish suzerainty at about the same time, the three Romanian countries entered a new stage in their history.

3. Beginnings of Ottoman Domination

THE beginnings of Ottoman domination over the Romanian countries, for which different forms of dependence in the past had paved the way, but which had been delayed by the struggles waged for a century and a half, was the result of international politics, of the disproportion between the forces of the two contenders, and of the constant struggles between the boyars and the ruling prince, which prevented any joint effort being made and enabled the Turkish Empire to act as arbitrator in domestic conflicts.

In this new stage of relationships with the Ottoman Empire, Moldavia and Wallachia could no longer pursue a foreign policy of their own. Their military forces, which had deteriorated on account of the new situation and of internal socio-political transformations, were obliged to participate in the expeditions of the Ottoman Porte under Turkish commanders. The very throne of the ruling prince was in the hands of the Sultan who confirmed the boyars' election of a prince or the succession to the throne, or else chose and appointed a prince, the latter practice tending to come into general use with time. A new prince was usually invested with his dignity at Constantinople and the ceremonial there was designed to emphasize his dependence on the Porte.

Any departure from the fulfilment of his obligations meant dethronement and sometimes the payment of yet more serious penalties. The ruling princes continued to be elected from among the members of the ancient princely families, even though the kinship with former ruling princes was sometimes fictitious. Before long, however, the Sultans began to appoint princes without taking into consideration their origin. Peter the Lame, for example, a descendant of the Wallachian princes, came to rule Moldavia (1574). Prompted by caution, for a long rule opened the possibility of independence, and by interest, for the prince that was appointed to the throne had to pay for the dignity, the Turks frequently changed the princes and this detracted from their authority which was, moreover, undermined by continued conflicts with the boyars. And it was also the boyars who encouraged the tendencies of the Porte to interfere in the domestic problems of the two countries.

The dominant feature in the history of the two Romanian states in the sixteenth century was their autonomy at a time when the Balkan peoples had for long been under the direct rule of the Ottoman authorities, their territories having been turned into *pashaliks*. And yet in course of time the Sultan tended increasingly to consider the two countries as provinces of the Empire and their ruling princes as his beys. Nevertheless, even the Turks preserved the consciousness that these "provinces" of the Ottoman Empire had a different status. There was no longer any danger of their being turned into Turkish *pashaliks* and this was the consequence of the line the Empire took and of the economic progress of the Romanian countries, which made it clear that it was more profitable to exploit them through the agency of local bodies. The long resistance of the Romanian countries had taken place at a moment when the threat of their being suppressed as states had been most serious.

Consequently the Romanian states continued to preserve their internal system, their laws, a social pattern of their own, without the superimposition of a dominant Ottoman class. The Romanians thus enjoyed better conditions of political and cultural development and were a rallying point of the Christian peoples in the Empire — a centre of support.

Transylvania's relations with the Porte were generally similar to those of the other two Romanian countries, with certain differences in favour of Transylvania, which were mostly due to the competition between the Habsburgs and the Ottoman Empire over its territory. Hence there was more freedom in foreign relations, far less Ottoman interference in domestic affairs and in general a political life that the suzerain power did not narrow down much. The prerogative of the diet to elect the prince of Transylvania was mostly observed, though the election had to be confirmed by the Sultan and a representative of the Porte was to be present when the prince was enthroned.

In Moldavia and Wallachia the Turkish ruling circles oscillated between applying conditions specific to the countries "conquered by force of arms" or to those that had submitted to them and had agreed to certain conditions and obligations.

The economic obligations enforced by the Porte on the three countries were generally the same, the difference being only the severity of their enforcement.

The main obligation, which was a sign of dependence of the state, was the payment of the tribute. Established before the period of actual Ottoman domination, like certain other political obligations, the tribute increased gradually, in particular in Wallachia : from 24,000 gold coins in 1542 to around 155,000 in 1593. In Moldavia it rose from 10,000 gold coins during the first reign of Petru Rareș to 35,000 under Bogdan Lăpușneanu (1568-72), further rising to 65,000 for a brief span in 1593. In Transylvania the tribute was of 10,000 gold coins in 1541 — and had only risen by 50 per cent by the end of the century, the rise taking place in 1575.

Apart from paying tribute and making emergency contributions to meet the Empire's military needs, the ruling princes of the Romanian countries were under the obligation of annually sending gifts (*peshkesh*) to the Sultan and the Turkish high officials. In the latter half of the sixteenth century those gifts equalled the tribute in value.

Important gifts were also sent to Constantinople whenever there were changes among the high dignitaries of the Empire as well as on the occasion of outstanding events in the Sultan's family. The envoys of the Porte to the Romanian countries also received rich gifts.

But the greatest expenditure for Moldavia and Wallachia was occasioned by the appointments to the throne and the struggle of the princes to keep the throne. It was a time when most offices were bought in many parts of Europe and the throne of the Romanian countries became the object of transactions for the benefit of the Sultan and of the grand vizir in the first place but also for the benefit of other influential personages. Between 1581 and 1590 Wallachia paid at least 3,500,000 ducats when Mihnea and Petru Cercel contended for the throne.

Furthermore, annual supplies in kind were made, though these were of comparatively low value, as well as war supplies, either unpaid or paid at prices established by the Porte, and labour contributions: transportation, and workers for the maintenance of Turkish citadels, etc. Finally, the Romanian countries had to supply Constantinople with foodstuffs so that their trade was being increasingly monopolized by the Empire. Turkish and Eastern traders generally were frequently in Transylvania and very frequently in Moldavia and Wallachia, where their transactions were concluded under a privileged régime. Indeed a monopoly régime was gradually established for certain products, the exports of which to other countries were forbidden as long as the requirements of the Porte had not been met.

The living conditions of the peasantry deteriorated during the latter half of the sixteenth century. In both Moldavia and Wallachia those peasants who were still free were the butt of the boyars' attack, overburdened as they were with taxes that compelled them to sell their cattle, then the plots of land that were no longer joint property, and finally to become serfs.

The boyars' estates increased considerably, simultaneously with the increase in the number of dependent peasants, whose living conditions were greatly worsened. The serfs had to fulfil their obligations to the state, which were even more oppressive than those to the boyars, even though the taxes paid by the serfs were lower than those levied on the free peasants. As a result, most of the peasant homesteads fell into ruin by the end of the century.

The peasantry, whether free or dependent, strove their utmost to offer resistance. They opposed the landowners by going to law to shake off serfdom, redeemed themselves whenever it was in their power to do so, made use of the right to change their place of habitation — a right that was gradually restricted by the landowners — and even rose in revolt as they did in Moldavia in 1536-64, as also in 1581 and in 1591. Flight from the landowner's estate was most frequent, sometimes whole villages breaking away to seek safety in other parts of the country, to become outlaws or to go into exile beyond the country's borders. From Moldavia, they preferred to go over to the Cossack lands, and from Wallachia, across the Danube or into Transylvania.

Continuing their efforts to enslave the peasantry, the dominant class suppressed the right of displacement by tying men to the land for all time. This was the stage of servitude current also in other countries of Eastern Europe as well as in Russia during the sixteenth century. "Michael's tie", the act enforcing this measure, probably dates from the first years of the reign of Michael the Brave. It applies not only to the serfs but also to the free but landless peasants who had settled on the boyars' estates and who were also deprived of the right of leaving the estate they had settled on. A similar decision was issued about the same time in Moldavia, though certain provisions were less hard on the peasants there. By tying the man to the land it became easier to levy the state taxes.

In Transylvania, where the peasantry had been tied to the land after Doja's uprising of 1514, labour service was thereafter greatly increased. This came as a result of the enlargement of the nobleman's reserve, which had to meet the increasing requirements of the main estate with its entire non-productive civil and military population, and also to supply the market.

The economic position of the nobility as a class was strengthened in all the three Romanian countries and this enhanced its preponderance in political life and accounts for the continuation of the feudal system in these countries for a long period.

In Transylvania ten years of frequent Turkish interventions after the Peace of Oradea in 1538 were unable to give any stability to the reign of John Sigismund on whose behalf Isabella, his mother, ruled in the capacity of regent. The only authority that succeeded in imposing itself was that of Bishop George Martinuzzi, appointed governor by the Turks and won over by the Austrians. Habsburg rule, as exercised by General Castaldo (1551-6), was unable to ensure internal stability and to prevent the establishment of the Timișoara *pashalik* in 1552.

When John Sigismund returned to Transylvania in 1556 with the support of Alexandru Lăpușneanu, Prince of Moldavia, and Pătrașcu the Kind, Prince of Wallachia, he was faced by the same unsteady internal situation which he was unable to dominate, and also by conflicts with the Habsburgs. When he died in 1571, the pro-Ottoman group with the Sultan's support brought Stephen Bathory to the throne. The prince's authority was strengthened after several years' struggle against the imperial forces and their partisans. At the close of 1575 Stephen Bathory was elected King of Poland, again with the support of the Porte. His brother, Christopher, ruled Transylvania with the title of voivode, but the country was actually under the effective leadership of Stephen. The throne was to be inherited by Sigismund, Christopher's son, heir apparent since 1581.

Stephen Bathory's reign was important insofar as Transylvania's autonomy was strengthened. During Bathory's rule in Poland (1575-86), the principality became a reserve of military forces for Poland's policy in the east as well as of material resources. At the same time Transylvania was then able to assert itself on an international basis.

4. The Struggle for the Recovery of Independence

DESPITE Ottoman domination, Moldavia and Wallachia continued within the focus of European diplomacy. The many plans of anti-Ottoman struggle, made especially in the Habsburg camp, took into account the military assistance that might be given by the Romanian countries, for their warlike tradition, as well as their desire to recover their independence, were well known. Furthermore, the power of the Roman Catholics was offset by Protestant proselytism among the peoples of the Orthodox religion. These converging tendencies resulted in the appointment of Iacob Eraclid, also called Prince Despot (1561-3), to the throne of Moldavia with the support of the Habsburg Empire, the German Protestants, and the Polish noblemen. Although Despot tried to stimulate the boyars by reminding them of the Romanians' Roman origin and of theirs to freedom, he came into conflict with them and was unable to rise against the Ottoman Empire. Nor could Petru Cercel (1583-5) build up a precise political orientation in Wallachia despite his generally admitted desire for independence. This prince had been trained in Western Europe and had become Prince of Wallachia with the support of Henry III, King of France.

It was only Prince John the Terrible (1572-4) of Moldavia who brought things to a head by appealing to the forces of the entire country. Refusing to accede to the demand of the Porte to increase the tribute twofold, the Moldavian prince made ready to resist and even attacked Peter the Lame at Jiliştea when the latter was approaching the country's border with a Turkish-Wallachian army to oust him from the throne. The Moldavians reached Bucharest, where they enthroned a prince for a few days, then went over to Brăila and burned down that town which was under Turkish suzerainty. Hard blows were also dealt to the Turkish forces in the Lăpuşna district, and in the vicinity of Tighina and Cetatea Albă. In early summer the Ottoman armies moved towards Moldavia in force, while the Tartars made their way from the East. At the Danube the Turks were able to cross the river, for Hetman Eremia did not defend the ford, according to the duty assigned to him. And once again the boyars betrayed their trust, for during the night that preceded the Battle of Lake Cahul (June 10, 1574) a group of them crossed over to the Turkish camp and when the battle began the cavalry abandoned the prince and went over to the enemy. Prince John was left with the peasantry, the Cossacks who were fighting on his side, and a sound artillery, which was to prove of good use before torrential rain ruined his ammunition. The Moldavians and Cossacks stood their ground before the successive attacks of enemy forces and even counter-attacked successfully. In the end, however, they were forced to retreat, which they did in good order, despite the heavy losses they had sustained. At Roșcani, they fortified their position, digging ditches all round and making a camp of wagons. Surrounded by Turks and Tartars, they resisted without water for three days, when the prince decided to surrender. Although promises had been given on oath, he was brutally killed and his body was tied by the legs to two camels driven in opposite directions and thus quartered. The Tartars overran the country, laying it waste.

The anti-Ottoman struggle did not come to an end on the death of Prince John. A whole series of princes — brothers, sons, or nephews of Prince John, some of them real and some presumed — successively tried their luck during the rule of Peter the Lame. And this with Cossack support, for they put their hopes in the common people who were eager to shake off oppression both within and outside the country. Under the socio-political conditions prevailing at that time, their attempts had no chance of success.

5. The Three Romanian Countries Unite under Michael the Brave

MICHAEL the Brave (1593-1601) came to Wallachia's throne at a time when the exactions of the Ottoman Empire and of its representatives were putting the economy of the country in frightful jeopardy; at the same time ever more serious infringements of its autonomy heralded the installation of a new form of Turkish domination, here as in Moldavia. The only way out of the difficulty was to fight, and for a long space of time, with few exceptions, all strata of society rallied to the cause. An anti-Ottoman coalition — The Holy League — set itself the aim of driving the Ottoman Empire out of Europe, and the participants in the League counted on the assistance of the Balkan peoples who had been constantly on the move during the last decade of the century. The forces concentrated by the allies — who included the Pope, Spain, and the Austrian Habsburgs, with support given by the German princes and by certain small Italian states, including Tuscany — were of unequal force and insufficient to reach their objective. A great impulse was given to the war by the Romanian countries joining in the conflict. A new front was thus opened, and the Christian peoples of the Balkan Peninsula now cherished hopes of liberation.

Early in 1594 Sigismund Bathory, Prince of Transylvania, joined the League, and in the summer of the same year an alliance for an offensive was concluded between Michael the Brave on the one side and Sigismund and Prince Aron of Moldavia on the other. In August, 1594, Prince Aron also concluded a treaty with Emperor Rudolf II. A joint action of the three Romanian countries could thus be undertaken.

Before the end of the year, on November 13, Turks in Wallachia were killed and war was declared. Similar acts occurred in Moldavia. While the Transylvanian and imperial forces struck at the Ottoman forces in Banat, the two Romanian princes attacked the Turkish citadels along the Danube and carried the war beyond the river into Dobrudja and Bulgaria. The Turkish and Tartar forces coming to appoint new princes faithful to the Sultan were defeated in the battles fought at Putinei, Ștefănești, Șerpătești, Rushchuk, and Silistra.

Taking advantage of this difficult moment, the boyars concluded a treaty with Sigismund Bathory on May 20, 1595, subordinating Wallachia to the Transylvanian prince. They thus minimized Prince Michael's authority, and took upon themselves the much coveted right of ruling the country. This was to be carried out through the agency of a council of twelve boyars whom Sigismund alone could change, and the latter's agreement was also necessary when death sentences or confiscation of fortune had to be carried out. Between the Prince of Transylvania and this Council, Michael had little authority, while the boyars, counting on the fact that the new master was a long way off, believed they had established the boyars' rule and provided a legal basis for it. The treaty included other provisions: Greeks were not allowed to hold any high offices in the country and no foreigner could own landed estates. The boyars thus removed all competition from abroad. At the same time Ștefan Răzvan, appointed Prince of Moldavia by Sigismund in place of Aron, signed a similar treaty. Consequently, just before the great Turkish campaign began, Sigismund could call himself Prince of Transylvania, Wallachia, and Moldavia. Subsequent developments, Michael the Brave's policy, and the war that followed with the demands and situations it created, prevented that title from becoming an actual fact and also delayed the establishment of the rule of the nobility in Wallachia.

In the summer of 1595 the Porte sent to Wallachia an expedition to re-establish its authority. Heading it was the new grand vizir, Sinan Pasha, for Ferhad Pasha had previously proved unable to cross the Danube.

Michael chose to give battle at Călugăreni, where the River Neajlov flowed into Cîlniştea, a place bordered by wooded hills and furrowed by streams and fens. The battleground diminished the disproportion between the two forces. The Romanians fought bravely, the prince himself setting the example of gallantry, so that the Turks were finally compelled to withdraw, having incurred severe losses (August 23, 1595). But Michael could not risk a new battle without support from abroad. He withdrew to the mountains in expectation of Sigismund's arrival while Sinan Pasha fortified the cities of Bucharest and Tîrgovişte in preparation for a long rule which seemed to herald the transformation of the country into a Turkish *pashalik*.

Early in October Sigismund came to Wallachia with Transylvanian troops as well as with German soldiers sent over by Archduke Maximilian, and three hundred Tuscan horsemen. Ştefan Răzvan, Prince of Moldavia, soon joined him with his own forces. Having defeated the Turkish garrison at Tîrgovişte, Ştefan Răzvan made for Bucharest while Michael and Sigismund advanced towards Giurgiu where Sinan's army was crossing the Danube. The Turkish rearguard was smashed and the Turks' prisoners, who had been reduced to slavery, were released. The citadel of Giurgiu was conquered after a two-day siege during which the technique of the Italians had proved of great help. The Ottoman expedition was an utter failure.

Wallachia had regained freedom and simultaneously her Danube boundary. On the other hand, in Moldavia Polish armies headed by Chancellor Ian Zamoyski installed Ieremia Movilă as prince at the end of August. The latter was the representative of the great Moldavian boyars faithful to Poland. It was thus that the régime of the nobility was installed in Moldavia under the patronage of Poland, where it had also triumphed. But the juridical statutes of the rule of the nobility were not so well defined in Moldavia as in the treaties concluded by the Wallachian boyars with Sigismund. Having recognized Poland's suzerainty, Ieremia Movilă also asked for this ascendancy to the throne to be confirmed by the Porte. This he did with the consent of the Polish king who did not wish to be at war with the Ottoman Empire. In expectation of better times to come, the Porte was glad to confirm Ieremia Movilă as Prince of Moldavia and, consequently, for about two decades Polish intervention restricted Ottoman domination in these parts. The anti-Ottoman front had suffered greatly as a result of Moldavia's defection. The attempt made by Ștefan Răzvan in December, 1595, to recover his throne, was defeated.

In continuation of the war against the Ottoman Porte, Michael's forces, together with Serbian and Bulgarian outlaws, fought the Turks south of the Danube as far as the passes of the Balkan Mountains. Romanian resistance prevented the Tartars from crossing Wallachia and thus crowning the Ottoman victory at Keresztes over the Habsburg forces and Sigismund by laying waste the country. Turnu was the last Turkish citadel in Wallachia to be conquered. At the close of 1596 the Porte sent Michael the princely banner he had earned by his military actions, thereby acknowledging its incapacity to oust him from the throne and accepting a situation which had to be regarded as inevitable for the time being. Michael himself was content to cease hostilities against the Turks for a time so as to shake off all subjection to the prince of Transylvania as well as to better his relations with the boyars.

In order to strengthen his position, Michael established direct and lasting relations with Emperor Rudolf II, who in the summer of 1597 contributed to the upkeep of 4,000 mercenaries. On June 9, 1598, a treaty was concluded at Tîrgoviște whereby Michael accepted the emperor's suzerainty without the obligation to pay tribute and without the emperor being entitled to interfere in the country's internal affairs. The emperor also undertook to observe the right of hereditary succession to the Wallachian throne for Michael's family. The Wallachian prince was to receive continued military aid and an important role was assigned to him in the anti-Ottoman war.

Michael was forced to continue in his anti-Ottoman policy in order to strengthen his country's independence and his connections with the Balkan peoples, who awaited liberation. So in the autumn of 1598 Michael sent an army corps to Sigismund — now back in Transylvania after having ceded that province to Rudolf II a few months previously — to defend Oradea, which was besieged by the Turks. But a more important battle was being fought along the Danube where Michael repelled a Turkish inroad into Wallachia, crossed the Danube and during a two-month campaign defeated the Turkish forces at Vidin, Nicopolis, and Cladova and laid waste the territory between the Danube and the Balkans.

Sigismund's new withdrawal from the principality of Transylvania in March, 1599, caused Michael to focus his attention on that province, for the new prince, Cardinal Andreas Bathory, was carrying on a policy designed to bring him nearer to the Ottoman Empire. In this he had Poland's support. Combined Polish and Turkish support was to bring Simeon Movilă, brother of the Moldavian prince, to the throne of Wallachia. Michael was therefore under the necessity of conquering Transylvania to make safe his throne threatened from all sides, and also in order to enable Wallachia and Transylvania to continue their anti-Ottoman policy in the Balkans. Michael turned for support to the emperor, but the latter delayed sending forces, and he decided to undertake the conquest alone.

Well organized, the campaign for the conquest of Transylvania unfolded according to Michael's plans : on October 30, 1599, Andreas Bathory was defeated at Şelimbăr and on November 13 Michael entered Alba

Iulia, and henceforth for eleven months Transylvania was under the rule of the Romanian prince.

In order to build up the old coalition of the three Romanian countries, it was necessary to conquer Moldavia, a pawn in Poland's policy, where Sigismund Bathory, who wished to recover the throne of Transylvania, found shelter. The campaign of May, 1600, took only a few days. The citadel of Suceava surrendered and Ieremia was pursued up to Hotin where he was defeated in a short battle. Subsequently Ieremia withdrew into the citadel of Hotin and then crossed into Poland. Michael was now entitled to call himself "Prince of Wallachia, Transylvania, and Moldavia".

Back in Transylvania, Michael had to face the uprising of the Transylvanian nobility supported by the Saxon patriciate [rich townsmen]. The rebels moreover obtained the assistance of Georgio Basta, the emperor's general, and succeeded in defeating Michael's armies at Mirăslău (September 18, 1600). Simultaneously Zamoyski marched into Moldavia, re-installed Ieremia Movilă, and in early October continued his way to Wallachia with Simeon Movilă in his train. Michael was defeated by Zamoyski at Bucov on the River Teleajen on October 20. Another victory won on the River Argeș resulted in Simeon ascending the throne of Wallachia. The latter rallied the boyars round him and was confirmed in his office by the Porte.

Michael headed for Vienna and Prague in an effort to obtain the Empire's support. Developments in Transylvania, where Sigismund was re-elected as prince, favoured him. Now supported by Basta, a general of Albanian origin in the Habsburg army, Michael set out to reconquer Transylvania. Together they won a victory at Gorăslău over Sigismund's forces (August 3). In early July, Simeon Movilă had been driven out of Wallachia. Conditions again appeared to be favourable to Michael. But on August 19, 1601, he was killed by Basta's men in his camp at Cîmpia Turzii.

During the eight years of his reign Michael had liberated Wallachia from the domination of the Ottoman Porte, had enabled it to play an outstanding part in South-east Europe and had achieved the political unity of the three Romanian countries. It was outstanding work with most important consequences.

The Romanian countries had united as a result of their joint struggle for the recovery of their independence. But over and above immediate circumstances, it was the result of historical solidarity built up over the centuries and for this reason it had been attempted in various forms : by Sigismund Bathory before Michael and was to be attempted by others after him. Michael, it is true, relied on the fact that the majority of the population in the three countries spoke the same language and had the consciousness of belonging to the same people. But this could not have been a decisive factor at the time, and Michael, whose political activity included certain measures favouring the Romanians in Transylvania, did not base his rule on it, for this would have required the overthrow of the entire system of political privileges on which the Transylvanian constitution depended, and the inception of a social revolution which Michael, himself the representative of a feudal state, had no means of achieving. For all these reasons, Michael's rule in Transylvania could never have been the rule of the Romanians for the Romanians. If made permanent, it would naturally have assumed an ever more pronounced Romanian character. The same holds true for the unification achieved by Michael. Unification had to take into account the historical realities of the three political bodies that were to be ruled by one supreme leader. Obviously, here again time alone would have allowed the consequences of a unitary rule to mature. But to make it long-lasting, it would have had to resist the pressure of the decisive social forces within the three principalities, and these were bound up with the ancient traditions of autonomy represented by Sigismund Bathory in Transylvania and by Ieremia Movilă in Moldavia. And the political forces outside them — Poland and the Ottoman Empire — also had to be taken into account. Michael could only have resisted such pressure by his own solidly built up power or by efficient aid received from the Habsburg Empire.

But Wallachia could not offer Michael the necessary power. The boyars' opposition there increased steadily, undermining the authority of the ruling prince, and Wallachia was the main support of his power. The country was exhausted by wars and by the effects of prolonged exploitation by the Porte, and the masses, who had supported the anti-Ottoman struggle, could not wish a system, exclusively in the service of the landowners, to be strengthened. To the very end Wallachia provided Michael with military forces, but the country could not be relied upon to provide sufficient forces to hold the two other principalities in subjection. A permanent army equipped with the war engines used at the time meant not only having a considerable number of men at one's disposal but also great material resources for the men's upkeep and for armament.

Michael received no assistance from the Habsburgs: no military support to supplement his own forces, no moral support such as a great power could have provided. The Habsburg Empire, supposing it had a purpose overruling its constant hesitations, only aimed to extend its rule, and Michael did not intend to act merely as a tool. Consequently, his fall was to be expected, and it was also to be expected that the fruits of the crime Basta had ordered to be perpetrated would not be reaped by the Empire.

On Michael's death a new situation was created in the relations of the Porte with Wallachia and the two other countries. For a century the effects of the united struggle of the Romanian countries, whose main leader had been Michael the Brave, made themselves felt, and all subsequent attempts at resistance were inspired by Michael's feats of arms. And unification, though achieved for such a brief space of time, also left its traces. Secretly it made its way into the people's consciousness and was added to everything that had brought the Romanians together, until it finally became a symbol, heralding the building up of a unitary Romanian state.

R. W. Seton-Watson states that although the political results of Michael's reign were almost instantly effaced, "It fired the imagination of the Romanian race and acquired a legendary, well-nigh mythological, significance which cannot be extracted from contemporary records, but which in modern times played a very real part in the evolution of the race towards cultural and political unity."

6. Restoration of Ottoman Domination

THE tragic death of Michael the Brave brought in its train the restoration of Ottoman domination over the three Romanian countries, though in each one of them this was achieved only by dint of great efforts.

The new wave of Ottoman domination that swept over the Romanian countries came under conditions that were altogether different from those prevailing at the close of the sixteenth century. There was no longer any danger of their being turned into *pashaliks,* and although princes were frequently sent from Constantinople without the boyars being consulted, this did not create a permanent system. Representatives of the Porte came more rarely than before to the Romanian countries, and direct interference of the Turks in domestic affairs was less harsh.

The economic obligations of the Romanian countries to the Porte changed to a certain extent. When Radu Şerban of Wallachia resumed relations with the Porte, the tribute amounted to 32,000 ducats, or about 20 per cent of its maximum value at the close of the sixteenth century. The tribute paid by Moldavia was about 30,000 ducats. The annual gifts made to the great dignitaries of the Porte had also decreased in value. At the end of the sixteenth century the heaviest expenditure was incurred by the prince on his accession to the throne. In the first decades of the sixteenth century conditions in this respect were quite different. When Radu Mihnea was ousted from the throne in the spring of 1611, Radu Şerban offered up to 100,000 ducats to be recognized as ruling prince. In 1623 it is estimated that no more than 100,000 gold ducats were paid by Radu Mihnea for his own installation as Prince of Moldavia and that of his son, Alexandru Coconul, in Wallachia. A few years later, however, in 1629, Radu Leon paid 200,000 ducats to obtain the throne.

It is obvious therefore that after Michael's mighty struggle for independence, the obligations of the Romanian countries towards the Porte were much less onerous than at the end of the sixteenth century. As for Transylvania, the tribute was again reduced to 10,000 ducats which was the sum paid before 1575. It is true that when Matei Basarab became Prince of Wallachia through force of arms, the tribute was doubled and the investiture expenses, which also included the debts incurred by his predecessor, rose to 400,000 ducats according to certain authorities. But this was in payment for a reign that was to last for more than two decades. As in the sphere of political relations, the second half of the century was to bring about an increase in material impositions to the Porte, without ever reaching the level of the days preceding the reign of Michael the Brave, until the eighteenth century.

7. Economic and Social Life

LIGHTER obligations towards the Ottoman Empire enabled on one hand a comparatively fair rebuilding of the Romanian economy, which had been on the brink of ruin at the close of the preceding century, and, on the other hand, some progress, though slow as yet, in certain branches of production. Documents mention that land had been cleared, this indicating an increase in the areas under crops, though travellers who came to these countries were amazed to see wide expanses of most fertile land lying fallow. Human settlements increased in number, which was a sign of demographic as well as of economic growth. Winter wheat sown after the land had been ploughed twice, was superseding spring wheat. Vine-growing was also developing. During the latter half of the seventeenth century maize began to be grown and was to become the peasants' staple food. In Transylvania maize had been grown since the beginning of the century. Tobacco was also grown in the Romanian countries at the time.

Sheep, pigs, and cattle were bred for foreign trade and were also a main source of income for both the peasant homestead and the feudal landowners. Preda Brâncoveanu, it is said, sent 1,000 oxen to Constantinople every year.

From the sixties of the century there were indubitable signs of progress in the production of craftware : new branches emerged and the crafts were organized in guilds. As a result, the towns of the Romanian countries developed into traders' and craftsmen's centres, though most of them were still small and relying on agriculture. There were weekly fairs and also large fairs that drew buyers and sellers from distant countries. In the seventeenth century inns were built for the traders, who also had their guilds. The most important towns were Jassy in Moldavia and Bucharest in Wallachia. Under Constantine Brâncoveanu, Bucharest was reported to have had 50,000 inhabitants. With a busy trade and an advanced cultural life as its main features, it was one of the important centre of South-east Europe.

In the seventeenth century, Transylvania continued to be a land of grain, wine, and cattle. Its craftware production with an organization of older date than in the other Romanian lands was also of greater proportions — a supplier of the home and foreign market. The guilds already had long-standing traditions behind them and constituted powerful bodies, although social contradictions were rife within them and the central power occasionally took measures to curtail their privileges. There was a busy city life in Brașov, Sibiu, Cluj, Bistrița, and Sighișoara. More advanced forms of production of a manufactory nature were occasionally met with: at Alba Iulia there was a workshop casting big guns and at Porumbacul de Sus a glassware shop. Similar glassware shops were founded in Wallachia by Matei Basarab and Constantine Brâncoveanu.

In Moldavia and Wallachia salt mining was carried on extensively and from the reign of Matei Basarab the ore deposits at Baia de Aramă and Baia de Fier were also mined. Exploitation of the subsoil held a far more important place in the economic life of Transylvania than in the other Romanian countries. Salt was extracted here as well as silver, iron, and gold, the latter being obtained in Moldavia and Wallachia only from the mountain streams. In the second half of the century mercury was also extracted, in particular at Abrud and Zlatna. Trade capital was invested in the mines which used equally serf and paid labour.

Foreign trade in Moldavia, Wallachia as also in Transylvania was carried on mostly with the Ottoman Empire and with one other, though relations were maintained also with other countries, for example Poland, the Habsburg Empire, and Venice. This was the time when in Transylvania trading companies were set up: Greek traders founded a company in Sibiu in 1636, while similar companies were started in other towns. In 1672 the Oriental Company was founded — a powerful concern playing an important part in Transylvanian foreign trade. Such associations included Romanian traders, whose importance was to increase considerably during the following century.

Economic progress in the seventeenth century did not involve a rise in the living conditions of the bulk of the population, which was made up of peasants. In Wallachia the peasants were tied to the land with great strictness, as established by Michael the Brave's deed. In Moldavia a serf who ran away from the boyar's estate could no longer become a free peasant after a number of years, that right having been abolished in the second half of the century. The Code of Laws printed during the reign of Vasile Lupu confirmed the right of the landowners to pursue the runaway peasants.

While the process of enserfing the free peasantry continued and feudal estates grew more extensive (although certain villages succeeded in freeing themselves in the first half of the seventeenth century), serfdom became ever more oppressive. The serfs could be moved from one estate to the other by the landowner, and could even be sold without their holding, being consequently separated from their land and reduced to a condition of sheer slavery. There were cases when serfs recovered their freedom by giving the landowner gypsy slaves, one head for another.

In the second half of the century the cases of serfs being released from serfdom became more frequent, in particular in Wallachia, but the conditions of the men thus freed did not change greatly ; a few of them recovered their land also, the remainder being obliged to settle on the boyars' estates and work for them. Initially they were bound to give the landowner a share of the crops but with time they had also to perform labour services, a practice which came into almost general use towards the end of the century. Consequently, their dependence on the landowners was increased.

In Transylvania also the powerful feudal structure of society was preserved and this prevented a switch over to a more advanced stage of organization of production relations. Part of the peasantry remained free, as in Moldavia and Wallachia. This occurred especially among the Szeklers, and on the lands of the emperor and the king, where the Saxon *sedes* were located and where there were also many Romanians. Făgăraş, Haţeg, and Zarand were districts where the ancient freedom of the Romanians was preserved.

But even in these districts serfdom made great strides so that the number of free Romanian and Szekler peasants diminished and even the free Saxon peasants on the emperor's lands were becoming increasingly dependent on the dominant class. The right to pursue runaway serfs was laid down in the codes of law drawn up in those days : *Approbatae constitutiones* (1653) and *Compilatae constitutiones* (1669).

After the disturbances of the first decade of the century, Gabriel Bethlen installed a régime of internal political stability, which was mostly maintained by his successors — George Rakoczy I (1630-48) and George Rakoczy II (1648-60). The Transylvanian prince thereby acquired much freedom of action and Transylvania was thus able to play an important international part during the decades that followed.

8. Transylvania during the Thirty Years' War

MAINTAINING relations with the Porte, to whom he was compelled to cede Lipova and to give support in its military campaigns against Poland, Gabriel Bethlen first put an end to the Habsburgs' attempts to undermine his rule ; this he did by concluding the Treaty of Tyrnavia in 1615 and subsequently starting an offensive on the territories of the Habsburg Empire. The outbreak of the Thirty Years' War (1618-48) was an opportunity for him to carry out his plans of conquering Habsburg Hungary and of weakening the Catholic forces while supporting the Protestants, he himself being a Calvinist, and endeavouring to strengthen that faith in Transylvania

Allied to the Czechs, Bethlen marched to the ramparts of Vienna in the autumn of 1619. Although there was nothing real about the title of king of Hungary bestowed by a diet that autumn, nor about the title of king of Bohemia received from another diet a year later, Gabriel Bethlen succeeded in the annexation of seven counties of the western regions. This was stipulated in the Peace of Mikulov in 1622, which was successively renewed after fresh military interventions, at Vienna in 1624 and at Bratislava in 1626.

Relations with Moldavia and Wallachia played an important part in Gabriel Bethlen's foreign policy. He even worked out a plan — suggested no doubt by the attempts previously made by Sigismund Bathory and Michael the Brave — of building up the kingdom of Dacia, which would include the three Romanian countries, to be placed under his rule with the consent of the Porte.

Gabriel Bethlen's death was followed by the struggle for power made by the various factions of the nobility, as well as by Habsburg attempts to reconquer Transylvania or at least to recover the seven counties. When George Rakoczy I's throne became more secure, he put an end to these disturbances and Transylvania was able to participate again in the Thirty Years' War. Following negotiations, an alliance was concluded by Transylvania, France, and Sweden in 1643. Supported by the main anti-Habsburg powers and subsequently by forces from Moldavia and Wallachia, George Rakoczy started a campaign early in 1644, Transylvania taking an active part in the war for a year and a half. Intent on getting rid of one adversary, the Habsburgs were glad to conclude peace at Linz in 1645 on terms similar to those of the Treaty of Mikulov. At the close of the war, Transylvania sent delegates who stood alongside those of the other powers, when the Peace of Westphalia was concluded in 1648.

9. The Régime of the Nobility

WHILE in Transylvania a comparatively powerful central authority was exercised by the prince — Gabriel Bethlen and subsequently the two Rakoczy princes — the régime of the nobility — of the boyars — was installed in Moldavia and Wallachia ; the great boyars dominated the political life of those countries through the intermediary of the Prince's Council and by holding the main public offices. It was a régime that relied on accepted practices rather than on definite institutions so that it had no uniformity while it was enforced. The authority of the ruling prince was occasionally enforced more potently, when the internal balance of forces, or the personality of a prince, made this possible.

Installed in Moldavia under the aegis of Poland at the close of the sixteenth century, the boyars' régime began to be patronized by the Porte when Radu Mihnea came to the throne. This prince succeeded in co-operating with the great boyars, the prince being allowed a fairly wide margin of power. This was achieved especially during Radu Mihnea's second principate (1623-6), when the throne of Wallachia was occupied by his son, Alexandru. In Wallachia, where the efforts of the great boyars to monopolize the power were of long duration, the new political régime acquired greater stability after the restoration of Ottoman domination. In both countries a prince would rule for a brief spell, from a matter of months to several years, for frequent changes suited the interests of the Ottoman Empire and of his dignitaries as well as the régime itself, competition aligning the boyars in rival factions or parties, which in support of another claimant to the throne occasionally offered open battle to the ruling prince. The struggle between the various factions was fanned by the different trends adopted in foreign policy. In Moldavia, for example, there was a group of boyars attached to Poland, in particular under the Movilă princes and their kinsman, Miron Barnovschi Movilă (1626-9, 1633).

Consolidation of Ottoman domination in Moldavia with the discarding of Polish interference, formed the basis of Turco-Polish conflicts which culminated in the expedition of Sultan Osman in 1621. The latter, however, was unable to advance further than Polish-occupied Hotin, where the Poles supported by the Cossacks offered bitter resistance.

The attempt made by Gaspar Graziani to free Moldavia by force of arms was also part of the Turco-Polish wars. Appointed ruling prince by the Porte in 1619, the Dalmatian Graziani joined the Poles and, despite the opposition of his Council, decided to end Ottoman domination. At Tuțora on the Prut, the Polish-Moldavian forces were surrounded by the Turks and Tartars, and before the Polish army, in a desperate situation and having incurred heavy losses, could retreat, Gaspar Graziani with only a few followers had already left the camp. He was killed by two of his boyars in the vicinity of Jassy in September, 1620.

An internal problem with most serious consequences was the appointing of Greeks to high offices and their coming into possession of landed estates. Plots in great numbers were then hatched and even open battles fought against the ruling prince. The number of Greeks about the prince — kinsmen, creditors, reliable collaborators, clients, etc. — had greatly increased as a result of the restoration of Ottoman domination in the early seventeenth century and the frequent appointment by the Porte of princes who had lived among the Greeks in Constantinople. There was consequently much competition from foreign elements in the exercise of high offices and, moreover, the prince was thus offered instruments that were independent of the great boyars so that the system was a threat to the boyars' régime. To a certain extent, insofar as the throne represented the authority of the Ottoman Empire, it was also a blow dealt at the autonomy of the country.

In Wallachia the movement against the Greeks began when plots were hatched by them against Radu Mihnea and Alexandru Iliaș. When the second plot was revealed the Greeks were bitterly attacked, elements from wide sections of society taking part in the movement, which occasionally assumed the aspect of a peasant uprising against the boyars.

In Moldavia there was a general resistance movement against Alexandru Iliaș, the boyars also calling upon the courtiers and the peasantry to support them. The latter congregated in large numbers under the impulse of fiscal oppression. A number of Greek boyars were killed and the prince was compelled to leave the country (1633). It was Vasile Lupu who was to benefit by this movement for he was appointed by the Porte without any of the boyars being consulted.

Anti-Greek reaction was also shown in the boyar opposition, with a wider popular movement joining in, against Prince Leon Tomșa (1629-32) in Wallachia. In 1631 under pressure of the anti-Greek current, the prince was compelled to promulgate a law giving satisfaction to the boyars. A number of measures were taken against the Greeks : all Greeks, with the exception of those married to Romanian women, were to leave the country and their estates to be confiscated and given over to the prince. Fiscal decisions were made for the benefit of the boyars, of the mercenaries, the prince's chancellors and the priests. Other decisions were made concerning the election of Metropolitans and bishops, the aim being that the Patriarch of Constantinople should not send Greek prelates ; Greek monks were to quit the monasteries, and the Romanian monasteries which had been dedicated to religious institutions in other countries were to shake off their dependence.

Apart from fiscal and juridical privileges and the elimination of Greek competition, the boyars, who profited most by the decisions of 1631, also strengthened their title of ownership over the landed estates through extension of the right of bequeathal. Despite these concessions, Matei of Brâncoveni continued the struggle against the prince and finally obtained the throne with the help of internal forces and of the pasha of Silistra. Not far from the monastery of Plumbuita on the outskirts of Bucharest, Matei, subsequently to be called Matei Basarab, defeated an army of Moldavians, Tartars, and Turks who were on their way to install Radu Iliaş, newly appointed by the Porte. The latter recognized the change made on the initiative domestic factors — which meant recognition of the country's autonomy and of the stand taken against the increasing part played by the Greeks — and granted the banner of the principate to the new ruler.

10. Matei Basarab and Vasile Lupu

THE reigns of Matei Basarab (1632-54) and Vasile Lupu (1634-53) are noted as periods when the prince's authority was increased — though within the limits of the boyar system and of Ottoman domination; when intensive political activities brought about an extension in foreign relations, and when culture and art showed outstanding achievements. These reigns were of long duration, due to a certain stability in the relations between the prince and the political forces of the country as well as to generally favourable international circumstances. Doubtless the resumption in 1635 of the war of the Ottoman Empire against Persia, which ended in 1639, and the Turkish campaigns against Venice for the conquest of Crete, which began in 1645, were favourable to the Romanian countries.

It is important to note that comparatively large military forces were built up in the Romanian countries at this juncture. Thus Matei Basarab had a strong army made up of the lesser gentry with offices at Court, and

THE BEGINNINGS OF OTTOMAN DOMINATION 235

of horsemen and mercenaries, which included infantrymen called *seimeni*, as permanent forces. To these were added the hosts of the great boyars and the peasants recruited in time of war. The army of Vasile Lupu, when his power was greatest, was not far below that of his neighbour. The economic progress made during the first decades of the century gave the prince the means of keeping up these forces but, nevertheless, the expenditure required for the purpose, the increased obligations towards the Ottoman Empire, the wide constructive activities, and, in Moldavia, the great pomp of the prince's court, greatly increased taxation.

The relations among the three Romanian countries were also one of the factors of stability, though oscillations were not infrequent. Finally, the personality of the two princes, varying greatly but both remarkable, should be taken into account. Matei Basarab must be regarded as the type of the "local prince" with a realist political outlook and relying on tradition. Vasile Lupu, impelled by the will to conquer — with his eyes also on Wallachia — found it suitable to establish close connection with the Greeks at Constantinople, supporting and, at the same time, dominating them. Out for prestige, the rigorous ceremonial of his court savoured of the "imperial". Both princes desired their country's independence and were skilful enough to ensure a certain amount of freedom. Both succeeded in asserting the existence of their states in the polity of Central and Eastern Europe. They were great military commanders always at the head of their armies, indefatigable in founding religious institutions, and showing much interest in culture.

The three Romanian countries continued to foster relations through the bilateral agreements between Transylvania and each of the two other Romanian countries, but the conflicts between Moldavia and Wallachia decreased their efficiency. Wider possibilities arose when the princes of Moldavia and Wallachia made peace in 1644. In 1640 Matei Basarab had contacted the Habsburg

Empire to induce it to begin a war against the Ottoman Empire, but Emperor Ferdinand III refused to act. With the same aim in view, Matei approached Venice as well as Poland.

When George Rakoczy II (1648-60) became Prince of Transylvania, the relations of Moldavia and Wallachia with that province continued. But in 1650 Moldavia was attacked by the Cossacks allied to the Tartars, pressure being thus exercised on Vasile Lupu to draw him away from Poland and into the alliance of Hetman Bohdan Chmielnicki. Ultimately an alliance was concluded and in 1652 Vasile Lupu's daughter, Princess Ruxandra, married Bohdan's son, Timuş. An understanding was also reached between Matei Basarab and the Cossacks. Vasile Lupu was shortly after compelled to take refuge in Poland (1653), for part of the boyars, rallying around Chancellor George Stephen, brought the latter to the throne with the assistance of George Rakoczy II and Matei Basarab.

A few weeks later, however, the new Moldavian prince was driven away by the Cossacks and, resuming the throne, Vasile Lupu with Cossack support marched against Wallachia, also having his eyes on Transylvania. Matei Basarab's hard-fought but crushing victory at Finta again brought George Stephen to Moldavia's throne and Vasile Lupu spent the rest of his life in Constantinople. In 1654 Matei Basarab died after a long rule, and Constantine Şerban (1654-8), Radu Şerban's illegitimate son, succeeded to the Wallachian throne. The Porte accepted the two princes.

11. Uprising of the Seimeni. The Anti-Ottoman Struggle

POLITICAL relations among the three Romanian countries were resumed, with Transylvania as the centres; they were used mainly as an instrument of repression to serve class interests. During the last year of Matei Basarab's reign the Dorobanți foot soldiers and the *seimeni* mercenaries had caused a number of disturbances and the *seimeni* of Moldavia undertook a similar action in 1654. On February 17, 1655, the most violent uprising of the seventeenth century broke out in Wallachia. It was known as the Seimeni's uprising, the latter being its most active elements. The uprising included vast sections of the people, which shows that through feudal and fiscal exploitation social antagonism had reached an acute stage.

Because of Constantine Șerban's decision to abolish the Seimeni corps, the Dorobanți, in sympathy with the latter, rose in protest although the Seimeni were mercenaries and mostly of Balkan origin while the Dorobanți were natives of the country. The movement of protest assumed quite early the most violent forms and a considerable number of boyars — the most powerful and richest — were killed and their houses plundered. Other mercenaries and local soldiers, including the numerous cavalry corps, joined in the movement which extended rapidly to various towns — Bucharest, Tîrgoviște, Ploiești, and Buzău — as well as to the villages. Numerous craftsmen, the poorer population of the towns, and the dependent peasantry took action alongside the rebel troops, being prompted by interests of their own, though related to those of the soldiers. The rich merchants and the boyars in their country houses were attacked; the rebels refused to carry out their feudal obligations and destroyed the deeds of ownership; and hostility was also shown against the clergy and the church. As the state and the dominant class were deprived of the means of suppressing the rebels, the latter were able to hold out for more than four months, preventing meanwhile any action on the part of the prince who, though not deposed, was kept under close watch. Although of long duration and enlisting large sections of the population, the uprising did not become a homogeneous and unitary movement.

There was no unity of command of the military forces participating in it and the forces did not co-operate to the same extent. The most active were the Dorobanți foot soldiers and the Seimeni.

Finally an expeditionary force was sent out to end the uprising. At the request of the boyars and of Constantine Șerban, and with the consent of the Porte, a Transylvanian army under the command of the prince himself and Moldavian troops commanded by George Stephen, who also had Tartar support, marched into Wallachia in June and defeated the rebels at Soplea (June 26, 1655). Centres of resistance continued their action until the autumn.

After the Soplea battle there seemed to be a stronger link between the three countries. But Constantine Șerban was compelled to accept a new treaty with George Rakoczy II, which recalled the one Sigismund Bathory had forced upon Michael the Brave rather than the pacts that had linked Matei Basarab to the two neighbouring princes beyond the mountains. The Transylvanian prince was given the right to control Wallachia's foreign policy and even to have his say in the appointment of the prince's dignitaries. George Stephen, on the other hand, while observing his alliance with Rakoczy, also sought support in Moscow, concluding a treaty to this end in 1656.

In 1657, in opposition to the Porte, the princes of Moldavia and Wallachia assisted George Rakoczy II in his unsuccessful attempt to take the throne of Poland. In the early months of the following year, the two Romanian princes were deposed, Mihnea III being appointed by the Porte in Moldavia and Gheorghe Ghica in Wallachia.

In Transylvania where George Rakoczy II — dethroned in the autumn of 1657 to be replaced by Francisc Rhedey — had succeeded in recovering the throne, the Grand Vizir Mehmed Köprülü at the head of an expeditionary force enthroned Acatiu Barcsay the following year and annexed Inău, Lugoj, and Caransebeş to the Timişoara *pashalik*. But George Rakoczy II again recovered the throne and, relying on him, as well as on Venice and the Pope, Mihnea III, who had also taken the name of Michael, now a symbol, on coming to the throne, decided to liberate Wallachia from the authority of the Porte. On his accession to the throne, Mihnea began to act for the benefit of the peasantry, helping the serfs to redeem their freedom and selling the peasants the estates that had been confiscated from the boyars. At the same time he built up his army and made efforts to co-operate with the soldiers. The prelude to the anti-Ottoman struggle, which began in September, 1658, was the assassination of a considerable number of great boyars who might have opposed the struggle. The signal was the slaughtering of the Turks at Tîrgovişte and in other towns. The pasha of Silistra was defeated, Giurgiu and Brăila were conquered, and audacious blows were inflicted on the right bank of the Danube. In October a new treaty was concluded with George Rakoczy II, which did not include the hard terms forced upon Constantine Şerban. Clashes with the Turks continued in the districts along the Danube and a victory was won at Frăţeşti in November. But Constantine Şerban having failed in his attempt to obtain the throne of Moldavia, and George Rakoczy II having been defeated, Mihnea was compelled to withdraw from Giurgiu to Tîrgovişte and make his way to Transylvania.

The anti-Ottoman campaign headed by Mihnea III ended in Wallachia, after a month and a half of heroic efforts which were not aided by sufficient military forces nor by favourable circumstances. In Transylvania George Rakoczy resisted for another six months, but the defeat inflicted on him at Floreşti in May, 1660, and the prince's subsequent death ended the struggle. At the end of August, Oradea, which had continued to resist, being supported by the population of the surrounding districts, surrendered. The town became the centre of a new *pashalik* which was to ensure Turkish domination in Transylvania. A new attempt on the part of John Kemeny to shake off Ottoman domination was defeated in January, 1662.

12. Struggle between Boyar Factions. The Habsburg Régime is Installed in Transylvania

THE efforts of the Ottoman Empire to defeat the Romanian countries' attempts at liberation and to curtail the autonomy the latter had enjoyed for two decades, as well as to increase the income it derived from them, were characteristic of the late sixties of the seventeenth century. The ability of the Porte to carry out its policy with success was due primarily to the period of restoration it was going through under the leadership of the grand vizirs of the Köprülü family ; on the other hand, the Romanian countries' military forces were on the decline after the reigns of Matei Basarab and Vasile Lupu.

Hence, as a result of stronger Ottoman domination, the terms of office of the ruling princes became shorter and their appointment was, with rare exceptions, made directly by the Porte without any previous election in the country ; the system of triennial and annual confirmation came into general use (called *mucarer*, which meant the tribute paid the Porte on such occasions) ; the activities of the princes were closely watched, and there was Turkish interference in domestic affairs. Economic pressure also intensified : extraordinary contributions had to be made, the office of prince had to be bought, and the countries had also to make the Porte gifts of produce and to provide free labour. The total volume of demands was greater in Wallachia but weighed more heavily on Moldavia, the latter's resources being more restricted.

Considerable changes also occurred in Transylvania, the Porte showing a tendency to subject it to the same conditions as the other two countries: economic and political oppression increased, though the situation in that province still differed from that of the other two. The territorial losses incurred by Transylvania weighed heavily on the province.

Increased Ottoman domination decreased the authority of the ruling princes and increased the part played by the nobility in the management of state affairs. Divided into factions, the noblemen contended violently for power. Permanent internal disturbances and frequent appeals to the Porte enabled the latter to increase its authority.

Intensive political struggles were waged in Wallachia for two decades between the parties of the Cantacuzino and the Băleanu families, the former being considered as representatives of the native boyars and the latter of the Greek boyars, although there were also Greeks in the first grouping.

The struggle for supremacy between the different factions assumed a most violent character: in 1663 Court Marshal Constantine Cantacuzino, a confidential counsellor of Matei Basarab and married to Radu Șerban's daughter, was killed on orders from Grigore Ghica (1660-4). The conflict caused frequent changes of the ruling princes until ultimately the Cantacuzino faction, relying on the vast estates of Constantine Cantacuzino's ten sons and sons-in-law, proved victorious, bringing Șerban Cantacuzino to the throne in 1678.

Similar events were taking place in Moldavia where the great boyars were the leading authority and the ruling prince was often tutored by one or the other of them. Here, too, the various factions showed different political trends, inclining either to Poland or to the Ottoman Empire. Chronicler Miron Costin and his brother Velicico fell victims in 1691 in the struggle between the Costin and Ruset families.

In Transylvania, too, the prince's authority decreased during the reign of Michael Apafi (1661-90), and the domination of the great noblemen intensified. The noblemen's faction headed by Michael Teleky, after dispersing the anti-Ottoman-minded faction which had supported John Kemeny, finally took the reins of government and defeating all attempts at overthrowing it made by Dionisie Banffy and Paul Beldy, the Szekler commander, enjoyed a long reign.

Socially, the political power of the noblemen favoured the extension of feudal estates, many of which merged for the benefit of one owner, and there was also a trend towards more intensive exploitation of the dependent peasantry — those who had settled by agreement on the estates and were now being reduced to serfdom — with new labour obligations being exacted. As has been said, however, there were frequent cases of release from serfdom.

In Wallachia, the economic development of the early years of the century continued at a steady rate, though hampered by socio-political conditions, while in Transylvania it came to a standstill altogether in certain sectors, as, for example, in mining and craftware production. Transylvania's economy was seriously affected by the military campaigns that led to the restoration of Ottoman domination (1657-62), and later by the prolonged struggle between the Austrians and the Turks as a result of which the domination of the Habsburg Empire was enforced upon that principality.

But it was in Moldavia that the situation was most serious. After the devastation of the territory in 1650 and the developments of the last years of Vasile Lupu's reign, the country became the theatres of war between the Ottoman Empire and Poland ; this war was brought about by Hetman Doroshenko's acceptance of the Porte's protection in Western Ukraine, which he needed in order to cope with Poland. From 1672 to 1676 five successive campaigns took place and five times the Turkish armies

THE BEGINNINGS OF OTTOMAN DOMINATION

passed through Moldavia on their way to the Ukraine and Podolia. And until 1681 there were further expeditions to the Ukraine against the Cossacks and the Russians, for the Cossacks had asked the Tsar's protection to help free them from Turkish interference. In 1672 the Turks conquered the Kamenetsk citadel which they retained as they also did Podolia, until the Peace of Karlowitz in 1699. Turkish-controlled territories north of Moldavia, with a strong citadel to support them, was a new means of dominating Moldavia and placing an extra burden upon the country, for it was through Moldavia that the Ottoman Empire effected the connection with its new possession.

The Polish-Habsburg victory at Vienna in 1683 and the anti-Ottoman coalition — the Holy League of 1684 — in which the Habsburgs, Poland, Venice, and Malta, and a little later Russia joined, made of Moldavia an everlasting battleground in the Polish sector. The war broke out in the winter of 1683-4 when the former prince, Ștefan Petriceicu, marched into Moldavia with Polish support. Ștefan Petriceicu, however, only held the throne for a few months. In 1684 the Polish campaigns began but made little headway — Hotin being the farthest point reached that year. In 1684 and 1691, under the reign of Constantine Cantemir (1685-93), Sobieski, the Polish king, and his army marched deep into Moldavia though the two expeditions failed in their purpose. Apart from these royal expeditions, small armies carried on periodic raids and Polish garrisons were established in north-west Moldavia, namely at Suceava, Neamțu, and a number of monasteries and were kept there until the Peace of Karlowitz. The Polish campaigns were the cause of frequent Tartar inroads, which also made their contribution to the ruin of Moldavia. As a result of these long periods of precarious conditions, of plunder and of exhaustive material contributions, Moldavia's economy lagged far behind that of Wallachia, though its material possibilities had been greater in the past. Consequently, it came to be considered more advantageous for a prince to pass from the throne of Moldavia to that of Wallachia.

After the relief of Vienna, the Habsburg armies marched into Hungary and settled there for a number of years, defeating the Ottoman forces and organizing the conquered territories. Buda, the main city of the Turkish *pashalik* for 145 years, and a key stronghold of Ottoman rule, was stormed in September, 1686. A year later, in 1687, the victory won at Mohács opened a way south of the Danube and the Drave and made possible the liberation of the rest of Hungary. Belgrade, the second fulcrum of Ottoman domination in the Danube area, fell in 1688. In 1691, after the Turkish successes of the preceding year, including the recovery of Belgrade, a crushing defeat was inflicted on the Sublime Porte at Szalankemen.

In the meantime the Habsburg forces had entered Transylvania. Early in 1685 negotiations had begun with a view to the emperor assuming authority in Transylvania, though its ancient privileges were to be maintained. The Făgăraş Diet, under the pressure of the imperial forces, decided on May 13, 1688, to free itself of the vassalage of the Porte and accept the emperor's protection. Leopold's Diploma of December, 1691, recognized the position of Transylvania as distinct from Hungary and its political organization as based on the union of the three privileged nations and on the four accepted religions. The diet was maintained, as was also the administrative and judicial organization and the entire legislation. The last prince of Transylvania, Michael Apafi II, although recognized by the diet, was taken to Vienna on his father's death in 1690, where he ended his life without ever having ruled. Leopold's Diploma thus ensured the further existence of the Transylvanian principality while enforcing the class privileges of the leading sections of the population.

For a time operations on the battle front came to a standstill. Subsequently there were some Ottoman successes, but after the Zenta victory on the Tisa in 1697 the destinies of war finally favoured the Habsburg Empire. Under the Peace of Karlowitz of 1699 the Ottoman Empire gave up its suzerainty over Transylvania which, except for Banat, passed under the authority of the Habsburg Empire.

The situation created along the northern border of Wallachia and the serious crisis in the Ottoman Empire determined the political trends of Wallachia where Şerban Cantacuzino reigned from 1678, for the Cantacuzinos had finally triumphed.

While lavishly serving the interests of those nearest to him and taking rigorous measures against opponents, the new prince wished to be more than the crowned head of a boyar faction. Therefore he made it his aim to raise the principate above the boyars and to take over as much authority as possible. A family alliance with the opposite camp — the Băleanus — was intended to strengthen the throne.

His attempts to recover authority at home went hand in hand with his striving to liberate the country from dependence on the Ottoman Empire. After having participated together with the Moldavian and Transylvanian princes in the siege of Vienna on the Turkish side, Şerban Cantacuzino started negotiations with the Habsburgs while at the same time establishing connections with Poland and Russia. While preparing his army for war, he sought, by means of understandings with the Bulgarians and the Serbs to rally the Balkans to the campaign he was planning. His negotiations with the Austrians, however, during which he demanded that his authority be fully recognized and his family have the right of succession, were concluded only in 1688; and while the envoys, who were to confirm Wallachia's acceptance of the emperor as its suzerain and the country's decision to shake off its dependence on the Ottoman Empire were still on their way to Vienna, he died.

13. The Reigns of Constantine Brâncoveanu and Demetrius Cantemir

HIS successor, Constantine Brâncoveanu (1688-1714), his sister's son, enjoyed one of the longest reigns in the history of Wallachia. This was largely due to his immense fortune, to the revenue he derived from the country, to his political ability, and to external circumstances favourable for a considerable time. It was a reign of economic progress and of great cultural and artistic achievements, with the personal initiative of the prince and of the Cantacuzinos as a whole playing an important part. The country won international prestige at the time, in particular in the countries of the Orthodox faith, but its state of dependence continued to bring humiliation upon the crown and country, though the suzerain occasionally showed that he valued his vassal. In his domestic policy Brâncoveanu no longer showed the authoritativeness prevailing during the reign of Şerban Cantacuzino and, surrounded by members of the Cantacuzino family, who shared his responsibilities, he succeeded in obtaining the support of most of the boyars and consequently in ending their opposition.

For a quarter of a century Constantine Brâncoveanu kept the autonomy of Wallachia intact, though three empires were contending for supremacy in South-east Europe. The treaty with the Habsburgs prepared by Şerban Cantacuzino was accepted by Brâncoveanu, but its execution was delayed. He succeeded in preventing the penetration of Austrian troops into Wallachia in the autumn of 1689 and he himself, together with Turkish and Tartar troops, marched into Transylvania in 1690, showing himself a factor in the defeat of the Habsburg General Heissler, at Zărneşti. But Brâncoveanu resumed relations with the Habsburgs and in 1695 he received the title of Prince of the Empire, though still remaining a subject of the Porte, which in 1699 bestowed on him the office of prince for the rest of his life. Notwithstanding this, in 1703 he was summoned to Adrianople and it was only on payment of large sums of money and by agreeing to pay a much higher tribute that he was able to save his throne and his life. During the last part of Brâncoveanu's reign the economic pressure of the Porte was increased, foreshadowing a new period of maximum exploitation of Wallachia's resources for the benefit of the Ottoman Empire and of its dignitaries.

While maintaining relations with the Porte, Constantine Brâncoveanu and the Cantacuzinos kept in close touch with Moscow with whom a treaty was concluded providing for Peter the Great's assistance in shaking off Ottoman domination. A similar agreement with the Tsar was concluded by Demetrius Cantemir, Prince of Moldavia, in the autumn of 1710. The Treaty of Luck concluded in April, 1711, stipulated that Moldavia had agreed to become the Tsar's protectorate, that the country's autonomy was recognized, that the prince was to have full authority in ruling the country and to enjoy the right of succession in his family. Demetrius Cantemir's principles of government, which he had no time fully to put into practice, are set forth in his writings. Essentially his aim was to do away with the political instability specific to the régime of the nobility by ensuring the prince's freedom of government and by the heredity of the throne. For these reasons the main points concerning the country's internal organization were set forth in the Treaty of Luck, similar to those Șerban Cantacuzino demanded when negotiating his treaty with the Habsburgs. In both Romanian countries these provisions met with the opposition of the great boyars who realized that their political privileges were being jeopardized. The attempt to end the boyar régime had no chance of success unless it were undertaken in close connection with the Porte, and primarily for its benefit, or else, against the Porte. The latter solution, which was in keeping with the general interests and with the liberation tendencies manifest in the two countries, was adopted both by Șerban Cantacuzino and by Demetrius Cantemir, who also tried to put it into practice.

Tsar Peter I started his campaign immediately after the conclusion of the Treaty of Luck. The great Moldavian boyars mostly kept out of the war ; thus, the army hastily brought together by Demetrius Cantemir included only country gentry, petty dignitaries, craftsmen, and some of the boyars' men. The Tsar's armies came by way of the Prut Valley. Brâncoveanu camped at Urlați, not far from Ploiești, awaiting further developments — not joining the Turkish camp, as he had been requested, and not giving the Russians any assistance, as he was expected to do. Thus the Battle of Stănilești, fought in July, 1711, was lost by the Russians whose war preparations had proved insufficient. Brâncoveanu's small army could not have changed the situation.

While the long era of Phanariot rule began in Moldavia about this time, Nicholas Mavrocordat being the first of the line. Brâncoveanu succeeded in keeping his throne until 1714. R.W. Seton-Watson relates how on April 4, 1714, a Turkish emissary, Aga Mustafa, with a small detachment of troops and written orders from the Sultan, arrived in Bucharest and proceeding to the palace, flung a black handkerchief over Brâncoveanu's shoulder and pronounced him to be "Mazil" (deposed). The prince called desperately from the palace windows for aid, but neither his guards nor his boyars dared to lift a hand. Two days later he and his family were sent away by road to Constantinople, the whole population following his carriage with sincere but impotent lamentation. On arrival the old man was thrown into the prison of the Seven Towers, and tortured in front of his children. He was invited to save himself by a forfeit of ten million piastres, but as this fantastic sum was far beyond even his utmost resources, he was executed, with his two sons and son-in-law, in presence of the Sultan himself, outside a summer kiosk on the Bosphorus. A French traveller gives a touching account of the execution. The younger son, a boy of sixteen, terrified at the sight of his relatives' death, offered to accept Islam in return for his life : "on which the father exhorting him to die 1000 times, if it were possible, rather than deny Jesus Christ, to live a few years longer on the earth. He said to the executioner. 'I wish to die a Christian : strike', and at once the latter cut off his head, as he had done to the others. At last he beheaded the father, on which their bodies were thrown into the sea and their heads exposed for three days above the great gate of the Seraglio."

"The longest reign in two centuries of Romanian history thus ended, as it was bound to end, in disaster (said Seton-Watson). Constantine Brâncoveanu had always tried to be on the side of the strongest, to balance between contending forces, to reinsure against every accident : but his lack of all principle or moral force left him in the end without friends."

However, he died bravely. His palace at Mogoşoaia, ten miles north-west from the centre of Bucharest, stands in a noble park and may be visited by the public. Brâncoveanu's successor, Stephen Cantacuzino, was also executed, together with his father, High Steward Constantine Cantacuzino, in 1716, when the throne of Wallachia was entrusted by the sultan to Nicholas Mavrocordat, who then abandoned the throne of Moldavia.

14. The Habsburg Régime in Transylvania

LEOPOLD'S Diploma, upon which the new régime of Transylvania after its annexation by the Habsburgs was based, made no mention of the Romanians. The reason is that the Diploma was a political instrument designed to win over the privileged classes, and the Romanians were not among the privileged. The Constitution of the principality, which the Habsburgs had maintained, overlooked them and their religion entirely, and the *Approbatae* of 1653 had already declared them to be merely tolerated.

A long process had created three political "nations" : the noblemen, and their allies — the Saxon communities and the privileged Szeklers. The noblemen ultimately came to mean the Hungarian nation, for it was the noblemen of that nation who held the political power. The term "nation of the nobles", which had a social and political significance, thus acquired an ethnical significance, with a tendency to exclude the Romanian nobility of Transylvania, few of whom remained. The religious reform, with the struggles it had brought about, had caused the three religions of most of the leading strata of the population, and also those of the Hungarian, Saxon, and Szekler masses, to be included in the Constitution and to be recognized by the state side by side with Catholicism, which had few supporters. The three religions were Calvinism, Lutheranism, and Unitarianism. The notion of "Romanian nation" had an ethnic significance. The social condition of the bulk of the Romanian population at a time when the consciousness of nationality was growing among the Hungarians as well as among the Romanians, affected their situation as a people. Although the masses continued their joint social struggle as a result of their similar living conditions, the Hungarian nobility came to consider the Romanians, who made up the bulk of the serfs, as a danger to their class privileges. Hence the measures taken repeatedly against them. Ultimately the entire people were declared to be merely tolerated while the aristocratic constitution of Transylvania, based on privileged conditions and orders, became increasingly aristocratic in character.

It was under these circumstances that the idea of the Eastern Orthodox Church of Transylvania joining the Roman Catholics was born. This was part of the far-reaching programme of extending the Pope's authority and the Catholic faith in Eastern Europe, and also belonged to the arsenal of the Habsburgs' government system. Metropolitan Theophilus accepted the union in the synod convened at Alba Iulia in February, 1697, express mention being made that the faithful were to preserve the Orthodox rites and that the Romanian priests should enjoy the same privileges as the Catholic priests, while the laymen of this faith should be "recognized sons of the homeland" and no longer merely tolerated. Theophilus's successor, Athanasie Anghel, confirmed the union in two new synods held at Alba Iulia in 1698 and 1700. The Union was put on a legal basis by two imperial diplomas in 1699 and 1701, the latter diploma providing that the faithful who had joined Rome should be considered as equal before the laws to the other citizens. This, an essential provision, remained a dead letter. Supported by the clergy, whose social condition was thus being improved, the union with Rome yet progressed slowly, having aroused much reaction among the masses and causing the ruling princes and the Church in Wallachia as well as the Eastern Orthodox Patriarchs to intervene against it. Catholic control over the Uniate Church was strengthened, a Jesuit theologian assisting the Metropolitan, who was made bishop of the Uniate Romanians. However, R.W. Seton-Watson comments that "Humiliating as the methods employed to achieve it may have been the union proved to be one of the most memorable events in the rise of Romanian nationality."

The union with the Catholic Church, like the whole imperial rule in Transylvania — for the latter was bound up with the union — had for a long time against it a wide anti-Habsburg and social movement that started in the territory of the kingdom of Hungary and swiftly swept over Transylvania. The movement was headed by Francis Rakoczy II from 1703 and rallied Hungarians, Romanians, Slovaks, and Ruthenians, though it never had real unity and was mostly spontaneous in its organizational forms. There was a fundamental contradiction between the aims the participating elements had in view, for their class conditions were different. The nobility wished to shake off Habsburg domination while the mass of the people were against the Habsburgs because of the heavy impositions and because they also wanted liberation from feudal servitudes. In Transylvania the rebels' aims were mostly social and for that reason few of the nobility joined the movement, although Rakoczy was proclaimed Prince of Transylvania by the diet of 1704.

The struggle ended in 1711 when the nobility signed the Peace of Satu Mare which re-established Habsburg authority in Transylvania. At this time, when Moldavia and Wallachia came under Phanariot rule, Transylvania witnessed the lasting installation of an Austrian régime after a period of crisis in the rule of the Habsburgs. The union of the church lasted until 1948 when the administrative union with Rome was severed by new legislation.

CHAPTER EIGHT

THE PHANARIOT RÉGIME IN MOLDAVIA AND WALLACHIA. HABSBURG ABSOLUTISM IN TRANSYLVANIA (1711-1821)

IN the eighteenth century the two empires which competed for domination over Romanian territory — the Ottoman and Habsburg Empires — consolidated their dominion of Moldavia, Wallachia and Transylvania respectively, restricting their autonomy and subjecting them to increased exploitation.

The reforms of the absolutist régime in Transylvania and of the Phanariot system in Moldavia and Wallachia leading towards centralization gradually gained their objectives. In Transylvania where a great power strove to develop its economic basis and to adjust itself to the progress of the advanced countries of Europe, the reforms were bolder than in Wallachia and Moldavia, where they were more restricted in character. The economic development of the two latter countries was hampered by the régime of brutal spoliation iinstalled by the Ottoman state which proved unable to make a systematic effort towards internal renewal.

This chapter includes some of the most depressing pages in Romanian history. R.W. Seton-Watson says that "The new princes were almost always rapacious, often treacherous, and thought only of their material interests... It is impossible to conceive a more disheartening task than that of recording in detail the history of these hundred years in Wallachia and Moldavia, and the western reader would only read it with impatience and under protest... The incredible nature of the regime is perhaps most eloquently expressed in a few bald statistics. Between 1714 and 1821 there were forty-one changes on the throne in Wallachia, between 1711 and 1821 thirty-six in Moldavia : in the one case there were twenty-three, and in the other twenty-four, princes, several being appointed more than once, and as several passed from one throne to the other at different times, the total number of reigning princes was not seventy-seven, but thirty-three, and all of these were drawn from twelve families... These men were continually intriguing against each other, in particular the Moldavian princes in order to obtain the richer prize of Wallachia, and they often paid for their ambition with their heads, yet fear of punishment did not deter their successors and intrigue was rife to the end. We thus reach the surprising result that the average duration of a reign in either Principality during the whole century was about two years and a half."

1. Salient Features of the Phanariot Régime

THE local princes had always proved inclined to join the anti-Ottoman struggle and therefore did not inspire the Turks with confidence. As it was impossible to turn Moldavia and Wallachia into *pashaliks* formula which had proved to be inapplicable to the Romanian countries also in the past, the Turks used the Phanariot princes as instruments to reduce them to obedience.

The Phanariot princes were mostly recruited from the top section of Greek society at Constantinople, residents of the Phanar, or lighthouse, district. Their political ambition depended upon the fortune they had acquired in the preceding centuries from trade and the management of the Porte's incomes. In the latter half of the seventeenth century the Porte saw its territorial expansion checked for good and was compelled to seek support in the Christian states of the West and to take as associated in state leadership the most active of the subjugated peoples — the Greeks. The high offices of Grand Dragoman of the Fleet and Grand Dragoman of the Porte were entrusted exclusively to the Phanariots, and this was the beginning of their political influence which increased as the crisis of the Ottoman Empire became more serious.

The Phanariot régime seriously restricted the autonomy of Moldavia and Wallachia, for it had been installed to keep these countries under subjection. Appointed directly by the Porte, the ruling princes of the two countries belonged to the Ottoman administrative hierarchy. The interference of the Porte in domestic affairs made itself increasingly felt ; repeatedly the Ottoman Empire took the initiative in ordering that certain measures should be applied in social and political organization, though these were matters of the exclusive competence of the local authorities.

Henceforth Moldavia and Wallachia no longer had a foreign policy of their own : the Phanariot princes carried on intensive diplomatic activities to serve the interests of the Porte. Under the circumstances, there was a further decline in the military power of Moldavia and Wallachia, which had already been obvious in the preceding period ; the armies of the two countries were gradually being reduced to the prince's guard and to a small number of troops strictly necessary for the keeping of public order and for guarding the frontiers.

The Porte needed faithful tools in Moldavia and Wallachia not only in order to reduce them to obedience but also to exploit their resources more systematically, for this was a time when the upkeep of the large Ottoman army and administration could no longer be met from the spoils of conquest but had to be obtained from the economic and demographic potentialities of the empire's territory which was gradually being restricted by the defeats of the Turkish armies in the wars waged against the European powers. Consequently, during the reigns of the Phanariot princes Moldavia and Wallachia were cruelly exploited. The tribute, the Bairam gifts, the gifts for the annual and triennial renewal of the prince's appointment, the taxes instituted in favour of the Sultan *(geaigea)*, amounted to immense sums. The struggle between the claimants to the throne and the rapid succession of princes were among the main means of squeezing the Romanian countries dry, for they assumed the form of actual auctions.

Furthermore, in wartime products and labour service were supplied free of charge, causing the countries immense losses, and certain products were bought by the Porte at its own prices. The Turkish Empire enforced a strict monopoly over certain products and the princes were frequently warned that no exports were to go to other countries ; thus Moldavia and Wallachia should fulfil their duty as granaries of the Ottoman Empire.

The mere substitution of Phanariot princes for the local princes was not sufficient to attain the double aim — political and economic — which had determined the Porte to constitute the régime. A programme of reforms was also implemented in the social and political institutions of the countries in order to consolidate the central power, now strictly subordinated to the Porte. These reforms were to the detriment of the boyars.

In the eighteenth century the flight of the dependent peasants from the estates they were tied to assumed proportions which completely disorganized the system of taxation and of social exploitation, compelling the authorities to change their methods of government.

The many fiscal, social, administrative and judicial reforms by which by the policy of the Phanariot régime was carried out were designed to end the flight of the peasants, to eliminate the factors that caused it, and to provide the state with the means of implementing the new programme of government.

A product of the crisis of the Ottoman society of the seventeenth and eighteenth centuries, the Phanariot régime experienced all the vicissitudes that attended the decline of the Turkish Empire as well as the struggle of the great powers to take over the might it had wielded.

While the political and military power of the great European states depended upon the development of production and trade, the Ottoman Empire confined itself to intensifying the fiscal exploitation of its subjects in order to meet its obligations. But oppression gave rise to increased resistance of the oppressed peoples, and this was a significant aspect of the crisis of the Ottoman Empire in the eighteenth and nineteenth centuries.

Ever on the defensive and incapable of resisting Austrian and especially Russian expansion by its own strength, the Ottoman Empire survived only through the competition and opposing interests of the great European powers.

The wars waged by Austria and Russia against the Ottoman Empire had greatly weakened the latter and helped to create new conditions for the liberation of the Romanian people. Romanian volunteers took part in the anti-Ottoman wars and Romanian boyars submitted memorials at Petersburg and Vienna asking that the autonomy of the two countries and of their fundamental institutions should be respected. In this manner Romanian people asserted their will to be free from Ottoman domination. On the other hand the Russo-Austro-Turkish wars turned the territories of the two countries into theatres of war and resulted in overall destruction and plunder, and, what is more serious, they were deleterious to the territorial integrity of the Romanian countries.

2. Installation of the Phanariot Régime and the First Reforms (1711-68)

NICHOLAS Mavrocordat, member of one of the most outstanding Phanariot families, who embodied the policy of Turco-Greek co-operation, was chosen by the Porte to re-establish Ottoman domination in Moldavia after the Stănilești victory and to prevent the desertion of Wallachia on the eve of a new war against Austria. Nicholas Mavrocordat inaugurated the Phanariot régime in Moldavia in 1711 and in Wallachia in 1716.

The unrestricted tasks Wallachia had to carry out after the outbreak of the Austro-Turkish war (1716-18) and the decisive victories won by the Austrian forces under the command of Eugene of Savoy at Petrovaradin in 1716 and at Belgrade in 1717, gave a vigorous impulse to Wallachian resistance to the newly founded Phanariot régime. Under the threat of the prince's domestic policy and especially of fiscal exploitation, which no longer spared them, the Wallachian boyars pinned their hopes on the Austrians with whom they started negotiations. The memorials submitted during the war by the boyars and the upper clergy to the court in Vienna demanded that the country's autonomy should be recognized within the Habsburg Empire and its institutions should be allowed to govern themselves. This naturally implied that the social and political domination of the great boyars was to be enforced.

Though violently suppressed by Nicholas Mavrocordat, the opposition of the boyars ultimately triumphed, not without some victims, among whom were Metropolitan Antim Ivireanul and a number of great boyars. Answering the call of the boyars, the Austrians, who had previously occupied Oltenia with the support of volunteers recruited from the Romanian peasantry, marched into Bucharest and captured the Phanariot prince by surprise. A simultaneous attempt on the part of the Austrians to take prisoner Michael Racoviță, the Moldavian prince, with the support of a number of Moldavian boyars, failed (1717).

In order to restore its control over Wallachia, the Porte resorted to John Mavrocordat, Nicholas's brother. Ruling under the title of Caimacan, John repudiated the internal policy of the captive prince, thus succeeding in partially defeating the hostility of the boyars and in consolidating his authority.

The Peace of Passarowitz, concluded in 1718, recognized the territorial gains of the Austrians. Serbia, including Belgrade, the Banat of Timişoara, and Oltenia, then came under Habsburg rule.

During the two decades of Austrian rule in Oltenia (1718-39) a number of reforms were introduced, which gradually extended over the main fields of social and political life. The fiscal system was reorganized, fiscal assessment was established on strict demographic evidence, the privileges of the boyars were restricted, agrarian relations were established on the basis of definite rules, and reforms were introduced in the administration and in the juridical system, all of which were designed to incorporate Oltenian society into the political system of Habsburg absolutism. The very narrow margin of autonomy initially allowed to the province was suppressed in 1726, when the office of *ban* was abolished and Ban George Cantacuzino, son of the former ruling prince, Şerban Cantacuzino, was ousted from his office.

Again appointed Prince of Wallachia after peace had been concluded, Nicholas Mavrocordat (1719-30) endeavoured to create suitable conditions for stabilizing the peasantry, whose constant displacement handicapped the system of fiscal exploitation. Abolishing the numerous taxes levied throughout the year under various names as a result of Turkish demands, the prince instituted one fixed tax levied four times a year. The fiscal reform carried out by Gregory Ghica (1726-33) in Moldavia relied on the same principle. But these measures shared the fate of most Phanariot reforms, which had scarcely begun to be applied when they were infringed in order to meet the Porte's demands. With the Russo-Austro-Turkish war again turning the territory of the two countries into a theatre of war (1736-9), their implementation was abandoned.

Russia availed herself of the favourable opportunity offered by the war. Having conquered Azov and the Crimea, the Russian forces reached the Dniester in 1739, occupied the citadel of Hotin and marched into Moldavia. Under the convention that the Moldavian boyars concluded with the commander of the Russian forces, the country's autonomy was recognized and its institutions were maintained. After a few initial successes, the Austrians failed to take Vidin and were defeated a number of times. In 1737 they had to abandon the Wallachian counties they had conquered a short time previously, and, at the same time, the hope of subjecting the whole of Wallachia to their rule. At the end of the year they were also compelled to abandon Oltenia, where the Habsburg régime had estranged all sections of the population : boyars, clergy, and peasants. In consequence of the Peace of Belgrade of September, 1739, the Austrians lost Serbia and Oltenia.

Oltenia's reincorporation into Wallachia following the Peace of Belgrade, and the necessity of creating a uniform régime for the two provinces made it imperative to speed up the policy of reforms. It was Constantine Mavrocordat (1735-41) who was at the helm of the country at the time. During nearly four decades of ruling alternatively Wallachia and Moldavia (1730-69), Constantine Mavrocordat, the most remarkable personality among the Phanariot princes, reorganized the fiscal, social, administrative, and judicial institutions of the two countries in the same spirit.

Laid waste by the wars of many years, Moldavia and Wallachia required suitable conditions to increase their population, and only fiscal stabilization, as in the past, could create such conditions. The Law of 1740 was primarily designed to meet this necessity. Under the provisions of the law, the numerous taxes were superseded by a fixed tax levied four times a year ; at the same time an attempt was made to suppress the joint and several responsibility of village communities towards the treasury — a feature specific to the medieval fiscal system.

In order to make the fiscal reform effective, it was necessary for all taxpayers to be registered in the treasury books. The lists drawn up for the purpose by Constantine Mavrocordat and later by his successors to the throne made it their aim to keep a strict demographic record, before this the number of taxpayers and their assessable capacity were but imperfectly known.

The administrative reorganization carried out by the Law of 1740 was designed to create an executive and control body which the state required if the success of the reforms, and primarily of fiscal reforms, was to be ensured. Constant control of village life that the prince was to exercise henceforth, required a suitable administrative machinery, and consequently country officers *(ispravnic de judeţ)* were appointed, with administrative, fiscal, and judicial duties. This was the most important and most durable of the administrative reforms of the Phanariot prince, Constantine Mavrocordat. He was the first to introduce paid civil servants in Wallachia, thus trying, though without success, to end the traditional practice whereby officials paid themselves from levies on the inhabitants under their authority.

The reforms were first experimented on in Wallachia and subsequently extended to Moldavia when Constantine Mavrocordat was transferred to that country (1741-3). The new prince of Wallachia, Michael Racoviţă (1741-4) infringed the fiscal reform of his predecessor and instituted one of the fiercest fiscal exploitations of the Phanariot period, levying taxes at many different periods of the year. The peasantry reacted promptly : over 15,000 peasants emigrated south of the Danube while many others went into hiding in the country, jeopardizing the incomes of the treasury and of the Porte. The Ottoman Empire was alarmed and again appointed C. Mavrocordat (1744-8), assigning to him the task of bringing back the runaways and investing him with the authority necessary to break the resistance of the boyars who opposed the application of the reforms. Mavrocordat restored the fiscal régime he had introduced during his previous reign and set about preparing for one of his most important reforms : the abolition of serfdom.

Already during his preceding reign, Constantine Mavrocordat had issued state rules governing the relations between landowners and peasants ; in 1744 he established that the peasants were to do twelve days' labour service for the boyars and monasteries. As the law applied only to those peasants who had settled on the estates of the boyars and monasteries by agreement, and not to the serfs whose obligations were at the landowners' discretion, the serfs refused to respond to the prince's call to return to the villages from where they had fled (October 26, 1745). Under pressure of their refusal, Mavrocordat enforced a new rule on March 1, 1746, whereby the serfs who returned to their villages were freed. Instead of putting an end to the peasants' flight, this measure intensified it, for the serfs who had not left their homes now did so in the hope of being freed from serfdom according to the provisions of the law. In order to end this state of affairs, Mavrocordat issued the Charter of August 5, 1746, abolishing serfdom. The serfs were entitled to redeem their freedom for the sum of 10 thalers, if their masters refused to free them free of charge.

Three years later, on April 6, 1749, Mavrocordat also abolished serfdom in Moldavia under pressure of the masses of serfs who had gathered in Jassy. In Moldavia as well as in Wallachia, the struggle of the dependent peasantry and the new policy of the Phanariot princes converged to put an end to the most oppressive form of personal dependence of the peasantry. Economic dependence, however, continued, for it was bound up with land ownership and land continued to be owned by the boyars and monasteries.

The stability which Mavrocordat endeavoured to establish in the two Romanian countries could not resist the régime of Ottoman exploitation. Shortly after the prince had restored the fiscal reform, Ottoman demands compelled him to infringe his own rules. The four yearly levies were increased and rose to twenty under the following princes. But as the Porte's requirements could not be met even in this way, the old taxes were enforced. The cow tax aroused the most bitter resistance as it had to be paid by the boyars as well. The consequence could only be a mass flight of the peasantry, and this disorganized exploitation and greatly reduced its efficiency. And then the princes were again compelled to enforce the reform. The Phanariot age was a constant alternation between fiscal oppression without precedent in the history of the Romanian countries, and short respites when the reforms were enforced.

The Russo-Turkish War of 1768-74 offered the Romanian countries a new occasion to free themselves from the Ottoman rule whose exploitation was so oppressive. Russia's armed intervention in Poland with the aim of consolidating Russian political influence induced the Porte to declare war in 1768. Being poorly equipped and without discipline, the Ottoman forces suffered a number of grievous defeats. In 1769 the Turks were driven out of the Romanian Principalities with the assistance of Romanian volunteers. When peace negotiations started at Focșani and Bucharest in 1772, delegations of Wallachian and Moldavian boyars demanded the re-establishment of the two countries' autonomy, with the guarantees of Russia, Prussia, and Austria.

The Peace of Kuchuk Kainarji in 1774 established the preponderant part to be played by Russia in Eastern and South-eastern Europe. Having obtained independence for the Crimean Tartars and freedom of navigation for her merchant vessels in the Black Sea and through the straits, Russia put an end to the exclusive rule of the Porte in the Black Sea, which thenceforth ceased to be a Turkish lake.

In exchange for her services to Turkey during the war, Austria obtained a considerable part of Moldavian territory — Bukovina — which she had actually occupied before having received the consent of the Porte (May 7, 1775).

3. End of Phanariot Rule (1774-1821)

THE Peace of Kuchuk Kainarji restored Ottoman domination in Moldavia and Wallachia and simultaneously the Phanariot régime. Turkish rule continued its oppressive policy, the two countries being ruthlessly exploited, but internal disintegration and the new defeats inflicted in the wars with the Christian powers made it ever more difficult for it to enforce its will.

The transformations wrought in South-east Europe, where a bourgeoisie was beginning to develop, gave a new impetus and new significance to the national liberation struggle. Swept along with the general current, part of the Phanariot aristocracy joined the anti-Ottoman struggle, supporting the Greek patriots and getting in touch with the countries hostile to the Porte. The Turko-Phanariot symbiosis continued, though with rifts that were to cause deep disruptions in 1821.

Military defeats and Russia's political pressure compelled the Ottoman Empire to change its relations with Moldavia and Wallachia and allow them a new juridical status. A number of documents issued by the Ottoman Chancellery in 1774, 1783, 1791, 1798, and 1802 included concessions to the demands of the two countries, which Russian diplomacy supported with the aim of weakening the power of the Porte.

Much the same effect was obtained by the setting up of foreign consulates, an expression of the new balance of power in international affairs, which ended the exclusive domination of the Porte in South-east Europe. Russian consulates were established in Moldavia and Wallachia in 1782 and Austrian consulates in 1783, while Prussia had her own consulates in the principalities in 1785, France in 1796 and Great Britain in 1803. These consulates showed that the Great Powers were interested in the resources of the Romanian countries and considered their geographical and political position of importance. Russia availed herself of the concessions forced upon the Porte, whereby the Romanian countries obtained some privileges, in order to undermine Ottoman domination in these countries and interfere in their domestic affairs. The consulates she had established in Bucharest and Jassy enabled her to supervise the application of the conventions concluded with the Porte and to exert her influence on the principalities.

Being reinstated in 1774, the Phanariot régime resumed its policy of reforms under the difficult conditions created by the havoc of war. A new effort towards the reorganization of Wallachia was made by Alexander Ypsilanti (1774-82) who fixed definite dates for the payment of the tribute and gave the country a few years of prosperity. He was the first to try to separate justice from administration, created new courts of law, and gave the country a Code of Laws (*Pravilniceasca Condică*) in 1780, which opened a new stage in the slow process whereby common law was replaced by the written law. A similar policy, though on a more restricted scale, was carried out by Prince Gregory Ghica in Moldavia (1774-7). It was during his reign that rules were worked out under which civil servants were paid a salary. This was a new effort to do away with corrupt practices, the venality of state officials, and the exploitation of the population by State officials. Gregory Ghica was killed by the Turks, a victim of his conflict with the boyars and of his relations with the Russians.

This time again the peaceful respite offered the two countries was a short one. Breaking its engagements only a few years after the conclusion of peace, the Porte again made excessive demands which undermined the reforms. The new Russo-Austro-Turkish War (1787-92) proved ruinous to the economy of the two countries. The occupation of the Crimea by Russian troops in 1783 and Russian shipbuilding for navigation in the Black Sea caused the Porte to declare war on Russia in 1787. On the basis of the treaty of alliance concluded in 1782, Austria fought alongside Russia. Having conquered the region between the Bug and the Dniester, the Russian troops marched into the Romanian countries under the command of Suvorov and won the Battles of Focșani and Rîmnic in July, 1789. In their turn, the Austrians occupied Wallachia and the counties between the Carpathians and the River Siret in Moldavia. But developments in Western Europe — the insurrection of the Netherlands and the French Revolution — compelled Austria to conclude the Peace of Shishtov in 1791 under which she waived all territorial claims. Russia concluded peace at Jassy in January, 1792, thereby obtaining the territory between the Bug and the Dniester from the Porte.

The French Revolution and the Napoleonic Wars which overthrew feudal institutions in Western and Central Europe brought their influence to bear also in East and South-east Europe. Exposed to the attacks of the French army, Austria was compelled to give up her programme of expansion in South-east Europe, thus leaving room for the play of Russian policy. As France's influence increased in the Ottoman Empire, the effects of her policy made themselves felt also in the Romanian principalities, which now entered the sphere of French interests. Intent on supervising the moves of the Russians and the Austrians, France extorted the Porte's assent to her appointing a consul in Bucharest and a vice-consul in Jassy.

Placing their hopes for the moment in France, the Romanian boyars submitted memorials to Napoleon, demanding the re-establishment of the country's autonomy and the removal of the Phanariot régime. Napoleon, however, looked upon the two Principalities as an object of compensation. In 1806, in order to create difficulties for Russia along the Danube, he prompted the Porte to recall Constantine Ypsilanti, Prince of Wallachia, and Alexander Moruzi, Prince of Moldavia, both of whom favoured Russia. Having been won over to Greece and her struggle to shake off the domination of the Porte and restore her own freedom, Constantine Ypsilanti organized an army of Romanians and Balkan people, got in touch with the leaders of the anti-Ottoman uprising which had broken out in Serbia 1804, and maintained close relations with Russia.

The removal of the two princes by the Porte infringed the provisions of the agreement of 1802, and in 1806 Russia availed herself of the opportunity to occupy the principalities. And when Napoleon concluded peace with the Russians at Tilsit the following year, the Porte remained alone to wage war on Russia (1806-12).

Romanian participation in the anti-Ottoman war again made a considerable contribution to its victorious end. The Russian forces remained in Moldavia and Wallachia until 1812 when, war with France being imminent, Tsar Alexander I concluded peace with the Porte. Following the Peace of Bucharest (May 28, 1812), the Romanian principalities were evacuated by Russian troops, with the exception of the territory between the Rivers Prut and Dniester (Bessarabia), which was incorporated into Tsarist Russia.

The Phanariot régime survived the Russo-Turkish War of 1806-12. Unable to find another formula for ruling the Romanian countries, the Turks again appointed Phanariot princes, although in recent times they had repeatedly proved disloyal to the Porte.

During the reigns of John Caragea (1812-18) and Alexander Șuțu (1818-21) Wallachia was again subjected to fierce fiscal exploitation. Overwhelmed by unbearable taxation and by a fiscal machinery that derived enormous benefits from the offices bought from the princes, whole villages, and occasionally whole districts, were deserted by their populations. The efforts of the executive bodies to check the peasants' flight were of no avail for, though some of the runaways could be brought back to their villages, a movement that had spread throughout the country could not be entirely checked. The reports sent in to the authorities also brought to their attention the emergence of centres of active resistance foreshadowing the events of 1821.

The Phanariot régime was the most oppressive stage of Ottoman domination in Moldavia and Wallachia. Exacting from the two countries through the agency of the Phanariot princes great sums of money and immense quantities of products, the Porte delayed the development of the productive forces and the breaking up of feudal structures.

At court there was the greatest luxury. The prince and his family rarely received even boyars at their own table, and at the divan, or council, or at audiences the most humiliating ceremonies were observed. It was the function of high officials to support the prince under the shoulders as he moved from room to room : and he affected the motionless pose of Turkish dignitaries. Only a few of the highest boyars were allowed to seat themselves in his presence, most of them might not even kiss his hands, but were happy to kiss his foot or the hem of his garment. One of the first Austrian residents in the Principalities, writing in the eighties of the eighteenth century, tells us that he had often seen a boyar making the sign of the cross before he was received in audience. For there was virtually no check upon the prince's merest whim, and even a boyar had little remedy against disgrace or the seizure of his fortune. Prince Constantin Rakoviţa (1753-6) on one occasion ordered the arrest of a German doctor who had offended him, and had him stripped and flogged before him night after night until he died.

"The princes of this period deserve nothing better from the historian than the pillory and the branding iron," said R.W. Seton-Watson. Worst of all perhaps was Constantine Hângerli, a Greek of the Archipelago, who in 1797 succeeded the relatively estimable Alexander Ypsilanti in Wallachia, and promptly doubled all the taxes, adding on his own behalf a vacarit or cattle tax which had been abolished sixty years earlier, in the reign of Constantine Mavrocordat by a solemn oath of hospodar, metropolitan and boyars. The metropolitan of the day had spirit enough to refuse a dispensation for so monstrous a betrayal, whereupon Hângerli obtained what he required by sending a bribe of fifty purses to the patriarch in Constantinople. So exorbitant was this demand as virtually to amount to confiscation of all the herds of all Wallachia. The collectors were ordered to levy the increased tax within the brief space of ten days and employed very severe measures, not stopping short of torture. When at length despairing protests were made before the palace — in itself a most unusual event — the prince appeared at a window and called out angrily, "Pay the taxes and you won't be killed."

Two incidents will serve to illustrate the depths of degradation reached under the wretched Hângerli. In 1798 Hussein Pasha, who commanded the Turkish army at the siege of Vidin, suffered a severe reverse at the hands of Pasvan Oglu and made his way to Bucharest, where Hângerli received him with great servility and kissed his hand in public. Noting that the boyars, when they attended a reception in his honour, did not bring their wives with them, the Pasha ordered them to appear at the palace at an early date. The boyars were shrewd enough to suspect a trap, but too subservient and cautious to disobey. They therefore dressed up a number of the prostitutes of Bucharest and presented them at the ceremony as their wives. At the end of the evening the Pasha ordered that the best-looking among these women should be removed to his quarters and told his attendants that they might make their choice from those that were left.

The treacherous Hângerli was meanwhile denouncing Hussein to the sultan as responsible for the disaster before Vidin : but he was not sufficiently versed in the secret scandal of the court to realize that Hussein's wife was the mistress of Selim III, and so this intervention brought disaster on his head. An emissary was sent from the Porte to Bucharest, accompanied by a tall negro executioner. Forcing his way into the palace he produced a *firman* (edict) of the sultan and ordered the negro to strangle the wretched Hângerli then and there, before the eyes of his terrified guards (March 1, 1799). When some of the boyars rushed in they found that the prince's head had already been hacked off, and the room was deluged with blood. His naked body was then thrown into the street and left there till evening. "An admirable picture of Turkish culture in the dying century," Seton-Watson commented.

4. Transylvania under Habsburg Absolutism

LIKE Moldavia and Wallachia under the Phanariot princes, Transylvania, now subjected to the Habsburg régime, experienced a new form of government with the same centralizing tendency as its main feature, the difference being that the reorganization programme was more far-reaching here and more consistently carried out.

After the Peace of Satu Mare of 1711, the Austrian régime greatly restricted the autonomy of the principality, which was to conform itself increasingly to the pattern of the absolutist state. While the letter of the Leopold Diploma was observed, its provisions were in actual fact being gradually infringed. The institutions embodying the autonomy of the principality were maintained but they were converted into bodies carrying out an absolutist policy. The Diet had an increasing number of representatives appointed by the Court (royalists) and was gradually deprived of its fundamental prerogatives : the right to elect the prince and the other high dignitaries and to make laws. The government *(regium gubernium)* headed by a governor who, with time, came to be directly appointed by the emperor without the Diet being consulted, became one of the most efficacious tools of the Habsburg policy. The revenues of the country were forestalled by the Empire and used for its own aims ; they were levied, as they had been in the past, through the agency of the Treasury, now reduced to a body carrying out the fiscal policy worked out in Vienna. The activities of the local bodies of power were subordinated to the control of the central ruling bodies : the Aulic Chancellery, the War Council and the Aulic Chamber (the Imperial Treasury).

With time the principality had no longer a military force of its own. First integrated in the imperial army under imperial command, the Transylvanian military force ultimately disappeared altogether. The Austrian forces stationed in the province were the safest guarantee of its loyalty. Imperial commanders frequently interfered in the politics of the principality and were sometimes even appointed as governors. The dominant classes allowed themselves to be dispossessed of part of their political power because the absolutist state allowed the exploitation régime in force to continue. Politically, this meant that the constitutional system established in the preceding centuries was maintained, the only active factors in the principality being considered the "constitutional nations" and the "accepted religions". Socially, it meant continued exploitation, which weighed most heavily on the Romanian serfs.

Banat, conquered by the Habsburg troops and incorporated in the Empire after the Peace of Passarowitz (1718), had a régime different from Transylvania's. No previous pact hindered Austrian policy here as it did in

Transylvania. Ruled by military governors and later — in the latter half of the eighteenth century — by civilian presidents, the province was under the double authority of a War Council and of an Aulic Chamber (the central institution for leading the Habsburg Empire). A colonization policy, the result of the demographic views of the Austrian authorities, brought numerous German, Italian, French, and Bulgarian people into the province. Fiscal exploitation, the removal of the Romanians from their settlements in order to make room for the settlers, the labour required to implement a public works programme of wide range, the unfair practices of the administration, and the excesses of the troops stationed in the province, were the causes of a great uprising that broke out during the Austro-Turkish War (1736-9). It was only during the last year of the war that the imperial army in a large-scale campaign was able to defeat the rebels.

New trends in the Habsburg policy during the latter half of the eighteenth century brought about changes in the compromise that had been reached between the absolutist régime and the privileged estates, a compromise on which the government system of Transylvania was based in the first half of the twentieth century. The Habsburgs revised their method of government and endeavoured to introduce a new social and political pattern. In order to cope with the new realities cropping up in the Empire as a result of the development of a capitalist economy, the state worked out a new formula for its government — an enlightened absolutism — which, while preserving the essential trends of the trends of the absolutist policy, now more comprehensive, more far-reaching, and applied at a swifter rate — brought to the fore the rationalist ideology of the eighteenth century, the philosophy of enlightenment, with the idea of progress at its core.

The reforms carried out by the régime of enlightened absolutism — more timidly under Maria Theresa (1740-80) and more systematically under the impulse of

Joseph II, co-regent from 1765 and subsequently emperor (1780-90) — made it their aim to enlarge the foundations of absolute power and eliminate the out-of-date institutions of feudal society in order to enable absolutism to adjust itself to the new economic and social realities and thus protect it from revolutionary outbursts.

As a result of the Empire's prolonged military efforts during the eighteenth century, domestic policy had to make it a main concern to procure the financial resources required for foreign wars. The greatest source of funds was taxation, but the state also endeavoured to increase its revenues by implementing a systematic programme of modernizing production and stimulating trade.

In both mines and factories paid labour was gradually superseding the servile labour of the serfs carried out as part of their feudal obligations. Feudal enterprises soon became joint enterprises and then capitalist. Extensive mining called for an increasing number of paid workers (over 1,000 men were employed at Săcărîmb and Băiţa in the latter half of the eighteenth century). Child labour, specific to early capitalism, was widely used.

The evermore exclusive tendencies of craftsmen's guilds restricted the Romanians' participation in production in that sphere. On the other hand, the Romanians made up the bulk of the workers in factories and mines.

An important part was played in the Transylvanian economy by domestic crafts, which in certain sectors proved to be dangerous competitors of the production of the guilds.

Agriculture also became the concern of state policy, which supported the extension of the land under crops and the modernization of agricultural techniques. The increase in urban population and the presence of imperial military units raised the demand for agricultural produce and stimulated the landowners' interest in farming. But as the landowners increased their output by extending their lands and not by improving farming techniques, which were still primitive, they lessened the holdings (*sessiones*) of the serfs, limited the right of their using pasture land and forests and increased the labour obligations of the dependent peasantry. In 1820 the nobility availed themselves of the favourable opportunity offered by a new conscription to extend their estates on a large scale to the detriment of the holdings of the serfs.

Focusing its attention on the problems raised by material production and trade, whose development was considered as a first condition of raising the fiscal capacity of the bulk of the population, the Habsburg state naturally changed its social outlook. The nobility, having no longer any military duties, were now considered to possess a privilege that was no longer justified: exemption from taxation, which kept immense fortunes out of the imperial treasury. That privilege was first attacked during Maria Theresa's reign, when the nobility was taxed for the first time. Joseph II later introduced the principle of equality of public obligations in the fiscal policy of the Habsburg state, thus continuing and strengthening the measures taken by Maria Theresa. In Transylvania this new fiscal policy proved ineffective.

Enlightened absolutism also took a new stand on the problem of the dependent peasantry, its policy evolving in the eighteenth century from the regulation and restriction of serf obligations under Maria Theresa, to the suppression of some of the fundamental features of serfdom under Joseph II.

But the nobility found refuge in the ancient autonomy and the ancient institutions of the counties against the attack of absolutist power, and this induced Joseph II to reorganize the administrative system. The principality was divided into eleven counties, no longer autonomous but subordinated to the central power, with its administrative machinery made up of paid officials.

Dismantling the institutions on which the political power of the nobility depended, subjecting the régime of exploitation by the nobility to state regulations, and abolishing religious discrimination, enlightened absolutism paved the way for the disruption of the traditional system of government in Transylvania.

5. Struggle of Transylvanian Romanians for Political and Social Emancipation

THE policy of the Habsburgs created a new background for the Romanians' struggle for social and political emancipation. Their first occasion to evade the ruling principles which had kept them outside political life for centuries was the adoption of the Catholic faith encouraged by the imperial authorities. For the Habsburg state Catholicism was an ideological formula designed to give spiritual unity to the many provinces and peoples that made up the Empire. In Transylvania union with the Catholics had a political aim. Having aroused the hostility of the privileged, the absolutist régime needed domestic support to consolidate its rule and sought to find it among the Romanians who formed the bulk of the population. By winning the Romanians over to the Catholic faith, the Habsburg monarchy intended to create a means of exerting pressure on the privileged and, if necessary, a means of undermining their power.

The Uniate rite was an instrument of political domination for the imperial authorities, while for the Romanians, who accepted it, it was a political act: a means of discarding the condition of a tolerated people that the constitution of the principality had imposed upon them. The struggle for political rights, which was the aim of those who had first joined the Catholic faith, became an actual fact under the leadership of the Uniate Bishop Ioan Inochentie Micu-Klein (1728-51).

The claims which Micu set forth in the many memorials he submitted to the Vienna authorities, and which he supported against the fury of the privileged in the Diet — Micu being a member of the Diet — voiced the aspirations of the whole Romanian population without any social or religious distinctions. In Micu's views the Romanian nation was not identified with a privileged minority but comprised all the people; consequently, his claims were not confined to demanding privileges for the Romanian clergy and gentry but embraced the bulk of the Romanian population, including the serfs, for Micu demanded that the number of days of labour service be reduced and that the serfs should have the right of apprenticing their children to a trade.

Micu not only raised the banner of the Transylvanian Romanians' political struggle and established its programme, but also gave it a historical and political foundation. The Roman origin of the Romanians and their continuity on Transylvanian soil, which had been latent in their consciousness since ancient times, now became a political weapon in Transylvania, where the right to political existence was denied this people. The claims of Micu and of the leaders who succeeded him in the Transylvanian Romanians' struggle against national oppression were for fair treatment founded on the Roman origin of the Romanian people, their uninterrupted existence on the territory since ancient times, their number so much larger than that of the other nationalities living there, and their wide participation in public obligations.

But Micu's programme exceeded by far the intentions of the Court of Vienna, which wished to exercise strict control over the religious union and to use it only as far as it suited its interests. The gap between the claims of the Romanian bishop and the policy of the Austrian Court was further widened after the outbreak of the war of Succession to the Austrian throne (1740-8). In its struggle for survival, the Habsburg monarchy was saved mostly through the support of the Hungarian magnates, which was obtained by great concessions to them. In order to end the movement created by Micu, which increasingly hindered its policy, the Court summoned him to Vienna. After a short stay in the capital of the Empire, Micu took refuge in Rome where he continued to guide his people until his death.

The failure of the political struggle begun under cover of a religious union and in the hope of radical changes for the Romanians gave rise to a wave of popular reaction against the Uniate faith. Promoted by the Serbian monk Visarion Sarai in 1744 and, on a larger scale and more threateningly for the régime, by monk Sofronie of Cioara in 1759, disturbances arose in South Transylvania which, though first begun as religious reactions, became occasions for making social claims.

A joint movement of the Romanian and Szekler peasantry in 1762-3 was the result of the setting up of border regiments : two Romanian regiments in Transylvania with their headquarters at Năsăud and Orlat, three Szekler regiments also in Transylvania, and two Romanian regiments in Banat.

At first viewed with hostility by the peasantry, who rose in revolts quelled with much shedding of blood, the Romanian regiments subsequently became factors of social emancipation for the serfs who had enrolled as well as an instrument for the Romanians' political gains. As officers had to be trained, the authorities opened schools in the border districts, whereby the ranks of the Romanian intelligentsia were strengthened in Transylvania.

6. Horea's Uprising

THE implementation of the agrarian programme of enlightened absolutism created new conditions for the struggle of the serfs. There is no doubt that the attempt made by the absolutist régime to restrict the exploitation of the dependent peasantry by the nobility through well-defined regulations, thus making the peasantry available for exploitation by the state, did not yield the results that had been expected of it. Ignoring the imperial ordinances or evading their provisions, the nobility succeeded in maintaining their positions and even in increasing their exploitation of the peasantry. Oppression became intolerable as a result of increased taxation which, however, did not affect the noblemen's incomes. At the same time, the serfs came to believe that the imperial authorities sided with them in their struggle against the nobility. Their belief was based on the agrarian policy of the state, the successive attempts to put order in agrarian relations, the interest shown in the peasantry and the inquiries undertaken by Joseph II during his journeys to Transylvania. The exasperated peasantry were thus made hopeful, and this state of mind was a factor in the great uprising of the Transylvanian serfs of 1784.

The first signs appeared in the Western mountains, which were to become a centre whence the uprising radiated ; at the Cîmpeni Fair in 1782 the peasants around Zlatna, whose obligations had been unduly increased through the extension and modernization of the mines and the rise in taxation, attempted to assert their traditional rights by forcibly opposing one of the most damaging innovations of the revenue office : the sale of the right to open taverns. The repression that followed prevented the incident from spreading, but two years later a similar uprising swept over most of the country.

The emperor's decision to increase the number of border regiments as a result of the new stage in the eastern crisis foreshadowed by the plans of Empress Catherine II was an occasion for the serfs to show their feelings. The Romanian and Szekler regiments set up during Maria Theresa's reign — the stress of their installation apparently forgotten — now appeared as a means to freedom, enrolling being the safest and quickest way of breaking free from serfdom obligations. Consequently, the peasants enrolled in large numbers, thus becoming exempt from all obligations to their landlords.

Scared by the proportions of the movement and the refusal of the serfs to fulfil their obligations, the noblemen demanded that the government cease their enrolling of them, and were given satisfaction. The movement was, however, too strong and the peasants' hopes of liberation too deep-rooted for the movement to be stopped once under way. On the pretext of orders from the emperor, Horea, the main leader of the peasants, encouraged them to resist. Several hundred peasants marched from Mesteacăn — to where they had been called by Horea on October 31, 1784 — to Alba Iulia, in order to enrol. At Curechiu the march turned into an open revolt, the peasants killing the officials sent by the authorities to end the movement. R.W. Seton-Watson comments that "mystery will always surround the figure of Horea, for all we know of him comes through the medium of his highborn and hidebound enemies".

The uprising spread quickly, having behind it a background of centuries of cruel exploitation. Before long it had swept over Zarand, the county of Hunedoara, the Abrud Mountains, and the Turda county, and hotbeds of revolt also cropped up in the north. In the final stage the whole country was involved. The fury of the rebel serfs razed the noblemen's country houses to the ground and turned the archives showing their debts and the noblemen's deeds of ownership into heaps of ashes. A programme was worked out which became ever more radical in its demands. On November 11, the peasants of Zarand sent the noblemen besieged at Deva an ultimatum calling for the abolition of the nobility and the division of the noblemen's estates, and demanding that the noblemen be subjected to taxation. The peasantry demanded not only that their obligations be restricted, but also that feudal relations be suppressed.

Taken aback by the violence and the proportions of the uprising, the government temporized and began negotiating with the rebels, meanwhile awaiting orders from Vienna. Having taken refuge in the towns, the nobles armed themselves and attempted to put up a defence, thus reviving an old institution : the noblemen's insurrection.

In November the imperial authorities began negotiations to end the conflict. A number of conventions agreed upon by the envoys of the authorities and the rebel groups gave satisfaction to the peasantry, granting their main claims. The most important of the conventions — concluded at Tibru on November 12 — admitted the peasant's right to enrol in border regiments and suppressed serfdom. But both the authorities and the nobility carried on negotiations only in order to gain time for reprisals.

Adverse to mass movements, which hastened the course of reforms, Joseph II determined to use force against the rebels. The latter's staunch resistance continued until mid-December when, realizing the hopelessness of their struggle, the peasants spread through the countryside and their leaders took refuge in the mountains. Betrayed to the authorities, Horea and his main collaborators, Cloşca and Crişan, were imprisoned at Alba Iulia and tried. Horea and Cloşca died on the wheel, and were disembowelled alive while Crişan committed suicide.

As a result of the uprising, letters patent abolishing serfdom were issued on August 22, 1785 : the peasants' personal dependence was done away with ; the dependent peasantry were again allowed to change their quarters, to practise a craft and to marry without the consent of their landlords. The uprising and the measures that followed it were an important stage in the breaking up of feudal relations in Transylvania.

7. Supplex Libellus Valachorum

THE end of the reign of Joseph II also meant an end to the policy of reforms. The peasants' uprisings in the Habsburg Empire, and subsequently the bourgeois revolution in France, foreshadowed the collapse of the entire régime in which the power of the dominant class was vested. The nobility reacted vigorously and the Empire gave up the experiment of enlightenment. Threatened to be swept away, the absolutist power again forged an alliance with the nobility in order to oppose the revolutionary wave. Joseph II himself cancelled his reforms, the tolerance edict and the patent on serfdom excepted. After the short reign of his brother Leopold, the reactionary nobles definitely triumphed under Francis I, and a régime was instituted with secret police and censorship as essentials.

Relying on the concepts of enlightenment and invoking the reforms of Joseph II, the spokesmen of the Romanian bourgeoisie in process of formation and mostly made up of small office-holding gentry, intellectuals, and officers in the border regiments, tried to oppose the reactionary wave and demanded that the Romanians' political claims be given satisfaction. In March, 1791, a general memorial — *Supplex Libellus Valachorum* — was forwarded to the Court of Vienna. Among those responsible for it were Samuil Micu-Klein, Ion Budai-Deleanu, Petru Maior, and Gheorghe Șincai. Resuming Inochentie Micu's arguments — now founded on the historical and philological investigations of the Transylvanian School — *Supplex Libellus* demanded that the Romanians be allowed equality with the other nations. The memorial further asked that the name and condition of tolerated people should be abolished, that the Romanians — clergy, noblemen, townspeople, and peasants — should enjoy rights equal to those of the corresponding estates of the other nations, and that the Romanians should have access to state offices in proportion to their number. The memorial was of outstanding importance, for it proposed to abolish the medieval constitution of the principality and give political promotion to the Romanian nation. Although rejected by the Diet of the principality to which it had been sent by the emperor, *Supplex Libellus* was an important stage in the struggle of the Romanians of Transylvania for emancipation from the régime of national and social oppression to which they had been condemned by the constitution.

CHAPTER NINE
THE REVOLUTION OF 1821.
THE RULE OF NATIVE PRINCES IS RE-ESTABLISHED

THE revolution of 1821 meant a great stride forward in the development of the Romanian people. It was a movement essentially different from the spontaneous, unorganized peasant uprisings of the Middle Ages : its programme demanded national independence, personal freedom, equality before the law, and removal of all impediments to the free exercise of industry and trade ; its motive power was the liberal boyars, the bourgeoisie — at the time in its formative process — and the free peasants, whom Karl Marx considered as belonging to the middle class ; it aligned itself within a European revolutionary movement ; and its organization and leadership as well as the wide response it called forth in all the countries inhabited by Romanians also made it different from the peasant uprisings of former times.

The abolition of the Phanariot régime and the restoration of the rule of the native princes after Tudor Vladimirescu's revolution did not amount to a mere change of figureheads but was a genuine national revolution. The immense resources that had gone to the maintenance of the ruling princes and the Phanariot court surrounding them were now left in the country and served to modernize Romanian institutions. In 1829, by the Treaty of Adrianople, the Romanians obtained freedom to trade and the right to open factories and mines ; they recovered the citadels along the Danube and thenceforth the frontier between the Principalities and Turkey was the Danube. All this was achieved as a result of Tudor Vladimirescu's movement and in conformity with the demands of the boyars. Even though Tudor's comprehensive programme was not implemented, the more restricted programme set forth in the boyars' memorials was carried out in part immediately after the movement had been defeated and the other part between 1821 and 1831. Like any other national liberation movement, the revolution of 1821 caused all classes of Romanian society to join forces in the struggle against Ottoman domination. And this genuine social and national liberation movement opened a new age in Romanian history : the modern age.

In the period between Tudor Vladimirescu's revolution and the revolution of 1848, the crisis of feudalism was aggravated, the social background of a national policy became more comprehensive, and the intellectuals trained in the schools of the country or abroad worked out a political programme and adopted the ideas of the Transylvanian School, turning them into a ready weapon. To begin with, Greek culture supported by the great boyars, the high clergy and the educational system, lost its prestige. After 1821 Greek schools were closed and replaced by Romanian ones, many teachers coming from Transylvania.

In the second place, the abolition of the Ottoman trading monopoly gave a powerful impulse to the national economy while the *Règlement Organique,* which will be dealt with in the next chapter, putting some order into political life, gave it greater stability and created favourable conditions for the development of capitalism and for the movement towards independence and unification. On the other hand, with the preponderance of the great boyars in state affaires, the *Règlement Organique* aggravated the antagonism between the main classes of society as well as the crisis of feudalism. In all three Romanian countries the crisis was punctuated by a number of revolts which ultimately led to the revolution of 1848.

1. Causes of the Revolution of 1821

FROM the latter half of the eighteenth century, the independence movement of the Christian peoples in European Turkey, being favoured by the military defeats of the Turks and the revolutionary agitation fomented by France, had made unceasing progress and, as a result of the growth of economic and social forces, assumed revolutionary proportions in the early years of the nineteenth century. The Serbians rose in revolt in 1804 and, after ten years' fighting, achieved their autonomy in 1815. With the Romanian people's national consciousness strengthened, their struggle for the preservation of the autonomy of the Principalities was given a new impetus. Upon the Bulgarians, Paisy's writings (1762) had the effect of setting them at variance with Greek culture and awakened their national feelings. But despite these tendencies to be free from Ottoman rule, their objective could not be attained as their efforts were sporadic and disconnected.

A secret society — *Etaireia* — founded at Odessa in 1814 by three Greek merchants, resolved to unite all the Christian peoples in European Turkey in a joint struggle for their independence. The society gained popularity in all the Mediterranean and Black Sea ports, where Greek colonies were to be found, as well as in the main towns of European Turkey. In Bucharest, Jassy, and Galatz, branches of the society were set up which were joined not only by Greeks but also by a number of Romanian boyars, merchants, and prelates.

The revolutionary movement of 1821, which started in Oltenia, spread throughout the Romanian Principalities, and, though suppressed in the Principalities, continued in Greece, was no local, spontaneous uprising as the feudal rebellions had been. By its causes, aims, and results it was part of the wider movement which threatened the reactionary régimes of Central and Southern Europe.

In the Romanian Principalities the first two decades of the nineteenth century saw the oppression and exploitation of the people ruthlessly practised and the awakening of national consciousness. The war of 1806-12 had exhausted the two countries, but they quickly recovered after peace had been concluded. Years of abundant rainfall caused farming output to rise. But although the balance of trade was favourable, the balance of payments showed a deficit that increased with every passing year : gold flowed out of the countries to the Porte and to build up a stock abroad for the ruling princes.

The financial crisis further emphasized the drawbacks of the Turko-Phanariot and feudal régimes. Both producers and merchants complained that Customs duties, home taxation, and export licences, which were sold by the ruling princes, absorbed nearly all their profits. The dependent peasants had additional feudal burdens to bear and, moreover, there were boyar and monastery monopolies, and fiscal extortion, which had become all the more oppressive as the total of taxpayers had been reduced to half the previous figure owing to the increase in the number of those exempted from taxation : peasants, who paid dues to the landowner, and merchants newly risen to the rank of boyar.

The free peasants, who made up one-third of the rural population, complained that though the exports of pigs, wool, and wine were permitted, obstacles were raised in the way of prohibitive taxes. The *pandours,* a military category of the Romanian army enlisted mainly from Oltenia, who were enlisted from among the free peasantry, had been exempted from taxation as a reward for their military services. But Prince Caragea cancelled their exemption and consequently they became receptive to revolutionary propaganda and joined Tudor Vladimirescu's army.

There was also discontent among the merchants and tradesmen. Even the great boyars, who realized that they could increase the incomes they derived from their lands now that limits had been set to the supplies to the Porte, became partisans of free trade which could not be achieved without the suppression of Ottoman monopoly. In the various memorials they submitted to the imperial cabinets in St. Petersburg and Vienna, they demanded that the citadels on the Danube be restored to Wallachia, the tribute to the Porte be cut, trade should become free, and the right to open factories and mines be guaranteed.

The union of the various sections of society in the struggle for freedom from foreign domination became possible only after a national consciousness had been formed. And this national consciousness was built up by the movement of the intelligentsia known by the name of the Transylvanian School which came into being at the close of the eighteenth century as an expression of the struggle of the Romanian people of Transylvania to have themselves recognized as a fourth political nation. Samuil Micu-Klein, Gheorghe Șincai, and Petru Maior, the most outstanding representatives of this school, gave historical and philological proof of the Roman origin of the Romanian people and language, and consequently of their being the first inhabitants of Transylvania.

They used the heroic name of Dacia as a sum total of the aspirations of all Romanians towards political and cultural unity, and it was on it that they based their reasons for nurturing such aspirations. As part of the community of Latin peoples, the Romanians could defy the so-called superiority of the other political nations and religions as well as the Greek culture in the two Principalities. The word Dacia became a manifesto in the historical and literary publications of the three Romanian countries.

Shortly before the insurrection of 1821 all sections of society had been prepared to rise against the Turks. Such was the background against which the *Etaireia* propaganda worked, and as the propagandists, who were mainly Greeks working in the Russian consulates, had been given assurance of support from Russia, many people joined the *Etaireia,* among them the high clergy, the great boyars with Grigore Brâncoveanu at their head, as well as shopkeepers and artisans. Tudor Vladimirescu, who was to give the signal of a general insurrection, had been initiated into the *Etaireia* shortly before the outbreak of the revolution.

2. Tudor Vladimirescu's Movement

BORN into a family of free peasants in the village of Vladimiri in the Gorj country around 1780, Tudor Vladimirescu, through education, trade, and the offices he filled, rose above the condition of his parents and became part of those new men whom a memorial of the boyars of Oltenia described as a permanent revolutionary ferment.

In 1806 he was appointed sheriff *(vătaf de plaiu)* at Cloşani in the Gorj country, an office which he held until the revolution. During the war of 1806-12 he fought at the head of a corps of *pandours* and was awarded St. Vladimir's Order for gallantry and his services in the field, and was subsequently promoted to the rank of lieutenant and placed under Russian protection.

On January 15, 1821, when Prince Alexander Şuţu had just died or was about to die, a Protection Committee was made up of the highest boyars, all affiliated with the *Etaireia.*

The same day the most outstanding among them — Grigore Brâncoveanu, Grigore Ghica (the ruling prince to be), and Barbu Văcărescu — concluded an agreement with Tudor Vladimirescu under which the latter assumed the obligation of "raising the people to arms" while the boyars undertook to supply the necessary means for war. Tudor Vladimirescu's action was to be the signal for a general insurrection, when a diversion would be created

14. Michael The Brave, Copperplate by Egidius Sadelav, made at Prague on the visit of the Romanian Prince to Rudolph II in 1601.

15. Statue of Michael the Brave at Bucharest.

16. Constantin Mavrocordat, Copperplate by Georg Friedrich Schmidt after Jean Etienne Liotard.

17. Constantin Brâncoveanu.

18. Matei Basarab, contemporary Copperplate by Marco Boschini, Venice.

19. Horea.

20. Cloșca.

21. Crișan.

22. Tudor Vladimirescu.

23. Avram Iancu. Painting by Barbu Iscovescu.

24. George Baritiu.

25. Nicolae Bălcescu, revolutionary leader of 1848.

26. Public Assembly in Blaj.

27. Mihail Kogălniceanu.

along the Danube in order to draw the Turkish forces there and thus make it easier for Alexander Ypsilanti to reach Greece.

During the night of January 19, 1821, Tudor began a march upon Oltenia in the course of which, at the head of a group of mercenaries, he called to arms all the counties in that part of the country, promising justice and freedom. Within a few days he had accomplished his aim. From the Tismana Monastery he issued a manifesto which ran : "Brothers living in Wallachia, whatever your nationality, no law prevents a man to meet evil with evil... How long shall we suffer the dragons that swallow us alive, those above us, both clergy and politicians, to suck our blood ? How long shall we be enslaved ?... Neither God nor the Sultan approves of such treatment of their faithful. Therefore, brothers, come all of you and deal out evil to bring evil to an end, that we might fare well... And you should come to wheresoever you will hear that the Assembly convened for the good and the benefit of the country is to be found, and whatsoever the leaders of the Assembly advise you to do, do it faithfully and wheresoever they will summon you to come, there you should come !"

The proclamation claimed a legal basis for the uprising — the right to oppose an oppressive government ; the army was the "Assembly of Release" organizing a movement for the good and benefit of the community. In conclusion, there was a warning that no one should touch "even a grain" of another's property except for "the ill-gotten property and wealth of the tyrant boyars, which were to be destroyed". For tactical reasons the boyars who joined the movement were to be exceptions, "as promised".

The peasants, however, did not make distinctions. For them all boyars were tyrants and their fortunes ill-gotten, and so all boyar and monastery property was to be destroyed. Possessed by "the spirit of revenge" they "sped blindly" under Tudor's banners. In a few days the uprising had spread over the whole of Oltenia and "the entire Principality began to totter". Wherever he went, Tudor was greeted like "a protective god". The people called him "Prince Tudor".

From Oltenia the uprising extended over the whole of Wallachia and also called forth a powerful response in Transylvania, where the Romanians were sure that the noblemen would soon be exterminated, that Tudor would be coming to mete out justice and rid them of the nobility. In Moldavia there were only local, isolated incidents. There the mass of the people were less stirred because no one had promised to rid them of Ottoman rule and the boyars' exploitation.

Tudor's proclamation was made known throughout Wallachia as well as in Transylvania; it was like a declaration of war addressed to the boyars and to the whole feudal system. The Moldavian Court Marshal, Iacovache Rizo Merulos, wrote to Ypsilanti: "Tudor Vladimirescu had raised all the counties beyond the Olt by the day before yesterday, proclaiming liberty and equality and the abolition of boyar privileges, avenging those unfairly treated and returning the plunder. His proclamations call upon all to take up arms."

Throughout Oltenia the revolutionary spirit turned the formerly "kindly and submissive population" into ruthless avengers of oppression and extortion. The villagers attacked the estates of the boyars and monasteries, broke into the barns and divided the stores among themselves. But the fury of destruction struck especially at the centre of the landowners' power, the country houses, where, apart from the fruit of the serfs' labour, the books with the unjust accounts were kept. The books were burned by the rebels. These outbursts against long stored-up injustice threatened to turn the movement into a "blind" uprising and to compromise everything. Tudor consequently severely punished the acts of plunder committed by some of the men in his army.

In order to lull the vigilance of the Turks and forestall their military intervention, Tudor sent the Porte a statement to the effect that he was faithful to the Ottoman rule and that his movement was against the Phanariot princes who, jointly with the boyars, "robbed and flayed us so that we are left only with our souls". Simultaneously, however, he gave the emperors of Russia and Austria the reasons that had caused the people to rise against their oppressors and "he made bold to demand the support and intervention of the two emperors".

For as long as it was possible, the Protection Committee kept Tudor's uprising and his proclamations secret from the Porte and, when they had to send a report, they minimized the events, describing them as if they had all been a plundering undertaking for the suppression of which the internal military forces sufficed. But the forces the Committee sent to Oltenia to bring the rebels back to "their holy duty of obedience" merely strengthened Tudor's camp. The heads of the mercenaries were members of the *Etaireia*. Having left sufficient defence forces at Craiova, Tudor took the bulk of his army — 5,000 Oltenian foot soldiers, among them many Transylvanian deserters, and 1500 Albanian mercenaries — to Bucharest. Marching through mud and slush at the rate of 25 kilometres a day, an excellent performance for the best organized armies in those days, he reached Bolintinul din Vale near Bucharest on March 16.

Here he learned that the Tsar had condemned the events in Wallachia, threatening to join forces with his allies to put down the revolution and declaring Tudor Vladimirescu to have forfeited the title of Knight of the Order of St. Vladimir and his position as a Russian protégé. This shattered the hopes of success of the *Etaireia*. The principal members of the Protection Committee took refuge in Transylvania.

Although Bimbasha Sava, commander of the Bucharest garrison, tried to prevent Tudor from entering Bucharest before Ypsilanti's arrival, Tudor entered "his capital" where he was received with great enthusiasm by the population. From Bolintinul din Vale, he launched a call to all those inhabitants of Bucharest who had not forgotten that they were "part of the same nation" and had not allowed "the holy love of the homeland" to die in their hearts, asking them to join him in order to restore "our rights". He asked that two delegates be sent him by every guild. Each guild sent ten delegates.

The Tsar's disapproval and the flight of the boyars who had made Tudor join the *Etaireia* movement left him without any "legal justification" and compelled him to conclude with the boyars an agreement whereby he acknowledged "the temporary rule of the country", while the boyars admitted that his movement was "useful and redeeming, and advantageous to the people". The boyars also vindicated Tudor's movement in a report sent to the Porte. Actually they were waiting for Ypsilanti's arrival before taking a stand.

3. Alexander Ypsilanti's Intervention

IN the evening of March 6, Ypsilanti crossed the River Prut and, escorted by 200 mercenaries of the prince's guard who had come to meet him, entered Jassy as a master and took the reins of public administration and the command of the military forces. The Russian consul, Andrea Pisani, did not even make a pretence of arresting him or of protesting against his incursion, and this strengthened the general conviction that he would be followed by a great Russian army. Provisions were prepared for that army; the Metropolitan of Moldavia girded Ypsilanti with a sword during a ceremony officiated at the Three Hierarchs' Church, and the great boyars and the bankers supplied him with money, men and weapons. During the night the Turkish merchants in Jassy as those of Galatz had been killed. The next day Ypsilanti issued two proclamations: one to the

Greeks calling them to arms for the liberation of the homeland, another to the Moldavians to set their minds at rest, assuring them that "should the Turks dare to penetrate into Moldavia, an all powerful force was ready to punish them for their audacity".

These "fatal acts of rashness" overthrew the plans of the Imperial Cabinet, turning Russia into the instigator and organizer of the movement. Tsar Alexander I was consequently compelled to repudiate Ypsilanti.

With the forces and the funds collected in Jassy, Ypsilanti marched slowly towards Bucharest, as if to permit the Russian army to overtake him. He reached Colentina only on April 18 at the head of a mob of some 5,000 men, of whom barely a hundred were in uniform. The Metropolitan and the boyars hastened to pay their respects to him. But Tudor could be persuaded to visit him only a week later.

The interview yielded no results. Ypsilanti could not persuade Tudor to accept the fact that he had "obeyed higher orders" and that a Russian army would soon arrive. Nevertheless, Tudor Vladimirescu did not break with him for fear of "thwarting the plans of a greater power". He promised to procure the provisions necessary for the *Etaireia* army against payment. The agreement, however, did not last. Tudor complained that Ypsilanti was trying to hire his troops and that the *Etaireia* army was plundering a country which Ypsilanti had promised to cross only on his way to the homeland he meant to liberate.

It was a state of tension. This was the moment when a letter arrived from the Tsar condemning Ypsilanti's movement and authorizing Turkey to send troops to the two Principalities. Threatened by a Turkish attack, and in danger of being abandoned by his partisans, Ypsilanti removed his camp to Tîrgoviște, near the Transylvanian frontier, in the hope that Turkey would make a serious mistake and thus justify Russia's military intervention in the Principalities. He had to gain time. When Ypsi-

Ianti had left Bucharest, Tudor occupied the monasteries of Mihai-Vodă and Radu-Vodă and the Metropolitan church, which dominated the town, and arrested the Protection Committee, which was making ready to go to Tîrgovişte; he imprisoned them at Belvedere Dinicu Golescu's country house. For a month and a half, he was master of Bucharest and of the greatest part of Wallachia.

The flight of the boyars who had involved Tudor in the *Etaireia* movement, and Russia's disavowal of the entire movement, gave Tudor freedom of action. Relying exclusively on the masses of the people, he fully endorsed their claims and took measures and issued orders, both within and outside the country, like a sovereign. The people called him openly "Prince Tudor". He promised to cut down the taxes and to defend the peasantry from boyar oppression, and this gained him the support of the masses and enabled him to strengthen his army.

Although the people's "Assembly" was the only organized force capable of defending the country from a disastrous Turkish occupation, Tudor did not proclaim himself as ruling prince, but sought to gain the co-operation of the high clergy and of the boyars in order to conclude an agreement with the Turks. Through the intermediary of the government, Tudor got in touch with the pashas of Vidin, Silistra, and Brăila assuring them, as he had done in his previous reports, that he had risen only against the Phanariot princes and had not departed one inch from his submission and faithfulness to the Porte. Before treating with him, the pashas demanded that he should lay down his arms for "no request of privileges and justice can be made with armed hands".

Realizing that the country could not be saved without the use of arms, Tudor prepared to resist. He made it a general rule that each fiscal grouping should provide two armed men, as the prefect of Olt had done. This was tantamount to a mass levy. After this he surrounded the Cotroceni camp with fortifications and trenches and trained his army.

Tudor furthermore tried to win over Sava, who commanded a corps of Albanian mercenaries. Sava, however, whom Ypsilanti had appointed generalissimo of the *Etaireia* army along the Danube, as he had also appointed Iordache the Olympiot, came to an agreement with the Turks and contributed to the suppression of the followers of the *Etaireia*. When the Turks approached Bucharest, Tudor withdrew towards Pitești in order to spare the capital from fire. It was his intention to reach the fortified monasteries in Oltenia. At the bridge over the River Argeș he came up against Iordache, Ypsilanti's chief lieutenant, who obliged him to stop at Golești where he took Tudor from the midst of his army and surrendered him to Ypsilanti at Tîrgoviște. The latter put Tudor to death without a trial. This was the end of the *Etaireia* insurrection in Wallachia and Moldavia.

4. Consequences of the Revolution

THE two Principalities were occupied by the Turks and the repression and plunder they were subjected to for the next sixteen months ruined and depopulated them. Most of the boyars and merchants emigrated to the neighbouring countries and only returned long after the Turks' departure. The peasants took refuge in the woods, at least as many of them as could do so, and when they returned they had to pay their dues to the landowners.

After the extermination of the *Etaireia* followers, the reorganization of the two principalities became actual.

Under the pressure of Britain and Austria, the Porte gave up the idea of turning them into *pashaliks* and ruling them through the intermediary of military commissars *(muhafizes)*, so as not to give Russia cause to interfere. Having decided to appoint native princes, the Turks summoned a delegation of seven Moldavian and seven Wallachian boyars to Constantinople. The Wallachian boyars brought with them a memorial drawn up in Bucharest and comprising 24 points stating the essential grievances that had been included in the memorials addressed to the Russian and Austrian emperors during the revolution.

The Porte took no account of the memorials and demanded that the two delegations should give them written proposals. The demands of the two delegations were almost identical: native princes, a native guard instead of the Albanian mercenaries, a ban on the purchase of real estate by foreign subjects, the removal of Greek monks, the right of holding high office to be reserved exclusively for the natives of the country, and freedom to complain to the Porte.

The Porte only admitted part of these demands and on July 1, 1822, appointed Ioniță Sandu Sturdza as Prince of Moldavia and Grigore Ghica as Prince of Wallachia, according to the delegates' demand. The other claims in the boyars' programme — freedom of trade, industry, and mining, and reforms concentrating all political power into the hands of the great boyars — were postponed until the conclusion of the Treaty of Adrianople.

The re-establishment of the native princes' rule did not only mean a change of persons. It amounted to the overthrow of a régime — the Phanariot régime — and with it went all the burdens laid upon the country for enriching the Phanariot princes' relatives in Constantinople.

As many of the boyars had taken refuge in Transylvania to return only in 1826, the reprisals against the participants in the revolution were not so severe as was usual after peasant uprisings.

Farming produce having become more profitable, the boyars asked that the number of work days a year should be increased from 12 to 14. Their demand was, however, ineffective on account of the peasants' opposition, who refused to work even the usual number of days, and of the scarcity of labour. The public debt increased during the revolution and the Turkish occupation, and payment was exacted now not only from the usual taxpayers but also from the sections of society exempted from taxes, thus diminishing the boyars' income and instituting a precedent that threatened their privileges.

In Wallachia the ruling prince was attacked by some of the great boyars who wished to take his place and who sent reports to the Porte criticizing his financial administration. However, such intrigues were easily terminated by the prince.

The Wallachian gentry claimed the same rights as the great boyars but there were among them some that foreshadowed future events. Thus Eufrosin Poteca proposed that a bourgeois republic should be proclaimed and all citizens be equally taxed.

The intervention of the Russian consuls ended such plans for reform and the Porte was compelled to sign the Akkerman Convention on October 7, 1826, whereby the rule of a prince was to last for a term of seven years and certain rules were to be made to improve economic conditions in the Principalities.

In the meantime the Turks were about to put down the uprising in Greece, which had lasted since 1821. European public opinion, however, forced France and Britain to intervene. The Turkish fleet was sunk at Navarino, and the Russian armies crossed the River Prut and after a number of brilliant victories forced the Porte to capitulate.

The Peace Treaty signed at Adrianople (September 14, 1829) gave Russia the Caucasus area of the Black Sea coastline and the Danube mouths up to where the Prut flows into the Danube ; declared navigation to be free on the Danube, in the Black Sea and in the Straits ; and confirmed the autonomy of Greece and Serbia.

A separate act, which was an integral part of the treaty, returned to Wallachia the citadels on the left bank of the Danube and established Wallachia's frontier with the "Ottoman States" along the river. The inhabitants of the two Principalities were exempted from providing the supplies that had previously been sent to the Porte and were given full freedom of trading in all the products of the land and of their work. The princes were to be elected for the term of their lives and were to administer the country freely together with a "Divan" council. The Porte agreed to confirm the *Règlement Organique* which was to be worked out during Russia's occupation of the Principalities. The occupation was to last until all war reparations amounting to 11,500,000 ducats had been fully paid.

The stipulations of the Treaty of Adrianople, which concluded the struggle started by the *Etaireia*, gave the Romanian Principalities nearly everything the boyars had claimed in their memorials during the revolution of 1821 : freedom of trade, once considered by the Turks as the greatest threat to the Empire, the opening of the Danube ports, and the restriction of the Ottoman government's right to interfere in the internal affairs of the Principalities. The suzerainty of the Porte was thus reduced to payment of a tribute and the confirmation of the appointment of the ruling princes.

Considering its consequences, the insurrection of 1821 was a genuine national revolution for Moldavia and Wallachia.

CHAPTER TEN

THE AGE OF THE RÈGLEMENT ORGANIQUE AND THE REVOLUTION OF 1848 IN THE ROMANIAN COUNTRIES

THE *Règlement Organique* passed by the Public Assemblies in 1831 was actually a constitution, Romania's first, which gave the Romanian Principalities institutions liable to favour the development of capitalism. However, on account of its revolutionary connotations the term "constitution" was replaced by the word *Règlement*.

The régime created by the *Règlement Organique* concentrated all power in the hands of the great boyars ; they thereupon instituted what the villagers called "the slavery of compulsory service". Freedom of trade and the fact that offices were no longer sold confined the boyars' sources of income to the exploitation of their estates. The boyars consequently sought to extort as much as possible from the work of the dependent peasants on their estate and to tie them to the land.

Having abolished the monopoly of the guilds, the *Règlement Organique* favoured the development of industry, which was also stimulated by the greater profits brought in by agricultural production. Paid labour was used to an increasing extent. In pace with economic progress, the Romanian bourgeoisie increased in number. More and more young people were being sent for higher education to establishments in the West, especially in France. On their return, they headed the renewal movement under way in the country, organizing secret societies and drawing up programmes of struggle for social and political emancipation. Despite the repression of all forms of liberalism by the Protecting State, the national movement made decisive progress during that period, paving the way for the solidarity of the three Romanian countries in the revolutionary struggle of 1848.

1. The Règlement Organique

UPON the conclusion of peace, the Romanian Principalities were to be occupied by Russia until all war reparations had been paid. General Paul Kiselev, a man of high character, broad outlook and marked ability, was appointed President Plenipotentiary of the Divans of the two Principalities, an office which he held from November 12, 1829, to April, 1834, when the Russian forces left the Principalities. In the exercise of the extraordinary powers with which he had been invested for the reorganization of the Principalities, he used tact and moderation.

The Principalities were in a desperate state. The population, partly decimated by the war, was threatened by plague and starvation. Kiselev organized a sanitary cordon along the Danube as well as a medical service to control the plague. By the close of 1829 the epidemic had been stamped out. In order to fend off starvation, grain was imported from Odessa, and after 1830 granaries were built and corn was stored to prevent the recurrence of such calamities.

The campaign Kiselev organized against the plague and starvation, visiting the hotbeds of disease in person, revealed to him the vices of the administration, which he remedied even before the *Règlement Organique* had been worked out. He issued decrees whereby justice was separated from the administration, abolished the exemption of dependent peasants from taxes to the state, whereby 40,000 families were at the service of the boyars, built up a national army, and established definite taxes which were brought to the knowledge of the taxpayers. All these measures were to be incorporated in the *Règlement Organique.*

The *Règlement Organique,* which did duty for a constitution until 1859, was drawn up by two committees, each made up of four Moldavian and four Wallachian boyars, with the Russian Consul General, Mintchiaky, as chairman.

The text was amended by Kiselev, after which it was examined by the Imperial Cabinet and subsequently submitted to the Divans, who discussed it without having the power to change it. The *Règlement* was promulgated in July, 1831, for Wallachia and in January, 1832, for Moldavia.

State organization relied on the principle of the separation of powers. The executive power was the prerogative of the rulling prince who was elected for the term of his life from among the great boyars by an Extraordinary Public Assembly. In the exercise of the executive power, the prince was assisted by six ministers. In the event of a conflict with the Assembly the prince had no right to dissolve it but only to prorogue it. Legislative power was vested in the Public Assembly, made up of 42 deputies in Wallachia : the Metropolitan, who was also Chairman of the Assembly, the three Wallachian bishops, twenty great boyars chosen by seventy boyars of the same rank, and eighteen deputies elected by the boyars of the second and the third rank. The Moldavian Assembly was made up of 35 deputies elected according to the same rules. The judicial power was exercised by tribunals, of which there was one in every county. The courts of appeal were two (Judicial Divans) in Wallachia, one in Bucharest, and another in Craiova, and one in Jassy in Moldavia. They were independent of the ruling prince and the Assembly. "Courts of conciliation" were set up for the settlement of local conflicts in the villages, mostly cases of damages caused by stray cattle. The magistrates and civil servants were to be appointed for a term of three years and could be confirmed in their posts every three years. The *Règlement* did not lay down the principle of the irremovability of judges. Controlling the Assembly and the tribunals, the great boyars could solve all questions referring to agrarian relations to suit their class interest.

Despite the narrow class spirit that had inspired it, the *Règlement Organique* meant great progress in the modernization of the Principalities. The historian and revolutionary, N. Bălcescu, admitted that "despite all their evils, the *Règlement* enacted some useful principles and became an instrument of progress". Separating justice from the administration and investing judicial sentences with authority, they introduced order and abolished the right of the plaintiff who had lost his case under one prince to re-open it under the following prince. Property and economic transactions were thus consolidated.

The innovatory nature of the *Règlement Organique* was apparent especially in fiscal matters which had not been solved by the Phanariot reforms, frequent as they were. To begin with, the *Règlement* reduced the chaotic diversity of taxes to one — capitation — which became a fixed one. For the first time all the people were taxed, for all exemptions had been done away with and a strict record of the population was kept, the registers being far more accurate than in the past and reducing the number of inhabitants whose existence the boyars concealed from the authorities. With the Porte no longer making repeated and unexpected demands, the fiscal régime showed a stability which was reflected in the stability of the population. The *Règlement* abolished indirect taxation, the supplies to the Porte, requisitioning and domestic custom duties, and adopted the modern principle of a state budget based on balanced revenues and expenditure. The budget was debated by the Public Assembly and audited by a special body. But the *Règlement* exempted the boyars and the clergy from taxation.

Furthermore the *Règlement Organique* set up civil registry offices and state archives as well as colleges in Bucharest and Jassy for the training of civil servants. To guard the frontiers, a militia was created which was to constitute the embryo of the national army.

With a view to the unification of Moldavia and Wallachia, the *Règlement* incorporated almost identical provisions in the two countries. More than that : articles 317 in Wallachia and 429 in Moldavia proclaimed that by virtue of their common language, religion, customs, and interests, "the inseparable unification" of the inhabitants of the two Principalities was a "redeeming" necessity.

The *Règlement Organique* wrought radical changes in the structure of landed estates and of agrarian relations. The historian R.W. Seton-Watson commented that "Kiselev's rule marks an epoch in Romanian history. It is the transition from chaos and decay to the first rudiments of ordered and decent government". Boyars took advantage of the protection of the Russian army to force upon the peasants the conditions required to produce grain for the market. The feudal estate, on which the peasants enjoyed various rights — the right to cultivate fallow land, to gather firewood and building timber, to use pasture land for their needs — now tended to be turned into an absolute property of the bourgeois type.

In the second place, the peasants were deprived of land whose possession they had enjoyed before the *Règlement* came into force. On the basis of a so-called reciprocity of rights and uses, the land was not distributed according to the needs of a family and the hereditary right over the land, but according to the labour expended for the landowners.

Restricting to a maximum five head the cattle for which the landowner was obliged to give land, the *Règlement* struck a blow at animal husbandry which was still the peasants' main source of income. For apart from draft cattle, the villagers kept up to forty head of cattle. Consequently, the dependent peasant who wanted to keep more cattle or to till more land than the *Règlement* admitted had to come to terms with the landowner. "Willing agreements" were to be a terrible instrument of enslavement in the hands of the landowners and their main means of exploiting the villagers.

In exchange for the land, the *Règlement* demanded that the people contribute twelve days' work a year, which were counted according to the work done per day as established by the *Règlement*: so many square yards ploughed a day, so many square yards hoed, so many mown, etc. The established day's work could only be effected in two or three days. According to Bălcescu, the number of days' work was actually 56 in Wallachia and 84 in Moldavia per annum.

Such measures strengthened the boyars' economic and political position and, paradoxically, ensured the evolution of society towards capitalism, though on the basis of what were mostly feudal relations. Having in their hands all the political power as well as the means of compulsion of a modernized state machinery, the boyars increased the exploitation of the peasants on their estates, thus creating conditions which the peasants described as "the slavery of labour service".

There was general opposition among the peasants to the Labour Service Law. In Moldavia the agitation assumed such serious proportions that Cossack squadrons had to be brought into action in order to put it down. The main reason for dissatisfaction was the recruiting carried out for the army newly created by the *Règlement Organique*. But the law on labour service gave almost equal dissatisfaction to the peasants, proof of which is the fact that after the suppression of the uprising, the struggle continued — the reason now being that "the small holdings assigned them were insufficient for subsistence". The villagers on the bank of the Prut emigrated to Bessarabia, upon which the government was forced to enact a new law suspending the application of the labour service law in the border districts until 1848.

2. Economic Life

THE increase in marketable agricultural production was hampered by feudal privileges and the slow development of transport and communication routes and of the home market. Although feudal relations dominated the economy, a number of innovations heralded the growth of capitalism. Ploughing and threshing machines began to be imported and later to be manufactured in the country. Selected seed was now used and new plants were being cultivated extensively. Pedigree cattle were imported in order to improve the native breeds. Art and trade schools were opened in Jassy and Bucharest. In Transylvania fodder and industrial plants were introduced and vineyards and orchards were extended.

Despite the economic restrictions of feudal relations, which still predominated, the output of marketable agricultural products increased in the Romanian countries. In Transylvania crop rotation and irrigation were introduced as a contribution to the modernization of farming.

The profits that could be made on marketable agricultural products gave a spurt to industry. The government supported industrial expansion by awarding "stimulating bounties"; it further set up technical schools and did much towards the spread of the technical Press and literature. The *Règlement Organique* abolished the monopoly held by the guilds.

In Moldavia and Wallachia the manufactory stage was reached in the food industry (pastes, edible oil, sugar, cured meats) for which there were low-priced raw materials in quantities. The shipyards at Galatz and Giurgiu, the brick yards and breweries, the distilleries, candle factories, paper mills and tanneries, the tobacco and glass plants employed a large number of workers, some of them brought from other countries. The factories producing earthenware, textile fabrics, and rope found it more difficult to meet foreign competition. There was an increasing number of paid workers but they often continued their farming, for work was intermittent in the factories and these establishments often closed down.

The most developed industry was mining, while one of the most important exports was salt from all three Romanian countries. Oil was beginning to be exploited on an ever larger scale. It was in Transylvania's mining industry that the capitalist way of production reached its highest development level, mining becoming the most important source of capitalist accumulation. In the gold mines, which had been worked from ancient times, techniques were improved. In 1838 a steam engine was already working at Zlatna and the Baia Mare mines soon followed suit. Joint stock companies were set up in order to obtain the capital required for great depth mining.

Farm production was stimulated by the opening of the Danube ports and the access to world markets, while the abolition of various feudal ducs and the development of communication routes enlarged the home market. The customs union of 1846-8 was a further step forward.

With the development of the means of transportation and trade routes, the home market grew steadily. In 1846 the construction of roads linking Bucharest with Orșova, Focșani, Brăila, Sibiu, and Brașov was begun. This was done by means of the labour services of the dependent peasants and of budget appropriations.

As river navigation would inevitably be an improvement on transport by means of ox-drawn carts, work was begun in order to make the main rivers of Wallachia and Moldavia navigable. The cost, however, proved to be beyond the means of the two Principalities and the venture was abandoned. Sea navigation, on the other hand, progressed steadily. It was during this period that a national fleet of merchant ships began to be built up. In 1834 the first ship flying the Romanian flag unloaded 100 tons of wheat at Constantinople, while another carried oak staves to Marseilles. In 1839 the Galatz shipyards launched seven ships and in 1840 ten. Integration into international trade, though on a small scale as yet, would have been impossible before the Treaty of Adrianople.

Freedom of trade gave a powerful impulse to the fairs, where traders purchased goods for export and for town supplies. The main exports of the two Principalities were cattle, horses, sheep, grain, and building timber. Now that Romanian exports went to a larger number of countries, there was a tendency for Britain and France to replace Turkey and Austria as the main customers of the Principalities. A favourable balance of trade clearly showed that trade had expanded. From 1835 to 1844 Wallachia's exports increased threefold, from 21,500,000 lei to 64,400,000 lei, while Moldavia's exports rose from 26 million lei to 52 million from 1843 to 1847. After 1840 grain exports rose above cattle exports in value.

The bulk of Moldavian and Wallachian exports was carried on via Galatz and Brăila. In 1837 449 vessels entered the port of Brăila and in 1847 their number rose to 1,383, of which 418 were British. The port of Galatz developed along the same lines, with 236 vessels calling in 1833 and 1,064 in 1847. In 1833 the Porte had acknowledged the right of the Principalities to fly a national flag on their ships.

The trading houses and companies of Sibiu and Brașov played a considerable part in trade expansion. The Romanian commercial company of Brașov with a membership of one hundred handled nearly the entire trade of Brașov. Out of a total number of 139 Brașov traders, 118 were Romanian.

3. Political Life

THE first princes to ascend the throne during the implementation of the *Règlement Organique* were Alexandru Ghica and Mihai Sturdza. They were not elected as the

Règlement laid down, but were appointed by the suzerain and the protecting courts on the basis of the Petersburg understanding of January 17, 1834. Alexandru Ghica, Prince of Wallachia (1834-42), was the brother of the former Prince Grigore Ghica, during whose reign he had held the highest offices as he had also done during Kiselev's administration. He was reputed to be a well-informed man, of outstanding integrity, and a great patriot.

Mihai Sturdza was Prince of Moldavia until 1849. With a penetrating mind and well-informed, he was also an excellent organizer and a skilled diplomat able to parry all the blows dealt by internal opposition and by the suzerain and the protecting courts. These qualities were, however, overshadowed by his insatiable greed, as well as by excessive pride and an imperious will.

Both princes were from the first faced by great financial difficulties, the result of the deficit left by Count Kiselev's administration, the tribute which the Treaty of Adrianople had fixed at three million piastres which had not been paid during the Russian occupation, and the expenditure required by the princes' investiture at Constantinople. The Bucharest and the Jassy assemblies voted for an increase in the Civil List from 1,200,000 to 1,600,000 piastres and for a contribution of 1,200,000 piastres to cover the expenses incurred at Constantinople. The 1835 budget could not be balanced. In order to cover the deficit, the poll tax was increased by thirty per cent.

A misunderstanding arose between the Assembly and Ghica over the so-called additional article. During the negotiations carried on at Constantinople for the ratification of the *Règlement Organique* by the Ottoman government, the Russian ambassador had introduced certain amendments and had added on the last page an article stipulating that no law passed by the Assembly and sanctioned by the prince could be promulgated unless it had been approved by the suzerain and the protecting courts. Baron Rückman, Russia's Consul General, demanded that the article "which had been omitted by mistake" should be passed by the Assembly. In 1835 Sturdza had the article passed. In Wallachia, however, the problem envenomed the relations between the Assembly and the prince for three years. Ghica would have liked the article passed without public debates. The opposition, however, contested the authenticity of the article and refused to pass it. Rückman went to Constantinople and returned with a decree *(firman)* compelling the Assembly to introduce the article in the *Règlement*. Both the prince and the Assembly did so in May, 1838. The legislative right belonged to the Assembly only within the limits fixed by the protecting court.

The misunderstandings between the Assembly and the throne were to paralyse both parties and to subordinate them to the protecting court. It was against this state of affairs that a national opposition was built up which obtained the majority in the election of 1837. The opposition was supported by the liberal youth who had been studying abroad from where they returned with a programme of liberal reforms. A far more radical movement was subsequently organized by Mitică Filipescu, who, relying on the radical elements of the bourgeoisie at the time in process of formation, made it his aim to overthrow the entire social order. A secret society was formed to which Bălcescu also belonged. The society counted on the aggravation of the Eastern Question in 1840 and the disruption of the Ottoman Empire, which would have allowed the Romanian Principalities to obtain their independence and to abolish the feudal régime. The conspirators' plans were overthrown when the latent conflict between England and France was smoothed out, and the treachery of some of the members of the society delivered the leaders to the authorities.

The suppression of the revolutionary movement of 1840 did not strengthen Ghica's position. The election of 1841 showed the great boyars to be most powerful and the latter started a ruthless campaign against the prince whom they reproached with the measures taken in favour of the peasantry, especially with the intention of changing the stipulations of the *Règlement Organique* referring to the peasants' freedom to change their place of habitation and to the right to graze their cattle.

The boyars used against Ghica the two attempts made by some Bulgarian immigrants in Wallachia and Bessarabia, to return to Bulgaria in order to stir up revolt against the Ottoman rule. Denounced to the suzerain and the protecting courts, Ghica was deposed on October 7, 1842, after a biased inquiry.

His successor, Gheorghe Bibescu (1842-8), who had studied law in Paris, was a scholarly man and one of the richest boyars of the country. He was the first prince to be elected in keeping with the stipulations of the *Règlement* by an Extraordinary Public Assembly in which the masses of town and village were not represented. Bibescu owed his election to the campaign he had set afoot, together with his brother, Barbu Ştirbei, against Alexandru Ghica.

The agreement between the Assembly and the prince was of short duration. In 1834 national opposition was built up again in the form of a secret society — *Brotherhood* — headed by Ion Ghica, Christian Tell, and Nicolae Bălcescu, who was just out of prison. The opposition fought not only for the bourgeoisie and the liberal boyars, but also for the lesser bourgeoisie, the workers and the peasants. The conflict between the Assembly and the prince broke out over the concession given to the Russian engineer Trandafilov to explore and exploit the metal mines of the country. Instead of making an unbiased inquiry, the Assembly showed the whole affair to be a form of foreign exploitation and demanded that the concession be cancelled. With the assistance of the Russian ambassador, Bibescu obtained a decree from the court entitling him to prorogue the Assembly for the rest of its mandate and to govern for two years by means of decrees. The Assembly elected in 1846 was made up of Bibescu's partisans so that "the age of perfect union between the administration and the Public Assembly" would have lasted for five years if the revolutions of 1848 had not ended Bibescu's reign.

Bibescu's attempt to solve the problem of the monasteries under Greek patronage and administered by Greek monks, who derived an income equal to a fifth of the state's revenue, was unsuccessful on account of the opposition of the Russian ambassador, who defended the monasteries. The most important event of Bibescu's reign was the customs union of 1848 between Moldavia and Wallachia, which made of the territory of the two Principalities an economic unit as a prelude to political union.

Mihai Sturdza, the Moldavian prince, retained his throne from 1834 to 1849, although he met with the same difficulties as the two princes of Wallachia. His reforms prepared Moldavia for the great struggle for the union of the two Principalities. Under his rule Moldavia enjoyed fifteen years of stability which were decisive in the modernization of the country. The modern roads and bridges built at the time with the serfs' unpaid labour as also through appropriations from the state budget enabled northern Moldavia's wheat to reach the Galatz market and linked the most isolated districts with the national market. He organized an efficient postal service, created the first modern hospitals, and improved the prison régime. In 1834 he declared Galatz a free port, thus advancing the town's demographic and economic development. Traffic in the port increased, enabling the local merchants to improve the port, raise a dike to protect it against floods, and rebuild the town in stone.

Sturdza paid great attention to administration and education. With the educational system developing and large numbers of young people being sent to study abroad, the prince was able to provide better informed and more energetic prefects and mayors for the different districts and towns of the country.

Throughout his reign Mihai Sturdza had three parties opposing him. The great boyars, who considered themselves his equals and consequently entitled to supersede him, hatched intrigues in the Assembly and in drawing-rooms and sent complaints to the suzerain and the protecting courts. Sturdza parried by dispatching counter-demands and taking disciplinary measures.

The little and middle boyars, among whom were many merchants whom Ioniță Sandu Sturdza had raised to the rank of boyar, now clamoured for full equality with the great boyars and for their privileges, their claims based on the principles of the French Revolution.

The intelligentsia opposed Mihai Sturdza's reactionary régime by every possible means : the Press, literature, and meetings. A systematic movement for the union of the two Principalities and for democracy was set afoot by M. Kogălniceanu, C. Negruzzi, Alecu Russo, Vasile Alecsandri, Anastase Panu, V. Mălinescu, C. Negri, and others. Sturdza fought them by suppressing their publications and exiling the authors to monasteries or, more efficiently, by partly carrying out their programme.

Opposition was also forthcoming from the secret society styled the Patriotic Association, which counted Theodor Rășcanu, V. Mălinescu, Alexandru Ioan Cuza, Ion Lambrior, and Gr. Carp among its members. The programme of the Association was to overthrow Sturdza's régime, set free the boyars' gypsy slaves, obtain juridical equality, and introduce taxation of landed estates — that is, suppress the boyars' exemption from taxes. The Association was influenced by the powerful peasant upsurge of the winter of 1845-8. Ultimately the Association was discovered and its members arrested or compelled to emigrate.

4. Transylvania during the "Age of Reforms"

THE age of the *Règlement Organique* was an "age of reforms" during which the changes wrought during the eighteenth century, as set forth in the preceding chapters, continued. During the first half of the nineteenth century, Vienna was bent on strengthening its economic and political domination over Transylvania. Supported by the Hungarian aristocracy, the imperial cabinet governed here through the agency of central bodies — the Vienna chancellery, the governor of Transylvania and the high officials appointed by the emperor direct — which established the taxes to be paid, the military contingents to be made available, and defended public opinion from the contamination of subversive ideas by means of censorship. The Diet was not convened from 1811 to 1834 — a span of twenty-three years. The lesser nobility backed the system, for it had preserved its administrative and juridical monopoly.

Subjected to a double exploitation — social and national — the Romanian people had much to suffer from the system. The process of economic and social emancipation was checked by the fact that Romanians were not entitled to settle in towns, practise certain trades or attend schools; and this also heightened the antagonism between Romanian serfs and the Magyar nobility. The Romanians' revolutionary trends and their desire for political union found efficient support in the activities of the Polish revolutionaries who had taken refuge in Transylvania. It was under the impulse of the Pole Adolf David that propaganda was begun in 1834 for "a republic of the united Romanians".

Even the liberal Magyar nobility admitted the need for reforms and the Vienna Court was thus compelled to convene the Diet. The bourgeoisie, which had risen to some importance in economic life, was also eager to gain political power. Though they acted jointly when the aim was to remove the barriers that prevented the free development of industry and trade, they split into factions when it came to sacrificing their own privileges. With national conflicts intensifying, some of the Magyars supported the idea of Transylvania being incorporated within Hungary, while the Romanian bourgeoisie and intelligentsia joined issue with the Romanian serfs in order to defend Transylvania's autonomy.

The serfs were also active. The parcelling-out of the peasant holdings, the seizure of the cleared land by the nobility, the oppressive labour service that had to be performed, and the confiscation of pasture land and forests were the causes of strong movements of protest, with the miners joining in, for they also were fighting for social and national emancipation.

The Diet of 1846-7 considered that putting agrarian relationships in order would end the discontent of the peasant masses. But this was a belated concession. The peasants now wanted full ownership of the land they used. The majority in the Diet passed a draft law which gave the serfs the land they had declared at the census. The draft relied on Cziraky's conscription of 1819-20. But the peasants, fearing that their taxes would be raised, had then declared areas smaller than those they actually used. The draft was passed by the Diet and sanctioned by the emperor but was never applied. It was the main task of the revolution of 1848 to make order in the relations between serfs and landowners.

5. A National Ideology Is Evolved

IN the Romanian Principalities the defeat of the revolution of 1821 did not weaken the national movement; quite the reverse, the movement was strengthened and came to be more closely connected to international developments. The constitutional projects made during the reign of native princes aimed at emancipation from Ottoman rule. During the Russo-Turkish War of 1828-

29 Iordache Catargi and Mihai Sturdza "dared to think of restoring a Dacian monarchy" under a foreign prince that did not belong to a dynasty reigning in the neighbouring countries. When it became known what immense war reparations Turkey had to pay under the Treaty of Adrianople (11,500,000 ducats) — reparations deliberately calculated to justify a ten-years occupation of the Principalities — the partisans of the union offered to pay the sum provided the country was given full independence guaranteed by the Great Powers. By organizing the two Principalities almost identically, the *Règlement Organique* furthered the national movement and justified its bringing to the fore the identity of the language, the people's national consciousness, and the common economic interests of the population in the two Principalities.

The French and British consuls constantly drew their governments' attention to the importance of the economic resources and geographical position of the Principalities and pleaded for their union. "The wish for independence", the French Consul in Bucharest wrote, "increases with every passing day. The enlightened Romanians do not doubt that a great change will occur in their situation". The Moldavians thought of a confederation made up of Moldavia, Wallachia, and Serbia under the guarantee of the Great Powers, and the Wallachians supported the plan. About 1839-40 the desire for independence had become general. "More than ever boyars and peasants cherish their homeland as they see in this state of affairs, which is new for them, promises for the future ; and the Prince leaves nothing undone to inspire the Moldavians with a feeling of nationality". The words are those of the French consul in Jassy.

When Prince Albert of Prussia stopped in Bucharest for a few days on his return journey from Constantinople, he was thought to have the intention of getting to know the city where he was to rule "as King of restored Dacia", according to the will of the Great Powers.

Dacia was like a magic word summing up all the aspirations for freedom, union and independence of the new generation in the two Principalities. Petru Maior wrote his *History of the Romanians' Origin in Dacia* (1812), M. Kogălniceanu followed suit with his *Literary Dacia* (1840) and A. Treboniu Laurian and N. Bălcescu with *Historic Magazine for Dacia* (1845). The word passed from the sphere of science and literature into the political language. And another word which assumed the same significance at the time was Romania : Aron Florian published *România,* M. Kogălniceanu, *Romanian Archives,* and there was also Romania's Literary Association. Later the phrase Daco-Romania came to be used by the national movement and also the word Romanianism. Romanians and other nations alike spoke of the Kingdom of Dacia and of the Romanian people's constant wish for independence and of turning the two Principalities into a buffer state such as Belgium, but making a connection between West and East.

During the fourth and fifth decades of the nineteenth century, there were profound changes also in the concepts of the Romanians of Transylvania. The conspiratorial programme of the people of Banat in 1839 included the setting up of "a united Romanian Republic" made up of Moldavia, Wallachia, and Transylvania.

With cultural ties with the West becoming closer and the number of young people studying abroad increasing, these tendencies were strengthened. This alarmed the Russian cabinet. In the main towns of Transylvania — Brașov, Sibiu, and Cluj — the intelligentsia within the budding bourgeoisie stiffened its backbone and assumed leadership of the national movements formerly in the hands of the clergy, investing it with a militant political character. While starting from the ideas of the first generation of the Transylvanian School — Roman origin of the Romanians and their continuity on the territory of ancient Dacia — the leaders of the new generation, Timoteiu Cipariu, Simion Bărnuțiu and George Barițiu, based their arguments on the demographic preponderance of the Romanians and the great extent to which they fulfilled their fiscal and military obligations. They drew the masses into the struggle, arousing in them the consciousness of a common cultural heritage and of their national rights. The language itself assumed a new significance ; it was not only considered as proof of the Romanian people, and as the closest tie between the people speaking it. It was the duty of the writers to enrich and polish it so that it might express the loftiest ideas and the deepest feelings. The Latin character of the Romanian language was no longer contested. Another important feature of this period was the toning down of religious controversies between the Romanians of the Orthodox faith and the Uniates, and the co-operation of the heads of the two faiths for the promotion of the national movement.

A third means of furthering the national struggle in Transylvania was the educational system. In order to raise the cultural level of Romanian priests, the Orthodox and the Uniate bishops founded seminaries with a two-year and later a four-year curriculum. The curriculum of the Blaj Lycée, where the first representatives of the Transylvanian School began their education, was greatly enlarged. It included the study of national and world history and of the exact sciences. Some of the graduates of the Lycée continued their studies in Cluj, Vienna and Rome, and thus proficient people were trained for the Romanian educational system and Press in Transylvania.

During the period of the *Règlement Organique* all the main points of the programme of the union had already crystallized. They included the idea of Romania acting as a buffer state to soften the clashes between the three empires — the Russian, Austrian, and Turkish — (thus making of the union of the two Principalities a European problem) ; the principle of nationality ; and a constitutional régime under a foreign prince with the joint guarantee of the Great Powers. It was left for the generation that followed to build up these ideas into one concept and to make them triumph.

The revolution of 1848 came as a result of the transformations wrought in Romanian society after the revolution of 1821. Its programme, which was more complex and more radical than that of 1821, made it its aim to promote the new capitalist structure of Romanian society, to strengthen its unity, and to prepare it for the struggle for independence. The experience stored during this period and the influence of the revolutionary ideas crystallized into a programme of bourgeois-democratic reforms, which was further developed and made specific during the revolution. The revolutions of 1848 in Paris, Vienna, Berlin and Budapest undoubtedly brought their influence to bear on the outbreak and unfolding of the revolution in the Romanian countries. But, as N. Bălcescu said, the European revolutions were only "the occasion and not the cause of the Romanian revolution". The fact that the revolution broke out almost at the same time in all the three Romanian countries was in itself proof of the unity and solidarity of the Romanian people everywhere.

6. The Revolution

WHILE continuing the revolution of 1821, the revolution of 1848 in the Romanian countries forms an integral part of the great effort of revolutionary renewal which swept over Europe in the late forties of the last century. When pointing to the historical roots of the revolutionary events of 1848 in Moldavia, Wallachia, and Transylvania, N. Bălcescu observed that the Romanian revolution was no "ephemeral phenomenon, without a past and a future, and without other causes than the fortuitous wish of a minority, and the general European movement... It originated in the past centuries and was hatched by eighteen centuries of toil, suffering, and communion of the Romanian people with themselves".

On the eve of 1848 Romanian society was in a state of acute effervescence as a result of the unrest of the masses and of the young bourgeoisie who claimed that feudal privileges should be abolished, that the peasants be given land and that conditions be ensured for a free development of capitalism.

In March, 1848, the revolutionary ferment in the two Principalities caused Nesselrode, the Russian chancellor, to bring to the attention of the ruling princes that the Tsar would not permit anarchy to worm its way into "the Ottoman states under his protection". And before long considerable armed forces had been concentrated on the left bank of the Prut. At Jassy an appeal was made calling for the overthrow of Sturdza and the election of a liberal prince. In Wallachia attempts were made to cause "disorders", as Prince Gheorghe Bibescu reported to Kiselev, and a revolutionary programme entitled *What Are Artisans?* was distributed. The programme called for the abolition of boyar privileges, equality of rights, and land for the peasants. The Romanians in Transylvania experienced much anxiety when the Hungarian Diet decided to annex the Principality. Encouraged by the victory of the revolution in Vienna, Simion Bărnuțiu issued a proclamation demanding that a national congress be convened in order to defend Transylvania's autonomy, obtain equality of rights for the Romanians with the other nationalities, and demand that serfdom be abolished. Bărnuțiu's programme reflected the deep unrest of the peasantry who threatened to revolt.

Made anxious by the many meetings held in private houses in Jassy and which consequently could not be controlled, Sturdza allowed the partisans of freedom, among whom were V. Alecsandri, Al. I. Cuza, and Zaharia Moldovanu, to meet at the Petersburg Hotel in the evening of April 8. Some thousand people were present, most of them townspeople from various sections of society, but also many liberal boyars and a number of conservative boyars hostile to Sturdza. After some vehement speeches during which the prince's abusive rule was attacked and freedom eulogized, a committee was elected to draw up a petition to be submitted to the prince for approval and subsequently to be distributed to the people by way of a proclamation.

The petition comprised thirty-five articles, the first being "religious observance of the Règlement" — this in order to give the movement a semblance of legality. Most of the claims were moderate: personal freedom, the organization of the educational system on a national basis in order to spread culture among all the people, ministerial responsibility, irremovability of civil servants, the setting up of a national bank, and public hearings at the tribunals. Although the peasants had not been invited to the Assembly, it was laid down that their condition should be improved speedily, in their relations with the landowners as well as with the administration. It was not specified, however, whether their improved condition also meant their emancipation and the granting of land. The petition also included more radical claims: that political prisoners, civilian or military, should be released; that the Public Assembly should be dissolved and a new Chamber be formed "without the administration influencing the electorate, so that the chamber should really represent the nation"; that the censorship of home news should be abolished and civil guards formed in all towns. The guards were to be "made up of Romanians as well as of foreigners possessing an estate". The realization of these claims would have resulted in the overthrow of the prince. The general moderation shown in the petition is to be accounted for by the fear of the leaders of the revolutionary movement that Tsarist Russia should find it a pretext to occupy the country.

The petition was signed by several hundred people, among them the Metropolitan and a number of ministers who had resigned. In the afternoon of April 10 it was submitted to the prince for approval. Sturdza declared that he could not accept the dissolution of the Public Assembly and civic guards being set up, and when asked whether he could accept the petition as it was, he refused to answer, took refuge in the barracks and ordered the army to put down the rising. The leaders of the movement called upon the people to join in the fight and to raise barricades, but it was too late. Over 300 persons were arrested, some of the boyars were exiled to their country estates or to monasteries and thirteen of the leaders were sent to Galatz under escort to be exiled to Turkey.

Although the movement was suppressed, it was the first step in the Romanian Revolution of 1848. In Moldavia, as well as in Transylvania and Bukovina, the Moldavian revolutionaries supported by the Romanians of Transylvania, Bukovina, and Wallachia, continued their struggle for the overthrow of the feudal system and of Sturdza as well as for the unity of the Romanian countries into a single state.

Although there was great unrest in Wallachia, Ion Ghica and C. A. Rosetti, who had organized the revolt, waited for the return to the country of N. Bălcescu, I. C. Brătianu, and other Wallachians who had participated in the February Revolution in Paris. On their arrival, a revolutionary committee was formed, and Bălcescu proposed that the insurrection should be on April 23. Most of the committee, however, opposed the plan, hoping for assistance from the French revolutionary government and from the Romanians of Transylvania. Some weeks later, the brothers Ştefan and Nicolae Golescu and I. Eliade Rădulescu, with great influence among the rich sections of the bourgeoisie and the liberal boyars, joined the revolutionary committee. A number of officers and of high administrative officials were also members of the conspiracy.

7. The National Assembly at Blaj

AFTER Simion Bărnuţiu had issued his proclamation, Aron Pumnul, a Blaj teacher, in conjunction with Avram Iancu and other young intellectuals, called a meeting of the Transylvanian Romanians at Blaj to claim national and social rights. Despite the opposition of the governor, Teleky, 4,000 peasants assembled at Blaj on April 30 under the leadership of Avram Iancu, Simion Bărnuţiu, Ioan Buteanu, A. Papiu-Ilarian, and other young intellectuals called "tribunes". In his speech Bărnuţiu said that the time had come for serfdom to be abolished and for the Romanians to enjoy all rights. He called for larger numbers to be present at the National Assembly convened in the meantime at Blaj in May. The first Blaj Assembly had paved the way for the revolution in Transylvania. In preparation for the National Assembly, a conference was held at Sibiu between April 26 and May 8 with Timotei Cipariu and August Treboniu Laurian, who had come from Bucharest for the purpose, taking part. The conference approved Simion Bărnuţiu's plan of issuing a proclamation to the Romanian nation, exacting a national oath and protesting against union with Hungary.

Some 40,000 people participated in the National Assembly at Blaj, the overwhelming majority being peasants though there were also many intellectuals, members of the clergy and bourgeoisie as well as some of the gentry. Also present were some Saxon serfs from the villages between the two Tîrnava Rivers with the Saxon scholar Stephan Ludwig Roth at their head. Among the Moldavian refugees were Alecu Russo, Al. I. Cuza, Gheorghe Sion, Lascăr Rosetti, N. Ionescu, and others. Bălcescu was not permitted to come. D. Brătianu came as the representative of the revolutionary committee in Bucharest and Transylvanians residing in Wallachia also turned up. The representative of Banat, Eftimie Murgu, who had been invited to preside over the Assembly, was unable to do so but other intellectuals from Banat and Crișana were present.

On the eve of the appointed date, Sunday, May 14, a conference was held in Blaj Cathedral after the service in order to fix the programme of the Assembly. The three currents that had been formed among the Romanians were : loyalists, who proposed that negotiations be carried on with the Vienna Court — among them the bishops Andrei Șaguna and Ioan Lemeni ; democratic liberals under the guidance of Timotei Cipariu and George Barițiu ; the revolutionary democrats headed by Simion Bărnuțiu, Avram Iancu, and A. Papiu Ilarian. Simion Bărnuțiu's speech was decisive for the orientation of the conference. While welcoming the news of the abolition of serfdom in Hungary, he declared himself against the union of the Principality of Transylvania with the kingdom of Hungary and proposed that the Romanian nation should be recognized in an autonomous Transylvania.

The next day, May 15, the National Assembly opened in the Blaj plain, thereafter named the "Field of Freedom". The two bishops — the Orthodox and the Uniate — were proclaimed presidents while Simion Bărnuțiu and George Barițiu were vice-presidents. On Bărnuțiu's initiative, a motion was passed declaring the Romanian nation "an independent nation" and "an integral part of Transylvania, based on equal freedom". An oath of loyalty to the emperor was taken, as also for the recognition of the Romanian nation and for liberty, equality, and fraternity. Included in the oath was a declaration that they should all "cooperate according to their possibilities, to obtain the abolition of serfdom, freedom for industry and trade, and safeguarding of justice...".

The next day A. T. Laurian submitted to the Assembly for approval a petition of rights — the National Petition — comprising sixteen articles, the most important of which were: independence for the Romanian nation with the right to be represented in the Diet of the country and in public offices proportionate to their number, and with the right to use the Romanian language in legislation; independence for the Romanian Church; abolition of serfdom without the serfs making any payment; freedom of industry and trade and abolition of guilds; freedom of speech, writing, and printing; personal freedom and freedom to meet; the setting up of courts of judge and jury; arms for the people and the establishment of a national guard; salaries for the Romanian clergy; a Romanian educational system of all grades, including a Romanian university; taxation proportionate to one's means and the abolition of privileges; the convening of a Constituent Assembly; postponement of the union with Hungary until an assembly had been convened, where the Romanians should be represented according to their number and the importance of their contribution to public obligations. The Assembly approved the National Petition enthusiastically, it being in keeping with the aspirations of the Romanian people.

A delegation headed by Bishop Andrei Șaguna and the Romanian nobleman Alexe Noptsa (Nopcea) was entrusted with the task of pleading for the national petition before the emperor; and the Uniate Bishop Ioan Lemeni, the only Romanian in the Diet, was entrusted with the task of demanding that the Cluj Diet postpone the question of Transylvania's union with Hungary until a Diet had been convened in which the Romanians should be represented proportionately to their importance. A permanent Romanian National Committee was formed at Sibiu. On the third day a protocol was passed and the first Romanian national guard was set up.

The Blaj National Assembly established the programme of the Romanian revolution in Transylvania. It rejected the union with Hungary and, as Bălcescu reported, the people clamoured : "We want to unite with the country", that is with Wallachia, for the Romanians had always called Wallachia the Romanian Country *(Țara Românească)*. Carol Szasz, the commissar of the Hungarian government, showed in his report that the Transylvanian Romanians were anxious to unite with Wallachia and Moldavia.

The delegation headed by Andrei Șaguna did not obtain the sanction of the National Petition from Emperor Ferdinand, for the latter had approved the April Laws which included the union of Transylvania with Hungary. Nor could Lemeni prevent the Transylvanian Diet from passing the union so that in early June Transylvania was considered by the imperial authorities as part of the kingdom of Hungary. The April Laws, which provided for the abolition of serfdom, were also being applied on the territory of what had been the Principality of Transylvania, despite the resistance of the Magyar nobility. This brought about armed conflicts of a social as well as of a national nature, for most peasants were Romanians while the overwhelming majority of the landowners were Hungarian. The Romanians did not recognize Transylvania's union with Hungary for it had been voted by a Diet where they had a single representative, Ioan Lemeni.

The Romanians in Banat as well as those in Crișana and Maramureș — outlying districts of the Transylvanian Principality, so-called Partium Districts depending on the kingdom of Hungary — fought for the national freedom as demanded by the Blaj Assembly. The Lugoj Assembly of June 27 decided that the people should immediately be armed and Eftimie Murgu be appointed as great captain of the people's army of Banat. Elected deputy in the Caraș County, Eftimie Murgu upheld this decision in the Budapest Diet, but Kossuth rejected it vehemently.

8. The Moldavian Revolutionaries Evolve a New Programme

AFTER the defeat of the March movement, the National Party in Moldavia continued its struggle by means of memorials and lampoons, with the aim of overthrowing the Sturdza administration. At Jassy a secret committee was formed which acted in close connection with the revolutionary leaders who had taken refuge in Transylvania and had removed to Cernăuți in Bukovina in June.

On May 24 a group of Moldavian revolutionaries drew up at Brașov a programme more radical than the one adopted in March. It was called "Our Principles for Reforming the Homeland", and provided for the abolition of feudal servitudes : land to the peasants without payment ; abolition of boyar privileges and equality before the law ; the union of Moldavia and Wallachia "into a single independent Romanian State". The programme was influenced by the National Petition which had been passed by the Blaj National Assembly. When the revolution broke out in Wallachia the Moldavian exiles, who had formed a Moldavian Revolutionary Committee at Cernăuți, contacted the Wallachian revolutionaries through the agency of I. Alecsandri, brother of the poet of the same name, and elected an Executive Committee to which Costache Negri and Al. I. Cuza also belonged. Under the influence of revolutionary propaganda, the peasant upsurge in Moldavia intensified and might have turned into a revolution if the Russian army had not occupied Jassy on July 10.

Being shadowed by the administration, M. Kogălniceanu crossed the frontier into Bukovina where he drew up a draft constitution and at the end of August published a new revolutionary programme : "Wishes of the National Party of Moldavia". He had been entrusted with the task by the Moldavian Revolutionary Committee. The programme demanded full autonomy for the country, equality in civic and political rights, a public assembly made up of the representatives of all estates, a prince elected by all the estates, responsibility exacted from the ministers and civil servants, freedom of the Press, all meetings of the Public Assembly and of the tribunals to be held in public, the country's representatives at Constantinople to be Romanians, individual freedom and inviolability of the home, equal access to education for all Romanians, with schools free of charge, civil guards in town and countryside, courts of judge and jury for issues of the Press and for political and criminal cases, abolition of the death penalty and of corporal punishment, irremovability of judges, religious freedom, political rights for all citizens irrespective of race and religion, secularization of the estates of the monasteries dedicated to religious institutions in other countries, councils controlling the administration in the provinces, towns and villages, abolition of ranks and privileges, general contribution to public obligations, abolition of slavery, abolition of the peasants' feudal obligations, land to be given to all peasants against payment. And over and above these reforms — the union of Moldavia and Wallachia, considered as the "keystone, failing which the whole national edifice would have collapsed".

9. The Islaz Proclamation. The Progress of the Revolution

IN May, 1848, the Revolutionary Committee in Bucharest worked out a programme and a proclamation to the people and elected an Executive Committee made up of N. Bălcescu, I. Ghica, and A. G. Golescu. Later, Ghica having been sent to Constantinople to convince the Porte that the revolution was not directed against it, C. A. Rosetti was elected to replace him. As decided by the Committee, the revolution broke out at Islaz in the

Romanați county on June 21. Eliade Rădulescu, Golescu, and Tell launched a call, and a numerous assembly, mostly made up of peasants, heard the revolutionary programme, which called for equal taxation, an assembly with all classes of society represented, a prince responsible before the law and elected for a term of five years (actually a president of a republic), ministerial responsibility before the law, freedom of the Press, the right for every county to elect its administrators, a national guard, secularization of the monasteries dedicated to religious institutions abroad, emancipation of the dependent peasants and the granting of land to them against payment (article 13, considered as the main claim of the revolution by Bălcescu), freedom for the gypsy slaves, free access to education, abolition of the ranks without any offices attached to them, abolition of corporal punishment and of the death sentence, rights for the Jews and political rights for all citizens without discrimination in regard to race and faith. Without demanding the country's independence, the Islaz Programme laid down that it was to enjoy full administrative and legislative autonomy. The programme rejected the Russian protectorate and the interference of "any foreign power in internal affairs", and demanded that the country's representative at Constantinople should be a Romanian. The whole of Oltenia came under the leadership of the revolutionaries.

In Bucharest the insurrection was fixed for June 22 at dawn but did not take place owing to the arrest in the afternoon of the preceding day of many revolutionary leaders following an unsuccessful attempt upon the life of Gh. Bibescu. The following day, under the pressure of thousands of townspeople and of peasants from the neighbouring villages, Gh. Bibescu sanctioned the programme of the revolution and accepted the ministerial cabinet forced upon him, with the exception of Chr. Tell as head of the army, the latter being replaced by Colonel Ion Odobescu.

After two days' reign on the terms forced upon him by the revolution, intimidated by the protest of Kotzebue, the Russian consul, Gh. Bibescu abdicated and left for Braşov. The Wallachian revolutionaries organized a provisional government on June 26. On June 27 the government and a great crowd took the oath of loyalty to the Revolutionary Programme, in the Filaret Plain, thenceforward named the *Plain of Freedom*.

Dissension arose within the government when the programme came to be implemented. Dissatisfied with the prominent part played by I. Eliade Rădulescu and Chr. Tell, the radical liberals C. A. Rosetti and I. C. Brătianu resigned. On the other hand, Bălcescu and A. G. Golescu were disconcerted by the delay of the peasantry's liberation and their coming into possession of land. The landowners, with the co-operation of Colonels Ion Odobescu and Ion Solomon organized a counter-revolutionary *coup d'état* on July 1. Most of the government members were arrested at their offices on the Mogoşoaia Road, but a forceful gathering of the people released them, arresting the two traitor colonels and Major Locusteanu, their accomplice.

A few days later a rumour spread that a Russian army had crossed the Prut and was making for Bucharest. In the evening of July 10, the government decided to withdraw northward to Rucăr to oppose the invaders with the support of the Transylvanians. Metropolitan Neofit remained in Bucharest and together with boyars Theodor Văcărescu and Emanoil Băleanu formed a government and re-established the régime of the *Règlement Organique*. The arrested officers were released and resorted to their posts. Because of the protest of the other European powers Russia withdrew her troops to the other side of the Prut and I. C. Brătianu, one of the secretaries of the provisional government, aroused the people of Bucharest, overthrew the boyar government, and called back the revolutionary government from Rucăr.

On June 26 with the programme of the revolution already beginning to be put into effect, the death penalty and corporal punishment were abolished, as also were the boyar ranks and the censorship, the political detainees were released, and new administrators were appointed in five counties of Oltenia and later in other counties.

On July 8 the government issued a decision proclaiming the gypsy slaves free and set up a committee to see that this decision was enforced. In order to make fundamental reforms a constituent assembly had to be convened. The assembly was not convened owing to the divergences that arose concerning the representation of the various classes as well as to the foreign threat.

In May, 1848, when Talaat Efendi stopped in Bucharest on his way to Jassy, the moderate liberals handed him a memorial with a number of proposals, among which was the wish of the Moldavians and Wallachians to merge into a single state. In support of this idea, *Pruncul Român* launched an appeal, "To our brothers in Moldavia", and *Poporul Suveran* published the article "Moldavia's Union with Wallachia", which described the union of Moldavia with Wallachia as "one of the main problems". Agents were sent to Moldavia to rouse the people to revolt and to demand union with Wallachia.

On July 6, the revolutionary government decreed that commissars recruited from among the radical intelligentsia would be sent about the country to explain the revolutionary programme and to incite the peasantry to support the cause of the revolution. Many of the commissars were Transylvanians who considered the revolution in Wallachia as part of the general Romanian revolution.

In order to strengthen the revolutionary movement, the provisional government contacted the Porte and the revolutionary governments in the other European countries. Before the outbreak of the revolution, Ion Ghica had been sent to Constantinople to win the support of the Porte for the revolutionary programme. He sought to persuade the Porte that it was in its own interest to strengthen the economic and political power of the Principalities. Dimitrie Brătianu was sent to establish co-operation between the Hungarian and the Romanian revolutionary movements but failed in his purpose. Later A. G. Golescu went to Transylvania with full powers to represent the revolution in Central as well as in Western Europe, and was subsequently appointed diplomatic agent to the French government. I. Maiorescu was sent to the German parliament in Frankfurt as representative of the two Principalities. Thus did the Romanian diplomatic agents bring the Romanian revolution and the cause of the Romanian people generally to the attention of the main European states.

10. The Revolution Fails in Wallachia

THE Wallachian revolution had carried the day inside the country. The counter-revolutionary boyars, however, demanded support from the Porte and Russia. But the Porte had been persuaded by Ion Ghica, supported by the Polish emigrants and the British and French ambassadors, not to regard the Wallachian revolution with hostility. On the other hand, a Tsarist army marched into Moldavia and prepared to occupy Wallachia. In order to check the advance of the Russian armies, the Porte sent Suleiman Pasha to Wallachia with an army to re-establish order. After prolonged negotiations, the provisional government on August 9 agreed to be superseded by a triumvirate committee given the name of "Regency". Made up of I. Eliade Rădulescu, Chr. Tell, and N. Golescu, all three moderate liberals, the Regency declared that it would submit all the changes made from June 23 on to the Sultan for approval. Suleiman Pasha declared himself satisfied, recognized the Regency and came to Bucharest on a short visit. The consuls of the European states resumed their official relations with

Wallachia, which had been interrupted since the inception of the revolution. In order to consolidate the present state of affairs, a delegation, which included Bălcescu, was sent to Constantinople to submit the reforms to the Sultan for approval.

The Tsarist government protested and demanded that another commissar be sent to Bucharest. The Sultan did not receive the Wallachian delegation and ordered Fuad Efendi to take an army to Bucharest and reinstate the *Règlement Organique*. The Regency invested Gh. Magheru with extraordinary powers and sent a large part of the army to Rîureni to put up armed resistance in Oltenia in the event of Fuad Efendi occupying Bucharest.

On September 25, 1848, the Ottoman army reached the outskirts of Bucharest. Fuad Efendi summoned 200 leaders of the country to Cotroceni and read a proclamation branding the revolution as a "rebellion" sprung from the spirit of "communism" and informing them that the *Règlement* had been re-established. Bălcescu protested that the rights of the country had been infringed upon, and the revolutionaries cried : "Death rather than the *Règlement*". Fuad Efendi ordered the arrest of the protesters, some of whom were eventually exiled. The leaders of the revolution, sent up the Danube beyond Orșova, succeeded in making their escape and reaching Banat.

On September 25 the Ottoman army entered Bucharest. One of its columns advancing up the Spirea Hill came up against a firefighting company strengthened by an army detachment. In the clash that followed there were many casualties on both sides. Eliade Rădulescu and Chr. Tell fled to Transylvania where they were followed by numerous revolutionaries. The Russian commissar, Duhamel, who had joined Fuad Efendi, ordered the Russian army to march into Wallachia. With the co-operation of the occupants and of the reactionary boyars, Constantine Cantacuzino re-established the régime of the *Règlement*.

In Oltenia, Magheru having determined to oppose the invading armies, maintained the revolutionary régime for another fortnight, but Eliade Rădulescu and Chr. Tell, who had reached Sibiu by that time, sent word not to oppose the two foreign armies far superior in number. The British consul in Bucharest, R. Colquhoun, gave advice to the same effect. Magheru accepted their decision, dissolved the camp in Trajan's Field on October 10, 1848, and withdrew to Transylvania with a number of officers, thus ending the revolutionary struggle which had began on June 21, 1848 in Wallachia. The new régime set up by the foreign armies, as well as the orders issued by Constantine Cantacuzino, came up against the staunch resistance of the peasants who refused to perform labour service.

11. The Revolution in Transylvania Continues

AFTER Transylvania was incorporated within Hungary, feudal servitude was abolished in both Hungary and Transylvania. The administration, however, continued to be in the hands of the Magyar and Saxon nobility, and the Romanians who did not recognize Transylvania's union with Hungary were subjected to a reign of terror. In August, A. T. Laurian and N. Bălcescu, both on the Romanian National Committee, were arrested by the Magyar authorities. Simion Bărnuțiu could only escape their fate by seeking the protection of the First Frontier Guards' Regiment. Soon after, the First and Second Frontier Guards' Regiments, made up of Romanians, refused to take orders from the War Ministry in Budapest. The Romanian National Committee convened a new assembly at Blaj, which was in session for ten days, from September 15 to 25, 1848. This time the Romanians who came to the assembly were armed with lances and hayforks and some of them with guns. There were over 20,000, mostly peasants, and their leaders — Avram Iancu, Axente Sever, and Iovian Brad — formed them into a military unit. Simion Bărnuțiu, August Treboniu Laurian, and A. Papiu Ilarian joined the Assembly on the last day. A new resolution was passed protesting against Transylvania's union with Hungary and demanding that a diet and a provisional government should be elected, with Romanians represented proportionately to their number. It was also demanded that an end be put to the pressure exercised upon the peasants to force them to do farm labour for the benefit of the nobility. A memorial was sent to the liberal parliament in Vienna seeking support for the Romanians' claims and for the Principalities. In October the armed struggle for the removal of Magyar administration began in Transylvania : fifteen Romanian legions had been formed, each under the command of a prefect and vice-prefect. When war broke out between Hungary and Austria the Romanians demanded arms and officers of General Puchner, the imperial military commander in Transylvania, but their claims were only partly met. Nevertheless, the Romanian legions — an army of peasants supported by the Frontier Guards' Regiments — defeated the Magyar National Guards who were sustained and influenced by the Transylvanian nobility. Saxon peasants from the district between the Tîrnava rivers fought alongside the Romanians under the leadership of Stephan Ludwig Roth. In October the Szeklers held a meeting at Lutița, following which they took up arms against the imperial forces. The most powerful resistance was organized by Aron Gabor in the Trei Scaune district, which remained under Szekler administration. In the Romanian districts that had been liberated a Romanian administration was established. The Romanian National Committee in Sibiu was considered to be the real government of the country. Late in December, the Romanians followed Bălcescu's prompting and a meeting in Sibiu proposed that a Romanian principality should be created out of all the Romanian districts in the Habsburg Empire, including Bukovina.

When General Puchner occupied Cluj he ordered the return of all the guns he had distributed, threatening to use his cannons against the Romanian legions if his order was not obeyed. It was obvious that not only the Magyar nobility but also the House of Habsburg were against the Romanians in their desire for national and social freedom. In the meantime the Magyar revolutionary government had sent an army to Transylvania under the command of the Polish General Joseph Bem. The latter had come to Hungary with other Polish emigrants hoping to subdue Transylvania and then go to Poland to liberate his own country. Having defeated the poorly equipped Romanian legions and the few imperial troops at Ciucea on December 25, Bem conquered Cluj, where he advised the Romanians and Saxons to accept the Magyar authority, and gave an amnesty. He obtained new recruits for his army, especially Szeklers, and by March, 1849, had occupied the greater part of Transylvania. Alba Iulia and the district of the Western Mountains remained under the Romanians' rule with Avram Iancu as leader. When the town of Sibiu had been conquered, the Romanian National Committee and many other Romanian revolutionaries took refuge in Wallachia where eighty of them, including Simion Bărnuțiu and later also George Barițiu, were under arrest for a few weeks. A delegation of Romanians from Transylvania, the Banat and Bukovina under Andrei Șaguna went to Olmütz in Moravia to submit to Emperor Francis Joseph a memorial proposing that all Romanian districts in the Habsburg Empire be united into a single autonomous principality. Francis Joseph promised to keep count of the Romanians' claims, but the constitution of March 4, 1849 only recognized the Romanian's national existence without creating a state for them.

Bem's amnesty was not observed. As the Magyar army advanced southwards, punitive expeditions were organized and "blood tribunals" were set up.

12. Romanian Revolutionary Resistance in the Western Mountains

IN April, 1849, Bem took his forces to Banat where a mass uprising of the Romanian peasants had dislodged the Magyar local authorities from August to October, 1848. He conquered the towns of Caransebeș and Lugoj and later Mehadia but could not take Timișoara. In the Western Mountains, where many Central Transylvanian peasants had taken refuge, the Romanians continued to resist successfully under Avram Iancu's command against the numerous Magyar detachments which had encircled them.

As the imperial armies were advancing, the Magyar parliament and government removed to Debreczen, where on April 14 the Habsburgs were proclaimed dethroned and Hungary to be independent. Kossuth was appointed governor of the Hungarian kingdom. Intent on concentrating all his forces against the Austrian armies, Kossuth determined to sweep away the Romanian resistance in the Western Mountains. He delegated the Romanian deputy Ioan Dragoș to persuade the Romanians to lay down their arms, but the latter would only accept a truce and refused to allow the Hungarian soldiers within their mountain stronghold.

While negotiations with Dragoș were in progress, the Magyar commander Hatvani attacked the Romanians by surprise and occupied Abrud in the evening of May 6. In the days that followed he was compelled to withdraw, suffering great losses. A week later Hatvani again attacked the Romanians and occupied Abrud but two days later was again defeated. The two attacks cost the Hungarians some 5,000 men. In May and June heavy fighting continued in the Western Mountains, but neither Colonel Kemeny's forces nor those of Paul Vasvari succeeded in defeating the resistance of Avram Iancu's men (the Moți, residing in the Western Mountains). The divergence between the Magyar and the Romanian revolutions in Transylvania, fostered by the mistakes of the Magyar revolutionary government who refused to recognize the Romanians' right to self-determination, as well as by the partly well-founded suspicions of the Romanian leaders and by the manoeuvres of the Vienna Court, caused considerable harm to both revolutionary movements. The Romanian revolutionaries of Transylvania, as well as the Wallachians Bălcescu, Ghica and Cezar Bolliac, endeavoured to co-operate with the Hungarian revolutionaries. Bălcescu went to Debreczen and discussed with Kossuth the problem of the relations between the Romanian and the Hungarian revolutionaries, but it was only on July 12, 1849, that Kossuth agreed to sign at Szegedin the *Pacification Project* and the treaty whereby a Romanian legion was formed. On July 28, 1849, the Magyar Lower Chamber passed a bill recognizing the national rights of the Romanians and Slavs in Hungary. On Bălcescu's advice, Avram Iancu agreed not to attack the Magyar army as long as the latter was fighting the counter-revolutionary forces of Austria and Russia. In his turn, Kossuth issued a decree whereby the Magyar army was to cease fighting the Romanians. But it came too late. Some days later, on August 13, 1849, General Görgei, commander of the Magyar forces, surrendered to the Habsburg and Tsarist armies at Șiria. The Romanians in the Western Mountains were compelled to lay down their arms when the imperial forces penetrated into Transylvania. The revolution had come to an end in Transylvania.

Although the revolution had been suppressed, it induced the House of Habsburg and the Magyar government to recognize the national existence of the Romanians in Transylvania.

13. Importance of the Romanian Revolution of 1848

ON the whole, the Romanian revolution of 1848-9 was a bourgeois revolution for its programme tended to consolidate capitalist relationships in the three Romanian Principalities. The programme included radical claims of interest to the masses, especially the granting of land to the peasants and a wider franchise. Such claims, as also the participation of the masses of townspeople and peasants in the revolutionary struggle, invested the revolution with a democratic character.

From the national point of view, the Romanian revolution of 1848-9 made it its aim to unite Moldavia and Wallachia into an independent state, to have the Romanians of Transylvania recognized as a nation and thereafter to unite all the Romanian districts in the Habsburg Empire into an autonomous principality. A more far-reaching aim was the creation of one Romanian state.

The revolutionary forces had achieved a stage of maturity great enough to defeat the counter-revolutionary resistance inside the country but they were unable to repel the armed intervention of the three reactionary empires of Europe.

In historical perspective, the Romanian revolution was the most advanced eastern outpost of the European revolution of 1848, and part of that revolution. It helped to spread the principles of the bourgeois revolution in South-east Europe.

CHAPTER ELEVEN

THE UNION OF THE TWO PRINCIPALITIES AND THE WAY IN WHICH THEY ACHIEVED THEIR INDEPENDENCE

DESPITE the military occupation of nearly three years' duration, the Principalities made great strides in all fields of activity after the revolution of 1848. The national movement advocating union of the Principalities was strengthened. The bourgeoisie increased in number and gave decisive support to the struggle for a national state. Apart from their militant activities inside the country, the revolutionary emigrants spread their propaganda in the capital cities of Europe, succeeding in winning the sympathy of liberal circles and making the cause of the union of the Principalities an integral part of the European movement for the emancipation of the oppressed peoples. During the Crimean War the union of the Principalities became a factor in the European balance of power. The Treaty of Paris, under which the Russian protectorate was superseded by the joint guarantee of the Great Powers, did not bring about the union of the Principalities, which was left for the Romanians to do. When in 1859 Al. I. Cuza was elected as Prince of the two Principalities, the Romanian people achieved their unity, which was consolidated by 1862. The representatives of the Romanian people then created the institutions of a modern state, while the land reform of 1864 turned all dependent peasants into free citizens. Cuza's deposition was partly due to the activities of the boyars expropriated under the land reform.

In Transylvania the laws of 1853 and 1854 made of the dependent peasants free owners of the holdings they used. Under the "Liberal Empire" which recognized the autonomy of its provinces, the election of 1863 gave the Romanians of Transylvania a relative majority of the mandates so that reforms favouring their development were made. Nevertheless, faced with the obstructions of the Magyar nobility and affected by its defeat, the Imperial Cabinet abandoned the cause of the Romanians and left it to the mercy of Hungary.

1. Development of the Romanian Countries after the Revolution of 1848

AFTER the revolution of 1848 was put down, the economy of the three Romanian countries expanded at a more lively tempo owing to the development of capitalist methods of production.

Though serfdom was abolished in Hungary and Transylvania by the laws of April, 1848, the problem of giving land to the former serfs was left in abeyance and was only solved by the patents of 1853 and 1854, when the rulers were compelled to apply the laws of 1848 and to give the peasants titles of property to their holdings.

New relationships between peasants and landowners were enforced in the two Romanian Principalities by the Porte and the Tsarist government under the Convention of Balta Liman of May 1, 1849, the aim being to forestall a new uprising of the peasantry. The land laws worked out by the committees that revised the *Règlement Organique* were approved in 1851 and applied in 1852. Under them the peasants were considered as free tenants while the boyars were owners of the land. The peasants' right to change their place of habitation was still restricted. Venal officials were removed from office in Wallachia and the tithe in kind was abolished in Moldavia; labour service was defined and the peasants were given access to new pasture grounds for their cattle.

Farming made notable strides, some of the landowners and big lessees even using machinery. As a result of the increase in manpower, cattle, and improved implements and machines, the agricultural output, particularly wheat, rose considerably. Wallachia's exports, which consisted mainly of wheat, went up from 76,310.38 lei in 1850 to 164,135.10 lei in 1852, further to rise to 177,010,800.20 lei by 1855.

The increase in farm products stimulated the growth of industry, more vigorously in Transylvania where there was an old industrial tradition, and more slowly in the two Principalities. Although the competition of the more developed regions of the Empire hindered an intensive expansion of Transylvanian industry, the mining industry excepted, Transylvania nevertheless progressed owing to the markets the two Romanian Principalities offered.

Economic expansion extended the home market, which brought about an increase in town population. In 1860 Bucharest, the most important town in the territory inhabited by the Romanian people, had a population of 121,734, Jassy had 65,745 inhabitants, and the less important towns under 30,000.

In order to prevent fresh disturbances in the Principalities, the suzerain and the protecting courts concluded the Convention of Balta Liman on May 1, 1849. The princes were no longer to be appointed for life but only for a term of seven years. The appointment was to be made by the Sultan after having reached an understanding with the Tsar. The Ordinary and the Extraordinary Public Assemblies were to be superseded by Divans *ad hoc* made up of boyars and members of the high clergy appointed by the ruling prince. The *Règlement* was to be revised. The Ottoman and the Russian armies remained in the Principalities until 1851. Grigore Al. Ghica was appointed Prince of Moldavia and Barbu Știrbei of Wallachia. Both princes made it their aim to improve public administration, the communication system, the educational system, and the army.

After the revolution, the Principality of Transylvania once again became a distinct administrative unit, depending directly on the imperial government in Vienna. Banat was united with the Serbian Voevodina to form a province whose capital city was Timișoara. Crișana remained part of Hungary, while Bukovina became a Grand Duchy depending on Vienna direct. The project of the national committee to unite all the Romanian territories of the Empire into one single principality was never realized.

The constitution issued by Francis Joseph on March 4, 1849, was abrogated in 1851, when a so-called neo-absolutist régime was installed. The administration was controlled by the Vienna government which carried on a policy of centralization and Germanization.

The national claims of the Romanians of Transylvania were not satisfied, and neither were some of their socio-economic claims, such as the claims of the peasants of the Western Mountains to the forests and pasture land. These claims had been upheld by Avram Iancu. The revolutionary leaders continued their struggle for the implementation of the programme worked out in 1848. Exiled or having emigrated, most of them had gathered in Paris, Brussels, and Vienna where they carried on rewarding and intensive activities in favour of the reforms for which they had fought in 1848, with emphasis on the union of the Romanian countries.

2. Struggle for the Union during the Crimean War

IN the summer of 1853 Moldavia and Wallachia were occupied by the Russian armies. France and Britain formed an alliance with Turkey and declared war on Russia. The Crimean War was to make of the union of the Principalities a problem on which the balance of power in Europe depended. In the autumn of 1853 and up to the spring of the following year the Russians and Turks fought each other along the Danube. The Romanian exiles taking advantage of this state of war sought to stir the people to revolt in Oltenia.

Following the Turco-Austrian Convention of June 14, 1854, the Principalities were evacuated by Russia and occupied by the Austrians who remained in occupation until March, 1857, during which time their investments in these countries show that they regarded the territory as their own. In October, 1854, Barbu Ştirbei and Grigore Al. Ghica were re-instated on the thrones of Wallachia and Moldavia, where they reigned under the occupation of the Austrian armies until the end of their seven-year term of office.

Believing that the European revolution on which they had pinned their hopes of union was not possible in the near future, the Romanian exiles in the summer of 1854 approached Napoleon III, Emperor of France, the British government and Cavour, Prime Minister of Sardinia, asking them to declare that Moldavia and Wallachia should be united into a single state under a foreign prince, which to them meant independence. Their demand was upheld by many progressive personalities in Europe, who considered that a Romanian national state would be a factor of progress in South-east Europe.

At the Congress of Paris, which ended the Crimean War, Count Walewski, foreign minister of France, proposed that the Principalities should be united under a foreign prince, and he was supported by Britain, Prussia, Russia, and Sardinia. The strong opposition of Austria and the Porte compelled the Congress to propose that the population of the two Principalities should first be consulted on the subject of union and that special assemblies should be constituted for the purpose. A European commission was formed to find out what the population desired. The Congress also decided that Russia's protectorate should be superseded by the joint guarantee of the great powers, that South Bessarabia should be joined to Moldavia, a commission of the Danube riparian states should be set up, in addition to a commission for the dredging of the Danube from Isaccea to where the Sulina arm joins the sea so that high tonnage vessels could navigate the river.

In order to encourage the movement favouring the union, Grigore Ghica enacted a liberal Press law and appointed partisans of the union to the main state offices. The movement favouring the union was openly organized. At Socola not far from Jassy a Union Society was set up on June 6, 1856, with a membership of bourgeois, liberal boyars, and moderate conservative boyars. The purpose of the society was to co-ordinate the action for the union of the Principalities under a foreign prince. A few days after, a union committee was set up in Jassy which sent delegates to the capital cities of the various districts in order to make up similar union committees. The delegates were welcomed enthusiastically everywhere so that the union movement assumed a mass character.

Austria and Turkey, soon joined by Britain, bent their efforts at Constantinople on preventing the inclusion of the union problem in the edict *(firman)* convening the *Ad Hoc* Assemblies. Their efforts were of no avail owing to France's opposition. They used the complicity of Toderiță Balș and Nicolae Vogoride, the *Caimacams (Prince Lieutenants)*, to forge the election lists so as to ensure the victory of the anti-union party.

At the same time the pro-union Press was suspended and a fierce persecution of the pro-union people began.

In Wallachia, the Porte appointed as Caimacam the former prince who reigned while the *Règlement Organique* was in force : Alexandru Ghica. The latter sought the support of the richest section of the bourgeoisie, supported the pro-union movement, and allowed the moderate emigrants to return to the country.

3. The Ad Hoc Assemblies

IN the first half of March, 1857, after the Austrian troops had withdrawn from the Principalities, the European Commission arrived in Bucharest.

Vogoride continued his persecution of the pro-unionists, arresting them and resorting to terror, deleting the names of those who were declared, or suspected, unionists from the election lists, and preventing them from sitting for public office and from casting their vote. The National Party protested to the European Commission and made pro-union demonstrations when the Commissioners came from Jassy to investigate. Al. I. Cuza, prefect of Galatz, refused to carry out the order to rig the election, and resigned his office, thus creating a sensation. The pro-unionists published in the West compromising correspondence between the Caimacam and his relations and the Vizir and decided to boycott the election.

Vogoride, ignoring the protests, carried through the election, which having been manipulated resulted in an anti-union majority. The powers supporting the union — France, Russia, Sardinia, and Prussia — demanded that the Porte should cancel the election but the latter, supported by Austria and Britain, refused. As a result, on August 5, the pro-union powers severed diplomatic relations with the Porte. In order to avert the danger of a European war, and perhaps of a revolution, Napoleon III accompanied by Walewski met Queen Victoria, Lord Palmerston, the British Prime Minister, and Lord Clarendon, the Foreign Secretary, at Osborne House on August 6. A compromise was reached after three days' talks. Great Britain agreed to convince the Porte to cancel the election and to revise the election lists, and France agreed to give up the plan of a union of the Principalities under a foreign prince.

Pressed by the British government, the Porte cancelled the election. The election was then carried out with untampered election lists and gave a complete victory to the National Party. All the leaders of the pro-union movement were returned, among them M. Kogălniceanu, V. Mălinescu, Costache Negri, A. I. Cuza, and Anastase Panu. In Wallachia it was the most important of the exiles who were returned : C. A. Rosetti, I. C. Brătianu, Şt. and N. Golescu, and Chr. Tell, who were allowed to enter the country late in June, 1857, and also Gh. Magheru and A. G. Golescu.

At the *Ad Hoc* Assembly in Moldavia, Kogălniceanu, as spokesman of the National Party, submitted a proposal in which it was pointed out that "the first, the greatest, most general and most national wishes of the country" were : 1. autonomy ; 2. union of the Principalities in a state bearing the name of Romania ; 3. a foreign hereditary prince ; 4. neutrality of the territory of the Principalities ; 5. a public assembly "where all the interests of the nation should be represented". Only two of the 83 deputies declared against the union of the two countries. The other 81 voted enthusiastically for Kogălniceanu's proposal.

In Wallachia the *Ad Hoc* Assembly unanimously passed a proposal which included all the points of the Moldavian resolution, this being proof of the perfect unity of views of the pro-unionists in the two Principalities.

As regards internal organization, the *Ad Hoc* Assembly in Wallachia considered that the problem should be postponed until after union had been effected. The deputies of the peasantry demanded that the peasants should be represented in the future legislative assembly. The Moldavian *Ad Hoc* Assembly debated upon the more important problems of internal organization, which if liberal reforms had been made, would have modernized the whole structure of the state. The solutions advocated were : assurance of personal freedom, equality before the laws and in regard to taxation, abolition of consular jurisdiction, re-organization of the army, freedom of religion, and independence of the Romanian Orthodox Church.

The deputies of the peasantry, considering the programme of reforms incomplete, submitted a proposal to the assembly in which, after pointing out that the peasants bore most of the public burden and were oppressed, demanded rights equal to those of the other citizens, abolition of corporal punishment, of the labour service for the administration, and of capitation, the right to elect village officials, abolition of the farming work due to the boyars for which they agreed to pay, the granting of land "up to two-thirds of the estate", and representation in the public assembly. The overwhelming majority of the *Ad Hoc* Assembly rejected the claims of the peasantry.

At the end of 1857 the Guaranteeing Powers agreed that the Porte should close the *Ad Hoc* Assemblies. The European Commission drew up a report to the Conference of the Guaranteeing Powers which included the conclusions drawn from the proceedings of the Assemblies and from other information, proposing the re-organization of the Principalities on a bourgeois basis and making known the vote of the *Ad Hoc* Assemblies in favour of the union.

4. The Convention of Paris

THE report of the European Commission was discussed by the Paris Conference in accordance with the directions of the treaty of 1856 (22 May-19 August 1858). Based on that report, the Conference passed a convention on the international and internal status of the Principalities.

The demand for the union of the two Principalities into one state was not satisfied. It was decided that they should be united under the name of the United Principalities of Moldavia and Wallachia. Full autonomy of the Principalities was, however, recognized under the joint guarantee of the seven signatory powers. The Sultan's suzerainty was maintained but the Porte was not entitled to send armed forces to the Principalities unless "disturbances" arose, and this could be done only with the agreement of the signatory powers. But the treaties the Ottoman Empire concluded with other states also bound the Principalities "in everything which did not infringe their immunities". Each Principality was to be ruled by an elected prince and by an elective assembly. At Focșani a Central Commission was to be set up for the purpose of working out the draft laws of common interest, which, however, only became laws after they had been approved by the two elective assemblies. Each elected a prince for life, whose father was to be Moldavian or Wallachian and who must have an income of three thousand gold ducats from his estate. With the exception of the laws of local interest, all the legislation was to be common to both Principalities, which were to have one single Court of Justice and of Cassation. The armies of the two countries were each to have a flag with a blue stripe in token of unity. The Moldavians and Wallachians were equal before the law and could be admitted to public functions in either Principality. This made it possible for the Principalities to elect the same prince.

In accordance with the decisions of the Paris Conference, at the end of October, 1858, three Caimacams were appointed in each Principality : Ștefan Catargiu, Vasile Sturdza and Anastase Panu in Moldavia, and Emanoil Băleanu, Ioan Manu, and I. Al. Filipescu in Wallachia.

5. Election of Alexandru Ioan Cuza in the Two Principalities

THE three Moldavian Caimacams were in favour of the union, but Ștefan Catargiu was bent on becoming prince at any cost. The election for the Elective Assembly took place in December.

Six of the sixty deputies who had been elected were invalidated and one — Costache Negri — resigned as he could not agree with the moderate conservatives in the National Party. Together with the Metropolitan, who was deputy by right, there were now 54 deputies, 31 of them belonging to the National Party and the others supporting the group of Grigore Sturdza or of his father, Mihail Sturdza. The success of the National Party appeared to be certain but at least five unionists stood for the dignity of prince without having asked the approval of the Party. Among the five were Lascăr Catargiu, M. Kogălniceanu, and Costache Negri, upheld by friends to oppose Lascăr Catargiu. Early in January, 1859, the deputies of the National Party met in the Natural Sciences Museum in order to establish who the one candidate should be. It was considered that he should be either M. Kogălniceanu or Lascăr Catargiu. The former was not accepted by the moderate conservatives on account of his democratic views, the latter was rejected by the democratic and the radical liberals, as he was known to oppose liberalism and the giving of land to the peasants. When Kogălniceanu left, the unionists finally declared Colonel Alexandru Ioan

(Alexander John) Cuza, the commander of the army, as sole candidate of the National Party. Cuza was not present and nobody had thought of him until then. Cuza was still under forty, his somewhat scanty education had ended in failure to graduate at the Sorbonne, and according to R.W. Seton-Watson, his private morals were far from exemplary. "Nor did his early career suggest any high standard of political integrity. As a member of the 'Young Moldavia' group, he had been mixed up in the movement of 1848, and it is interesting to note that curiosity had brought him to the Field of Liberty at Blaj... He was a well-meaning man, a keen Romanian patriot, with an all too thin veneer of liberalism, but self-indulgent, weak, an easy prey to favourites and parasites, lacking in experience, resources and method. He is reported to have greeted his election with the phrase, 'Gentlemen, I fear you will not be satisfied with me'."

The election of Cuza aroused great enthusiasm among the crowds awaiting the result of the vote, for the newly elected prince voiced the people's will to freedom and progress. Cuza was later elected Prince of Wallachia. After his election as Prince of Wallachia, Cuza intended to proclaim in Bucharest the complete union of the Principalities but refrained on account of the cautious attitude of France and the reserved attitude of Russia. The Porte considered that the election had gone against the provisions of the Paris Convention and in this was supported by Austria. In order to get the election recognized, Cuza sent the Moldavian Foreign Minister, V. Alecsandri, to seek the backing of Napoleon III, the British government and Cavour, Sardinia's Premier. Napoleon III and Cavour, whose good will was known to the Romanians, promised to help and the British Foreign Secretary was won over by Cuza's cautious and moderate policy after the election. At the conference of the representatives of the Guaranteeing Powers held in Paris on April 7 and April 14, 1859, the representatives of France, Britain, Russia,

Sardinia, and Prussia declared for the recognition of the election, while the representatives of the Porte and of Vienna opposed it. Having been defeated by France and Sardinia in the war in Italy, Austria no longer opposed the election when the Conference opened again on September 6 of the same year, and the Porte, now isolated, gave in, too.

When Cuza's election in the two Principalities had been recognized, the Romanians made it their aim to complete the union and build up a single state. Already in 1859 the telegraph offices had their centre in Bucharest and in the summer of the same year, at the time of the war in Italy, the armies of the two Principalities assembled at the Florești camp with the aim of defending the union and possibly of marching into Transylvania. A single general staff was organized for both armies under the prince's command. The following year, 1860, the course of the national currency, the *leu,* was unified, a single War Ministry was set up, the capitation tax was levied also on the privileged, and corporal punishment was abolished in both Principalities. The Central Commission at Focșani, which had begun functioning on May 22, 1859, drew up a draft constitution, as well as a draft land reform law in 1860 emancipating the peasants, though without giving them land, and a draft electoral law in 1861, which gave the franchise to the majority of the citizens who were of age.

In December, 1860, Cuza sent the Guaranteeing Powers an appeal asking that the union of the Principalities under one single cabinet be completed and a new electoral law be approved. Since the Porte postponed its answer to these requests, the Elective Assemblies asked the prince that they should be convened in April, 1861, to debate the draft land reform law of the Central Commission at Focșani. The real aim, however, was to proclaim the complete union of the Principalities. Prompted by Costache Negri, the diplomatic agent of the United Principalities at Constantinople, Cuza threatened the Porte by saying he would achieve the union by way of revolution.

The Guaranteeing Powers, concerned by the prospect, were prepared to satisfy the requests of the Principalities and for this purpose a conference of their representatives was convened at Constantinople. As the conference debates were protracted, in November Cuza apprised the Porte that he would call both Elective Assemblies and proclaim the union complete unless his requests were approved. On December 5 the Porte issued an edict *(firman)* approving the unification of the two Principalities' administrations but only for Cuza's lifetime. On December 23 Cuza announced that the union had been completed, and the two Elective Assemblies decided to meet in Bucharest on February 5, 1862, thus forming one single National Assembly.

Romania's government — for the United Principalities were now being given that name — was formed on February 3, 1862, with Barbu Catargiu, spokesman of the conservative majority in the Assembly, as Prime Minister. The cabinet included representatives of the conservative groups, both Moldavian and Wallachian. On February 5, Alexandru Ioan I read a message to the National Assembly and the cabinet announcing the complete and final union of the two Romanian Principalities. About the union he said : "As I have said, it will be such as Romania wishes it, such as she feels it should be." He pointed out that a new age was opening up for the country and demanded that the union should be strengthened by "the progressive development of institutions". The Romanian national state was thus formed, although it did not comprise all the territory inhabited by Romanians. However, the conservatives forming the cabinet were a source of anxiety for the masses of townspeople and peasants, as also for the progressive groups which three years before had imposed the election of Cuza in both Principalities. After the solemn meeting, the crowds cheered the prince and the progressive deputies and booed the conservative cabinet members and deputies. The peasant movement headed by Mircea Mălăieru, who sought to overthrow the conservative cabinet with the help of the masses in Bucharest and to compel the country to form a liberal radical government, had been put down the day before with the assistance of the Bucharest regiments.

6. Bourgeois Reforms.
Alexandru Ioan Cuza Is Deposed

THE conservatives intending to consolidate the capitalist system had meant to do so by dispossessing the peasants of the holdings they used and maintaining the political preponderance of the landowners. On April 6, 1862, the conservative cabinet submitted to the Assembly the draft land reform law worked out by the Central Commission of Focșani under which the peasants were released from feudal obligations but lost the holdings they used. M. Kogălniceanu opposed the bill with numerous arguments drawn from history, both that of Romania and of other European countries, and denouncing it as an obstacle to the consolidation of the Romanian nation and to progress. The conservative majority, however, passed it with a few amendments on June 23. The amendment proposed by Kogălniceanu and endorsed by 22 progressive deputies, including Ion Ghica, N. Golescu, Al. G. Golescu, and George Adrian, had been rejected. It provided for the peasants to be given their freedom and the holdings they used upon some payment made to the landowners as compensation for the labour services and the tithe which had been abolished.

On June 20 Barbu Catargiu was shot. The assassin was never discovered. Catargiu had left the Assembly in the carriage of N. Bibescu, Chief Commissioner of the Bucharest Police, after declaring his opposition to the convening of a committee to arrange a meeting to celebrate the anniversary of the revolution of 1848. The conservative majority was baffled both on account of the death of their former leader and because the prince had not sanctioned the bill passed by them.

Shortly after, Cuza entrusted the formation of the cabinet to N. Crețulescu, a moderate liberal and a partisan of bourgeois reforms effected by "a middle way" that would eschew internal difficulties and external complications. After an unsuccessful Press campaign against Cuza, the radical liberals, through the agency of Ion Ghica, came to an understanding with the conservative groups and formed "the monstrous coalition" against the prince's tendency to rule with authority.

Unable to stand its ground against the opposition and to proceed to carry out the land and the electoral reforms, the cabinet presided over by Crețulescu was superseded by a cabinet with Kogălniceanu as premier in October, 1863. On December 25, 1863, the estates of the monasteries were secularized, including those of the monasteries dedicated to institutions abroad. More than a quarter of the country's territory thus became state property. The law for the organization of the armed forces was also approved by the radical liberals after Kogălniceanu had accepted the introduction of an amendment providing for the setting up a civic guard. This strengthened the position of the government and weakened the co-operation between radical-liberals and conservatives. Cuza, however, opposed the bill and refused to sanction it. Kogălniceanu took advantage of the situation and on March 28, 1864, submitted to the Elective Assembly a land-reform bill against which on April 25 the majority of the Assembly gave a vote of censure. The radical-liberals had not voted against the government but I. C. Brătianu had submitted a land-reform bill which differed, though not greatly, from the government's. Cuza did not accept Kogălniceanu's resignation on May 14, 1864, and made a *coup d'état* dissolving the conservative-controlled **Assembly**.

A plebiscite approved the new constitution which was called "Statute enlarging on the Paris Convention". The prince's prerogatives were greatly increased, he alone being able to put forward bills, which were to be drawn up by a State Council whose members were appointed, though their appointment could be revoked.

Cuza went to Constantinople to have the new constitution sanctioned. The representatives of the Guaranteeing Powers and also the Porte approved the constitution, and Cuza also obtained recognition of the right of the United Principalities to amend their laws without the consent of the Powers. On August 26, 1864, Cuza promulgated a land law based on Kogălniceanu's bill of March of the same year. The peasants were thereby freed from feudal obligations and put in possession of the holdings they had used, supplemented, if necessary, to reach the number of hectares fixed for the various regions of the country. In fixing the area of the holdings given to the peasants, the number of their cattle was taken into account. The peasants who had been given land were to pay the landowners, through the intermediary of the state, a sum of money which was considerable, but which turned them into owners of the land in the bourgeois meaning of the word. The payment was to be spread over fifteen years. The peasants without cattle received smallholdings insufficient for their existence and they were thus compelled to sell their labour power. Over 48,00 peasant families (newly married couples, peasants living on "narrow" estates) who were to receive land from the state received it only in 1878. In many villages, with the complicity of the state machinery, the peasants were allotted the poorest land: marshland, sandy soil, and land in precipitous places. The landowners together with the state held about 66 per cent of the country's land while the peasants, including the free peasants of old, owned only a little over 33 per cent. Making the peasants independent of the landowners' estates, the land reform concluded the process of abolishing the feudal system and paved the way for the swift-paced development of capitalism in the United Principalities while contributing to the strengthening of "the nation", as Kogălniceanu had said.

Bourgeois institutions, first set up in 1859, continued to spring up. A law was enacted for the organization of the educational system which made elementary education compulsory, general and free of charge, and developed secondary and higher education. In 1864 the University of Bucharest was established, after the University of Jassy in 1860.

By the close of 1865 the capitalist system had triumphed in the main sectors of the United Principalities and a modern national state had been built up.

Kogălniceanu was unable to see the enforcement of the land law through as he was compelled to resign in January, 1865. C. Bosianu then headed a cabinet for several months, after which Cuza again entrusted the reins of government to the moderate liberal N. Crețulescu. Encouraged by Kogălniceanu's removal from office and the critical financial situation, the radical liberals and the conservatives came to an understanding and decided to work for the overthrow of Cuza, who was to be replaced by a foreign prince. The conservatives opposed Cuza because he had carried through the land reform and had widened the franchise; and the radical liberals opposed him because of the authoritarian régime he had installed in 1864. On August 15, while Cuza was on holiday at Ems in Prussia, the radical liberals incited the shopkeepers in Bucharest to revolt. Though easily defeated by the army, the uprising created a climate of distrust in Cuza both at home and abroad. When he wrote to Napoleon III listing his achievements and declaring himself ready to give up the throne, the answer was discouraging. Feeling isolated, he made it clear in a message he read on December 16, 1865, when the session of the legislative bodies opened, that he intended to abdicate.

An atmosphere had been created and on February 23, 1866, his opponents, with the assistance of a number of officers, obliged him to do so. Cuza's reign, though short, was among the richest in achievements in the history of the Romanian people.

R. W. Seton-Watson adds some details to the above account. He said that the famous Agrarian Law of 1864 and that on education will always stand to the credit of Cuza, "but they were his last solid achievements. Power demoralised him, though it was certainly no mere pose when he publicly reaffirmed his readiness to make way for a foreign prince, and he was too genuine a patriot to plunge his country into civil war. But he was surrounded by a camarilla of the worst kind, the finances again fell into disorder, salaries were in arrears, corruption was rampant, and there was much peculation with army contracts. Foreign commercial firms obtained concessions which enabled them to exploit the country. Meanwhile Cuza's private life became a public scandal, even in the lax society of Bucharest, and his treatment of his wife 'Domnea Elena' — a Rosetti by birth and noted for her high character and devotion to charity — caused much offence. His mistress, Marie Obrenovic — a daughter of Costin Catargiu and widow of a younger brother of Prince Miloš of Serbia — lived with him in the palace, but had many rivals to his favour, ... As Elena had no children, Cuza made his children by Marie his heirs, and it was even rumoured that he thought of the succession for one of them."

Sunk in indolence and self-indulgence, Cuza made no attempt to escape from the impasse he had created, and even disregarded an urgent secret warning of his danger. A number of prominent officers, won over by the Central Committee, carried out a successful palace revolution. Cuza was roused from his bed after midnight, and forced to dress hurriedly while his mistress hid behind an improvised screen ; an officer knelt and offered his back as a rest for the act of abdication, and no sooner had Cuza appended his signature, than he was hurried to a carriage and driven off to Cotroceni, whence, after an interval of some days, he was escorted to the frontier.

7. Transylvania from 1859 to 1865

THE peoples of the Habsburg Empire being dissatisfied with the neo-absolutist policy, which included Germanization took advantage of the defeat of the imperial armies in Italy in 1859 to show their desire for freedom. In fear of a new revolution, Emperor Francis Joseph dissolved the government in August 1859, and convened a reinforced Imperial Council in March, 1860, with representatives of the various peoples participating in the proceedings. The Romanians of Transylvania were represented by the Eastern Orthodox Bishop Andrei Şaguna, those of Banat by Andrei Mocioni, and those of Bukovina by Nicolae Petrino. After several months' talks, the Vienna Court, fearing lest the principle of nationality should dismember the monarchy, decided to set up again the autonomous states such as they had been prior to the revolution but on the basis of liberal bourgeois institutions. On October 20, 1860, Francis Joseph issued the October Diploma whereby the principality of Transylvania became again an autonomous state, and the old feudal constitution was to be drawn up on the basis of equality of all the people before the law, for which purpose a representative assembly of the nations and confessions was to be convened. In order to draw up an electoral law, a government headed by the Magyar Count Miko Imre was then formed and the *comitats* and *sedes* were re-established.

In November, 1860, the Romanians in Banat held a congress at Timişoara demanding autonomy for Banat or its incorporation into the principality of Transylvania. Andrei Mocioni submitted a Memorial to this effect to the emperor, but the demands of the Romanians in Banat were not satisfied and the emperor ordered that the province should be incorporated within Hungary.

In January, 1861, the Romanians of Transylvania under the leadership of Metropolitan Alexandru Sterca Şuluţiu and of Bishop Andrei Şaguna, held a national congress at Sibiu. The Congress demanded that the Romanian nation should be recognized and the electoral census be reduced, and it appointed a permanent commission of four to represent the Romanians.

The conference of the representatives of the various nationalities of Transylvania, who were to draw up the electoral law, was held at Alba Iulia on February 11, 1861, with the Magyar Catholic Bishop, Haynald, in the chair. It was made up of 124 Hungarians, 8 Saxons, and 5 Romanians. Three Romanians refused to come. Instead of drawing up the electoral law, the Magyar majority headed by Haynald proclaimed Transylvania's union with Hungary and closed the conference. The Vienna Court did not approve the decision and maintained the autonomy of the principality.

To replace Count Miko Imre, Folliot de Crenneville was appointed as Premier, with two Vice-Presidents, one of whom was a Romanian: Vasile Pop. The convening of a Transylvanian diet was postponed.

The Romanians demanded the right to call an advisory assembly with a view to setting up "the Transylvanian Association for Romanian Literature and the Education of the Romanian People" (A.S.T.R.A.), which was to "enhance the education of the people and promote literature with united powers." The assembly was held at Sibiu in March, 1861, when draft statutes were drawn up. The statutes were then approved and the new society was inaugurated at Sibiu on November 4, 1861.

When the great Polish uprising of 1863 broke out, the partisans of Kossuth planned to stir up an insurrection in Hungary, and General Türr came to Bucharest to effect an understanding with Cuza. As a result, the Vienna Court sought to give satisfaction to the Romanians in Transylvania in order to win them over. In April, 1863, the Romanians were allowed to hold a congress in Sibiu. Under the influence of the government the congress accepted an electoral law based on a yearly income of 8 florins at least. Based on the same law, elections for the diet were made and 46 Romanians were elected as compared with 42 Magyars and 32 Saxons. When the Diet opened its proceedings at Sibiu in July, the Magyar deputies refused to participate on the ground that they considered Transylvania to be part of Hungary. Being predominately Romanian, the Sibiu Diet passed bills providing for equal rights to the Romanian nation and its religion and the right to use equally the three languages spoken in the country: Romanian, Hungarian, and German. The two bills were not sanctioned by the emperor who, being paralysed by Magyar obstruction, had effected a *rapprochement* with the Magyar aristocracy who demanded Transylvania's incorporation within Hungary. On September 1, 1865, Francis Joseph decreed that the Sibiu Diet should be closed and a new diet be convened on the basis of the electoral law of 1791 which had been slightly changed to enable the bourgeoisie to vote. The result of the elections was naturally unfavourable to the Romanians although they formed an absolute majority in the province. The diet, now dominated by the Hungarian nobility, opened in Cluj in November and hastened to proclaim Transylvania's annexation to Hungary. The next month, the emperor ordered the Transylvanian government to send the diet deputies to the Hungarian Diet and cancelled the bills passed by the Sibiu Diet. But in order to give the Romanians some satisfaction, on December 24, 1864, he raised the Orthodox Bishopric of Sibiu to the rank of an independent Metropolitanate with two bishoprics: at Arad and Caransebeş, and with Andrei Şaguna as Metropolitan.

As the revolution of 1848 had not been successful, the union of the Romanian people into a single democratic and independent State was delayed, but social and economic development and the Romanians' perseverance in their struggle laid the foundations for a modern national state through the union of Moldavia and Wallachia. The revolutionary aspirations of 1848 were thus partially achieved.

The Land Law of 1864 did not completely do away with feudalism in agriculture. In Romanian economy as a whole, however, the fact that capitalist production tipped the balance created favourable prerequisites for economic, social, and political progress, though the landowners remained politically preponderant.

In the period which followed Cuza's fall the landowners — still a considerable economic force on account of their vast landed estates — held strong positions also in politics and consequently sought to enforce conservative views in accordance with their class interests.

Simultaneously, the extension of capitalistic methods of production increased the part played by the bourgeoisie in social and political life. Intent on developing industry and transport and using science and technique in production, the bourgeoisie within certain limits furthered the progress of society. Considering the special line followed by capitalist development in the country, the bourgeoisie accepted that the large landed estates should be maintained and to a certain extent also feudal relations, and this had unfavourable consequences for the economic development and the social and political evolution of the country. The compromise reached during the last years of Cuza's reign between the landowners and the bourgeoisie was consolidated by the installation of the Hohenzollern dynasty and formed the foundations of the political régime installed in 1866. Despite the changes wrought in the ratio of forces within this coalition, the régime continued until the Romanian national state was set up. But the compromise on which the political régime of the years after 1866 was built did not rule out contradictions and diverging interests among the participating forces.

The evolution of the ratio of social and political forces found expression in the Constitution of 1866, which was subsequently modified.

After Moldavia and Wallachia had united to form one state based on bourgeois institutions and with an international status which gave it full autonomy, the Romanian people still had to achieve Romania's independence and complete political unity in pursuance of the general programme of the revolution of 1848. From 1866 to 1878, owing to internal and external conditions, they were able to achieve only their country's independence. The situation of the Romanians of Transylvania was aggravated when the Austro-Hungarian monarchy was created by the Compromise of 1867, for it raised new obstacles to their struggle for national freedom. A complex process of economic, social, cultural, and political factors, however, enabled them to gain their independence.

8. Economic Development

THE economic development of Romania and of the Romanian territories in the Habsburg Empire helped to strengthen the capitalist system. At the same time Romania's economic development enabled her to free herself from her dependence on the Ottoman Empire. As most dependent peasants had been freed and given land, capitalist forces in Romania's agriculture made headway and the labour force needed for industry, transport, and trade increased. Part of the funds received by the landowners from the emancipated peasants were invested in farming implements and machinery or went to pay the workers, whether seasonal or day workers. A law on agricultural arrangements came into force in March 1866, under which village administrative bodies were obliged to ensure that the farm work they had engaged to carry out was effectively done. The law had been issued in order to compel the workers to perform farming work. On the other hand, the landowners and great lessees did not possess sufficient capital, implements and machines, and neither were they used to capitalist exploitation of the land, so that they came to pass on to the peasants part of their estates in exchange for a tithe on the produce and a number of days' work. Apart from this system, there was another which consisted in dividing the estate into holdings, some of which were tilled for the benefit of the landowners or lessees and others for providing the pay for the peasants' work on those holdings. In 1872 the law on farming arrangements was modified and it then became possible to use soldiers to compel the peasants to carry out their obligations. These were practices supposed to be founded on free contracts, but actually they ensured the intervention of state bodies for the benefit of the landowners. Such practices and the improvement of farming techniques doubled farming output from 1866 to 1878 and helped capital accumulation in the country through steadily increasing grain exports.

The peasants' struggle against the landowners continued, often assuming most violent forms. The rebellion of the frontier guards in May, 1866, the disturbances caused by the peasants who had not been given land, the suits for the marking off of the holdings, often accompanied by revolts and cruel repression, the unfair practices and illegality in the enforcement of the law on agricultural arrangements, especially after 1872, constituted landmarks during this period of unrest.

From 1866 to 1878 the number of industrial enterprises increased two and a half times, but small shops and factories predominated. The food industry took pride of place, followed by the textile industry — with four cloth factories — and by the timber industry. There was a considerable rise in salt extraction and the output of crude oil rose nearly threefold from 1866 to 1878. Simultaneously, refineries were set up, of which there were twenty in 1878. Industrial expansion was checked by the competition of foreign commodities and the trade treaties of the Ottoman Empire, which Romania was obliged to observe. After the opening of railway lines, the competition of foreign commodities was still greater. The industrialists asked the government for a protectionist policy. They were upheld by the theories popularized by Haşdeu and Xenopol and later by P. S. Aurelian. Protectionism implied removal of what was left of Ottoman suzerainty.

In Transylvania industry was more advanced than in Romania. During this period it made further progress but at a slow tempo, being checked by the industrial products of the western provinces of the Habsburg Empire. The most important was the mining industry which mainly belonged to foreign capitalists. Next came the food and the textile industries. After the construction of the main railway lines, the timber industry went ahead rapidly in both Transylvania and Bukovina.

In order to meet requirements, and also to enhance the unity of the state and for strategic purposes, nearly 1,000 miles of railway lines were constructed from 1867 to 1879. Most of the railway network was owned by foreign firms intent on making high profits and not on improvements. However, despite the difficulties encountered in constructing them, the railways proved of good use in the economy and in the struggle for achievement of Romania's independence.

In April, 1867, a law was enacted creating *a new monetary system and providing for the minting of national coinage.* The nominal *leu* circulating at the time was superseded by a real coin which was also named *leu* and was guaranteed by a gold reserve. However, it was only after the country had become independent that a national bank could be created with the right to issue money.

9. Prince Charles I of Romania

ON Cuza's abdication a regency was formed on the morning of February 23, 1866. It consisted of N. Golescu, a radical-liberal, Lascăr Catargiu, a conservative, and Colonel N. Haralambie. The Premier was Ion Ghica, a moderate liberal, the Minister of the Interior Dimitrie Ghica, a conservative, the Minister of Public Education and Cults, C. A. Rosetti, a Liberal and the Minister of War, Major D. Lecca. The legislative bodies met to proclaim Count Philip of Flanders, brother of the Belgian king, as prince. The latter, however, did not accept the throne. A conference of the representatives of the Guaranteeing Powers met in Paris and declared against the election of a foreign prince and eventually for the separation of the Principalities. With the tacit consent of Napoleon III, to whom he was related, Prince Charles of Hohenzollern Sigmaringen was proclaimed Prince of Romania. The separatist movement at Jassy was easily defeated by the army. Faithful to Cuza's memory, the peasants opposed the election of a new prince, who was not to become king until 1881.

Prince Charles (Carol), brought up as a Prussian officer, was a member of the elder South German and Roman Catholic branch of the Hohenzollern family. His father, Karl Anton, had voluntarily renounced his position as a reigning monarch, and had acted for three years as Prussian premier until Bismarck took his place in 1861.

According to R. W. Seton-Watson, the exact manner in which the candidature of Prince Charles first emerged is even today obscure, but the statesman Ion Brătianu took a leading part in the approaches to him. When Charles's mind was at last made up, there was still a very practical difficulty to overcome : how was the Prince to reach his new principality ? The sea route took three weeks, and led through Constantinople : the Russian route was equally impracticable. The sole alternative was through Austria : but hostilities between Austria and Prussia might break out at any moment, and Charles would be in danger of arrest as a Prussian officer, and, if identified, would certainly not be allowed to proceed to Romania. He therefore made his way to Zürich, procured a Swiss passport in the name of "Karl Hettingen" bound for Odessa, and travelled for some days across Austria and Hungary, in trains overcrowded and disorganized by the order of mobilization : he wore goggles and went second class (evidently for the first and last time, to judge by his naïve diary comments on the dirty carriages), and he narrowly escaped recognition by Austrian officers whom he had known in the Schleswig campaign. After an anxious wait of forty-eight hours for a Danube steamer at Buziaș, he was joined by Ion Brătianu, who had travelled direct from Paris, and now sat in the first class, studiously ignoring the bogus Swiss "drummer" (commercial traveller). When the steamer at last reached Romanian soil at Turnu Severin, Charles was in too great a hurry to land, and the captain, who knew he had a ticket for Odessa, called out to him to stop. But Brătianu and his suite hustled him unceremoniously down the gangway, and he landed in his future kingdom with an angry voice ringing in his ear, "By God, that must be the Prince of Hohenzollern". But Brătianu had already turned hat in hand to greet his new sovereign, who after a two days' drive in an open carriage with postilions and eight horses, across the still primitive Wallachia roads, was greeted with joy in Bucharest on May 22, 1866. The torrential rain that welcomed his arrival after a drought of three months was accepted in oriental fashion as a happy open. In 1869 he married Princess Elisabeth of Weld, the future "Carmen Sylva", who brought him great domestic happiness.

The Elective Assembly was dissolved after the law on farming arrangements and that on the organization of the civic guard had been passed. The Moderating Body also went out of session. The new Assembly proclaimed Charles I as prince, after which it became a constituent assembly and passed the new constitution.

The new constitution which gave the country the name of "Romania" and did not mention her dependence on the Ottoman Empire was liberal in character. It protected personal property and the means of production and ensured individual freedom. Courts of judge and jury were set up for cases dealing with the Press, for crimes and other suits. The head of the state was the prince. His dignity was hereditary and he was to reign in accordance with the provisions of the constitution. The government was appointed by him but had to enjoy the confidence of the Assembly of Deputies and of the Senate. The government and the legislative bodies made the laws. The prince had the right of absolute veto for he could refuse to sanction a bill passed by the legislative bodies. He was supreme commander of the army. A complicated electoral system ensured political domination of the bourgeoisie and landowners in the state.

After the constituent assembly was dissolved a new cabinet presided over by Ion Ghica was formed. The cabinet was made up of moderate liberals and moderate conservatives. In October, after protracted negotiations and with France's diplomatic support, the Porte recognized Charles I as hereditary prince.

10. Political Life in Romania from 1866 to 1877

THE cabinet presided over by Ion Ghica, having been unable to obtain the necessary majority in the parliamentary election of the autumn of 1866, was compelled to resign and make way on March 13, 1867, for a cabinet of a liberal coalition with C. A. Crețulescu as Premier but actually led by I. C. Brătianu, the Minister of the Interior. Counting on the outbreak of a new war between the Habsburg Empire and Prussia and on a general insurrection of the Balkan peoples, the new Romanian government interrupted the negotiations which Ion Ghica had started with Austria-Hungary and replaced the French military mission brought over during Cuza's reign by a Prussian military mission. This caused Napoleon III to assume a hostile attitude.

The Romanian cabinet allowed groups of Bulgarian revolutionaries to organize themselves this side of the Danube and carried on vigorous propaganda among the Romanians in Transylvania, supporting their Press and political and cultural organizations. Under the law on the organization of the army of 1868, efforts were made to increase to the utmost the country's military strength. When Napoleon III proposed an alliance with Francis Joseph against Prussia, Andrassy, the Hungarian Prime Minister, opposed it, desiring an understanding between Austria-Hungary and Prussia in the hope that the latter would force Romania to cease her revolutionary propaganda in Transylvania. Charles and the Conservatives were dissatisfied with the massive arming that was going on and the strengthening of the civic guard, and this resulted in the dismissal of Colonel George Adrian from the War Ministry. And when the Legislative Bodies had passed the law entitling a Prussian consortium headed by Strousberg to construct and exploit the railways, Bismarck demanded that Charles dismiss the radical-liberal government, which the Romanian prince hastened to do on November 28, 1868.

The new government with Dimitrie Ghica as Premier and Kogălniceanu as Minister of the Interior effected a *rapprochement* with Austria-Hungary who agreed to Romania's sending a semi-official diplomatic agent to Vienna. Seeing the failure of their plans, the radical-liberals started an ever more violent campaign for the removal of Charles. The Strousberg affair had strengthened the current opposing Prince Charles. The outbreak of the Franco-Prussian War in July, 1870, encouraged the radical-liberals, who believed that France would be victorious, to organize a conspiracy to depose Charles.

The insurrection that followed was premature and insufficiently prepared and was consequently a failure. The anti-dynastic current assumed a republican character, particularly after a republic was proclaimed in Paris. Being brought to court, the 41 leaders of the Ploieşti insurrection were acquitted by the court of justice and jury of Tîrgovişte, and on December 26 the Assembly gave a vote of censure to the government and showed hostility towards Charles. Ion Ghica was appointed prime minister again.

After threatening to abdicate in a letter published in the *Augsburger Allgemeine Zeitung,* Prince Charles took advantage of the republican demonstrations on the evening of March 22, 1871 against the banquet given in honour of William I, recently proclaimed Emperor of Germany at Versailles, to dismiss Ion Ghica's cabinet and to appoint a conservative cabinet under Lascăr Catargiu. Fear of the disturbances that a change of prince would cause, and also Prussia's victory over France, tempered the opposition of the radical liberals for a few years, so that in 1877 the conservatives were able to change the law on agricultural arrangements and the law on the organization of the armed forces. The changes in the former law favoured the landowners. Friction between the conservative groups — old right wing, young right wing, and centre — was aggravated in 1875-6. It was only fear of the liberal coalition organized in the spring of 1875 that still rallied the conservatives around Lascăr Catargiu. The economic crisis of 1873-7 further weakened the position of the conservative government.

Throughout this period Romania's foreign policy was still focused on obtaining her independence. When in November, 1870, Charles tried to persuade the Guaranteeing Powers to consent to the proclamation of Romania's independence, he met with opposition on the part of Chancellor Bismarck. In June, 1873, when visiting the Universal Exhibition in Vienna, Charles demanded Andrassy's support in exchange for a trade treaty favourable to the Habsburg Empire. Andrassy accepted the offer and a trade convention was concluded with Austria-Hungary in 1875. When Gorchakov, the Russian foreign minister, was asked for his consent to the proclamation of Romania's independence in 1873, he refused to give it. But in March, 1876, Russia concluded a commercial and Customs convention with Romania, wishing to cancel all the remaining provisions of the Treaty of Paris of 1856 and of the Paris Convention of 1858.

The peasant uprising in Herzegovina and Bosnia in July 1875, re-opened the Eastern Question. The Romanian people sympathized with the struggle of the rebels, But the conservative government, the moderate liberal group headed by Ion Ghica, and the independent liberal faction under N. Ionescu were afraid that the Russian armies might march through Romania to attack the Ottoman Empire. The government decided upon neutrality but began to make military preparations. On January 16, 1876, Lascăr Catargiu sent the Romanian diplomatic agent a note to the effect that Romania was not part of the Ottoman Empire and would oppose occupation by a foreign army by force of arms. At the same time he expressed his regrets that under the Treaty of Paris of 1856 Romania had not become "a powerful, fully independent state."

11. Transylvania from 1866 to 1876

DEFEATED in the Austro-Prusso-Italian War of 1866, Emperor Francis Joseph, eager to take his revenge, hastened to end the talks with the leaders of the Magyar nobility who demanded among other things that Transylvania should be incorporated within Hungary. The Romanians protested in a memorial drawn up on the initiative of George Barițiu and Ioan Rațiu in October, 1866, and signed by 1,493 intellectuals. Francis Joseph, however, did not take the Romanians' opposition into account and on February 17, 1867, when the first government of the kingdom of Hungary was appointed, with Julius Andrassy as Premier, Transylvania was incorporated within Hungary. On June 8, 1867, Francis Joseph was crowned King of Hungary and on that occasion sanctioned the law whereby Transylvania was united with Hungary.

Since 1865 there had been two camps among the Transylvanian Romanians : the active party headed by Metropolitan Andrei Saguna thought that the Romanians should participate in political life as they had no state machinery of their own nor a constitutional basis for their demands as the Hungarians had — for the latter could invoke the decisions of the Diet of 1848 sanctioned by the emperor before the Vienna Court. The passive party under George Barițiu and Ioan Rațiu refused to participate in the election and to run for the Budapest parliament. On May 15, 1868, after celebrating the anniversary of the national assembly of 1848 in Blaj, the passive party drew up a document — *The Blaj Pronouncement* — protesting, as they had done in 1848, against Transylvania's incorporation within Hungary against the will of the Romanians, demanding that autonomy be maintained, the laws passed by the Sibiu Diet of 1863-4 be enforced, and a democratic diet be elected so that it should really represent the population of Transylvania. The *Pronouncement* was widely publicized and caused deep unrest among the Transylvanian Romanians. Its authors were brought to trial, but the case was quashed some time after for fear that the Romanians might revolt. In December, 1868, the Hungarian Parliament passed the law of nationalities which laid down that there was a single nation — the Hungarian nation — throughout Hungary and that the "nationalities" were part of it. It was also in 1868 that the law on education was passed under which Hungarian, the official state language, had to be studied in all the schools.

The Romanians of Banat and Crişana started organizing their ranks with a view to resistance against the denationalization policy. At the conference held in Timişoara in January, 1869, a national party of the Romanians in Banat and Hungary was formed, with Alexandru Mocioni as president. In February, 1869, the passive party of the Transylvanian Romanians, meeting at the conference held in Miercurea, set up the Romanian National Party with I. E. Măcelariu as president. The Party demanded autonomy for Transylvania and adopted passive tactics. Though the Royal Hungarian Commissioner dissolved the party, it continued to function underground.

12. The Beginnings of the Working Class and Socialist Movement

WITH industry developing steadily, the number of workers increased and so did their resistance to the employers' exploitation. The working class movement assumed the form of spontaneous strikes, some of them violent, as was the case in March, 1873, when the carters of the port of Giurgiu clashed with the army and there was a great deal of bloodshed. In pursuance of previous efforts, the workers formed associations. In 1858 the Printers' Mutual Benefit Fund was founded in Bucharest, and in 1865 the printers' vocational organization issued the first working class paper : *Tipograful Român (The Romanian Printer)*. In 1867 and 1869 associations of craftsmen, journeymen, and apprentices were founded at Sibiu and Braşov and later in other Transylvanian towns. In 1868 the *General Association of Timişoara Workers* was founded. Its programme of action included social and political claims, which meant progress in the workers' class-consciousness. The association was to join the First International created and headed by Marx and Engels and a First International Section thus arose at

Timișoara under the leadership of Carol Farcaș and Gheorghe Ungureanu. Four years later the section was wound up by the Budapest Government, which was afraid of its democratic policy.

The socialist movement had its beginning in 1875. A student, Eugen Lupu, set up the first socialist nucleus at Jassy, drawing in a fellow student, Ioan Nădejde. About the same time the *Society of Culture and Solidarity between Students* was founded in Bucharest, an important part in the society being played by C. I. Istrati and N. Codreanu, both medical students. Codreanu was a Romanian refugee from Russia. On June 7, 1876, *Socialistul (The Socialist)*, the first socialist gazette to be printed in Romanian, appeared in Bucharest.

13. The War of Independence

A coalition of the liberal political groups against the conservative government compelled Charles on May 9, 1876, to form a liberal government with Em. Costache Epureanu as Premier, M. Kogălniceanu as Foreign Minister, and I. C. Brătianu as Finance Minister. The liberals were returned in the election for the Assembly of Deputies.

After the defeat of the Bulgarian uprising in April, 1876, the crisis of the Ottoman Empire was intensified owing to disturbances caused by the Young Turks, partisans of bourgeois liberalism, which culminated in the overthrow and assassination of Sultan Abdul Aziz. Thinking that the Porte would be more liberal under the circumstances, Kogălniceanu sent a note to the Romanian diplomatic agents together with a memorial demanding recognition of Romania's independence under the joint guarantee of the Great Powers. The Porte did not answer Kogălniceanu's note. Following Serbia's military action against the Ottoman Empire, Tsar Alexander II met Emperor Francis Joseph at Reichstadt in Bohemia on

July 8 with the aim of reaching an agreement on the Balkan problems. Fearing lest Romania's territory might be encroached upon under Reichstadt arrangements, Kogălniceanu sent the Porte a new note demanding peremptorily that the country's independence be recognized. But the Ottoman armies gained a victory over Serbia and the European powers were divided in two camps owing to the alliance between the three emperors brought about by Bismarck.

The liberal coalition government was not united and since the proposal to indict the former conservative government, headed by Lascăr Catargiu, accentuated the divergences within it, Epureanu resigned his office. On July 24, 1876, Charles asked I. C. Brătianu, one of the spokesmen of the radical liberals, to form a cabinet, with N. Ionescu to replace Kogălniceanu. The new cabinet continued to prepare the way for the proclamation of independence. During the last ten days of August a government delegation headed by Brătianu went to Sibiu to pay a "courtesy visit" to Emperor Francis Joseph, thus making known Romania's good neighbourly feelings. A month later another Romanian government delegation, again headed by Brătianu, was received by Tsar Alexander II and Gorchakov at Livadia in the Crimea to discuss the conditions under which the Russian army might march through Romania against the Ottoman Empire. The Romanian delegation demanded that a convention be first signed to ensure Romania's territorial integrity.

In the second half of September Romania, made anxious by the victories of the Ottoman armies in Serbia, mobilized her army which was made up of four permanent divisions and their reserves, with a brigade at Calafat to prevent a possible Ottoman attack. Simultaneously, the auxiliary army of foot soldiers composed of sixteen regiments was organized into four territorial divisions.

The army did not have sufficient guns, rifles, equipment, and officers, and finances of the state grievously felt the effects of the economic crisis.

In November, 1876, a Russian diplomat, Nelidov, escorted by Colonel Mihail Cantacuzino, came to Bucharest to draft a Romano-Russian convention. The convention was drawn up but was never signed, Russia having decided to postpone the war until the spring of the following year.

In October a Turco-Serbian truce was made. A conference of the 1856 Paris Treaty signatory powers was convened at Constantinople in December to re-establish peace in the Balkans. The Romanian government sent a delegate to the conference to obtain Romania's independence under the formula of absolute neutrality, with a special guarantee in the event of a war between the Ottoman Empire and one of the neighbouring states. The conference refused to discuss Romania's demand and was unable to convince the Porte to make Bosnia, Herzegovina, and Bulgaria autonomous. On December 23, 1876, the Sultan promulgated a liberal constitution which made mention of the right of investiture of "the heads of the privileged provinces", meaning Romania, Serbia, Montenegro, and Egypt. The Romanian government protested energetically against this provision of the Ottoman constitution. The current favouring the securing of the country's independence by force of arms was thereby greatly strengthened, despite the opposition of the moderate liberals headed by Ion Ghica, and of the independent liberals to a possible co-operation with Russia.

The Porte rejected the protocol concluded in London on March 31, 1877, by the representatives of the European Powers, demanding that the Porte accept the proposals of the Constantinople Conference. After concluding a secret convention with Austria-Hungary, under which the latter promised neutrality in exchange for the annexation of Bosnia and Herzegovina, Russia decided to declare war. On April 12, 1877, Baron D. Stuart, Russia's Consul General in Bucharest, demanded that Romania sign the convention whereby the Russian armies were permitted to cross her territory.

With the prospect of grave developments ahead, the Foreign Ministry was entrusted to Kogălniceanu who, in accordance with the decision of an enlarged Council presided over by Charles, signed the convention with Russia on April 16, 1877. The Russian armies were to be allowed to pass through Romania, paying for all they required, whether for services or materials. The Russian Government agreed to maintain and observe "the political rights of the Romanian state resulting from the domestic laws and the existing treaties, and to maintain and defend Romania's present integrity". A special convention defined the relations between the Russian army and the Romanian authorities.

On April 18 the permanent army as well as the territorial army with their reserves were mobilized and it was decided that, if necessary, a militia and civic guards would be raised for the defence of the towns. The third and the fourth divisions were massed south of Bucharest between Oltenița and Giurgiu, while the first and the second divisions were stationed at Calafat and in the neighbourhood of that town to prevent the Turks from crossing the Danube.

Russia declared war on the Ottoman Empire on April 24 and her forces crossed into Romania, making for the Danube. Convened in an extraordinary session on April 26, the Legislative Bodies approved the Romano-Russian Convention. Britain and France opposed the Convention. The Porte attacked the left bank of the Danube, the town of Brăila was bombed on May 8. The Romanian artillery bombed Vidin on the same day. Turkey and Romania were in a state of war. As a result of great demonstrations of national solidarity and for independence, on May 11, 1877, a group of radical-liberal deputies proposed that a motion should be passed for severing the country's dependence on the Porte and for declaring a state of war. After long debates another motion was passed which declared that a state of war had been created with the Ottoman Empire and demanded that the Cabinet obtain recognition of Romania's independence from the Great Powers at the next peace conference. A similar motion was passed by the Senate the next day. On May 21 Kogălniceanu, on behalf of the government, declared that Romania was "an independent nation". The Assembly of Deputies, like the Senate, voted for "Romania's absolute independence" with an overwhelming majority.

When mobilization had been completed, on May 8 the Romanian army numbered 58,700 men with 190 big guns, apart from the frontier guards, the militia, and the civic guards. In June the field forces were organized into four permanent army divisions and reserve divisions. After having covered the advance of the Russian armies towards the Danube, the third and fourth division made for southern Oltenia to ensure the defence of the Danube from the mouth of the Olto Gruia. In the first days of the war the Romanian navy had helped to put torpedoes along the Danube and to destroy two Turkish monitors in the neighbourhood of Brăila.

Grand Duke Nicholas, commander of the Russian armies along the Danube, proposed that the Romanian army should co-operate south of the Danube though without specifying the conditions of co-operation. On May 19, the Romanian government asked to have its own base of operation, with the left wing of the army along the Isker. A note from Gorchakov warned Romania that, should she intervene in the war, she was to do it "at her own expense, risks, and perils".

In order to mislead the Ottoman command, a Russian army corps crossed the Danube between Brăila and Galatz on June 22. It was a mere diversionary tactic. The bulk of the army crossed the Danube only four days later from Zimnicea to Shishtov, whence General Gurko marched south and crossed the Balkans at Shipka, reaching Stara Zagora in south-east Bulgaria on July 26. Another army advancing eastward was stopped on the River Lom. A third army attacked Nikopol facing the mouth of the Olt, and occupied it on July 16, being supported by the Romanian artillery and infantry on the left bank of the Danube. On July 20 the Russian army acting in the west attacked Plevna where Osman Pasha had recently installed a large army. Being inferior in numbers, the Russians were repelled. With a view to a new attack on Plevna, the Russian commander demanded that the Fourth Romanian Division should cross the Danube and occupy Nikopol and its surroundings. Although no convention had as yet been signed, the Romanian government agreed and occupied Nikopol. A new Russian attack on Plevna was repelled with heavy losses. At the same time Gurko was driven back to Shipka, which he was able to hold. There was a danger of the front advancing north of the Danube and of the war being protracted. Grand Duke Nicholas wired Charles to the effect that the Romanian army should demonstrate against the Turks on the Danube and if possible cross the river. The Romanian cabinet ordered the remainder of the Fourth Division to cross the Danube, after which, following a verbal understanding with Tsar Alexander, they sent another two divisions, altogether about 38,000 men. During an interview with Tsar Alexander, it was decided that the Romano-Russian armies which were to attempt a third attack on Plevna should be placed under the command of Charles, assisted by Russian General Zotov in the capacity of Chief of Staff, and by the Romanian General Al. Cernat, commander of the Romanian corps.

The Tsar insisted that the third attack on Plevna should be launched on September 11. Osman Pasha had brought fresh troops and had built strong redoubts on the hills north, east, and south of the town. The Grivitza I and Grivitza II, the strongest, were in the sector of the Romanian forces.

THE UNION OF THE TWO PRINCIPALITIES

The general attack was launched at 3 p.m. It was only at nightfall and after the fourth attack that the Romanians, helped by the Russians, succeeded in conquering Grivitza I. It was the only victory of a day of many casualties. It proved impossible to conquer Grivitza II. Two attacks launched by the Romanians on September 18 and October 19 were repelled with heavy losses. The Russian command brought in new troops, including the Imperial Guard. It was decided to encircle the redoubt until the Turks in the citadel ran short of food and ammunition.

In order to prevent a Turkish attack from the north, a Romanian detachment of 5,000 men and a Romano-Russian one of 1,200 men attacked Rahova on the Danube on November 19 and conquered it after two days with the assistance of some Romanian battalions which crossed the river from the north.

Intending to break through the encirclement and withdraw towards Sofia, on December 10, 1877, Osman Pasha attacked the Russian forces from the southwest and left a large number of troops along the Opanez to defend his right flank, where Romanians were to be found, as well as other forces at Crishin, where the Russians were stationed. The Turkish attack had chances of success in the early hours of the morning, but the Romanians conquered the redoubts along the Opanez, taking 7,000 Turkish prisoners and entering Plevna where they made Osman Pasha himself prisoner. Osman Pasha ordered his troops to surrender. The main battle of the war against the Ottoman armies had been won.

While the Russian armies were advancing towards Sofia and Philippopolis and crossing the Balkans at Shipka, the Romanian units started an offensive against the Turkish fortresses in western Bulgaria, their main targets being Vidin and Belogragic, both of which were soon surrounded. On January 24, 1878, the outside fortifications of Vidin were attacked, the fiercest fighting taking place for the conquest of Smîrdan which was protected by three redoubts. On January 31, 1878, when Vidin was about to surrender, an armistice was concluded between the Russians and the Turks, and the fighting ended in consequence also at Vidin and Belogragic. Romania's war of independence had ended.

On March 3, 1878, the Peace of San Stefano was concluded between Russia and the Ottoman Empire : the independence of Romania, Serbia, and Montenegro was recognized, the autonomous principality of Bulgaria was created, and an autonomous administration was introduced in Bosnia and Herzegovina. Dissatisfied with the provisions of the peace, which considerably enhanced Russia's prestige and position in South-east Europe, the other great powers convened a congress to regulate the status of south-eastern Europe. Russia could not oppose the plan and consequently renounced the Treaty of San Stefano and accepted participation in the Berlin Congress convened and presided over by Bismarck. On July 1, Brătianu and Kogălniceanu defended Romania's rights at the Congress, basing their contentions on the Romano-Russian Convention of April 16. The Treaty of Berlin of July 13, 1878, recognized Romania's independence, the country also incorporating the Danube Delta, Snake Island, and Dobrudja from east of Silistra to south of Mangalia. The Congress allotted South-west Bessarabia to Russia (R. W. Seton-Watson said that "the attitude of the powers was one of complete cynicism"). Romania was forced to grant civic rights to the non-Christian inhabitants in her territory.

Romania had achieved her independence at the cost of a heavy toll of life on the battlefield and great material sacrifices. The overwhelming majority of the people had enthusiastically backed the war of independence.

Having won her independence, Romania, now a sovereign state, was equal in rights with the other independent states. Henceforward she could set Customs tariffs to protect her economy and thus encourage the development of the big industry necessary for a modern economy.

The number of the proletariat increased with the growth of big industry. The armed forces necessary for the defence of Romania's territory and the liberation of the Romanian districts still under foreign rule were increased. The country sent diplomatic representatives abroad to protect its interests. Romanian culture was given a great impetus, for the Romanian people had gained confidence after securing their independence by their own sacrifices. The political régime slowly evolved along the path of liberalism towards a bourgeois democracy. On the whole, Romania's independence was the result of the progress achieved and at the same time a basis for her development along the path of capitalism.

CHAPTER TWELVE

THE ROMANIAN NATIONAL STATE MAKES GREAT STRIDES

THE period between the achievement of independence and the outbreak of World War I was marked by a great development of the Romanian state in all spheres. In the economic field the foundations were laid for a great mechanical industry, and the oil industry went ahead: agricultural output was increased through capital, but the manner of exploiting the land caused deep discontent which resulted in widespread rebellions such as those of 1888 and 1907. Foreign trade expanded steadily, providing the necessary resources for intensified modernization of institutions, and the strengthening of the army led to industrial development. The changes wrought in the economy and in the class pattern of society at the end of the nineteenth and the beginning of the twentieth centuries affected the ratio of forces between the two governing parties. While the Conservative Party primarily expressed the landowners' interests, the National-Liberal Party represented mainly the interests of the bourgeoisie, though this delimitation was not absolute. With the country making steady headway along the capitalist path, the National-Liberal Party gained more ground in politics, to be accounted for by the fact that the bourgeoisie, in full process of ascension, still had a part to play in Romania's economic and social life. We should also note the tendency towards diversification in political life, the creation of dissident liberal and conservative groups, which did not bring about essential changes, yet had a certain part to play in political developments.

During this period the advanced forces of Romanian society held an important place. It was the first time in the country that the proletariat, with its vocational and political organizations, asserted itself. The peasantry continued its struggles against the landowners' exploitation and what it regarded as the oppression and unfair practices of the state machinery. Other sections of Romanian society — the progressive intelligentsia, the craftsmen, and traders — worked side by side with these main social forces.

The progressive forces — in the first place the working class and socialist movement — made it their aim to solve democratically the fundamental problems facing the Romanian people. Going beyond the stage of workers' clubs, these forces set up a political party of the working class: the Social Democratic Party of the Workers of Romania.

Once Romania's independence had been recognized and the country proclaimed a kingdom, she played an important part in the policy of South-east Europe. This was a period when the national culture flourished, with some representatives of the Romanians in the oppressed provinces contributing also. The potent national liberation movement of this period paved the way for the union of all Romanians into a national state.

1. Economic Growth

POLITICAL independence enabled Romania to adopt a policy protecting the national industry. The spokesmen of this policy — M. Kogălniceanu, P. S. Aurelian, and A. D. Xenopol — were against free trade, they were supported by the economists siding with the landowners and demanded that the state subsidize the industries of the country. P. S. Aurelian declared that a national industry was "a vital condition for our state". The laws for the promotion of the paper industry (1888) and of the sugar industry (1882) favoured the development of industry in these branches, in particular after the customs tariff law of 1886 extended protectionism to the industrial enterprises that used local raw material. When the trade convention of 1875 expired in 1886. Austria-Hungary refused to agree to a new convention based on a protectionist tariff and began a customs war against Romania. On the other hand other countries — France, Russia, the Ottoman Empire — agreed to the customs conventions based on the new tariff, which were concluded between 1866 and 1891. Persevering in the creation of a big industry, the National-Liberal Government promulgated the law of 1887 : General Measures for the Promotion of the National Industry. The industrial enterprises that made use of machinery and had a capital of at least 50,000 lei or employed at least 25 workers were exempted from direct taxation, customs duties on imports of machinery and raw materials and in part from the transport costs for such machines and raw material going by rail. Consequently, industry zoomed even after the Conservatives had reduced the customs duty on imports of industrial products in 1891 and 1893. The protectionist system was further strengthened by the new customs tariff of 1904 and the law for the promotion of industry of 1812. The food industry still took pride of place followed by the mining industry, oil refining, and the timber industry. Next came the textile, leather, paper, and building materials industries. After 1900 metal works became of increasing importance.

Transylvanian industry was developed at a still higher rate owing especially to its exports to Romania. The customs war, however, slowed down its tempo of development after 1886 owing to the narrowing down of the Romanian market. The mining industry, especially coal mining in the Jiu pits, held the first place, followed by the food, timber, metal-working, textile, and building materials industries. Capital accumulation progressing at a slow rate, and most of the enterprises being small or only of medium size, the rate of growth was also slow, and on the whole the economy did not exceed the first stage of capitalist expansion.

Romanian agriculture progressed owing to the increase in manpower, to the use of improved implements and of machinery, and to the credit allowed it. In 1878 48,342 newly married couples were allotted 228,328.9 hectares, and under the law of April 6, 1889, 106,714 peasant families received 549,593 hectares. Nevertheless, in the early years of the twentieth century there existed an agricultural proletariat of over 300,000 families, and 1,015,302 peasants with 10 hectares at most, making up a total of 3,319,695 hectares. On the other hand, some 6,552 landowners owned 3,000,437 hectares, and the village bourgeoisie, made up of 36,318 families, owned 695,958 hectares. Consequently, a considerable part of agricultural land continued to be the property of the big landowners, most of whom still preserved semi-feudal production relations. Some 60 per cent of the landed estates were leased and some of the big lessees in Northern Moldavia made up genuine trusts after 1900.

In Transylvania, where part of the land passed into the hands of the well-to-do peasants through the agency of the banks, a number of landless peasants were forced to become factory workers or miners while others took up domestic service, worked by the day on the landowners' estates, or emigrated to America or to Romania.

The expansion of the economy made it necessary to extend the telegraph, road, and railway network and to use river and sea navigation to a greater extent. From 1887 to 1895 a bridge was built over the Danube at Cernavodă by engineer Anghel Saligny, Bucharest being thus linked to Constantza by rail. In 1890 Romanian

River Navigation, a state enterprise, was set up, and 1895 saw the establishment of the Romanian Maritime Service whose vessels plied between Constantza and Western ports. The port of Constantza was modernized at the turn of the century.

In 1880 the National Bank of Romania was established as a discount and currency circulation institution, with two thirds of its capital private and one third provided by the state. The National Bank promoted the expansion of industry and trade and lent the state funds at a reasonable rate of interest. Considerably increasing its reserves of precious metals and capital, it became the greatest credit institution in the country. The shareholders of the National Bank, mostly liberal-minded bourgeoisie, were able to influence political life by means of the Bank. During the last decade of the nineteenth century and the first decade of the twentieth, quite a number of banks were founded, some of them with foreign capital. The Romanian Bank, whose shares belonged mostly to liberals, was opened in 1911 and became the most important credit institution.

In Transylvania there were subsidiaries of Vienna and Budapest banks, and also local banks, such as Albina, which flourished remarkably after 1878.

Romania's foreign trade grew steadily. After 1900 the balance of trade was favourable again, owing especially to growing exports of oil and oil products and of grain and timber.

2. Continued Liberal Rule

INDEPENDENCE and a policy designed to promote economic expansion strengthened the position of the National-Liberal Party which ruled the country until 1888.

Fulfilment of the conditions laid down by the Congress of Berlin — the granting of full civic rights to

Jews and the redemption of the Railway Company bonds — resulted in the recognition of the country's independence and of the Kingdom of Romania. On March 26, 1881, the Legislative Bodies passed a law which was also approved by the spokesmen of the Conservative Party, whereby Romania was proclaimed a kingdom and its sovereign a king.

Dissidence and defection in the National-Liberal Party induced I. C. Brătianu to rely on the radical wing of the Party and to give the Ministry of Home Affairs to C. A. Rosetti, who advocated reforms in favour of the peasantry and of the democratization of the country (1881). Rosetti brought before the Legislative Bodies a new bill amending the agricultural arrangements law and another bill stipulating how magistrates were to be appointed. The opposition he met, secretly encouraged by Brătianu, compelled him to resign in 1882. The bill on agricultural arrangements was, however, passed after being slightly modified. Enforced execution of agricultural contracts was abolished, the solidarity of those hired for the performance of work was no longer demanded, and two days a week — Friday and Saturday — were left to the peasants for work on their own holdings.

The Treaty of Berlin of 1878 had extended the authority of the European Danube Commission up to Galatz and decided that the Commission, assisted by delegates of the riparian states, should work out the rules governing navigation, policing, and supervision along that portion of the river. In 1879 Austria-Hungary demanded that a joint commission under her leadership should take over these tasks but the proposal came up against Romania's opposition. In June, 1882, Austria-Hungary accepted France's proposal which provided for the setting up of a joint commission of the lower Danube riparian countries plus Austria-Hungary, with the participation of a delegate of the European Commission and presided over by the Austro-Hungarian delegate. Romania alone opposed this proposal, demanding that Austria-Hungary, which was not a riparian country in the reaches of the Danube over which the joint commission was to exercise its authority, be excluded. In order to solve the problem, the powers that had signed the Treaty of Berlin held a conference in London in March, 1883, to which Romania was not admitted. A treaty was concluded, the Conference deciding to extend the authority of the European Commission up to Brăila. The Commission was to function for another 21 years and the rules governing navigation, river policing, and supervision worked out by the European Commission in June, 1882, were to be applied to the Danube between the Iron Gates and Brăila. Romania opposed this treaty.

P. P. Carp, Romania's Minister in Vienna, who favoured a *rapprochement* with the powers of Central Europe, realized that the Danube question was settled in accordance with Romania's interests and then carried on talks for Romania's joining the Triple Alliance. I. C. Brătianu at Gastein met Bismarck and Kalnoky, the Austro-Hungarian Minister of Foreign Affairs, in Vienna, and on October 30, 1883, the Romanian Minister of Foreign Affairs, D. A. Sturdza, signed together with Kalnoky at Vienna, a secret treaty of mutual assistance in the event of an unprovoked attack, for a term of five years to be extended for another three years if not denounced in due time. The treaty was joined by Germany and was repeatedly extended, the last time being January, 1913. Romania thus had a firm position in the international relations of South-east Europe, which were occasionally strained. The radicals and the conservatives attacked the treaty when they knew about it, the radicals in fear that it might prevent the liberation movement of the Romanians of Transylvania and the conservatives out of sheer opportunism.

3. The Working Class and the Socialist Movement in the Last Decades of the Nineteenth Century. The Peasant Uprising of 1888

THE strides made in industry, transport facilities, and trade brought about an increase in the number of workers, and a corresponding rise in the number of strikes, owing to hard living conditions. After 1879 new vocational organizations were created in various branches of production and it is on them that the Romanian trade union movement was to rely during the last decade of the nineteenth century. The socialist movement, now legal, asserted itself vigorously. In 1887 workers' circles were organized in Bucharest and Jassy, these political organizations helping towards the adoption of scientific socialism by the working class movement and thus raising the movement of the Romanian proletariat to a higher stage. The propaganda some of the Bucharest socialists made in the villages in March and April, 1888, intensified the militant spirit of the peasantry.

After the granting of land to the newly married couples in 1878, many peasants had petitioned the government and the Legislative Bodies for land, but in vain. And with the drought that had played havoc in almost the entire country in 1887, the villagers were faced with starvation. The government distributed maize on credit but the quantities provided were insufficient, while the oppressive methods practised by the landowners and the great lessees were aided and abetted by the village and county authorities. The peasants' exasperation grew. The socialists as well as the United Opposition made propaganda in the countryside against the government. A revolt broke out at Urziceni and in a matter of days had spread to the villages in the neighbourhood. The peasants entered the town of Călărași. Before a week was over the uprising had spread throughout the counties of Ilfov, Dîmbovița, and Moldavia. In order to put it down, the Cabinet of Theodor Rosetti, formed on April 3, 1888, from members of the Junimea movement, young intellectuals, mainly conservative, sent the army against the peasants, many of whom were killed, injured, or arrested. By April 23 the uprising had been quelled in the counties around Bucharest, but the peasants resisted in other counties for another month.

The growth of the working class movement from 1888 to 1899 was evidenced by two great strikes : the strike of the workers employed at the Central Railway Shop of Bucharest and the strike of the printers (1888). The socialist movement also developed, in particular after Ioan Nădejde and D. Gh. Morțun were returned in the election of 1888. The next year five Romanian socialists, including C. Mille, Dr. D. Voinov, and Emil Racoviță, participated in the congress held in Paris which instituted the Second International. In 1890 the Bucharest Workers' Circle became the Workers' Club with a Press organ of its own — *Munca (The Labour)*. Other workers' clubs were set up in other towns and some of them had their own papers. With the working class movement developing, the first class party of the Romanian proletariat — the Social Democratic Party of the Workers of Romania — was formed in March, 1893. From 1890 on, local social democratic organizations were formed in Transylvania with a membership of Romanian, Hungarian, and German workers. With the number of workers increasing, workers' trade unions were started in Transylvania, but a law of the Magyar Parliament forbade railway workers and miners to join them. In the last decade of the nineteenth century the influence of the socialists increased in the ranks of agricultural labourers in Transylvania, who were being exploited by the landowners and the big lessees.

4. The Conservative Cabinets

IN order to prevent the indictment of the former cabinet under I. C. Brătianu and the denunciation of the alliance with Austria-Hungary, which the United Opposition had threatened to do, the king entrusted the Junimea group with the formation of the cabinet although this group had no electoral backing. The Premier, Theodor Rosetti, was also Minister of Home Affairs, P. P. Carp, the real leader of the Junimea group, was Minister of Foreign Affairs, Titu Maiorescu was Minister of Public Education and Cults, and Al. Marghiloman, a former liberal who had joined the Junimea, was Minister of Justice. The Cabinet was accepted by the Liberal majority in the Legislative Bodies and continued the building of fortifications and the alliance with Austria-Hungary. In October there was a new election which returned a majority of members of the Liberal-Conservative Party headed by Lascăr Catargiu and Gh. Vernescu. Theodor Rosetti had to reshuffle his cabinet and bring in a number of Conservative-Liberals. On December 30, 1891, Lascăr Catargiu formed what Titu Maiorescu described as "the real and final Conservative cabinet", which also included Junimea members headed by P. P. Carp. The Cabinet was in office until October 15, 1895. It strengthened the economic and political position of the landowners; built up a stronger repressive machinery in the villages by means of a special law passed in 1892, whereby the prefects and sub-prefects were entitled to repress any movement that undermined the public order and public safety; in 1892 a rural gendarmerie was set up for the same purpose and a new law on agricultural arrangements was passed. The last important measure taken under the "great Conservative cabinet", as it was described, was the Law on Mines promulgated in April, 1895, on the initiative of P. P. Carp. The law created advantages for foreign, especially German, capitalists, and with the aim of weakening the workers' movement, provided for the creation of assistance and pension funds for the workers. Having become President of the National-Liberal Party in 1892, D. A. Sturdza took advantage of the public opinion in Romania in favour of the national movement in Transylvania and set afoot great street demonstrations against the Conservative government. After the Law on Mines had been passed, the Liberals accused the Conservative government of having created advantages for foreign capitalists. In October, 1895, the cabinet of Lascăr Catargiu resigned under pressure of the demonstrations organized by the liberals.

5. The National Movement of the Transylvanian Romanians

IN Transylvania the Magyar government carried on a policy designed to denationalize the other nationalities living there. A law passed in 1879 enforced the use of the Hungarian language in all schools in town and village. The few Romanian deputies to the Budapest Parliament and the two Romanian Metropolitans of Blaj and Sibiu protested to the emperor against this law. A conference held in Sibiu in May, 1881, with the participation of 153 delegates — both Transylvanian and Banat delegates — decided that the two Romanian parties should merge into one single party and be called the Romanian National Party. The programme of the party raised a number of claims: autonomy for Transylvania, the use of the Romanian language in administration throughout the territories inhabited by Romanians, amendments to the Law of Nationalities, the appointment of state officials who knew Romanian in the territories inhabited by Romanians, a wider franchise, and the abolition of the measures resulting in national oppression. Since the divergences between those advocating an active and those declaring for a passive policy persisted, it was impossible to establish a single policy. However, both sides agreed that a memorial should be drawn up to show at length the unfair conditions created for the Romanians in Hungary. In 1882, in pursuance of that decision of the Sibiu Conference, G. Barițiu published at Sibiu a memorial in Romanian, Hungarian, French, and German, which was given a warm reception by the Press organs and the progressive political circles of Europe.

The damaging consequences for the Transylvanian economy of the customs war waged by Austria-Hungary against Romania in 1886 increased the resistance of the Transylvanian Romanians against the oppression of the Magyar government. A conference of the Romanian National Party held at Sibiu in 1887 decided that a new memorial should be drawn up to protest against the persecution of the Romanians. The memorial was to be handed to Emperor Francis Joseph and was also to be published. A favourable climate for launching the memorial was the creation in Bucharest of the League for the Cultural Unity of all Romanians as well as the *Memorial of the Bucharest Students* printed in French and the *Answer* written by Aurel C. Popovici. The memorial of the Transylvanian Romanians was published in Romanian, German, and Hungarian showing at length and with definite examples the injustice and oppression to which the Romanians were subjected by the Magyar government and its officials. It was signed by Ioan Rațiu, President of the Romanian National Party, Gh. Pop de Băsești, and Eugen Brote, Vice-Presidents of the Party, Vasile Lucaciu, Secretary General, Septimiu Albini, Secretary, and Iuliu Coroian, reviewer. A delegation of 300 Romanians led by Ioan Rațiu and made up representatives of all social strata went to Vienna to hand the memorial to the Emperor. On May 28, 1892 Francis Joseph, at the request of the Hungarian government, refused to receive the delegation. The delegation filed the memorial with the Imperial Chancellery, but the emperor sent it to the Hungarian Minister attached to the Imperial Court, without reading it. The Budapest government ordered that the memorial should be sent to the Prefecture of the country of Turda to be returned to Ioan Rațiu and that the signatories should be indicted. In May, 1894, the Cluj Tribunal judged the case for 18 days and sentenced the signatories of the memorial to imprisonment. Ten thousand Romanians, most of them peasants, demonstrated in sympathy with the accused. The national movement of the Transylvanian Romanians had gained much prestige; it was supported by the entire Romanian people and called forth a powerful response both in Europe and in America.

6. Conservatives and Liberals Rule the Country in turn

DESPITE the Liberals' violent demonstrations against the Conservative government, the two "historical" parties had come to a tacit agreement in accordance with which they were each in turn to form a cabinet. The system was upheld by King Charles and was applied until 1914 but, with the Conservative Party gradually falling apart, it functioned in favour of the Liberals. It was often described as the "Governmental Merry Go-Round".

7. The Arrangement between Liberals and Conservatives continues to Work

THE National-Liberal Party having been strengthened by the "generous ones" joining its ranks, as C. Stere, spokesman for the Populist Movement, had done a few years previously, was again in office with D. A. Sturdza as Premier in February, 1901. The economic crisis abating, the state was able to balance its budget, partly by cutting the civil servants' salaries. The Trades Law passed in 1902 gave rules and regulations establishing the mode of work in small workshops and created corporations which both employers and workers were obliged to join. As the corporations had been created to prevent the workers from forming trade unions based on the class struggle, the workers began to fight against them as well as for the abolition of the Trades Law. In 1903 a Law on Popular Banks and a Central Fund was passed in order to strengthen the influence of the bourgeoisie on the well-to-do and middle peasants. In 1904 a law on the management of agricultural communities was sanctioned under which the representative of such a community was able to obtain loans on mortgage from the Rural Land Credit Fund. Misunderstandings arising between various groups, brought about the resignation of Sturdza's cabinet in December, 1904. A Conservative cabinet then came in, with Gh. Gr. Cantacuzino as Premier but without any members of the Junimea movement, the latter having formed a party of their own. The main part in the cabinet was played by Take Ionescu, Minister of Finance, who was upheld by a bourgeois wing of the Conservative Party. In order to strengthen its relations with the king, the Conservative government celebrated a Forty Years' Jubilee of Charles' reign in May, 1906, with much pomp and at great expense. The Liberals refused to participate and a socialist circle — "Working Romania" — published the anti-dynastic pamphlet: *Forty Years of Poverty, Slavery, and Shame*. Nearly two months before, on March 26, 1906, a great street demonstration of the students had taken place in Bucharest at the prompting of the great historian, Nicolae Iorga; this was joined by the townspeople. The demonstration was against the cosmopolitanism of the Conservative landowners whom Iorga also criticized in his gazette, *Neamul Românesc (The Romanian People)*. The withdrawal of the Conservatives from the cabinet on March 25, 1907, was the immediate political effect of the great uprising of that year.

8. National Movement of the Transylvanian Romanians from 1894 to 1914

IN Transylvania the Romanian National Party continued its activities although its leaders were in prison and the party had been dissolved. In November, 1894, a conference held at Sibiu protested against the ordinance whereby the party had been dissolved. The Romanian National Party continued its activities, participating in a Congress of Nationalities made up of Romanians, Serbs, and Slovaks, which was held in Budapest in 1895 and where a programme was drawn up to oppose the policy of Magyarization. Upon Rațiu's death in 1902, Gh. Pop de Băsești, one of the leaders of the Transylvanian movement, was elected president of the Romanian National Party. In January, 1905, a National Conference was held, which decided that the passive policy be abandoned and an active one of a more comprehensive character be taken up, and demanding that the peasants on state-owned estates should be given land, and universal suffrage be allowed. In the Parliamentary election of 1906, 14 Romanian candidates were returned. In Budapest the Romanian deputies, together with the Serbian and Slovak formed a group with Teodor Mihali, a Romanian, as president, and Milan Hodza, a Slovak, as secretary. There were two trends in the Romanian National Party : national-radical under the leadership of Ioan Russu-Șirianu, and moderate-national headed by Teodor Mihali and Al. Vaida Voevod. When the monarchy came to be discussed, various forms of federalization were proposed to solve the problem of the nationalities which was creating increasing difficulties. In 1906 Aurel C. Popovici published *Die Vereinigten Staaten von Gross-Österreich (The United States of Greater Austria)* proposing that the Habsburg Empire should be turned into a federation of the various nationalities.

The Budapest government, realizing that this would minimize Hungary's position in the monarchy, responded by the Apponyi Law which stipulated that all denominational and private elementary schools should be closed. The schools, in which all subjects were taught in Romanian, were denominational. And the reason given by Apponyi for their closing was that the schoolchildren did not master the Hungarian language satisfactorily. A large meeting of Romanians was held at Sibiu to protest against this law, and their protest caused a number of famous writers to attack the Apponyi Law. Among these writers were Leo Tolstoy and Björnsterne Björnson.

9. The Socialist Movement in the Early Years of the Twentieth Century. The Peasant Uprising of 1907

AFTER the Workers' Social Democratic Party was disbanded in 1899, the socialist movement went through a transient period of stagnation until 1902, when a new stage in the development of the working class movement began in Romania simultaneously with the issue of the gazette *România Muncitoare (The Working Romania)*. Before 1907 the main objective of the movement was the struggle against corporations and for the setting up of trade unions. In 1906 a General Trade Union Commission was created as a nucleus for the Romanian trade union movement, with the participation of delegates from all territories inhabited by Romanians, including those under foreign rule.

In 1905 the *România Muncitoare* was published again after having been banned for some time, and this gave a new impetus to the working class movement. Strikes were called, in particular in Bucharest, Galatz, and Turnu Severin, where the strike movement was led by the local socialist circles and the trade unions. When the bourgeois democratic revolution broke out in Russia in 1905, the Romanian workers showed their sympathy for the revolutionary struggle of the Russian proletariat and peasants against the autocratic Tsarist government by holding a mass meeting in Bucharest and issuing a gazette *Jos Despotismul (Down with Despotism)*. The Romanian socialist movement gave material and moral support to the 700 sailors on the Russian cruiser *Prince Potemkin,* which had landed at Constantza and asked political asylum from the Romanian government.

In Transylvania a Romanian section of the Social-Democratic Party of Hungary was formed in 1903, the Romanian socialist movement thus assuming a national form. In December, 1905, an independent congress of the section was held at Lugoj. After the Romanian socialist section had been set up, the ties between the Romanian socialists on both sides of the Carpathians became closer.

The peasant movement developed in Transylvania at the close of the nineteenth century as a result of the proletarianization of an important part of the peasantry and of socialist propaganda among agricultural labourers. In Crişana and Banat there was an increasing number of strikes at harvesting time. Prompted by the workers of Oradea, the peasants of Aleşd and the neighbouring villages rose in 1904 against the authorities who favoured the landowners. The gendarmes fired at them and killed 33 peasants and wounded many others, most of them Romanians. In token of solidarity, the workers of Oradea went on strike. In their anxiety, the Magyar landowners caused the Daranyi Bill to be passed in April, 1907, establishing the relations between landowners and agricultural labourers : agricultural strikes were banned and the agricultural labourers who opposed the landowners and big lessees were severely punished.

In Romania a great uprising broke out in February, 1907, as a result of intensified exploitation of the various strata of peasants. This was a genuine peasant war, which started at Flămînzi in the country of Botoşani against Mochi Fischer, a lessee who had created a great land trust in northern Moldavia.

In March 1907, masses of peasants devastated the houses of certain lessees in the town of Botoșani. The army went into action and a considerable number of peasants were killed and injured. The uprising spread over the counties of Dorohoi and Jassy. The peasants demanded that the rent for the land they held from the big lessees should be reduced. Before long the rebellion had swept over the southern part of Moldavia and then on March 22 it flared up in the counties of Rîmnicu Sărat and Buzău and a little later extended to the county of Teleorman, where it rose to its greatest height. In the days that followed, the villages of the counties of Vlașca, Olt, and Romanați were in arms to be followed by the counties of Dolj and Mehedinți. The peasants set fire to the landowners' country houses and divided the grain, cattle, and land among themselves. In the towns of Vaslui, Galatz, Rîmnicu Sărat and Buzău, they sought out the landowners, the big lessees and the prefects of the counties. The ruling classes, especially the landowners, were panic-stricken. On March 25, 1907, the Conservative cabinet presided over by Gh. Gr. Cantacuzino, unable to put down the revolt, resigned. A Liberal cabinet was then formed with D. A. Sturdza as Premier, Ionel Brătianu as Minister of Home Affairs, and General Averescu as Minister of War. The next day the two historical parties — the Liberals and the Conservatives — pledged in Parliament to support each other until the revolt had been put down. Brutal repression followed. Many peasants were killed or taken into custody and maltreated, and some of them were tried and sentenced. By the 20th of March, 1907, the uprising had been quelled. Many thousands of peasants had been killed; estimates go as high as 11,000.

The workers of Pașcani, Galatz, Bucharest, the Prahova Valley, and other parts of the country supported the rebel peasants. On March 24, 1907, a large meeting of the Bucharest workers protested against the exploitation of the peasantry and the oppression of the administrative bodies. The young socialist M. Gh. Bujor published a call in the *România Muncitoare*: "To the Conscripted Soldiers and Those in the Reserve", directing the soldiers not to fire at the peasants but to side with them. Many intellectuals spoke or wrote in defence of the peasants. The uprising of 1907 called forth wide response in Transylvania, in the ranks of the intelligentsia as well as in those of the workers and peasants, and was not without an impact on various countries in Europe. Lenin compared its consequences with those of the bourgeois-democratic revolution in Russia. At the Congress of the Second International, held in Stuttgart in the summer of 1907, the Romanian delegates introduced into the discussion the reasons for the peasant revolt and the manner in which it had been repressed.

After the uprising had been put down, the Liberal cabinet went in for Parliamentary elections and submitted to the legislative bodies bills which, in their view, would solve the land problem. In December, 1907, a law on agricultural arrangements was passed establishing the minimum wages of agricultural labourers and the maximum rent that could be asked of the peasants who rented land. The Rural Fund Law, passed in 1908, provided for the creation of a bank that was assigned the task to purchase landed estates to be sold to the peasants in smallholdings. It was also in 1908 that a law was passed forbidding anyone to rent more than 8,000 acres. The next year another law was passed under which the state-owned estates and those which were church, county, or village property or belonged to charitable and cultural institutions, were to be leased to peasant associations. All these measures reduced the landowners exploitation of the peasants but did not solve the land problem.

D. A. Sturdza having resigned for reasons of health, Ionel Brătianu was elected president of the National-Liberal Party and was asked to form a cabinet in 1908.

With the number of strikes increasing and the Workers' Party being reorganized, the Liberal government, in its anxiety, passed a law — the Orleanu Law — in 1909 forbidding state employees to join trade unions.

10. The Social-Democratic Party of Romania is Reorganized

THE Socialist Conference held at Galatz in June, 1907, created the Socialist Union of Romania as the centre of the socialist circles and sent four delegates to the Congress of the Second International at Stuttgart. The statutes of the Union were sanctioned by a new conference held in Bucharest in January, 1908, when a draft programme was also discussed. With the socialist movement developing at a swift tempo it became necessary to reorganize the Social-Democratic Party, which was done at the Congress of February 15, 1910. The aim of the Party was "to do away with labour exploitation of any kind and to replace exploitation by the socialization of the means of production". In regard to the agrarian problem, the programme confined its aim to "compulsory redemption of as large a part of the big estates, as will be necessary". Other aims were universal suffrage, a lay educational system, and in the national problem "solidarity with the Romanian proletariat of Transylvania".

In 1912 and 1913 the Social-Democratic Party fought against Romania's participation in the Balkan Wars, supporting the decisions made by the Congress of the Second International held at Basel in November, 1912. In January, 1914, a Trade Union Congress was held in Bucharest. The Romanian Socialists demanded universal suffrage and also that the state purchase the big landed estates and rent them to the peasants. A general strike was announced for the summer of 1914 with the aim of compelling the Revision Chambers to make the democratic reforms demanded by the socialists. Subsequently the strike was postponed until autumn but never took place on account of the war.

11. Romania on the Eve of and during the Balkan Wars. World War I in the Offing

AT the close of the year 1910 the Conservatives were in office again with P.P. Carp as Premier, the latter having been elected President of the Conservative Party in 1907. In 1908 the group headed by Take Ionescu had formed a separate party — the Democratic-Conservative Party — whose programme voiced especially the interests of the middle bourgeoisie. The new Parliament elected in 1911 passed a new Trades Law which determined the hours of work for women and children. Apart from the obligation imposed on all employers and workers to join the guilds and consequently the corporations, workers' insurance funds were created for cases of illness and disability as well as a fund for old age pensions. In 1912 a new law was promulgated encouraging the industries that used agricultural produce, native oil, or minerals as raw materials. When the government wished to close the streetcar company in Bucharest, they came into violent conflict with the Liberals who held most of the shares, and P. P. Carp was compelled to resign in April, 1912. The new cabinet was formed with the participation of the Democratic-Conservative Party, with Titu Maiorescu as Premier.

On October 9, 1912, the First Balkan War broke out between Bulgaria, Serbia, Greece, and Montenegro on the one side, and the Ottoman Empire on the other. Romania declared her neutrality. In June, 1913, Bulgaria attacked Serbia and Greece. On July 10, Romania declared war on Bulgaria, and, without encountering any serious resistance, her army reached the outskirts of Sofia and the Bulgarian government sued for peace. Peace was concluded on August 10, 1913, between Romania, Serbia, and Greece on the one side, and Bulgaria on the other. Romania annexed Southern Dobrudja down to a line linking Turtucaia to Ekrene. As peace had been concluded without the participation of Austria-Hungary, the latter's prestige in South-east Europe dwindled.

Undermined by the misunderstandings between the two Conservative Parties whose alliance had been achieved forcibly by the king, the government presided over by Titu Maiorescu resigned in January, 1914. Ionel Brătianu who some six months previously had announced his programme of democratic reforms, with more land for the peasants and a unique electoral college, then formed a Liberal cabinet. The Liberals' success in the Parliamentary election was ensured to a great extent by the democratic reforms previously announced. After the new Legislative Bodies had voted for the Constitution to be revised in April, 1914, they were dissolved and new elections were made for the Revision Chambers though the revision of the Constitution was postponed on account of the war having broken out in the summer.

The period between 1878 and 1914 was a comparatively quiet one in foreign affairs, but it was shaken by two big peasant uprisings in 1888 and 1907 in Romania, and by the National Movement activities from 1892 to 1894 in Transylvania. It was, moreover, a period of considerable capitalist development of Romanian society, in particular in the economy and in culture. Romania's independence was strengthened and conditions were created for the union of all Romanians into a national state.

CHAPTER THIRTEEN
ROMANIA IN THE FIRST WORLD WAR

DURING the period 1859-62 Moldavia and Wallachia united to form a single state that in 1862 was named Romania, and was recognized by the powers which had signed the Treaty of Paris. In 1878 the new Romanian state won its independence and in the decades that followed modern institutions strengthened the state. The First World War and the great October, 1917, Socialist Revolution — which paved the way for the general crisis of capitalism and for great changes in social and international relations — created objective conditions for the union of all Romanians into a national State.

1. Romania Remains Neutral (1914-16)

WHEN the war for a new division of the world among the great powers broke out, Romania, which had concluded a treaty of alliance with Austria-Hungary, was forced to make a decision. On August 3, 1914, a Crown Council was called together at Sinaia under the chairmanship of King Charles with the participation of the cabinet and of the heir apparent, Prince Ferdinand, as well as the President of the Assembly of Deputies, former Premiers and the Presidents of the various parties. The King, supported by P. P. Carp, was in favour of Romania joining Germany and Austria-Hungary, to which she was bound by a treaty of alliance which had been extended not long before. Theodor Rosetti declared for neutrality while Al. Marghiloman and Take Ionescu proposed an armed neutrality, a point of view subscribed to by Brătianu, Chairman of the Council of Ministers, who had previously come to an understanding with them and was also upheld by Ion Lahovari, M. Pherekyde, and others. When a telegram announced Italy's decision to remain neutral, Italy also being an ally of Austria-Hungary and Germany, Charles I accepted armed neutrality, having to submit to the will of the majority in his capacity as constitutional king. Both Italy and Romania felt bound by treaty of alliance only in the event of an unprovoked attack, but now it had been Austria-Hungary which had opened hostilities.

The defeat of the Austro-Hungarian armies in Galicia and of the German armies on the Marne strengthened the current in favour of the Entente, and hopes were raised of liberating the Romanian territories under Habsburg oppression. The Liberal government secretly acted to this end. With the king's knowledge, Brătianu obtained an agreement that Russia, in exchange for Romania's benevolent neutrality, "should oppose any change of the territorial status quo of the present frontiers" of the Romanian state and should acknowledge her right "to annex the regions of the Austro-Hungarian monarchy inhabited by Romanians". In September, 1914, a secret convention was concluded with Italy under which the two countries agreed not to abandon neutrality without advising each other.

In ill health and having experienced great spiritual anxiety, with the thought of abdicating always uppermost, Charles I died on October 10, 1914. His successor was his nephew, Ferdinand, whose wife, Marie, was closely related to the British and Russian dynasties and did not hide her inclination towards the Entente. Ferdinant wanted to declare war in order to liberate Transylvania.

R. W. Seton-Watson, referring to the death of the monarch, said that:

> The utterly abnormal situation of the moment dwarfed an event which would otherwise have been recognized as ending the most prosperous and pacific era in all the troubled history of the Romanian race. The nation was not in a mood for calm estimates and retrospects: it was holding its breath before a plunge which instinct told it was sooner or later inevitable, into murky waters whose depth it could not fathom, and for the moment it felt out of sympathy with the dead monarch. But today there is no sane Romanian who would deny the essential greatness of its first king, his untiring efforts to raise and fix the standards of public and private life in a country demoralised by corrupt alien rule, his rigid insistence on the example that the court must set, his rare qualities as an administrator and as a soldier, his devotion to duty, the realist methods which he applied to problems of foreign policy, his constant encouragement of intellectual effort in every sphere. His weak points... were the artificial balancing by which he sought to retain his control of politics, the exaggerated secrecy in which he shrouded his relations with other Powers, above all his narrow outlook towards the peasant masses, which he scarcely admitted as a factor in his political calculations. But these were limitations due to the environment from which he came and to a period which had created the illusion of permanence upon contemporaries, but was in reality essentially fluid.

The new king, Ferdinand, lacked his uncle's prestige and political associations. Though well-read, versatile and a good judge of character, he was deficient in will power, slow to reach a decision: a natural diffidence made him uncertain in the expression of opinion, and he was much amenable to the influence of a powerful minister.

The Romanian National Party in Transylvania suspended its activities when the war broke out. Following the advice given by King Charles and by Brătianu, its leaders did not oppose the war started by Austria-Hungary; some of them even declared their loyalty. Although the German government advised Hungary to make concessions to Romania in order to induce her to enter the war, the Hungarian Prime Minister, Istvan Tisza, only proposed that some territories not belonging to the Hungarian kingdom should be ceded to Romania.

Having signed the agreement with Russia, the Liberal Cabinet decided to prolong the country's neutrality until the military situation would enable Romania to make a decisive contribution entitling her to incorporate the Romanian territories of Austria-Hungary. In the meantime Romania was to acquire war materials and the Entente to organize an expedition to the Balkan Peninsula and to create a favourable situation on the Eastern Front.

In order to endow the country with sufficient quantities of modern armament, orders were placed in Italy, Britain, and France, credit being allowed by the suppliers. In November, 1915, a General Board was created in the War Ministry to arrange that 30 per cent of the ammunition necessary should be produced within the country, the remainder to be imported. As the fortifications around Bucharest and along the Focşani-Nămoloasa-Galatz line were out of date, because of the firing range of the artillery, 250 heavy cannons were taken from the forts to build up a heavy artillery. The armament and ammunition that had been ordered arrived in the country only at the close of 1916, so that when Romania entered the war her army was poorly equipped with modern armament.

Although conscription reduced the manpower available for agriculture, the farming output was maintained at the level of the previous years. When Turkey entered the war in October, 1914, and closed the Bosphorus and the Dardanelles, Romania could no longer export grain, oil products, and timber to the Western countries and was compelled to accept the terms of the Central Powers whose share in Romanian exports increased greatly. The government took measures against excessive exports by organizing in October, 1915, a central commission for the sale exports of grain and grain by-products, and a commission for wine exports. In order to prevent the Central Powers from getting grain supplies from Romania, Britain opened a British Bureau in Bucharest in January, 1916, which bought 800,000 tons of grain, though the grain could not be taken out of the country. Owing to the rise in the price of farm produce, the landowners and grain brokers made considerable profits.

Take Ionescu and N. Filipescu declared openly for Romania entering the war on the side of the Entente, and created the organization named National Action which arranged large street demonstrations. Simultaneously, the *League for the Cultural Unity of all Romanians,* under the leadership of N. Iorga since 1906, was acting in unison. On December 27, 1914, the Cultural League, as it was called for short, was reorganized and renamed The League for the Political Unity of all Romanians, with a new governing board made up of the Transylvanian Vasile Lucaciu, Chairman, and of N. Filipescu, Take Ionescu, N. Iorga, Dr. C. I. Istrati, Barbu Delavrancea, Simion Mândrescu, and Octavian Goga. The two organizations co-operated, drawing the people into the struggle for the liberation of Transylvania and Banat. The following year two more organizations were formed which agitated for Romania to join the war against Austria-Hungary; the *Unionist Federation* presided over by N. Filipescu, and the *Patriotic Action,* with C. I. Istrati as president.

While keeping up appearances of neutrality, Brătianu continued his negotiations for an alliance with all the Entente powers, which Italy had joined in May, 1915, without informing Romania, as she had engaged to do. In the autumn of 1915 there was an increased clamour for Romania to enter the war against Austria-Hungary, though there was also some Press propaganda in favour of co-operation with the Central Powers, led by Carp, Marghiloman, and their followers. On December 29 and 30, 1915, Take Ionescu in a speech to the Assembly of Deputies demanded that the cabinet carry on "a policy of national instinct" and declare war on Austria-Hungary. Brătianu answered briefly saying that he had assumed responsibility for the political situation of the country but refused to go into details. Carp alone violently attacked Take Ionescu's arguments.

2. The Socialist and Working Class Movement during Neutrality

FAITHFUL to the decisions made by the Stuttgart and Basel Congresses of the Second International, the Romanian Social-Democrats declared against Romania joining in the war. An extraordinary Congress of the Social-Democratic Party and of the trade union movement held in Bucharest on August 23, 1914, declared for absolute neutrality and for defending the territorial integrity of the country.

After the extraordinary Congress of August, 1914, there were numerous workers' meetings which debated the decisions that had been made and pointed to the baneful consequences of the armament drive on the workers' living conditions. At the meeting held in Bucharest on November 29, 1914, when the session of the Legislative Bodies opened, the Socialists launched the slogan: "Make war on war". In May, 1915, a demonstration against the war took place in Bucharest and in July of the same year the Social-Democratic Party held an Inter-Balkan Socialist Conference in Bucharest with the participation of Romanian Socialists, and of delegates of the left-wing Bulgarian Socialists and of Greek Socialists. The Conference pointed to the imperialist nature of the war between the Central Powers and the Entente and condemned the voting for war credits by the leaders of the Socialist parties in the belligerent countries.

With Romania's entry into the war in the offing, the workers' demonstrations against war increased in number. The most important took place under the leadership of the Social-Democratic Party at Galatz on June 26, 1916, on which occasion nine demonstrators were killed, among them Spiridon Vrânceanu and Pascal Zaharia. Decrying the Galatz slaughter, the workers of the main towns of the country demonstrated anew against war in the following days.

3. Romania Joins the War

BY August, 1916, neither the armies of the Central Powers, which had been joined by Bulgaria in October, 1915, nor those of the Entente had succeeded in obtaining a decisive victory in the war. Serbia had been defeated and her government had been compelled to withdraw to the island of Corfu with what was left of her army. The great German offensive which began at Verdun in February, 1916, ended after six months of heavy fighting without the victory that had been expected. The French armies had not been defeated, but in August, 1916, they were very weak and needed a long respite in order to renew their forces. On the Eastern Front the great Russian offensive of the spring of 1916 was prolonged into the summer, but was checked in mid-August. The Entente countries, finding themselves in a situation which threatened to become dangerous, for the Central Powers could resume their offensive at Verdun or start a counter-offensive on the Eastern Front, forced Romania to enter the war, threatening her that she would not be accepted as an ally unless she decided then and there. Russia was the first to order Romania to attack Austria-Hungary in June, 1916, and France followed suit in early

July. Hard-pressed, the Romanian government gave in although the country's military preparations had not been completed. On August 17, 1916, Romania signed a treaty of alliance and a military convention with the Entente Powers. She was admitted as an ally with rights equal to those of the other allied powers and was given the right to obtain the Romanian territories in Austria-Hungary. Russia engaged to support Romania in Dobrudja by sending one cavalry and two infantry divisions. An offensive was to be undertaken in Galicia and at Salonika in order to help Romania in her military operations against Austria-Hungary. It was decided that Romania was to enter the war on August 28, 1916. When the two documents had been signed, Stürmer, Russia's new Foreign Minister, demanded that the great allied powers should revise their treaty with Romania at the end of the war.

A Crown Council held in the Cotroceni Palace on the evening of August 28, 1916, decided that Romania was to join in the war against Austria-Hungary. That night the Romanian armies marched into Transylvania. Concurrently, Romania's representative in Vienna submitted his country's declaration of war to the Austro-Hungarian government. Romania went to war for the liberation of Transylvania and of the other territories whose majority population was indisputably Romanian. The war Romania undertook against Austria-Hungary in 1916, like the war of independence of 1877-8, was welcomed by the Romanian population in Transylvania.

4. The First Phase in Romania's War: August-December, 1916

ON declaring war on Austria-Hungary, the Romanian government mobilized 833,601 men, 522,890 of them in the fighting units, which consisted of 23 infantry divisions and two cavalry divisions, apart from other units.

The army did not possess sufficient modern armament. The time of her entry into the war was unfavourable as there were no great battles being waged on the Western or the Eastern Fronts and the offensives promised by the Entente in Galicia and at Salonika did not take place. The Central Powers were able to withdraw a sufficient number of well-trained divisions from the Western, the Eastern, and the Salonika fronts to send them against Romania.

The government had decided that the troops should advance into Transylvania but General Averescu and other senior officers, as well as the French command, thought it preferable to keep on the defensive along the Carpathians and to march into Bulgaria in order to join the Allied armies at Salonika from where modern armament and ammunition could easily be brought. The viewpoint of the government, who considered it necessary immediately to liberate the territories inhabited by Romanians, prevailed. During the first days the 1st, 2nd and 3rd Romanian armies liberated Orşova, Braşov, St. Gheorghe, Gheorghieni, and Miercurea Ciucului, crossing the Perşani Mountains in the north-eastern part of the county of Făgăraş, as well as the Volcanic Mountains towards the town of Tîrgu-Mureş. On September 3, 1916, an army made up of Bulgarian, German, and Turkish units under Field Marshal Mackensen attacked Romania along the Dobrudja Front, took Turtucaia after three days' fighting and advanced northward without meeting any opposition, conquering Silistra on its way. The Romanian armies suffered heavy casualties and by the end of September they had been forced to withdraw along the Carpathian Line. The German and Austro-Hungarian troops took the way of the Oituz Valley in order to encircle most of the Romanian army in Oltenia and Muntenia, and possibly to capture the government. Their attacks were, however, repelled. Similar attacks were repelled at Predeal and along the Olt Valley. At the end of October, after an unsuccessful attempt, seven German divisions under General Kühne's command started an offensive along the Jiu Valley against a single Romanian division and forced it to withdraw south-east; the Germans then took Craiova and crossed the Olt. Mackensen conquered in turn, Constantza and Cernavodă late in October and advanced the front to North Dobrudja. On November 24 another five German, Bulgarian, and Turkish divisions crossed the Danube at Zimnicea advancing towards Bucharest while the Germans south of Sibiu entered the Olt defile making for Pitești and Bucharest. In early October, a French military mission under the command of General Berthelot had arrived in the country to help the Romanian units. Advised by General Berthelot, the Romanian general staff had started a counter-offensive along the Rivers Argeș and Neajlov, but the Romanian units were attacked by the Germans from the west and were forced to withdraw eastward. On December 6, Bucharest was occupied only a short time after the King and the government had left for Jassy. Despite her losses, Romania was not out of the fight. Coping with an enemy superior in number, and with better armament and more military experience, the Romanian armies had, nevertheless, inflicted heavy losses on the Central Powers. Romania's sacrifices in men and territory enabled the allied armies, especially the French, to rebuild their forces. General Ludendorff wrote in his *War Memoirs*: "We defeated the Romanian army, but were unable to destroy it. Despite our victory over the Romanian army we were weaker than we had been."

While the front was being maintained, the government was reorganized, Take Ionescu as a minister without portfolio and some of his followers coming in on December 24, 1916. When the Parliamentary session opened in Jassy, the Message of the Crown again pointed to the necessity of land reform and of a wider franchise. This was done in order to raise the morale of the soldiers.

In the territories that had been occupied — Oltenia, Muntenia, and most of Dobrudja — the Germans imposed a state of military occupation the aim of which was to collect as many agricultural and industrial products as possible to sustain the war of the Central Powers. There were requisitions of grain, cattle, wine, oil products, industrial installations, machines, and various materials. The Romanian General Bank, with German capital, was authorized to issue paper money. By the time the Peace of Bucharest was concluded, the bank had flooded the market with 2,172 million lei, more than half for the German occupation armies and the remainder for the Austro-Hungarian, Bulgarian, and Turkish armies. It was with this money that the occupants paid for part of the agricultural and industrial products taken from the population. A Romanian administration was organized under the leadership of the Conservative Kostaki Lupu, a follower of P. P. Carp. The latter, together with Maiorescu, Marghiloman, and Stere, had remained in the occupied territory. In the summer of 1917 Stere published *Lumina (The Light)*, a paper which decried Romania's entry in the war beside the Entente. The occupation forces issued a paper in Bucharest: *Gazeta Bucureștilor (The Bucharest Gazette)*, with an edition in German: *Bukarester Tageblatt*. Part of the population, especially townspeople, had withdrawn to Moldavia.

5. Military and Political Developments in the First Half of 1917

A balance of forces was created when the Romanian Front was along the lower reaches of the River Siret and the Eastern Carpathians. In the winter of 1916-7 the fighting continued on the Western and Russian Fronts without any decisive results, though Germany had started a great submarine war in order to force Britain and France to their knees. The Russian Revolution of

February, 1917, which removed Tsarism and installed a republic weakened the Eastern Front of the Entente. The U.S. armies came into the war on the Western Front only in the summer of 1918. The Central Powers availed themselves of the lull in the fighting to try to put Romania and Russia out of action, then Italy and finally France, and thus obtain a decisive victory.

Living conditions were very difficult in Moldavia, where the government had withdrawn with a large part of the state machinery, the army, part of the organization for waging war, and part of the population of the occupied territory, and where numerous Russian military units were also to be found. There was a shortage of housing, fuel, and food, particularly in the winter of 1917, which was unusually long and severe. The agglomeration, malnutrition, and insufficiency of hospitals as well as lack of medicines caused an epidemic of typhus which took a toll of tens of thousands of people, especially soldiers and children. In the spring massive requisitioning of cattle and the mobilization of the peasantry brought about farming difficulties, so that it was thought necessary to extend the requisitioning law to agricultural labourers and women. Food supplies eventually improved owing to the Russian government's consent to the Romanian state's organizing storehouses administered by its own officials east of the Prut. From October, 1916, to May, 1918, the state borrowed large sums from the National Bank of Romania and obtained a credit of 40 million pounds sterling from the Bank of England in order to meet war requirements. As the National Bank had issued large quantities of bank notes, the Romanian currency began to fall. Afraid that Jassy, too, might be taken by the enemy, the government sent the treasury of the National Bank, to the value of over 300 million lei in gold, plus other state and private valuables, to Moscow for safekeeping. This was done on the basis of agreements concluded with the Russian government.

The outbreak of the bourgeois-democratic Revolution in Russia on March 10, 1917, called forth a response also in Romania, where numerous Russian troops, whose commander was under King Ferdinand's nominal authority, were also to be found. The left wing of the National Liberal Party, though with only a small membership, founded a new party in April — the Labour Party — which numbered among its members the former socialist G. Diamandi, Dr. N. Lupu, Gr. Trancu-Iași, Professor M. Carp, and others. The new party pledged itself to agitate for the granting of a sufficiency of land to the peasants before long, for workers' legislation reducing the hours of work, for universal suffrage and the country's democratization. With the consent of the government and in pursuance of N. Iorga's advice, King Ferdinand issued a proclamation on April 5 promising the peasants land and universal suffrage. The proclamation, whose aim was to forestall revolt in the ranks of the peasants serving in the army, was repeated on May 6, 1917. The King's solemn promises were welcomed by the soldiers and helped to raise their morale. In June the Constituent Assembly passed the amendments to the Constitution whereby the land reform and universal suffrage came into force. On July 23 the cabinet was reshuffled, Take Ionescu becoming Vice-Chairman of the Council of Ministers. During the winter and later, many deputies and intellectuals, on the advice of the Chairman of the Council of Ministers, had gone to Odessa and Kherson and even to the United States and France in order to defend the interests of the country.

Following the outbreak of the Russian bourgeois-democratic revolution, soviets were organized among the soldiers of the Russian army at the Romanian front. In March and April, conferences were held between the Romanian Social-Democrats and the soviets of Russian soldiers in Jassy and in other towns not occupied by the Germans. Fearing that an insurrection supported by the

Russian soviets might break out, King Ferdinand went to the front on May 1, and gave another proclamation promising reforms.

When the front had been fixed, the Romanian government proceeded to reorganize the army, now made up of two instead of three army corps, with fifteen infantry divisions, two cavalry divisions, and a number of independent units. They were equipped with the modern armament that had been bought from France, Britain, and Italy two years previously but which had only reached the country in the winter of 1917. During the winter and spring soldiers and officers were trained to use the new armament and to master the new fighting techniques. The experience gained during the war had raised the military standards of the soldiers and officers, and of the commanding officers of large units. The self-seeking commanders were replaced by officers who had given proof of ability, courage, and patriotism. The French military mission was of great help in the reorganization of the army. The general staff came under the command of General C. Presan, former commander of the third army, while General C. Christescu was appointed commander of the first army though he was subsequently replaced by General Eremia Grigorescu. General Al. Averescu remained in command of the second army.

In the spring, summer, and autumn of 1917 Romanian volunteers from the Austro-Hungarian monarchy who had become prisoners in Russia increased the ranks of the army. On April 26, 1917, the organization of Romanian prisoners with its headquarters in Kiev (Darnitza) launched an appeal calling on all Romanian prisoners in Russia to fight for Romania, to enable her to bring about the union of the provinces under Habsburg rule with the mother country. The first batch of 1,500 volunteers, both soldiers and officers, reached Jassy on June 9, 1917, where they were given an enthusiastic welcome.

6. The Romanian Front in the Summer of 1917

THE Allies having demanded that an offensive should be launched in June on the Romanian and Russian Fronts, the First Army occupied an area along the lower reaches of the Siret between the Fourth and the Sixth Russian Armies, ready for an offensive at Nămoloasa, with the help of the Fourth Russian Army, to liberate Wallachia. The German command had also planned an offensive at Nămoloasa with the intent of encircling the Romanian and Russian armies in Moldavia after having broken the front with the assistance of the German-Austro-Hungarian troops in Galicia and Bukovina who were to start an offensive towards Cernăuți-Hotin-Chișinău at much the same time. When numerous Russian units were withdrawn from the Romanian Front to be sent to Bukovina and Galicia to check the German-Austro-Hungarian drive, the First Army changed from the offensive to the defensive in the Nămoloasa area. The Second Army under General Averescu's command went into action at Mărăști, together with the Fourth Russian Army, on July 24, 1917. The enemy lines were broken through along 30 miles to a depth of 20 miles, and the Romanians reached the River Putna. Compelled as they had been to give up their offensive at Nămoloasa when their front north-west of Focșani was threatened, the armies of the Central Powers attacked vigorously in the Mărășești and Oituz area on August 6, 1917, in order to encircle and wipe out the Second Romanian Army. For a fortnight the Germans attacked the Romanian-Russian positions but were repelled at every attack, counter-attacked and forced to retire. By September there was peace on the Romanian front.

The victories won at Mărăști, Mărășești, and Oituz inflicted heavy losses in men and materials on the Central Powers and enabled the Romanians to keep Moldavia.

7. Armistice with the Central Powers. The Treaty of Bucharest

THE Great October Revolution changed the situation in Eastern and South-eastern Europe. On November 21, the Soviet government issued a decree ordering that hostilities on all fronts should cease immediately and peace be concluded without any annexations or war reparations. On November 26, 1917, Soviet Russia proposed to the Central Powers that negotiations for a truce be started. The talks began at Brest-Litovsk on December 3, 1917, and a truce agreement was signed on December 15, 1917, followed by the signing of the peace treaty on March 3, 1918, between the Central Powers and Soviet Russia. General Scherbachev, Commander of the Russian armies on the Romanian Front, did not observe the cease-fire order given by the Soviets but lacked the necessary authority to carry out the plans of the Russian armies on the Romanian Front. On December 11, 1917, the Romanian government concluded a provisional armistice. The Brătianu cabinet resigned and was superseded by an Averescu cabinet on February 8, 1918, in preparation for the negotiations with the Central Powers. The main purpose was to gain time in the hope that the Allies would soon defeat the Central Powers. A Romanian delegation sent to Bucharest for talks demanded that the armistice be extended for at least another twenty days. Mackensen, Commander of the Forces of the Central Powers on the Romanian Front, would hear of no extension and demanded that the delegations for the conclusion of peace should meet on February 20, 1918. Carp and Stere manoeuvred with a view to replacing the dynasty with another which would be satisfactory to the Central Powers, so as to obtain better conditions.

General Averescu met Mackensen at Buftea, where he was informed of the terms of peace. Romania was required to demobilize her army but no territorial concessions to Bulgaria and Austria-Hungary were demanded.

On March 5, 1918, the preliminaries of peace were signed at Buftea. The Central Powers annexed Dobrudja to the banks of the Danube leaving to Romania a commercial way of access to the Black Sea through the port of Constanza. The frontier was changed in favour of Austria-Hungary and economic concessions were made to her. Eight divisions were to be demobilized immediately. The foreign military missions were to be repatriated as soon as possible. The French mission left for France by way of Russia.

The terms set by the Central Powers at Buftea were onerous, and General Averescu being unlikely to obtain better ones even if the negotiations were prolonged, a new cabinet under Marghiloman was formed on March 18, the latter being in favour with the Berlin and Vienna governments. After protracted negotiations, Marghiloman and von Kühlman-Burian, the new Foreign Affairs Minister of Austria-Hungary, jointly with the Bulgarian and Turkish delegates, signed the Treaty of Bucharest on May 7, 1918. Bulgaria was to have southern Dobrudja up to the Cernavodă-Constantza railway line, with the rest of Dobrudja becoming a condominium of the four conquering powers until Bulgaria and Turkey came to an understanding; Austria-Hungary was to have a large number of villages in the country of Suceava together with the Carpathian slopes up to the summits; the Romanian army was to be reduced to 8 divisions of peace-time strength; the two infantry divisions and the two cavalry divisions in Bessarabia were to keep their complete wartime strength; the country's exports of grain, cattle, and other foodstuffs were to be the monopoly of a German-Austro-Hungarian company soon to be set up; the shipyards at Turnu Severin were to go to Austria-Hungary; petroleum was to become the monopoly of a German enterprise for thirty years; navigation on the Danube and woodworking were to become a German and Austrian monopoly; the National Bank and public finances were to be under the control of German commissars; the Central Powers were to keep six divisions in the occupied territories as well as "the bodies required for economic exploitation", until the peace had been ratified. The Romanian government at Jassy would exercise its authority over Muntenia and Oltenia under German control when the treaty had been signed. In short, the Treaty of Bucharest was intended to turn Romania into a German colony.

8. Romania Joins in the War again

HAVING signed a peace with Soviet Russia, Germany started a new offensive on the Western Front in the hope of defeating France before the American armies went into action. Her early victories raised the confidence of the supporters of the Marghiloman Conservative cabinet. The Parliament, now incomplete, as many deputies, including Take Ionescu, had left for Western countries, was dissolved, and in May new elections were organized on the basis of the election lists of 1916, after the Peace Treaty of Bucharest. The Liberals not wishing to oppose the Conservative Government, the latter were returned.

The new Parliament had a number of bills to debate but its main task was to ratify the Treaty of Bucharest, which was finally done after long discussions. The king, however, had systematically put off the ratification of the treaty. Amendments to the Constitution were to be made by a Constituent Assembly after the termination of war.

The counter-offensive of the Entente on the Western Front, which had begun in July with continuous victories created an atmosphere unfavourable to the Marghiloman government. The Central Powers reproached Marghiloman with postponing the indictment of the Brătianu cabinet ministers, who were considered guilty of having declared war on Austria-Hungary. The matter was debated in Parliament and Al. Constantinescu, former Minister of Home Affairs, was taken into custody but was released after a few weeks. The command of the occupation forces moreover reproached the Romanian cabinet with postponing the ratification of the Peace Treaty of Bucharest. When Bulgaria succumbed after her defeats on the Salonika Front in September, 1918, Mackensen changed his stand and was prepared to alter the Treaty of Bucharest in Romania's favour.

On August 28, 1918, Marghiloman submitted his resignation to the king, who did not accept it. But the minister understood that defeat was awaiting the Central Powers and that he had played his part in politics. With the military collapse of Austria-Hungary and Germany imminent, the king demanded the resignation of the Marghiloman cabinet on November 6, 1918, upon which General Coandă, supported by the Liberals, formed the new cabinet. On November 10, 1918, military units on their way from Salonika crossed the Danube at Zimnicea under General Berthelot's command and were welcomed by the population as liberators. On the same day, the Romanian cabinet mobilized the army which again crossed the Carpathians, now to submit a memorial to the ministers of the Entente at Jassy, asserting that Romania "was entitled to make good her claims" and demanding that the Treaty of Bucharest be cancelled. At the same time the memorial declared that the Romanian state was resuming operations with the Allies. Concurrently, a declaration of war on Germany was sent to Mackensen who was asked to evacuate the country immediately. The following day Germany and the Allies concluded an armistice and World War I came to an end. Mackensen began his retreat on November 12, 1918. Three envoys of the Romanian National Party of Transylvania arrived in Jassy to inform the Romanian cabinet how matters stood in Transylvania and ask for their support and the help of the army. The Romanian National Committee also sent a delegation to Jassy with the same purpose in view. The Parliament that had been elected in May and the laws it had promulgated were cancelled.

The political representatives of the Romanian population in the provinces under Austria-Hungary had fought for liberty as had done the other nationalities, basing their claims on the principle of the right of self-determination.

9. Transylvania Unites with Romania

THROUGHOUT the duration of the war the measures taken by the Hungarian government in Transylvania caused much hardship for the working masses of all nationalities. With men being mobilized by the hundreds of thousands there was soon a shortage of manpower in both industry and agriculture. The right to strike was denied the workers and the hours of work were increased. Agricultural as well as industrial production decreased so that starvation was rife in the towns in 1917. The terrorizing of the working masses, and of the population generally, became worse after Romania's entry into the war, many Romanians being taken to concentration camps in Western Hungary, at Sopron, and even as far as Styria. Some were accused of treason. The review *Luceafărul (The Morning Star)* of Sibiu and the paper *Românul (The Romanian)* in Arad were both suspended. On August 2, 1917, the Hungarian government implemented a number of measures designed to Magyarize the denominational Romanian schools in the vicinity of the Hungarian frontier. The overwhelming majority of Romanian intellectuals, including Iuliu Maniu, St. Ciceo-Pop and Vasile Goldiș, refused to sign the declaration of loyalty demanded by the Tisza cabinet in December, 1916. The threat of famine, the cruel exploitation and police measures, to which should be added the encouragement given by the Russian revolution of February and especially by the October Socialist Revolution, impelled the workers and peasants to take a stronger stand against the dominant classes in the winter of 1917. There were many strikes, although they had been banned, organized by the trade unions, which had become active again.

The peace treaty that was concluded in March, 1918, with Soviet Russia and the Ukraine, and in May with Romania, did not shake the confidence of the masses in the forthcoming collapse of the Austro-Hungarian monarchy. Two general strikes caused the very foundations of Austria-Hungary to totter. In their turn the peasants agitated for land from the big estates. On February 1, 1918, there was mutiny on the warships in the port of Cattaro; the sailors demanded that peace talks should begin and the right to self-determination of the peoples in the Austro-Hungarian monarchy be recognized. Though the mutiny was repressed, the climate in the navy and the army was ominous. Many Romanians participated in the mutiny.

In October the revolutionary movement of the oppressed nations suddenly flared up: Romania, Czech, Slovak, Croatian Serbian, and Ukrainian soldiers were deserting from the front. On October 18, 1918, President Wilson recognized the right of the peoples of Austria-Hungary to national self-determination and less than a fortnight later — on October 28 — Prague was in revolt and the Czechoslovak Republic was proclaimed. Refusing to fire at the Czech demonstrators and, handing over to them their armament stores, the Romanian military units helped towards the victory of the revolution. The next day revolution broke out in Vienna and shortly after, on October 31, the autonomous state of the Serbs, Croatians, and Slovenes was created; revolution flared up in Budapest while on the Italian front the

Austro-Hungarian armies were being routed. The revolutionary movement had given rise to a bourgeois-democratic revolution in Transylvania as well, where the local authorities were ousted from office and the measures the Budapest government had previously enforced were ignored. Workers' Councils were organized at Timișoara, Oradea and Petroșani. The soldiers released their imprisoned comrades and the villagers forced the Austro-Hungarian authorities to flee. Everywhere national guards were formed, replacing the Habsburg military units. In many rural districts the peasants rose against the landowners and lessees. In November the membership of the Romanian socialist section amounted to 100,000.

On October 29 the Romanian Socialist Central Committee and the leaders of the Romanian National Party agreed to form a Romanian National Central Council to represent all the Romanians of Transylvania. Two weeks later the Romanian National Central Council was set up. It consisted of six Social-Democrats, Tiron Albani, Ion Flueraș, and Iosif Jumanca among them, and six members of the Romanian National Party, who were Theodor Mihali, Ciceo Pop, Vasile Goldiș, Vaida Voevod, Aurel Vlad, and Iuliu Maniu. The Romanian National Central Council moved from Budapest to Arad to assume leadership of the national liberation struggle of the Transylvanian Romanians. Country, town, and village national councils were officially constituted and the old Magyar authorities were ousted from office.

A manifesto called together the Grand National Assembly at Alba Iulia for December 1, 1918, and the regulations for the election of deputies were published. Every electoral constituency was to elect five delegates by universal suffrage, apart from which the clergy of the two Romanian denominations, the cultural associations, and all public organizations, as well as the two Romanian parties — the Romanian National Party and the Social-Democratic Party — were also entitled to send delegates. The people were requested to come in numbers to Alba Iulia.

The participants in the Grand National Assembly held in the building of the Alba Iulia Casino on December 1, 1918, amounted to 1,228 delegates elected by the electoral constituencies, and the other organizations of the Romanians of Transylvania, Banat, Crișana, and Maramureș. While the meeting of the Great National Council was being held in the Casino, 14 mass meetings took place in various parts of the town, with the participation of some 100,000 people from all over Transylvania, Banat, Crișana, and Maramureș. There were also a number of representatives from Romania. The Romanian army was still a long way from Alba Iulia although it had crossed the Carpathians nearly three weeks before.

Vasile Goldiș submitted a political report at the session of the Great National Council as well as a draft declaration to be approved by the Council. The first article of the declaration stated: "The National Assembly of all the Romanians of Transylvania, Banat, and the Hungarian country, whose rightful representatives were assembled at Alba Iulia on December 1, 1918, decree that those Romanians and all the territories inhabited by them should unite with Romania". Article 2 stated that these territories were to be autonomous only until the Constituent Assembly elected by universal suffrage should meet. Furthermore the Declaration promised that all the peoples living together in the area would enjoy national liberty, all religious denominations be equal and autonomous, and universal suffrage, freedom of the Press, a radical land reform, and an advanced labour legislation would be ensured. Article 9 created a Great National Council to designate Transylvania's representatives to the Peace Conference. Iuliu Maniu on behalf of the Romanian National Party, and Iosif Jumanca, on behalf of the Social-Democratic Party, made declarations demanding that Transylvania should unite with Romania. In his declaration, Iosif Jumanca stated : "...We are here today, as the true representatives of the Romanian workers of Transylvania and Banat, to declare before you, before the Socialist International and before the whole world that we want all Romanians to be united". After these speeches the Declaration was passed unanimously by the Great National Council whose enthusiasm knew no bounds. The fourteen meetings held in the town approved the union with Romania, cheering joyfully. Many representatives of the Romanian National Party and of the Social-Democratic Party spoke at these meetings.

Before winding up its proceedings, the Great National Council elected 150 deputies, who were to make up the new Great National Council, and also a Directing Council, which was to rule Transylvania until the Constituent Assembly had been convened. Shortly after, a meeting of the Saxons at Mediaş also demanded that Transylvania should be united to Romania.

The decision made by the National Assembly at Alba Iulia terminated the process of the national union of the Romanian people into a single independent state. In their struggle for unity and national independence, the Romanian people had been urged forward by the progressive elements of modern Europe. The flame of the revolution lit in Europe in 1848 constantly upheld the Romanian people in their efforts and finally loosened the cruel reins which checked their natural development.

CHAPTER FOURTEEN

ROMANIA BETWEEN THE TWO WORLD WARS (1918-39)

AFTER the Romanian national state had been recognized by the peace treaties, a process of comparative consolidation took place in Romania through economic rehabilitation, agrarian reform, and unification of the legislative system.

In the years following World War I new political parties and groupings came into being. The working class, the revolutionary and progressive movement in the country, took a growing part in politics. An important event was the creation in May, 1921, of the Romanian Communist Party which was to lead the great political actions of the proletariat, culminating in the fighting at Lupeni, Grivița, and in the Prahova Valley. After the crisis of the years 1929 to 1933 the national economy recovered, and in 1938 some industries attained the highest production level ever known.

In February, 1938, when a royal dictatorship was established, the functions of Parliament were greatly narrowed while at the same time a number of laws restricted civil rights and liberty.

In foreign policy Romania pursued the general line promoted by the League of Nations which guaranteed the territorial *status quo* and proclaimed the principles of international law guaranteeing self-determination and equality of rights between countries — principles which the Romanian state has always endorsed.

1. Romania from 1919 to 1929

THE Romanian national state, in the creation of which the entire people had taken part, was recognized by the Peace Conference in Paris which opened on January 18, 1919, to settle the many economic, financial, and territorial problems which the nations of Europe now had to face, and especially the political organization of post-war Europe. All Romanian provinces were now united, and a national, socio-economic and political framework had been created for the more rapid development of the productive forces, for the stimulation of the energy and creative capacities of the people.

The dominant position of the Allied Powers at the peace conference made them in effect an international caucus dictating their views to the whole world. They imposed onerous conditions upon the defeated states, and even the smaller allied countries were deprived of rights previously enjoyed. This was also the case of Romania. Under the pretext that the Romanian government had concluded a separate peace with the enemy in 1918 and the United States had not signed the secret treaty with Romania in 1916, the great powers allowed her only the status of a country with "special interests" at the peace conference.

The sort of treatment meted out to Romania at the peace conference is clearly shown in the memorial which the Romanian governmental delegation submitted to the Supreme Allied Council on July 21, 1919 : " ... From the first Romania's representatives to the peace conference were surprised to see that, without any valid reason, the number of delegates allowed to Romania was inferior to that of other allied states such as Belgium and Serbia. The Romanian delegation, however, abstained from objecting to a decision which might seem merely formal at that moment. But they were still more surprised to find that the frontiers recognized in the treaty concluded with France, Great Britain and Italy in 1916 now disputed."

N. Titulescu who had studied "all the correspondence and talks between France, Britain, the United States and Italy" at the peace conference and had quoted from the "famous talks between the Four — Clemenceau, Wilson, Lloyd George and Orlando — taken down in shorthand by Mantoux," telegraphed King Carol II : "To begin with I was affected to see how little space Romanian problems were allowed among so many other much less important ones. In the second place I must confess that Romania's position in the light of these documents is exasperating."

During the peace conference problems of the greatest concern to Romania were discussed and settled without the participation of her delegates. Only after repeated protests from the Romanian delegation were they allowed to participate in the conference working committees. The delegation was first headed by Ionel Brătianu, then by Nicolae Mişu, General Coandă, Al. Vaida Voevod, and Nicolae Titulescu. The Romanian protest was supported by the French delegation from political and economic motives.

The Peace Treaties of Versailles (June 28, 1919), Saint-Germain (December 9, 1919), Neuilly (November 27, 1919), Trianon (June 4, 1920), and Sèvres (August 10, 1920) were of the utmost importance to Romania's international position. Although on the whole those treaties imposed the domination of the victorious great powers over the capitalist world, they recognized the creation of a number of national states and the rounding-off of others (such as Romania, Yugoslavia, and Czechoslovakia) in Central and South-East Europe. These profound transformations in the life of the European peoples were the result of the struggle of those peoples against the old retrograde empires of the Habsburgs and the Tsars.

The great powers recognized Romania's northern and western frontiers, but their policies often infringed the independence and sovereignty of the country by interference in its internal affairs.

Romania was obliged to assume financial obligations amounting to over 5,000 million francs in gold on the grounds that the Romanian state was liable for part of the debts of the Austro-Hungarian state, or as a "liberation" contribution. Important advantages, mainly of an economic nature, had to be conceded to the great western powers.

Bessarabia's incorporation into the Romanian state was sanctioned on October 28, 1920, by the treaty concluded by Britain, France, Italy, and Japan on the one side, and Romania on the other.

The provisions of the treaties, and also the policy of concessions promoted by the representatives of the Romanian exploiting classes, caused Romania to be dependent on the great western imperialist powers.

This also accounts for the affirmative answer given by the Romanian rulers to the leaders of the Entente, who asked them to provide armed forces in order to help put down the Hungarian proletarian revolution in March, 1919. Alarmed at the possibility of the spreading of revolutionary ideas and of the growing struggle of the working class, as a result of which the revolutionary movement might be victorious in Central and South-East Europe, the Allied Powers overthrew the power of the Hungarian proletariat, drawing the armies of the neighbouring bourgeois states — in the Romanian, Czechoslovak, and Yugoslav states — into interventionist action and supporting the counter-revolutionaries in Hungary.

Romanian reaction consequently responded to the call of the Hungarian reactionaries and helped them to put down the proletarian revolution, although Bela Kun, in his capacity as foreign affairs commissar in the Hungarian revolutionary government, in a proclamation to the Czechoslovak, Yugoslav, and Romanian governments declared "repeatedly and solemnly that we do not uphold the principle of territorial integrity and now bring to your knowledge that we recognize unreservedly all your national territorial claims." On August 4, 1919 the Romanian royal army entered Budapest and remained there until the spring of the following year.

The Romanian proletariat, the revolutionary movement of Romania, opposed this intervention with determination, firmly denouncing it and supporting the Hungarian councils.

Romania's main problems after World War I were economic recovery and the internal consolidation of the state, primarily by the unification of legislation throughout the country. In foreign affairs the country's territorial integrity had to be defended and the *status quo* maintained.

A serious economic crisis with deep-lying social and political implications arose from the loss of men and materials, the destruction and disorganization of production and transport, the occupation of the greater part of the country by the central powers, and not least from war expenditure.

The prices of principal foodstuffs had increased from four to six times compared with prewar, and some of them had gone up to twenty times what they were in the first year of the war. Inflation and expenditure in support of the counter-revolutionary intervention in Hungary made everything dearer still. The condition of the working class grew worse following the declaration of a state of emergency and the militarization of industries.

The revolutionary upsurge grew in intensity, and strikes were frequent in various branches of industry and in different areas, culminating in the country-wide general strike of 1920 in which over 400,000 workers were involved.

One of the important problems to be settled was that of the peasants. Under pressure of the masses, in particular of the villagers, the rulers were compelled to take certain measures. The land reform was partially enacted in December, 1918, when a decree was issued expropriating a considerable part of the great landed estates. Land had been promised to the peasants at the front in the spring of 1917 and the land reform had been laid down in the Constitution in the summer of that same year, though without practical effect. The law was finally passed in 1921. Out of the 12,240,000 acres expropriated, with compensation, during the period following the passing of the land reform law, 6,928,000 acres were divided between nearly 1,500,000 million families, and the remainder of over 4 million acres of grass land and forest became village property to be used by the peasants on payment of a tax.

The land reform momentarily improved the condition of the peasant masses, restricting the power of the big landowners. It was an important step forward, ensuring as it did the development of the country. Nevertheless, social progress was checked by the fact that considerable areas still remained in the hands of the big landowners, by limitations in the law itself, and by the fact that it was not properly enforced.

In the same year an old claim of the masses for which the most advanced forces headed by the proletariat had agitated for many decades was met. The turnover tax was introduced, this being the main indirect tax.

Another important bourgeois democratic reform concerned the electoral system. In November, 1918, the census system was abolished and "universal suffrage by equal, direct, compulsory and secret ballot" was introduced, with provision for the representation of the minorities in every constituency. The election reform considerably enlarged the right of the masses to act in political life.

The statutes of co-existing nationalities were passed, equality in rights of all citizens, irrespective of nationality, being thus recognized in Romania.

Other measures which helped to strengthen the state and to palliate the material condition of the masses were the unification of the currency — the four coinages circulating in the country without cover were converted into lei — and the reorganization of railway transport through centralization and unification of railway administration.

These reforms and measures dealt a blow at the economic and political power of the most retrograde forces in the country and met some of the claims of the working masses ; and they were actually achieved as a result of the action of the masses. A process of democratization was thus under way in various fields of political and economic life. The right to strike of the workers in state or private enterprises considered to be of public interest was limited, and the Trancu-Iași Law of September 5, 1920, banned the organization of workers in trade unions overtly directed by a political party.

On March 29, 1923, radical amendments were made to the Constitution, with a number of new articles and paragraphs introduced so that the Constitution could rightly be considered a new one. The four parts and 138 articles of the new Constitution, on the whole, voiced the views of the dominant classes, namely the bourgeoisie and landowners. At the same time it laid down a number of important claims put forward by the masses : the land reform, the electoral system, freedom of speech and assembly, freedom of the Press, and equal rights for all citizens irrespective of nationality. There were, however, no real guarantees that the provisions of the Constitution would be put into effect.

A new period began in Romania after 1922 : industry and the economy as a whole developed more rapidly, and there was comparative political stability.

Throughout the period of economic recovery, and in the years that followed it, a great struggle took place for the dominant positions in the national economy between Romanian capital — the National-Liberal Party — and the monopoly capital of the great western powers. The Romanian state endeavoured to limit the penetration of foreign capital but was unable to resist the economic force and the means of political pressure of the big monopolies. Although the economic positions of the Romanian bourgeoisie were generally strengthened, Romania continued to be dependent on foreign capital.

From 1923 to 1928 Romanian industry was considerably advanced and diversified, although the consumer goods and the extractive industries still predominated. The share of industry in the social product and in the national revenue increased as a result of increased capital investments and of better equipment on the factory floor. By 1928 industrial output had gone up 56 per cent as against 1919.

The growth of the economic potentialities of the country is best shown by the figures referring to the extractive industries. In 1930 extracted crude oil amounted to 5,792,311 tons as against 968,611 tons in 1918, Romania taking the sixth place in the world. In 1927 lignite extraction amounted to 2,850,011 tons compared with 1,594,719 tons in 1921. In the same year output of natural gas reached nearly 217 million cu.m., and was to rise to 1,200 million cu.m. in 1930, compared with 144,242,051 cu.m. in 1921.

The state allotted subsidies to the industrial undertakings using at least 20 hp or employing at least ten workers. In 1919 there were 2,747 big enterprises in Romania whose aggregate capital totalled 2,834 million lei and which employed 117,424 hands; in 1928 there were 3,966 big enterprises aggregating a capital of 39,770 million lei and employing 206,547 people.

The process whereby production and capital were concentrated and centralized was speeded up after World

War I. From 1924 to 1928 the total of socio-industrial capital rose from 18,800 million lei to 46,100 million lei — an increase of nearly 250 per cent. The number of companies with a capital of over 100 million lei also went up, accounting for 7.5 per cent of the total number of companies in 1928 and for over 73 cent of the overall capital available in the country.

The rise in industrial production brought about a considerable increase in the numbers of the working class. During the three years from 1922 to 1926 the number of people employed in the extractive and the processing industries grew from 234,000 to 306,500, further rising to 450,000 in 1930.

Despite her industrial growth Romania continued to rank among the poorly developed industrial countries. Medium, small, and artisan enterprises still accounted for a considerable share of industrial production.

Although Romania's industrial potentialities increased perceptibly, her economy continued to be predominantly agricultural, with a low development level of productive forces.

Agriculture still accounted for the greatest share of the national economy. Grain production increased with every passing year, from 7,127,000 tons in 1921 to 12,083,900 tons in 1926 and 13,670,900 tons in 1929.

Romania's livestock amounted to a considerable figure: in 1922 there were in the country 5,700,000 head of cattle, and in 1924 there were 13 million sheep. Romania thus held fifth place in the world after the U.S.A., the U.S.S.R., Britain and Spain.

Although Romania's agricultural production had developed considerably during the interwar period, the material and social conditions of the working masses were most precarious. The land reform carried out by the bourgeoisie accentuated social differences in the countryside, increased the number of poor peasants and of the agricultural proletariat while strengthening the ranks of the kulaks. There were large numbers of landless peasants who continued to have a hard time working for the landowners, while those peasants who had been given land on the implementation of the land reform got into debt in order to pay for the land received, and this further aggravated their situation.

The enslaving loans granted by the great international monopolies, no less that Romania's public debt incurred during World War I, resulted in a considerable increase in taxation, a great burden for the working masses.

Romania's political régime during the period between the two World Wars became involved in the tightening of the domination of the big industrial and financial bourgeoisie, and this gave a reactionary character to the power of state.

Unable to adopt constructive, democratic ways of solving the great problems facing the country, some of the bourgeois parties were nevertheless compelled to consider Romania's new situation and the revolutionary struggles of the masses, and to include a number of democratic provisions in their programmes. The political situation in interwar Romania can best be gauged by the widening front of the struggling masses dissatisfied with their socio-economic and political conditions, and by the intensive struggle carried on by the masses headed by the Communists against the exploiting classes and the leaders of the country.

Carrying on their activities against the background of a general crisis of capitalism, the bourgeois and landowner parties of that period made anti-Communism a main feature of their policy.

Significant changes were made in Romania's political configuration in those days following the adoption of the general suffrage, which brought the masses into the political arena and caused the regrouping of political forces.

The land reform which weakened the economic basis of the Conservative Party and of the kindred groups —

the Progressive Conservative Party, the Democratic Conservative Party — soon caused these parties to go out of the picture.

The National-Liberal Party, headed by Ionel Brătianu, president of the party, Vintily and Dinu Brătianu, M. Pherekyde, Al. Constantinescu, C. Anghelescu, and I. G. Duca, was the greatest political force of the bourgeoisie actively participating in all the political and social reforms made during the first years of the post-war period. However, the reactionary character of the National-Liberal Party was to be brought out even more strongly as the socio-economic and political positions of the Romanian bourgeoisie, particularly of the big bourgeoisie, were strengthened.

The Romanian National Party, relying on the leaders and the masses of Transylvania, held an important place in political life. Headed by I. Maniu, Al. Vaida Voevod, V. Goldiş, Ştefan Ciceo-Pop, and M. Popovici, this party included nearly all those who had struggled for Transylvania's union with Romania. Now that new conditions prevailed, these militants still considered their party as a force that would carry out the radical democratic changes listed in the Declaration of Alba Iulia of December 1, 1918. The leaders of the Romanian National Party, and in the first place Iuliu Maniu and Al. Vaida Voevod, advocated that those reforms were to be made in a conservative spirit.

The National Party of Transylvania, which had a regional character, merged in February, 1923, with what was left of the Conservative parties now grouped under Take Ionescu's leadership ; in 1925, with the Democratic National Group led by N. Iorga ; and in October, 1926, with the Peasant Party headed by I. Mihalache. The National Peasant Party sprang up as a consequence of the merger. It was a powerful party which inspired broad masses with confidence for it carried on propaganda against the Liberal government and flaunted bourgeois-democratic slogans, some of them fairly advanced.

In time a number of groups seceded from the party which was heterogeneous from the social and ideological standpoint and within which there were ceaseless conflicts in connection with tactics and occasionally with political interests in the election of the leaders. Thus, shortly after the Party had been formed, Iorga's group separated to form the Democratic National Party, and in February, 1927, a considerable number of members of the former Peasant Party created a new Peasant Party under the leadership of Dr. N. Lupu.

The active presence of the Romanian people as a whole in political life, the great revolutionary effervescence which followed World War I, the assertion of democratic, progressive currents, as also the contradictions in the ranks of the old parties of the Romanian bourgeoisie and landowners, all contributed to the creation of new political parties and groups.

Founded in December, 1918, the Peasant Party was made up of heterogeneous groups. The social basis of the party consisted of part of the peasantry and of the lower town bourgeoisie, while among the leaders there were bourgeois democratic elements, mostly coming from the Liberal Party, such as C. Stere, Pavel Bujor, and Gr. Iunian. Other leaders, among them Simion Mehedinți, had belonged to the Conservative Party. There were few new personages, among them I. Mihalache and V. Madgearu. The Peasant Party's aim was to turn Romania into a democratic country, to satisfy a number of fundamental claims of the working peasantry ; among other things the expropriation of landed estates (half of the compensation to be paid by the state), graduated income tax, abolition of the gendarmerie, and, for the workers, the right to organize themselves and to have a Press of their own. The party also intended to give a democratic character to the state machinery and to nationalize the National Bank, thus asserting itself as a democratic, progressive party. Along the line of the peasant-favouring concepts prevailing in Romania since the close of the nineteenth century, the theoreticians of the Peasant Party, in particular Mihalache and Madgearu, upheld the notion of a "peasant state", contending, despite evidence to the contrary, that the peasantry should play the main part in the state. Although they spoke about the community of interests between workers and peasants, they opposed the idea that the working class party might defend the interests of the peasantry and considered that the peasants should form an independent class party.

In 1918 the People's League was founded under General Al. Averescu's leadership. In April, 1920, it changed its name to the People's Party, becoming a bourgeois political formation which created a diversion and at a certain moment gained exceptional popularity owing to its vague promises of carrying out a number of democratic reforms. During the battles of the summer of 1917 General Averescu had become widely popular among Romanian soldiers and among the peasantry generally, promising the soldiers in the 20s to struggle for two fundamental reforms : agrarian and electoral.

Among the leaders of the People's Party there were also landowners such as C. Argetoianu and Matei Cantacuzino, who had seceded from the Conservative Party, and some generals, among whom were Gr. Crăciuneanu and C. Văleanu.

These men were reactionary figures but the party also included some outstanding personalities of Romanian political and cultural life with democratic, progressive views, such as Vasile Kogălniceanu, M. Sadoveanu, Petru Groza, and Victor Babeș, all eager to help improve the condition of the peasants and make of Romania a genuinely democratic country.

In March, 1920, Averescu formed the cabinet, when it was seen that he had made skilful use of his popularity and authority in order to strengthen the precarious sociopolitical position of the exploiting classes. The democrats in the ranks of the People's Party, disappointed with the political trends supported by Averescu and Argetoianu, left the party, causing its prestige and popularity to suffer greatly.

Other bourgeois parties in existence at the time were of lesser importance. For instance, the National Democratic Party headed by Nicolae Iorga, the Labour Party under O. Pancu-Iași's leadership, and the Magyar and German Parties, which represented the interests of the dominant classes in the ranks of the co-inhabiting nationalities. This was the time when certain extreme right-wing organizations came into being : the National Christian Defence League with A. Cuza as president, and Archangel Michael's Legion, a fascist-type organization which was later to assume the name of the "Iron Guard". These last two political organizations exerted little influence on Romanian public opinion.

Unlike all the other political parties and groups, from the most reactionary to the most democratic and progressive — all of which intended to maintain the existing system — the Romanian Communist Party played a new and most important part in Romanian political life. Continuing the ideals of social and national liberation of the workers of town and countryside, of the genuine democratization of the country and of its socialist transformation, the Workers' Party, which assumed the name of Socialist Party in 1918 to show its opposition to the reformist social-democracy of the Second International which had proved a failure, organized demonstrations and strikes in various enterprises and branches of production as well as the general strike of 1920 which involved the whole Romanian proletariat. The party carried on intensive political and ideological activities, exposing the exploitation and oppression of the masses of town and country. The Workers' Party struggled for certain aims of the masses to be satisfied immediately and for radical changes in the country.

In the heat of the workers' great struggles of 1918, 1919 and 1920, years of intensive revolutionary action, the working class movement in Romania reached a speedy ideological maturity, with the reorganization of the Socialist Party on a revolutionary basis as its main concern.

The creation in May, 1921, of the Romanian Communist Party, based on Marxist-Leninist ideas, as an avantgarde detachment of the working class, was a historic turning point in the development of the working-class movement and a most important moment in the history of the Romanian people. From its very first steps in the political arena, the Communist Party, led by Gh. Cristescu, Secretary General, Alexandru Dobrogeanu-Gherea, D. Fabian, E. Köblös, and others came up against numerous difficulties but asserted itself as an influential political force. During the period between the two World Wars the political arena of the country was greatly influenced by the revolutionary movement of the proletariat, which, headed by the Communist Party, fought for democratic rights and liberties and against the exploiting régime and for the satisfaction of the aspirations of the working people's.

When the Socialist Party became the Communist Party in May, 1921, part of the right-wing social-democratic leaders — I. Jumanca, Gh. Grigorovici, I. Flueraș, E. Gherman, and I. Pistiner, who had withdrawn from the Socialist Party early in 1921 — formed regional social-democratic parties in Muntenia and Moldavia, in Transylvania and Bukovina. In June 1921 these Social-Democratic groups formed the Federation of Socialist Parties of Romania, which, however, lacked mass support. Consequently, its leaders tried to exert an influence on the Trade Unions and this broke up the unity of the Trade Union movement of Romania in 1923.

In May, 1927, the Federation of the Socialist Parties of Romania was dissolved and the Social-Democratic Party was created with a leadership which included Ilie Moscovici, C. Titel-Petrescu, Ion Flueraș, Iosif Jumanca, L. Iordache, Lothar Rădăceanu, etc.

In June, 1928, a group of Romanian Socialists among whom were L. Ghelerter, Ştefan Voitec, Constantin Mănescu and Zaharia Tănase, disapproving of the tactics of the Social-Democratic Party in a number of problems, withdrew from the Party and created a new Workers' Party, the Socialist Party of the Workers of Romania.

All through these years the Romanian Communist Party asserted itself strongly in Romania's political arena. After the imprisonment of the delegates who had voted for the creation of the Marxist-Leninist Revolutionary Party in 1921, the Romanian Communist Party, carried on intensive political work among the masses with the aim of reorganizing the local sections and of rallying the working masses in its struggle for the recognition of its organizations and of the Party itself, and for the defence of the Communists and of the other revolutionaries who had been imprisoned.

Although working under most unfavourable conditions, the Romanian Communist Party decided to stand for the Parliamentary election to be held early in 1922. To this end the Party organized many popular meetings and submitted its lists of candidates in several counties.

The Dealul Spirei Trial of May 23 to June 4, 1922, of 271 revolutionary militants, many of whom had been delegates to the First Congress of the Party, was a political event of prime importance focusing as it did the attention of the working class and of the progressive political circles upon the Communist Party. The trial was proof of the strength and vitality of the young Communist Party and also showed that it was deeply rooted in the Romanian working class and the Romanian people as a whole.

On July 27, 1924, the Romanian Communist Party, the Communist Youth Union, and the revolutionary mass organizations were dissolved and their offices closed, their archives were confiscated, and their leaders arrested. With the Romanian Communist Party outlawed, the leaders of the Party were faced with very complex tasks.

The Party had no experience in organizing underground activities for a long period ahead.

Hugh Seton-Watson has pointed out in his book *Eastern Europe 1918-1941* (Cambridge, 1945) that in Romania and the Balkans the trade unions were never strong. The absence of a large body of skilled workers, and the low cultural and economic level of the peasant recruits to industry made the task of organization almost impossible. Moreover, the governments were terrified of trade unions and "nests of Communism", and used every excuse to repress their activities, organizing strike-breakers, constantly backing up employers and putting down strikes by armed force. Two examples of the latter were the "massacre" of the Jiu valley, carried out by the "progressive" government of Iuliu Maniu in 1929, and the railway strike of Bucharest (Grivitsa workshops) in 1934, suppressed by Vaida Voevod and Călinescu at heavy cost of life, after complete violation of promises which had been made in order to secure the evacuation of the shops by the workers.

In the autumn of 1925 the Peasants' and Workers' Bloc was created following a decision made by the Central Committee of the Romanian Communist Party. The Bloc was conceived of as a legal political organization guided by the Romanian Communist Party with a membership of Communists, socialists, social-democrats, and left-wing members of the Peasant Party. Its aim was to fight for civic rights and the freedom of organization, assembly, and speech. Apart from these claims, the programme of the Peasants' and Workers' Bloc included expropriation without payment of the landowners, who were to be left only 100 acres, and the granting of land to the peasants.

A realistic programme and flexible tactics worked out by experienced revolutionary militants enabled the Bloc to achieve important successes : it concluded an understanding in the elections of 1925 and 1928 with the Socialist Party, the Social-Democratic Party, and the Peasant Party.

Greater economic power in the hands of the big banking and industrial bourgeoisie enabled the latter to strengthen their political domination for a time.

In January, 1922, the Liberal Party, as spokesman for the most powerful groups of the dominant class, took the reins of government and kept them with a short interruption (March, 1926 to June, 1927) up to the end of 1928. A new electoral law was passed on March 27, 1926, introducing an "electoral premium" and thereby ensuring the overwhelming majority of the mandates for the Government and thus seriously violating democratic principles.

In order to remain in office the Liberal Party resorted to many kinds of arbitrary practices, creating terror through the gendarmerie, enforcing states of emergency, and holding electoral campaigns during which blood was shed and ballot boxes were stolen. The reactionary policy carried on by the Liberal government aroused dissatisfaction in all sections of society, and this further strengthened the alliance between the opposition parties.

Under pressure of the masses roused by its profoundly anti-popular policy, the Liberal Party in March, 1926, had to hand over the reins of government to the People's Party led by General Averescu. In June, 1927, a transition cabinet was formed with Prince Știrbei as Premier but, less than three weeks later, on June 22, 1927, a new Liberal government was formed under the leadership of Ionel Brătianu who continued to exert a decisive influence in politics.

With King Ferdinand's health deteriorating, the Liberal Party considered it necessary to take a number of measures designed to defend and maintain its political domination. With the assistance of Queen Marie and Prince Știrbei, the Liberals in December, 1925, forced Prince Carol to give up his claims to the throne. This course of action was facilitated by Prince Carol's adventurous and immoral life.

When King Ferdinand died in 1927, a regency was formed. The Regents were Prince Nicholas, Miron Cristea, Patriarch of Romania, and G. Buzdugan, President of the Court of Cassation, who supported the Liberal government.

The opposition parties intensified their activities. In the Press and by their spoken statements, the leaders of the National Peasant Party revealed the unfair practices of the Liberal administration. Concurrently, the deputies of the National Peasant Party, in order to obstruct the policy of the Liberal cabinet, did not appear in Parliament. On the initiative of the National Peasant Party, a great public meeting was held at Alba Iulia on May 6, 1928, to demand the resignation of the Liberal government. The meeting was an occasion for the Communist Party to rally great numbers of workers and peasants and force the National Peasant Party to enlarge its programme of struggle along democratic lines. The impressive demonstration of a hundred thousand people upholding the slogan of "a march on Bucharest" forced the National-Liberal Party to hand over the reins of government to the National Peasant Party in November, 1928.

Romania's foreign policy after World War I bore the seal of the interests of the Romanian bourgeoisie and landowners. The ruling circles forged a system of international relations and agreements designed to ensure the class domination of the bourgeoisie and landowners inside the country and at the same time to guarantee its territorial integrity which had been achieved by virtue of the international principle of the right of the peoples to self-determination. The ruling circles consequently turned toward France and Britain, whom they considered as likely to defend Romania's interests. The Romanian state also strengthened its relations with the neighbouring countries — Czechoslovakia, Poland, and Yugoslavia — which were formed, or whose territories were rounded off, after disintegration of the Habsburg and the Tsarist Empires. Romania also fought the policy tending towards a revision of the peace treaties. The stand taken by bourgeois Romania in her foreign relations was also influenced by the fact that the country was a borderland between the capitalist world and the Soviet Union, and difficulties in Romania's foreign policy were also created by the policy of concessions of the great Western Powers towards Germany.

When Romania signed the peace treaties, which also included the League of Nations Covenant, she became a member of that international organization. In 1921 the "Final Statutes of the Danube" came into force. Britain, France, and Italy, although having no frontier along the Danube, became members of the bodies entrusted with regulating navigation along the great European river.

Although Romania never took part in any of the actions of certain Western powers against Soviet Russia, the relations between the two countries were strained. Nevertheless, the strain in Romano-Soviet relations eased after 1920. On January 15 of that year, the Soviet government proposed that talks should be held in order to settle the differences between the two states, but the conference that took place in Vienna between March 27 and 29, 1924, during which the differences between the two countries were discussed, was a failure.

In order to counteract the revanchist intentions of the defeated countries, Romania, Czechoslovakia, and Yugoslavia concluded bilateral treaties in 1920 and 1921, thus laying the foundations of an alliance known as the Little Entente. The Romanian politician Take Ionescu tried without success to enlarge the Little Entente by drawing in Poland and Greece. Take Ionescu's plans failed because of the contradictions existing between Poland and Czechoslovakia on the one hand and Yugoslavia and Greece on the other. In spite of this a treaty of alliance was concluded between Romania and Poland in 1921 with the aim of ensuring the defence of the frontiers of the two states. The treaty was extended in March, 1926.

Romania endeavoured to establish good relations with Hungary and Bulgaria despite the fact that the Hungarian reactionary circles kept up an atmosphere of agitation over the new frontiers of the neighbouring countries. Under the influence of the policy of domination carried on by the Austro-Hungarian monarchy, the leaders of Admiral Horthy's Hungary hoped to build up again St. Stephen's kingdom by including some foreign territories.

Nevertheless, agreements of local interest and trade connections were concluded between Romania and Hungary during that period, and the problem of the Hungarians choosing to move to Hungarian territory was settled amicably.

Romania was one of the fourteen states which signed the Geneva Protocol of October 2, 1924, unanimously adopted by the League of Nations Assembly and recommending the peaceful settlement of international disputes.

At Locarno on October 12, 1925, Britain, France, Italy, Belgium, Czechoslovakia, and Poland signed arbitration and conciliation treaties with Germany. The same countries minus Czechoslovakia and Poland concluded the multilateral guarantee pact — the Rhineland Pact. This was among the first moves in the Anglo-French policy of concessions to German imperialism, a policy designed to ensure the security of Western Europe. Romania showed hostility toward the Locarno Agreement for it gave Germany a free hand to expand eastward.

In June, 1926, Romania signed a treaty of alliance with France together with a military convention, and on September 16, 1926, a treaty of friendship and cooperation with Italy which provided mutual assistance for the defence of the frontiers of the two countries in accordance with the treaties concluded after World War I.

The signing of the Paris Pact better known as the Kellogg-Briand Pact, on August 27, 1928, was an important moment in international affairs. The fifty states which had joined the pact bounded themselves to settle all differences by peaceful means. Romania joined the pact and voiced her wish for its speedy enforcement. This is also shown in the Moscow Protocol of February 9, 1929, concluded by the governments of the Soviet Union, Romania, Poland, Estonia, and Latvia. The Protocol laid down the decision of the signatory states "to contribute to the safeguarding of peace between their countries and to put into force without delay between the peoples of these countries the Treaty of Paris concluded on August 27, 1928, whereby war ceased to be an instrument of the national policy". The Romanian Parliament unanimously ratified the Moscow Protocol with the assent of all political parties and groups.

2. Romania during the 1929-33 Economic Crisis

THE effects of the world economic crisis, the symptoms of which from 1928 were felt in Romania on a wide scale, owed their intensity to some specific factors, among which were a preponderance of backward agriculture in the economy, with vestiges of a semi-feudal production, a considerable foreign debt, the taking over of important enterprises by foreign capital, and a sharp reduction in the prices of products designed for export concurrently with the high prices of imported goods.

The various branches of production were unequally affected as regards intensity and duration. The oil industry, for example, was even able to increase its output, and the textile and leather industries also produced more goods. Nevertheless, the total volume of industrial production decreased by nearly 50 per cent during the crisis. Coal and the processing industries in particular registered a substantial decrease in output. In 1933 production capacities were left idle to the extent of 73 per cent for pig iron, 43 per cent for steel, and 77 per cent in the timber industry.

The crisis also affected agriculture, the value of foodstuffs produced decreasing from 15,300 million lei in 1928 to 8,500 million lei in 1933.

Hundreds of banks, including two of the biggest — Marmorosch Blank & Co, and the Bercovici Bank — failed, causing a large number of small depositors to lose their savings and at the same time making money scarce.

In order to ward off economic disaster, the National Peasant government of those days promoted a policy of "opening wide the gates" to foreign capital and contracted a number of loans from the West on usurious terms (stabilization, issue and other loans). The result was an increase in the public debt and control of the imperialist powers over the country's policy and economy, as well as deterioration of the living conditions of the working masses in town and village.

In agreement with the foreign monopolists, who had their own experts and supervisors in the country, the Romanian bourgeoisie and landowners tried to remedy the crisis by substantially reducing wages, cutting down the number of the staff ("sacrifice curves" was the term used for this), and by increasing taxation.

During the economic crisis the workers of Romania went in for labour disputes, strikes, and revolutionary action against the exploiting classes and their political régime in the hope of putting an end to the crisis by these means.

From 1929 to 1932 there were 377 strikes in 1,054 enterprises, with nearly 830,000 work days lost, while in more than 4,000 enterprises there were some 840 latent labour disputes. The first great class battle during this period was the strike of the Lupeni workers in August 1929. With the revolutionary wave sweeping the country, the Fifth Congress of the Romanian Communist Party held at the end of 1931 was an important moment in the life of the Party and the working class movement.

The government headed by Vaida Voevod signed the Geneva Agreement of January, 1933, under the auspices of the League of Nations, which guaranteed loans at exorbitant interest to the foreign monopolists; while in the country wages were being cut (this being the third sacrifice curve), 30 per cent of factory and office workers were dismissed and consumption taxes were increased. It was then that the Romanian Communist Party called upon the working people to start the greatest class struggle in interwar Romania: the battles of the railway and oil workers of January-February 1933. It was a stirring demonstration of the spirit of struggle, self-denial, and sacrifice of the Romanian workers. Although much blood was shed on their being quelled, these great social battles were an important political victory of the Romanian working class through their immediate results and vital consequences for the political and social life of the next period. These battles were fought immediately after Hitler's dictatorship had been installed in Germany (1933) and were consequently of great international significance, being as they were among the first large-scale activities to be undertaken by the proletariat against Nazism.

It was as a result of the workers' battles that the government had to give up applying the Geneva Agreement and cutting wages.

The economic crisis also brought about political instability: the cabinets were repeatedly changed or reshuffled, and the political parties of the dominant classes, in particular the two great so-called historical parties — the National Liberal Party and the National Peasant Party — were wearied by internal dissensions. As a consequence, new political groups were formed and the old parties were greatly weakened. In 1929 a Liberal Democratic Party was made up under the leadership of I. Th. Florescu. In 1930 a National Liberal Party was headed by Gh. I. Brătianu and a Peasant Democratic Party was headed by C. Stere. In 1932 a Radical Peasant Party was formed under the leadership of Gr. Iunian. During the same period, the group headed by Octavian Goga seceded from the People's Party to form the National Agrarian Party.

The Iron Guard and the Christian National Defence League — fascist organizations — were strengthened with the support of the reactionary members of the dominant classes, the aim being to oppose the workers' activities.

Taking advantage of the people's dissatisfaction with the Liberals' policy, the National Peasant Party was returned in November, 1928. Its home policy was, however, as reactionary and antagonistic to the people as that of the Liberal governments, all promises made while the party was in opposition being forgotten. In order to strengthen its position against the Liberal Party, the National Peasant Party, together with other political groups, helped to bring Prince Carol back, and he was proclaimed King on June 8, 1930.

From the early days of his accession to the throne. King Carol appeared anxious to instal "an authoritarian régime" which meant a personal dictatorship.

In his book on this period Hugh Seton-Watson said that King Carol II showed that he had no intention of remaining a mere colourless constitutional king. "Superficially brilliant and basically ignorant, gifted with enormous energy and unlimited lust for power, a lover of demagogy, melodrama and bombastic speeches, he was determined to be a Great Man, the Saviour and Regenerator of his country. His impressionistic mind was filled with admiration for Mussolini, then still the most picturesque figure on the European political stage, and he set himself to imitate him."

Carol's first aim was to break up the political parties, by winning over to himself the younger and ambitious politicians, pushing out the weak and old, and eliminating those who stuck by their principles by a judicious combination of terror and calumny. He was helped by the attitude of Maniu, who unfortunately chose as the ground on which to fight Carol the latter's private life. During his exile the king had become attached to a Jewish lady named Magda Wolf or Lupescu. Despite an undertaking to Maniu to sever the connection, the king was no sooner installed in the palace than he brought her from France to Bucharest. This was too much for Maniu, who resigned the Premiership in favour of an insignificant member of his party, a lawyer named Mironescu with business connections.

"Bourgeois sexual morality is probably less esteemed in Romania than anywhere else on the Continent," Hugh Seton-Watson wrote in 1945. "It was not the right issue on which to base the whole conflict between Democracy and Dictatorship. Moreover the resignation of Maniu, far the strongest personality in his party, left the field open for royal intrigue."

After a National Peasant cabinet headed by G. G. Mironescu, an Iorga-Argetoianu cabinet followed on April 17, 1931. The latter cabinet began to put into practice the king's projects : it passed a law on the suspension of compulsory enforcement of judgements concerning landed property (December 18, 1931) and a law on the reduction of agricultural debts (April 19, 1932) — measures which favoured the well-to-do peasants and the big landowners. Nevertheless, the government was unable to pay the salaries of its employees and was obliged to resign on May 31, 1932 and give way to a National Peasant cabinet headed by Vaida Voevod.

During the years of the economic crisis the National Peasant cabinets presided over by Iuliu Maniu, G. G. Mironescu, and Vaida Voevod increased Romania's economic dependence on the big foreign monopolies, helped to aggravate the political crisis, and favoured the activities of fascist and pro-fascist organizations.

3. Romania Faces the Fascist Peril (1933-39)

AFTER the economic crisis of 1929-33, there was a change for the better in the Romanian economy: industrial and agricultural production rose steadily reaching in 1938 the highest level ever to have been known in capitalist Romania. The level reached at the time is an eloquent illustration of Romania's creative capacities: having united all the Romanian-inhabited provinces within its boundaries, the country made of them an economic whole with high indicators in its development within the limits of the capitalist régime. During this period the process of the concentration of capital and production was accentuated as was also the formation of monopolies, which began to play a dominant part in the country's economic and political life.

A salient feature of the Romanian economy after the economic crisis was the development of industry as a whole.

From 1932 to 1937 the value of Romania's industrial production increased by 100 per cent, from 32,400 million to 64,500 million lei.

The expansion of heavy industry in interwar Romania was also illustrated by the increase in iron ore from 6,000 tons in 1928 to 122,000 tons in 1938, while imports of metallurgical semi-fabs decreased from 189,000 tons in 1929 to 23,000 tons in 1937 and the imports of rolled metal from 87,000 tons to 12,000 tons. Capital investments in the metal-working industry went up from 2,100 million lei in 1927 to 5,700 million lei in 1938.

The country's industrial development during the period that followed the economic crisis may also be observed from the following data: electric power output rose from 410 million kw in 1926 to 1,077 million kw in 1936 and to 1,148 million kw in 1938; the value of food production went up from 14,959 million lei in 1926 to 15,577 million lei in 1938, while the value of metal-working production rose from 7,058 million lei to 11,363 million lei, the value of textile production from 6,656 million lei to 14,692 million lei, and of electrical engineering production from 114 million lei to 675 million lei.

Mining output also increased considerably during the period that followed the economic crisis: the crude oil output, which amounted to nearly 5 million tons in 1929, had risen to 8,703 million tons by 1936.

The capital required for the expansion of Romanian industry was mainly supplied by the state in the form of substantial advances, anticipated payment for the orders placed, and bounties from the budget. Nor should the funds provided by the foreign capitalists, whether private capitalists or monopolists, be underestimated.

King Carol II had a personal interest in the expansion of the heavy industry for he held 30 to 35 per cent of the shares of the Malaxa works, about the same amount of shares of the I.A.R. Plant (Romanian Aeronautical Industry) and Astra-Vagoane Works, and a smaller amount in the Reșița and Auschnit plants. The king also had an interest in a number of sugar factories, in breweries, in the Mica gold mines, the Buhuși and Scherg textile mills, and the telephone company.

The country's economic dependence on the imperialist powers increased during that period. It was estimated that on the eve of the Second World War, foreign capital held 38 per cent of the capital of the joint-stock industrial companies.

Although agricultural production also developed after the economic crisis of 1929-33, Romanian agriculture as a whole was still lagging behind. In 1935 the number of tractors used was only 7 per cent more than in 1927.

Economic expansion during that period did not perceptibly improve the lot of the masses. The living and working conditions of the working masses of town and country lagged far behind the progress of capitalist economy and caused numerous conflicts. A few conclusive facts will illustrate the poor conditions under which the working people were labouring : the workers' general wage indicator decreased from 2,760 in 1929 to 1,705 in 1937 ; from 1934 to 1937 the cost of living increased by 27 per cent, while income tax rose by 23 per cent, and wages went up by only 6 per cent.

Nor were conditions any better for the peasants during that period. They had not sufficient land, the overwhelming majority of the peasantry laboured under increasing exploitation, both direct and indirect, and chronic diseases spread at a rapid rate as a result of the lack of the necessities of life and of medical assistance. In 1938 the National Agrotechnical Institute ascertained that out of about 3,000,000 peasant homesteads, two million had not a single cow, 1,7 million had not a single pig, and a quarter of a million not a single chicken.

In 1929 the Ministry of Public Health ascertained that nearly 70 per cent of the village cottages were built of logs plastered over with clay. The floors were of beaten earth and dung, and the roofs were covered with shingles or thatch.

The conditions of the poor generated great discontent which resulted in local movements and rebellions among the Romanian peasants and those of other nationalities, as for example the revolt in the Ghimeş Valley in 1934 and the strikes and demonstrations of the workers in a number of industrial branches.

Political life was in ferment — the result of economic and social processes, of the increasingly radical trends of the working masses, and of the international situation. This situation was reflected in the antagonism and the struggles between the working masses and the exploiting classes and in the unceasing conflicts between the bourgeois-landlord parties and political groups.

The divergences between the political parties and groups of the exploiting classes were fanned by Carol II, whose manoeuvres and backstage combinations were aimed at disorganizing the political parties and installing a royal dictatorship.

The Liberal cabinet formed in November, 1933, with I. G. Duca as Premier banned the Iron Guard. Duca was a representative of the "old Liberals" who wanted to maintain the bourgeois parliamentary forms of government and the Franco-British, anti-Nazi trend in the country's foreign policy. In answer to the ban, a group of legionnaires assassinated the prime minister, described by Hugh Seton-Watson as a man of personal honesty and democratic convictions who distrusted Carol's intentions, on December 29, 1933, on the platform of the Sinaia railway station.

On December 30, 1933, Carol II designated C. Anghelescu as Premier but replaced him on January 2, 1934, by Gh. Tătărăscu, leader of the "young Liberals" who held the helm of the country supporting the king and being supported by him.

In his four years' administration Tătărăscu increasingly used decrees as a method of government, thus restricting parliamentary activities. In April, 1934, the Parliament passed a law on "the defence of order within the state" which enabled the government to dissolve any political group that jeopardized the political and social order. This had been done in order to check and suppress all revolutionary and democratic movements.

While special laws were being passed against the revolutionary movement, King Carol and his main collaborators tolerated and even supported terrorist and fascist organizations, such as the Iron Guard, with the aim of using them for their own purposes. It is significant to note in this respect that those who had made the attempt on Duca's life were treated leniently and the legionnaires were able to organize congresses and fascist demonstrations.

With a growing internal and external tension, all the political forces in the country gave their views on the policy to be adopted. The fascist organizations, and primarily the Iron Guard which was supported by Nazi Germany, were exposed and branded as obscurantists, mystical organizations jeopardizing the very existence of the Romanian state.

The right-wing political groups and circles led by Vaida Voevod, Gh. Brătianu, and C. Argetoianu, on the other hand, supported and encouraged the fascist organizations, thus undermining the country's resistance against the fascist peril.

The working masses headed by the Romanian Communist Party rose against fascist organizations and their supporters inside the country, as did also the other workers' parties, the Social-Democratic, the United Socialists, and wide circles of the lower bourgeoisie and the intelligentsia, and indeed all outstanding democratic political personages, who showed anxiety at the activities of the legionnaires and the increasing danger of the country being dismembered and enslaved by Nazi Germany. From among them were Nicolae Titulescu, Nicolae Iorga, Gr. Iunian, Virgil Madgearu, Victor Iamandi, Armand Călinescu, and Dem. Dobrescu.

As a result of the intensive activities carried on by the Romanian Communist Party, the Trade Union movement formed into a united whole in 1936, and for the first time since the Romanian Communist Party had been created, May Day demonstrations were held under the banner of the Workers' United Front.

An important place in the anti-fascist struggle of the Romanian people was held by the Ploughmen's Front, a democratic organization set up in 1933 under Petru Groza's leadership. Tens of thousands of peasants of the Hunedoara, Cluj, and Timiș-Torontal counties had joined the Ploughmen's Front, whose leaders were people who had risen from the peasants.

The anti-fascist struggle was also vigorously carried on by a number of mass organizations, such as the Democratic Students' Front, the Bloc for the Defence of Democratic Liberties, the Democratic Union, the League of Labour, and the Friends of the U.S.S.R.

Dissatisfied with the reactionary policy of the leaders of the Magyar Party in Transylvania — a bourgeois party dominated by counts and capitalists — the democratic elements in the same party created the Hungarian Working People's Union in 1934 (MADOSZ). This was an organization opposed to the fascist peril and Horthy's revisionism and chauvinist instigators, and fighting for a democratic régime, for the promotion of unity of action of all working people irrespective of nationality.

The first important success in the rallying of all democratic forces against fascism was achieved on December 6, 1935, when a solemn covenant was concluded at Țebea under Horea's legendary holm oak, between the Democratic Bloc, the Ploughmen's Front, MADOSZ, and the Socialist Group headed by C. Popovici. The Țebea covenant called forth a wide response throughout the country and promoted a great movement among all those who were hostile to fascism and reaction.

It was along the line of achieving anti-Nazi unity, as advocated by the Communist Party, that the Democratic Front was created in February, 1936, on the occasion of the local parliamentary election in the counties of Mehedinți and Hunedoara. The local organizations of the National Peasant Party in those counties then rallied to the joint front made up of the Democratic Front, the Ploughmen's Front, MADOSZ, and the Socialist group. Election returns were a victory of the People's Front and a defeat for the right-wing parties and organizations.

In August, 1936, the Central Committee of the Romanian Communist Party drew up a programme for the people's anti-fascist front which provided for the dissolution and banning of all fascist organizations in the country, the defence of the constitutional régime and of all democratic institutions, the conclusion of a mutual assistance pact with the Soviet Union, and closer relations with France and with the countries of the Little Entente and the Balkan Entente.

The Communist Party also declared it was prepared to have talks with any party and organization with a view to organizing a joint struggle against Nazi and Horthy revisionists. "Should Nazi Germany when unleashing war in Europe and against the U.S.S.R., attack Romania with the assistance of Horthy's Hungary," it was stated in the protocol, "the Communists will consider it necessary to defend every inch of the country's soil."

Starting from the idea that the main object of the democratic struggle was to overthrow the Tătărăscu government, and, from the consideration that the National Peasant Party was bent on overthrowing that government, the leaders of the Communist Party called upon the masses to vote for the candidates of the National Peasant Party in the parliamentary election of December, 1937, so that the party might be the representative of all democratic forces. However, Iuliu Maniu, President of the National Peasant Party, together with the Liberal group headed by Gheorghe Brătianu, concluded the so-called "non-aggression pact" with the Iron Guard. Under the circumstances, with the democratic forces unable to form a coalition, the savage campaign carried on by the Iron Guard in the election could not but seriously affect the election returns. For the first time in the political history of the country, the election did not result in a stable parliamentary majority for any of the political parties to enable it to form a cabinet.

In order to gain time before installing a personal dictatorship, Carol II called upon the National Christian ultranationalist Party, headed by Octavian Goga and A. C. Cuza, who had had a small number of votes, to form the cabinet. Also were included some bourgeois of note, such as Armand Călinescu, who voted for a foreign policy opposed to the expansion of Nazi Germany.

The installation of Nazism in Germany on January 30, 1933, had the most serious consequences for the destinies of many peoples in the world. Germany withdrew from the League of Nations on October 14, 1933, made military service compulsory in March, 1935, and openly declared for a revisionist and revanchist policy, demanding that the German colonial empire should be built up again. This meant that Germany's relations with other states were deteriorating, Germany was becoming an immediate danger to the national independence of many countries, including Romania, while jeopardizing human culture and civilization.

The ascension and consolidation of the Nazi régime in Germany, of fascism in Italy and Hungary, and of Japanese militarism, all of which helped to increase the danger of war, no less than the policy of the great western powers — Britain and France — who tolerated aggression and made concessions to the revanchist-revisionist forces, made it necessary for Romania to evolve an independent foreign policy. In that period, too, Romania promoted peace in this part of Europe and acted with determination within international bodies in defence of the European *status quo*, and for an understanding among nations, for disarmament and collective security in Europe.

The Romanian cabinets of that period carried on a policy of friendship and co-operation with France and Britain who, despite their inconsistency, declared in defence of the *status quo*, though they gave way before aggression. Romania belonged to the group of anti-revisionist countries and to the system of political and military alliances based on the participation of the great western powers. For years Romania made a considerable contribution to the international conferences which debated the problems of disarmament, of the safeguarding of peace in Europe and throughout the world. The Romanian representative at the Geneva Disarmament Conference, Nicolae Titulescu, accepted and backed the proposal of the Soviet Union that aggression should be defined, as submitted by Litvinov on February 6, 1933, considering it to be "the clearest document in the course of the length discussions within the Security Committee".

Besides the Little Entente member-countries, the representatives of France, Spain, and China declared in favour of the definition of the notion of aggression. Anthony Eden, the British delegate, considered the Soviet proposal "as too rigid", while the delegates of Mussolini's Italy and Horthy's Hungary rejected the definition considering it as "doubtful" and "unrealizable". The Disarmament Conference reached no decision for the Great Western powers adopted a hesitating attitude. When the various points of view were somewhat reconciled, the first convention defining the aggressor was signed in London on July 3, 1933, by the U.S.S.R., Romania, Poland, Estonia, Latvia, Turkey, Iran, and Afghanistan. An identical convention was signed on July 4, 1933, by the representatives of the Soviet Union, of the members of the Little Entente, and of Turkey.

The London Convention was an event of outstanding importance as it continued the Kellogg-Briand Pact. It was a guarantee of the territorial integrity of the signatory countries, opening new prospects in international life in the safeguarding of peace in this part of the world.

Together with the other countries of the Little Entente, Romania rose with determination against the draft Quadripartite Pact inspired by Mussolini — to which Britain, France, Italy, and Germany were to belong. The pact was an infringement of the principle of equal rights for all states in international relations, and implied an amendment to the statutes of the League of Nations and the revision of peace treaties, being consequently against the interests and rights of small-and medium-sized European countries. The four Great Western powers were to constitute a directorate which would decide the destinies of Europe. It was considered by Romania to be a gross infringement of the League of Nations Charter and direct encouragement of the revanchist policy of Nazi Germany and her allies.

Nicolae Titulescu, in his capacity as Romania's Minister of Foreign Affairs, tabled a protest of the Little Entente against the agreement, which he described as a plot against peace and a danger to the independence of small countries. He definitely demanded that the clauses referring to the revision of existing treaties should be cancelled. The firm stand taken by the Little Entente and the divergences among the four powers prevented the ratification of the pact.

With the stand of the U.S.S.R. and of the Little Entente member countries being very much the same with regard to the increasing danger of Nazi Germany, and also considering the *rapprochement* between the U.S.S.R. and France, the Romanian, Yugoslav, and Czechoslovak governments showed a wish to bring their diplomatic relations with the Soviet Union back to normal.

After talks held at Geneva, Warsaw, and Ankara, the U.S.S.R. resumed diplomatic relations with Romania in 1934. The Romanian-Soviet *rapprochement* created a climate propitious to the negotiations of a mutual assistance pact between the two countries.

Foreign Affairs Minister Nicolae Titulescu was empowered by the Romanian government to proceed with the conclusion of a mutual assistance pact with the U.S.S.R. At Montreux in Switzerland in July, 1936, Titulescu and Litvinov drew up a Romanian-Soviet protocol which included the main provisions of a mutual assistance treaty between Romania and the Soviet Union based on mutual observance of national independence and sovereignty.

Litvinov, however, suggested that the signing of the mutual assistance pact should be postponed. The talks were not resumed and the two countries continued only to maintain good neighbourly relations.

This was also the period when the Romanian government concluded and strengthened regional pacts designed to consolidate peace in Eastern and South-Eastern Europe. Despite the opposition of the revisionist powers, a Balkan understanding — the Balkan Pact — was signed at Athens on February 9, 1934, by Romania, Greece, Yugoslavia, and Turkey, the signatory powers "mutually guaranteeing the security of the Balkan frontiers" and "engaging not to undertake any political action towards another non-signatory Balkan state without the mutual advice of the other signatories, and not to assume any political obligation to any other Balkan State without bringing it to the knowledge of the other parties." The Balkan understanding was a means of fighting against the plots of the revisionist states in this part of Europe and an important step in safeguarding peace and security among the peoples.

Through the efforts of her representative, Nicolae Titulescu, Romania made her contribution within the two organizations as well as at the League of Nations, by asserting the point of view of small and medium countries, defending their independence and national sovereignty and thus safeguarding peace.

Romania's representatives rose against the aggressive activities of the fascist and revisionist states as well as against the policy of encouraging the militarization of Nazi Germany. Romania protested against the Anglo-German naval agreement of July 18, 1935, under which Nazi Germany was permitted to build up her navy. Romania, like other small and medium countries, was greatly worried by the re-militarization of the Rhineland in March, 1936, and France's passive stand when the Treaty of Versailles was thus infringed. Romania's stand which branded fascist Italy's aggression against Abyssinia and demanded that the sanctions listed in the League of Nations' Pact be applied called forth a powerful response.

In August, 1936, Titulescu made a statement whereby Romania joined the committee of non-interference in Spain. The Romanian government specified that should a legal republican government seek its support, it reserved for itself the right to decide. During that period Romania maintained economic and diplomatic relations with Republican Spain and allowed weapons and ammunition designed for the Spanish Republican government to pass through Romanian ports. On October 22, 1937, Romania signed the Nyon Pact on the joint measures to be taken to fight the piratical activities of the submarines of the fascist states in the Mediterranean at the time of the Italo-German interference in Spanish affairs. Nevertheless, the Tătărăscu government checked the activities of Communist, anti-fascist organizations which struggled in support of Republican Spain and tolerated pro-fascist demonstrations.

Although influenced by bourgeois concepts, Titulescu adopted an advanced foreign policy. Aware of the danger of Nazism to world peace, he rose in defence of the principle of equal rights and of state sovereignty and against the tendencies of the Great Western powers to disregard the rights and interests of the other nations. Carrying on intensive work, Titulescu made a considerable contribution to the Romanian people's struggle in defence of their independence and national sovereignty and for safeguarding peace in the world.

In August, 1936, Titulescu withdrew from the cabinet as a consequence of the attacks and intrigues of international reactionary forces and of the right-wing forces within the country. Titulescu's withdrawal weakened the influence of the political circles which opposed the revisionist plans of Nazi Germany and Horthy's Hungary, and also disrupted the unity of the Little Entente.

The Goga-Cuza cabinet called together by King Carol II in preparation of a royal dictatorship was short-lived, lasting only 44 days. On February 10, 1938, King Carol II became a dictator. The cabinet was headed by

Patriarch Miron Cristea. It was made up of many reactionaries and of a number of notable members of the old bourgeois parties who were anti-Nazi and considered the royal dictatorship as a means of checking the ascension to power of the Iron Guard.

The royal dictatorship put an end to democratic parliamentary life. It narrowed down the existing bourgeois democratic liberties and banned the activities of the political parties. Leadership was concentrated in the hands of the king.

The new Constitution of February 24, 1938, suppressed all the provisions of the 1923 Constitution which had a general democratic character and vested power entirely in the hands of King Carol II. Parliament had only a formal part to play.

In October, 1938 a decree was issued whereby the workers' trade unions were dissolved and guilds were created, which were considered as vocational bodies subordinate to the aims of the royal dictatorship.

In order to give the impression that the country was governed in the name of the nation, the National Renaissance Front led by members of the royal clique was created in December, 1938. In June, 1940, the National Renaissance Front was named the Nation's Party and was the only legal party in the country.

During King Carol's dictatorship the country was ruled by special decrees. The state intervened more energetically in economic life, favouring a protectionist customs tariff, which further strengthened the positions of the bankers and financiers around Carol II.

During the period of royal dictatorship the economic situation of the working class worsened. Strikes took place among the workers, and there was general unrest among the peasantry throughout the country.

The leaders of the National Peasant and the National Liberal Parties, I. Maniu and D. Brătianu, took no definite measures to prevent the installation of King Carol's dictatorship, but merely confined themselves to protest while carrying on their activities within a more limited framework, in spite of the fact that all parties had been banned.

The Romanian Communist Party considered King Carol's dictatorship as a profoundly anti-popular régime and the expression of Romanian reactionary circles. The Party documents, however, pointed out that Carol's dictatorship should not be taken for a fascist dictatorship and that the main enemy was the Iron Guard.

Starting from this premise, the Communist Party established in June, 1938, a programme of action which included a number of economic, social, and political measures designed to re-establish the political picture of 1936 and unite all the patriotic forces in order to strengthen the resistance capacity of the Romanian people against the danger of a joint Nazi-Horthy aggression.

When Austria was annexed by Nazi Germany in March, 1938, the gates were opened for Germany's penetration into South-east Europe. This was an event that had a direct impact on Romania, which was valued by Nazi Germany as a source of raw materials. In order to gain new positions in Romania, the Nazi government sought to take advantage of the difficulties Romania was having in her trade with Great Britain and France, in particular in the spring and summer of 1938. Furthermore, by incorporating Austria, Nazi Germany had gained control of the communications between Eastern and Western Europe.

Under these circumstances the Romanian government did its utmost to maintain and consolidate its regional alliances. After lengthy consultations, the states which had joined the Balkan Entente concluded an agreement with Bulgaria at Salonika on July 31, 1938, under which disputes among the Balkan states were to be settled without force.

Intensified economic pressure on Romania by Nazi Germany caused friction among the Romanian dominant classes. Important financial and industrial circles, to which some of the leaders of the main bourgeois parties also belonged, opposed Germany in her efforts to strengthen her position in the country. The Iron Guard and other pro-Nazi groups as well as some important monopolist reactionary leaders (N. Malaxa and I. Gigurtu) sought to tighten Romania's relations with Germany.

During the Czechoslovak crisis of March-September, 1938, which created favourable conditions for Polish and Hungarian revisionist claims, the Romanian government consistently supported its ally Czechoslovakia.

Romania refused to consider Hungary's offer of a bilateral understanding as long as the Horthy government was not prepared to come to an understanding with Czechoslovakia as well. At the session the Little Entente held at Sinaia in May, 1938, the Romanian Minister of Foreign Affairs stated once again that the clauses of the Romanian-Czechoslovak Treaty would immediately be applied if the Hungarian ruling circles resorted to force.

Continuing along the line of compromising with Germany, Britain and France sacrificed Czechoslovakia. The Munich agreements of September, 1938, opened the way for Nazi Germany towards the countries of Eastern and Southern Europe. Romania's foreign situation was thus aggravated. She had lost an ally in Czechoslovakia, which was also one of her main armament suppliers. The Little Entente actually ceased to exist when Czechoslovakia was occupied.

In a stern indictment of all dictators who believed in the "old theory that small states had no right to independence" as they were included in the vital areas of the big states and were only named on the maps "in order to show to which of the big States they fell", the historian Nicolae Iorga wrote : "All those who believe that the small States have been done away with are mistaken ; they will die and the nations will survive ;

and it is they who observe their independence and not the madmen who think they can rise against the will of the centuries and do away with them, that are wise...."

The Nazi government increased its pressure on Romania. At the same time, the royal dictatorship government, faced with economic difficulties and the pressure of pro-Nazi circles inside the country, received no effective assistance from Britain and France and began to make economic concessions to the Reich during the last months of 1938, demanding in exchange that the leading German circles should guarantee that they would not support the claims of Horthy's Hungary to Romanian territories. The German economic delegation led by Clodius carried on negotiations in Bucharest in November and December, 1938, but made such excessive demands that Romania's representatives were forced to reject them.

Hoping to obtain effective support, King Carol went to France and Britain in November, 1938. Not obtaining the support he expected in Britain, he passed through Germany on his return. Hitler refused any guarantee against a change of frontiers.

Germany's occupation of Czechoslovakia in March, 1939, created great tension between Romania on the one hand and Germany and Hungary on the other. There were plans for a joint German-Hungarian invasion of Romania.

The conciliatory attitude of Britain and France and their treachery towards their smaller allies — for they gave free rein to Germany to invade Czechoslovakia and extend its domination in Central and South-east Europe, and this actually meant that Romania was isolated — induced the Călinescu government to conclude an economic agreement with Germany on March 23, 1939, in the hope of thus avoiding a conflict. The agreement came into force during the last months of 1940 and was followed by other onerous treaties which subordinated Romania's economy and policy to the aggressive interests of Germany.

Many progressive political forces, and primarily the Communists, voiced their ardent patriotism, attacking the Romanian-German agreement of March, 1939, and proving to be active defenders of the country's interests. A document of the Romanian Communist Party stated: "The Communists will fight in the first ranks. Unite in a single powerful front against Hitler and his revisionist allies!".

The patriotism of the masses was proved beyond a doubt by their attitude during the great anti-Nazi demonstration held on May Day 1938 when workers and craftsmen marched through Bucharest chanting the slogans: "For a free and independent Romania!" "Down with Fascism!" "Let the Romanian-German economic pact be abrogated!" "Down with the Nazi aggressors!"

Such demonstrations were held in all the more important towns and industrial centres of the country, showing that the Romanian people had rallied to the anti-Nazi movement and that it was their will to fight against the aggressor and against fascism.

Romania's position was becoming increasingly critical owing to Nazi and revisionist pressure, which continued in the spring and summer of 1939; to the reactionary policy promoted inside the country by the exploiting classes; and to the oscillations and even the mistakes made by the ruling political circles in foreign affairs. Under such circumstances, in order to ward off foreign dangers, Prime Minister Armand Călinescu and other ministers hostile to Nazi Germany sought to consolidate Romania's systems of alliances and create fulcrums against the country's political and economic encirclement by the fascist states. In April, 1939, the Romanian government, together with Poland and Greece, accepted the guarantees of Britain and France on the assumption that Anglo-Franco-Soviet negotiations, which were being carried on in Moscow with a view to the conclusion of a mutual assistance pact, would change the international ratio of forces to the detriment of the Nazi aggressors. Furthermore, the Romanian government sought to strengthen its ties with the countries of the Balkan Entente, especially with Greece and Turkey, which seemed ready to resist Nazi aggression in South-east Europe.

No understanding was reached between the Western Powers and the U.S.S.R., and this had a baneful influence not only upon Romania's situation but also upon the whole of Europe, and even the whole world. On August 23, 1939, an economic convention and a non-aggression pact were concluded between the U.S.S.R. and Germany.

Romania's situation further deteriorated when the Second World War broke out, bringing in its train ruinous consequences for the country, for many peoples of Europe and, indeed, the entire globe.

CHAPTER FIFTEEN

ROMANIA DURING WORLD WAR II
(1939-45)

THE Second World War had a number of profound consequences on the situation of Romania. During the first part of the war the Romanian leaders adopted a neutral policy. Faithful to the traditional orientation toward France and Britain, they sought to ward off the danger of the country being isolated, to keep the country out of the military operations that were unfolding in the immediate neighbourhood, and to protect their territorial integrity. Developments in Europe, and in particular the defeat of France, shattered the hopes Romania had pinned on this line of orientation.

Without any foreign support, Romania saw her territory reduced in the summer of 1940 and was compelled to submit to Nazi Germany. A fascist military dictatorship was installed and German forces marched into the country. Finally Romania was drawn into the anti-Soviet War.

The Romanian people showed almost unanimous hostility to Nazism, and the resistance movement developed unceasingly from 1940 to 1944, assuming various forms according to the specific conditions prevailing in the country. The movement culminated in the anti-fascist insurrection of August, 1944, organized on the basis of a wide coalition of the anti-Nazi patriotic forces, from the most consistent and most determined of them — the Romanian Communist Party — to King Michael and the entourage of the royal palace. Overthrowing the fascist military dictatorship on August 23, 1944, and taking up arms against the Nazis, the Romanian people made an important contribution to the war waged by the antifascist coalition, until the capitulation of Nazi Germany.

1. Romania's Neutrality

AFTER the outbreak of World War II, with the armies of Nazi Germany at the country's borders, the Romanian ruling circles made it their aim to see that Romania should not be isolated and to defend her territorial integrity, which was threatened by Germany and the countries which wanted the peace treaties reviewed. In the hope that the economic and military potentialities of Britain and France would ultimately make up for their insufficient forces in the first stage of the war, Romania's rulers sought to keep the country out of war. A communiqué was issued by the Council of Ministers on September 4, 1939, stating that Romania would carry on a neutral policy and follow a "line of balance". Practice showed that the balance was most precarious and that the right-wing circles were to gain ground as the influence of Germany increased in South-east Europe.

Eager to secure the integrity of her frontiers, Romania sought to improve her relations with Hungary and proposed that the two countries should conclude a non-aggression pact. The Hungarian government rejected this proposal.

In the autumn of 1939 the Romanian government approached the Soviet Union with a view to reaching an understanding.

Concurrently, circumstances being unfavourable to the small States, Romania strove for the formation of a "block of neutral countries" in South-east Europe. Germany undertook many activities to halt this initiative. Despite the risks she incurred, Romania supported the Poles who were undergoing great trials. She permitted war materials designed for the Polish army to cross Romanian territory; received some 50,000 Polish refugees, both civilian and military, into the country; allowed the President of the Polish Republic and the Government members to settle in Romania as private people; and saved and dispatched to the West the Polish treasury.

Germany protested vehemently against these measures.

Prime Minister Armand Călinescu, spokesman of the bourgeois circles which opposed the expansion of Nazi Germany and which were intent on preserving Romania's integrity and independence, was assassinated on September 21, 1939, by the Iron Guard, a Nazi agency.

Every effort made by Romania to improve her relations with the neighbouring countries, to bring them back to normal came up against the opposition of the revisionist states.

Romania strove to develop her economic relations with all countries — Britain and France, as well as Germany and Italy — but the consequences were not such as had been expected by the Romanian Government. For Nazi Germany economic relations were mere levers helping her to achieve Romania's economic and political subordination.

Romania's isolation and her complete abandonment to the hands of Berlin caused serious prejudices to Germany's opponents, for many resources, in particular Romanian oil, were thus placed at the disposal of the Germans. France's capitulation and Britain's defeat on the continent, no less than the threatened Nazi invasion of Britain, further aggravated Romania's situation.

On June 26, 1940, Bessarabia and Northern Bukovina were incorporated within the U.S.S.R.

Foreign developments and the ever more brutal interference of Nazi Germany in Romania's internal affairs favoured the rise of pro-German groups in political life. On July 4, 1940, a cabinet was formed with I. Gigurtu as premier and many representatives of the fascist groups holding important positions.

The new cabinet took stern repressive measures against the democratic forces, sending the Communists and anti-fascist to concentration camps. Such measures weakened the Romanian people's capacity to resist at one of the most serious moments in their history.

On July 15, 1940, Hitler asked King Carol II to accept the policy of the Nazis and consent to territorial changes, threatening that non-acceptance "sooner or later, the sooner more likely, would mean Romania's annihilation".

These were difficult moments for the destinies of the country. Alone, without any outside support, a prey to Nazi Germany and her allies, Romania had to submit to the onerous conditions of the Vienna Fascist Diktat at the end of August, 1940. Northern Transylvania, with over 2,500,000 inhabitants, most of them Romanian, went to Horthy's Hungary.

The whole of Romania protested against the Vienna Diktat; every social section, all the political groups and figures of note expressed their revolt and anger at seeing the country's territory mutilated. Great demonstrations against the Vienna decision took place throughout the country with citizens, often the local authorities, and military units protesting. International public opinion attacked the Vienna Diktat, and Great Britain issued an official statement showing that she did not recognize the arbitrary Ribbentrop-Ciano statement.

Commenting on the Vienna Diktat in *Eastern Europe 1918-1941,* Hugh Seton-Watson said that excitement among the Romanians of Transylvania reached a feverish pitch. "The people wished to fight, however desperate the odds, and expected Maniu, the Grand Old Man of Romanian Transylvania, to lead them. But Maniu did not move... Popular indignation was intense, and even obtained expression in parts of the country...."

Faced with such an impressive demonstration of revolt on the part of the Romanian people the Romanian historians said, the Nazi Reich encouraged the Iron Guard and the Nazi Party of the Germans in Romania, intensified the activities of the German Legation and of the Gestapo, and made preparations to invade the country in the event of an armed resistance.

Such were the prevailing internal and external conditions under which a fascist-military dictatorship was installed in Romania with the direct participation of Hitler's emissaries. The dictatorship was followed by the penetration of German forces into the country.

On September 4, 1940, the Gigurtu cabinet resigned and General Ion Antonescu was designated prime minister by royal decree. Two days later Carol II, whom the Reich did not trust, was forced to abdicate in favour of his son Michael. General Antonescu then became "Leader of the State" with dictatorial powers.

Hugh Seton-Watson said in his book that although of German origin, the king undoubtedly had a strong Romanian patriotism, but this in the course of years become inextricably identified with his own ambition. Convinced from the beginning that party politicians were the curse of his country, and that only his personal rule could benefit her, he was at a loss what to do. Surrounding himself with flatterers and intriguers, and relying on the most flexible, irresolute and incapable of the politicians, he found himself without trustworthy advisers at a time when the tense international situation complicated every problem of home politics. The single powerful personality, Călinescu, who, in a ruthless manner, genuinely attempted to serve his country, was removed by assassination in September 1939. "Carol saw that the country was rotten, that drastic reforms were needed, and he neither saw what reforms to apply, nor was personally suited to apply them... The régime solved nothing, it maintained its order by its bayonets, collected with extreme brutality taxes urgently needed for rearmament, and produced a plethora of extravagant speeches which provoked silent laughter and hatred. No one took the régime seriously, not even its apologists..."

According to the plan worked out jointly with the German Legation, and at the latter's express demand, General Antonescu formed a military-legionary cabinet with legionnaires, as Nazi agents, holding key positions. The military fascist régime was the most reactionary, most anti-popular, and most anti-national form of government in the history of the country, enforced by the fascist and pro-fascist Nazi circles in Romania.

2. The Military-Fascist Dictatorship in Romania

THE military fascist dictatorship was based politically on the Iron Guard until January, 1941, with the mighty support of the Nazi Wehrmacht whose units filtered into the country from October, 1940, to rise to half a million men by January, 1941. Actually Romania had been occupied by Nazi Germany and this was confirmed both by the activities of the Nazi forces and officials and by the appreciations to be found in the documents of the time. In one such document it is stated : "The United States consider Romania as an occupied country for although the German forces entered the country with the assent of the Romanian government, the Romanian people would never have freely admitted it except under duress."

The fascist rulers installed a régime of terror and fierce repression. The laws issued at the time provided for stern sanctions, which included the death penalty, for any act showing resistance to the military-fascist régime and the Nazi war. New concentration camps and prisons were created for thousands of anti-fascists.

Legionnaires closely co-operating with the Gestapo killed many opponents of fascism, including outstanding militants, Communists (Constantin David), and prominent scientists and men of letters (the world-famous historian Nicolae Iorga and the university professor Virgil Madgearu).

With the military-fascist régime installed, the representatives of the main parties which had held the reins of government before 1938 adopted a stand which suited their class interests and tried to save their positions now threatened by the new internal situation and by the development of the war. Maniu, D. Brătianu, and other politicians were generally for a bourgeois, constitutional form of government. As a result of their ties with the West, they were still partisans of France and Britain and believed that the western powers would be victorious. However, the international situation from the political and military points of view, the isolation of Romania in this corner of Europe, Germany's brutal pressure, and sharp internal contradictions convinced these political leaders that some concessions should be made to German pressure and to the pro-Nazi internal circles. Considering Germany's domination as temporary, they felt that the only acceptable solution to Romania's problem was the formation of a cabinet enjoying the confidence of Nazi Germany.

Counting on General Antonescu's pro-British feelings — he had been military attaché in London — and on the General's aversion to King Carol II, while at the same time fearing that a dictatorial Legionary government might be set up, the leaders of the National Peasant and of the National Liberal Parties agreed that the government should be headed by a person acceptable to Hitler who might to a certain extent defend their interests. But beyond the calculations of those politicians there was a most cruel reality : Romania's utter subordination to the interests of the Nazi Reich.

The presence of the Nazi forces in Romania and the country's political subservience created conditions that enabled the German monopolies systematically to get hold of the Romanian economy.

According to the plans of Nazi Germany, Romania's economic subordination was gradually to result in the seizing of her national industry, the country being thus turned into an outlet for the products of German industry and into a source of raw materials and foodstuffs. "Romania had better give up the idea of having an industry of her own," Hitler declared at the time. "She should direct the wealth of her soil, primarily wheat, towards the German market... Romania's proletariat, which is infected with Bolshevism, would thus disappear and our country would never lack for anything."

Under the agreement of December 4, 1940, the government of the Third Reich obliged Romania to adapt her economy to the requirements of Nazi Germany, to have her various branches of activity controlled by German "experts", and to make payments under the "Central Clearing House in Berlin".

By consenting to this agreement, General Antonescu won the goodwill and support of Hitler to the detriment of the Iron Guard. The dissensions between the majority of the military forces and the pro-Nazi Legionnaires assumed violent forms.

On January 21-23, 1941, the Legionnaires' rebellion broke out, its aim being to remove General Antonescu from office and to instal an Iron Guard administration for good and all. The Romanian army, hostile to the Legionnaires — Nazi agents and a hotbed of anarchy and terror — put down the rebellion. The Iron Guard had received no support whatever from any internal political or social groups.

Germany, which was preparing for the anti-Soviet war and needed peace and order behind the front-to-be, supported General Antonescu, though on the other hand it gave asylum to Horia Sima and other Legionary leaders and used them as a political reserve and to blackmail Antonescu.

After the rebellion of January, 1941, a cabinet of officers and technicians was formed. Though the Nazis insisted, Antonescu opposed the plan to rebuild the Iron Guard. However, Antonescu's military dictatorship continued its profoundly anti-popular internal policy and the enslavement of the country to Nazi Germany and drew the country into the war of the Reich without the approval of the Romanian general staff, government, or King.

★

When the German forces marched into Romania in the autumn of 1940, they were given a hostile reception by the people who considered them as so many bayonets supporting a fascist dictatorship and as a main instrument in ensuring the Reich's domination over the country. The terrorist methods instituted by the Iron Guard in the autumn of 1940 were continued with the support of the Nazi divisions. All this induced the Romanian people to speed up the organization of a resistance movement against the fascist dictatorship of the Nazi invaders.

Faced with disaster, the patriotic forces of the country organized a resistance movement which developed under new conditions into the anti-fascist and anti-Nazi struggle of the Romanian people.

The resistance movement involved the most different social strata and classes. The working class, being the most combative, best organized and keenest in fighting fascism, rallied round it the great patriotic forces of the peasantry, the progressive intelligentsia, and the patriotic elements in the army and drew them into an ever more active struggle.

Many scientists opposed the offensive of fascist ideology, defending the traditions of the national culture and making their contribution to the struggle of the people for removing the fascist yoke. Outstanding Romanian intellectuals repudiated Antonescu's dictatorship and the alliance with the Nazi Reich. They declared for the defence of Romania's national interest and her extrication from the anti-Soviet war.

The same spirit that prevailed among the masses was also to be found in the army, who were almost wholly against the Nazi war and regarded with hatred the Nazi armies which had violated the country's sovereignty. Clashes took place at the front between Romanian and Nazi soldiers. The German commanders sent in reports stating that they were profoundly dissatisfied with the lack of enthusiasm of the Romanian units and the difficulties made by the Romanian officers in carrying out operations under German command. The anti-Nazi feelings of the Romanian army increased as a result of the plundering carried out by Nazi Germany in Romania, of the heavy casualties at the front, and of the behaviour of the Nazi troops, who, not infrequently, struck down the Romanian soldiers in their retreat, crushed the wounded under their tanks, and bullied, humbled, and attacked the Romanian soldiers. As a consequence, many Romanians refused to leave for the front or deserted and went over to the Soviet or the partisan army, or engaged in armed clashes with the German soldiers. Romanian and Nazi officers could not come to an understanding, the reasons being those which had determined the anti-Nazi feelings of the soldiers.

A number of army commanders, generals, and chiefs of staff opposed the anti-Soviet war. The anti-Nazi Romanians in France, the U.S.S.R., Czechoslovakia, Belgium, and elsewhere joined in the struggle of the patriotic forces of those countries, thus making their contribution to the common cause of the peoples of the world. Alongside the brave French resistance fighters, many Romanians fought and died for the liberation of France from Nazi occupation. In the Soviet Union tens of thousands of prisoners formed divisions to fight the Nazi armies.

A stimulus was given to the anti-fascist resistance when in 1943 an anti-Nazi patriotic front was formed, uniting the Communist Party, the Ploughmen's Front,

MADOSZ, the Socialist Peasant Party, the Patriots' Union, and the local organizations of the Social-Democratic Party.

Wide circles, which included members of the bourgeois parties and of the Royal Palace, opposed Antonescu's dictatorship and Nazi Germany, showing their hostility to the German occupants and their revolt to see the country plundered by them. They demanded that the economic treaties concluded with the Reich be revised and German interference in the country's internal affairs be restricted.

The defeats suffered by Nazi Germany at the hands of the anti-fascist coalition, in particular on the Soviet Front, the increased dissatisfaction of the masses, and the upsurge of the people's anti-fascist struggle struck the dominant classes with panic, aggravating the political crisis of the military dictatorship. Nor was the army very eager to support Antonescu's government, and this led to the disorganization of the fascist state machinery.

In 1943 and 1944 sabotage intensified among the workers in industrial enterprises and in the transport services, as did also the opposition of the peasantry to requisitioning and conscription. There were protests from the intelligentsia, and the soldiers refused to go to the front, all of which showed the people's hatred for the Nazi war and their desire to shake off the fascist yoke.

There were partisans in the Banat Mountains as well as in the Bucegi and Vrancea Mountains, in Maramureș, in the Suceava county, in the Danube Delta, and in Oltenia.

The difficulties that Antonescu's dictatorship laboured under and the victories of the Soviet armies, who bore the brunt of the war in Europe, as well as the victories of the British and American armies, led the leaders of the National Peasant and National Liberal Parties to renew their contacts and negotiations with the Western diplomats, the aim being to conclude a secret peace and thus extricate Romania from the war.

Talks took place to this effect in Cairo in March and May, 1944, and hopes were placed on the "Balkan version" of the Second Front in Europe as advocated by Winston Churchill.

When military operations began on Romanian territory in Northern Moldavia, the Nazi command turned the country into a devastating theatre of war.

With this turn of events, the entire nation made it its aim to save the country from a disastrous total war. All sections of society, all classes, political parties, and persons of note opposed the dictatorship and the Nazi war, rallied to the cause, but definite measures had to be taken for the overthrow of Antonescu's government and the turning of the country's arms against Nazi Germany.

The National Peasant and National Liberal Parties sought to extricate Romania from the war by carrying on negotiations with the anti-fascist coalition powers, though they gave a wide berth to the Soviet Union. Their approaches overlooked the fact that the United States, Britain and the U.S.S.R. acted in unison in the war, nor did they take into account the prospects that might open up at the conclusion of the war. Hoping that an Anglo-American front would be made in the Balkan Peninsula, or that airborne Anglo-American forces would land in Romania, the politicians who represented these circles opposed for a long time the unification of all anti-fascist patriotic forces in the country. Subsequent developments showed the weakness of their orientation.

The king and the leaders of the National Peasant and National Liberal Parties had finally to submit to factual evidence and admit that the only political group able to switch over to definite action was the Communist Party. Consequently the circles in the royal palace, and a number of generals and party leaders, agreed to co-operate in one form or another with the Communists, despite their anti-Communist feelings.

The Communist Party, having considered the situation in the country and abroad, worked out a plan for unifying all the forces hostile to dictatorship and to the Nazi war, from the Communists to the royal palace, from the workers to the generals, and drew them all into a carefully prepared, well co-ordinated plan which was to end in the anti-fascist insurrection of August 1944.

In April, 1944, an understanding was reached between the Communist Party and the Social Democratic Party for the creation of a Workers' Single-Front, for building up a united action of the working class in wartime and under a military dictatorship. This was of considerable importance in speeding up the coalition of all democratic and patriotic forces with a view to overthrowing the fascist régime.

In May, 1944, an agreement was reached between the Communist Party and the Liberal group headed by Gheorghe Tătărăscu.

On June 20, 1944, the leaders of the National Peasant and National Liberal Parties subscribed to the creation of the National Democratic Bloc made up of the Communist Party, the Social-Democratic Party, the National Peasant Party, and the National Liberal Party.

Intensive activities were simultaneously being carried on in the ranks of the army, as patriotic officers and generals were induced to make military preparations for the insurrection. The military committee which was formed after the conference held by the representatives of the Romanian Communist Party, the royal palace and the army in the night of June 13, 1944, was assigned the task of preparing the military units for their participation in the insurrection.

In the summer of 1944 a comprehensive coalition of forces had been formed in Romania which included the working class and its parties, the bourgeois parties, and the royal palace entourage. This alliance was an essential factor of success in the overthrow of Antonescu's military dictatorship and in Romania's joining the antifascist coalition.

3. Armed Insurrection

THE creation of armed working class detachments designed to fight in the patriotic struggle was of great importance in the success of the insurrection. Organized in the factories of Bucharest and in certain districts of the country (Prahova Valley, Oltenia, Banat), armed and well-trained, these detachments were to rally all the patriots determined to fight against the fascist régime and the Nazi forces.

The plan for the overthrow of the fascist dictatorship was carefully worked out from the military standpoint as well as from the political. The insurrection was to begin in Bucharest in the latter half of August and at the same time in Ploieşti and in the Prahova Valley oilfields.

Bucharest was a fitting place to start the insurrection for it could bring in the support of the masses. A surprise attack would cripple, from the start, the German command and the fascist repression bodies, for it was in Bucharest that the government of the military dictatorship had its headquarters; it was there that the central state institutions and the main Nazi military command for Romania were to be found.

While these measures were to be taken inside the country, certain units of the Romanian army, under the command of generals who had enthusiastically consented to help overthrow the dictatorship, were to check the penetration of Nazi forces from Northern Transylvania and over the western and southern frontiers of the country. The Romanian forces on the Moldavian front were to separate from the Nazi units and join the forces fighting against Nazi Germany.

Military developments during the last ten days of August, 1944, created favourable conditions for the insurrection. Along the Jassy-Kishinev Front a strong offensive of the Soviet Army began on August 20, 1944. The bulk of the Nazi forces were putting up a hard fight, suffering heavy casualties. Romanian regiments and divisions withdrawing from the front produced gaps in the defence line. However, the Nazi forces were far from being defeated, and the German command had prepared their withdrawal over a long period.

In the fortified area of Focşani-Nămoloasa-Galatz and along the Danube up to its confluence with the Black Sea, the Nazi command and Antonescu's government had taken special defence measures for a strong resistance line. The area between the bend of the Carpathians and the bend of the Danube at Galatz, some sixty miles long, was the only place where the Soviet armies could penetrate to make their way to the Danube plain, Bulgaria, and Yugoslavia. But the area which was fortified 40 miles deep was considered to be impregnable. The Nazi command banked on prolonged resistance in that area. Other successive lines of resistance along the larger rivers and the mountains were to have been built up within the country in order to delay the advance of the Soviet armies.

However, the armed insurrection was to overthrow all those plans. In accordance with the plan worked out by common agreement by the Communists and the representatives of the royal palace, it began on August 23, 1944. On orders from the King, the heads of the military fascist government, Ion and Mihai Antonescu, were arrested by members of the royal guard. A group of patriotic fighters headed by Communist leader Emil Bodnăraş removed them from the palace and imprisoned them in one of the secret houses of the Communist Party. Other ministers, including the Home and the War Ministers, were summoned to the palace to participate in a Crown Council and were arrested the same evening.

During the night of August 23, 1944, a government was formed. It was made up of officers and technicians, with General Sănătescu as Premier and representatives of all the parties of the National Democratic Bloc (the Romanian Communist Party, the Social Democratic Party, the National Peasant Party and the National Liberal Party), as ministers without portfolio.

During the night the army and the patriotic forces disarmed the German military units. The insurrection quickly swept over the country, from Moldavia and the Black Sea coast to Banat and Central Transylvania.

The fiercest fighting took place in Bucharest and along the Prahova Valley, where strong Nazi military units and commands were to be found.

The order Hitler sent General Friessner, commander of the Southern Ukraine armies, on August 24, 1944, to resist at any cost, "to destroy the capital and instal a new pro-German government" resulted in violent attacks by German air and motorized units. Though an understanding had been reached between the King and the German General Gerstenberg, according to which the German army was to be allowed to withdraw from the country provided it abstained from destructive action, the Romanian patriotic fighters and the army had begun to clear the towns of Nazi units. When the Germans launched their air attack on Bucharest, the fighting became general wherever Nazi units were to be found.

Apart from the mortality figures during the fighting, over 50,000 of the Nazi army were made prisoners, including fourteen generals, and immense quantities of war materials were taken.

The armistice convention signed in Moscow between the governments of the Soviet Union, the United Kingdom, and the United States of America, on the one hand, and the Romanian government on the other, stated :

"At 4.00 a.m. on August 24, 1944, Romania ceased entirely her military operations against the Union of

Soviet Socialist Republics in all theatres of war, ceased to make war against the United Nations, severed relations with Germany and her satellites, joined in the war on the side of the Allied Powers and fought against Germany and Hungary with the aim of restoring Romania's independence and sovereignty..."

By August 26, Bucharest was cleared of German troops. On August 30 and 31, 1944, the first Soviet units reached the outskirts of Bucharest, which had been liberated by the insurrection, and were welcomed by the population. By August 31, in barely eight days, the Romanian insurrectional forces had defeated the Nazi troops over most of the country's territory.

As a result of the collapse of the government of military-fascist dictatorship and of the German Command in Romania, the country did not become a ravaged territory, hundreds of thousands of lives were saved, and many towns and villages were left untouched. Industrial enterprises and particularly the installations in the Prahova Valley oilfields, were also saved. Since the Nazis had planned to destroy these installations in their withdrawal, their survival was of great importance because fuel could be supplied to the anti-Nazi front.

During the night of August 24, 1944, Soviet troops encircled the bulk of the South-Ukraine Nazi armies in the centre of Moldavia and Bessarabia and by the end of August had thoroughly routed them, and even succeeded in taking some of the passes in the Moldavian Carpathians. Other important Soviet units proceeded at a swift pace, making their way towards Bulgaria, Yugoslavia, and Northern Transylvania, without having to fight on Romanian soil.

The insurrection had an anti-fascist character for the forces that had achieved it had anti-Nazi aims. Antonescu's military dictatorship was overthrown, and Romania joined the anti-fascist coalition, fighting against Germany and her fascist allies with a view to the liberation of the homeland and to ensuring full national independence. Vast numbers from all sections of society took part in the overthrow of the military fascist dictatorship and in pushing the Nazis beyond the country's frontiers, for the liberation of the homeland from the fascist yoke was an aim that rallied all the forces of the nation.

At the same time, the insurrection and Romania's joining the anti-Nazi coalition were of the utmost importance in international affairs. The way was thus opened to the Soviet army toward the Danube Valley, a strategic area, as well as through the passes of the Eastern Carpathians, and a contribution was thus made to the collapse of the Nazi forces in the Balkans. The military and economic potentialities of the Allies were increased by Romania joining the anti-fascist coalition, and the war in Europe was thus shortened. The character and role of the insurrection in the anti-fascist struggle and the contribution of the Romanian people to the common cause are brought out by numerous documents originating in many countries.

Before the end of the day on August 23, 1944, developments in Romania were already commented upon. That evening the BBC pointed out that "Romania's move would have marked effects..." and the United States radio station in Europe stated that "henceforth Romania was a new ally in the United Nations' camp for she had asserted her will to join in the struggle against the common enemy".

The following day and for many days thereafter the Soviet, French, British, American, Turkish, Swedish, and Swiss radio stations and daily papers gave special attention to Romania's move on August 23, and to her joining the anti-fascist coalition.

The foreign Press described the spirit of the population which was definitely hostile to Nazism. The Swedish paper *Svenska Morgenbladet* recorded that in Romania there had always been a great feeling of sympathy with the United Nations in all sections of society.

In accounting for this state of spirit and attitude, a number of papers spoke of the consequences of Romania's dismemberment in the summer of 1940, of the dissatisfaction and great hatred of the people for the Vienna Diktat whereby the Axis Powers had ceded to Hungary Northern Transylvania, where nearly 150,000 Jews, more than were killed in all the other countries in Southeastern Europe, were assassinated by Horthy's régime.

Le Figaro wrote that Romania had been the only one of Germany's satellites which had "not received any territories in exchange for its alliance, but on the contrary had been compelled to cede to Hungary one of its most fertile provinces — Northern Transylvania".

The Nazi Press, in its turn, pointed out that this was no putsch of the royal palace circles, nor a mere change of government, but a revolt that meant to change the line followed thus far.

With reference to the character and significance of the move of August 23, 1944, and to the part played by the Romanian Communist Party in preparing for and organizing that move, *L'Humanité* noted: "The Romanian people are setting an example. After Antonescu's removal from power, they immediately turned against the Germans. In Romania, as well as in France and Yugoslavia, the Communist Party, though working underground, was one of the main factors in this change of allies."

Pointing to the decisive significance in the country of the move of August 23, the Swedish paper *Ny Dag* wrote: "The Romanian people are now taking their destinies in their own hands and proclaiming a democratic order."

The *New York Herald Tribune* of August 24, 1944, showed that what was left of the sixth and eighth German armies had been trapped between the Russians and the Romanians, the latter attacking the Germans from behind according to orders received from Bucharest, adding that it was the second time that the Wehrmacht had had its sixth army trapped.

The civilian and military insurrectional forces prevented the Nazis from organizing resistance along the narrow and strongly fortified line between the Eastern Carpathians, Focşani, and the Danube — one of the strongest strategic points, a gate toward the heart of the Balkans, the key to the Balkan plains, as it was described in the documents of those days.

The success of the insurrection also prevented the Nazis from resisting along the Southern Carpathians. The Romanian forces organized the defence and repelled the German-Hungarian attacks from the Transylvanian plateau, and this was of considerable importance for the subsequent development of the war. This operation of the Romanian army was widely commented on abroad. In its broadcast of August 28, 1944, a New York radio station declared that Romania had enabled the Allied forces to crush the German resistance along the Carpathians, thus making a decisive contribution to the victory of the Allied Powers.

The withdrawal of German forces from favourable positions held in Romania had serious consequences for Nazi Germany.

Moscow Radio pointed out : "Nowhere on Romanian territory did the Germans succeed in repeating the events which took place in Northern Italy in the summer of 1943. They did not succeed in disarming the Romanian army or occupying the main strategic positions."

The documents of those days also brought out the influence which the victory of the anti-fascist insurrection in Romania had on other countries and on the general progress of the war. They laid stress on the consequences abroad of Romania joining the anti-fascist coalition : military, strategic, economic, and moral-political consequences.

With reference to the effects achieved by Romania's joining the United Nations, the BBC stated in its broadcasts of August 24, 1944, that Romania's move was an act of great courage which should speed up the end of the war and that Germany's situation in the Balkans would soon be a fearful catastrophe.

Indeed, according to the directions given on August 29, 1944, 27 divisions of the second and third Ukrainian fronts were placed at the disposal of Soviet headquarters, which was thus in a position to increase the pressure on the enemy along other fronts.

Moscow Radio pointed out that Romania leaving the Axis was of overwhelming importance not only for her but also for the whole Balkan Peninsula for it was a blow that caused the entire German domination system in South-east Europe to collapse. The significance of this move should not be underestimated, it was remarked. On August 27, 1944, the British *Sunday Times* pointed out that Romania breaking away from the Axis to go over to her traditional allies might be a deadly blow to Germany, for the latter thus lost her last important oil reserves and, at the same time, three ways were being opened for the Russians' advance : towards Bulgaria, whose position would probably be modified the moment the first Russian soldier appeared on her frontier ; toward Yugoslavia and the Adriatic, where the population was sure to rise everywhere against what was left of the German army ; and toward the Hungarian plain, Budapest, and Vienna, which would cause the pro-Nazi Magyar régime to collapse and bring about a revolt in Czechoslovakia. The *Sunday Times* concluded that Romania could be described as a keystone.

A communiqué of the Allied Headquarters in the Mediterranean stated that the Germans' withdrawal from the Peloponnesus had been considerably speeded up by Romania's defection and by the consequences of that move on the Germans' position throughout South-east Europe.

The United Nations more than once expressed their gratitude for the contribution made by the Romanian people to the general cause of the anti-fascist, anti-Nazi struggle.

The documents of those days also spoke of Germany's losses in Romania as disastrous and catastrophic, and also of the collapse of the South-Eastern Front. The events that took place in Romania in August, 1944, have gone down in history and their consequences for the Nazis have always been described as shown above.

The Nazi High Command was compelled to admit that the developments in Romania had serious consequences on the position of Germany and her associates. In a report to Hitler drawn up by Keitel and Guderain, it was pointed out that these events, apart from their immediate military consequences, at the same time brought about a reversal of fronts which was extremely dangerous, and would lead not only to the loss of Romania but also of Bulgaria, Yugoslavia, and Greece, and jeopardize the position of the whole German army in the Balkans.

The authors of the report suggested "that every measure should be taken to wipe Romania off the map of Europe and to annihilate her people as a nation".

The August insurrection is a landmark in the history of the Romanian people, a national and social turning point, the beginning of a new age, the result of the people's struggle for freedom, of their will to freedom, with roots going deep into their history. It is a link with the other turning points in the life of the Romanian people.

4. Romania's Participation in the Anti-Nazi War

DURING the first days of September, 1944, most of the Romanian units which had taken part in the insurrection were sent north-west of the Southern Carpathians to strengthen the positions of the Romanian forces along the western frontier of the country. Two enemy offensives were thus repelled : one on the Transylvanian plateau between September 5 and September 8, and another in Crişana and Banat on September 18. Furthermore, the Romanian army ruined the plan of the Nazi command to establish the front line on favourable defensive positions from Slovakia's mountains, along the Eastern and Southern Carpathians, and along the Balkans down to Greece. The mountain passes and routes in the Banat plain and across the Transylvanian plateau were now accessible so that a link could be established with the rest of the country, and Soviet and Romanian tank divisions and motorized and infantry forces could be grouped unhindered with a view to operations in the plain towards Debreczen, Budapest, and Vienna.

The advance of the Soviet forces across the Eastern Carpathian passes toward the front held by the Romanian army changed the ratio of forces to the detriment of the enemy, conditions being thus created for a new large-scale offensive. By early October, 1944, the joint action of the Soviet and Romanian forces advanced the front to the upper reaches of the River Mureş, while in Crişana and Banat the enemy was repelled to the Romanian-Bulgarian and Romanian-Yugoslav frontiers.

On October 6, 1944, the Romanian and Soviet armies, in order to liberate North-west Transylvania and the Hungarian territory up to the River Tisza, engaged in a powerful offensive known as the Debreczen operation. The Romanian units taking part in that operation totalled 260,000 men.

On October 25, 1944, enemy resistance was crushed in the Satu Mare and Carei areas and Romania was completely freed from the fascist yoke. Northern Transylvania, which had been seized from Romania by the Vienna Diktat, was again incorporated within the country. The news was welcomed by the entire Romanian people. Meetings and demonstrations were held, the masses showing their gratitude for the heroism and sacrifices of the soldiers at the front and pledging to increase their efforts in the war until the capitulation of Nazi Germany.

Co-operating with the Soviet forces beyond the country's frontier, the Romanian troops took part in the liberation of Hungary and Czechoslovakia until the final defeat of Nazi Germany and the victorious conclusion of the war in Europe.

The Romanian forces fighting on Hungarian territory included seventeen infantry and cavalry divisions, an aircraft detachment, two anti-aircraft artillery brigades, a railway brigade and other units, totalling over 210,000 men. The Romanian forces had their share in the liberation of Budapest, Debreczen, Miskolcz, and other towns.

On December 18, 1944, Soviet and Romanian units crossed the Hungarian-Czechoslovak frontier. On Czechoslovak territory Romanian troops, as part of the great operative units of the Soviet army, fought bravely in the Javorina, Lower Tatra, the Slovak Metallic, and Higher Tatra Mountains. The winter was severe and the terrain unfavourable for action. Nevertheless, the resistance of the enemy was gradually broken down and many towns were liberated, among them key centres such as Lucenec, Zvollen, and Banska Bistrica.

The Romanian units taking part in operations in Czechoslovakia totalled more than 248,000 men. They were made up of sixteen infantry and cavalry divisions, an aircraft detachment, an anti-aircraft artillery division, a railway brigade, a tank regiment, and other units.

By the end of the Second World War in Europe Romania's entire military and economic potential was engaged alongside the anti-Nazi coalition.

The Romanian military units fighting in the anti-Nazi war from August 23, 1944, to the capitulation of Nazi Germany amounted to nearly 540,000 men. Some 170,000 Romanian officers and men were killed or injured in the battles waged against the fascist invaders. From August 23, 1944, to May 12, 1945, the Romanian army defeated over fourteen Nazi and Hungarian divisions.

Many orders of the day of the Romanian Ministry of War and General Staff showed the gallantry in the field of the Romanian troops, as did also seven orders of the day of the Soviet High Command and twenty-one Soviet war communiqués. Over 300,000 soldiers, non-commissioned officers, and officers were awarded Romanian, Soviet, and Czechoslovak orders and medals.

Romania's entire national economy worked for the front. Although the Romanian people made every effort and sacrifice to support the anti-Nazi war, yet the economy suffered in the extreme as a result of the Nazi plunder, the destruction caused by bombing and military operations, the blocking of Romanian foreign currency in the western countries, and the expenditure on the support of the anti-Nazi front and the war reparations. All this amounted to more than 3.5 times Romania's national revenue of 1938.

Official representatives in various countries, political and military figures as well as the foreign Press often pointed to the important contributions made by Romania toward the defeat of Nazi Germany. On September 29, 1944, Anthony Eden, the British Foreign Secretary, pointed out that Romania had substantially helped the Allied cause.

W. M. Molotov, Minister of Foreign Affairs of the Soviet Union and head of the Soviet delegation to the Paris Peace Conference, said on October 10, 1944 : "We all know that Romania, by a decisive move, shook off Antonescu's fascist régime and joined the Allies... Together with ourselves and with the Allied troops, the new democratic Romania engaged in the fight for Hitler's defeat and made considerable sacrifices in that fight. We all recognize the services the Romanian people have made for the cause..."

28. Alexandru Ioan Cuza.

29. Entrance gate at Alba Iulia.

30. Conquest of the Grivița Redout.

31. Inauguration of the Romanian Academic Society (August 13, 1867).

32. The Mărășești Mausoleum erected to the Romanian heroes fallen in battle.

33. Nazi officers captured in Bucharest during the Insurrection.

34. Dr. Petru Groza

35. Meeting in Bucharest on March 6, 1945.

36. Nicolae Titulescu.

37. Dr. Constantin C. Parhon.

38. Mihail Eminescu.

39. Tudor Arghezi.

40. George Coşbuc and Ion Luca Caragiale.

41. Lucian Blaga.

On January 7, 1945, the BBC reported that among the nations fighting against Nazi Germany Romania had the fourth largest number of men fighting for the destruction of Nazism.

In an article headed "Romania Alongside the United Nations", French General Cochet and Lieutenant Colonel Paquier pointed out that the Romanian forces fighting side by side with Soviet forces had advanced more than 800 miles through enemy positions along the River Mureș and up to Bohemia, liberating 5,830 towns and villages and taking 100,000 prisoners. They concluded : "The French who fought together with the Romanians during the 1914-18 war were able to appreciate their power of resistance, moral unity and fervent patriotism.

"Romania has given her best to the cause of the Allies."

Because of her contribution to the anti-Nazi war, it was proposed to give Romania the status of co-belligerent. Thus, in January, 1945, Ivor Thomas, a British M.P., said in the House of Commons that Romania having the fourth greatest number of men fighting against Germany, should be given this status.

The delegations of France, Czechoslovakia, the Ukrainian Soviet Socialist Republic, and the Byelorussian Soviet Socialist Republic submitted similar proposals to the Peace Conference in the autumn of 1946. But Romania was not given the status of co-belligerent.

CHAPTER SIXTEEN

CREATION OF SOCIALIST ROMANIA

THE victory of the anti-fascist insurrection of August, 1944, opened up a new era in Romania's history. It was the beginning of a popular revolution in the course of which Romanian society underwent constant transformations which led to the installation of the socialist system. The Romanian Communist Party, which had been formed in 1921 but was forced underground, was now in a strong position to influence events with the help of the Russian liberators.

1. The Struggle for the Installation of a Democratic Régime

THE people's revolution went through two distinct stages in Romania: a stage during which bourgeois-democratic changes were made, and a stage of socialist transformations, the two forming an uninterrupted revolutionary process.

After August 23, 1944, Romanian was again a constitutional monarchy based on the Constitution of 1923.

In a statement to the country, the cabinet of General C. Sănătescu, which had been formed at the very beginning of the anti-fascist insurrection, pledged itself to ensure the continued struggle of the Romanian army side by side with the Allied armies and to establish a democratic régime of public liberties and civic rights.

Measures were taken to abolish the fascist legislation and to reinstate the constitutional democratic institutions. A general amnesty was granted to political prisoners.

Romania joined the anti-fascist coalition with all her forces, the Romanian army fighting side by side with the Soviet army in the war against Hitler's and Horthy's troops. On September 12, 1944, the representatives of the Romanian government signed in Moscow the armistice convention between Romania and the United Nations, recording Romania's extraction from the anti-Soviet war and her turning against Nazi Germany. Under the armistice convention the frontier between the U.S.S.R. and Romania was re-established along the line of June 28, 1940 ; at the same time the Vienna Diktat of August 30, 1940, was declared to be null and void.

An Allied Control Commission, acting in accordance with the general directives and orders of the Soviet High Command on behalf of the Allied powers, was formed for the purpose of checking on the carrying-out of the provisions of the armistice convention until such time as the peace treaty was to be signed.

The liberation of the country created new conditions for a political life, with all the democratic parties and organizations finding a wide scope for their activities. An important part was then played by the working class parties — the Romanian Communist Party and the Social Democratic Party — acting within the framework of the United Working Class Front. No longer working underground, the Romanian Communist Party was reorganized, increased, and strengthened in town and country. The Social-Democratic Party adopted an identical or nearly identical position in the fundamental problems raised by democratic changes to be made in Romania. Simultaneously, the trade union movement was reorganized. On September 1, 1944, representatives of the Central Committee of the Romanian Communist Party and the Social-Democratic Party adopted by common agreement the principles and measures of organization of the

Workers' Trade Unions. A commission for the organization of a United Trade Union movement was formed and subsequently in January, 1945, a congress took place during which the General Confederation of Labour was formed.

The parties making up the National Democratic Bloc had a common aim — the liberation of the country's territory — but they had different views regarding the socio-political régime to be installed in the country. Whereas the King and the leaders of the National Peasant and the National Liberal Parties wished to reinstate the old régime, a large part of the political forces declared for the installation of a genuine democratic régime and for the implementation of socio-economic reforms.

The economic situation of the country was most precarious, for industry was hardly developed, and the consequences of German domination and of the havoc wrought by war had also made their impact. In 1944 industrial output was about 40 to 50 per cent of the pre-war level; railway transport had decreased to 30 per cent of the 1943 level; grain production was less than half the 1939 figure. Moreover, the economic situation was aggravated by inflation, by the great difficulty of obtaining raw materials, and by the blocking of Romania's foreign currency in the western countries.

The country's expenditure as a result of its participation in the war alongside the states of the anti-Nazi coalition and the war reparations of 300 million dollars to the U.S.S.R. it had to start paying in September, 1944, weighed heavily on the Romanian economy. There were further economic difficulties as a results of the stocking of considerable quantities of products and of speculation. Taxation was heavy, primarily on the workers and peasants; during the 1944-5 financial year income tax derived from salaries and wages accounted for nearly 50 per cent of the budget revenue, while trade and industry contributed only about 25 per cent. There was a great housing shortage because of the destruction wrought by war. The very large number of disabled and war widows and orphans, the scarcity of medicines and the lack of medical staff to remedy the deplorable health situation which was aggravated by malnutrition, all made their impact on the economic and social situation of the country and called for speedy remedies.

The first cabinet of General Sănătescu, composed of generals, resigned on November 5, 1944, as a result of a protest from the Soviet General Vinogradov on alleged non-fulfilment of the armistice terms. Almost immediately a new government was formed, again with General Sănătescu as Premier, but this time the cabinet included a large number of representatives of the democratic forces grouped in the National Democratic Front: the Vice-Chairman of the Council of Ministers, Dr. Petru Groza, belonged to the Front as did also six ministers and three under-secretaries of state. According to Hugh Seton-Watson in *The East European Revolution,* this new government passed some long overdue political measures. In particular it decided to arrest former Iron Guardists, and repealed all anti-Jewish legislation. The Government fell as a result of disputes about the Ministry of the Interior, held by the national peasant Penescu. He was bitterly attacked by the communists as a protector of fascists. Sănătescu was replaced as Premier by General Rădescu. This elderly officer (said Seton-Watson) had been well known for his anti-German attitude during the war, and had been for a time interned. He enjoyed the confidence of the Soviet command, which had pressed for his appointment as Chief of the General Staff. The main changes in the new cabinet were that Rădescu himself took over the Ministry of the Interior and that the ministries without portfolio were abolished.

Land reform was a pressing problem at this time. The new Premier set up a commission for the study of land reform, but it was composed mostly of landowners and little progress was made. In the draft programme of the National Democratic Front published in January, 1945, immediate implementation of land reform was a fundamental point. As the government postponed carrying out the reform, the Ploughmen's Front launched a campaign early in February of that year for the forceful occupation of the landowners' estates by the peasants. Peasant committees came into existence in all parts of the country. Often facing the bullets of the gendarmes, the peasants divided the estates with the support of teams of workers without waiting for the law which refractory ministers continually postponed. In a matter of weeks the drive for the division of estates became a general phenomenon throughout the country.

Concurrently, the remnants of the administration dating from Antonescu's dictatorship were ousted from power as were also other anti-democratic elements heading the local bodies of state power. The prefectures in 52 out of the 58 existing counties came under the control of the National Democratic Front. Occasionally, this took place after violent clashes between the masses and the forces of repression acting on orders from General Rădescu, as for example at Craiova, Constantza and Caracal.

Political tension was running high at the close of February, 1945. Popular demonstrations, often ending in violent clashes with the authorities and pro-fascist elements, took place throughout the country. Hundreds of thousands of people-workers, peasants, members of the intelligentsia, office clerks and members of the army-took part in the demonstrations held on February 24 throughout the country. In certain areas the demonstrators were fired on. In Bucharest they were fired on from some public institutions, and there were a number of casualties, killed or wounded. However, the attempt to use military units against the demonstrators on a large scale was unsuccessful.

Hugh Seton-Watson said in his *East European Revolution* that

During these months public order was in a curious condition. In Moldavia and southern Bukovina the old officials had fled before the Red Army's advance. There had also been a panic flight of the greater part of the large landowning and bourgeois class. Consequently not only had the old administration broken down, but the old political parties — national peasants and liberals — had lost what little organisation they had been able to retain under the dictatorships of Carol II and Antonescu. The Russian authorities had to ensure order, and it was they who chose its Romanian exponents. These were for the most part communists or persons willing to obey communist orders...

It was only in Wallachia and southern Transylvania that the government's writ ran. Here the old bureaucracy which had served Carol II and Antonescu was still in charge when King Michael brought Romania out of the war. There is no doubt that many of the old officials had fascist sympathies, and that many were hated by the people for their corrupt and brutal behaviour in the past. A purge was urgently needed. But the purge became in fact a struggle between the parties, each wishing to replace those dismissed with its own supporters and to keep in their jobs those who were willing to serve it. The communists had two great advantages: they were supported by the Soviet authorities, and they were able to point to the mistakes of the other parties when they had been in power in the past, but themselves, having never been in power, were not open to similar attack. In the first few months they won some genuine support from the poor and oppressed. In the cities they appealed not only to workers but to small shopkeepers and lower officials, who suffered great economic hardship. In the countryside the Ploughmen's Front made some genuine progress at the expense of the National Peasant Party.

This organisation, founded in 1934 in the south Transylvanian town of Deva, had never before had more than local importance. But it was a genuine movement of radical peasants, actually managed by the peasants themselves with the advice of some intellectuals, including the former minister Dr. Petru Groza. The Front now spread outside the small area where it had previously existed. Its spokesmen in the villages had considerable success when they stressed the past failures of the National Peasant Party, its tendency to help only the richer peasants' interests, and its domination by non-peasants. But success damaged the Front. As it spread to new regions it became dependent on people who knew nothing of its former aims and struggles. It tended to rally only the village malcontents, willing to follow any demagogic slogan, the same people who earlier had formed the rural support of the Iron Guard. For its organisation it depended on communists. Soon its cadres consisted mainly of communists, and its leadership was filled with avowed or concealed communists, many of whom were not only not peasants, but had little interest in peasants. It became, and was generally regarded as, the rural branch of the Communist Party...

The crisis came in February 1945. Rădescu, unable to express himself in the censored press, made fierce attacks on the communists at public meetings. The Malaxa metallurgical works in Bucharest was the scene of a bloody battle between national peasant and communist workers. Many of the latter had been brought to the works from outside in lorries, and some were armed. The Malaxa works had been before the war an Iron Guardist stronghold, which gave the communists a chance to accuse the government of encouraging fascists to attack "democratic workers". There were probably in fact quite as many Guardists among the communist contingent in this fight as among their opponents. On February 24 the communists organised a mass demonstration in the Palace Square. There was some shooting. The communists blamed the police, Rădescu the communists. The same day Rădescu made a bitter broadcast, calling the communist leaders Anna Pauker and Vasile Luca "foreigners without God or nation" and "horrible hyenas". (Anna Pauker was a Jewess and Vasile Luca a Hungarian from the Szekely country in Transylvania.)

Coming up against the opposition of the masses [the Romanian history continues], General Rădescu was compelled to resign on February 28, 1945. Ultimately the King agreed to the formation of a government proposed by the National Democratic Front. On March 6, 1945, a government of wide democratic interests was formed, with Dr. Petru Groza as Premier. The National Democratic Front held preponderant positions in the Cabinet: the chairman of the Council of Ministers and fourteen Ministers belonged to the Front. The Liberal Party headed by Gh. Tătărăscu was represented by the Vice-Chairman of the Council of Ministers and three ministers.

2. The Bourgeois-Democratic Revolution is Completed

AS soon as the democratic government was in office it proceeded to legalize and complete the main reform, that of the land. Under the law published on March 23, 1945, all landed estates exceeding 100 acres were expropriated, as were also the estates belonging to collaborationists, war criminals, those guilty of the country's disaster, and those who had not themselves tilled their land during the previous seven years, an exception being made for estates of less than 20 acres.

The law stipulated that special village committees were to draw up a list of those who were to receive land. The list was to include only landless peasants or peasants owning less than 10 acres. The order in the lists was as follows: soldiers; those mobilized and those who had fought against Nazi Germany; landless peasants, agricultural labourers, and crop sharers who had worked on the estates being expropriated, irrespective of the village they lived in; and peasants owning less than 10 acres.

Over 900,000 peasant families, accounting for about one third of the total population of the country, received land by virtue of the Land Reform Law. As a result, the proportion of poor peasants was considerably reduced and the number of middle peasants increased. Over 400,000 families of landless peasants now had their own homesteads and another 500,000 improved their economic position. The land reform solved the fundamental problem in the process of bourgeois-democratic changes in Romania — a process which had been left incomplete in the stage of the revolution of 1848 and during the subsequent period. An age-old dream of the Romanian peasantry, for which they had waged unceasing battles, had come true.

The landowners as a class disappeared and this undermined the very foundations of the old socio-political régime. The Romanian people's national independence and their democratic gains were closely bound up with the final victory over Nazi Germany. As soon as it had been installed, the democratic government took a number of measures designed to step up the country's war effort. However, there were internal difficulties. Speculation and inflation were at their height, and economic difficulties were aggravated by the consequences of two years' drought. Incited and supported by the western imperialists outside the country, the King and leaders of the National Peasant Party (Maniu) and of the National Liberal Party (Brătianu) started a virulent campaign against the government.

Beginning in August, 1945, the King severed all contact with the Groza cabinet and refused to sign the decrees, thereby hoping to induce him to resign. The "royal strike", begun under the impulse of foreign forces, ceased on account of lack of mass support and of the compromise reached in Moscow in December, 1945, at the conference of the Foreign Ministers of the United States, Britain and the U.S.S.R. In answer to the request of the United States and British representatives, this conference demanded that the Romanian government should include a representative of the "historical" parties. The Groza cabinet agreed to this request, and Emil Hațieganu and Mihai Romaniceanu thus became ministers without portfolio to represent the National Peasant Party and the National Liberal Party respectively. According to Hugh Seton-Watson, the circumstance in which Groza was put in power enraged the British and American governments. In spite of the obligation under the Yalta Declaration to consult the Allied Powers, the Soviet government had taken unilateral action. The Soviet authorities were consistently unfriendly, even offensive, to their colleagues on the Control Commission. Thus the British and Americans inevitably grew more hostile to the pro-Soviet elements in Romania and more friendly to the opposition. The conflict between the Groza government and the oppositional "historic parties" became an international issue. Following the agreement on the two additional ministers, the new government took office on January 7, 1946, and American and British recognition was granted on February 4. The Soviet Union had earlier recognized the new government.

The agreement reached in Moscow at the conference of the Foreign Ministers of the three powers did not end foreign pressure and interference; in certain respects it increased them, and this was facilitated by the presence of the reactionary parties in the Romanian cabinet. As a result of such pressure and interference, the right-wing leaders of the Social Democratic Party, headed by Titel Petrescu, diverged from the line of the United Workers' Front and proved hostile to the co-operation in the election of all the political forces that made up the government of a wide democratic nature. Repudiating such an orientation, the extraordinary congress of the Social-Democratic Party of March, 1946, decided to co-operate with the Romanian Communist Party and with other progressive parties. On the other hand, a new group headed by Dr. Nicolae Lupu made up the Democratic Peasant Party, after seceding from the main opposition party, the National Peasant Party.

The developments bound up with the electoral campaign took place in a most complex and contradictory climate. The Peace Conference was held in Paris from July 29 to October 15, 1947. Showing the position of the Romanian government, the declaration headed *Romania's attitude towards the Peace Conference*, published on August 12, 1946, pointed out that Romania, on the basis of her overall contribution to the anti-Nazi war was entitled to demand and obtain : recognition of her status as co-belligerent, the removal from the treaty of the economic clauses which affected the situation of the country and her economic policy, and limitation of the restrictions concerning armament and the armed forces necessary for the country's defence.

Moreover, the Romanian government proposed that the problems of Danube administration, which were to be debated by the conference, should be settled by a special convention concluded by the countries bordering upon the river.

The Romanian delegation had to fight against numberless difficulties raised not only by the contradictory interests of the Great Powers but also by the attempts made by certain states to recover the positions they had lost as a result of the defeat of fascism and the post-war socio-political transformations. Although the Great Powers unanimously appreciated the effort made by the Romanian people in the fight for the defeat of Nazi Germany, and the human sacrifices they had made for the victory of the United Nations, the Peace Conference did not give Romania the status of co-belligerent. At the same time, the peace treaty included onerous clauses of war reparations to be paid for the damages caused by Antonescu's dictatorial régime which had drawn the country into the anti-Soviet war during which 350,000 Romanians lost their lives.

However, the Romanian delegation did obtain recognition of Romania's "having taken an active part in the war against Germany"; the cancellation of the Vienna Diktat, and engagements on the part of the Allied and Associated Powers to back Romania's application for membership in the United Nations Organization. This application was not granted at the time but Romania was admitted to the organization in 1955. The signing of the peace treaty between Romania and the Allied and Associated Powers took place on February 10, 1947.

Nearly 7 million citizens took part in the parliamentary election of November 19, 1946, the greatest number of votes ever cast in the history of the country. Election returns showed an indisputable victory for the bloc of democratic parties, which gained 79.86 per cent of the votes. The government coalition held 376 of the 414 mandates in the Assembly of Deputies. Parliament issued a number of laws designed to strengthen the régime and Romania's independence and national sovereignty. On December 20, 1946, Parliament passed the law for the nationalization of the National Bank of Romania, the most important financial and money-issuing institution of the country. The state now had control over credit and money issues and over all credit and banking institutions, whether public or private. This enabled the state to improve the financing of industry, agriculture and transport and to step up commodity circulation in the general interest of the country.

In May, 1947, Parliament passed a law for the setting up of industrial offices, whose task it was to guide, supervise and control economic activities of both state and private capitalist concerns. The offices were joint bodies of co-ordination of economic activities in certain branches of industry; they were made up of representatives of the Ministry of Industry and Trade, of Trade

Unions, and employers. The state, through the agency of its representatives in the management of industrial offices, was able to intervene in the activity of enterprises, to indicate a production programme, establish the quotas of raw materials required and their distribution, and fix the profit percentages, the distribution and circulation of products, and wage and salary levels.

Another major step was currency reform, which took place on August 15, 1947. This was a hard blow struck at speculative capital and it ensured a new distribution of the national revenue in favour of the working masses. The reform put an end to economic chaos and inflation and created the prerequisites for a rapid recovery of the economy. Carried out on the basis of internal resources, without any foreign loans, the reform of the currency made a substantial contribution to the strengthening of national independence.

Defeated in the election and compromised by their political views, with roots in the past, the "historical" parties were isolated from the masses. They found no place in the arena of legal activities and were increasingly engaged in clandestine plots whereby they wrought their own destruction. On November 6, 1947, the representatives of the National Liberal Party of Gh. Tătărăscu within the government were repudiated by the Assembly of Deputies for having diverged from the political line of the government and had to resign. They were not the only political casualties in that troubled year. According to Hugh Seton-Watson in *The East European Revolution* "In June a group of National Peasant Leaders, including Mihalache, the former chairman of the party, were arrested as they prepared to leave Romania by air. Some days later Maniu was arrested, and the National Peasant Party was formally banned. The trial of the leaders on a charge of conspiracy began in October. From the evidence given it would seem that there was some truth in some of the charges. American officers had made plans for subversive action with some members of the National Peasant Party, who had passed some information to them. The plans were childish and the information poor : neither seriously threatened the government. There was no evidence that Maniu was involved in any of the plans, and it seemed probable that among the plotters and among the organisers of the escape by air there were agents provocateurs of the government. Maniu and Mihalache were sentenced to solitary confinement for life. It was a terrible end to the career of the great Transylvanian patriot, who despite all his faults and hesitations in past years was still regarded by the majority of his countrymen as the greatest living Romanian."

Now the stage was set for the abolition of the monarchy. King Michael had, in effect, retired from politics. The Soviet government had shown appreciation of his role in 1944 by awarding him its highest decoration, the Order of Victory. As Hugh Seton-Watson pointed out, "There was no republican propaganda. But as the successive liquidation of the anti-communist and independent non-communist parties turned Romania into a 'popular democracy', it became clear that the days of the monarchy must be numbered. In November, 1947, the King came with his mother to London for the wedding of Princess Elizabeth and then stayed abroad for some weeks, during which he became engaged to Princess Anne of Bourbon-Parma. On his return to Bucharest he was presented with a demand for abdication. All power was already in communist hands, and it was clearly impossible to resist."

In the morning of December 30, 1947, King Michael signed the act of abdication in the presence of Dr. Petru Groza, Chairman of the Council of Ministers, and of Gh. Gheorghiu-Dej, Secretary-General of the Romanian Communist Party. In the afternoon of the same day, the King's abdication was made known to the Council of Ministers and a proclamation to the country was issued.

Speaking at the meeting of the Council of Ministers, Dr. Groza pointed out that the abolition of the monarchy "had been achieved by agreement with the king, who was aware that monarchy was a serious obstacle in the path of the people's development. History will record a friendly abolition of the monarchy without any convulsions, much against the wishes of our enemies. To use the phrase of the Queen Mother, the people achieved today a decent and elegant divorce from the monarchy".

That evening the Assembly of Deputies met to pass the law whereby Romania became a People's Republic and to elect the Presidium of the Romanian People's Republic. The Presidium was made up of C. I. Parhon, Mihail Sadoveanu, Ştefan Voitec, Gheorghe Stere and Ion Niculi.

The historic act of the proclamation of the Romanian People's Republic marked the transition to a new historical stage in Romania's development — a stage of economic and socio-political changes of a socialist nature.

3. Building up Socialism in Romania

THE Romanian people were faced with a number of fundamental objectives, primarily with outstripping the stage of economic development of those days and of turning Romania into a country with a well-developed industry and a modern agriculture. The prerequisites of the rise of the people's living standards and the prosperity of the homeland along the path chosen by the new system were to be achieved by means of economic progress, the creation of an advanced technical basis, and the rise in labour productivity.

Organizational and political unification of the working class played a most important role in the building up of a Romanian socialist society. Unification was the result of an evolutionary process whereby closer relations were forged between the parties and organizations working within the working class movement — a remarkable experience of internal as well as of international significance. In February, 1948, a congress took place for the unification on Marxist-Leninist principles of the Romanian Communist Party and the Social Democratic Party. A single working class party — the Romanian Workers' Party — was thus created. The party had this name until the Ninth Congress of the Romanian Communist Party in July, 1965. The 1948 Congress gave the main lines of the programme of socialist, economic and political construction.

The economic policy of the people's democratic state was focused on the industrialization of the country. In June, 1948, the main industrial, mining, banking, transport and insurance companies were nationalized, the foundations thus being laid for a powerful socialist sector of the economy. This made it possible to switch over to planned development of the national economy — a decisive step in the furtherance of the general progress of the country.

Well aware that electrification was an essential factor in the industrialization process and in raising the welfare and degree of civilization of a country, the Romanian Communist Party and the people's democratic state worked out the directives of a Ten-Year Electrification Plan (1951-60). The plan, which was drawn up with the contribution of many specialists and was debated by the Academy, established the guiding lines for rational capitalization of the power resources of the country.

During the period that followed, socialism was built up at a steady rate : industrialization was consistently carried out on the basis of new techniques. All the districts of the country were turned into important economic and cultural centres. Districts such as Moldavia, Oltenia and Dobrudja, which had lagged in the past, were drawn into an active economic life through judicious use of the prevailing economic and natural conditions, the creation of an industrial background in the towns, and a rational use of the labour forces.

In working out its agrarian policy, the state started from an analysis of the particular features of Romanian farming, the main one being the existence of a large number of small peasant homesteads of poor productivity. The peasantry, which accounted for two-thirds of the population of Romania, was one of the main problems of the age of socialist construction. The switchover from millions of small, poorly-equipped rural homesteads to the organization of big co-operative farms using modern agricultural machinery was tantamount to a revolution. It was not an easy matter and results of the switchover were only gradually felt because many deficiencies had to be overcome. The expansion of industry was one of the basic conditions for the socialist reorganization of agriculture.

The reorganization of Romanian agriculture was based on a programme worked out in 1949 in accordance with which agricultural production co-operatives were created. Material incentives, which were insufficient during the first years, played an ever more important part during the last two decades. A policy was evolved for the gradual economic restriction of the well-to-do peasants, who were deprived of the possibility of exploiting the other peasants and were subsequently induced to join the co-operatives.

In Romania the building up of the co-operative system in agriculture has resulted in a gradual but appreciable rise in farming output. This increase is due to the fact that agriculture has been equipped with modern machines, chemical fertilizers, and advanced technical methods have been used. In 1965 there were 81,336 tractors; by 1980 this number had increased to 146,500; in 1965 there were only 292 self-propelled combines, but by 1980 there were 39,100; the 23,241 mechanical cultivators in 1965 had been increased to 37,992 in 1979; and the number of chemical fertilizer-spreaders has more than trebled since 1965 (4,363 to 14,739 in 1979).

Private farming has not been eliminated. The state owns 30 per cent of the farms; 60.6 per cent belongs to agricultural production co-operatives, with 6.2 per cent allotted to members for household needs, and 9.4 per cent of the land is farmed privately.

When Romania embarked upon socialist economic development a great disadvantage was a disproportionately big population active in agriculture (74.1 per cent in 1950). Even as late as 1979 there was still a discrepancy between the number of the population active in agriculture (30.7 per cent) and its share of the country's social product (13.7 per cent). This explains the need to cut down the number of people active in agriculture to 12-15 per cent of the country's total population until 1990. The increase of agricultural production changed more or less its pattern, so, if in 1950 field crops were 61 per cent and livestock and meat production was 39 per cent, in 1979 the respective figures were 56 per cent and 44 per cent. Since 1950, farm production has increased 3.5 times. However, despite this growth, the provisions set failed to be completely fulfilled in agriculture, and this side of the economy is receiving fresh attention.

As compared to 1938, the year with the most advanced economy prior to the Second World War, Romanian industry produces 48 times more than it did then. It is telling that in the past decade (1971-80), while in the developed countries the gross national product grew at an annual rate of 3.3 per cent and in the developing countries at an annual average rate of 5.1 per cent, the social product grew in Romania at an annual average rate of 8.7 per cent, the national income by 9.2 per cent, the net industrial production by 10.7 per cent and farm production by 4.7 per cent. Between 1950 and 1980 the number of jobs increased by five million and the nominal net average remuneration rose 5.6 times. The nominal net monthly income of the peasantry rose from 167 lei to some 1,400 lei.

In 30 years of socialist construction, the per capita consumption rose 3.7 times with meat, 1.6 times with milk, 4.5 times with eggs, 4 times with sugar, and more than twofold with vegetables. Most telling is the fact that these rises were attained in conditions of the fast growth of urban population — from 3.7 million in 1948 to 11 million in 1980.

Between 1950 and 1980 4.6 million dwellings were built, which means that about 70 per cent of the country's population live in new homes. The health of the population has been radically improved; the average span of life has risen from 42 years in 1932 to 70 years during 1976-80.

Whereas in 1950 the per capita income in Romania was 15-20 times lower than that in the developed countries, it is today 4-5 times lower at the most. Romania is still a developing country, belonging to the category of countries with a per capita income of 1,500 to 2,000 dollars, but one of the targets in the current 5-year plan (1981-5) is to turn Romania from a developing country into a medium-developed one, so that the gap between it and the economically advanced countries in per capita income should be narrowed down to 2-3 times in 1985.

Between 1950 and 1979 Romanian foreign trade expanded 34 times. In 1980 the volume of foreign trade was twice as big as the 1975 one, and Romania was engaged in economic, technical and scientific relations with 150 states, compared to 131 in 1975.

Romania's foreign trade has been well diversified between East and West. In 1979 the Soviet Union was the chief export partner, taking 16.9 per cent of Romania's exports, followed by Federal Germany (9.2), East Germany (5.8), the People's Republic of China (5.7), United States (4.9), Czechoslovakia (4.8), Italy (4.1), Hungary (3.5),

Poland (3.3), Holland (3.2), France (3.0), Turkey (2.3), Egypt (2.3), Great Britain (2.2) and Yugoslavia (1.9).

In imports, Romania took 14.7 per cent of the total from the Soviet Union, Federal Germany (8.9), Iran (8.5), East Germany (6.4), United States (6.0), People's Republic of China (4.6), Czechoslovakia (4.4), France (3.6), Iran (3.3), Poland (3.3), Hungary (3.1), Italy (2.8), Libya (2.7), Austria (2.6) and Bulgaria (2.0).

The estimated average annual growth rate for foreign trade between 1981 and 1985 is of the order of 8.5 to 9.5 per cent, with exports increasing at even higher rates (10 to 11 per cent). Measures have been taken for a certain qualitative restructuring of industry by developing fuel and energy low consumption branches, and by particular attention paid to the expansion of the energy and fuels basis for Romania to be able by 1990 to rely on her resources in these fields ; in 1980 she was still compelled to import 58 per cent of her crude oil necessities.

A feature of Romania's economic development in the period of socialist reconstruction has been that of co-operation with more than 100 developing countries ; these have grown rapidly in recent years (10 times in the 1965-76 period). In 1976 they represented 21 per cent of the total trade exchanges of the country. Romania has concluded 121 co-operative ventures with developing countries in Asia, Africa and Latin America, out of which 86 concern economic units to be built and complex installations to be delivered to these countries and 27 refer to joint production companies to be constituted.

CHAPTER SEVENTEEN
CULTURE AND SCIENCE

THE Romanian lands from the earliest times have produced some particularly gifted sculptors, culminating in Constantin Brâncuși (1876-1957) who gained world fame. But who was the sculptor who made The Thinker *(Ginditorul)*, a clay statuette unearthed in a grave in the Neolithic necropolis of Cernavodă, belonging to the Hamangia civilizations (5,000-3,000 B.C.), which extended almost throughout the territory of Dobrodja, and spread to the south-east as well ? It is a masterpiece of world value and anticipates, by at least five millennia, *The Thinker* of August Rodin (1880), symbolizing the creative genius of human thought.

Another testimony to the brilliant civilization on Romania's territory in early times is the Dionysian panther (2nd and 3rd centuries B.C.), unearthed in the region of the Iron Gates. In the museums in Romania there are a great many objects of Greek and Roman origin, but when we turn to the original inhabitants of the land we find that the most representative category of products showing the progress achieved by Geto-Dacian cultures is earthenware. Besides the traditional hand made types, whether porous or burnished, a considerable number of wheel made types showing great craftsmanship and an advanced technique have been found in Geto-Dacian settlements. Among the luxury ware made by Getian potters there are in particular cups and bowls decorated in relief with dies in imitation of the Hellenistic model but with elements suggesting local imagination. In the first century A.D. remarkable progress was made by the shops at Sarmizegetusa (Grădiştea Muncelului), where painted ware showing realistic figures was being produced apart from other types of ware.

The Geto-Dacians also gave proof of their craftsmanship in their jewellery. Their bone tools are engraved with fine geometrical motifs. In Roman Dacia the crafts were of great variety, relying for the most part on local raw materials. Vestiges and indications have been found everywhere attesting to the existence of shops where metals, wood, fabrics, and hides and skins were processed. Ceramics needed for building purposes were being produced in quantities. They included roofing tiles, bricks, pipes as well as pottery, lamps and figurines. Jewellery was made out of metal and engraved semi-precious stones.

Under the Romans there was a high level of cultural progress in the province. All the inhabitants, irrespective of their ethnical origin or social status, spoke only Latin among themselves and with the authorities. Writing was in general use, as proved by the many inscriptions, of which some 3,000 (all Latin, with the exception of about 35 in Greek) have been discovered so far. The waxed tables preserved in a mine at Roşia (Alburnus Major in Roman times) showed that writing was in daily use, even among the lower strata of the population. The verse on funeral monuments showed a prevailing interest in literature and lofty thoughts. A taste for immortalizing thoughts, deeds, and persons in inscriptions and through artistic representations was widespread. From among the fine arts sculpture, in particular relief, was mostly practised. It was *par excellence* the art of the province and often assumed summary and rustic forms, though always reflecting a robust, realistic spirit identical with that of the art of the western Danubian provinces and also having affinities with the sculpture of Moesia Inferior. Painting found expression on less durable materials and as a result there are no important vestiges of it left. To form some idea of what it was like we can only make deduction from the polychrome mosaic of those days, of which some remarkable specimens with heroic or mythological representations have been preserved at Ulpia Sarmizegetusa and Apulum.

Romanian culture in the Middle Ages reflects not only the economic structure that generated it and which it served but, naturally, the role of the princes and the church. In the early years of the sixteenth century Radu the Great, Prince of Wallachia, brought the printing press into the country, the printer being the Serbian monk Macarie, who, after an apprenticeship at Venice, had printed a number of Slavonic books at Cetinje. The first printing press in Transylvania was introduced in 1528, and *A Treatise on the Plague* was printed in Sibiu by the Saxon Luca Trapoldner in 1530. In was also at Sibiu that the first book was printed in Romanian in 1544. This is *The Romanian Catechism*, printed by Filip the Moldavian, to whom the printing of the Slavo-Romanian Gospel of 1551-3 is also ascribed.

The writings in Romanian were of great importance for the development of Romanian culture. The Chancellery and the Church used the Slavonic language in Wallachia and Moldavia and Latin in Transylvania. Though in the past the appearance of the first writings in Romanian was ascribed to the influence of the Hussite doctrine or of the Reformation, it was actually a direct consequence of the transformation wrought within Romanian society which enabled the lesser Romanian gentry and the townspeople to gain access to culture. These were sections of society that had no knowledge of the ancient Slavonic culture and consequently used the national language and encouraged its use. The first text in Romanian known to have appeared in Wallachia is the letter of a Cîmpulung townsman, Neacşu, to the mayor of Braşov in 1521. In Transylvania and Maramureș, the first writings in Romanian appeared at the end of the fifteenth century and the beginning of the sixteenth.

In the seventeenth century Romanian was adopted in the writings of the age. In 1688 a Romanian translation of the Bible was printed, the translation being the work of a team of scholars which included the brothers Șerban and Radu Greceanu. Great attention was paid to works of history. In Moldavia the first historical writing in Romanian was *The Chronicle of the Land of Moldavia* by Court Marshal Grigore Ureche.

In Transylvania, occupied by the Hungarian kingdom, the Romanian population, despite adverse political and social conditions, carried on artistic activities according to popular and orthodox tradition and kept up its connections with the sister countries on the other side of the mountains, Wallachia and Moldavia. The most precious gems of Romanian art in Transylvania are the wonderful wooden churches of a later date which the peasants built with impressive craftsmanship down the centuries. Combining traditional Eastern Orthodox and Gothic elements, with the image of the peasant house predominating, these anonymous craftsmen of the Romanian villages scattered all over Transylvania, and especially in Maramureș, produced elegant constructions considered by specialists to rank among the most original creations of wooden architecture in Europe.

Moldavian art was to reach its culminating point in the age of Stephen the Great (1457-1504), an age of maximum economic and political, as well as cultural, progress of the Moldavian state. Stephen was a great builder of churches, as was his son Petru Rareș. The creative imagination of fifteenth-century builders is shown by a new, indeed unique system of construction devised by them and not met with elsewhere, either in the East or the West. The most impressive example is the so-called Moldavian vault. Instead of raising the tower of the churches of triconch design on the ring obtained from the four usual pendentives of an Eastern Orthodox Church, the Moldavian craftsmen encased in that ring a second row of smaller diagonal pendentives over which they raised a much slimmer tower than the traditional Byzantine type.

Unlike its architecture, where Western elements played an important part, Moldavian painting was faithful to the Byzantine tradition. Slav and Byzantine elements, to which a creative impulse was added by the brilliant local craftsmen, inspired the first great period in the early years of the fifteenth century, though nothing much has been left of the churches thus decorated, except the lovely miniatures made by Gavril Uric. During the reign of Stephen the Great, Moldavian painting appears as the work of a fully crystallized national school. Recently the signature was discovered of the most remarkable painter of those days — Gavril, the monk of Bălinești, (1493) — which proves that the craftsmen were Romanian.

The famous painted monasteries in Moldavia were built in an age when towns and crafts were developing apace and the greatest artists were no longer members of the clergy, as in the fifteenth century, but laymen, such as the painters Toma of Humor (1535) and Dragoș Coman of Arbure (1541). In these most original specimens of Romanian medieval art frescoes are on the exterior and interior walls.

While the paintings inside the churches were dedicated to a religious purpose, as everywhere throughout the Middle Ages, their main aim being to save the souls of the faithful, exterior painting was something like a prayer designed to inspire the people in the struggle for the independence of their country.

In the early half of the eighteenth century painting on glass, often for icons, became popular in Transylvania, and the result may be seen in many museums and monasteries today. In the centres of the west and east of Central Europe, glass painting was based on an old tradition of folk handicrafts. In Transylvania it was grafted on an ancestral fund of folk art never altered by any influence on a peasant art to the purest essence. Romanian icons on glass are the individual creation, specifically national, of the master painters who rose from among the peasantry. The Romanian peasant in eighteenth and nineteenth-century Transylvania lived in almost total isolation from any urban centre, preserving intact his own spiritual and material universe, mirrored in his icons as well. The entire glass painting in Central Europe tackles lay themes besides those predominantly Roman Catholic. Moreover, Transylvania is the only place where icons on glass adopted an Orthodox iconography of Byzantine origin, though it is situated in Central Europe.

Modern Romanian literature began in the latter half of the eighteenth century and was the product and expression of the Age of Enlightenment. A national literature did not mean a tendency towards isolation but signified a link with Western literature, first made manifest by the Transylvanian School. From the late 1870s until well after the first years of the 1880s the Junimea Society, to which the first truly great writers belonged, was the centre of Romanian literature. It was owing to the Junimea Society and in particular to Titu Maiorescu (1840-1917), the founder of Romanian literary criticism, that literature was rigorously set apart from culture as a whole and, at the same time, rose to the level of world literature, thanks to such writers as Eminescu, Creangă, Caragiale, Slavici, and Coșbuc.

The poet of love and death, and great emotion before the secrets of the universe, a brilliant mind tortured by the eternal problems of existence, a heart seething with emotion, and an intense feeling for the transient glory of the world, and with an ardent, overwhelming love for the country, Mihail Eminescu (1850-89), who may be regarded as the national poet, invested the Romanian language with an unexpected splendour and expressiveness. Eminescu reached a level beyond that of any other Romanian poet so far with his poems on love, satires, the poem "Evening Star" and a number of great unfinished poems, among them "Memento Mori" and "Mureșeanu".

At the close of the eighteenth century and during the first decades of the nineteenth profound transformations occurred in the evolution of the fine arts as a result of a more accentuated trend in Romanian society towards a modern culture of European type. In architecture the neo-classical style predominated as an expression of the new tendency. Sculpture, after a promising start, had for a long time played a secondary part, being confined to the decoration of residences of the ruling princes and of boyars or of the funeral monuments carved by native craftsmen. The revolution of 1848 was decisive in the history of Romanian sculpture as it gave rise to an art with loftier cultural and aesthetic aims. The first Bucharest sculptor to create works of notable artistic interest was Karl Storck (1826-87), who was also the first professor of sculpture at the Bucharest School of Fine Arts. One of his pupils, Ion Georgescu (1856-98), became the most celebrated Romanian sculptor of the nineteenth century.

In painting as in architecture, the decisive moment for modern Romanian art was that of the contact with neo-classicism. In was in Moldavia that religious painting first entered upon a period of neo-classicism, illustrated especially by the works of Eustatie Altini (*ca.* 1772-1815). A pupil of the Vienna Academy, Altini painted from 1802 to 1814 a number of altar screens, the most remarkable being in St. Spiridon Church in Jassy (1813). Altini took up and developed the traditions of the easel portrait which were spread in the Romanian countries in the eighteenth century. Gheorghe Tattarescu (1818-94) was for a number of years the best known artist in the country after his return from Italy in 1852. With him, neo-classical religious painting was finally crystallized, even dropping into stereotyped methods. His revolutionary ideas found expression in his canvas "Romania Awakes" and in the portrait of Nicolae Bălcescu, which he painted in Paris in 1851 when the great historian was in exile. When he exhibited a self-portrait at the Paris Salon in 1853 Theodor Aman (1831-91), who was to remain in the French capital until 1853, won a reputation afterwards brilliantly confirmed. In the years that preceded the Union he sent to Bucharest canvases such as "The last night of Michael the Great" (1852) which also brought him well-deserved fame. After the Union, Aman and Tattarescu obtained from the authorities the establishment of a school of fine arts in Bucharest (1864). In Jassy a similar institution had been created in 1860, with G. Panaitescu, a noted painter, as director.

The first exhibitions of living artists organized in Bucharest (1865-8) were given an indifferent reception, the critics confining themselves to conventional comments, but in 1870, when Nicolae Grigorescu (1838-1907) exhibited there for the first time things were altogether different. Heated discussions were aroused by the work of the young painter, similar to those which Manet and his friends, the Impressionists, gave rise to in France. Two concepts then assumed different forms in Romanian art and were to face each other for several decades: those of Aman and the followers of academic painting, and those of Grigorescu under whose influence the most gifted pupils of the School of Fine Arts were to develop. Grigorescu's canvases exhibited in Bucharest aroused the vocation for painting of Ion Andreescu (1850-82). He began painting in 1873 and his artistic skill, especially in landscape painting, won him a place among the European masters of his generation.

Ștefan Luchian (1868-1916) is generally considered to have blazed the path of twentieth-century Romanian painting. After studying at the academies in Bucharest and Munich he found in Paris in 1891-2 an environment that proved to be most favourable to his development. Impressionism was on its way to being finally accepted by the public, in particular Manet's art, Degas's pastels, and the symbolist primitivism of Gauguin. It was here that he discovered his own personal path, far removed from the routine of the Salon and definitely modern, as was shown in "The Last Autumn Race" (1892).

The changes which occurred in social life in the early nineteenth century brought about the emergence of a musical art which was national and no longer only religious. Even closer contact with Western Europe caused music to shed its oriental links, transforming public taste. The foundations of an artistic education were laid by the School of the Philharmonic Society (1834) and by the Philharmonic and Dramatic Conservatory (1836). When the Music and the Declamation Conservatories were founded in Jassy in 1860 and in Bucharest in 1864, Romanian musical training evolved systematically and continuously and no longer haphazardly.

The objectives were shortly reached in full. In 1866 the first symphony concerts were held and in 1868 a permanent orchestra, conducted by Eduard Wachmann, was inaugurated in Bucharest. This orchestra performed with fair regularity up to the War of Independence and then resumed its activities in 1881. Choirs were formed, the most important of which was The Carmen Society (1901) as well as the first chamber music orchestra (Constantin Dimitrescu's string quartet, 1880). The first Romanian opera company was built up on the initiative of George Stephanescu (1843-1925). The first composers were Alexandru Flechtenmacher (1823-98), who composed the first Romanian operetta "The Old Witch", I. A. Wachmann (1807-63), Carol Miculi (1821-97), Ludovic Wiest (1819-39) and Eduard Caudella (1841-1924), composer of the first Romanian opera, "Petru Rareș". It is to the credit of these composers that they combined popular melodies with a classical harmonic system, thus achieving a synthesis which was to prove its viability towards the close of the century when the choirs of Gavril Muzicescu (1847-1903), inspired by peasant folklore, gave the first adequate interpretation of the modal particularities of folk songs and paved the way for a specific musical language.

All sectors of literature went through a period of unusual creative effervescence during the span between the two world wars. Modernism, incorporating the currents derived from symbolism, dominated lyrical poetry. Greeted as a new Eminescu on the publication of his first volume, "Words that Fit", Tudor Arghezi (1880-1967) made unprecedented transformations in poetical syntax and in the language generally. Another fine lyrical poet was Lucian Blaga.

The fine arts went through a period of remarkable achievement between the wars. Among the outstanding artists was Camil Ressu (1880-1962), an excellent portrait painter but also a landscapist and painter of grave, true-to-life pictures of the peasant. This was a time, too, when the great painter G. Petraşcu (1872-1949) attained fulfilment. His landscapes, interiors, still-lifes and portraits show poetical awareness, a brilliant colour scheme and exceptional richness.

Foremost among the representatives of Romanian sculpture and of world sculpture generally is Constantin Brâncuşi. Already in 1907 when he produced his "Prayer", Brâncuşi had departed from traditional sculpture, endeavouring to produce archetypes to reach primordial forms. Brâncuşi gained world fame by such works as "Eve" (1921), "Girl's Torso" (1922), "Socrates" (1923), the many versions of the bust of Miss Pogany, and of the "Wonder Bird" and "The Cock" (1921), in which there are echoes of Romanian folk art. Tourists make a pilgrimage to Tîrgu Jiu to see Brâncuşi's noted works "The Infinite Column", "Gate of the Kiss", and "Table of Silence", set in the landscape.

During the period between the two world wars many of the Romanian sculptors who still do credit to their country began their activity. Among them are Ion Jalea (b. 1887), Cornel Medrea (1894-1964) and Oscar Han (b. 1891).

It was in the early years of the twentieth century that the first generation of composers with a sound training of high standard emerged from the magic circle of the eminent symphonist and teacher Alfonso Castali (1874-1942). Among them were Dimitrie Cuclin (1885), Alfred Alessandrescu (1893-1959), Ion Nonna Ottescu (1888-1940) and Constantin C. Nottara (1890-1951). Symphonic music thus made new strides, going beyond the limits of a certain "provincialism".

However, it was Georges Enescu (1881-1955), who laid the foundations of the modern Romanian musical school. As a composer, violinist, conductor and teacher (Yehudi Menuhin was among his pupils), this brilliant musician achieved a synthesis of specific national features and the universal. Borrowing and assimilating elements from the national *melos*-modalism, intervallics, rhythm and heterophony, as well as from the German symphony and from the French musical school, Enescu succeeded in creating a climate that was genuinely Romanian in forms of perfect originality. His works, from the "Romanian Poem" (1898) and the two "Romanian Rhapsodies" (1901) to "Oedypus", first played in Paris in 1936, and his "Chamber Symphony" (1954), integrate Romanian spirituality with its most characteristic features into the musical culture of Europe. They are a perfect synthesis of Romanian music and of the musical culture of our century.

Another figure of international reputation was the playwright Eugène Ionesco, born on November 13, 1912, at Slatina. He was educated in Bucharest and Paris, and was a lecturer and critic in Bucharest before settling in Paris in 1938. The plays of Ionescu, now a member of the French Academy, have been performed all over the world. His work was foreshadowed by that of "Urmuz" (Demetru Demetrescu-Buzău), creator of a brand of absurd humour which made him a leader of the avant-garde movement not only in Romanian but also in world literature.

During the age of socialist reconstruction 240 houses of culture have been built and 7,800 cultural clubs organized. An impressive number of new artists have become known. Among them are Corneliu Baba, portraitist and painter of compositions of great expressive force, Al. Ciucurencu, still painting landscapes and still lives but who now engages enthusiastically in historical compositions, Ion Tuculescu, who uses folklore motifs in his highly expressive paintings, Ion Musceleanu, a sensitive and subtle landscape and portrait painter, and St. Szonyi (1919-66) a painter of vast compositions illustrating the people's revolutionary struggle.

Romania's reputation as a land of sculptors has been continued by Ion Jalea, Cornel Medrea, Oscar Han, Gh. D. Anghel, Romulus Ladea, Constantin Baraschi, Ion Irimescu, Boris Caragea, Mac Constantinescu, and Geza Vida.

An outstanding novelist is Mihail Sadoveanu (1880-1961), whose home in Jassy is now a place of pilgrimage. He has been compared to Thomas Hardy as a depictor of village life.

Now for science. Between the wars there was a galaxy of mathematicians, a number of whom opened up new prospects in this field. Thus Gh. Țițeica (1873-1939), one of the creators of a special form of affine geometry, left his name to a class of curves and to a class of surfaces he studied. At Jassy, research on differential geometry made remarkable progress under the guidance of Al. Myller, who was also the author of the motion of concurrent directions. S. Stoilov (1887-1961) was the first mathematician to have given a topological characterization of the functions of a complex variable, introducing the notion of "interior transformation" for the purpose.

Romanian physicists, although working in laboratories that were poorly equipped — they were often compelled to work in foreign laboratories for that reason — made discoveries of note. H. Hulubei became an authority on X-rays and was elected corresponding member of the Paris Academy of Science. In aerodynamics. H. Coandă discovered the possibility of deviation of a fluid jet flowing into another fluid (the Coandă effect) and E. Carafoli became known for his studies on aerodynamic profiles.

The medical sciences benefited by the contributions of scholars of prestige, among them Fr. Rainer, supporter of a dynamic functional orientation in anatomy, C. I. Parhon, one of the founders of endocrinology and the discoverer of the syndrome named after him, C. Levaditti, who made a valuable discovery in the field of infra-microbiology, D. Danielopolu, who first used the viscerographic method, and Mina Minovici, head of the Romanian school of forensic medicine.

Romanian researchers made a number of technical inventions and discoveries, some of which have been applied throughout the world. T. Vuia devised a steam generator, Gh. Constantinescu a mechanical sonar convertor, A. Persu an aerodynamic car without differential, and T. Negrescu made a quantitative spectrographic analysis of alloys.

Romania has a number of "firsts" in aeronautics. Traian Vuia (1872-1953) flew a self-propelled plane for the first time, H. Coandă (1886-1972) was the inventor of the jet plane (December 14, 1910) and Aurel Vlaicu (1882-1913) designed the first metal-built plane.

During the age of socialist reconstruction mathematics continues to be distinguished by the work of scholars of world renown whose reputation was already established during the inter-war period, D. Pompei and S. Stoilov among them. Important results have been obtained in the theory of ideals (D. Barbilian), in the theory of probabilities and mathematical statistics (Gh. Mihoc and O. Onicescu), in the logic and algebraic study of the schemes of automatic relay mechanisms (Gr. Moisil), in the study of polyharmonic and polycolonic functions (M. Nicolescu), of equations with partial derivatives (N. Teodorescu), of non-holonomic spaces (Gh. Vrînceanu), and in the mathematical analysis and mechanics of fluids (C. Iacob).

Research in physics has been given a great impetus, especially after the Physics and Atomic-Physics Institutes were set up, the Atomic-Physics Institute being endowed with an experimental reactor and a betatron. Researchers here have studied in particular elementary particle physics and nuclear physics (Șerban Țițeica), radioactive isotopes and their application (H. Hulubei) and gas discharge physics (E. Bădărău and Th. V. Ionescu). The first laser which was built in 1962 under the guidance of I. Agârbiceanu gave credit to Romania as one of the first countries to have created such a device.

The outstanding results scored in chemistry are due to a considerable extent to the Chemical Research Institute. Among the achievements of Romanian chemists of great importance to the economy should be mentioned those in the field of plastics.

Continuing their research in medicine, an old tradition in the country, a number of scholars of note with their collaborators and disciples have enhanced the reputation of the Romanian medical school. The main fields in which Romanians have made their mark in furthering medical knowledge and advocating efficient treatment are : endocrinology (C. I. Parhon, St. Milcu, A. Aslan), infra-micro-biology (St. S. Nicolau), neurology (A. Kreindler and O. Sager), internal medicine (N. Gh. Lupu), bacteriology (M. Ciucă), physiology (Gr. Al. Benetato, D. Danielopolu), and surgery (D. Bagdasar, I. Hațieganu, N. Hortolomeiu).

Finally, no chapter on Romanian culture would be complete without a tribute to that great historian, Nicolae

Iorga, who, as has been pointed out, was murdered by the Romanian fascists. He had a world reputation as a historian. In the ten volumes of his *History of the Romanians*, a monumental work relying on extensive documentation, Iorga gave priority to the political and cultural life of the Romanian people. A visit to the Institute of History which bears his name in Bucharest, gives an indication of his immense output.

Another Romanian historian of international reputation is Mircea Eliade, who was born in Bucharest in 1907. His speciality is the history of religions and he has written on occultism, witchcraft and cultural fashions. He has held professorhips in Bucharest, Paris and the United States, where he now lives.

COMMENTARY

THE two most prominent leaders of the Communist Party in modern Romania have been Gheorghe Gheorghiu-Dej and his successor Nicolae Ceaușescu, and the study of their early lives gives an insight into the conditions in the last decades before the coming of the new order. Gheorghiu-Dej was the elder of the two. He was the son of a worker, born in 1901 in the Moldavian town of Bîrlad. As was common with so many other children of his time he was obliged to earn his own living from the age of 11. He worked in various factories, became a skilled electrician, and was first employed at the Danubian port of Galatz; later he worked on the Romanian railways. Although he was always active in trade union politics he did not join the Communist Party until 1930. He was transferred to the Transylvanian town of Dej as a punishment for political activities when he was a railway worker, and from that time integrated the name of the town with his own. For his part in the Grivița railway workshops strike in Bucharest in 1933 he was sentenced to 12 years hard labour, but, despite his confinement in various prisons, he maintained control of the banned Communist Party.

A struggle took place between pro-Russian and pro-Romanian elements in the leadership. Gradually the Muscovites were removed from power, but in the "in fighting" that took place in the Communist Party, and in Communist relations with other parties, certain excesses were committed and these are regretted today, although such regrets are not officially voiced.

Nicolae Ceauşescu, who was to succeed Gheorghiu-Dej as leader of the Romanian Communist Party on the latter's death in 1965, was born in January, 1918, in the village of Scorniceşti in the Olt region. Ten years later he was working as an apprentice shoemaker in Bucharest. His revolutionary activity started early. He was first arrested when he was 15. After that he was frequently in and out of prison, helped to organize violent strikes, and plotted with other communists to sabotage his own country's military, transport and shipping installations when Romania was allied with the Nazis. In 1936 he was in the notorious Doftana Prison with other political prisoners, including Gheorghiu-Dej, who was later to become prime minister of Romania. Ceauşescu was released from Doftana in 1938, but in 1939 he was back in prison, this time in Jilava, in the south of Bucharest. While he was there the prison was invaded by members of the Iron Guard, who massacred 64 of the prisoners, but the bulk of the political prisoners were saved by the intervention of soldiers guarding the prison who had been inactive in the earlier part of the raid.

Ceauşescu, with other political prisoners, was tranferred to other prisons and ended up in a concentration camp in Tîrgu Jiu, where he remained until Romania was liberated by the Russians, helped by the Romanians themselves. Ceauşescu and Gheorghiu-Dej had thus spent the whole of the war in prison, which was not as safe as it might seem, when the massacre at Jilava is taken into account.

For two years, during 1946 and 1947, Ceauşescu was away from Bucharest for long periods at a time, working mainly in Constantza and Oltenia. Many parts of the country were close to famine as a result of the years of fighting and requisitioning of stocks by the Germans, and it was Ceauşescu's job to ensure that production was re-established and supplies of food and vital equipment were distributed evenly. Then, in 1948, he was given his first ministerial position, as Deputy Minister of Agriculture. This involved him in organizing the collectivization of agriculture — a daunting task when the peasant's love of the land is taken into account. Many of the peasants had welcomed the agrarian reforms which had given them their own land, but now, after only a few years, it seemed to many that it was to be taken away again. It took all Ceaușescu's oratorical skill, all his power of persuasion, to convince the peasants that collectivization could serve the nation's best interests and still leave them their own plot of land for household purposes.

After this Ceaușescu's rise was rapid. He had proved himself in the field, his Marxist orthodoxy was beyond reproach, and he was, above all, a patriot. In 1950 he was given the sensitive post of Deputy Minister of the Armed Forces and made chief of the army's political section.

Although Gheorghiu-Dej and Ceaușescu had their differences in internal matters, they shared a common belief in an independent and united Romania. For this they had to start loosening the economic bonds with the Soviet Union. Under Stalin, Soviet-Romanian companies, known popularly as Sovroms, were established to manage the important Romanian industries, such as transport, aviation, timber, banking, oil, manufacturing, chemicals, gas, metals and coal. It was agreed that the Soviet Union and Romania should each contribute half the share capital and have an equal say in the running of the companies and their products. But it soon became clear that the Soviet contribution was more often than not merely a rechannelling of the heavy reparations fixed in the Armistice settlement (from September 1944 to June 1948 the Soviet Union appropriated the whole of the Romanian navy and the best part of its merchant fleet, a total of 700 ships. In addition, they took a vast amount of equipment from the oil industry and half the rolling stock of the Romanian railways, as well as timber, grain, industrial equipment and livestock). The Soviet Union made little contribution in real terms, took half the profits, and at the same time ensured that Romanian industry was geared to Soviet interests. Gheorghiu-Dej and Ceauşescu arranged for the Soviet shares to be bought by the Romanian government. By 1954, all except two of the Sovroms had been bought back by the Romanian government. The others, petrol and quartz companies, were dissolved a year later. As Donald Catchlove points out in his book *Romania's Ceauşescu* (London, 1972), "Of all the countries in the communist bloc, Romania had been most involved with the joint companies, and buying out had cost her more than any other country. It was an expensive operation for a country already crippled by the war but for Gheorghiu-Dej and Ceauşescu it was an investment in an independent Romania, and on that basis, eminently worthwhile."

The next step was to arrange for the withdrawal of Russian troops from Romanian territory. By July 25, 1958, the Romanians were able to announce there were no more Soviet troops on Romanian soil. Romania's independent position was outlined after a week-long meeting of the Central Committee of the Party in April, 1964. A statement from the meeting laid down some basic guidelines for behaviour: "national independence and sovereignty, equal rights, mutual advantage, comradely assistance, non-interference in internal affairs, observance of territorial integrity and the principles of socialist internationalism". Ceauşescu had been the architect of the statement, and it contained many of the sentiments he has since voiced in speeches and writings.

For a number of years before Gheorghiu-Dej's a death in March, 1965, Ceauşescu had been the acknowledged draughtsman of Gheorghiu-Dej's major policies, so it was not difficult for him to take over the leadership of the party and the country. He was elected First Secretary of the Central Committee of the Party in March, and in July, at the Ninth Congress of the Party, he became a member of the Executive Committee and the Standing Presidium and General Secretary of the Central Committee.

Nicolae Ceauşescu's triumph was sealed when he was elected President of Romania in March, 1974. In a message to the *Guardian* from Bucharest on March 28 the journalist Jonathan Steele, a specialist in East European affairs, said that

> Nicolae Ceauşescu was today elected the first President the Socialist Republic of Romania has ever had. With all the trappings of a centralised State from the unanimity of the vote to the huge portraits of him which appeared on the front of Bucharest's main public buildings during the night, the proceedings had a clock-work inevitability.
>
> It is easy to be cynical about the procedure in which a constitutional amendment is proposed on Tuesday, reported in the newspapers on Wednesday, and ratified on Thursday. The central fact is that although the 55-year-old Romanian party leader now has more power within his country than any other East European leader he also has more popularity.
>
> In spite of his enormous prestige, not even President Tito is as universally liked at home as is Ceauşescu.
>
> The reason is simple. Romania's struggle for independence is more recent and more precarious than Yugoslavia's. By coincidence, this week's events come almost exactly ten years ofter the historic statement put out by the party's Central Committee.
>
> To most Romanians the document is known as the Declaration of Independence even though the party, in its sober and deliberately unprovocative way, prefers to give it its full name — "a statement on the stand of the Romanian Workers' Party concerning the problems of the world Communist and working class movement".
>
> The statement emphasised Romania's refusal to join in Khrushchev's condemnation of China or his

> scheme for a supranational planning body for Comecon and it affirmed every party's right to manage its own affairs.
>
> Since then by a series of cautious steps Romania has continually extended its independence. Its most dramatic move was its refusal to join its Warsaw Pact allies in invading Czechoslovakia.
>
> In the process Romania has developed a whole philosophy of international relations geared to what Ceauşescu calls "the democratisation of international life".
>
> Romania has relations with almost every State in the world and wants to build up the role of small and medium sized nations on the grounds that size should not matter in international affairs. Every State should have equal rights and be free of outside interference...

As Mr Steele has indicated, Romania's refusal to join other Warsaw Pact countries in the invasion of Czechoslovakia was a dramatic move. It was also a dangerous one. There was a fear at the time that the Soviet Union would also invade Romania — a fear that has been resuscitated once or twice since. If this happened, Romania has given notice in advance that she would meet force with force, something which the Czechs were not prepared to do. Not only did Romania not take part in the invasion of Czechoslovakia but she condemned it in strong terms. Addressing 100,000 people in the Piaţa Republicii on August 21, 1968, President Ceauşescu said that "The penetration of the five socialist countries into Czechoslovakia is a great mistake and a grave danger to peace in Europe, to the fate of socialism in the world. It is inconceivable in the world today, when peoples are rising to the struggle for their national independence, for equality of rights, that a socialist state, that socialist states, should transgress the liberty and independence of another state."

Romania has also criticized Soviet intervention in Afghanistan.

Ceauşescu has travelled incessantly, visiting heads of state in Africa, Europe, and Asia. Such visits are not mere courtesy calls. They are mostly followed by agreements on political, scientific, cultural and trade matters. One such visit was to London in June, 1978, as the guest of the Queen. He was the first Head of State from a Warsaw Pact country to stay at Buckingham Palace. An invitation to the Queen to visit Romania was accepted, and at the time of writing (mid-1983) it is expected to take place in 1985. Ceauşescu took the unprecedented step of inviting President Nixon to Bucharest in mid-1969, and Nixon became the first American Head of State to visit a communist country. A "most favoured nation" trade pact has been achieved between Romania and the United States.

Romania is in a unique position to influence international events because of her contacts in areas of conflict. For instance, alone of the Warsaw Pact countries, she maintained diplomatic contacts with Israel after that country's war with the Arab States in 1967, but this has not affected her friendship with the Arabs. President Ceauşescu is widely believed to have played an important role behind the scenes in arranging the meeting between Prime Minister Begin of Israel and the late President Sadat of Egypt that led to the Camp David agreement. Romania has also managed to maintain good relations with the Soviet Union and China when the two giants of the communist world were at loggerheads.

President Ceauşescu's skill as a negotiator has been recognized by a number of states, including some in the West. In the *Observer* news service from London, dated June 23, 1983, Jim Morenno said that "Romania seems to be trying to mediate in a dispute about the expulsion of 2,000 ethnic Chinese from Outer Mongolia — the pro-Soviet Mongolian People's Republic. The Mongolian strong-man, Jumjaghin Isedenbal, visited Bucharest recently for talks with President Ceauşescu, two weeks after a similar visit by the Chinese Deputy Foreign Minister, Quyan Quychen. Romania's relations with both countries are good, and Ceaușescu has tried to mediate between China and other states on several occasions: Ceaușescu played a role in America's *rapprochement* with China and in the recent thaw in relations between China and Albania. China's Prime Minister Zhao Zhyang has described Romania and Yugoslavia as China's "best friend."

In all disputes in which his advice is sought President Ceaușescu's advice is always the same — get round the table and negotiate. War is not the answer.

Romania has taken an independent line in a part of Europe under the influence of Russia, which has urged member states in the Warsaw Pact to spend more on armaments. For several years Romania decreased her spending on arms by 10-15 per cent and has now frozen expenditure. In the section on Foreign Policy in the 1981 Year Book, the authorities say that "Focusing all attention on the fundamental aspects of continuing the course of detente in Europe and in the World, Romania particularly stresses the need to take effective measures in the field of disarmament, particularly nuclear disarmament. Now, when mankind is still living under the dark sign of the arms race, any significant progress towards a new international political and economic order, based on cooperation and collective responsibility, depends also on the course taken by disarmament. The generations of today and of tomorrow are faced with no loftier responsibility or more important duty than to take effective steps towards disarmament as the main guarantee of peace and international security. To this end, Romania believes that all efforts should be rallied for putting a stop to the stationing and development of new nuclear rockets in Europe, for organizing a Conference on Disarmament and the initiation of negotiations on restrictions of deployment and development of new rockets."

Romania has urged that the two military blocs in Europe, NATO and the Warsaw Pact, should be dissolved. Unlike some of her neighbours, she has sponsored disarmament demonstrations on her soil.

Worldwide attention to Romania's distinctive place in the Warsaw Pact countries followed after the meeting of the Pact's leaders in Moscow on June 28, 1983, to discuss Soviet plans to deploy new nuclear missiles at strategic sites in Eastern Europe if the West went ahead with its missile plans. The heading in the *Guardian's* report of the conference was "Romania thwarts Soviet plan to counter Cruise" and, commenting on the summit meeting, Michael Simmons said that

> As in previous years, it was the Romanians who blocked the call for a more aggressive final document. President Ceaușescu has consistently thwarted the Warsaw Pact supranational tendencies, cutting his defence spending in the past three years and refusing to have Pact forces stationed on Romanian soil.
>
> Some sources in Moscow last night said he had attended this summit with the greatest reluctance. He chose yesterday to publish his discordant views.
>
> While one press release in Bucharest announced President Ceaușescu's departure for Moscow, another giving details of a presidential interview granted to Swedish journalists a month ago, showed continued opposition to fundamental pact thinking.
>
> Military manoeuvres, the Romanian leader said, were unnecessary shows of force which in no way contributed to detente or mutual confidence, and Soviet troops, he said, should get out of Afghanistan, which should be left free to sort out its own problems.

A major effect of President Ceaușescu's visits abroad and reception of world leaders in Bucharest has been the acknowledgment that Romania is an independent state. This is particularly important because of the world reactions that would follow if Russia were tempted to intervene in Romania as she has done in Hungary and Czechoslovakia. At the time of writing this possibility is considered to be rather remote because of the continuing turmoil in Poland and the international pressure on the Soviet Union to withdraw from Afghanistan.

There have, of course, been criticisms. President Ceaușescu has been condemned for encouraging a "Cult of Personality". This, I feel, should be considered in the light of realities in Eastern Europe. Tito was also a cult figure. Ceaușescu and Tito, who were close friends, became the embodiment of their nations' hopes and aspirations. While they were there (and Ceaușescu is still there) the world took notice of them in a way that would not have been possible if they were candidates for office placed in power by the Russians. Ceaușescu still remains a popular figure. When he speaks at conferences in Romania, often at great length, he is accorded standing ovations, with applause lasting several minutes, at key points in his speech. This is hardly likely to happen to a Western statesman. Sustained applause on such occasions should be interpreted as a sign of endorsement of the policies of the Party and the leader.

Another criticism concerns what is regarded by some Western critics as Romania's too strict internal régime. The régime is strict for a very good reason: to be otherwise would be to invite intervention by the Russians on ideological grounds. There is, of course, some internal dissent, as there is in any country, but the bulk of the people seem to be satisfied. There is no unemployment. If someone is out of work he or she is offered a number of jobs in succession. If none is accepted the person concerned is fined. There is no unemployment pay, as there is in the West, but provision is made in the system for the sick and the handicapped. Remnants of the "cold war" still linger in Romania, as they do in other socialist countries, but these are gradually disappearing under the influence of tourism and Western books and films.

A small amount of hard currency is now available to enable Romanians to travel to the West on holiday.

A question frequently asked in the West is "Why can't the people in Eastern Europe leave their country if they want to ? Are they in some sort of prison ?" Efforts are made in Romania to persuade people to stay to help in the reconstruction of their country. The economy is still expanding and jobs are there, unlike many countries in the West. Some who have left the country illegally return in chastened mood, but to others the lure of the West, particularly the United States, is irresistible. A certain amount of emigration is allowed, particularly to ethnic minorities. Hungarians do not experience much difficulty if they want to go to Hungary and there has been a steady flow of Romanians of German origin to Germany. The number of Germans in Romania before the war was 800,000, but many were conscripted by the Germans to fight against the Russians, and those that survived were brought to Germany during the retreat. These have been joined by relatives. At present there are about 340,000 Germans in Romania and about 10,000 a year leave for the country of their origin. According to the *Guardian* of May 30, 1983, the number of Romanian emigrants to the United States has averaged 2,400 a year.

It is obvious to me, as a visitor to Romania for 17 years, that conditions have greatly improved there and the régime is more relaxed than it was. This is not just a personal view but one confirmed by many talks with Romanians, often in informal surroundings. The régime, untroubled by the sort of internal opposition so obvious in Poland, is now looking to the future as the world economy gives signs of recovery. In common with other countries throughout the world, Romania found herself in a difficult position as the world recession, still very much in evidence at the time of writing, deepened. The result was that she had to ask for her debts to be rescheduled. At the end of 1981 Romania's debts totalled 10.1 billion dollars. This sum was reduced to 9.5 billion dollars by the end of 1982 and it was expected that a further 1.6 billion dollars reduction in debt would take place in 1983. It is hoped that the country will be free of debt at the end of the decade.

The depression has helped to draw attention to some weaknesses in the Romanian economy, primarily in agriculture and in the energy systems. The population continues to be well fed, as is to be expected in such a rich agricultural country, but bread, sugar and cooking-oil were rationed in the autumn of 1981 : sugar because excessive quantities were used for wine-making, a popular home industry in a country where there are plenty of grapes ; bread because it was being fed to animals, particularly pigs, in large quantities instead of animal foodstuffs (there is the same problem in the Soviet Union) ; and cooking-oil because it was hoarded for fear of possible future shortages. In January 1982 there was a good deal of comment in the Western Press because food prices in Romania had been increased by 35 per cent, but the previous increase in the price of food had been 32 years earlier! There are no long queues for food such as one sees in television pictures from Poland, but some consumer goods are scarce and when a supply of them arrives in the shops a queue quickly forms. Because of the shortage of hard currency, the Romanians have evolved an ingenious way for paying for goods from the West : the seller is required to take Romanian goods of equivalent value in exchange. No doubt this requirement will be modified as the country's financial position improves.

As oil production falls on the mainland fresh supplies are being sought by off-shore drilling in the Black Sea, but it is too early yet to report on possible results of this operation. Outside the Soviet Union, the biggest hydro-electric power station in Europe is at the Iron Gates on the Danube at a point separating Romania and Yugoslavia. This was operating at full capacity in 1971 and the output will be stepped up when a second barrage and power station which are being built fifty miles down the river are completed in 1985.

The largest project in the current Romanian five-year plan, and also one of the largest at present being undertaken in Europe, involves the construction of a new deep-water port at Agigea, just south of Constantza the country's largest port, and a link by a forty-mile canal with Cernavodă, a port and important railway station on the Danube. When the canal is finished in the year of writing (1983) there will be a significant saving of 250 miles for ships engaged in trade between the Danube and Constantza. Another important result will be the development of industry at a number of smaller ports along the canal. The Romanians hope that the building of the Cernavodă-Agigea canal, in parallel with the Nurnberg-Regensburg canal (Rhine-Main-Danube) which is also under construction, will provide a flowing shipping course between the Black Sea and the North Sea, linking Constantza with Rotterdam. When this is finished, the canal will be finally linked with the Rhine, Elbe, Oder, North Sea and Baltic Sea.

A further point that has loomed large with the planners is that eventually, possibly in the 1990s, a canal linking Bucharest with the Danube at Giurgiu will be developed so as to be able to carry a substantial amount of goods from the capital to the sixteen ports on the Danube. More than this, such a canal could provide valuable recreational facilities for the people of Bucharest and tourists.

The developments outlined here should greatly improve Romania's economy.

Now to return to the political and international scene. No other issues draws more unfavourable attention to Romania than the continued agitation by Hungarian *émigrés* and other Hungarian groups abroad about the alleged persecution of the Hungarian minority in Romania, particularly Transylvania. As I have been unable to find any confirmation of such persecution in the course of extensive inquiries within the country, it is worthwhile setting out the legal position. Article 17 of the Constitution states that "The citizens of the Socialist Republic of Romania, irrespective of their nationality, race, sex, or religion, shall have equal rights in all fields of economic, political, juridical, social and cultural life. The State shall guarantee the equal rights of the citizens. No restriction of these rights and no difference in their exercise on the grounds of nationality, race, sex, or religion, shall be permitted. Any attempt at establishing such restrictions, at nationalist-chauvinist propaganda and at fomentation of racial or national hatred shall be punished by law." Article 22 states that "In the Socialist Republic of Romania the co-inhabiting nationalities shall be assured the free use of their mother tongue, as well as books, newspapers, periodicals, theatres and education at all levels in their own languages. In territorial-administrative units also inhabited by population of non-Romanian nationality, all the bodies and institutions shall use in speech and in writing the language of the nationality concerned and shall appoint officials from its ranks or from other citizens who know the language and way of life of the local population."

As any sophisticated person understands, a Constitution can lay down a certain requirement but the reality may be something rather different, even in matters of degree. In my opinion, the reality of life for the minorities in Romania conforms to what is set out for them in the Constitution. Repeated visits and conversations with Hungarians, in particular, and Germans fail to bring to light examples of the persecution alleged by their fellow countrymen abroad. A possible reason for this continued Hungarian agitation is the belief that Transylvania really was part of territorial Hungary, first settled by the Magyars and ruled by them, except for periods when it came under Turkish or Austrian control. This assumption does not accord with the findings of independent historians, let alone Romanian ones, findings confirmed by archaeological discoveries in the past fifty years. Despite this, the agitation continues, fanned by nationalism and by the Soviet Union, who want to lure the Romanians back to a closer collaboration with them.

Another possible reason for Russian background support for the Hungarian agitation about her minority is a fear that the Romanians might reclaim Bessarabia and northern Bukovina. This, I gather, is not a Romanian intention, but if it were, Russia could have a useful card in reserve by implying that she could hold the Hungarians in check if a dispute developed over Transylvania but only, of course, if Romania did not press her claims to what is now Soviet territory.

A most unfortunate aspect of the Hungarian agitation about the minority in Romania is that it has spread to the New World, particularly the United States and Canada, where former Hungarian citizens have urged Congress not to renew Romania's most favoured nation trade status with the United States. As a result of this, a crowd of Americans of Romanian origin agitated against this Hungarian intervention for over three hours in front of the United Nations headquarters in New York on February 26, 1983. A recital of facts such as those outlined here may irritate some Western readers who think, sensibly, that old animosities should be forgotten and people of different origins should learn to live together in peace, but as Professor Hugh Seton-Watson points out in *The East European Revolution*

> Westerners should be careful in their denunciation of East European nationalism. The dreary rivalries and territorial squabbles of small nations should indeed be condemned as a nuisance to peace and tragic waste of national energies. But defence of national individuality against an alien totalitarian Moloch is neither ignoble nor ridiculous. Western

nations have never faced such a threat. No one questions their nationality, they do not have to defend it. The East European nations have their backs to the wall. If the West cannot help them, it need not insult them.

I will now set out a few facts about the position of the 1,706,874 Romanians of Hungarian origin ("Hungarians") in the country. Out of the total number of deputies elected to the Grand National Assembly, the country's Parliament, 8.2 per cent are Hungarians. From the total of 51,441 deputies elected to the county, municipal, town and commune people's councils, 3,774, i.e., 7.3 per cent, are Hungarians.

When I was in Cluj-Napoca, the capital of Transylvania, I had an interview with members of the People's Council. The deputy chairman, Mr Josif Gavrea, declared that there was no discrimination against Hungarians or any other minority. The Council had 70 deputies of whom 21 were Hungarian; five of the 17 members of the Executive Committee of the Council were Hungarians, and of the five vice-chairmen of the Council two were Hungarians. The chairman of the Council of Working People of Hungarian origin in Cluj-Napoca, Dr András Dancsuly, Professor of Pedagogy and Psychology at the local university, explained to me that he and his Council represented 23 per cent of the whole population of the district of Cluj-Napoca, consisting of over 160,000 Hungarians. No one had ever complained that he had been discriminated against because he was not of Romanian origin.

Mrs Maria Bisztrai, Director of the Hungarian State Theatre in Cluj-Napoca, pointed out that the city was unique in offering entertainment in separate Hungarian and Romanian opera houses. On any evening you could go to the opera because, if there was not one at the Hungarian opera house, there would assuredly be one at the Romanian opera house. There were six theatres for Hungarians in the whole country and also Hungarian touring companies. The culture of the Hungarians has not suffered in Transylvania, she said.

Later I talked to Professor Camil Mureşan, Dean of the Faculty of History at Cluj University, and asked him for his views on the Hungarian problem as presented in some Western newspapers. Had there, for instance, been resentment among Hungarians about what could be called the 'lost lands' ? He replied that, apart from disgruntled *émigrés,* there was no evidence of any such resentment, but, on psychological grounds, he would not exclude resentment, although there was no modern evidence for it. In his own faculty, 25 per cent of the teachers and researchers were Hungarians, and of the students studying history 240 were Romanians and 52 were from minorities, mostly the Hungarian minority. Courses were in Romanian and Hungarian. The two races "fitted in" properly, and when there was disagreement between them, it was not on grounds of nationality.

Officials point out that the State ensures the training of the necessary teaching staff for education in the Hungarian language and in addition provides the required text books free of charge.

In the 1981-2 school year for children who were being taught in the Hungarian language there were 1,086 crèches and kindergartens which accommodated 55,609 children ; 1,391 elementary schools with 190,196 pupils and 156 secondary schools with 36,083 students were provided. During the same period, in higher education, of the total number of students (176,889), 9,593 were Hungarians who studied mainly in the Hungarian language. For instance, at the Babeş-Bolyai University at Cluj-Napoca, 77 out of a total of 207 courses were given in Hungarian. At the Medical-Pharmaceutical Institute at Tîrgu Mureş 126 of the 132 courses were delivered in Hungarian as well as Romanian.

In Romania books in the Hungarian language are issued by 12 publishing houses, which printed 217 titles with 2,314,695 copies in 1981. In addition, 266 books in Hungarian, with a total of 335,391 copies, were imported.

The Hungarians in Romania are provided with nine daily newspapers, with 96,221,205 copies, a year ; eight weekly magazines with 7,117,658 copies a year ; two fortnightly magazines with 1,944,117 copies a year, and another six magazines with a total of 181,133 copies a year. The Romanian government spent 16,432,000 lei in 1980 in subsidizing the publication of printed material in Hungarian.

The Central Radio and Television stations have broadcasts in Hungarian. For television, there are three hours in Hungarian weekly and on the radio seven hours daily. In addition, the radio studios at Cluj-Napoca and Tîrgu Mureş broadcast an average number of 1914 hours in Hungarian every year.

At the beginning of 1982 the Hungarians in Romania had 240 choral groups, 220 folk music orchestras, 56 brass bands, 390 folk dance groups and folklore ensembles, 660 theatre groups, and 270 artistic groups.

Hungarians in Romania, who mostly belong to the Roman Catholic and Reformed Churches, worship in their own language.

These facts, I hope, speak for themselves, and are the answer to the allegations of persecution spread by Hungarian circles abroad.

Now we return to the broader sweep of history. We have seen how the Romanian nation slowly emerged during centuries when the territory comprising modern Romania was under the domination of Turks, Austrians or Hungarians, with occasional incursions of other peoples such as the Poles and Russians or, as during the last war, the Germans. Adjustments have been made to boundaries and some territory lost. No country is immune from the effect of developments in neighbouring countries and what happens in the Soviet Union, with which Romania shares the longest of its frontiers, is bound to affect Romania.

At present relations between the Soviet Union and Romania are reasonably good and there are hopes that this will continue.

As Hugh Seton-Watson pointed out in *The Imperialist Revolutionaries*, "The Soviet empire was not confined to the republics of the USSR. The conquests of 1945 enabled the Soviet rulers to establish their domination over a hundred million Europeans — a domination much more comprehensive than that once exercised by Western 'capitalist' empires over 'semicolonial' lands like the old China and Turkey. Eastern Europe became an area of indirect rule, or of Soviet neo-colonialism... Direct domination extended also to the cultural field: national histories had to be rewritten and falsified, as those of the non-Russian peoples of the USSR had been rewritten and falsified, for the greater glory not only of the CPSU and the great Stalin but also of the great Russian nation, from the time of Peter the Great or earlier."

After Stalin's death these controls were substantially loosened, but they are still there, reinforced by the presence of Soviet divisions in such countries as Hungary, Czechoslovakia, East Germany and Poland. If conditions get out of hand in these countries, and they are at present on the boil in Poland, the Soviet troops on the spot can soon make their presence felt.

Although tension has lessened in Eastern Europe, apart from Poland, in recent years, it could be revived at any time, such as by the artificial agitation over the "plight" of the Hungarians in Romania or of Albanians in Yugoslavia. East Europe in the twentieth century has been a storm centre. In it two world wars have started, Hugh Seton-Watson states in *The East European Revolution*. He develops this theme in *The "Sick Heart" of Modern Europe* (University of Washington Press, 1975) in which he discusses the relationship of the Danube peoples to the "imperial power".

Officially, he said, this is today based on the so-called Brezhnev Doctrine. If socialism is in danger in any of the socialist states of Eastern Europe, it is the right and duty of the other socialist states to help the endangered state to restore socialism. This has to be done regardless of whether the socialist leaders — that is to say, the leaders in power in the communist party — ask for the help or not. Whether socialism is danger is decided by the other socialist states' rulers, under the leadership of the Central Committee of the Communist Party of the Soviet Union.

Not only must the ideological infallibility of the CPSU be recognized, but all aspects of Soviet reality must be represented, in all forms of public expression in the Danube lands, according to the detailed requirements of the current orthodoxy, and lavishly praised. National history must be rewritten wherever it touched on Russian history, not only in the Soviet period but in the distant past. Thus Empress Catherine's treatment of Poland must be interpreted according to the views of the Central Committee of the CPSU today.

Hugh Seton-Watson said in the book from which I have been quoting that

> It is only fair to admit that one attempt at rewriting history and remoulding culture was abandoned. After 1945 Romanians were forced to sever cultural relations with France and Italy, to play down the role of France in the liberation of the Romanian nation and to show that throughout their history, the Romanians' best friend had been the great Russian people (even though it could be admitted that one or two Tsars had perhaps not always behaved impeccably). Attempts were made to transform the usage of the Romanian language, stressing the words of Slav origin and minimizing those of Latin origin, the ultimate aim no doubt being to show the Romanians were not "Latins" but "Slavs". This was given up in the mid-1960s, when the insistence by the Romanian communist leaders on Romania's economic and cultural sovereignty was accepted.

After giving a brief outline of what happened to the reputation of President Thomas Masaryk, of Czechoslovakia, after the Russian intervention of 1968, when Masaryk was declared to be an unperson again, "and for good measure almost all prominent Czech historians were dismissed from their jobs", Professor Seton-Watson said that "To be deprived of one's national history, to see one's national identity threatened, is something which Americans or West Europeans can hardly imagine happening to them. Historians should not, of course, overrate their own importance, but from some experience I am fairly sure of one thing: in the Danube countries, national history, or if you like historical mythology, is something about which not only professors of history but also working men and women, in factories and farms, feel bitterly. Attacks on it create a smouldering resentment which does not die out and can easily turn into a flame."

Professor Seton-Watson points out that since 1945 we have seen the triumph over the middle of Europe of a great big imperial machine, just one, and not three this time. And in less than thirty years there have been revolutions or revolts again, not bourgeois or proletarian (though the proletariat has been rather fully involved), but triggered off by very much the same sort of people, from the thinking classes, the intelligentsia, as in 1848. There have been risings in Pilzen and Berlin and Poznan and Warsaw, and all over Hungary and Bohemia and Moravia, and in Gdansk and Szczecin; and all have been crushed. But the difference between now and a hundred years ago is that the solution of that time — war — cannot be used; or if it does come to that, it will destroy us all.

There is no easy answer to the problems outlined by Professor Seton-Watson. We are faced, he said, "with uncertainty, unbending imperial arrogance, and widespread loss of nerve... Europe remains the heart of the human race, and the heart of Europe is sick. The sickness will not be cured by pretending that it does not exist".

However, there is one point he makes in his book on which I would like to expand.

> Today about eighty million Europeans are subjected to national humiliation, and this makes Europe one of the most explosive parts of the world. It is within the power of the Soviet leaders to put an end to national humiliation, and to content themselves with mere domination. This the peoples of the Danube lands would gladly accept. However, the choice lies only with the Soviet leaders. Sometimes Western journalists and politicians speak as if it lay within the power of the United States to ensure to the Soviet's tranquillity in the Danube lands, as if they could grant or withhold some magic recognition of the status quo which would relieve Muscovite minds of fear. But the truth is that this is not within the power of the United States, and would not be even if George Washington or Abraham Lincoln were at the helm. The remedy for the tension in the middle of Europe lies in Soviet hands alone. Only they can defuse the time bombs which they have been busily piling up.

Calls from the West for more "freedom" in East Europe are unlikely to be heeded by those in power. It all depends on what is meant by "freedom". If it is interpreted as freedom to introduce a Western-style democracy, with accompanying capitalism, in Eastern Europe the Soviet Union will take steps, including armed intervention, as it did in Hungary and Czechoslovakia, to see that this does not happen. The Russians still have a very cautious eye fixed on Germany and regard the East European bloc countries and the Baltic states as buffers between them and the former enemy. Communism is the cement that binds them. If "freedom" is interpreted as the right for any citizen, Russian, Hungarian, Czech, Polish, Bulgarian or Romanian to pack his bags and depart with his family and friends for the West, this again would create fresh problems. No Western country, beset as they all are with financial and housing problems, could cope with a flood of immigrants. If, for instance, the Romanians flooded out of the country, and state industries started to break down for lack of labour, it is highly likely that the Soviet authorities would take steps to prevent what they would regard as a state of unrest and seal the frontiers again. It is far from certain that a Romanian, guaranteed a job in his own country, could find suitable work in a Western country. Many disillusioned Romanians who left the country, legally or illegally, have returned to report on the difficulties they faced in the West.

It will be seen that the problem of the East European countries is more complex than at first appears and that calls for more "freedom" are unlikely to influence the Russians, obsessed, as they are, with their own security. Just as the West feels threatened by the communist bloc headed by the Soviet Union, so do the Russians feel threatened by the West and particularly by the military power of the United States. What can be done to break this impasse?

The only answer which suggests itself to me is that the longer peace is maintained the more chance there is for confidence to grow between nations. This may sound trite but it is something which cannot be said too often. Tourism is helping people to see how others live. Russians who come to London can see for themselves that it is not the London of Dickens's day, as so many have been led to believe, and those who go from the West to the East European bloc will find people very like themselves living in very similar conditions. Films and television have brought the West, including the worst aspects of it, into most East European homes. This traffic is rather one way because few films made in Hungary, Poland, Romania or Bulgaria, let alone in Russia, are seen on Western TV.

In the early years after the Second World War so much of Eastern Europe had been devastated that there was every reason for the authorities to use the law to keep their citizens within their own borders to help in the work of reconstruction, but now, surely, it is time for the barriers to start coming down. The standard of living has risen so much in the East European bloc that the gap between it and the West is narrowing all the time and eventually will be abolished. It is no longer true that life in the East European bloc is one of grey, cheerless uniformity. What is lacking is the profusion of consumer goods we are accustomed to in the West, but gradually these will come as it becomes less necessary for trade surpluses to be ploughed back into industry.

These are general remarks and now it is time to turn to something more specific. Romania is a country under strict internal control for reasons I have already explained and this has given rise to misunderstandings abroad. Nazi sympathizers and elements of the Iron Guard who now live outside Romania have lost no opportunity to blacken the reputation of the country of their birth because they have lost their privileges. The same may be said of the Hungarian agitation. Hungarians were once a privileged minority in Transylvania. Now they are equal with the other races but being equal does not seem to be enough. This continuing agitation from outside the country about the alleged persecution of the Hungarian minority, for which I have found no evidence, can impose a threat to peace, for if Russia wants badly enough to bring Romania under the subjection imposed by force of arms on the Hungarians and Czechs here is a ready-made excuse.

The Romanians have shown other East European nations how, while remaining convinced communists, they can look after their own national interests in foreign policy, trade, and culture. This surely sets an example to others in the bloc, but, it must be admitted, Romania does not have Russian troops on her soil. It is greatly to be hoped that Soviet garrisons will gradually be reduced in other countries and eventually withdrawn. They are not very much in evidence when a visitor goes to Czechoslovakia or Hungary, as I have done, but the fact that they are there is enough to keep the government of the country concerned in line. While countries such as these are humiliated resentment will smoulder away below the surface like an underground fire. It is in the interests of the Soviet Union to show more consideration for national susceptibilities.

Another way to increase understanding between East and West would be for more awareness that the world cannot be divided into "goodies" and "badies", as in a Western film, with the capitalist West always good, and the Communist East always bad. There are good and bad features in both systems. Certain American publications stress only what has gone wrong with East European economic systems and ignore what has gone right. Surely the latest world recession has taught us, through the dole queues and millions denied the right to work in the West, that the capitalist system is not working as it should. Nor, of course, is the communist.

Now it is time to draw to a close. The Romanian historians have taken us from early times before the birth of the Christian era through to the period of socialist reconstruction and I have added some notes on features of the present day, closing at the end of 1983, which I hope will be of use to future historians and students of international affairs. In my comments I have tried to be unbiased. I can see perfectly well the Hungarian viewpoint on Transylvania but I believe it to be mistaken. Hungarians and Germans, the other significant minority in Romania, have their rights respected, as their leaders, civil and religious, tell me. I can quite understand that many Romanians want to emigrate, attracted by an easier life and the profusion of consumer goods in the West, and I can also understand why their leaders want to them to stay and help in the reconstruction of their country, pillaged for centuries by the Turks and, more recently, by the Nazis. How this will work out remains to be seen.

I have already quoted Professor R. W. Seton-Watson's statement at the end of his *History of the Roumanians* that "Two generations of peace and clean government might make of Roumania an earthly paradise, for she has great natural resources and all that is necessary to a well ordered economy. But her chief asset is the Roumanian peasant, who amid adverse political surroundings has shown a virility and endurance that border on the miraculous", but I will quote it again in closing. Romania is still grappling with her problems in these years of world recession, and her planners would be the first to admit that some aspects of the economy, such as those connected with energy and agriculture, show shortcomings that have yet to be overcome. If peace can be maintained, the future for Romania is surely bright.

Bibliography

The Bibliography that follows is the one given in "The History of the Romanian People" (Bucharest, 1970) and as such will be useful to students of history as well as others. I have added to this some books for suggested further reading. The ones by Professor Hugh Seton-Watson will be particularly useful for the light they throw on Romania's place in modern European history. Obviously, there are a great many books that could have been added to this list but I hope that the ones I have given will suffice for the average reader.

GENERAL WORK

Constantinescu, M., C. Daicoviciu et St. Pascu, *Histoire de la Roumanie*, Paris, 1970.

Iorga, N., *Geschichte des rumänischen Volkes im Rahmen seiner Staatsbildungen*, vol. I-II, Gotha, 1905.

Iorga, Nicolae, *Histoire des Roumains et de la Romanité orientale*, vol. I-X, Bucarest, 1937-1944.

Iorga, N., *La place des Roumains dans l'histoire universelle*, vol. I-III, București, 1935-6.

Istoria României (A History of Romania), I-IV, București, 1960-4.

Istoria României în date (A History of Romania in Dates), București, 1971.

Seton-Watson, R. W., *A History of the Roumanians from Roman Times to the Completion of Unity*, Cambridge, 1934.

Xenopol, A. D., *Istoria Românilor din Dacia Traiană* (A History of the Romanians in Trajan's Dacia), ed. a 3-a, vol. I-XIV.

Călinescu, G., *Istoria literaturii române de la origini pînă în prezent* (A History of Romanian Literature from its Origin to Date), București, 1941.

Din istoria Dobrogei (About the History of Dobrudja), vol. I-III, București, 1965-72.

Iorga, N., *Istoria armatei românești* (The History of the Romanian Army), vol. I-III, 2nd ed., București, 1929-30.

Iorga, N., *Istoria bisericii românești și a vieții religioase a românilor* (The History of the Romanian Church and the Religious Life of the Romaniarns), 2nd ed., vol. I-II, București, 1929-32.

Iorga, N., *Istoria comerțului românesc* (A History of Romanian Trade), 2nd ed., vol. I-II, București, 1937.

Iorga, N., *Istoria învățămîntului românesc* (A History of Romanian Education), București, 1928.

Iorga, N., *Istoria presei românești de la primele începuturi pînă la 1916* (A History of the Romanian Press from its Early Beginnings to 1916), București, 1922.

Istoria artelor plastice în România (The History of Fine Arts in Romania), vol. I-II, București, 1968-70.

Kirițescu, Costin, *Sistemul bănesc al leului și precursorii lui* (The Monetary System of the Leu and its Predecessors), vol. I-II, București, 1964-7.

Lupaș, I., *Istoria Unirii Românilor* (The History of the Romanians' Unification), București, 1937.

Pascu Ștefan, I. Ionașcu, C. Cihodaru, Gh. Georgescu-Buzău, *Istoria medie a României*, I (sec. X—sfîrșitul sec. XVI), (Romanian Mediaeval History), București, 1966.

Vătășianu, V., *Istoria artei feudale în țările romăne*, vol. I (A History of Feudal Arts in the Romanian Countries), București, 1959.

ANCIENT HISTORY

Berciu, D., *Contribuții la problema neoliticului în România în lumina ultimelor cercetări* (Contributions to the neolithic Problem in Romania in the Light of Recent Research), București, 1961.

Daicoviciu, C., *La Transylvanie dans l'Antiquité*, Bucarest, 1945.

Macrea, M., *Viața în Dacia romană* (Life in Roman Dacia), București, 1969.

Pârvan, V., *Dacia. An Outline of the Early Civilizations of the Carpatho-Danubian Countries*, Cambridge, 1928.

Păunescu, A., *Evoluția armelor și uneltelor de piatră cioplită pe teritoriul României* (Evolution of Chipped Stone Weapons and Tools on Romania's Territory) București, 1970.

Pârvan, V., *Getica, O protoistorie a Daciei* (Getica — An Early History of Dacia), București, 1926.

Pippidi, D. M., *Contribuții la istoria veche a României* (Contributions to Ancient Romanian History), 2nd ed., București, 1969.

Pippidi, D. M., *I Greci nel Basso Medio dall'éta arcaica alla conquista romana*, Milano, 1971.

Protase, D., *Problema continuității în Dacia în lumina arheologiei și numismaticei* (The Problem of Continuity in Dacia in the Light of Archaeology and Numismatics), București, 1966.

Protase, D., *Riturile funerare la Daci și la Daco-romani* (Funeral Rites Among Dacians and Daco-Romans), București, 1971.

Rusu, I. I., *Ilirii* (The Illyrians), București, 1969.

Rusu, I. I., *Limba traco-dacilor* (The Language of the Thraco-Dacians), București, 1967.

Tudor, D., *Oltenia romană* (Oltenia in Roman Times), 3rd ed., București, 1968.

Tudor, D., *Orașe, tîrguri și sate în Dacia romană* (Towns, Boroughs and Villages in Roman Dacia), București, 1968.

Zaharia, E., *Săpăturile de la Dridu. Contribuția la arheologia și istoria perioadei de formare a poporului român* (The Excavations at Dridu. Contribution to the Archaeology and History of the Period when the Romanian People was formed), București, 1967.

MEDIEVAL HISTORY

Brătianu, Gh. I., *Une énigme et un miracle historique : le peuple Roumain*, Bucarest, 1937.

Constantiniu, Florin, *Relațiile agrare din Țara Românească în secolul al XVIII-lea* (Agrarian Relations in Wallachia in the 18th Century), București, 1972.

Corfus, I., *Agricultura Țării Românești în prima jumătate a secolului al XIX-lea*, (Agriculture in Wallachia in the First Half of the 19th Century), București, 1969.

Cultura moldovenească în epoca lui Ștefan cel Mare (Moldavian Culture in the Age of Stephen the Great), București, 1964.

Giurescu, C., *Studii de istorie socială* (Studies of Social History), București, 1943.

Iorga, N., *Byzance après Byzance*, Bucarest, 1971.

Mihordea, V., *Relațiile agrare din secolul al XVIII-lea în Moldova* (Agrarian Relations in Moldavia in the 18th Century), București, 1968.

Nistor, I. I., *Handel und Wandel in der Moldau bis zum Ende des XVI. Jahrhunderts, nach den Quellen dargestellt*, Cernăuți, 1917.

Nistor, I. I., *Die Auswärtigen Handelsbeziehungen der Moldau im XIV., XV., und XVI. Jahrhundert, nach Quellen dargestellt*, Gotha, 1911.

Onciul, D., *Scrieri istorice* (Historical Essays), vol. I-II, București, 1968.

Panaitescu, P. P., *Introducere la istoria culturii românești* (An Introduction to the History of Romanian Culture), București, 1969.

Panaitescu, P. P., *Mircea cel Bătrîn* (Mircea the Old), București, 1944.

Panaitescu, P. P., *Mihai Viteazul* (Michael the Brave), București, 1936.

Papacostea, Ș., *Oltenia sub stăpînirea austriacă* (1718-39). (Oltenia under Austrian Rule), București, 1971.

Pascu, St., *Voievodatul Transilvaniei* (The Principality of Transylvania), vol. I, Cluj, 1971.

Popa, R., *Țara Maramureșului în veacul al XIV-lea* (The Maramureș Country in the 14th Century), București, 1970.

Prodan, D., *Iobăgia în Transilvania în secolul al XVI-lea* (Serfdom in Transylvania in the 16th Century), vol. I-III, 1967-8.

Prodan, D., *Supplex Libellus Valachorum*, București, 1967.

Stahl, H. H., *Les anciennes communautés villageoises roumaines. Asservissement et pénétration capitaliste*, Bucarest, 1969.

Stoicescu, N., *Sfatul domnesc și marii dregători din Țara Românească și Moldova* (The Prince's Council and the Great Dignitaries in Wallachia and Moldavia), București, 1968.

Ştefănescu, Şt., *Bănia în Ţara Românească* (The Title of Ban [Governor] in Wallachia), Bucureşti, 1965.

Vîrtosu, E., *Titulatura domnilor şi asocierea la domnie în Ţara Românească şi Moldova* (The Titles of the Ruling Princes and Association to the Ruling of the Country in Wallachia and Moldavia), Bucureşti, 1960.

MODERN HISTORY

Adăniloaie N. şi D. Berindei, *Reforma agrară din 1864* (The 1864 Land Reform), Bucureşti, 1967.

Bodea, C., *The Roumanian Struggle for Unification 1834-1849*, Bucureşti, 1970.

Copoiu, N., *Refacerea Partidului Social-Democrat din România (1910-11)*, Reinstatement of the Social Democratic Party in Romania (1910-11), Bucureşti, 1966.

Deac, A., *Internaţionala I şi România* (The First International and Romania), Bucureşti, 1964.

East, W. S., *The Union of Moldavia and Wallachia, 1859*, Cambridge, 1929.

Georgescu, Titu, *De la revoluţionarii democraţi la făurarii P.C.R.* (From the Democratic Revolutionaries to the Creators of the Romanian Communist Party), Bucureşti, 1971.

Hitchins, K., *The Rumanian National Movement in Transylvania (1780-1849)*, Cambridge, 1969.

Kiriţescu, C., *Istoria războiului pentru întregirea României, 1916-1919* (The History of the War for Romania's Unification, 1916-1919), 2nd ed., vols I-III, Bucureşti.

Liveanu, V., M. Rusenescu, Tr. Lungu, I. Kovács, V. Bogza, *Relaţii agrare şi mişcări ţărăneşti în România între 1908-1921* (Agrarian Relations and Peasant Uprisings in Romania between 1908 and 1921), Bucureşti, 1967.

Lungu, Tr., *Viaţa politică în România la sfîrşitul secolului al XIX-lea (1888-1899)* (Political Life in Romania at the Close of the 19th Century (1888-1899), Bucureşti, 1967.

Oţetea, A., *Tudor Vladimirescu şi revoluţia din 1821* (Tudor Vladimirescu and the Revolution of 1821), Bucureşti, 1971.

Oţetea, A. şi I. Popescu-Puţuri, *Marea răscoală a ţăranilor din 1907* (The Great Peasant Uprising of 1907), Bucureşti, 1967.

Popescu-Puțuri, I. (Redactor responsabil), N. Goldbergher, A. Deac, D. Hurezeanu, *Mișcarea muncitorească din România 1893-1900* (The Working Class Movement in Romania), București, 1965.

Riker, W., *The Making of Roumania*, Oxford, 1931.

Stan, A., *Le problème agraire pendant la révolution du 1848 en Valachie*, București, 1971.

Studii privind Unirea Principatelor (Essays on the Union of the Romanian Principalities), București, 1960.

Zane, G., *Le mouvement révolutionnaire de 1840. Prélude de la révolution roumaine de 1848*, Bucarest, 1964.

Ion Popescu-Puțuri, Augustin Deac, *Unirea Transilvaniei cu România 1918* (The Union of Transylvania and Romania, 1918), București, 1972, 2nd ed.

CONTEMPORARY HISTORY

Anescu, V., *Efortul economic al poporului român în războiul antihitlerist*, (The Economic Effort of the Romanian People in the Anti-Nazi War), București, 1964.

Ceaușescu, Ilie, *P.C.R., stegarul luptelor revoluționare din anii 1929-1933* (The Romanian Communist Party, the Standard-Bearer of the Revolutionary struggle of 1929-1933), București, 1971.

Campus, Eliza, *Mica înțelegere* (The Little Entente), București, 1968.

Constantinescu, M., E. Cimponeriu, V. Liveanu, M. Rusenescu, I. Chiper, *Études d'histoire contemporaine de la Roumanie*, Bucarest, 1970.

Fătu, M., *Din istoria politică a României contemporane* (On the Political History of Contemporary Romania), București, 1968.

Ioniță, Gh., *Pentru un front popular antifascist în România* (For an Anti-Fascist People's Front in Romania), București, 1971.

Matei, Gheorghe, *La Roumanie et les problèmes du désarmement, 1919-1934*, București, 1970.

Oprea, Ion, *Nicolae Titulescu*, București, 1967.

P.C.R., în viața social-politică a României. 1921-1944 (The Romanian Communist Party in Romania's Socio-Political Life. 1921-1944), București, 1971.

Petric, A., Gh. Țuțui, *L'instauration et la consolidation du régime démocratique populaire en Roumanie*, Bucarest, 1964.

Popescu-Puțuri, I. și A. Deac (redactori), *Crearea Partidului Comunist Român, mai 1921* (The Creation of the Romanian Communist Party, May 1921), București, 1971.

Popișteanu, C., *România și Antanta Balcanică* (Romania and the Balkan Entente), București, 1968.

România în războiul antihitlerist. 23 august 1944-9 mai 1945 (Romania in the Anti-Nazi War. 23 August 1944-9 May 1945), București, 1966.

Savu, Al., *Dictatura regală (1938-1940)* (The Royal Dictatorship), București, 1970.

Stănescu, M., *Mișcarea muncitorească din România în anii 1921-1924* (The Working Class Movement in Romania over 1921-1924), București, 1971.

Studii privind politica externă a României (1919-1939) (Studies on Romania's Foreign Policy (1919-1939), București, 1969.

Țuțui, Gh. și A. Petric, *Frontul unic muncitoresc în România* (The United Worker's Front in Romania), București, 1971.

Zaharia, Gh. (coordinator), I. Alexandrescu, M. Fătu, P. Nichita, C. Olteanu, Gh. Țuțui, V. Zaharescu, *România în anii revoluției democrat-populare, 1944-1947* (Romania in the Years of the Democratic Popular Revolution, 1944-1947), București, 1971.

SUGGESTED FURTHER READING

Boner, C., *Transylvania: Its Products and Its People*, London, 1865.

Forwood, W., *Romanian Invitation*, London, 1968.

Gerard, E., *The Land Beyond the Forest*, London and Edinburgh, 1888.

Jelavich, B., *History of the Balkans*: Vol. 1, Eighteenth and Nineteenth Centuries; Vol. 2, Twentieth Century, Cambridge, 1984.

MacKenzie, A., *Dracula Country*, London, 1977.

MacKenzie, A., *Romanian Journey*, London, 1983.

MacKenzie, A., *The History of Transylvania*, London, 1983.

Pascu, Ș., *A. History of Transylvania* (trans. D. R. Ladd), Detroit, 1983.

Seton-Watson, H., *Eastern Europe 1918-1941*, Cambridge, 1945.

Seton-Watson, H., *The East European Revolution*, London, 1950.

Seton-Watson, H., *The "Sick Heart" of Modern Europe*, Washington, 1975.

Seton-Watson, H., *The Imperialist Revolutionaries*, London, 1980.

Seton-Watson, R. W., *The Rise of Nationality in the Balkans*, London, 1917.

Starkie, W., *Raggle-Taggle. Adventures with a Fiddle in Hungary and Rumania*, London, 1933.

Walker, M. A., *Untrodden Paths in Roumania*, London, 1888.

Acknowledgements

I wish to thank the Director and staff of the "Nicolae Iorga" Institute of History, Bucharest, for the help they have given me in many hours of talk there ; historians at other universities throughout the country ; Cambridge University Press for permission to quoe from R.W. Seton-Watson's *A History of the Roumanians* and Hugh Seton-Watson's *Eastern Europe Between the Wars 1918-1941* ; The University of Washington Press for permission to quote from Hugh Seton-Watson's *The "Sick Heart" of Modern Europe* ; the Hutchinson Publishing Group Ltd. for permission to quote from *The Imperialist Revolutionaries* by Hugh Seton-Watson ; Associated Book Publishers Ltd. for permission to quote from Hugh Seton-Watson's *The East European Revolution,* and to the Minority Rights Group Ltd, of Benjamin Franklin House, 36 Craven Street, London ᵂC2N 5NG for permission to quote from Report No. 37 *The Hungarians of Romania* by Mr George Schöpflin (price £ 1.20).

LIST OF ILLUSTRATIONS

I. Section one

1. Neolithic statuette.
2. Neolithic statuette ("The Thinker").
3. Dacian Prayer Centre in Sarmisegetuza.
4. Dacian Helmet from Coțofănești Hoard.
5. Battle Scenes on Trajans's Column.
6. Dacian Peasant.
7. Bust of Trajan.
8. Stephen The Great's Statue at Jassy.
9. Voroneț Monastery.
10. The Three Hierarchs Church at Jassy.
11. Vlad the Impaler.
12. Vasile Lupu, Copperplate by Willan Hondias after Abraham van Vestereldt, 1651.
13. Demetrius Cantemir, Copperplate by Christian Fritsch, 1745.

II. Section two

14. Michael The Brave, Copperplate by Egidius Sadelav, made at Prague on the occasion of the visit of the Romanian Prince to Rudolph II in 1601.
15. Statue of Michael the Brave at Bucharest.
16. Constantine Mavrocordat, Copperplate by Georg Friedrich Schmidt after Jean Etienne Liotard.
17. Constantine Brâncoveanu.
18. Matei Basarab, contemporary Copperplate by Marco Boschini, Venice.
19. Horea.
20. Cloșca.
21. Crișan.
22. Tudor Vladimirescu.
23. Avram Iancu. Painting by Barbu Iscovescu.
24. George Barițiu.

25. Nicolae Bălcescu, revolutionary, leader of 1848.
26. Public Assembly in Blaj.
27. Mihail Kogălniceanu.

III. Section three

28. Alexandru Ioan Cuza.
29. Entrance gate at Alba Iulia.
30. Conquest of the Grivița Redout.
31. Inauguration of the Romanian Academic Society (August 13, 1867).
32. The Mărășești Mausoleum erected to the Romanian heroes fallen in battle.
33. Nazi officiers captured in Bucharest during the Insurrection.
34. Dr. Petru Groza.
35. Meeting in Bucharest on March 6, 1945.
36. Nicolae Titulescu.
37. Dr. Constantin C. Parhon.
38. Mihail Eminescu.
39. Tudor Arghezi.
40. George Coșbuc and Ion Luca Caragiale.
41. Lucian Blaga.

Index

An index should, in my opinion, be something more than a list of names, places, battles or treaties. Rather, it should serve as a guide to the book, so that the reader who wishes to establish some particular point should be able to find it by looking in the appropriate section of the index. Under the heading "Romania", or "Wallachia", "Moldavia", or "Transylvania" there are potted guides to the contents of this book. A great deal of attention is now being paid to archaeology and the light it throws on what happened to the original inhabitants of the Romanian lands, and the Romans who had settled there, after the imperial administration was withdrawn. Rather than give a list of obscure villages where important archaeological discoveries have been made I have given page references following the entry "Archaeological research". Place names have been restricted to events of significance associated with them.

Aron, Prince Petru I, 191, 195
Aron, Prince Petru II, 216-7
Abdul Aziz, Sultan, 373
Abrud, 227
Abyssinia, 464
Actium, Battle of, 80
Adamclisi, Battle of and monument, 86, 97-9, 124
Adrian, George, 353, 368
Adrianopole, Treaty of, 297, 307-8, 315
Aegean migrations, 51
Afghanistan, 538, 541-2
Agârbiceanu, I., 531
Agathocles, 72
Agathyrsi, 69

Agigea, 545
Agrippa, C. Fonteius, 88
Ahtum, Duke, 159-60
Alba Iulia (Apulum), 21, 107, 133, 165, 220-1, 250-1, 335, 359
Albania, 540, 552
Albert, Prince of Prussia, 315
Albani, Tiron, 425
Albini, S., 393
Albinus, D. Claudius, 112
Aldea, Prince Alexander, 189
Alecsandri, I., 326
Alecsandri, V., 312
Alessandrescu, A., 528
Alexander I, Tsar, 267

Alexander II, Tsar, 373-4, 378
Alexander the Good, Prince, 185, 188-9, 193
Alexander the Great, King, 60, 70, 72
Ali Pasha, Vizir, 172
Altini, E., 524
Anastasius, Emperor, 125, 140
Anatolia, 57, 203
Andrassy, Julius, 368-71
Andreescu, Ion, 525
Andrew II, King of Hungary, 161
Anghel, A., 251
Anghel, Gh. D., 529
Anghelescu, C., 438, 457
Anne, Princess of Bourbon Parma, 511
Antonescu, General Ion, 476-80, 482, 485-6, 488, 496, 502-3, 508
Antonescu, Mihai, 486
Apafi, Prince Michael, 38-9, 242
Apafi, Prince Michael II, 244
Apollodorus of Damascus, 99
Apollonia (Sozopoli), 78
Apponyi Law, 397
Arab states, 539
Archaeological research, 20-1, 49, 52, 74-6, 81, 114, 122, 128, 133-4, 136, 140-1, 143-4, 152, 155, 159
Archangel Michael's Legion see Iron Guard
Ardarich, King, 139
Arpad dynasty (Hungary), 166
Argedava, 76-7

Argeș, 11, 76, 221, 295
Argetoianu, C., 440-1, 453, 458
Arghezi, Tudor, 527
Arrian, 71
Aslan, A., 531
Asparukh, 146
Athanarich, 138
Attila, 139
Augustus, Emperor (Octavian), 80-1, 88
Aurelian, Emperor, 19, 120-22, 127, 135
Aurelian, P.S., 364, 383-4
Austria, 34, 307, 467 — also see Habsburgs
Avars, 67, 123, 126, 142-50
Avarescu, General, 339-40, 412, 419, 440-1, 445

Baal, 114
Baba, Corneliu, 529
Babeș, Victor, 440
Bădărău, E., 531
Bagdasar, D., 531
Baia, Battle of, 196
Baia Mare, 306
Balak, 153
Balc, Voivode, 171-2
Bălcescu, N., 302, 304, 310, 316, 318, 321-2, 325, 328-9, 332, 334, 337, 525
Balcic (Dionysopolis), 63
Băleanu, E., 329, 349
Băleanu family, 245
Balica, Despot, 171
Balkan Pact, 464, 467
Balș, T., 344
Banat, 105, 124, 143, 151, 204, 216, 259, 316, 322, 325, 335, 358, 371, 398
Banffy, Dionisie, 242

Bărăgan steppes, 72
Bărbat, 163
Barbilian, D., 530
Barcsay, Prince Acatiu, 238
Barițiu, G., 316, 323, 335, 393
Bărnuțiu, S., 316, 322-3, 333
Basarab I, Prince, 155, 157, 166-7
Basarab, Prince Laiotă, 196
Basarab, Prince Matei, 225, 227, 234-7, 241
Basarab, Prince Neagoe, 205
Basarab, Prince Nicholas, 167-8
Basarabi culture, 56, 58
Basești, Gh. Pop de, 393, 396
Basta, General G., 221
Bathory, Cardinal Andreas, 220
Bathory, Prince Christopher, 213,
Bathory, Prince John Sigismund, 213,
Bathory, Prince Sigismund, 216-22
Bathory, Prince Stephen, 213
Bayazid, Ilderim, Sultan, 187
Begin, M, 539
Béla, King (his anonymous notary), 153, 159
Béla IV, King of Hungary, 162
Béla Kun, 431-2
Beldy, Paul, 242
Belgrade, 108, 191, 203, 244, 258
Bem, General Joseph, 335-6
Benetato, Gr. Al., 531
Berlin, Treaty of, 380, 386-8

Berthelot, General, 422
Bessarabia, 27, 304, 310, 344, 380, 431, 474, 488, 547
Bethlen, King Gabriel, 229-30
Bibescu, Prince Gheorghe, 310-11, 319, 328-9
Bibescu, N., 353-4
Biharia citadel, 159
Bîrsa plain, 61
Bismarck, Chancellor, 365, 368-9, 380, 388
Bisztrai, Maria, 548
Bithynians, 54
Björnson, B., 397
Black Sea, origin of name, 56 ; ceases to be a Turkish lake, 264; drilling for oil, 544 ; plan to link by canal to North Sea, 545
Blaga, Lucian, 527
Blaj, 317 ; national assembly at, 322-5 ; new assembly, 333-4, 392
Blasi (Romanians north of the Danube), 153
Blow, D., 30
Bobîlna uprising, 179-81
Bodnăraș, Emil, 486
Bogdan, Prince, 155, 170-1, 187
Bogdan III, Prince, 204
Boii, 73
Bolliac, Cezar, 337
Boner, C., 22
Bosianu, C., 356
Bosnia, 375, 380
Borșa, Prince Roland, 162
Bosphorus, 407
Brad, Iovian, 334
Brăila, 10, 214, 307, 388
Brâncoveanu, Prince Constantine, 226-7, 246-9
Brâncoveanu, Grigore, 288

Brâncoveanu, Preda, 226
Brâncuși, C., 518, 527
Brașov, 175, 185-6, 227, 307, 326, 329
Bratei village, 133
Brătianu, Dimitrie, 322, 331, 438, 466, 478
Brătianu, Dinu, 438, 506
Brătianu, Gh. I., 451, 458, 460
Brătianu, Ion C., 321, 329, 346, 354, 365-6, 373-4 387-8, 391
Brătianu, Ionel, 399, 400, 403, 405, 408-9, 421, 430, 438, 445
Brătianu, V., 438
Britain, 295, 297, 307, 309, 315, 331, 333, 345-6, 376, 407-8, 415, 417, 430, 446, 461, 467, 472, 474-5, 483, 487-92, 507, 539
Bronze Age, 47-55
Brote, Eugen, 393
Brotherhood secret society, 310
Bucharest, 214, 218, 226; roads to other centres, 306, 327-9, 336, 383, 389, 395, 409, 413, 502, 504, 537; proposed link with Danube, 545; Treaty of Bucharest, 414, 420-1
Buda, 201, 204, 244
Budapest, 424
Buftea, 420
Bujor, M. Gh., 400
Bujor, Pavel, 439
Bukovina, 321, 326, 335, 342, 418, 474, 547
Bulgaria, 69, 89, 150, 155, 161-2, 166, 310, 368, 373, 375, 380, 402-3, 410, 412, 420, 422, 467

Burebista, King, 59, 63, 76-9
Buri, 94-6, 112
Buteanu, Ioan, 322
Buzdugan, G., 446
Byzantium, 66, 124, 143, 145, 147, 150, 152-3, 155, 159

Caesar, Julius, 78
Caffa, 197
Călărași, 10
Călinescu, A., 444, 458, 460
Callatis (Mangalia), 57, 63-7
Calvinists, 24-5, 229, 250
Canada, 547
Canacuzino, Court Marshal Constantine, 241
Cantacuzino, High Steward Constantine, 249
Cantacuzino, Prince Constantine, 332-3
Cantacuzino, George (Ban), 259
Cantacuzino, Gh. Gr., 395, 399
Cantacuzino, Matei, 440
Cantacuzino, Prince Șerban, 38-42, 241, 245-6, 248, 259
Cantacuzino, Prince Stephen, 249
Cantemir, Prince Constantine, 243
Cantemir, Prince Demetrius, 247-8
Caracalla (M. Aurelius Antoninus), Emperor, 113
Carafoli, E., 530
Caragea, Boris, 529
Caragea, Prince John, 267, 286
Caragiali, I. L., 523
Carinus, Emperor, 133

INDEX

Carol I, King-*see* King Charles I
Carol II, King, 445, 452-3, 455-6, 465-7, 475-6 (abdication), 478, 503
Carp, Gr., 312
Carp., P. P., 388, 391, 402, 404, 409, 414, 419
Carpi, 134
Casimir, King of Poland, 195, 198-9
Cassiodorus, 140
Castaldo, General, 213
Castali, A., 528
Catargi, Iordache, 315
Catargiu, Barbu, 352-3
Catargiu, Lascăr, 369-70
Catargiu, Ștefan, 349
Catchlove, Donald, 536
Catherine II, Empress of Russia, 552
Catholic (Roman) Church, 24-5, 250-1, 275, 550
Catus, S. A., 82
Caucaland, 138
Caudella, Eduard, 526
"Cavarna Country", 171
Cavour, Count Camillo, 343, 350
Ceaușescu, President Nicolae, 31, 33, 533-42
Celts, 51, 54, 59, 61-2, 71, 73-5, 77
Cercel, Prince Petru, 214
Cernat, General Al., 378
Cernăuți, 326
Cernavodă, 66, 385, 518, 545
Cetatea Albă, 198, 207, 215
Charlemagne, Emperor, 149-50
Charles V, Emperor of Austria, 203
Charles (Carol) I, King, 16, 365-70, 375-81, 394-5, 403, 404-6 (death), 407

Charles Robert, King of Hungary, 157, 167
Chilia (Lycostomo), 157, 166, 190, 195, 198
China, 32, 537, 539-40, 551
Chmielnicki, Hetman Bohan, 236
Christianity, 123, 137, 150
Churchill, Sir Winston, 483
Ciceo-Pop, Ștefan, 423, 438
Cimmerians, 55
Cîmpulung, 11
Cipariu, T., 316, 323
Ciucă, M., 531
Ciucurencu, Al., 529
Clarendon, Lord, 346
Claudius, Emperor, 82
Clemenceau, G., 430
Clodius, Carl, 469
Coandă, General, 422, 430
Coandă, H., 530
Coconul, Prince Alexandru, 225
Cochet, General, 497
Codreanu, N., 373
Coman, Dragos, 522
Commodus, Emperor L. Aurelius, 112
Convention of Balta Liman, 340
Convention of Paris, 348-50
Constantinescu, Al., 422, 438
Constantinople, 14, 124-5, 135, 146
Constantine the Great, Emperor, 124-5, 133, 135-6
Constantius II, Emperor, 125
Constantza (Constanța), 63-7, 385-6, 413, 420, 534, 545
Constantinescu, Gh., 530
Constantinescu, Mac, 529
Constitutio Antoniniana, 113

Copper and Bronze Ages, 47-54
Coroian, Iuliu, 393
Cossacks, 215, 236, 243, 304
Coșbuc, George, 523
Coson, 80
Costișa culture, 53
Costin, Miron, 241
Costin, Velicio, 241
Costobocae, 110-11
Coțofeni culture, 49
Cozia, 11
Crăciuneanu, General Gr., 440
"Craiova treasure", 60
Crassus, M. L., 80-1
Creangă, Ion, 523
Crenneville, Folliot de, 359
Crete, 234
Crețulescu, N., 354, 367
Crimean War, 339, 343
Criș culture, 46
Crișan (rebel leader), 280
Crișana, 61, 143, 151, 204, 325, 371, 398
Cristescu, Gh., 442
Curio, Proconsul Scribonius, 75
Czaky family, 183
Cumans, 152, 155, 160
Curtea de Argeș, 167
Cuza, A. C., 441, 460, 465
Cuza, Prince Alexandru Ioan, 16, 312, 319, 322, 326, 339, 345-6, 350-6 359, 361, 365
Czechoslovakia, 424, 430, 446-9, 495, 542, 553, 555 557

Dacia, 11, 14, 17-18, 50-1 ; war against Romans, 79-102 ; first mentioned in historical records, 74 ; culture and religion, 83-7 ; as organized after Trajan's victory, 103-6 ; inroads by free Dacians, 109-10; civilization under Romans, 114 ; religious beliefs, 118 ; abandoned by Imperial administration, 120 ; theory of continuity of people, 127-8 ; appeal of the name to nationalists 287, 315-6 ; culture 518-9
Daicoviciu, H., 20-1
Dan I, Prince, 169
Dancsuly, András, 548
Danielopolu, D., 531
Danube, 10, 14-15, 64-5, 75, free navigation 297 ; bridge at Cernavodă 385 ; river commission formed 387-8, 447 ; plans for link with North and Baltic Seas 545; big hydro-electric power station, 544-5
Dapyx, 81
Daranyi Bill, 398
Dardanians, 75
Dardanelles, 407
Darius, 68-70
David, Adolf, 313
Decaeneus, 76
Decebalus, King, 16, 59 ; wars against Romans, 88-102
Dej, 533
Delavrancea, Barbu, 408
Demetrescu-Buzău, D., 528
Desideriu, S., 28
Diamandi, G., 416
Dicomes, King, 80
Dlugosz's Chronicle, 161
Dlugosz, Jan, 197

INDEX 577

Dnieper, 52, 55, 57
Dniester, 61, 260
Dobrescu, Dem., 458
Dobrogeanu-Gherea, A., 442
Dobrotich, Despot, 171
Dobrudja, 14, 63-7, 72, 74, 81, 108 ; state founded 171 ; union with Wallachia, 172 ; 185-6, 411, 413 ; part annexed by Romania, 403 ; annexed by Central Powers, 420 ; developed by economic planning, 513-4
Doftana Prison, 534
Doja's uprising, 201-2
Domitian, Emperor, 89-91
Donat, I., 37
Dorians, 51, 57
Dorobanți, 237-8
Doroshenko, Hetman, 242
Dracula see Vlad the Impaler
Dragoș, Ioan, 336
Dragoș, Prince, 170-1
Dridu culture, 148-9, 152
Drobeta (Turnu Severin), 94, 96 ; destruction of bridge 108
Dromichaites, King, 60, 72-3
Duca Prince Gheorghe, 38
Duca, I. G., 438, 457
Duhamel (Russian commissar), 332
Duras, King, 89

Eden Anthony, 462, 496
Egypt, 203
Elagabalus, Emperor, 113-4
Eliade, Mircea, 532
Elizabeth, Princess (now Queen), 511, 539
Eminescu, Mihail, 523, 527
Enescu, Georges, 528

Epureanu, Em. C., 373-4
Eraclid, Prince Iacob, 214
Eregli (Pontiac Heraclea), 64
Etaireia, 285, 287-8, 292, 294-5
Evangelical Church, 24

Fabian, D., 442
Farcaș, Carol, 372
Ferdinand, King of Romania, 404, 406, 413, 416-8, 421, 446 (death)
Ferdinand of Habsburg, part ruler of Transylvania, 203, 206
Ferdinand III, Emperor of Austria, 236
Ferdinand I, Emperor of Austria, 325
"Field of Freedom", 323
Filip the Moldavian, 520
Filipescu, I. Al., 349
Filipescu, Mitică, 309
Filipescu, N., 408
Fischer, Mochi, 398
Flechtenmacher, Alexandru, 526
Florescu, I. Th., 451
Florus, 75
Flueraș, Ion, 425, 442
Foltești (union of tribes), 50
Foreign trade after World War II, 516
France, 203, 266, 297, 309, 315, 331, 344, 376, 387, 407, 410, 416-7, 430, 446, 461, 467, 472, 474, 497, 553
Francis I, Emperor of Austria, 281

Francis Joseph, Emperor of Austria, 335, 342, 358, 360, 368-70, 373-4, 393-4
French Revolution, 266, 312
Friessner, General, 487
Fronto, M. Claudius, 111
Fuscus, C., 89-90, 95

Gabor, Aron, 334
Galatz (or Galați), 292, 305, 307, 387, 401, 410, 533
Galicia, 77, 405, 412
Gallus, R., 88
Gauls *see* Celts
Gavrea, J., 548
Gelu, Duke, 158-9
Geneva Agreement, 451
Genoese, 14, 157, 172, 197
Genucla, 81
George, D. Lloyd, 430
Georgescu, Ion, 524
Geography of Romania *see* Introduction
Gepidae, 138-44
Gerard, Emily, 35-6
Germany, 457-8, 460-5, 471-97, 552, 555
Gestenberg, General, 467
Getae or Geto-Dacians *see* Dacians
Ghelerter, L., 443
Gheorghiu-Dej, Gh., 511, 533-6
Gherman, E., 442
Ghica, Prince Alexandru, 307-10, 345
Ghica, Dimitrie, 365, 368
Ghica I, Prince Grigore (Gregory), 241
Ghica II, Prince Grigore (Gregory), 259

Ghica III, Prince Grigore (Gregory), 265
Ghica IV, Prince Grigore (Gregory), 288
Ghica V, Prince Grigore (Gregory) Al., 342-4
Ghica, Ion, 310, 321, 327, 330, 337, 353-4, 365, 367-9
Gigurtu, I., 468, 474-6
Giurgiu, 239, 305
Glad, Duke, 158
Goga, Octavian, 408, 452, 460, 465
"Golden Horde" (Tartars), 155
Goldiș, Vasile, 423
Golescu, A. G., 327, 329, 331, 346, 353
Golescu, N., 321, 327, 331, 346, 353, 365
Golescu, Ștefan, 321
Görgei, General, 337
Gorchakov, Prince Alexander, 374, 377
Goths, 110, 123-4, 135-6
Gratian, Emperor, 133
Graziani, Prince Gaspar, 232
Grecianu, Radu, 521
Greceanu, Șerban, 521
Greece, 14, 51, 56-7, 64, 217, 232-3, 252-70, 284, 287, 293; uprising against Turks, 297, 493
Grigorescu, Nicolae, 525
Grigorovici, Gh., 442
Gritti, Aloisio, 206
Groza, Petru, 440, 458, 501, 504-5, 506-7, 511-12
Guderain, General, 493
Gurko, General, 377-8
Gyla, Duke, 159

Habsburgs, 203, 213-4, 223, 229, 243, 246, 253, 258-260, 266, 295, 335-7, 340-2 involvement in Transylvania, 550
Hadrian, Emperor, 106-8
Hagighiol barrow, 60
Han, Oscar, 529
Hângerli, Prince Constantine, 269-70
Hașdeu, 364
Hațieganu, Emil, 507
Hațieganu, I., 531
Hatvani, Hungarian commander, 336
Haynald, Bishop, 359
Heissler, General, 246
Henry III, King of France, 214
Herodotus, 59, 67-9
Herzegovina, 375, 380
Hinogu (Axiopolis), 66
Histria, 14, 56, 63-7
Hitler, A., 469-70, 475, 478-9, 487, 493
Hodza Milan, 396
Holy League, 216, 243
Horea (rebel leader), 277-80
Horthy, Admiral, 448, 459-60, 462, 468, 475, 490
Hortolomeiu, N., 531
Hulubei, H., 530
Hungary, 8 ; number of Hungarians in present-day Romania, 22 ; Hungarian views on their rights to Transylvania, 17-19 ; 30-2, 34, 150 ; origin of race and arrival, 150-4 ; efforts to subdue Wallachia, 167-8 ; divided between Habsburgs and Turks, 204 ; under Habsburg domination, 244-5 ; serfdom abolished, 340; 342 ; 405, 420 ; allied with Germany in World War I, leading to loss of Transylvania, chapter thirteen ; 431-2, 448, 462, 468-9, 473, 475, 488, 542 ; legal position of Hungarians under constitution in modern Romania, numbers and facilities for education, etc., 545-50, 552, 555, 557-8
Huns, 123, 133, 138-9
Hunyadi, John see Iancu of Hunedoara
Hussite ideology, 179 ; military tactics, 190

Iacob, C., 531
Ialomița, 10, 81
Iamandi, V., 458
Iancu, Avram, 322-5, 342
Iancu of Hunedoara (John Hunyady or Hunyadi to the Hungarians), 184, 189-91
Iazygians, 111-2
Ilarian, A.P., 323, 334
Iliaș, Alexandru, 233
Illyrians, 51, 75, 82, 104, 120, 145
Imre, Count Miko, 358
Indo-Europeans, 48, 55
Innocent XI, Pope, 39
Ionescu, Eugène, 528
Ionescu, Take, 395, 402, 405, 408-9, 413, 416, 421, 438
Ionescu, Th. V., 531

Iordache (Ypsilanti's chief lieutenant), 295
Iordache, L., 442
Iorga, Nicolae, 395, 408, 438, 441, 453, 458, 468-9, 477, 531-2
Irimescu, Ion, 529
Iron Gates, 10, 75, 518, 544-5
Iron Guard, 32, 441, 452, 457, 460, 466-8, 474-7, 501, 504, 557
Islaz proclamation, 327-8
Israel, 33, 539
Istrati, C. I., 373, 408
Italy, 405, 407-8, 417, 461, 553
Iunian, Gr., 452
Ivireanul, Metropolitan, Antim, 258

Jachint, Metropolitan, 168
Jalea, Ion, 529
Jassy, 226, 292, 319, 326, 365, 373, 389, 413, 415, 417, 422-3, 524, 529
Jews, 490, 501
Jilava Prison, 534
John Albert, King of Poland, 199
John V. Paleologus, Emperor, 171
John Sigismund, King of Hungary, 203-4, 213
John the Terrible, Prince, 214-5
Joseph II, Emperor of Austria, 273-4, 278, 280-1
Jordanes, 89, 140
Julianus, T., 90-1
Jumanca, Iosif, 425-7, 442
Junimea movement, 390-1, 395
Junius Brutus, 80
Justin I, Emperor, 141

Justin II, Emperor, 143
Justinian I, Emperor, 125, 140, 143
Justinus, Emperor, 125

Kaghan, 146
Kalnoky, Count 388
Kan, Prince Ladislau, 163
Kapolna Union, 180
Kara Mustafa, Grand Vizir, 39, 41-2
Karlowitz, Peace of, 245
Keitel, General, 493
Kellogg-Briand Pact, 448-9, 462
Khazars, 146
Kherson, 416
Kiselev, General Paul, 300, 303, 308
Klein, Uniate Bishop see Micu-Klein
Knights of St. John, 157 162
Köblös, E., 442
Kogălniceanu, M., 312, 316, 326, 349, 353-4, 356, 368, 373-4, 376, 383
Kogălniceanu, Vasile, 440
Köprülü, Grand Vizir Mehmet, 238
Kossovo, Battle of, 190
Kossuth, L., 325, 336, 359
Kouchuk Kainarji, peace of, 263
Kreindler, A., 531
Krum, Tsar, 149
Krushchev, N., 537
Kuvrat (or Kurt) see Kaghan, 146

Laberius Maximus, 94
Ladea, Romulus, 529
Ladislau, Duke of Oppeln, 167
Lahovari, Ion, 405

INDEX 581

Lake Capul, Battle of, 215
Lambrior, Ion, 312
Laonic Chalcocondil, 192
Lăpușneanu, Prince Alexandru, 213
Latène culture, 59, 73
Laurian, A. T., 316, 323, 333-4
League of Nations, 447, 461-2, 464
Lecca, Major D., 365
Lederer, L., 30
Lemeni, Bishop Ioan, 323, 325
Leopold I, Emperor, 25, 39, 41
Leopolda's Diploma, 244, 249, 270
Lepeș, Bishop G., 179
Leunclavius (German historian), 187
Levaditti, C., 530
Litovoi, Prince, 12, 162-3
Little Entente, 447, 462
Litvinov, M. M., 461-2
Locarno Agreement, 448
Locusteanu, Major, 329
London Convention, 462
Longinus, 100
Longobardi, 142
Lorraine, Prince Charles of, 39, 41
Louis of Anjou, King of Hungary, 167-8, 170-1
Louis II, King of Hungary, 203
Luca Abore, 206
Luca, Vasile, 504
Lucaciu, Vasile, 393
Lubin, Treaty of, 189
Luchian, Ștefan, 525
Lucius Aurelius Verus, 109
Luck, Treaty of, 247
Ludendorff, General E., 413
Lupescu, or Wolf, Magda, 453
Lupu, Eugen, 373
Lupu, Kostaki, 414
Lupu, N., 416, 439, 508
Lupu, Prince Vasile, 228, 233-6, 242

Macarie (Serbian monk), 520
Macedonia, 70-2, 75, 87
Măcelariu, I. E., 372
Mackensen, General, 412-3, 419, 422
Macrinus, Emperor, 113
Madgearu, Professor Virgil, 439-40, 458, 477
Magheru, Gh., 332-3, 346
Magyars see Hungarians
Maior, Petru, 287, 316
Maiorescu, I., 331
Maiorescu, Titu, 391, 402-3, 414, 523
Malaxi, N., 468
Mălinescu, V., 312, 346
Mândrescu, Simon, 408
Mănescu, Constantin, 443
Mangalia, 57, 63-7
Maniu, Iuliu, 423, 425-6, 438, 444, 453, 460, 475, 478, 506, 510-11
Maramureș, 18, 77, 152, 170-1, 325, 521
Marcomanni, 110-12
Marcus Aurelius Verus, Emperor, 109-11, 117, 119
Marghiloman, Al., 391, 405, 409, 414, 421-2
Margrave of Brandenburg, 169
Maria Theresa, Empress of Austria, 272, 274, 278
Marie, Queen of Romania, 445

Mark Antony, 80
Martinuzzi, Bishop G., 213
Masaryk, Thomas, 553
Matthias Corvinus, King of Hungary, 192-3, 195, 198-9
Mauricius Tiberius, Emperor, 145
Mavrocordat, Prince Constantine, 260-2, 269
Mavrocordat, Prince John, 258-9
Mavrocordat, Prince Nicholas, 248-9, 257-9
Mavropous, Metropolitan John, 154
Maximian, Emperor, 134
Maximilian, Archduke, 218
Medrea, Cornel, 529
Mehmed IV, Sultan, 39
Mehmed Köprülü, Grand Vizir, 238
Mengli-Ghirai, Tartar Khan of Crimea, 199
Menuhin, Y., 528
Merulos, Court Marshal I. R., 290
Mesopotamia, 107
Michael the Brave, Prince, 16, 200, 212, 216-224
Michael, King of Romania, 16, 472, 476, 483, 487, 503, 505, 511-12 (abdication)
Micu-Klein, Bishop I. I., 275-7, 281
Micu-Klein, Samuil, 281, 287
Miculi, Carol, 526
Mihalache, I., 438-40, 510-11
Mihali, Teodor, 396
Mihnea, Prince Radu, 225, 231, 233
Mihnea III, Prince of Wallachia, 239

Mihoc, Gh., 531
Mikulov, Treaty of, 230
Milan Edict, 137
Miletus, 57, 64
Milcu, St., 531
Mille, C., 390
Minority Rights Group, 27
Minovici, Mina, 530
Mintchiaky, Consul General, 301
Mircea the Old, Prince, 14, 43, 172, 175, 185-7, 189
Mironescu, G. G., 453
Mişu, Nicolae, 430
Mithridates, King, 75
Mocioni, Andrei, 358
Moesia, 19, 82-3, 88-9, 104, 119, 124
Mohács, Battle of, 202-4
Mohammed II, Sultan, 190-2 196-8
Moisil, Gr., 531
Moldavia, emergence as state, 156, 169-71 ; early economic life, 173-77 ; early social structure, 177-9 ; early political organization, 181-5 ; first silver coins minted, 188; Metropolitan Church founded, 188 ; reign of Stephen the Great, 193-99 ; passes under Turkish suzerainty, 207 ; tribute to Porte, 210-11, 224-5; under Phanariot régime, 248, 252-70 ; serfdom abolished, 262 ; foreign consulates established, 265 ; customs union with Wallachia, 311 ; first prince of united principalities elected, 349-50 ; first World War against Ger-

INDEX

many is mainly conducted from Moldavia, chapter thirteen ; developed through economic planning, 513 ; the painted monasteries, 522
Molotov, W. M., 496
Mongolia, 539-40
Monteoru Group, 52
Moravian Principality, 150-1
Moruzi, Prince Alexander, 267
Moscow Protocol, 449
Moscovici, Ilie, 442
Mosna, 59
Movilă, Prince Ieremia, 218-9, 221, 223
Movilă, Prince Miron, 232
Movilă, Prince Simeon, 220-1, 232
Muntenia see Wallachia
Murad II, Sultan, 197
Mureș, 61
Mureșan, Camil, 549
Murgu, E., 322, 325
Mușa, Sultan, 187
Mușat, Prince Petru, 177, 186, 188
Mușceleanu, Ion, 529
Mussolini, B., 452, 462
Muzicescu, Gavril, 527
Mycenaean civilization, 51
Myssians, 54, 68

Nădejde, Ioan, 373, 390
Nague, A., 179
Nămoloasa, 418
Napoleon I, Emperor, 266-7
Napoleon III, Emperor, 343, 346, 350, 356, 365, 368
NATO, 541
Navarino, Battle of, 297
Neanderthal man, 44

Negri, C., 312, 326, 346
Negrescu, T., 530
Negrussi, C., 312
Nelidov, A. I., 375
Neofit, Metropolitan, 329
Nero, Emperor, 88
Nesebar (Mesembria), 63
Nesselrode, Count Karl Robert, 319
Neuilly, Treaty of, 430
Nicea Empire, 161
Nicholas, Prince of Romania, 446
Nicholas, Grand Duke of Russia, 377
Nicodim (monk), 168-9
Nicolau, St. S., 531
Nicolescu, M., 531
Nicopolis, Battle of, 172
Nicopolis ad Istrum (Stari Nikiup), 97
Niculi, Ion, 513
Niger, C. Pescennius, 112
Nixon, President Richard, 539
Nokai Khan, 166
Noptsa, Alexe, 324, 351
Nottara, C. C., 528
Noua culture, 53

Obrenovic, Marie, 357
Odobescu, Colonel Ion, 328-9
Octavian (Emperor Augustus), 80-1
Oder-Vistula culture, 74
Odessa, 416
Odrysian tribes, 70
Oclu, Pasvan, 269
Olbia, 56, 63, 72, 78
Olt, 44, 104-5, 140-1, 162, 294

Oltenia, 73, 105, 124, 162 ; under Habsburg rule, 259 ; incorporated into Wallachia, 260, 328, 330, 333, 414, 513-4, 534
Onicescu, O., 531
Oradea, 165; Peace of, 213, 220, 239, 398
Orăștie Mountains, 95, 99, 101
Oriental Company, 227
Orlando, V.E., 430
Orleanu Law, 401
Orthodox Church, 24-5, 233, 250-1, 317, 347, 360, 522
Osman, Pasha, 378-9
Osman, Sultan, 232
Ostrogoths, 138
Oțetea, A., 7
Otomani groups, 52
Ottescu, Ion N., 528
Ovid, 81

Pachorus, King of the Parthians, 100
Palmerston, Lord, 346
Pancu-Iași, O., 441
Pandours, 286
Pannonia, 61, 82, 110, 146, 160
Panu, A., 312, 346, 349
Papiu-Ilarian, A., 322
Parhon, C. I., 512, 530-1
Paris, Treaty of, 1856, 370
Paris Peace Conference (1947), 508-9
Parthians, 106-7, 109-10
Pascu, Ș., 21
Passarowitz, Peace of, 259
Pătrașcu the Kind, Prince, 213

Patriotic Association, The, 312
Pauker, Anna, 504
Paul of Aleppo, 11
Pavel of Voivodeni, 179-80
Paquier, Lt.-Col., 497
Peace Conference (1946), 497
Peasants, 164-5, 178-81, 211-2, 228-9, 242, 256, 261-2 ; serfdom abolished, 262, 268, 277-80, 286, 296-7, 300, 303-4, 312, 314, 340-1, 353 ; land law passed, 355, 362-3, 370, 396, 398-400, 425, 433, 426-7, 456, 502, 506
Pechenegs, 151-2, 154-5, 160
Penescu, N., 501
Periam-Pecica group, 52
Persia, 234
Persu, A., 530
Peter II, Prince, 190
Peter the Great, Tsar, 247, 551
Peter the Lame, Prince, 208, 214-5
Petrascu, G., 527
Petriceicu, Prince Ștefan, 243
Petrino, Nicolae, 358
Phanariot rule, 248, 252-70, 302
Pherekyde, M., 405, 438
Philip of Flanders, Count, 365
Philippi, Battle of, 80
Phocas, 145
Phrygians, 51, 54, 68
Piatra Roșie, 95
Pick, H., 31
Pietroasa gold treasure, 139
Pindus, 20

Piscul Crăsanilor, 82
Pistiner, I., 442
Pius, Emperor T. Aelius Antoninus, 108
"Plain of Freedom", 329
Plevna, 378
Poland, 39, 40, 61, 161, 188, 193, 198-9, 213, 218-9, 227, 236, 243, 313, 359, 389-90, 446-7, 473-4, 542-3, 550, 552
Pompei, D., 530
Pompeius Trogus, 74
Pompey, 78
Poteca, Eufrosin, 297
Pop, Vasile, 359
Popescu-Puțuri, I., 7
Popești, 76, 82, 86
Prince Potemkin cruiser, 398
Proto-Bulgars, 67, 126, 141-8, 151
Prussia, 263, 344, 351
Ptolemy, 71
Puchner, General, 334-5
Pumnul, A., 322

Quadi, 110-11

Racovița, Prince Constantine, 268
Racovița, Emil, 390
Racovița, Prince Michael, 259, 261
Rădăceanu, Lothar, 442
Rădescu, General, 501, 504-5
Radu of Afumați, Prince, 205
Radu the Handsome, Prince, 176-7, 192

Rădulescu, I.E., 321, 328, 331-3
Rainer, Fr., 530
Rakoczy, Prince George I, 229-30
Rakoczy, Prince George II, 229, 238-9
Rareș, Prince Petru, 206-7, 521, 526
Rășcanu, Theodor, 312
Rațiu, Ioan, 370-1, 396
Rausimodus, King, 124
Răzvan, Prince Ștefan, 217-8
Reformed Church, 26, 550
Règlement Organique, 284, 298-315, 317, 332, 340
Religion, 24-6 ; "four received religions" in Transylvania, 24, 249-50 ; Uniate Church formed in Transylvania, 250-1
Ressu, Camil, 527
Rhedey, Prince Francisc
Rhineland Pact, 448
Rodna, 165
Roles, King, 80
Roman, Prince, 14, 188
Romania, geography, 8-15; area, 9; population, 9; boundaries, 9; theory of formation of language, 128-31, 154, 160, different names for Romanians, 153 ; feudal society and political bodies emerge, 155, 158; first coins minted, 168; three Romanian lands united under Michael the Brave, 216-24; *Règlement Organique* first constitution, 299-325; mer-

chant fleet established, 306; use of word "Romania", 316; first Romanian government of two united principalities, 352; estates of monasteries secularized, 354; land law passed, 355; fights with Russia against Turks and gains true independence, 373-81; national bank established, 386; Romania proclaimed a kingdom, 387; joins triple alliance, 388; the peasant revolt of 1907, 398-9; Romania defeats Bulgaria in first Balkan War, 402-3; World War I leads up to the link with Hungary being broken in Transylvania, chapter thirteen; frequent changes in government and King Carol II's dictatorship, chapter thirteen; Romania, having been forced to fight with axis powers against Soviet Union changes sides in August, 1944 and, allied with Russians, carries war against Germany beyond her own territory; Northern Transylvania is freed but land is devastated and heavy reparations have to be paid to Russia, 500; King Michael abdicates and People's Republic formed, 511-12; agriculture reorganized into co-operative farms, 514-5, expansion of foreign trade, chapter sixteen; withdrawal of Russian troops, 536; "most favoured nation" pact with U.S.A., 539; foreign debts, 543-4; universities established, 356

Romaniceanu, Mihai, 507
Romans, conflict with Dacians, 79-83; Trajan's two wars and conquests, 88-102; right to Roman citizenship of all free townsmen, 113; imperial administration abandons Dacia, 120-24
Românul, M., 179
Rosetti, C.A., 321, 329, 346, 365, 387
Rosetti, Lascăr, 322
Rosetti, Theodor, 390-1, 405
Roşia, 519
Roth, S.L., 322, 334
Rotterdam, 545
Rubobostes, King, 74
Rucar, 329
Rückman, Baron, 309
Rudolf II, Emperor, 219-20
Russia, 8, 28-9, 32, 257, 263, 266, 291-8, 309, 344, 375-80, 397, 404, 411, 415-9, 424, 447, 471, 473, 483, 487, 507, 533-6, 538-44, 547-56
Russo, A., 322
Russu-Şirianu, Ioan, 396
Ruthenians, 251

INDEX

Sabinus, C. Oppius, 89
Sadat, President, 539
Sadoveanu, M., 440, 512, 529
Sager, O., 531
Saguna, Bishop (later Metropolitan) Andrei, 323-5, 358-60, 371
St Germain, Treaty of, 430
Saligny, Anghel, 385
Salonika, 412
San Stefano, Peace of, 380
Sănătescu, General, 487, 498-501
Sarmatians, 51, 81-2, 88, 95, 107-8, 124
Sarmizegetusa Regia (Grădiştea Muncelului), 79, 83-4, 101
Satu Mare, Peace of, 252, 270
Saturninus, M. Aponius, 88
Sava, Saint, 137
Sava, Generalissimo Bimbasha, 291, 295
Saxon colonists, 24, 163, 180, 191, 193, 221, 250, 322, 334, 427
Scherbachev, General, 419
Schöpflin, G., 27-8
Scodisci Celts, 61, 73, 75
Scorniceşti, 534
Scythia and Scythians, 5, 10, 51, 55, 57-9, 60-1, 64-5, 81, 124-6
Seimeni, 235-8
Selim I, Sultan, 203
Selim III, Sultan, 270
Septimus Severus, Emperor, 112-3
Şerban, Prince Constantine, 11, 236-8
Şerban, Prince Radu, 225, 236, 241

Serbia, 83, 89, 166, 191, 259, 315, 373, 380, 410
Seton-Watson, Hugh, 8, 20, 28-30, 34-5, 37, 444, 452-3, 457, 475, 501, 503-4, 507, 510-11, 547-8, 551-4
Seton-Watson, R.W., 8, 16-20, 22-3, 36-7, 193, 199, 201, 206, 224, 248-9, 251, 253-4, 269-70, 279, 303, 350, 357-8, 365-6, 380, 558
Sever, Axente, 334
Severin-Banat, 161-2
Severus, Alexander, Emperor, 113
Sèvres, Treaty of, 430
Shishman, Tsar Michael, 166
Shishtov, Peace of, 266
Sibiu, 165, 185, 227, 307, 334-5, 359, 392-3, 396
Sighişoara, 201, 227
Sigismund of Luxemburg, King, 186, 188-9
Sima, Horia, 479
Simeon, Tsar, 150
Simmons, Michael, 541
Sinan Pasha, Grand Vizir, 217-8
Şincai, Gheorghe, 287
Sinoe, Lake, 64
Sion, Gheorghe, 322
Sitalces, King, 70
Sixtus IV, Pope, 196
Slavici, 523
Slavs, 36, 132, 141-51, 553
Snow, C.P. (Lord Snow), 36
Slovakia, 77, 93, 251
Sobieski, King John III of Poland, 41-2, 242-3
Sofia, 190, 403
Soliman Hadamb, 197

Soloman, Colonel Ion, 329
Someş Valley, 61
Sopron, 423
Sovroms, 535-6
Spanish Civil War, 465
Stalin, J., 535, 551
Stănileşti, Battle of, 248
Starhemberg, Count Ernst, 41
Steele, Jonathan, 537
Ştefan Lăcustă, Prince of Moldavia, 207
Ştefăniţă, Prince of Moldavia, 177, 204, 206
Stephanescu, George, 526
Stephen I, King of Hungary, 159-60
Stephen I, Prince of Moldavia, 188
Stephen, Prince George, 236, 238
Stephen the Great, Prince of Moldavia, 11, 43, 184, 193-9, 204, 521-2
Stephen Dushan, Tsar, 170
Stere, C., 394, 414, 419, 439, 452
Stere, Gheorghe, 512
Stînceşti, 59
Ştirbei, Prince Barbu, 310, 342-3
Ştirbei, Prince, 445
Stoilov, S., 529
Storck, Karl, 524
Strabo, 77
Strousberg (Head of Prussian consortium), 368
Stuart, Baron D., 375
Sturdza, D.A., 392, 394, 399, 400
Sturdza, Prince Ioniţă Sandu, 296, 312
Sturdza, Prince Mihai, 307-8, 311, 315, 319-21
Sturdza, Vasile, 349

Stürmer, Boris, 411
Styria, 423
Suceava, 199, 221, 243
Suleiman I, Sultan, 203, 206
Suleiman Pasha, 331
Şuluţiu, Metropolitan A.S., 359
Supplex Libellus Valachorum, 281-2
Şuţu, Prince Alexander, 267-8, 288
Syria, 203
Szalankemen, 244
Szekler colonists, 24, 163, 180, 195, 201, 229, 250, 277-8, 334-5
Szonyi, St., 529

Tacitus, C.C., 93
Tacitus, Emperor Marcus Claudius, 133
Talaat Efendi, 330
Tănase, Zaharia, 443
Tartars, 10-11, 155; invasion of 1241, 18, 162, 165-6, 169-70, 197, 204, 215, 217, 243, 263
Tătărăscu, Gh., 457, 460, 465, 484, 505, 510
Telegrad (citadel), 159
Teleky, Count, 322
Teleky, Michael, 242
Tell, Christian, 310, 328-9, 331-3, 346
Teodorescu, N., 531
250
Teurisci, 73
Teutonic Knights, 161, 163, 188-9
Theophanes, 131
Theophilus, Metropolitan, 250

Theophylact, 131
Thirty Years' War, 229-30
Thomas, Ivor, M.P., 497
Thrace and Thracians, 48, 50-2, 54-5, 57, 59, 60, 67-9 70-3, 75, 80-1, 83, 106, 145
Thucydides, 59
Tiberius, Emperor, 83
Timişoara, 204, 213, 342, 358, 372
Timur Lenk (Tamerlane), 187
Tinosul, 82
Tîrgovişte, 192, 218, 239, 293
Tîrgu Jiu, 527, 534
Tisa, 52, 145
Tisza, Istvan, 407, 423
Ţiţeica, Gh., 529
Ţiţeica, Şerban, 531
Titelescu, N., 430, 458, 461-5
Titel-Petrescu, C., 442
Tito, President, 537, 542
Tolstoy, Count Leo, 23, 397
Toma of Humor, 522
Tomis (Constantza), 57-67
Tomşa, Prince Leon, 233
Trade Unions, 442, 444, 500
Trapoldner, Luca, 520
Trajan, Emperor, 16, 63, 86; conquest of Dacia, 92-106; erection of column in Rome, 106; death, 106
Trandafilov (Russian engineer), 310
Transylvania, 16-20; incorporated into Hungary, 23, 333; privileged nations, 24; "four received religions", 24, 249-50; names of country, 160; invasion by Magyars, 151-60; early conquest completed, 160-1; how territory was divided, 183; vassal of Sultan, 204; tribute paid, 225; subjection by Habsburgs, 249-52; peasants' war, 277-80; serfdom abolished, 280; rise of Transylvanian school, 316; revolution and move towards nationhood, chapter ten; the Sibiu congress and its disregarded findings, chapter eleven; Romanian National Party formed, 392; Romanian National Central Council set up, 425; Grand National Assembly at Alba Iulia, 425-7; reunited with Romania, 427, 430; Vienna Diktat, 475; nearly 150,000 Jews killed, 490; northern Transylvania liberated, 494-5
Trianon, Treaty of, 430
Triballians, 71, 83
Tripartium Code, 202
Trogus Pompeius, 62
Ţuculescu, Ion, 529
Tumular grave culture, 52
Turanian invaders, 126, 155, 157, 160
Turks, 13-14, 30, 34, 184-99, 200-25, 235-40, 248-9, 253-70, 375-80, 407, 550
Türr, General, 359
155, 157, 160

Tyras (Cetatea Albă), 57, 63
Tyrnavia, Treaty of, 229

Udi, 152, 155, 160
Ukraine, 61, 242-3
Ulfilas, Bishop, 137
Ungureanu, Gheorghe, 373
Uniate Church, 24-5, 250-1, 275-7, 317
Unitarian Church, 24, 250
United Nations, 488-9, 491, 493, 508-9
United States of America, 415-6, 429, 477, 483, 487, 507, 543, 547
Universities established, 356
Ureche, Court Marshal Grigore, 193, 521
Uric, Gavril, 522
Urosh III, Prince, 166
Uzun Hasan, Khan, 196

Văcărescu, Barbu, 288
Văcărescu, Theodor, 329
Văleanu, General C., 440
Vandals, 112
Varna (Odessos), 63; Battle of, 190
Vasvari, Paul, 337
Venice, 196, 227, 234, 243
Verdun, Battle of, 410
Vernescu, Gh., 391
Versailles, Treaty of, 430
Vespasian, Emperor, 88
Vicina, 157
Victoria, Queen, 346
Vida, Geza, 529
Vienna, 38-40, 203, 230, 243-4, 257, 393, 423; Vienna Diktat, 475, 490, 509
Vinogradov, General, 501
Visigoths, 132-3, 135-6, 138

Vitalianus's rebellion, 125
Vitellius, Emperor, 88
Vlachs (Romanians), 153
Vlad, Aurel, 425
Vladimirescu, Tudor, 283-4, 288-95
Vladislav I, King of Hungary, 190
Vladislav II, King of Hungary, 199
Vladislav Iagello, King of Poland, 186
Vladislav, Prince Vlaicu, 168, 176
Vlad Țepeș (the Impaler), 43, 184, 191-3, 198
Vlaicu, Aurel, 530
Voevod, Al. Vaida, 396, 425, 430, 438, 444, 458
Vogoride, N., 344-5
Voinov, D., 390
Volga, 52
Volohi (early name for Romanians), 153
Vrînceanu, Gh., 531
Vuia, T., 530

Wachmann, Eduard, 526
Wachmann, I.A., 526
Walewski, Count, 343-6
Wallachia, emergence as state, 156, 166-9; foundation of church organization, 167-8; early economic life, 173-77; early social structure, 177-9; early political organization, 181-5; falls under Turkish sovereignty, 207; tribute to Porte, 210-11, 224-5; frequent changes of prince, 254; Phanariot régime, 248, 252-70; serfdom abol-

ished, 262; foreign consulates established, 265; customs union with Moldavia, 311; revolution and move towards nationhood, chapter ten; first prince of united principalities elected, 349-52
Warsaw Pact, 30, 33, 538, 541
Westphalia, Peace of, 230
Wiest, Ludovic, 526
William I, Emperor of Germany, 369
Wilson, President, 424, 430
"Wooden structure tomb" group, 52

Xerxes, 70
Xenopol, A.D., 383

Yalta Declaration, 507
Yugoslavia, 32, 430, 446-7, 493, 537, 544, 552
Ypsilanti, Prince Alexander, 265, 269, 289-95
Ypsilanti, Prince Constantine, 267

Zaharia, Pascal, 410
Zamolxis (Dacian god), 85
Zamoyski, Chancellor Ion, 218, 221
Zapolya, J., 201, 203, 206
Zenta victory, 245
Zhao Zhyang, Chinese P.M., 540
Zimnicea, 82
Zlatna, 227, 306
Zopyrion, 71-2
Zotov, General, 378
Zyraxes, 81